PennyPress®

PUZZLER'S GIANT BOOK OF CROSSWORDS 67

Penny Press is the publisher of a fine family of puzzle magazines and books renowned for their editorial excellence.

This delightful collection has been carefully selected by the editors of Penny Press for your special enjoyment and entertainment.

Puzzler's Giant Book of Crosswords, No. 67, August 2018. Published four times a year by Penny Publications, LLC, 6 Prowitt Street, Norwalk, CT 06855-1220. On the web at PennyDellPuzzles.com. Copyright © 2018 by Penny Publications, LLC. Penny Press is a trademark registered in the U.S. Patent Office. All rights reserved. No material from this publication may be reproduced or used without the written permission of the publisher.

ISBN-13: 978-1-59238-136-4

ISBN-10: 1-59238-136-7

Printed by LCS Communications, Dwight, IL, U.S.A. 7/10/18

PENNY PRESS PUZZLE PUBLICATIONS

◆ PUZZLE MAGAZINES ◆

- All-Star Word Seeks
- Approved Variety Puzzles
- Classic Variety Puzzles Plus Crosswords
- Easy & Fun Variety Puzzles
- Easy Crossword Express
- Family Variety Puzzles & Games
- Famous Fill-In Puzzles
- Fast & Easy Crosswords
- Favorite Easy Crosswords
- Favorite Fill-In
- Favorite Variety Puzzles
- Fill-In Puzzles
- Garfield's Word Seeks
- Good Time Crosswords
- Good Time Easy Crosswords
- Good Time Variety Puzzles
- Large-Print Word Seek Puzzles
- Master's Variety Puzzles
- Merit Variety Puzzles & Games
- Original Logic Problems
- Penny's Finest Favorite Word Seeks
- Penny's Finest Good Time Word Seeks
- Penny's Finest Super Word Seeks
- Quick & Easy Crosswords
- Spotlight Celebrity Word Seek
- Spotlight Movie & TV Word Seek
- Spotlight Remember When Word Seek
- Tournament Variety Puzzles
- Variety Puzzles and Games
- Variety Puzzles and Games Special Issue
- Word Seek Puzzles
- World's Finest Variety Puzzles

◆ SPECIAL SELECTED COLLECTIONS ◆

- Alphabet Soup
- Anagram Magic Square
- Brick by Brick
- Codewords
- Cross Pairs Word Seeks
- Crostics
- Crypto-Families
- Cryptograms
- Diagramless
- Double Trouble
- England's Best Logic Puzzles
- Flower Power
- Frameworks
- Large-Print Crosswords
- Large-Print Cryptograms
- Large-Print Missing Vowels
- Letterboxes
- Match-Up
- Missing List Word Seeks
- Missing Vowels
- Number Fill-In
- Number Seek
- Patchwords
- Places, Please
- Quotefalls
- Share-A-Letter
- Simon Says
- Stretch Letters
- Syllacrostics
- The Shadow
- Three's Company
- What's Left?
- Word Games Puzzles
- Zigzag

◆ PUZZLER'S GIANT BOOKS ◆

Crosswords   Sudoku   Word Games   Word Seeks

PUZZLE 1

• SOFT TOUCH •

ACROSS
1. Freudian topics
4. Helper
8. Cartoon chipmunk
12. April shower
16. Just bought
17. Some lingerie
18. October's jewel
19. Director Preminger
20. Comforter stuffing
22. Child's bruin
24. Choice
25. Baseball's Doubleday
28. Letters on a boot box
29. Rap's Dr. ___
30. Not mine
31. Coarse files
34. Fastens
37. Two to a qt.
38. Promise to repay
40. Partner of aah
41. Graceful waterfowl
42. Form or cycle starter
43. Wireless
44. Dimwitted
47. Blissful places
48. Pvt.'s superior
49. Ventilate
50. Dull pains
52. Train station
55. Buff
56. Thurman of "Pulp Fiction"
57. Sword haft
58. Minor falsehood
59. Shocking fish
60. ___ Newton
63. Log floats
65. Managed
69. Sailboat
71. Speculate
72. "Xanadu" rock gp.
73. Car style
74. Idolized
78. Sleeper's cushion
82. Fine goat wool
84. Unwritten
85. Bologna bread, once
86. Akron's state
87. CEO, e.g.
88. Infant
89. Export
90. Snow melter
91. Assortment

DOWN
1. Knowledge, briefly
2. Bottomless
3. Smack, as a mosquito
4. Hates
5. "Me, Myself & ___"
6. Patriotic assn.
7. Literary piece
8. Too-indulgent relatives
9. Parrots
10. Shaver
11. Deacon
12. Choir garments
13. Consumed food
14. Give-go link
15. Negative connector
21. Ocean motion
23. Affirmative answer
26. Strike, slangily
27. Kook
32. Talcum applicator
33. Wooer
34. Shrill
35. Of best quality
36. Silvery gray fur
39. "Dukes of Hazzard" deputy
41. Miss Hawkins
43. Crack a book
45. Exhausted
46. Otherwise
50. Tennis great
51. Tribal head
53. Exclude
54. Small flaps
60. Gushed
61. Debtor's abbr.
62. Republican inits.
63. Glowing
64. Power source
66. Retort
67. Inventor Whitney
68. Kewpies
69. Contempt
70. "___ Bill"
71. Aromatic herb
75. Guns the motor
76. Canal of song
77. Govt. branch
78. Short haircut
79. Geologic division
80. Wipe gently
81. Be deceitful
83. Cry of discovery

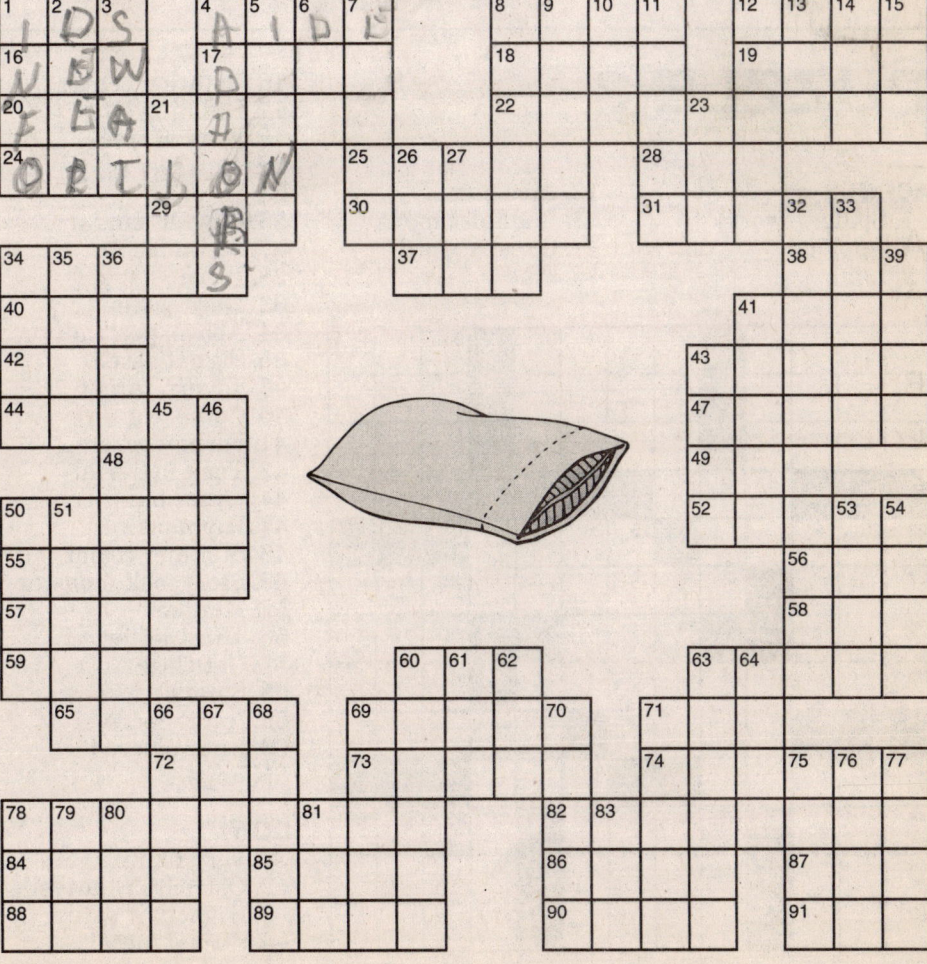

5

PUZZLE 2

ACROSS
1. ___ and haw
4. Unmannerly
8. Spur
12. "___ Got a Secret"
13. Molecule part
14. Highway division
15. Wrongdoing
16. Assist
17. Poker stake
18. Hit hard
20. Clear profit
21. Cease
22. Pack animal
24. Thanksgiving veggie
26. Hopelessness
30. Debris
34. Forest creature
35. Andean climber
37. Income
38. Joy
40. Refuse
42. Tidbit for Dobbin
44. Behold
45. Dog's pest
48. Kind of room
50. Broad valley
54. Security device
55. Quiz
57. Overcame
58. Pain
59. Majestic title
60. Compute
61. Destitute
62. At once, to a doctor
63. Okay!

DOWN
1. Snake's comment
2. Wicked
3. Bill of fare
4. Hooray
5. Tool
6. Distribute
7. Unoccupied
8. Blood part
9. Rave's partner
10. In the know about
11. Profound
19. Space
23. Mexican sauce
25. Knowledgeable
26. Society newcomer
27. Building annex
28. Glide down the slopes
29. Type of doll
31. Resort of sorts
32. Label
33. Sight organ
36. Lash enhancer
39. One who drenches
41. Sleeping place
43. Curl of hair
45. Move, as wings
46. Crazy
47. Bouncing sound
49. Leave
51. Not at home
52. Metal deposit
53. Finishes
56. Encountered

PUZZLE 3

ACROSS
1. Spiders' works
5. Applaud
9. Limb
12. Give out
13. Buddhist monk
14. Ghostly word
15. Pipe
16. Rotation center
17. Building site
18. Kind of tree
20. Molars, e.g.
22. Saunter
25. Clog or sandal
27. Scramble for
28. Pause
33. Hard water
34. Above, poetically
35. Signal assent
36. Tavern target
40. Collie, e.g.
41. Farm worker
42. Tusk material
44. Metal pin
47. Payment
48. Summer cooler
49. Storybook monster
52. Moniker
56. Third letter
57. Get close
58. Steers
59. Audio receiver
60. Embroidered
61. Repair

DOWN
1. Very damp
2. Ostrich's relative
3. Highchair attire
4. Strong metal
5. Chowder ingredient
6. Careless
7. Pierre's pal
8. Minister
9. Skillful
10. Origin
11. Wool-eater
19. Island necklace
21. Slippery swimmer
22. Eager
23. Flaky mineral
24. Lager
25. Place
26. German mister
29. Midday
30. Loosen
31. Portal
32. Fidgety
37. Article
38. Billy clubs
39. "___ Hard"
43. Poison
44. Run competitively
45. Plan
46. Swerve
47. Forest plant
50. Gosh!
51. Uncooked
53. Lumberjack's tool
54. Fellows
55. Conclusion

PUZZLE 4

ACROSS
1. Get lighter
5. Competent
9. Dangles
14. Depressions
15. Amtrak travel
16. WWII craft
17. Metallic deposits
18. Cooled
19. Cheerful
20. Broke a fast
21. Feline
22. Ready for print
24. Forbidden
26. Botched it
28. Holy cow!
31. Warning torch
33. Serious
35. African tours
37. Stretched the neck
38. Fix
39. Queeg's ship
41. Cans
42. Meeting plan
44. Gave away
46. Smoothed
47. Let loose
48. Geologic period
49. Strikes out
51. Salivate excessively
55. Ponder
56. Sooner than, in verse
58. Blubber
59. Art of illusion
62. Creeper
64. Suspect
65. Detached
66. Differently
67. Value
68. Words of agreement
69. ___ out (barely made)
70. Wad of Washingtons

DOWN
1. Bob on water
2. Blood line
3. Wimp
4. Road curve
5. Opera solo
6. Germs
7. Prevaricate
8. Church official
9. Cigar container
10. Help in crime
11. Neither hide ___ hair
12. Slender fish
13. Porky's abode
21. Popular soda
23. Plunge
25. Insult
27. Soot, e.g.
28. Wish-granter
29. Revise
30. Last bits
32. Game rooms
34. Second of two
35. Sweet stuff
36. Sports ring
38. Docket item
40. Baloney
43. Subtracts
45. Senate staffer
50. Flood wall
52. Briny body
53. Speak formally
54. Ancient instruments
55. Muck's partner
57. Oboe insert
59. Has permission to
60. Gorilla, e.g.
61. Pump purchase
63. Sort
64. Frizzy hairdo

Halftime
PUZZLE 5

Pair off the groups of letters to form ten 6-letter names of languages.

ALI	GAE	KOR	PAS	_____	_____
BRE	GER	LIC	REW	_____	_____
DAN	HEB	MAN	SLO	_____	_____
EAN	HTO	NCH	TON	_____	_____
FRE	ISH	NEP	VAK	_____	_____

PUZZLE 6

ACROSS
1. Complain
5. Stage object
9. Turncoat
12. Maturing agent
13. Bellowed
15. Heartache
16. Fashioned
17. Give some gas
18. 100%
19. College figure
20. Undo 14 Down
21. Paper's concern
23. Egyptian symbol
25. Pizzeria appliance
27. Jewish leader
30. Meanie
32. Scale syllables
35. Cast
36. Sandwich choice
38. Specters
41. Unusual
42. Gossip
44. Garden pond dweller
45. Afternoon break
47. Departed
48. Slip up
49. Have bills
50. Underwater sight
52. Art-class models
54. Wildcat
56. Small duck
58. Yucca fiber
61. Above
63. Pitfall
67. Baden-Baden, e.g.
68. Carrying
70. Chest sound
71. Wheel nut
72. Graceful waders
73. Distant
74. Half ems
75. Topped a cake
76. Recipe instruction

DOWN
1. Sleep under the stars
2. Lab gel
3. Change
4. Quickly assembled home
5. Profusion
6. Uncommon
7. Senate bore
8. Favorite
9. Mop
10. Battery terminal
11. Scream
13. Catch some rays
14. Remove from print
22. Scoop
24. Dark time
26. One with a strict diet
27. Greek letters
28. Soundtrack
29. Dampen
31. Canyon
33. Invited
34. Shop
37. Hunger
39. Serengeti scavenger
40. Gentlemen
43. Melted
46. Hawk
51. Foreign
53. Extremes
55. Legendary beast
57. Units of work
58. Capri, e.g.
59. Whirled
60. Names
62. Clamp
64. Huck's transport
65. Wings
66. Collar
69. Kimono sash

PUZZLE 7

Shuffle

Two 6-letter words with their letters in the correct order are combined in each row of letters. To solve the puzzle, separate both words. There are no extra letters, and no letter is used more than once. Helpful hint: the two words are related.

Example: S M Y E S T H T E O M D (SmYeSthTEoMd) = SYSTEM, METHOD

1. C P R E A N Y C I O N L _____ _____
2. B U Z I T T P O P N E R _____ _____
3. O Z R I N C H I N I A D _____ _____
4. G N I U N G T M E R E G _____ _____
5. M O U S Y S E S T E L R _____ _____

PUZZLE 8

ACROSS
1. Skyscraper
6. Burn slightly
10. Dirty air
14. Reflection
15. Healthy
16. Select
17. Swivel
18. Field of study
19. British nobleman
20. Home for swine
21. Among
23. Alpacas' kin
25. Tale teller
26. Getaway
27. Twist
29. Workout room
30. Elbow's site
33. Legume
34. Not certain
37. Pond growth
39. Ornamental edge
40. Bungle
41. Angers
42. Bread bakers
44. Swindle
46. Third letters
47. Tied the knot
48. Decade numeral
50. More frosty
52. Enthusiasm
53. Taunt
54. Part of speech
57. Snazzy
58. Military conflict
61. Sparse
62. Skunk feature
64. Comparable
66. Likewise
67. Fly alone
68. Ms. Day
69. Pretend
70. Wound cover
71. CIA employee

DOWN
1. Waiters' rewards
2. Fail to include
3. Uneven
4. Big head
5. Keep
6. Rocker, e.g.
7. Strenuous
8. Pub serving
9. No kidding?
10. Water vapor
11. Title of respect
12. Southern veggie
13. Firms up
22. Bethlehem trio
24. Tibetan monk
25. Flax product
27. Operate a loom
28. Scampered
29. Greek sandwich
30. Consent
31. Leaf gatherer
32. Eyesore
33. Squander
35. Flowerless plant
36. Frizzy do
38. Lawful
43. Rouse
45. Fuzzy fruit
49. Carve in relief
51. Buzzing insect
52. Snake poison
53. Pulsate
54. Word of lament
55. Printer's term
56. Florist's container
57. Float soda
58. Telegram
59. Related
60. Coffee break
63. Medic
65. Campfire item

Crackers

PUZZLE 9

Test your safecracking skills by rotating the four lettered dials until a common 8-letter word can be read across the middle of the dials.

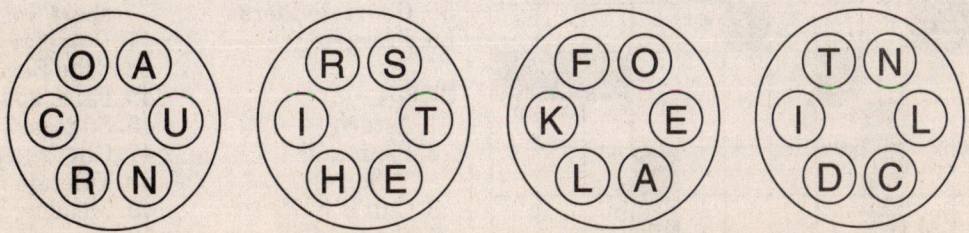

PUZZLE 10

ACROSS
1. Clothing
5. Stuff
9. Priest's robe
12. Place
13. "___ Comes the Sun"
14. Be untruthful
15. Group of birds
16. Theories
17. Informal shirt
18. ___ in a lifetime
20. "All ___ Eve"
22. Distribute
25. Basilica recess
27. Dance like Sammy
28. Empty
30. Adult tadpole
34. More wicked
36. Ready for service
38. Food list
39. Meaning
41. Electrified atom
42. Elderly
44. Unexpected defeat
46. Pantry staple
49. Billions of years
51. Buff
52. Dutch cheese
54. On vacation
58. Cuckoo
59. "Soap" surname
60. Metallic vein
61. However
62. Prayer word
63. Cat's call

DOWN
1. Chew the fat
2. Exist
3. Race, as a motor
4. "Blue ___"
5. Stylish
6. Close again
7. Branch
8. Buttes' kin
9. Choir voice
10. In ___ of (instead of)
11. Sugar source
19. Pacific goose
21. Greek letter
22. News flash
23. "___ the Tiger"
24. Washer cycle
26. Increased by
29. Compel
31. Oriental sashes
32. Healing plant
33. Auto imperfection
35. Maui cookout
37. Overwhelm
40. Think
43. Actress Garbo
45. Hymn
46. Ravel
47. Crescent-shaped figure
48. Final notice
50. Forewarning
53. Aswan or Hoover
55. Grief
56. Big fuss
57. Bow wood

PUZZLE 11

ACROSS
1. Citrus beverage
4. Settee
8. Harsh cry
12. Amusing
13. Footless creature
14. Of an epoch
15. Little kids
17. Mosaic need
18. Lessen
19. Greased
20. Entertained
23. Wisecrack
25. Workout aftermath
26. Went off the springboard
27. Genetic material
30. Plump
32. More creepy
34. Outer coat
35. Caboose's locale
37. Sentry's word
38. Curved line
39. Young horse
40. "Alice" star
44. Goatee's site
46. Did well on
47. Captive
51. Three voices
52. Mother's sister
53. Be in the red
54. Offer for cash
55. Court dividers
56. Procure

DOWN
1. Astern
2. Penn and Teller, e.g.
3. Call it quits
4. Tossed dish
5. Accessible
6. Precede
7. Yellow-pages fillers
8. Sherpa's sighting
9. Nutmeg covering
10. Knitting rib
11. Beseeched
16. Nerd
19. Double curve
20. Reality
21. Mountain feedback
22. Hoodlum
24. Affirm
26. Hair colorist
27. Gauge
28. Jodie Foster film
29. Pretentious
31. Grain husk
33. Horned mammal, for short
36. Accumulate
39. Boxers' weapons
40. Back muscles, for short
41. Property parcel
42. "The Seventh ___"
43. False god
45. Suggest
47. Chef's need
48. Yuletide drink
49. Meadow mama
50. Steep flax

CODEWORD

PUZZLE 12

Codeword is a special crossword puzzle in which conventional clues are omitted. Instead, answer words in the diagram are represented by numbers. Each number represents a different letter of the alphabet, and all of the letters of the alphabet are used. When you are sure of a letter, put it in the code key chart and cross it off in the alphabet box. A group of letters has been inserted to start you off.

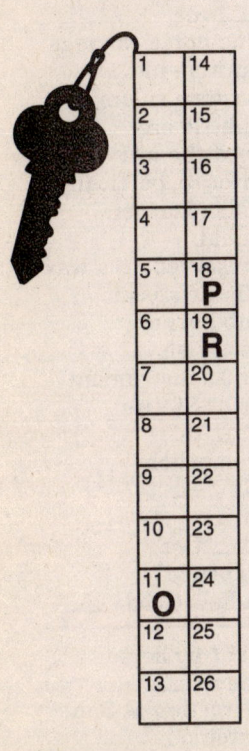

Drop-Outs

PUZZLE 13

The answer to each clue is the name of a famous person whose initials in the clue have been replaced with asterisks. For example, base*all g*eat (baseBall gReat, initials BR) is Babe Ruth.

1. Nehru's offspr*n* _____
2. Dyn*mite's i*ventor _____
3. Frankenstein's *on*ter creator _____
4. Grav*ty scie*tist _____
5. Jazz tru*pet legen* _____
6. Stand-u* come*y pioneer _____
7. Refor*ation *eader _____
8. Notab*e Aida *ortrayer _____
9. "Rhinoc*ros" wr*ter _____
10. A*eri*an impressionist _____

11

PUZZLE 14

• STAR TIME •

ACROSS
1. Anger
4. Actor Grant
8. Judge
12. Young boy
13. Medicinal plant
14. Spew
15. Star of "Adventure in Baltimore"
18. Close tightly
19. Altar vow
20. Wooden stakes
23. Rara ___
26. Cooling device
29. Star of "The Story of Alexander Graham Bell"
32. Mild oath
34. Storage place
35. Letter opener
36. Star of "Ruggles of Red Gap"
39. Colorant
40. Umpire's call
41. Place in office
43. Lawyer's charge
45. Shopping aid
48. Star of "Farewell, My Lovely"
54. German river
55. Church part
56. Actor Vigoda
57. Lairs
58. Mimicked
59. Journalist Rather

DOWN
1. "___ Impossible"
2. College cheers
3. Singer Brickell
4. Phoned
5. Pub order
6. Acuff or Orbison
7. Abominable Snowman
8. Deleted
9. Stereo component
10. Sesame seed
11. Summer, on the Somme
16. Knock sharply
17. Type of cheese
21. Asian desert
22. Tizzies
24. ___ tea
25. One-horse carriage
26. Turkish hat
27. Eastern rulers
28. Shuttle org.
30. Feed the kitty
31. Prior to, poetically
33. Links learners
37. Equal
38. Preserved, in a way
42. Muscle spasm
44. Lab burner
46. Food fish
47. Brass instrument
48. Actor Steiger
49. "___ to Melancholy"
50. Big ___
51. Chart
52. "___ Got Sixpence"
53. "A Few Good ___"

PUZZLE 15

• LI'L DARLING TEXAS •

ACROSS
1. Scarlett's home
5. Circle segment
8. Refrain start
11. Alack's partner
12. Feathery scarf
13. "Bali ___"
14. Part of Texas
17. Put a halt to
18. Pose
19. Majors or Remick
20. Detective Sam ___
22. Glass container
23. Etc.'s relative
24. Blanched
27. Church dignitary
30. English school
31. Ventilate
32. Love, to Pedro
33. Banner
35. Rock
36. Slippery
37. Golf ball mount
38. Rigatoni or spaghetti
40. Cravat
41. Texas export
44. Singer Garfunkel
45. Texas border river
48. Sargasso or Caspian
49. "___ to Joy"
50. Greek portico
51. Pitch
52. Neither's partner
53. 11th president

DOWN
1. Evening bugle call
2. Jai ___
3. Talk wildly
4. Fire remnant
5. "Li'l ___"
6. Went by horse
7. Silent ___
8. Attraction at San Antonio
9. Author Ayn ___
10. Helper
15. "When I was ___ ..."
16. Noble Italian family
21. Sense of taste
22. Female donkey
23. Misstep
24. Vigor
25. Dined
26. Texas symbol
27. "The ___ and the Pendulum"
28. Weight unit
29. Poet's before
31. Some
34. Winged
35. Fortune-teller
37. Striped cat
38. Gone by
39. Zone
40. Fuss
41. Wise in the ways of
42. False god
43. Plumber's problem
46. Charged particle
47. Venomous snake

BRICK BY BRICK

PUZZLE 16

Rearrange this stack of bricks to form a crossword puzzle. The clues will help you fit the bricks into their correct places. Row 1 has been filled in for you. Use the bricks to fill in the remaining spaces.

ACROSS

1. Faction
   Political group
   Venomous serpents
2. Grimm heavy
   Bellowing
   "___ Velvet"
3. Lumber
   Southpaw
   Nee
4. Put apart
   She-sheep
5. Promo spots
   Hunky-dory
   Depend (on)
6. Went frequently
   Records
7. Egg shapes
   Outspoken
   Brawl
8. Brains
   Car style
   Skirt type
9. Take steps
   Loud chimes
   Arctic
10. Piece of prose
    Gauge
11. Builder's map
    Poet's before
    A little bit
12. Astronaut's org.
    Curtail
13. Culture medium
    Meddle
    Like the Mojave
14. Cornmeal loaf
    Limber
    Pal, in Perth
15. Seasoned
    Spy
    Or ___!

DOWN

1. Piglet's mother
   Fragrance
   Wine valley
2. Self-importance
   Tool
   Amazed
3. Flaky rolls
   Rational
4. Danson and Kennedy
   Antique
   Pardoned
5. Dory sticks
   Lass
6. Earmark
   Asian legume
   Yosemite ___
7. Avoid surplus or debt
   Romantic dance
8. Raised bed
   Avoid
   Steam
9. Horse opera
   One-dish meal
10. Produce tears
    Flourish
    Rubbish
11. Diamond ___
    Dappled
12. Monasteries
    Dad's partner
    Pastime
13. Obtuse
    Three-sided
14. Undiluted
    "Moonlight ___"
    ___ a boy!
15. D.C. figs.
    Telegraphed
    Cee's follower

BRICKS

E D A		I		E S		E	A		I D G
N G S		A D S		T	E		D	M	P A

D	S	N A S		I N I		M I N		A
	G O	A G A		L A R		A C T		R S

E	M	E		A B R		R O A		E S
		E	R I D	N O O		E F T		

O R T		S A Y		A T E		S O L		E
L S		P L A		T A D		A O		E L Y

E	A	E D		A T E		O G R		W E S
D	L	V O C		K	R	W O O		

P O N		T S		A T E		R E S		N M
A G E		R O W		L S E		O V A		P O

L U E		R		B		T I M		L I S		G I L
O R N		Y	B		R E		A L		O L E

DIAGRAM

	1	2	3	4	5	6	7	8	9	10	11	12	13	14	15
1	S	E	C	T	■	■	B	L	O	C	■	A	S	P	S
2															
3															
4															
5															
6															
7															
8															
9															
10															
11															
12															
13															
14															
15															

PUZZLE 17

ACROSS
1. Info
5. Grimm monster
9. State further
12. Hubbubs
13. Target
14. Cry of disapproval
15. Abominable Snowman
16. Trademark
17. Shocking fish
18. Hair tint
20. Clergyman
22. MTV feature
25. Fleecy females
27. Before, in poems
28. Patron
30. Stored
34. Large amount
35. Fury
36. Batman and Robin, e.g.
37. Conscious of
39. Helsinki native
41. Mischievous youth
42. Poker-pot stake
44. Small amounts
46. Hooded jacket
49. One of Santa's helpers
50. Flightless bird
51. Fizzy beverage
54. V
58. Clump
59. Tease
60. Corrupt
61. Cloud's location
62. Strong desires
63. Deli breads

DOWN
1. Night's opposite
2. Lime beverage
3. Little one
4. Stage remark
5. Gape
6. Sticky stuff
7. Tatter
8. Wed secretly
9. Retired
10. Go-getter
11. Give (out)
19. Part of IOU
21. Inquire
22. Presidential rejection
23. Cast or wrought
24. Auto-mishap reminder
25. Scary
26. Little bird
29. Baking direction
31. Revise a manuscript
32. Mountain cat
33. Spinning toys
38. Acorn producer
40. Zilch
43. Mean
45. Make a bid
46. Small dowels
47. Berserk
48. Red stone
49. Enjoys lunch
52. Be indebted to
53. Commotion
55. Kind of league
56. Be competitive
57. Subways' cousins

PUZZLE 18

ACROSS
1. Switch positions
4. Frenzied
8. Crochet
12. Jungle snake
13. Low in fat
14. Give a job to
15. "Holiday ___"
16. Informed of
17. Toward shelter
18. Bus fare
20. Chinese skillet
22. Appendages
25. Ms. Laurie
29. Clothes line?
32. Volcanic flow
34. Dazzle
35. Hook's foe
36. Wicked person
37. Third letter
38. Go on stage
39. Virginia dance
40. Writing surface
41. The items here
43. Remove, in printing
45. One + one
47. Convent
51. Up to the task
54. Spent
57. How ___ you?
58. Fly high
59. Clock with a watch
60. Zipped
61. Song of praise
62. Shock
63. Highway curve

DOWN
1. Newspaper notice
2. Taboo
3. Plunged
4. Unaccompanied
5. Guys
6. Cereal grass
7. Be aware
8. Army fabric
9. Zilch
10. Hot temper
11. Ball holder
19. Tall tree
21. Whitish gem
23. Singing club
24. Put away
26. Rate of speed
27. Flock members
28. Foul smell
29. Small dispute
30. To ___ his own
31. Poker chip-in
33. Nasty
36. Sketched
40. Society gal
42. Ship section
44. Encumbered
46. Pitchers' goals
48. Unclothed
49. Important ages
50. Hankerings
51. Blond shade
52. Lad
53. Getaway
55. Command to Fido
56. Flightless bird

PUZZLE 19

ACROSS
1. Pale gray
4. Tumbled
8. Cassette, e.g.
12. ___ is me!
13. Location
14. Final, e.g.
15. Piece of corn
16. Cup's lip
17. List of options
18. Salivate
20. Egyptian snake
22. IOU
25. Seeped
29. Rant
32. Oboe's need
34. Mine deposit
35. Unit
36. Actress Blair
37. Capture
38. Broke a fast
39. Highly excited
40. Dilemma
41. Bus station
43. Change decor
45. Which person?
47. Put to use
51. Cry
54. Smart kid
57. Pro vote
58. Burn reliever
59. Pleasing
60. Sunday seat
61. Mar
62. Zoomed
63. Burro

DOWN
1. Dazzled
2. Float aloft
3. Brave person
4. Aesop's specialty
5. Bungle
6. Floral wreath
7. Tibetan monk
8. Rhythm
9. Wood cutter
10. Frying need
11. Australian bird
19. Poetic work
21. Pop
23. Military prison
24. Choir member
26. District
27. Important times
28. Young society entrants
29. Avenue
30. Feed the kitty
31. Al Gore, e.g.
33. Margin
36. Thin strip
40. Swab
42. Small hooter
44. Stunned
46. Holds
48. Mama's mate
49. Soap-making substances
50. Evergreen plants
51. Horrible
52. Ginger beverage
53. Overcame
55. ___-hop
56. Polar sight

PUZZLE 20

ACROSS

1. One on Santa's payroll
4. Understood
8. Pitfall
12. Spoil
13. Walk in the woods
14. Furor
15. "___ as directed"
16. Cut down
17. Atop
18. Arab chief
20. Rested
22. Verve
24. Top
28. Peppy
31. Vow
34. Rowing tool
35. Ginger ___
36. 1 + 1
37. Connection
38. Word of assent
39. Emeril Lagasse, e.g.
40. Battlefield vehicle
41. Hot sauce
43. Yuck!
45. Morsel for an aardvark
47. Melodic
51. Bite
54. Stereo
57. Raw metal
58. Helper
59. Sulfuric ___
60. Casino cube
61. Oozed
62. Had being
63. Winding curve

DOWN

1. Flightless birds
2. Actor La Rue
3. Liberate
4. Neutral color
5. Veto
6. ___ out
7. Gets hitched
8. Actuality
9. Thump
10. Back in time
11. Stockade
19. Poison ___
21. Cinder
23. Destructive insect
25. Bit
26. Drizzle
27. Excursion
28. States
29. Guilty, e.g.
30. ___ estate
32. Dumbfound
33. Bean curd
39. Preserve
40. "___ will be done..."
42. Cut
44. Soar
46. Melt
48. Took a howdah
49. Garden bloomer
50. Average grades
51. Gossip
52. Naught
53. Tangy beverage
55. "The ___ Storm"
56. Pine tree

PUZZLE 21

ACROSS
1. Deep sadness
4. Senseless
8. Like some wine
12. Build on
13. Wight, e.g.
14. More than a few
15. Egg drink
16. Therefore
17. Other than
18. Pick up the check
20. Decimal base
22. Bird of peace
25. Valuable thing
29. Begs
32. Withdraw
34. Wonderment
35. Frying utensil
36. Smidgen
37. Aggravate
38. ___ trip
39. Caesar's city
40. Compass point
41. Jewish cleric
43. Scarf
45. Elect
47. Looking at
51. Bewildered
54. Lined up
57. Bill and ___
58. Contented murmur
59. Walking aid
60. Wrap up
61. ___ off (angry)
62. Had unpaid bills
63. Two, to Pedro

DOWN
1. Crave
2. Scent
3. Sidle
4. The same
5. Speck of residue
6. Winter ailment
7. Pop quiz
8. Prayer finales
9. Maiden
10. Printers' measures
11. Color
19. Promos
21. Have a bite
23. President's no
24. Quizzes
26. Collect
27. Female wool growers
28. Writing
29. Impersonator
30. History
31. Door feature
33. Concept
39. Slit
40. How come?
42. Room and ___
44. Stitched
46. Mexican food
48. Froze
49. Taboo
50. Olympians
51. Skillful
52. Take legal action
53. Browning's before
55. Unrefined
56. Single

PUZZLE 22

ACROSS

1. More than
5. Nursery bed
9. French peak
12. In ___ of
13. Hippy dance
14. Flirt with
15. Farmer's locale?
16. Unattractive
17. Come to a close
18. Nog need
20. Desert stops
22. Ling-Ling, e.g.
25. Daylight source
26. Consume
27. Smeller
30. Small coin
34. Kind of room
35. Fence doors
37. Take a nap
38. Huron, e.g.
40. Spelling error
41. Haze
42. Subway posters
44. Pain
46. Comment
49. Lingerie item
50. Ventilate
51. Pinch
54. Gentle
58. Not con
59. Pairs
60. October gem
61. Make a quilt
62. Evergreen shrubs
63. Salesmen

DOWN

1. On in years
2. Compete
3. Slippery fish
4. Reigned
5. Train sound
6. Shag or plush, e.g.
7. Ailing
8. Louisiana marsh
9. Terrifies
10. The ___ Ranger
11. Seed vessels
19. Posse
21. Plus
22. Knit's opposite
23. Floating
24. Bottle part
25. Ooze
28. Feeling one's ___
29. Hog's home
31. Data
32. "Blue ___"
33. Irritable
36. Coast up high
39. Gobble
43. Goddess, e.g.
45. Croc's cousin
46. Plant juices
47. Wear down
48. Lined up
49. Deep tone
52. Be in hock
53. Draw behind
55. Impersonate
56. Outline
57. High tracks

19

PUZZLE 23

ACROSS
1. Mas' mates
4. Follow orders
8. Romp
12. Little demon
13. Lose interest
14. Prospector's find
15. Ostrichlike animal
16. Trumpet, e.g.
17. On the summit of
18. Evade
20. It follows Fri.
22. Give guns to
24. Fragrant wood
28. G-men
31. Per
34. ___ trip
35. Caustic material
36. Unwarranted
37. Preceded
38. Electric or moray
39. Without clothes
40. Choice word
41. Bracelet site
43. Burrow
45. Tree-trunk section
47. Flirted
51. Pale
54. Emend copy
57. One who excels
58. Fruit cover
59. Canned fish
60. "Murder, ___ Wrote"
61. Simple
62. Male descendants
63. Lay turf

DOWN
1. Like a certain piper
2. Bullets and bombs
3. Potato
4. Different
5. Life story, for short
6. Misstep
7. Yearns
8. License or dinner
9. Batch
10. "Much ___ About Nothing"
11. Nope's opposite
19. Ford fuel
21. Throb with pain
23. Waitperson's handout
25. Wooded valley
26. Matures
27. Went by horse
28. Soared
29. Observer
30. Corned-beef source
32. Total (up)
33. Hinted
36. Golden-rule word
40. Omelet necessity
42. Sneakily
44. Fragments
46. Fetches
48. Young lady
49. Mountain sound
50. Title of ownership
51. Zoo attraction
52. Baltic or Black
53. "___ So Fine"
55. Hall and Oates, e.g.
56. Country hotel

PUZZLE 24

ACROSS
1. Fruit pastry
4. Fit of temper
8. Bread unit
12. Do sums
13. Music system
14. Lion's pad
15. Flower wreath
16. Alternative word
17. Military
18. Not glossy
20. Barnyard male
22. Verbal
25. Luxury boat
29. Blemish
32. Wick
34. Deposit eggs
35. Cut
36. Curved line
37. Matterhorn, e.g.
38. Birthday number
39. Surface measure
40. Poker term
41. Actor Karloff
43. Fall behind
45. Place for clouds
47. Tiny bits
51. Sonnets' kin
54. Unpaid
57. Pitcher's stat
58. Doozie
59. Oxen team
60. Feel awful
61. Medicine amount
62. Small bills
63. Large rodent

DOWN
1. Tropical tree
2. Inkling
3. Rework text
4. Transparent
5. Zero
6. ___, ands, or buts
7. Row level
8. Andes climber
9. Rowboat need
10. Attempt
11. Saute
19. Skier's line
21. Yes, to Popeye
23. A long way off
24. Attracted
26. Family
27. Cease
28. Kind
29. Fat
30. Company symbol
31. Imitator
33. Battle memento
39. Query
40. Give it ___
42. Distribute
44. Clerks
46. String toy
48. Eye drop
49. Opera solo
50. Season
51. ___-fashioned
52. Couple
53. Overhead trains
55. Took the prize
56. ___ out (barely make)

PUZZLE 25

ACROSS
1. Atlantic fish
6. Cheerio
10. Boor
13. Minted
15. Skating jump
16. "___ Gang"
17. Electrical unit
18. Circle
19. Had pizza
20. Born as
21. Sashes
23. Radiant
25. Hoopla
26. Egg producer
27. Cover charge
29. Wight, e.g.
32. Refs
36. Creep
38. Angel's instrument
40. Stout
41. Dawdle
42. Front tooth
45. Connect
46. Trouble
47. Sod
48. Many times
50. Court response
52. Fable
54. Neath's opposite
55. Young bear
57. At all
60. Towels, e.g.
63. Diva Callas
65. River barrier
68. Lemon drink
69. Rock mass
71. Flee
73. Caspian ___
74. Olympic sled
75. Garden tool
76. Dupe
77. Head sheik
78. Rent contract

DOWN
1. Examine
2. Draw near
3. Primed
4. Buck
5. Horse race
6. Vinegary
7. Rotation center
8. Twice five
9. Water plants
10. Ember
11. Sedan, e.g.
12. Doodled
14. Not shallow
22. Oahu gift
24. African animal
25. Chop
26. Leading man
27. Delicate
28. Bald bird
30. Move
31. Scale notes
33. Dull finish
34. Gripping tool
35. Noticed
36. Applaud
37. Ignited
39. Tennis expert
43. Unfeeling
44. Shed tears
49. In favor of
51. Top card
53. That girl
56. ___ Sam
58. Regard
59. Tripod
60. Glasgow girl
61. Thought
62. Kind of tide
63. Wise men
64. Teen follower
65. Baby's father
66. Copies
67. Simple
70. Pirate's drink
72. Letter before dee

PUZZLE 26

ACROSS
1. Pads
6. Hornet
10. Boring tools
14. Correct
15. Female voice
16. Trench ___
17. ___ board
18. Objective
19. Oompah horn
20. Commotion
21. Frequently
23. Rent out
24. Charred
27. Pamper
29. ___ trip
32. Bro's sib
33. Charge
34. Pampered
36. Small fry
37. Yearn
41. Fair-haired
42. Demeanor
43. Pamphlet
44. Drip
45. Lemon drink
46. Court clown
47. Ball callers
49. Weed tool
50. Subways' kin
51. Magazine VIP
54. Angrily
56. Decay
57. Chomper
59. Stench
63. Stunned
65. Cheats
66. Clay brick
67. Partly
68. Grimm heavy
69. Immerse again
70. Choice word
71. Playthings
72. Congeals

DOWN
1. Brood
2. Luxury car
3. Ripened
4. Beat
5. Pigpen
6. Carriages
7. Soaring
8. RBI or ERA
9. Skunk
10. Take steps
11. Part of WWJD
12. Sticker
13. Say
22. Likewise not
25. Pre-owned
26. Free (of)
28. Contracts
29. Declines
30. Gust
31. Thin woodwind
33. Not anti
35. Data
36. Secure
38. Mention
39. Foot part
40. Fouls up
42. Promos
43. Detect
45. Peachlike fruit
46. Scribble
48. Horde
49. Colts, e.g.
51. Wipe clean
52. Wooden peg
53. Objects
54. Mr. Fonda
55. Alpine song
58. Takeout
60. Dummy
61. Final bio
62. Agts.
64. Casino cube
66. Rainbow

PUZZLE 27

ACROSS
1. Polynesian picnic
5. Snatch
9. Issued by Benedict XVI
14. Alike
15. Atmosphere
16. Coldly
17. Big rig
18. Jewels
19. Guide
20. Ski-lift type
22. Stolen
24. Poor grade
25. Finisher
28. Atomic bit
30. ___ whiz!
31. Junk mail
34. Most sick
37. Tear roughly
38. Leafy lunch
40. Thick
42. Inner selves
44. Blends
46. John Doe, e.g.
47. Ache
49. Some tides
51. Metal box
52. Potent
54. Situate
55. Certain dashes
56. Eden dweller
57. Push gently
59. Taxi
62. "___ De-lovely"
64. Circle parts
66. Abundance
68. VCR need
70. Phonograph
74. Foolish
75. Had debts
76. Level
77. Quarrels
78. Joins
79. Dark breads

DOWN
1. Spanish article
2. Hilo strings
3. Intent
4. Bond
5. Nuts
6. Regretful type
7. Give guns to
8. Pound
9. Revolvers
10. Play a role
11. Dappled
12. Skipper's command
13. Old harp
21. Lingerie items
23. Wildcatter's quest
25. Wading bird
26. Whinnies
27. Banish
29. Light stuff?
32. Flood control
33. Hurl
34. Flawless
35. Scheduled
36. It's everything!
39. Hewing tool
41. Heavily populated
43. Aching
45. Fitness club
48. Cows
50. Harmony
53. Web
58. Escort
59. Hairdo
60. Skin breakout
61. A Bridges
63. Store away
64. Imitated
65. Ohio team
67. Furthermore
69. Respectful fear
71. Yale climber
72. Charge
73. Not outs

PUZZLE 28

ACROSS
1. Hot tubs
5. Emerald ___
9. Croc's relative
14. Twist
15. Double
16. Knowledgeable
17. Singing voice
18. Seasoning
19. Advances
20. Mexican money
21. Insult
23. Goodness!
24. Pen part
27. Bee chaser
28. Wound
29. Disburden
32. Jazz job
34. Simple
36. "We ___ the Champions"
37. Christmas carol
39. Slogan
43. Apartment
45. Permit
47. Colder
48. Make certain
50. Nerve
52. Gear part
53. Passive
55. Gunk
56. Shady
57. Hinged fastener
60. Sass
62. Crooked
64. Lodge member
65. Dither
67. Certain gem
71. Lions' sounds
74. Precious
76. Give (out)
77. Drawn from a keg
78. Hosiery hue
79. Extra
80. Wanting
81. Remains
82. Gaze

DOWN
1. Substitute
2. "___ Rider"
3. Carney et al.
4. Ladle
5. Possessive pronoun
6. Clean the decks
7. Purple shrub
8. Main course
9. Lass
10. Amaze
11. Latin dance
12. Direct
13. Witness again
22. Balance ___
25. Snub
26. Personal history, shortly
28. Harmony
29. "Rat ___"
30. Heavy metal
31. TV rooms
33. Hairstyling aid
35. Seaman
38. Relay portion
40. Twitches
41. Not bogus
42. Military
44. Throw away
46. Ticket
49. Long fishes
51. Cow sound
54. More giving
57. Egret, e.g.
58. Marooned
59. Glide
61. Section
63. Alpine song
66. Covers a roof
68. Mallet game
69. Too
70. Bulb plant
72. Cool!
73. Bond, e.g.
75. Groove

PUZZLE 29

ACROSS
1. Rage
6. Small store
10. Large drum
14. Of sound
15. Mime
16. Border
17. Bend in prayer
18. Presented
19. "Of ___ I Sing"
20. Hook shape
21. Milk farms
24. Shelley poem
25. Rink judge
26. Fastened
28. Instinctive
32. Shabby
33. Masters
34. Massage
36. Pool of water
40. Small sausages
42. Sparkler
44. Mr. Karloff
45. Merchant
47. Yak
49. Twist
50. Pitcher
52. Harness track
54. Soundproofing
58. Terrible
59. Johnny ___
60. Films again
62. Can cover
65. Soprano's solo
67. Ripple
68. ___-baked potato
70. Long skirt
71. Barely makes
72. Tart fruit
73. Clairvoyant
74. Slight hollow
75. Dark wood

DOWN
1. Rouse from sleep
2. Operates
3. Summer coolers
4. Four-in-hand
5. Container
6. Wise travelers
7. Divided
8. Study
9. Elm's summit
10. Fly swatter
11. Loathe
12. Textured leather
13. Knight mare?
22. Miles away
23. Bush
25. Crinkled
27. Bestowed
28. Takes
29. Estate unit
30. Duck
31. Type of nut
35. Ask humbly
37. Shootout shout
38. Pisa dough, once
39. Spot
41. Drain
43. Blemish
46. Subscribed again
48. Newborn
51. Second shooting
53. King's home
54. Weight units
55. Strange
56. Remain
57. Crow's kin
61. Annoying thing
62. Celeb's transport
63. Church picture
64. Turn down
66. ___ conditioner
69. Entanglement

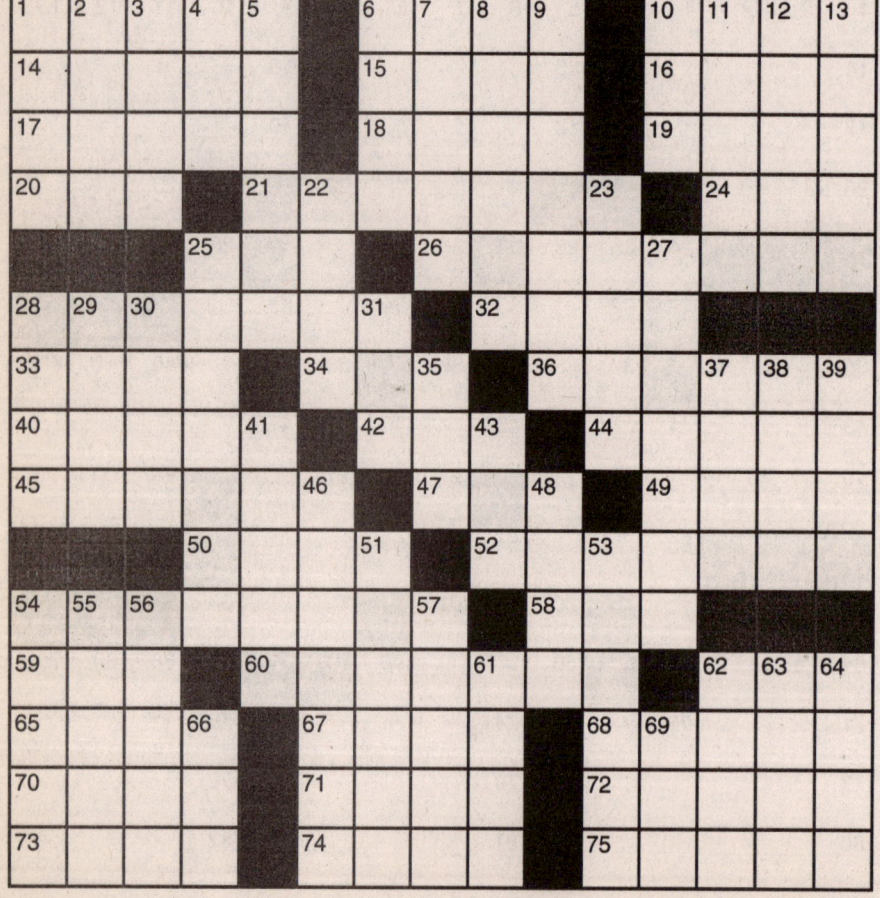

PUZZLE 30

ACROSS
1. Reserved
4. Noose
8. Assert
13. Mai ___
14. Entice
15. Called up
16. Heidi's mount
17. Liberal ___
18. Lengthen
19. Chest
21. Single unit
23. Pigpen
24. Distort
27. Final word
30. Pistol
32. Pledge
34. Clod
37. In shape
38. Keats' ajar
39. Drifting
41. Thin strip
43. Latin dance
45. Dilly
46. Uptight
48. Average
49. Backdrop
50. Honest
51. Shock
52. Mr. Kennedy
53. Buddhist monk
55. BLT spread
57. Ger. neighbor
60. Ref's cousin
62. Enter
66. Foreign
69. Otherwise
72. Goof up
73. Bake again
74. Film holder
75. Ripen
76. Familiar
77. Knotted
78. Cay

DOWN
1. Attempt
2. Light ring
3. Barks
4. Pack animal
5. "___ Gang"
6. Food scrap
7. Mexican coin
8. Half-dozen
9. Make lace
10. Pub pints
11. Pup ___
12. Whirl
15. Reckon
20. Admit
22. Slangy no
25. Spacious
26. Daddy
28. Pixie
29. Void's pal
30. Titan
31. Articulate
33. Cadence
35. Rodent
36. Blanched
37. Winter shot
39. Main artery
40. For shame!
42. Transport
44. Soothing salve
47. ___ urchin
51. Preserves
52. Great weight
54. Mire
56. Produce
57. Brew coffee
58. Farm team
59. Loony tunes
61. Bouncy
63. High point
64. Impulse
65. Poker three
67. Pull behind
68. Charged particle
70. Luau garland
71. Perceive

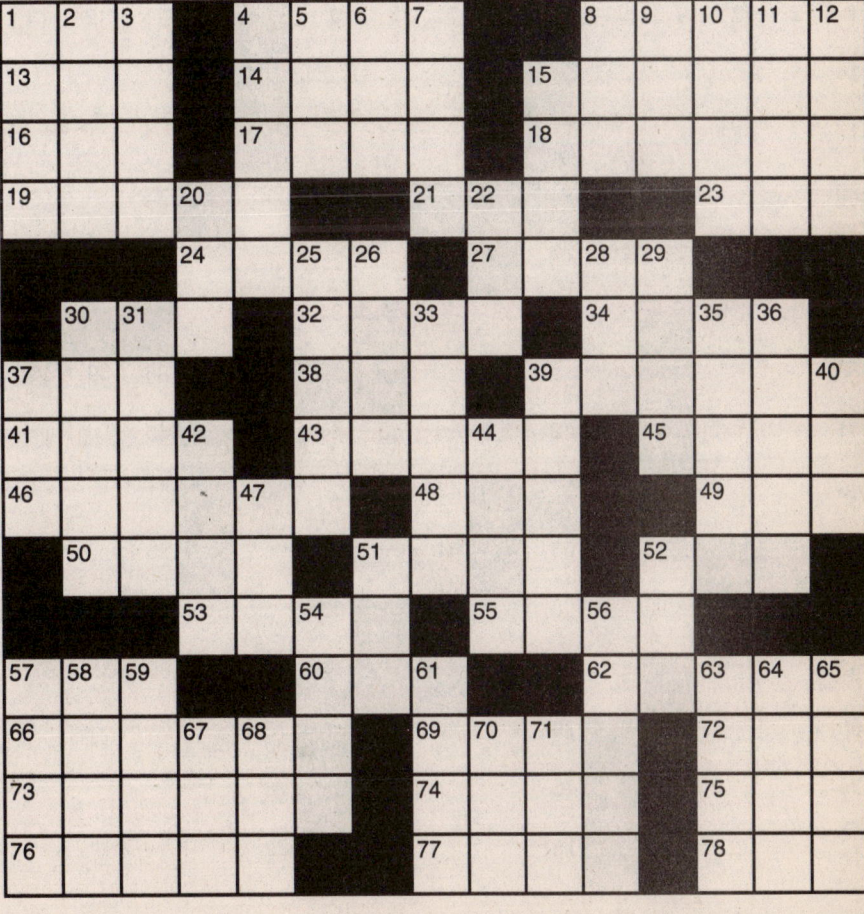

PUZZLE 31

ACROSS
1. Soccer, e.g.
6. Pulverize
10. Some vipers
14. Brief role
15. Female voice
16. Hone
17. Attentive
18. Sail pole
19. Erie or Huron
20. Computer list
21. Wrath
23. Heartbreak
24. Capture
27. Humbled oneself
29. Murky
32. Judge's garb
34. Dweller's bldg.
35. Fish eggs
36. Night orb
37. Expensive
41. Depot abbr.
42. Boxing period
45. Block
46. Electrical units
49. Eye part
51. Undies item
52. Rower's need
54. Mane site
55. Like a fox?
56. Frenzied rush
60. Make a quilt
62. Young boy
63. This lass
64. Eliminate
68. Press
70. Besides
73. Evaluate
74. Wrenched
75. Put aboard
76. Fall flower
77. Beef dish
78. Goldie ___
79. Hot vapor

DOWN
1. Ripoff
2. Whiten
3. Foretoken
4. TV repeat
5. Little child
6. More, to Juan
7. Matterhorn, e.g.
8. Step
9. Type of film
10. Hole punch
11. Wool wrap
12. Type of tea
13. Horse
22. Nights before
25. Coat sleeve
26. Dolt
27. Real
28. Boston winter hrs.
29. Sketched
30. Bit
31. Protein source
33. Heckler's call
38. Fades away
39. James ___ Jones
40. Speak to God
43. New Deal org.
44. Dunks
47. Huck's pal
48. Depletes
50. Behold
53. Discuss again
56. Narrow cuts
57. Gypsy's card
58. Cherish
59. River deposit
61. Most terrible
65. Companion
66. Notion
67. Semester
69. Just released
71. Pig
72. Have deed to
73. Furnace fuel

PUZZLE 32

ACROSS
1. Vamoose!
6. Hymn closer
10. Type of tennis court
14. Fuming
15. Fabric weave
16. Fireman's need
17. Autry et al.
18. Flirty look
19. Freshly
20. Once owned
21. Query
23. Districts
24. Way station
26. Acts
30. Effuse
32. Graduate, briefly
33. Go ___ better
36. Decree
37. Just say no
38. May queen?
39. Unfamiliar
42. Casino cube
43. Regretful people
45. Go wrong
46. Bee Gees, e.g.
48. Guys, not dolls
49. Fido, e.g.
50. Lively dance
51. Skilled
54. Flare-up
57. Dried mud
59. Play a guitar
61. Tack on
63. Bring to court
64. Engine noise
65. Bill collector?
68. Regularly
70. Breed of steed
71. Sported
72. Bird's perch
73. Be a moocher
74. Lady's man
75. Liquefies

DOWN
1. Groans
2. Make
3. Jumbled
4. Consumed
5. Butte
6. Came to
7. Periodical, briefly
8. House wing
9. Maiden-named
10. Bewitch
11. Homesick
12. Floundering
13. Some evergreens
22. Spit
23. Brink's car
25. ___ vault
27. Filled pasta
28. Skedaddle
29. Away
31. Frenzy
34. Neither
35. Middle of summer
39. Cleo's serpent
40. Falsity
41. Part of IRS
42. Slim down
44. No longer mint
47. Agent, shortly
48. Straight, e.g.
52. Revolver
53. Most loyal
55. English football
56. Rowed
58. Tepees, e.g.
59. Box
60. Radial, e.g.
62. Student's digs
65. It hoots
66. Pursue
67. Be in the wrong
69. Enemy

PUZZLE 33

ACROSS
1. Tall tree
4. Chilled
8. Hit a hole in one
12. Scarf
13. Cobras, e.g.
15. Dimwit
16. Vagrant
17. Dimple
18. Came to ground
19. Assert
21. Man's title
22. Liver spread
23. Certain viper
25. Fine rain
27. Most intelligent
32. Phonograph records
35. Pronoun
36. Map books
38. Lower limb
40. Song of praise
41. Elec. measure
42. Above, in poems
43. Needle's cousin
44. Fasteners
48. Snow blade
49. Rustic house
51. Kindest
53. Hideous
55. To's mate
56. Plunders
59. Have a bite
61. Utter
65. Border on
66. High pitch
69. Hound
70. Toppled
71. Trapped
72. Journal
73. Toddler
74. Narrow board
75. Subways' kin

DOWN
1. Fades away
2. Oaf
3. Papa's lady
4. Tourist's stop
5. Rascal
6. ___ out (barely earns)
7. Blue fabric
8. Conforms
9. Soda flavor
10. Fix copy
11. Love to excess
13. Nap
14. Step
20. Road material
24. Stroke gently
26. Bro's sib
27. Mart
28. Doc
29. Sports venue
30. Hockey shot
31. Pounds down
33. Seal a deal
34. Looks for
37. Erupt
39. Sand
44. Sharp turn
45. Coves
46. TKO caller
47. Waited on tables
50. Flurry
52. Excessive
54. Tales
56. River craft
57. Yield to commands
58. Majority
60. Type of duck
62. Out of action
63. Groovy!
64. ___ Benedict
67. Swimsuit top
68. Say yes to

OVERLAPS

PUZZLE 34

Place the answer to each clue into the diagram beginning at the corresponding number. Words will overlap with other words.

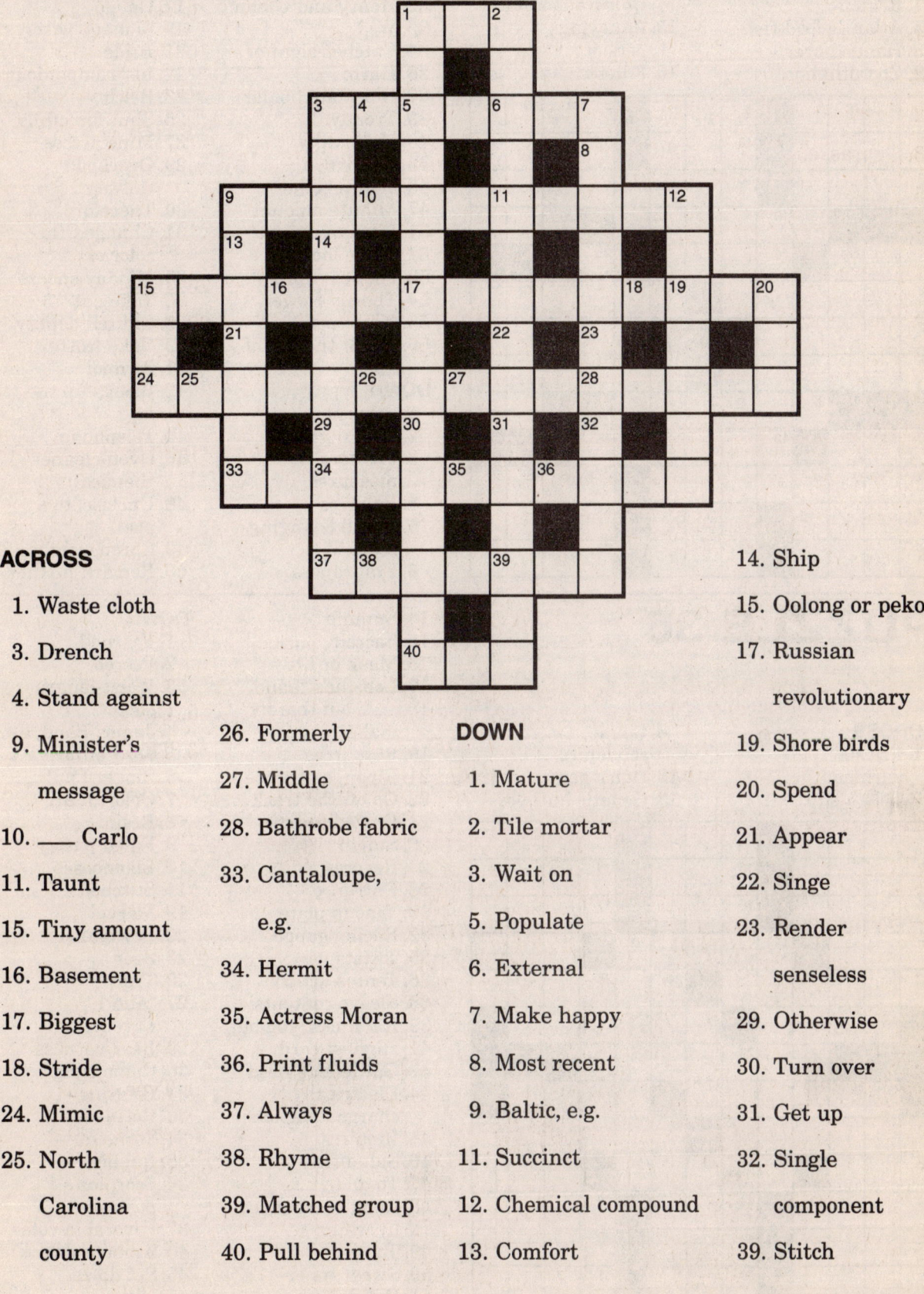

ACROSS

1. Waste cloth
3. Drench
4. Stand against
9. Minister's message
10. ___ Carlo
11. Taunt
15. Tiny amount
16. Basement
17. Biggest
18. Stride
24. Mimic
25. North Carolina county
26. Formerly
27. Middle
28. Bathrobe fabric
33. Cantaloupe, e.g.
34. Hermit
35. Actress Moran
36. Print fluids
37. Always
38. Rhyme
39. Matched group
40. Pull behind

DOWN

1. Mature
2. Tile mortar
3. Wait on
5. Populate
6. External
7. Make happy
8. Most recent
9. Baltic, e.g.
11. Succinct
12. Chemical compound
13. Comfort
14. Ship
15. Oolong or pekoe
17. Russian revolutionary
19. Shore birds
20. Spend
21. Appear
22. Singe
23. Render senseless
29. Otherwise
30. Turn over
31. Get up
32. Single component
39. Stitch

31

PUZZLE 35

ACROSS
1. Region
5. Atlantic food fish
8. Handed over
12. Coordination
13. Fuss
14. Culture medium
15. Annoying person
16. Filleted
18. Frightens
20. Movie backdrop
21. Spinner's work
24. Attacks
26. Green lizard
28. Like river mouths
32. Henry and Glenn
33. Wed
34. Catches sight of
36. Harm
37. Hot-plate holder
39. Trendy
40. Unhealthy
43. Concealed
45. Join together
47. Minute amount
51. Like an omelet
52. Make lace
53. Footless animal
54. Thorny flower
55. "Chances ___"
56. Grant the use of

DOWN
1. Serpent
2. Cereal grain
3. Printers' measures
4. Behaves
5. Beach changing-room
6. Fragrances
7. Gift receivers
8. "My ___ Sal"
9. Grows older
10. Flower jar
11. Formerly, formerly
17. Gauge
19. Manage wisely
21. Bride
22. Ids' companions
23. Belch
25. Shut forcefully
27. Mine access
29. Overhead railway
30. Therefore
31. Changed the color of
35. Midday snooze
36. Take out
38. Church deputy
40. Cake froster
41. Symbol
42. Brings up the rear
44. Telephone
46. Oven-cleaner chemical
48. Unclose, to a poet
49. Cargo weight
50. Remark further

PUZZLE 36

ACROSS
1. Priests' garments
5. Lobe's site
8. Luau souvenirs
12. Hen's pen
13. Genetic initials
14. Summit
15. Sacred
16. Mask or lift
17. Lobster's "hand"
18. ___ out (barely make)
19. Resources
21. Ripen, as cheese
22. Go off the track
24. Proved untrue
26. Sullen
27. Reveres
28. Entrance
30. Teacup plate
32. Racing gauge
35. Twists
36. Tennis action
38. Sleeve contents
39. It'll knock you out
41. Highest card
42. Gardener's need
44. Electrically charged particle
45. Inquires
46. Salad fish
47. To-and-___
48. Land surrounded by water
49. Tense
50. Sweet tuber
51. Deli loaves

DOWN
1. Yearned
2. Peered
3. Waist-length jacket
4. James Bond, e.g.
5. Ford failure
6. Singer Paul ___
7. Colorful arc
8. Resin
9. Filled pastry
10. Likenesses
11. Stitched
19. Marvel
20. Lawmaker
23. Seer
25. True
27. "And I Love ___"
29. Bear witness
30. Camouflage
31. Pointing
33. Refined
34. Torment
35. Rubbish
36. Scorpion's poison
37. Favorable votes
40. Kibbutz dance
43. Set down
45. Ditty

DOUBLE TROUBLE

PUZZLE 37

Not really double trouble, but double fun! Solve this puzzle as you would a regular crossword, except place one, two, or three letters in each box. The number of letters in each answer is shown in parentheses after its clue.

ACROSS
1. Thin tuft (4)
3. Loud uproar (6)
6. Sunshade (7)
9. Tune (4)
10. Country home (5)
11. Merry (7)
12. Native (8)
14. Leash (6)
16. Mailed (4)
17. Claim (6)
19. Keepsake (7)
21. Guard (6)
23. Ticket remnant (4)
25. Great commotion (7)
28. Pack away (4)
29. Tell (6)
31. Unable to move (5)
32. Set free (7)
35. Small valley (4)
36. Wee (5)
37. Pure (6)
39. Chore (6)
41. Final (4)
43. Impede (6)
45. Upright (8)
48. Apronlike garment (8)
50. Uttered (6)
52. Care for (4)
53. Hunting dog (6)
54. Troublesome (7)
55. Listen to (4)

DOWN
1. Sagacity (6)
2. Mooch (6)
3. Collarbone (8)
4. Pepper grinder (4)
5. Make a speech (5)
6. Time gone by (4)
7. Pay increase (5)
8. Acetone, e.g. (7)
11. Seethe (7)
13. Delay (5)
15. Subject (5)
18. Hand movement (7)
20. Guided trip (4)
21. Minister (6)
22. Mason's tool (6)
24. Sword part (5)
26. Dampen (7)
27. Fortunate (5)
30. Bank employee (6)
33. Apiece (4)
34. Coast (8)
36. Gentle (6)
38. Sports group (4)
40. Starving (8)
41. Slip-up (5)
42. Work shift (5)
44. Individual (6)
46. One-tenth tax (5)
47. Date chart (8)
49. Following (5)
51. Gambling game (5)

In the Middle

PUZZLE 38

Fill in the squares to form a word that is the missing link to connect the two given words. For example, if the two given words were CRAB and SAUCE, the missing link would be APPLE (Crab apple, Applesauce).

1. PICTURE / BOX
2. NEWS / HEAD
3. HORSE / STEERING

PUZZLE 39

ACROSS
1. Flex
5. Former European coin
10. Sour
14. Declare
15. Silly
16. Medieval weapon
17. Tour-de-France entrants
19. Once ___ a time
20. Large deer
21. Despise
22. Special ability
24. Grade
25. Counterfeit
26. Pointy tooth
29. Freedom of action
33. Expert
34. Breakfast sizzler
35. Buddy
36. Excellent review
37. Cavalry weapon
38. Await action
39. Notable era
40. Adjust
41. Fool
42. Depot
44. Boundary
45. Matinee ___
46. Misfortune
47. Fish catcher
50. Vanished
51. Lip
54. Heavy metal
55. Unable to read
58. "A Whiter Shade of ___"
59. Make fun of
60. High cards
61. Fight
62. European viper
63. Sapphires, e.g.

DOWN
1. Newborn
2. Sinister
3. Tie's location
4. Like some martinis
5. Expand
6. Merge
7. Lawsuit
8. Fire or army insect
9. One who writes a will
10. Charm
11. Horn or Hatteras
12. Sacred picture
13. Fender-mishap result
18. Intone
23. Similar
24. Ready to pick
25. Aspect
26. Jeweler's weight
27. Maxim
28. "___ Say Die"
29. Price tag
30. Topple
31. Jitterbug, e.g.
32. Church officer
34. Fundamental
37. Spanish maiden
38. Unadulterated
40. Theme-park feature
41. Gift recipient
43. Gentler
44. Witty repartee
46. Idaho's capital
47. Yodelers' mountains
48. Lowest tide
49. Celebration
50. Happy
51. Kentucky Derby, e.g.
52. Piece of gossip
53. Disarray
56. Preceded
57. Dust cloth

PUZZLE 40

Riddle Me This

Here are 5 riddles and their mixed-up answers! Unscramble each group of letters to form a word. Use those words to fill in the answer blanks.

WSCEHA   ALBMER   ANIHLGI   AMLE   TEOTPA   AECK   SACB   QRASEU

1. What's worse than raining cats and dogs?   ___ ___ ___ ___ ___ ___ ___ ___ ___ ___
2. What kind of nut sneezes the most?   ___ ___ ___ ___ ___ ___
3. What starts with a T, ends with a T, and is full of T?   ___ ___ ___ ___ ___ ___ ___
4. What dessert is as hard as a rock?   ___ ___ ___ ___ ___ ___ ___ ___
5. What does a mathematician like to eat?   ___ ___ ___ ___ ___ ___

PUZZLE 41

ACROSS
1. Whitewater vehicle
5. Highly impressed
9. Designer Chanel
13. Neutral shade
14. Flaming
15. Effigy
16. Skinny
17. Submarine detector
18. Old King ___
19. Hurricane center
20. Tinge
21. Special skills
22. Bellybutton
25. Previously owned
28. Confuses
30. Embrace
33. Brawl
34. Rice dish
35. Easter bonnet
37. Wading bird
38. Bottom point
39. Dial sound
40. Expected to arrive
41. Sublease
42. Sparkled
43. Bad pun
45. Overwhelm with noise
46. Iowa State's town
47. Creep
48. Winglike
51. Enemy
52. Certain evergreen
55. Bike or blind
56. Laughing ___
58. Colorful swimmer
59. Mexican worker
60. Western movie
61. Dreadful
62. Obstacle
63. ___ out (barely manages)
64. Auto imperfection

DOWN
1. Nerve network
2. "___ Breaky Heart"
3. Kinder
4. Large cask
5. In trouble
6. Sherry or port
7. Roaring Twenties, e.g.
8. Actor James Van ___ Beek
9. Buzzing insect
10. Scent
11. Foal
12. Bullring bravos
14. Cigar's residue
23. Brewed drinks
24. Neckline shape
25. Not illuminated
26. Injury mark
27. Sprite
28. In the thick of
29. Remove errors from
30. Downy duck
31. Brown sugar/molasses treat
32. Lustrous velvet
34. Blanches
36. Adolescent
38. Maui goose
39. Spring occurrence
41. Battering ___
42. Mediterranean, e.g.
44. Using a scull
45. Dismal
47. Ice-cream holders
48. Stereo components
49. Right to property
50. Wild ox of Sulawesi
51. Celebration
53. Make a living
54. Hone
56. Tilling tool
57. Chatter
58. Strange

You Know the Odds

PUZZLE 42

The names of six kinds of cheese are spelled out, but they are missing every other letter. It shouldn't be too difficult to fill in the even letters now that You Know the Odds!

1. M _ Z _ A _ E _ L _
2. C _ M _ M _ E _ T
3. M _ N _ E _ E _   J _ C _
4. L _ M _ U _ G _ R
5. P _ R _ E _ A _
6. G _ U _ E _ E

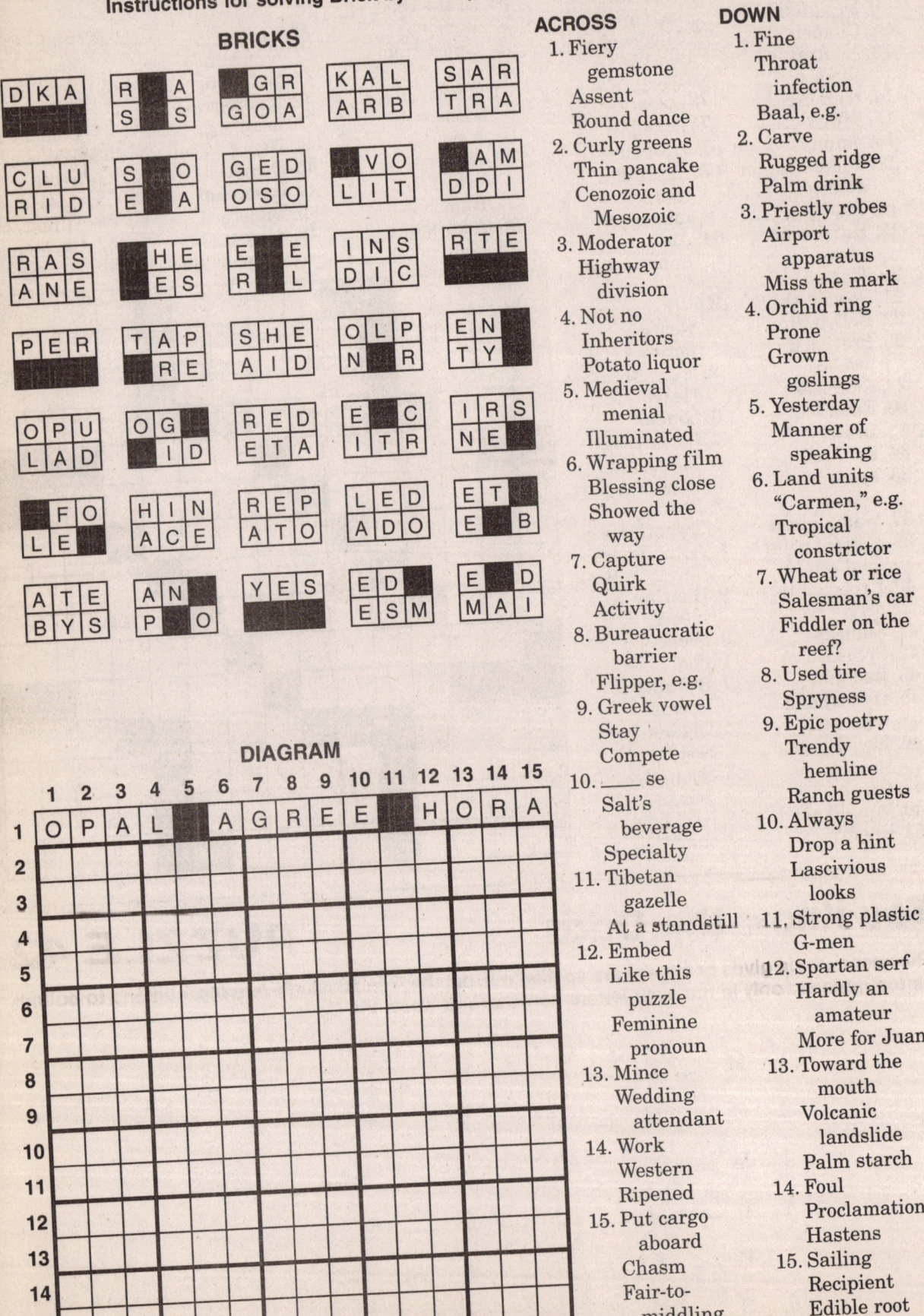

PUZZLE 44

ACROSS
1. Nimble
5. Loose flesh
9. Pinch
14. Hawaiian feast
15. Bowling path
16. Stallion
17. Expressed praise
19. Witness again
20. "Like ___ for Chocolate"
21. Cunning
23. Drum lightly
24. Child's game
27. Interlock
29. Con's counterpart
32. "___ It Romantic?"
34. Which person's?
37. Race circuit
38. Displayed
40. Carry on
42. Unable to react
44. Big boys
45. Surmise
46. Neutral shade
47. Transferred, as real estate
49. Flightless bird
50. Japanese verse
52. Invalid
53. Dark bread
54. Negative responses
56. Increase
57. Clever
60. Like a snail
62. Mentioned
67. Reluctant
69. Babbled
72. Free-for-all
73. Green fruit
74. Resounded
75. Take the helm
76. Diner sign
77. Stratagem

DOWN
1. Cabbage dish
2. Insect stage
3. Absorbed
4. Holiday season
5. Common ailment
6. Lass's mate
7. Once again
8. Darken
9. Separate grain
10. Deep sorrow
11. Hitherto
12. Away from the harbor
13. Retain
18. Degas, for one
22. Indecent
25. Cigar's remains
26. Elflike being
28. Cornucopia
29. Ballet bend
30. Creamy dressing
31. "Aida," e.g.
33. 'Twixt partner
35. Less hazardous
36. Opponent
39. Assume
41. Bona fide
43. Devastation
45. Most inactive
47. Fencing event
48. BPOE member
51. Authentic
55. Extremely impressive
57. Charity gifts
58. Pound or Frost
59. "A ___ of Two Cities"
61. Defeat sound
63. Criminal, slangily
64. Certain exam
65. Gambling ga
66. Nervous
68. Shirt style
70. Great respect
71. Cookie holder

Blips

PUZZLE 45

Place one of the given letters in each circle to form nine 3-letter words reading from top to bottom. Use each letter only as many times as it is listed.

A B B G G I N N O T W Y

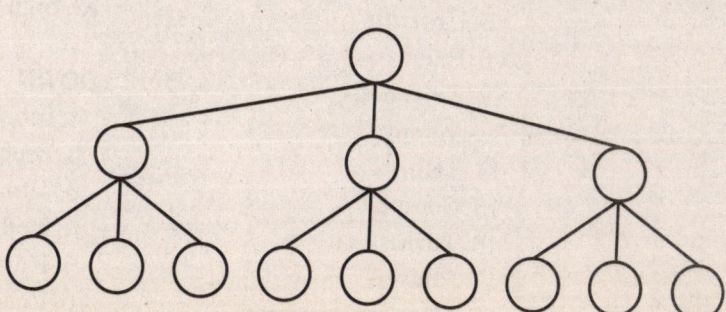

Puzzle 46

THREE-D CROSSWORD

Here's a crossword with a third dimension! Each of the three faces (A, B, and C) is a crossword with words reading across and down. As you solve this puzzle, you'll see that some of the answers from one face continue on another face of the cube. Watch your ABCs, and you'll find that this is a real blockbuster.

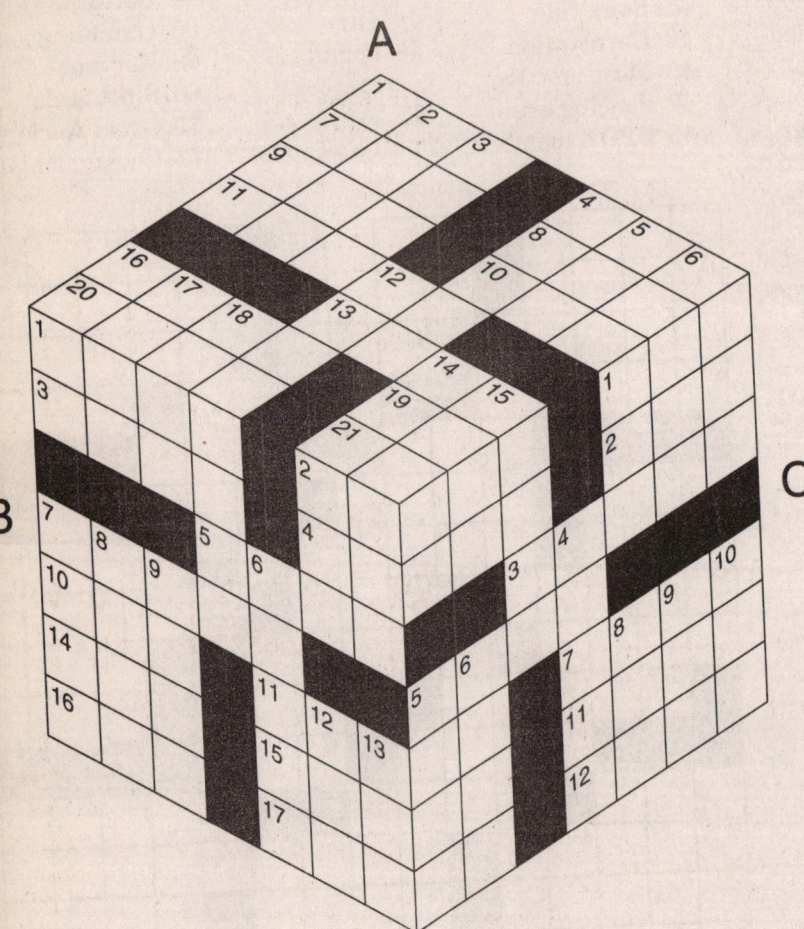

B CLUES

ACROSS
1. Largest continent
2. Got up
3. Vaccination
4. Firm belief
5. Frosted
7. Parking spot
10. Paving stuff
11. Jotted down
14. Boxing great
15. Threesome
16. Funnyman Skelton
17. Religious groups

DOWN
6. Pennies
7. Asterisk
8. Light-hued
9. Hot and dry
12. Miner's find
13. Muscle twitch

A CLUES

ACROSS
1. Pie ___ mode
4. Trees and shrubs
7. Hawaiian garland
8. Better ventilated
9. As well
10. Pin's cousin
11. Spirited horse
13. Covered, as floors
16. Commotions
19. Soothe
20. Gold leaf
21. Maned animal

DOWN
1. Word of sorrow
2. Pre-Easter season
3. ___-de-camp
4. Black and white "bear"
5. Untruth
6. Exist
12. Extremely happy
14. Tell
15. Coupled
16. Turkish rulers
17. Platter
18. Mixture

C CLUES

ACROSS
1. Loud uproar
2. Permit
3. Water jugs
5. Broad
7. Sunburn soother
11. Solemn promises
12. Sight orbs

DOWN
4. Intertwine
5. Proceeded
6. March date
8. Hollywood's Myrna ___
9. Have debts
10. Road curve

CODEWORD

PUZZLE 47

Codeword is a special crossword puzzle in which conventional clues are omitted. Instead, answers to words in the diagram are represented by numbers. Each number represents a different letter of the alphabet, and all of the letters of the alphabet are used. When you are sure of a letter, put it in the code key chart and cross it off in the alphabet box. A group of letters has been inserted to start you off.

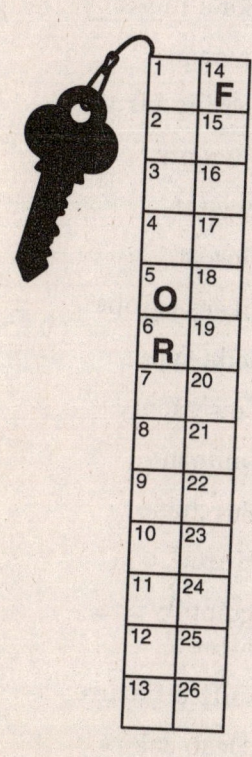

Disco

PUZZLE 48

Each numbered disc has a 5-letter answer (Clue A) and a 4-letter answer (Clue B) reading in a clockwise direction. Enter the first letter of each 5-letter answer in the circle in the preceding disc. For example, in disc 1: C + RUSH = CRUSH.

A
1. Mash
2. Marten
3. Intertwines
4. Barely earning
5. Shell lining
6. Get to
7. Terminate
8. Little bit

B
1. Hurry
2. Proficient
3. High pair
4. Monarch
5. Farm unit
6. Individually
7. Diminish
8. Bushel part

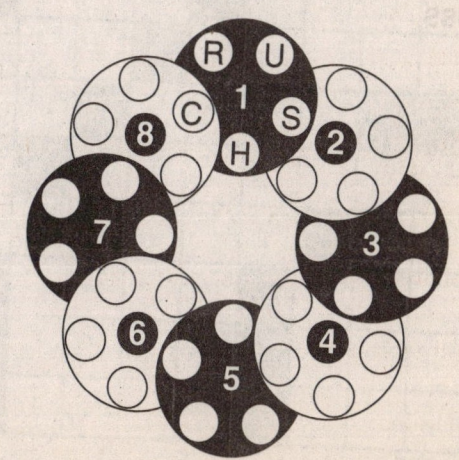

PUZZLE 49

ACROSS

1. Arrow part
. Drains
. Horse's dinner
. Hooded snake
. Foretelling sign
. Fall in droplets
. Deal out
. Doom
. Pickle vendor
. Garden buzzer
. Browning piece?
. Clear profit
. Haul behind
. Admirer's song
. Fish groups
32. Remove from print
33. Moneyless
34. Pinch hitter
36. Called up
40. Beside
42. Cup
44. Want urgently
45. African trip
47. Sweet tuber
49. ___ out (barely manages)
50. Beavers' projects
52. Frenzied
54. Pestering
58. Disintegrate
59. Caustic stuff
60. Slumped
62. Pitcher spout
65. Brewed drinks
67. Vocal solo
68. Sidestep
70. Vogue
71. Hiker's abode
72. Memo taker
73. Black stone
74. Hem
75. Adjust

DOWN

1. Wound cover
2. Hollow
3. Skillful
4. To's mate
5. Skin marking
6. Couch
7. Pile up
8. Stroked
9. Smirked
10. Unmatched
11. Gladiator's place
12. Like a mosaic
13. Revenge
22. Hooting birds
23. Souvenir
25. Twister
27. Closest
28. Fitness clubs
29. Soda type
30. Cow's foot
31. Quantity
35. Purchase
37. Huron, e.g.
38. Happily ___ after
39. Office fixture
41. Drab colors
43. Yak
46. Duplicate
48. Nothing more than
51. Slept noisily
53. Rat or mouse
54. Texas mission
55. Hosiery fabric
56. Impoverished
57. Leaving
61. Head
62. Not on time
63. Concept
64. Bonus
66. Gender
69. Oath

PUZZLE 5

ACROSS
1. Foreman
5. Subside
8. Collars
12. Unwrap
13. Rene's cap
15. Excursion
16. Tibetan monk
17. Please
18. 45 player
19. Touch ground
21. Smooth
23. Dunk
24. Carve
26. Strivers
28. Pine-family tree
31. Hearty bread
32. Mad
33. Intense
35. Periods of time
37. Bar order
38. Fairy
39. Switch positions
43. Meeting plan
46. Slink
47. Desire
49. Clear profit
51. Desertlike
52. Lyrical
53. Command to Fido
54. Walking on ___
55. Elegant
57. Tell
62. Rebuke
64. Lubricate again
66. Patron
67. Market
68. Robe fabric
69. Burn
70. Nelson or Duane
71. Billy ___ Williams
72. Bad actors

DOWN
1. Gaucho's tool
2. Milky jewel
3. Highway vehicle
4. Bottleneck
5. Snakelike fish
6. Cheeky
7. Alpha's follower
8. Utmost degree
9. Awakened
10. Prior to
11. Omits
13. Actress White
14. Resident
20. Not there
22. China item
25. Mortar
27. Bricklayer
28. The ___ Four
29. Road hazard
30. TV's McClanahan
32. Newborn
34. Quality
36. Long in the tooth
40. Gave food to
41. ___ and wide
42. Blue yonder
44. Grasp
45. Guide
46. Eyelid woe
47. Labored
48. Messenger
50. Premature
52. Dated
53. Ocean's edge
56. Rose starter
58. Luxurious
59. Floating
60. Athletic group
61. Fouls up
63. Thickness, as of lumber
65. Incense

PUZZLE 53

ACROSS

1. Stroll
. Flow back
. Disney deer
. Ethical
. Sound receiver
. Tree nut
. Explore
. Twist the truth
. Settee
. Do needlework
. View
. Gains
. ___ room (den)
. Swindle
. Temporary car
31. Gardening device
32. Pat
35. Rigid
36. Cloth coloring
38. Personality
40. Fall bloomer
42. Memorable time
44. Gin and ___
45. Blush
47. Equip
49. Feeble
50. Ace
51. House locale
53. Motorbikes
55. Songlike poem
57. Rembrandt work
58. Gawk at
61. Ring up
63. Fabric remnant
66. Small orchard
68. Dad
69. Purpose
71. Rants
72. Supplement
73. One who finishes
74. Watchers
75. Fox's home
76. Iron setting

DOWN

1. Bands' blasters
2. In addition
3. Forehead
4. Prof's workshop
5. XI
6. Squiggly swimmers
7. Lures
8. Glimmer
9. Faulty
10. Serving perfectly
11. Budge
12. Playgroup problem
13. Motels
22. Cooled
24. Evaluated
26. Charged particle
27. Bar request
28. Surgeon's beam
29. Exceed
30. Seeded loaf
32. Adjusted
33. Vocal solos
34. Bushel part
35. Field cover
37. Bungle
39. Drying aid
41. Depend
43. Ambition
46. And not
48. Hoodlum
52. Toppled
54. Parts
55. Pry bar
56. Clog
58. Shrek, e.g.
59. Dreary
60. Passion
62. Sincere
63. Impolite
64. Cruising
65. Infection carrier
67. Hook shape
70. Picnic pest

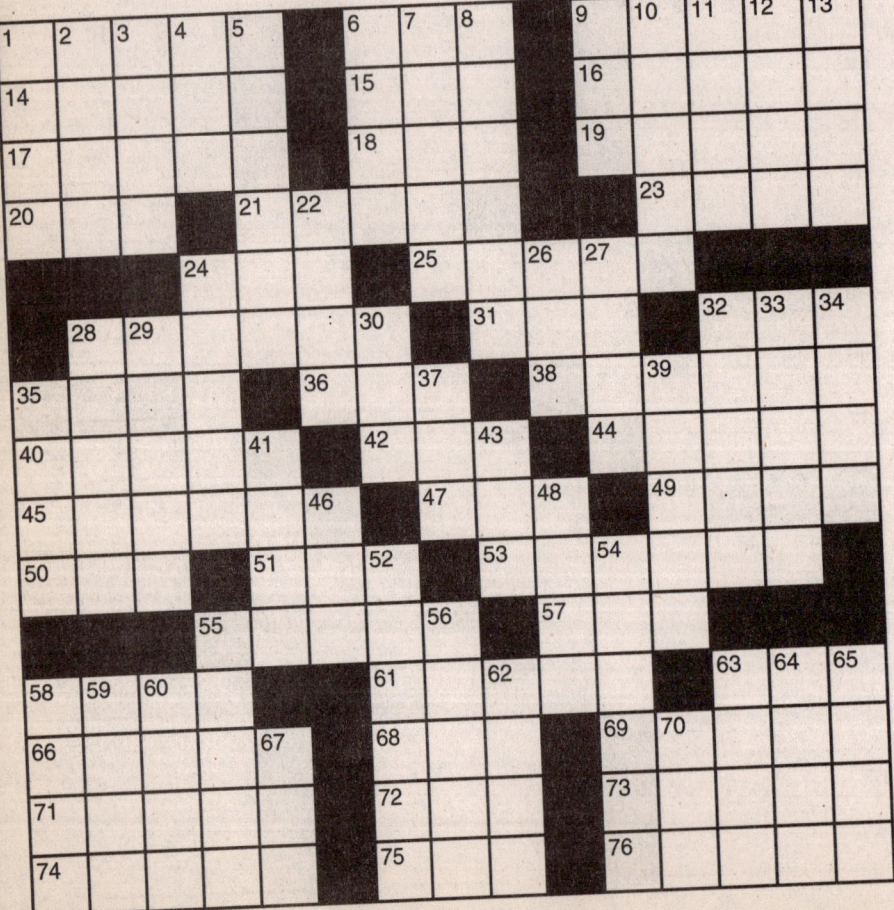

PUZZLE 5

ACROSS

1. Building lot
5. Early bird?
8. "Mary Poppins" song word
12. Beach toy
13. Band
15. Fail to win
16. Time pieces?
17. Spicy dish
18. Samovars
19. Spoil
20. Shred
21. Wave parts
23. Hockey shot
25. High card
26. In the buff
27. Heidi's peaks
29. Unearth
30. Feminine pronoun
33. TV dog
36. Rainbow shape
37. Sailor's howdy
38. Charm
39. Shout
40. Fumble
41. Prospect
42. Orange tuber
43. Some soups
44. Consumers' lures
45. Fashion line
46. Diner topping
47. Ember
49. Camp bunk
50. Word to a nag
54. Prawn's kin
56. Ditch
57. Both Begleys
58. Mr. Coward
59. Wipe out
61. Remnants
62. Protected, at sea
63. Stunned
64. Leg hinge
65. Hang fire
66. ___ diem
67. Walls have ___

DOWN

1. Mimics
2. Actress Kane
3. Gaucho's tool
4. High tracks
5. Principles
6. Squawk
7. Four qts.
8. Gave a hint
9. Good-luck token
10. "___ It Romantic?"
11. Chow hall
13. Abrasion
14. Ants' bash?
22. Welcome mat
24. Outmoded
28. Equivocate
29. Dehydrate
31. Desire
32. Sight-seers?
33. Tibetan holy man
34. Betwixt
35. Tanning lotion
36. Sleeve occupant
37. Cupid's dart
39. Engine shaft
40. Fellow
42. Barked
43. Caressed
45. Stage hog
46. Working-class cat?
48. Desqueaked
49. Derange
51. Hair tint
52. More bizarre
53. Burros
54. Fasten
55. Crater
60. Knock on wood
61. Barely earn

PUZZLE 51

ACROSS
- Cuban dance
- Little rascal
- Excess
- Grasping tool
- Forest ma[...]
- Folk stories
- Slumbering
- Vocabulary
- In fashion
- Tandoor
- Nonets
- Hummus holder
- Amusing
- Grand-scale tale
- Soybean product
- Understood
- 35. Derrick
- 36. Wholly
- 37. Money player
- 39. Large vase
- 40. Kitchen tool
- 44. Blacktop
- 45. Gangster's gun
- 46. Unlatch, in poems
- 47. Bill
- 49. Cloth scrap
- 51. Small seabird
- 53. Assembled
- 54. Onager
- 56. Mind
- 58. Preface
- 61. Bird or fruit
- 63. Cartoon unit
- 66. Blitzen, e.g.
- 68. Nary a soul
- 71. Man or Wight
- 72. Teeny
- 73. Ill will
- 74. Let it stand!
- 75. Some trains
- 76. Winding curves

DOWN
1. Junk e-mail
2. Furthermore
3. Gentle
4. Wax worker?
5. "Roses ___ red . . ."
6. Dormant
7. Bewail
8. Corral
9. Pasting
10. Bank deal
11. Beg
12. Golfers' pegs
14. Dot
19. Wildebeest
22. Barrel
24. Brooch
25. Glazes
26. Satisfied
27. Fallacy
28. Ling-Ling, e.g.
30. Cowboy flick
31. Winter illness
33. Selected
34. Hint
35. Nasty mutt
38. Planet for Mork
41. Cauldrons
42. Chimp
43. Pinnacle
48. Barn loft
50. Red stone
52. This instant
55. Turf
57. Cherry choice
58. Showy bloom
59. Swallow shelter
60. Floor square
61. Ship bottom
62. Makes mad
63. Atlantic fishes
64. Selvage
65. Sodium solutions
67. Sheepish she
69. Mining extract
70. City vehicle

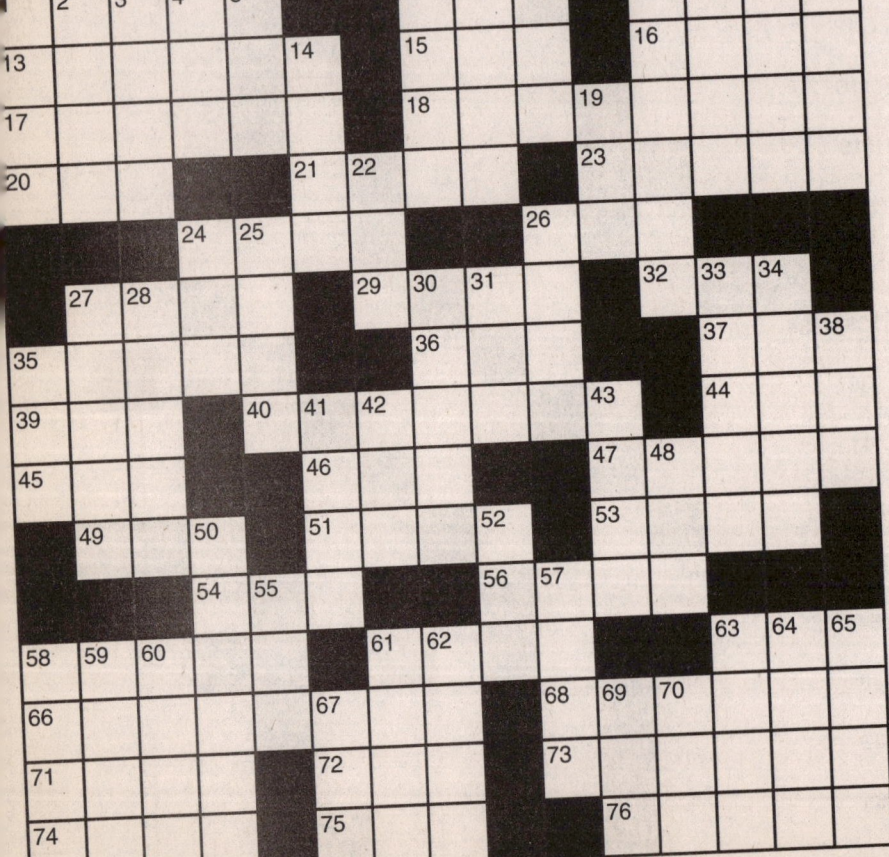

PUZZLE 5

ACROSS

1. Was very cold
6. Adages
10. Hair parter
14. Mooed
15. Nerd's kin
16. Scheme
17. Flirted
18. Hatha ___
19. Polenta grain
20. Feed lines to
21. Meringue's lack
23. Thundered
25. Comic's Etta ___
27. Itsy-bitsy
28. Junior
29. Enlarged
31. Messengers
35. Lifework
38. Make an album
39. Uncle Sam's target
40. Torment
41. Fitting
42. Not those
44. Supplied
45. Lend a hand
46. Prejudiced
47. Nature
50. Take no food
51. Game room
52. Cry noisily
53. Sharpen
57. Scribble
60. Victim
62. Use a paddle
63. Courts
64. Energy source
66. Slow down
68. Church recess
69. Little bit
70. Estimator
71. ___ off (irritated)
72. The majority
73. Trick out

DOWN

1. Congregate
2. Rascal
3. Young bird
4. Last letter
5. Current event?
6. Designed
7. Roused from sleep
8. Hairpiece
9. Ingenue
10. Buzzing insect
11. Stench
12. Nothing but
13. Ensemble
22. Debtor
24. Paddle
26. Young voter
30. West or Largo
31. Color
32. Drain cleaners
33. Application
34. Took legal action
35. Diner
36. Becomes older
37. Heaters
38. Cow chew
41. Craps cube
42. Not 'tain't
43. Biblical verb
45. Praise
46. Pig movie
48. Obliterated
49. Very recent
50. Layout
52. Blemishes
54. Speechify
55. Mentions
56. Water-servers
57. Whack
58. Handle well
59. Pasadena bloom
61. Grounds
65. As well
67. Obstruct

PUZZLE 55

ACROSS
1. Leave out
5. Fibbed
9. Pond plant
13. Not twice
14. More willing
15. Noodle
16. Humble desserts?
17. Burdensome
19. Emphasize
21. Speech impediment
22. Create a quilt
23. La followers
24. Ja and oui
26. Unstable
30. Fill again
33. Victory sign
34. Butter square
36. Playground items
38. Follow directly
41. Pursue
43. TV-replay method
44. Hurricanes
46. Curious
48. Massage
49. Robs
51. Pencils' ends
54. River sediments
56. Goal
57. Watering hole
60. Lop the crop
61. Principles
65. Relationship
68. Gobs
69. One opposed
70. Albacores
71. Grain
72. Intense
73. Palmist
74. Desist

DOWN
1. Drenches
2. Do the cable stitch
3. Bakery employee
4. 100 centimos
5. Luxury's spot?
6. Suggest
7. Creepier
8. Outfits
9. Stomach muscles
10. Garlands
11. Bestowed
12. All over again
14. Busybody
18. Signifies
20. Squat
25. Make dirty
26. Dusks
27. Sublets
28. Plant again
29. Harsh cry
31. Worship
32. Object
35. Also
37. Wails
39. "Trinity" writer
40. Realm
42. Certain poem
45. Nominates
47. Empties
50. Sculpture
52. Support
53. Smudges
55. Book back
57. Great number
58. Cornmeal bread
59. Pot bet
62. Landed
63. Crazy
64. Pace
66. ___ and tuck
67. Paddle

PUZZLE 56

ACROSS
1. Oafs
6. Church rite
10. Landed
14. Tax inspection
15. Voice range
16. Took a drive
17. Guide
18. Shortly
19. Cameo
20. Males
21. Escort
23. Hymn finale
24. Ham it up
25. Filthy
28. Strolled
31. Crafty
32. Wow!
35. Skirt type
36. Dad's lady
38. Central part
40. Sun-dried brick
42. Lump
44. Equip again
45. Band
47. Stir-fry pan
49. Eye part
50. Tea, in Paris
51. Anger
53. Silly laugh
55. Vamoose!
57. Beach color
58. District
61. Alter a skirt
63. Burst
66. Factual
67. Strong wind
68. Hurrah
70. Pedro's house
71. Wee particle
72. Pedal
73. Rocketed
74. Camera part
75. Occasion

DOWN
1. Money
2. Guitar's kin
3. Poems
4. Vegas cube
5. Hit
6. Alda's series
7. African shrubs
8. Shops
9. Child
10. Display
11. Weaver's need
12. Not in use
13. Adolescent
22. Plant stalk
24. Excuse
26. Antlered animal
27. One who colors
28. Distance across
29. Cherish
30. Collie, e.g.
32. Twist
33. Weird
34. Graceful trees
35. Spar
37. Crop
39. Royal rule
41. Spectacular
43. Marsh
46. Blunder
48. Flying toy
52. A martial art
54. Make a bet
55. Meal course
56. Honeydew, e.g.
58. Circle parts
59. Harvest
60. Diminish
62. ___ and haws
63. Tar
64. Baking need
65. Harbor town
67. Young woman
69. Gun an engine

PUZZLE 57

ACROSS
1. Book part
5. Targets
10. Drama divisions
14. Bart's dad
15. Pesky insect
16. Stop, Trigger!
17. ___ crust
18. Starcraft
20. Social event
21. Many times, to Keats
23. Little jump
24. Pops
25. Crowd number?
27. Circuit
29. Most frosty
31. Tumbling
35. "Let ___ eat cake"
36. Russian emperor
38. Flight unit
40. Long, long time
41. Therefore
43. Kind of league
44. Very tiny
47. Pain
48. Bligh's direction
49. Use again
51. Kings
53. Dainty
54. Ventilated
55. Had a bagel
58. Musician Charles
60. Coat holder
61. Moisture
64. Cruel
67. Call up
69. Con man
70. Ancient strings
71. Fresher
72. Movie lioness
73. Offspring
74. Apprehensive

DOWN
1. Closed
2. Bishop of Rome
3. Restlessness
4. Named, before marriage
5. Bloopers
6. Playing marble
7. Political electees
8. Arithmetic
9. Saunter
10. Hole piercer
11. Cleave
12. Nero's garment
13. Answers
19. Milky stones
22. Go and get
26. Shorten
28. Fruit stone
29. Thing
30. Chorus
31. Ornate
32. Bend
33. Made final
34. Donor
37. Eager desire
39. Deli loaves
42. Chilling
45. Not cooked
46. Music drama
48. Beer's relative
50. Oysters' outputs
52. Crucial
54. Church recesses
55. Efficient
56. Shadow
57. Historic ages
59. Child's toy
62. Barely makes do
63. Had being
65. Bikini part
66. Coffee server
68. Low neckline

PUZZLE 58

ACROSS
1. Alpine repeat
5. Supervisor
9. Hoof sound
13. Sketched
14. Dish
15. Acclaim
16. Sea flier
17. Metric quart
18. Freshly
19. Long fish
20. Hole
21. Dodgers
23. Motto
25. Borer
26. She cries uncle!
28. Salespeople
32. Prance
35. Teen spots?
37. Single unit
38. Cast
39. Extends
42. High note
43. Plus
44. Equine control
45. Rouse
47. Nuisance
50. Flower holders
52. Flavor
54. Sampled
58. Executive
61. Chip sauce
62. How ___ you?
63. Door sign
64. Less frequent
66. Steamer
67. Cafe list
68. Looks at
69. As well
70. Keats wrote them
71. Jealousy
72. Tints

DOWN
1. Hems
2. Mean
3. Howdy!
4. Hooting bird
5. Radar spot
6. Bread variety
7. Rodeo animal
8. Repaired
9. Infant's bed
10. Kent's coworker
11. Aloft
12. Church seats
14. 747, e.g.
20. Ways of walking
22. 100 percent
24. Large antelope
25. Trick
27. Mind
29. Granite
30. ___-slapper
31. Visualized
32. Iranian ruler, once
33. Salad fish
34. Crimsons
36. Granny
40. Maintain
41. Clean house
46. Stubborn animal
48. Position
49. Fail to keep up
51. Excites
53. Teach
55. Score
56. Cancel
57. Audition tapes
58. Office note
59. Felled
60. IX
61. Like morning grass
65. Gun a motor
66. Scoundrel

PUZZLE 59

MOVIES & TELEVISION

ACROSS
1. Lukas ___
5. Holbrook et al.
9. Asta's doc
12. Table doily
15. Moon ___ Zappa
16. A Hale
17. "Wings" abbr.
18. Julia Child's phrase
19. "___ Breckinridge"
20. Disney fish
21. A Harrison
22. Eve Plumb role
23. "The ___ Shoes"
25. Pontiff
27. Director James ___
29. Athletics
32. Poe, e.g.
34. Marie Wilson role
35. "___ Tac Dough"
36. "___ Copy"
39. Tatum ___
41. Vowel request to Vanna
42. "Anchors ___"
44. Mrs. Flintstone et al.
48. Woods or Grey
50. Hayward role
51. "Seinfeld" gal
52. TV's Florek
54. Stone and Reed
57. Ms. Swenson
58. Hams it up
60. "___ Got a Secret"
61. Singer DiFranco
62. Hugh Grant film
63. Berenger film
65. "El ___"
68. Mr. Ed's comment
70. Matthew Fox series
71. "Exodus" hero
72. Role for Oland
75. Kazan of films
77. Dreyfuss/DeVito film
79. TV legal drama
81. DeMille work
83. "Angie" actor
84. Yalie
85. Footed vase
87. Cola, e.g.
89. Silent
93. TV alien
94. Mr. Caesar
95. Pile on
96. Mr. Jannings
97. Born
98. TV's Alicia
99. Film lioness
100. Tyne ___

DOWN
1. Drone
2. "Ask ___ Girl"
3. Broadcast
4. "Brenda ___"
5. Wood cutter
6. Capp's order
7. Torch
8. Pry
9. Ben ___ of "Roots"
10. Gigi's summer
11. Rieger's vehicle
12. Houlihan's rank
13. Frighten
14. "Tuckerville" gal
24. Film's Hawke
26. Milne bear
28. Film heavy
29. RR depot
30. Needle's kin
31. Bunker's portrayer
33. "The Love Boat" actress
37. No joke
38. Ms. Conn
40. Suffer
43. Mr. MacLeod
45. Newsreel maker
46. Director Lee
47. Abundance
49. Rabbit ears

PUZZLE 59

52. ___ Plaines
53. A Dolenz
54. Actor Davis
55. "Resident ___"
56. Default result
59. Wind dir.
61. Ava's ex
63. "___ Ahoy"
64. "CHiPs" star
66. Exasperation
67. Loud clamor
69. A Jackson
72. "___ Slate"
73. Ms. Berry
74. "___ of Her Own"
76. Theater walkway
78. "A Guy ___ Joe"
80. Newman/Woodward film
82. "___ Runnings"
86. One-third of a TV do
88. "___ Boot
90. Ms. Thurman
91. "Dusk ___ Dawn"
92. TV Tarzan

PUZZLE 60

ACROSS
1. Is in the red
5. Film's Torn
8. Piercing tools
12. '60s lamp
13. Coops
15. Brunch, e.g.
16. Colorist
17. Small hooter
18. Mama's fellow
19. Feeling awful
21. Fine
23. Barnyard pen
24. Wary
27. Choir section
29. Western shows
31. Suffering
32. Lounge
33. Pup's cry
34. Skillfully
36. Cavity
38. Family member
39. Water sport
40. Turret
42. Strong desire
46. Expected
48. Food tin
49. Stubborn sort
50. Complain
52. "___ a Living"
54. Have regrets
55. Blob
57. Yacht spot
58. T-man
59. Eccentric
60. Divan
62. Pester
64. Piece of cake?
66. Tint again
68. Under cover?
72. Off-white
73. Hearing
74. Pay
75. Short pause
76. Mint
77. Door handle

DOWN
1. Vintage
2. Route
3. Palindromic mom
4. Bombay dress
5. Uncooked
6. Frozen abode
7. Quick look
8. Band aid
9. Sneaky person
10. Compact computer
11. Leaves 'em laughing
13. Deflate
14. Asterisk
20. Testing area
22. Cellist Ma
24. Barter
25. Drifter
26. Cheer
28. Excursion
30. Jacket fabric
35. Call for Heidi?
37. Personal quirk
38. Guardian
41. Fence
43. Sod
44. Inkling
45. Listen to
47. Alien ships
50. Dress part
51. Senior officials
53. Resort
55. Adorer
56. Sweet wine
57. Miss Hawkins
61. Feathery plant
63. Goggle
65. Road groove
67. Swerve, at sea
69. Prohibition
70. I topic
71. Society miss

PUZZLE 61

ACROSS
1. Imitating
6. Hold
10. Shrew
13. Beau
14. Nurse Barton
15. Mine product
16. Numbers game
17. Fortunate
18. Visualize
19. Dieter's resort
20. Speak formally
22. Crow's bill
23. Affirm
24. Abhor
27. Fireplace ledge
31. Deli meat
34. Lost
35. Annually
37. Breeze
39. Passes over
41. Junk mail, usually
42. Kind of comment
44. Powder ___
45. More immense
48. Broiler
49. Persuade
51. Most strange
53. Singer Nelson ___
54. Tone
55. Scold
58. Tempts
60. Corsage flower
63. Amiss
64. Heroic poems
66. Black
68. Simpleton
69. Wearies
70. Ignited again
71. Saute
72. Invites
73. Cogs

DOWN
1. Shoemakers' tools
2. ___ deck
3. Whit
4. Capture
5. Channel
6. Excess
7. Thoroughbred
8. Taunt
9. Reimburse
10. Scents organ
11. Locality
12. Nerd
14. Hammer end
21. ___-poly
22. Plead
25. The works
26. Dolls, e.g.
27. Conceal
28. Awry
29. Whinny
30. Faucet
31. Emblem
32. Green
33. Accomplices
36. Worm-getter
38. Housing fee
40. Winter glider
43. Gesture
46. Build on
47. Trounce
50. Skinny fish
52. Gobi, e.g.
54. Razz
55. Santa's runway
56. From a distance
57. Uncertain
59. Super serves
60. Birthmark
61. Item
62. Legend
64. Fade away
65. Hawaiian staple
67. Busy one

PUZZLE 62

ACROSS

1. Darn again
6. Make secure
10. Cost
13. Spare
14. Look forward to
16. Beam of light
17. Less corrupted
18. Type of bean
19. Dusk
20. Summer quencher
21. Office writer
23. Say
25. Some evergreens
27. Branch of math
29. Powder ___
31. Appearance
35. Rot
38. Tyne ___
41. Store news
42. Benefit
43. Biggest
46. Prosecute
47. Highbrow
49. Went auburn
50. Ingested
52. Manhattan square
54. Motel
55. Oboe's kin
59. Canine cry
63. Carved pole
66. Wreckages
68. Island gift
69. Mirror
70. Strawberry ___
72. Oil source
74. Duffer's goal
75. Because
76. Adorer
77. Graceful tree
78. Woodland animal
79. Skating jumps

DOWN

1. Settle a debt
2. Ooze out
3. Spread
4. Lyrical before
5. Conflicts
6. Blazer feature
7. Unpaid
8. Slender craft
9. Equipment
10. Worry
11. Icicle hanger
12. Observer
15. Journeys
22. Price label
24. Knocks
26. Take to the slopes
28. Inlets
30. Gym wing
32. Side of New York
33. Sleuth's guide
34. MTV watcher
35. Cummerbund
36. Yearn
37. Perfume
38. Withered
39. Develop
40. Was ahead
44. Inserts
45. Twice five
48. Movie swine
51. A few
53. Young sheep
54. Scribe's need
56. Gleamed
57. Small weight
58. Senior
60. Choice group
61. Flat
62. Docks
63. Record
64. Milky gem
65. Duration
67. Pop
71. Jar covering
73. Bagels and ___

PUZZLE 63

ACROSS
1. Litigates
5. Gun
8. Join
12. Gumbo vegetable
13. Legal
15. Shampoo ingredient
16. Lemon skin
17. Gung-ho
18. Soothing exercise
19. Milk type
21. Ump's compatriot
23. Dem., e.g.
24. Cross
26. Most recent
28. Chimp
29. Pixie
32. Intention
33. Hidden
36. Speech problem
39. Sandwich fish
40. Brandish
42. Christmas contraction
44. Semester
46. Soft drink
48. Sty cry
50. Coloring
51. Bit
52. Female college grad
55. Neck back
57. Brooch
58. "___ Got a Crush on You"
60. "Family ___"
62. Person opposed
64. Shows
66. Certain woodwind
70. Bridle strap
71. Hideouts
72. Dish
73. TV's "Star ___"
74. Convened
75. Geologic ages

DOWN
1. Douse
2. Luau instrument
3. Before, in poems
4. Kind of dip
5. Paper amount
6. Coop product
7. Challenger
8. Can
9. Flee to marry
10. Trademarks
11. Dispensed
13. Kauai gift
14. Movement
20. Joint
22. Sense
24. Nozzle
25. Pasta variety
27. Lingers
28. Feign
30. Regulation
31. Movie, slangily
32. Lounged
34. Billiard shot
35. Continuously, to Yeats
37. Plunge
38. Father
41. 24 hours
43. Held session
45. Tiny
47. Diner card
49. Bellybutton
52. Isolated
53. Ocean cruise
54. Loosen
56. Clay brick
59. Huge quiz
60. Dix or Bragg
61. Snaky curve
63. Scribe's need
65. Pizza ___
67. Hiss
68. Acknowledge
69. Chicago railways

PUZZLE 64

ACROSS

1. Shaping tool
4. Knock
7. Swiftly
11. Uninteresting
15. August sign
16. Baseball's Bonds
18. Cato's way
19. Aggravate
20. Lao-tzu's principle
21. Approve
22. Greek-salad topper
23. Off yonder
24. Warship fleets
26. Chimpanzee
28. Physicians' gp.
30. Snaky curve
31. Hair-care goo
32. GI's hangout
33. Equip
35. Yearn
38. Type of cracker
41. Accumulated
45. Bank transaction
46. Named, before marriage
47. Stiller's partner
49. Roof part
50. Crease
51. Attire
53. Very eager
54. Ring judge
55. Geographer's volume
57. Belly
60. Not moist
61. Activity
64. Soap ingredient
65. "Roses ___ Red"
66. Raised edge
69. Alpine warbler
71. Military coat
76. Lime or lemon
77. Forum wear
78. Part of a goblet
82. Pet in "Peter Pan"
83. Dawn, in verse
85. Deteriorate
87. Luau instrument, briefly
88. Rests
89. Marzipan nuts
91. Procedure
93. Lily species
94. Fill with wonder
95. Former French coin
96. Klutz
98. Sunbather's goal
100. Dainty
103. Mad ___ hornet
104. Apprehends
108. Had bills
110. Form of address
112. Lawful
114. Whopper
115. Oodles
116. Elba, e.g.
117. Israel's Shimon ___
118. Shelley offering
119. Group of computer bits
120. Young person
121. Spanish article
122. School wing

DOWN

1. Utah resort
2. "Yes, ___"
3. Type of lens
4. Follow closely
5. LAX postings
6. Historic starter
7. Certain flute
8. Had a cupcake
9. Bristle
10. Melbourne transport
11. Undergarment
12. Beach employee
13. Expression of regret
14. Towel-insignia word
16. Ordered
17. Bread ingredient
25. Program
27. Tennyson piece
29. Circle section
32. Operator
34. Bitter resentment
35. A, in communications
36. Water bird
37. Corridor
39. Team cheer
40. Primers
41. Scent
42. Hoops player
43. By any chance
44. Disobey
48. Past
52. Romantic songs
56. Pronounce
58. Short farewell

PUZZLE 64

59. Mesh fabric
62. Loved to excess
63. Fragrances
66. Shangri-la official
67. Matinee figure
68. Lasting
70. Selfish trip
72. Dangerous
73. Toe feature
74. Preposition
75. Container
79. Ballet skirt
80. ___ out a living
81. Recollections
84. At once
86. Hurricane centers
90. Fresh
92. Head part
97. Liberal ___
98. Mummy's place
99. Not in
101. Give forth
102. Relieve
103. So be it!
104. Indian city
105. Walk heavi
106. Shipshape
107. Appear
109. Hide the gray
111. Porter
113. Elusive swimmer

PUZZLE 65

ACROSS
1. Globe bearer
6. Fat
10. Norm
13. Angelic child
15. Mythology
16. Pride
17. Stove
18. Newspaper piece
19. Historical epoch
20. Desire
21. Certain adder
23. Roused
25. Aglow
27. Relaxes
28. Windstorms
32. But
33. Oneness
34. Pine product
36. Society girl
39. 8 bits
40. Air again
41. Skirt type
42. Wood cutter
43. Waffle topper
44. Check for fraud
45. Friend or ___?
46. Ponder
48. Rate
51. Catch a bus
52. Alarms
54. Sit-ups targets
55. Mire
58. ___ code
59. Antler
61. Invent
64. Actress Arden
65. Blue-pencil
66. Asian boat
67. Poor grade
68. Blocks
69. Sappy

DOWN
1. Sore
2. "How do I love ___?"
3. Slim
4. Sculpture
5. "Runaround ___"
6. Failure
7. Tennis stroke
8. Operatic song
9. Separating
10. Sneaks a look
11. Be in accord
12. Horses' colors
14. Plait
22. Hoarder
24. Type of meal
25. Chip in a chip
26. Set down
28. Brass instrument
29. Black gem
30. Ceremony
31. Truth ___
32. Yang's mate
35. Terrific
36. Crib word
37. Freeway sign
38. Gnash
40. Bread for pastrami
41. Muffle
43. Calmed
44. Relief
45. Conifer
47. LPs' successors
48. Knocked down
49. Dynamic
50. Indian home
53. Cola
54. Tiny colonists
55. Plans
56. Western state
57. Not accept
60. Cup's edge
62. Flock male
63. Flightless bird

PUZZLE 6

ACROSS
1. Lessens
5. Green
8. Brace
12. Han ___
13. Star, briefly
15. Cord
16. TV static
17. Alert
18. Complete
19. Bruised ___
20. Railroaded
21. Nice guy
22. Pancho's topper
24. Term of respect
26. Glimpsed
27. Nab
31. "All ___ Jazz"
34. Fresh
36. Recollection
37. Cool
38. Calmed
40. Stone
41. Barefoot
43. Fab!
44. Stretch wide
45. Vaporized water
46. Peel
48. Ms. Leoni
50. Connection
54. Hind appendage
57. Aunt's kid
59. Pair
60. ___ of thumb
61. Bakery items
62. Parry
63. Annoys
64. Begin
65. Frilly fabric
66. Go beyond
67. Sneaky
68. Puts to work

DOWN
1. Twisting turns
2. Drum type
3. Flourish
4. Female pig
5. Paid off
6. 1836 battle site
7. Had being
8. Show
9. Wander about
10. Available
11. Frisky
13. Swayed
14. Canopied items
20. Cook in oil
23. Wager
25. Like most cupcakes
28. Roman cloak
29. Personnel
30. Song of praise
31. In this way
32. Inkling
33. Altar area
35. Clash
36. Olympic winner
38. A few
39. Wall hangi[ng]
42. Bareheade[d]
44. As of now
47. Dashed
49. Plays a part
50. Rustic
51. Brainstorms
52. Unit of weig[ht]
53. Knots
54. Journey
55. Subtle air
56. Sorts
58. Mares eat 'e[m]
62. Winter shot

Puzzle 67

ACROSS

- Scatter
- Depletes
- Beseech
- Elegant headgear
- Requests
- Wood chopper
- Wedding site
- Dirt
- Offense
- Honey makers
- Paving goo
- Come about
- Takes one's gun
- Sublets
- Blessed
- 31. Increase
- 33. Woodwinds
- 34. Test tube
- 36. Exec's car
- 40. High peak
- 41. Flicker
- 44. Green
- 45. Nuisance
- 47. Stockings
- 48. Isolated
- 50. Superstar
- 52. Leveled
- 53. Hawker
- 56. Fall fruits
- 59. Easy to reach
- 60. Battering ___
- 61. Kind of dive
- 65. ___ man out
- 66. Baseball misplay
- 69. Soprano, e.g.
- 70. Dessert pastry
- 71. Broil
- 72. Beginning
- 73. Boston Red ___
- 74. Farewells
- 75. Pale

DOWN

1. Cut
2. Linoleum piece
3. Judge
4. Deletion
5. Combat
6. Asparagus unit
7. Startle
8. Apiece
9. Was located
10. Sink
11. Live
12. Heredity factors
15. Mako, e.g.
21. Small amount
23. Whirl
25. Wasp's home
26. Jiggle
28. Detergent
29. Adept
30. Police
32. Bedridden
34. String instrument
35. Electees
37. Wrought ___
38. Long hair
39. Unpaid
42. Owl's query?
43. Overhang
46. Tethered
49. Exercises
51. Laundry machine
52. Large tree
53. Cuts of pork
54. Boom box
55. Certain finger
57. Not poetry
58. Splits
62. Among
63. Farm division
64. Store sign
67. Actor Reiner
68. Beam
69. Passing through

60

PUZZLE 6

ACROSS
1. Short cuts?
5. Lump
8. Blind part
12. Touch
13. Round cap
15. Hurt sound
16. Folk tales
17. Glowing coal
18. After the bell
19. Kind of floss
21. Waken
23. Palermo res.
25. By means of
26. Baggier
29. Dated
30. Pen part
33. Title of respect
34. Deceive
36. Flaming
38. Rip apart
40. Bird of prey
41. Stones
42. Landscape
43. Had memorized
45. Hone
46. Tom and drake
47. Color
49. Bellowed
51. Wander about
52. Evasive
53. Study
57. Cancel
62. Keen
63. Gallant
67. Ambience
68. Plunged
69. More confident
70. Showy flower
71. Deuce beater
72. Running game
73. Line

DOWN
1. Beyond gray
2. Clarinet's kin
3. Char
4. Manuscript mark
5. Opal or ruby
6. Eye
7. Winged insect
8. Without aid
9. Maui feast
10. Behaves
11. "How do I love ___?"
13. Creed
14. Follow
20. Donkey
22. Guidance counselor?
24. Bent
25. Tennis shots
26. Jouster's weapon
27. Gobi stopovers
28. Sign
30. Nook
31. Bothered
32. Exceed
33. Team shout?
35. Have title to
37. 4-letter bird
39. Hoagie
44. Metalwork
48. Gapes
50. Pipe cleaner
53. Flat float
54. Anytime
55. Foul
56. Leisurely
58. Bear's burro
59. Lira replacement
60. Stumble
61. Relaxation
64. Inning ender
65. Swimsuit top
66. Stool support

61

PUZZLE 69

ACROSS

1. High cards
. Feel pain
. Pat dry
. Lounge
. "Gasoline ——"
. Cowboy's gear
. Serving aid
. Library no-no
. Cake decorator
. Type of snake
. Goblet feature
1. Rap
2. Save
4. Confuse
7. Sea swallow
8. Kind of rummy
29. Pod veggie
32. Request
34. Track and field event
36. Revise a manuscript
39. Knotted loop
41. Be next to
42. Romantic ballad
44. Barnyard animal
46. Florida island
47. Leatherworker's tool
48. Lode
51. Strong plastic
53. Dreary
55. Slug's cousin
58. Fibbed
60. Coconut cream ——
61. Opinion survey
62. Furious
64. Give (out)
65. Rotten
66. Celebrated
67. Patron
68. Statistics
69. Enjoyed a pool
70. Bunks

DOWN

1. Holy table
2. Old-time girdle
3. Pass by
4. Slick
5. Soothing plant
6. Scale
7. Stags and bucks
8. Scrutinize
9. Carry along
10. Daft
11. Oil org.
12. "Tarzan" ape
14. Penny ——
20. Basks
21. "King ——"
23. Packing box
25. Self-images
26. More exquisite
29. British bar
30. Flightless bird
31. Talented
33. Part of a.k.a.
34. Captain's book
35. Singer Brown
36. Deer's kin
37. Bambi's mom, e.g.
38. Trailing plant
40. Exclusively
43. Play ketch?
45. Anxious
49. Intrude
50. Hammered down
51. Country estate
52. Andean animal
53. Something done
54. Suggestive looks
55. Rushed
56. PBS science show
57. Got down
59. Topic of gossip
62. Conditions
63. Damp and cold
64. Name

FOUR-MOST

PUZZLE 7

The 4-letter entries in this crossword puzzle are listed separately and are in alphabetical order. Use the answers to the numbered clues to help you determine where each 4-letter entry goes in the diagram.

4 LETTERS

AWED
BRAT
CARL
CEES
DICE
DISC
DIVE
DOLE
DRAB
EDGY
EDIT
EELY
EVES
EYES
GLEN
GRAD
HIDE
IDOL
IOTA
ISLE
ITCH
LIEN
LOGO
LORE
ONCE
POLO
RELY
RYES
SWAB
SWAT
TO-DO
VEER
VENT
WHYS
YEWS
YOKE

ACROSS

1. Shady
12. Flirt with
15. Biblical vessel
18. Horn sounds
20. Be in hock
25. Shrub fence
34. Not young
35. Fish eggs
36. Sandwich sellers
37. Waikiki wreath
38. Finished dinner
41. Insults
45. Skilled person
47. Alternative
57. Clinging vine
60. 1.0 GPA
63. Road bend

DOWN

4. Explosive charge
5. Line of seats
6. Period in history
8. Shopping binge
9. Unhappiness
10. ___ aboard!
11. Plaything
19. Pumpkin dessert
24. Greetings!
40. Horse doc
42. Orbs
44. Campus people
51. Glacier material
52. Dawn to dusk
53. Crude metal
55. Intense anger
56. Crow sound

PUZZLE 71

ACROSS

1. La Scala shout
5. Droughty
10. Shopper's mecca
14. Mr. Pacino et al.
17. Downy duck
18. Lemon's kin
19. Uncertain
20. Explosive noise
21. Intermediary
22. Hemingway's nickname
23. Comedy routine
24. Zsa Zsa's sister
25. Talk wildly
26. Slanted font
28. Sultan's wives
30. Of the backbone
33. Cut a rug
36. Warhol's forte
39. "___ Good Cop"
40. Worshiper
42. Lauer of "Today"
46. Sake
48. Thrill
49. Not nearby
50. View
52. Superhero's logo
53. Larder
55. Documents
56. Edge of a roof
58. Unbarred, to a bard
60. Certain sprite
61. Pungent condiment
64. Untrained
67. Split ___
68. Ocean motion
69. Behave theatrically
71. Fragments
75. Proposal
76. Welsh ___
78. Partridge's tree?
79. Beginning section
82. Narrate again
83. Shotgun shells
84. Exhausting
86. Vice
87. Dirty place
88. Counted fat grams
90. Tycoon's property
93. Brooding type
96. Tranquilize
98. Curtsies
102. Shoemaker's device
103. Support a criminal
106. Field of study
107. Picture show
108. ___ whillikers!
109. Highway fee
110. Bassoon, e.g.
111. Lifeless
112. Turkey's Mount ___
113. Lessen
114. Pianist Duchin
115. Ancient instruments

DOWN

1. Grizzly, e.g.
2. Latvian capital
3. Yemenite port
4. Flues
5. Table scrap
6. Kind of skiing
7. Lariat
8. Horned antelope
9. Business arrangement
10. Eyelash enhancer
11. Pose a question
12. Island garland
13. Carpentry tool
14. Rich Little, e.g.
15. Passion
16. Did the crawl
27. Graven images
29. Jingle writer
31. Buffed
32. The lowdown
34. Butterfly snare
35. Thin pancakes
36. Dwelling
37. Fend off
38. Robber
41. Illicit absence
43. 1 p.m., for example
44. Asphalt
45. Endeavor
47. "Bonnie ___ Clyde"
51. Dull person
52. Cain's mother
54. Disciple
57. Stubborn beast
58. Curious
59. Dock
62. At the location

PUZZLE 7

63. Assist
64. Judges' garments
65. Leaning
66. Damply
70. Faced
71. Posh resort
72. Haw's partner
73. Crash into
74. Weaken
75. Newlywed
77. Operatic piece
80. Young louse
81. Railroad bridge
85. Furnished
86. Constant
89. Upset
91. Charger
92. Very dark wood
93. Bethlehem trio
94. Felt obligated
95. Prayer
97. Have courage
99. "Moon ___ Miami"
100. Install electricity
101. Positions
104. Feathery wra[p]
105. Golfer Ernie ___
107. 1,000,000, for short

PUZZLE 72

CLUES IN TWOS

Some of the Clues in this crossword are In Twos. Fill in two different answers to the same clue in the squares indicated.

ACROSS

1.] Light
9. Hoover ___
12. Cougar
13. Sulfuric and amino
15. Fellow
16. Military subdivision
17. Grill
18.] Bounce
19.] Bounce
21. Hautboy
22. Drat!
23. Quiche ingredient
25. Soft shoe
27. Fitness center
28.] Rim
31.] Rim
35. Bean curd
37. Window blind
39. Margarine
40. Mr. Onassis
41. Bad scent
42. Silly
44. ___ d'Azur
46.] Drink
47.] Drink
48. Hearth residue
50. Cease
52. Take legal action
53. Puts to sea
57. Qualified
60.] Leave
65.] Leave
66. Perfect
67. Ms. Turner
68. Salt Lake City's site
69. Proverb
70. Medical topic: abbr.
71. Withdrawal site: abbr.
72.] War god
73.] War god

26.] Train
27.] Train
28. Burden
29. Object of adoration
30. Sassy
31. Spiral
32. Radius's neighbor
33. Gather crops
34. ___ appetit!
36. To's counterpart
38. Fireplace shelf
43. Water in the Loire
45. Stores, as fodder
49. Old photograph tint
51. "___ Kapital"
52. Genesis man
54. Mideastern religion
55. Rain-forest vine
56. Detection device
57. Turquoise
58. Cigar remainder
59. Actor Neeson
61. Icelandic tome
62. Hindquarters
63. Wizard
64. Holman and Turner

DOWN

1. Urge
2. Melodies
3. Pennsylvania Dutch
4. Percentage
5. Environment
6. Square measure
7. Big cat
8. Lyrical
9. Smear
10. To boot
11. Allot
14. Doze
15. Synthesizer pioneer
20. Cut off
24. Petrol

PUZZLE 73

Slide-O-Gram

Place the seven words into the diagram, one word for each row, so that one of the columns reading down will spell out a 7-letter word that is related to the others. Each given letter is part of one word.

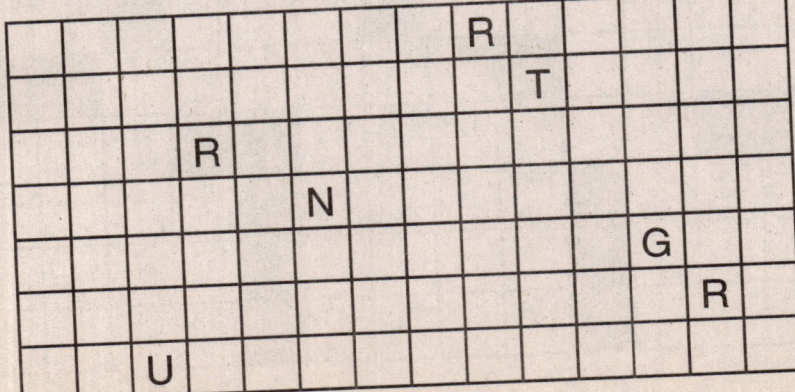

Artichoke
Asparagus
Cucumber
Eggplant
Endive
Escarole
Squash

PUZZLE 74

ACROSS
1. Hay-storage areas
6. Cancel
11. Eskimo houses
13. Wooer
14. Goober
15. Bowers
16. Gender
17. Chain of hills
19. Family animal
20. Brooks
22. Be generous
26. Alleged
30. Mountain cat
31. Go by plane
32. Not far
33. Greek vase
35. Take another stab at
36. Audio system
38. Yes, at sea
41. High schoolers
42. Pep
45. Wonderful thing
47. Split
49. Mean
50. Net user
51. Leg joints
52. Cover again

DOWN
1. Smooch spots
2. Curved molding
3. Linen-fiber origin
4. Coal measure
5. Reference
6. Cry of discovery
7. Tease
8. At the peak
9. Painful
10. Once, formerly
12. Arouse
13. In a wise manner
18. State
21. Trig term
22. Luxury hotel
23. Steady drone
24. Electrical unit
25. Stadium cheers
27. Greeted
28. Cup handle
29. Arid
31. Willingly
34. Weasel-like mammals
35. Pinker
37. Halts
38. Out of control
39. Knitter's need
40. Coastal flier
42. Metallic element
43. Brain wave
44. Criminal, slangily
46. Neckline style
48. Struggle

PUZZLE 75

ACROSS
1. Hacks
5. Yearning
9. "___ Alive!"
12. Brilliant fish
13. Small deer
14. Sigma's follower
15. Agile
16. Saving plans
17. Foamy brew
18. Sailor
19. South African money
20. Appealed
21. Skid
23. Salty solution
25. Rich soil
26. Subtract
27. Supervise
29. Rubbernecked
31. Indy event
34. Teetertotter
35. Dodge
37. Army vehicle
38. Mail
41. Apple seed
42. Capp and Capone
43. Bullets, to a GI
44. Musical tone
45. Grant's foe
46. Achieve
47. Sunburn soother
48. ___ "Kookie" Byrnes
49. Wise about
50. Taverns

DOWN
1. Charges
2. Horrify
3. Latin quarter
4. Introverted
5. Formal solo
6. Popping kernel
7. Earphones
8. Letter before tee
9. Of slanting type
10. Kind of scout
11. Soft leather
19. Marine hitchhiker
20. Multiple
22. Jacquard-weave fabric
24. Beloved
26. Accomplished
28. Dan Rather, e.g.
29. Made watertight
30. Became rigid
32. Roof topper
33. Magazine chief
34. Musty
36. Tools for duels
39. Throw off
40. Forbidden thing
43. Earlier
44. Capture

67

PUZZLE 76

CODEWORD

Codeword is a special crossword puzzle in which conventional clues are omitted. Instead, answer words in the diagram are represented by numbers. Each number represents a different letter of the alphabet, and all of the letters of the alphabet are used. When you are sure of a letter, put it in the code key chart and cross it off in the alphabet box. A group of letters has been inserted to start you off.

LOVE CODEWORDS? *Enjoy hours of fun with our special collections of Selected Codewords! See page 159 for details.*

PUZZLE 77

Two-Step

It's as easy as 1, 2! First, read across each row of words and cross off every letter that appears either twice or four times in that row. Then, reading down, do the same in each column of words. Once a letter is crossed off, it cannot be part of another pair or foursome. After you have crossed off all the pairs and foursomes in the rows and columns, read the remaining letters, from left to right, to reveal a punny caption for the picture. We have started the puzzle by crossing off the first pair of letters.

MULBERRY	INGOTS	ANTHEM	TOASTY
THUMB	ANSWER	MOOCH	CARING
RIPER	SHARPEN	WINTER	ABOVE
AXED	TOAD	WHICH	VICTOR

CAPTION: _ _ _ _ _   _ _ _ _ _ _ _ _ _

BRICK BY BRICK

PUZZLE 78

Rearrange this stack of bricks to form a crossword puzzle. The clues will help you fit the bricks into their correct places. Row 1 has been filled in for you. Use the bricks to fill in the remaining spaces.

ACROSS

1. Tease
   Knitted
   Exchanges
2. Radius's neighbor
   Stack
   Lofty pad
3. Dry up
   Marine eagle
   Fight with swords
4. Overthrow
   Athens vowel
5. Seep
   Arm joint
6. Settler
   One of two
7. Glistened
   Grow
   Trigonometric function
8. Seed coat
   Skating figure
   Pecan or filbert
9. Single entity
   Bride's headwear
   Cordwood measure
10. Go back on a promise
    Hate
11. Pine
    Inferior
12. Snacked
    Type of tantrum
13. Show off
    So long, in London
    Reduce
14. Pakistani coin
    Burden
    Baseball-team number
15. Perfume oil
    Close by
    Excursion

DOWN

1. Simply
   Goad
   Swimsuit part
2. Biscuit topper
   Fake
   Three strikes
3. Crisp cookie
   Certain antiseptic
   Befitting
4. Ahab's weapon
   "___ and Sympathy"
   ___ horse
5. Forsaken
   Cheese shredder
6. Gasp
   Incident
7. Above, to a bard
   Weird
   Kind of jacket
8. Pianist Cliburn
   Solid
   Tropical cuckoo
9. Duelist's choice
   Lug
   Harbor ship
10. Peep
    Fertilizer
11. African expedition
    Blackthorn fruit
12. Teeny
    ___ a boy!
    Agonize
13. Prince Valiant's son
    Black eye
    Duo
14. Photo
    Term of office
    Anglo-Saxon peon
15. Observe
    Nerve network
    Foul smell

BRICKS

| HER | | EIT | PER | POD |
| INE | ST | ES | ASE | UNI |

| RE | TA | EGE | AT | TEM |
| | WRI | ARN | ST | AE |

| ER | PI | RIE | T | REN |
| RIS | SHO | NCE | ST | YE |

| TOP | SN | ULN | DE | EAP |
| | HT | SEA | P | RNE |

| INE | IGH | PLE | NUT | ONE |
| REK | EIL | OOZ | ERE | NE |

| E | AH | RUP | E | AE |
| TAT | RE | ATT | TV | FE |

| | EE | E | PLO | ONU |
| BOA | AR | E | OOR | NIG |

DIAGRAM

	1	2	3	4	5	6	7	8	9	10	11	12	13	14	15
1	J	O	S	H	■	W	O	V	E	■	S	W	A	P	S
2															
3															
4															
5															
6															
7															
8															
9															
10															
11															
12															
13															
14															
15															

BRICK BY BRICK FANS! *Get a ton of Brick by Bricks—over 50 fun puzzles in each of our special collections! To order, see page 159.*

PUZZLE 79

ACROSS
1. Richard Harris film
5. Manly
10. Vatican leader
14. Dog's bark
15. Luminous
16. Figure-skating jump
17. Wicked
18. Rock's ___ Jam
19. Summit
20. Pass along
22. Bro's sibling
23. Picnic crashers
24. "Of Mice and ___"
26. Not neat
29. Tiny frog
32. Simmered
36. Lang. in Warsaw
37. Harsh
39. Iron source
40. Ancient
41. Discolored
42. Decorative container
43. ___ out a living
44. Sagest
45. Adjust, as a clock
46. Plaids
48. Repeated
51. Gabriel, e.g.
53. Buzz
54. Trucker's vehicle
57. Wrestler's pad
59. Flocks
63. Recuperate
64. Monastery head
66. Winnings
67. Low female voice
68. Pantry staple
69. Threatening word
70. Colorist
71. Absorbent fabric
72. Abound

DOWN
1. Debtor
2. Wander about
3. Spring
4. Blazing
5. Road diagram
6. Ripens, as cheese
7. Miner's stake
8. Shrewdness
9. Nocturnal bird
10. Tropical fruit
11. Draft animals
12. Type of moss
13. Part of BPOE
21. Slangy affirmative
25. Fitting together
27. Limber up
28. Finch food
29. Fast dance
30. Senior
31. Convene again
33. Mickey, e.g.
34. Made a boo-boo
35. Auto imperfection
36. Verse writer
38. Compete
41. "___ Lake" (ballet)
47. Seamstress
49. Cry of disbelief
50. Breakfast fare
52. Toil
54. Herringlike fish
55. Slippery
56. Aussie's buddy
58. Sightseeing trip
60. Audition prize
61. Patient's portion
62. Goblet feature
64. Toward the rear, nautically
65. Endeavor

PUZZLE 80 — Everything's Relative

Find the word that precedes or follows four of the five words in each group below. Then, find the bonus word that precedes or follows the five words you've eliminated.

1. TOE	DOOR	CANE	HANG	THUMB
2. STAIR	OIL	INK	MAPLE	FARE
3. NECK	BRUSH	NOSE	FEED	LOAF
4. COAT	DARK	PIPE	BLACK	FORK
5. HOME	PLUM	OFF	WHEEL	DATA

BONUS: _____

PUZZLE 81

ACROSS
1. Foe of the "Titanic"
5. Filled tortilla
9. Pullmans, e.g.
13. Curing chemical
14. More painful
15. Skip over
16. Soy product
17. Dexterous
18. Not on your ___
19. Of the North
21. Confuse
22. Enemy agent
25. Ignited
26. Leatherworking tool
28. Wiggly sea creature
29. Jeweler's glass
31. Bother
34. Wrapped up
36. Garden workers
39. Art ___
40. Summary of beliefs
42. Toll
44. Oral permission
46. Most likely
48. Fairy
50. Martini garnish
51. Beseech
54. Tourist lodging
55. Total
57. Rules to follow
58. Commence
60. String
63. Flounder's kin
64. Boom box
65. Chalet feature
69. Consistent
70. Rankle
71. Musical-staff sign
72. Experiment
73. Forest denizen
74. Course book

DOWN
1. Winged mammal
2. Self-importance
3. Game official
4. Chow
5. In unison
6. "Aida" highlight
7. Wine locale
8. Crude copper
9. Chilly
10. Organic compound
11. Infantry weapon
12. Hard metal
14. Kolkata clothing
20. Table spread
21. As well
22. Winter vehicle
23. Cornmeal cakes
24. Agave plant
27. Mackerel
30. Tactics
32. Highly skilled
33. Part of a calyx
35. Disdain
37. Bridge term
38. Round of gunfire
41. Bleaker
43. Corrosive liquids
45. Barbecue skewer
47. Presage
49. Mad
51. Thing of worth
52. Range
53. Cabbagelike veggies
56. Big name in fashion
59. Landlord's concern
61. Advantage
62. Denomination
64. Cool, man!
66. Pub potable
67. Provoke
68. Salamander

Lucky Clover

PUZZLE 82

Fit the seven words into the four-leaf clover. Each word starts in a circle and may go in any direction. Words sometimes overlap.

Chronic

Confidential

Crayon

Sacred

Steadfast

Stoic

Yonder

71

PUZZLE 83 — DOUBLE TROUBLE

Not really double trouble, but double fun! Solve this puzzle as you would a regular crossword, except place one, two, or three letters in each box. The number of letters in each answer is shown in parentheses after its clue.

ACROSS
1. Wizardry (5)
3. Setback (8)
6. Substitute (4)
9. ___ jacket (5)
11. Female urchin (6)
12. Small stream (5)
13. Singer Amos (4)
14. Nasty look (4)
15. Uncle ___ (3)
16. To wit (6)
18. Flock tender (8)
21. English coin (5)
22. Burn with water (5)
23. Vast timespan (3)
24. Sulks (6)
25. Dud (5)
26. Party giver (4)
27. British brew (3)
28. Explain clearly (6)
29. Respond (5)
30. Discontinuance (9)
32. Snicker (7)
33. Resident (6)
34. Vamoose! (5)
35. Relay ___ (4)
38. Mr. Disney (4)
40. Slumber (5)
41. ___ R. Murrow (6)
42. Vague idea (6)
43. Edible bulb (5)
44. Corn spike (3)

DOWN
1. Iron attractor (6)
2. Ethereal fluid (5)
3. With nobility (7)
4. Dutch painter (7)
5. Briny (6)
6. Rascal (5)
7. Armed fight (3)
8. Quick look (4)
10. Disastrous (7)
15. Shack (4)
17. Make right (5)
18. Lox (6)
19. Religious dissent (6)
20. "___ Look Now" (4)
21. Curly-haired dogs (7)
22. Incident (5)
24. Teeth straighteners (6)
25. Maned male (4)
26. Shouted (8)
28. Rebellious (7)
29. Bulletin (6)
31. Concentration (9)
32. Titleholder (8)
34. Silver ___ (6)
36. Mindful (5)
37. Fragrant tree (5)
38. Pale (3)
39. Fortune (3)
40. ___-mo (3)

PUZZLE 84 — Double Up

Each puzzle consists of four 5-letter words that use ten different letters exactly twice apiece. Thus, since there are already two T's in the first puzzle, you cannot use another T. There is only one C in that puzzle; think of a word using the second C.

1.
N	T	H
U		L
C	O	T
	I	G

2.
D	C	L
	D	R
M	L	H
	U	O

3.
R	B	N
	N	P
P	E	T
	A	O

4.
G	A	T
	L	I
L	N	O
	R	A

PUZZLE 85
• EZ PASS •

ACROSS
1. Commercials
4. Keanu Reeves flick
9. Peach stone
12. Sought office
13. Rigid
14. Sooner than, in verse
15. "Nana" author
17. Sun-bronzed
18. McIntosh, e.g.
19. Song or gab ending
20. MDs
22. Mai ___ cocktail
24. Green soup
27. Spunk
32. Region with a variable climate
35. Worrier
36. Cookie box
37. Egyptian snake
38. Ore.'s neighbor
41. Uneasy
44. Music hall
48. Taste
49. Last Aztec emperor of Mexico
53. Sticky substance
54. Speaker
55. Democrat's opp.
56. In the past
57. English weapons
58. First number

DOWN
1. Telephone code
2. Soggy
3. Prune
4. Beef animal
5. Candy brand
6. Rocker Brian ___
7. Exchange stud. class
8. Narc's org.
9. Folk's Seeger
10. Levin and Miller
11. Camper's home
16. Legal deg.
19. Effervesce
21. Paper currency
22. ___-frutti
23. Finished lunch
24. School gp.
25. Electric ___
26. "ER" organization
28. Owns
29. Flower container
30. Tropical bird
31. Chick's mom
33. Use rosary beads
34. Some dashes
39. Activists
40. Woodworking tool
41. Singer Jones
42. Race type
43. Greek hero?
45. Lira replacement
46. Peck film, with "The"
47. Neck back
49. Unset bks.
50. Mare's morsel
51. Comic Louis ___
52. Five and five

PUZZLE 86
• DIRECTOR'S CUT •

ACROSS
1. Upper limb
4. Best
9. Sp. misters
12. Scottish negative
13. Young chicken
14. Motorists' org.
15. Road signals
18. Trade for money
19. Furtiveness
20. Rainbow shape
23. "___ That Jazz"
24. Total collapse
28. Director Reiner
31. Photographic device with a tiny aperture
35. Fruity drink
36. Nail polish solvent
37. PC key
40. Number of cards in Cato's deck?
41. Kind of desk
45. Loose bag
49. Elusive maneuver
52. Golf score
53. Fido's strap
54. Couple
55. Pay ending
56. Sea raptors
57. Appropriate

DOWN
1. Picnic crashers
2. Hard to find
3. Brunch, e.g.
4. Switch word
5. Illusionist Geller
6. Muscle twitches
7. "___ Dawn" (Reddy song)
8. Bay window
9. Comedian Mort ___
10. "Round and Round" band
11. Miss America's garb
16. Glimmer
17. Maiden
21. It comes after pi
22. ___-de-sac
24. Resort of sorts
25. Center
26. Chemical suffix
27. Apiece
28. Race in neutral
29. Prospector's find
30. Piece of soap
32. Cartoon frame
33. Pierre's pal
34. Somewhat wet
37. Subways' cousins
38. Rural crossing
39. Lid
41. Default result
42. Track shape
43. Zhivago's beloved
44. Hymn of praise
46. Opera heroine
47. Sudden takeover
48. Tangle
50. Enzyme suffix
51. Book pts.

PUZZLE 87

Diagramless crosswords are solved by using the clues and their numbers to fill in the answer words and the arrangement of black squares. Insert the number of each clue with the first letter of its answer, across and down. Fill in a black square at the end of each word. Every black square must have a corresponding black square on the opposite side of the diagram to form a diagonally symmetrical pattern. Puzzles 87 and 88 have been started for you.

ACROSS
1. Spider's trap
4. Petty quarrel
8. Arabian prince
10. Carbonated drink
11. Albacore
12. Defect
13. Enormous
15. Secret
18. Less than many
21. Bustle
22. Family
24. Generation
25. Church bench
26. Rule
28. Dodge
30. Flick
32. Highway charge
36. Baking chamber
37. Bread spread
38. Role
39. Pat

DOWN
1. Soggy
2. Ostrich's cousin
3. Receptacle
4. Read hastily
5. Sulk
6. 100%
7. Make lace
9. Wrath
12. Weariness
14. Provoke
15. Jar top
16. Shelley work
17. Pledge
18. Retainer
19. Misjudge
20. Colorless
23. Bow
27. Kill, legislatively
28. Constantly
29. Carpet fluff
30. Floor washer
31. Germs
33. Archaic
34. Meadow
35. Tennis shot

PUZZLE 88

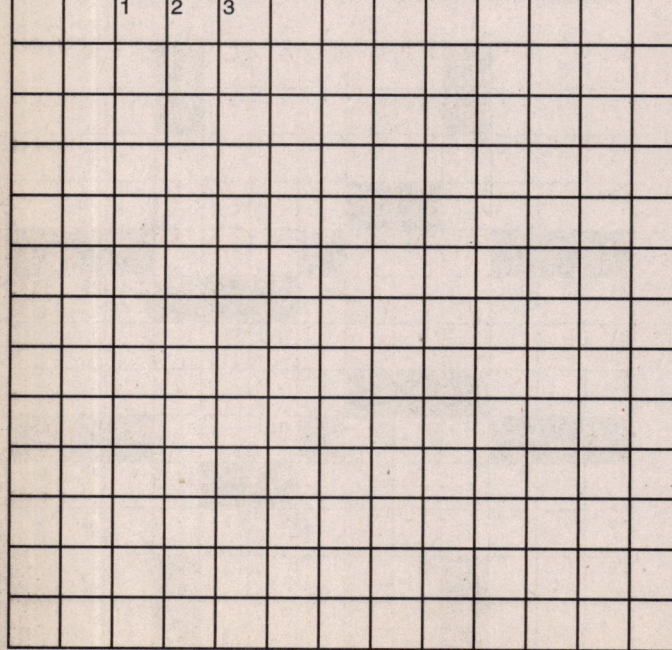

ACROSS
1. Casper's greeting
4. Buffoon
8. Cattle group
9. Gold fabric
10. Detested
11. Rainbow
12. Light breeze
13. Bird homes
14. Sharp blow
16. Candy unit
17. Okey-dokey
19. Motor disk
20. Bestowed
23. Slick
24. Father
26. Put to good ___
27. Manufactured
30. Swift horses
33. Blokes
34. Singer Perry ___
35. Lassoed
37. Hunch
38. Flabbergasted
39. Fender flaw
40. Finger count

DOWN
1. Double-cross
2. Neighbor of Wash.
3. Unusual
4. Circular
5. Sculls
6. Exclude
7. More or ___
8. Flag down
10. Contains
13. Christened
15. Sweet ___
16. Dreadful
18. Kind of cheese
19. Snivel
21. Maven
22. Block up
25. Moisten
26. Underwater menace
28. Heroic action
29. Football player
30. Lab fluid
31. Took a taxi
32. Mass response
35. Tattle
36. Be in the red

PUZZLE 89

ACROSS
1. Summer shirts
5. Downright
7. ____ and Ives
9. Fencing sword
11. Madrid's locale
13. Prior to, in verse
14. Fitness facility
15. Actress Sten
16. Sugary
18. Busy place
19. Leafy lunch
21. Frozen water
24. Poetic form
25. Conceals
26. Bit for Silver
27. Crony
28. Looked steadily
29. Poker stake
30. Make a speech
32. Word of lament
33. Hook's foe
34. Under the weather
35. Equip
38. Limber
40. Defensible
42. Recover
43. Ship off

DOWN
1. Authentic
2. Go astray
3. Corn servings
4. Cut with scissors
5. King topper
6. Taunted
8. Mature
9. Coastal flier
10. Garden veggie
12. Part of NFL
13. Letter holder
15. Verdi opera
16. Winter coaster
17. Used to be
18. Bunny's move
19. Small, medium, or large
20. Fruity drink
22. Broadway musical
23. Summer, to Pierre
25. Derby, e.g.
28. Male goose
29. Unify
31. Rave's partner
32. Tire filler
36. "The Defiant ____"
37. Salary
38. Slipped
39. Writing tool
41. Prohibit

Starting box on page 562

Crossblocks

PUZZLE 90

Insert the letters and letter groups into each diagram to form words reading across that answer the clues on the left. In each diagram, a bonus word will read diagonally down in the tinted blocks.

1.   A D DE END ER

ET EUR F FA H IC

LTE MA N RE T

Guard
Layman
Cultural
Wavered

2.   AB ABG AD AUT CR

EX IC LE MIR NG OC

ODI PL RA RAT SS

Lawn weed
Despotic
Bursting
Excellent

75

PUZZLE 91

ACROSS
1. Honest prez
4. Waiting-room word
6. Rips
8. Francis or Kendall
11. Shuteye
13. Heart
14. Domesticates
16. Little pies
17. Weary
19. Jazz's Davis
20. Small fleet
22. Put in order
23. Least refined
25. Grand canyon?
26. Ranch resident
29. Sassy
30. Furnish with funds
32. For fear that
33. Flavorful
35. So far
36. Communication channels
38. Fender-bender souvenir
39. Maiden-name indicator

DOWN
1. Formicary dweller
2. Honey makers
3. Glorify
5. Halloween option
7. Big rig
8. Divided nation
9. Humanities
10. Of course!
12. Take part in a concert
13. Phone
15. Peddles
16. Floor square
18. Metes (out)
19. Hand warmers
21. Aesthetic judgment
22. Pocket money
23. Bureau
24. Drying oven
25. Algonquian speaker
27. Cheese town
28. Used a lasso
29. Take to the skies
31. Expand
34. Break bread
37. Corroded

Starting box on page 562

PUZZLE 92

Triangle Sums

The two diagonals divide the diagram on the left into four large triangles. Place the nine squares on the right into the diagram so that the sums of the four numbers in those triangles are equal. If a square is divided, place it in the diagram in a square that is divided the same way.

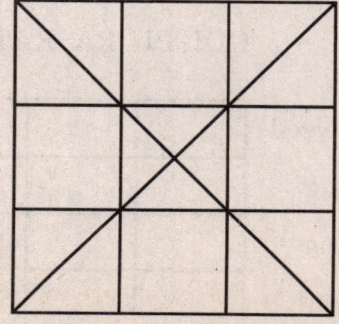
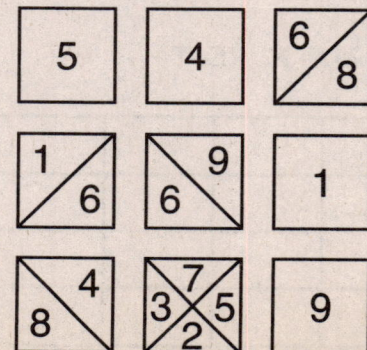

PUZZLE 93

ACROSS
1. Celebrity
5. Witnessed
8. Column
9. Bind
10. Dish dryer
11. Green shade
12. Before long
13. Yonder
15. Navy or pinto
16. Peak
17. Coastal soil
18. Gathered
19. Tot up
22. Sting
24. Trend
25. 1,440 minutes
26. Swell
27. Blame
28. Staff symbol
29. Fruit quaff
30. Purring pet
31. Weary
32. Certainly!
33. Stable food
34. Sheet of glass
35. Mongrel
36. Lawyer's concern
37. Jolt
38. Grotto
39. Small quarrel
41. Love on the run
43. Bungle
44. Clay square
45. Unite
46. Hardens

DOWN
1. Silverware item
2. Incorporated village
3. Brighton drink
4. Akin
5. Excitement
6. Direct at a target
7. Minuscule
10. Warty critter
11. Lick up
12. Mailed
14. Like a fiddle
15. Undraped
17. Rescues
18. Atlas page
19. Place on a pedestal
20. It may be blind
21. Hid the gray
22. Persuade
23. Concocted
24. Obese
27. Sunbeam
28. Nil
30. Rugs
31. Diamond corner
33. Steady drone
34. Tar
35. Nick
36. Ann and Cod
37. Troubadour
38. Young horse
39. Give a darn?
40. Historic starter
42. Golfer's concern

Starting box on page 562

Crozzle

PUZZLE 94

The 4-letter answers to the clues are to be entered into the diagram either from top to bottom or diagonally upward. The word MEAN has been entered as an example. When the diagram is correctly filled, you will be able to read an 8-letter word across the top row of letters.

1-2. Object
2-3. Average
3-4. Moniker
4-5. Throw off
5-6. Tessera
6-7. French pronoun
7-8. Scat queen
8-9. With wings
9-10. Knocks
10-11. Interval
11-12. Hammer target
12-13. In person
13-14. Tied
14-15. Cool!
15-16. Mission

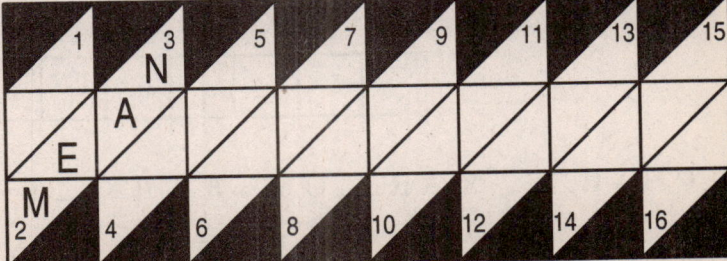

77

PUZZLE 95

ACROSS
1. NYC clock zone
4. Poet Millay
8. Wading bird
10. Not cooked
13. Reproduced
14. Downturn
16. Trick
17. Pacific island
18. Buck or doe
19. Operator
20. Flower
23. Thai
25. Trade
27. Sixth sense
28. Proves human
30. Pocket money
32. Car size
34. Oil, e.g.
35. Positive
37. Knox, e.g.
38. Airshow stunt
40. Suffer
41. Capture
43. Garden tools
47. Recuperates
50. Corridor
51. ___ mater
54. Soft drink
56. Hens' products
57. Devastates
59. Sinister
60. Teacher's org.
61. Exuberance
62. 18-wheeler
63. French summer

DOWN
1. Road curve
2. Convinced
3. Accurate
4. Kind of tide
5. Lackluster
6. Jodie Foster film
7. Bye, Pedro!
9. Iowa town
10. Deception
11. Imitates
12. "Wish You ___ Here"
15. Clergyman
16. Landfill
21. Have a debt
22. Artist Chagall
24. Hearth residue
26. Prim's partner
29. Clever
30. Erie or Panama
31. Director's cry
33. Peach center
35. Shirt feature
36. Ark builder
37. "Fee, ___, foe, fum!"
39. Dessert choice
40. Hole punchers
42. Intertwines
43. At that time
44. Seethe
45. Gymnast Korbut
46. Fake coin
48. Letter or potion
49. Slender
52. Marathon segment
53. Dill seed
55. Boxing champ
58. Understand

Starting box on page 562

PUZZLE 96 — Keyword

To find the Keyword, fill in the blanks in words 1 through 10 with the correct missing letters. Transfer those letters to the correspondingly numbered squares in the diagram. Approach with care—this puzzle is not as simple as it first appears.

1. C H A R __
2. S P __ R E
3. A R __ O R
4. B L __ N K
5. C R A __ E
6. A __ G E R
7. N A __ T Y
8. P __ N C H
9. S T O __ E
10. C H __ C K

PUZZLE 97

ACROSS
1. Consomme
6. Branch
9. Spokes
10. Traipse
12. Poetic form
13. Light ax
15. Skinny
18. Writer Waugh
19. Ancient dagger
21. "The Other" author
24. Distant
25. Doggie doc
27. Osculate
28. Moon goddess
29. Heraldic band
30. Tourist's aid
33. Regulated course
36. Singer Grant
37. Fabricated
38. Leer at
39. Nipa palm
40. Braggart's problem
41. Outfit
42. Beau
46. Quick cut
48. Eye layer
50. Short-billed rail
52. First-down requirement
56. Revenue
58. Weary
59. Complete mess
60. Soap chemical
61. Diners' lists

4. Fastens with cord
5. Beverly ___
6. Gallery display
7. Pooh's friend
8. Papa's lady
11. Beer ingredient
12. Lewd
14. Not him
16. Sickly
17. Contemptibly small
20. Celtic language
22. Female gamete
23. Island goose
26. Beige
27. Hawaiian acacia
28. Golfer's concern
30. Morning Prayer
31. Slow, in music
32. Energy
33. Beluga product
34. Quiche component
35. Incandescence
37. Earth's neighbor
43. Old French measure
44. It climbs
45. Well-groomed
47. Spectrum revealer
49. Nutmeg coat
51. Diarist Frank
52. Bean curd
53. Flightless birds
54. Dehydrated
55. Comprehend
57. Dismiss

Starting box on page 562

DOWN
1. Forehead
2. Grade
3. Curious

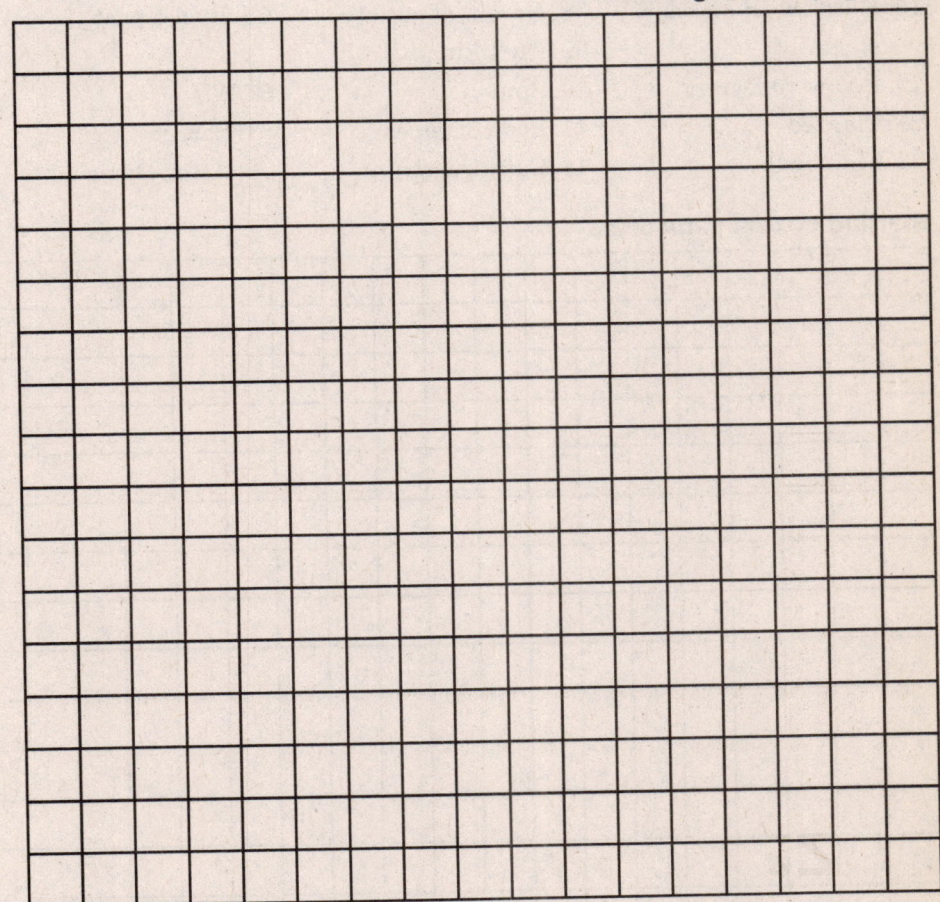

PUZZLE 98

Tiles

Imagine that these Tiles are on a table, each tile showing a 2-letter combination. Can you rearrange these Tiles visually to form a 10-letter word?

PUZZLE 99

ACROSS

1. Mischievous child
4. Honest ___
7. Knot
9. False move
11. Vanity
13. Car-patch material
14. Judge's wear
15. Arden and Brenner
17. Gold bar
18. Horse with an easy stride
19. Below, to Byron
21. Planted
23. Finished
24. Snooker stick
25. Watery-patterned fabric
27. Lots
29. Cut remnant
30. Dawdling
31. Unripe
33. Quote
34. Devours a book
35. Campfire treat
37. Oxygen tank?
38. Cream of society
39. Ale's kin
40. Spur
41. Loop of rope
42. Capture again
44. ___ Arbor, Michigan
45. Allied nations
47. Fixed a boot
51. Association
54. Tile-joint filler
55. Cold-cut shops
57. January forecast
58. Author Ayn ___
59. Fiber plant
60. Expunging
62. Paint type
63. Pharmacy measures
64. Commanded
65. Insect pest

DOWN

1. Secret
2. Actor Davis
3. Dress feathers
4. Eternities
5. Church game
6. Bestow
7. Like a teetotaler
8. Active
9. Crime-solving org.
10. Carved pole
11. Make do
12. Scone
14. Meanderer
16. Cram
18. Navigational aid
20. "___ So Shy"
22. Medicated
26. Frosts
27. Church steeple
28. Dove home
31. Romance, e.g.
32. Waste cloth
33. Bunk
34. Laments
35. Sluggish
36. Certain skirts
37. Kingly
38. Set up
39. Worker's reward
40. Arrogant
41. Shrew
43. Having a central point
45. Wheat and oat husks
46. Extended
48. Allowable
49. Delight
50. Submerged
52. British nobleman
53. Sneezy, e.g.
54. Dirty
56. Male or female
61. Gal of song

Starting box on page 562

DIAGRAMLESS DEVOTEES! Delve into a special collection with loads of challenging puzzles in every volume of Selected Diagramless. To order, see page 159.

PUZZLE 100

ACROSS
1. Annoy
4. Wager
7. Feathery scarf
8. Which person?
11. Secondhand
13. Frigid
14. Type of bagel
17. Inquire
18. Soccer shot
20. Arthur of "Maude"
22. Recipe meas.
24. Wide collar
26. Doze
28. Joseph Smith's gp.
30. Haunch
31. Cans, in London
32. Mass of hair
34. Akron's state
35. Relax, soldier!
37. Working
41. Instruct
42. Avenue crosser
43. Rescue
44. Cut of meat
46. Hole puncher
48. To and ___
49. Herbal brew
50. Troy, N.Y. school
51. Sticky stuff
52. Oahu neckwear
53. Noah's vessel
54. Part of BMOC
56. Primp, avian style
59. "M*A*S*H" setting
61. WWII craft
62. Knight's title
63. Terminus
64. Illuminated
65. Slugger's stat
67. Train unit
68. Seine
69. Mommy has three
70. Tire woe
72. Cyclones' hometown
74. Manifest
77. Join forces
80. Artifacts, perhaps
82. Cannon, e.g.
83. Sped
84. Annex
85. Kiwis' kin
87. Small fry
88. Turf
89. Nice summer
91. Fine dirt
92. Switch positions
93. Spread to dry
95. Bug
98. Rend
100. Black Hills locale
104. Zodiac sign
105. Sherpa sighting
106. Poor grade
107. Trigger's morsel
108. Horned viper
109. Volga feeder

DOWN
1. Heron's kin
2. Spacecraft
3. Bandleader Kyser
4. Purchase
5. Snaky letter
6. Summer shirt
8. FDR's relief agency
9. Brick carrier
10. Unlocked
12. Society miss
15. Punctual
16. City in India
17. Attraction
18. Sweetie
19. Tennis doubles?
21. Pedro's parting word
22. Not this
23. Position
25. Bind
27. Go-getter
29. Simple symphonies
33. Like better
34. Sarge's dog
36. Oak nut
37. Christiania, now
38. Cliff dwelling
39. Ward off
40. Plumbing problem
45. Puppy's bite
46. Like fine wine
47. Prevailed
52. Oodles
54. Home of the Heat
55. Stops
57. Kent portrayer
58. Whole
59. Actress Novak
60. Sandy's comment
61. Jungle vine
62. A pompano
64. Dregs
66. Fast-flowing talk
68. Firn
71. Excellent
73. Dart
75. Cairo's river
76. Boston player
78. Roger Rabbit, e.g.
79. Tolkien creatures
81. Command
82. Part of "TW3"
85. XL squared
86. Not at home
90. Writer Bagnold
94. Dawn to dusk
96. Fr. holy woman
97. Hurricane center
99. Small quantity
101. Pod legume
102. Part of TGIF
103. Cracker adjunct
104. Card game

Starting box on page 562

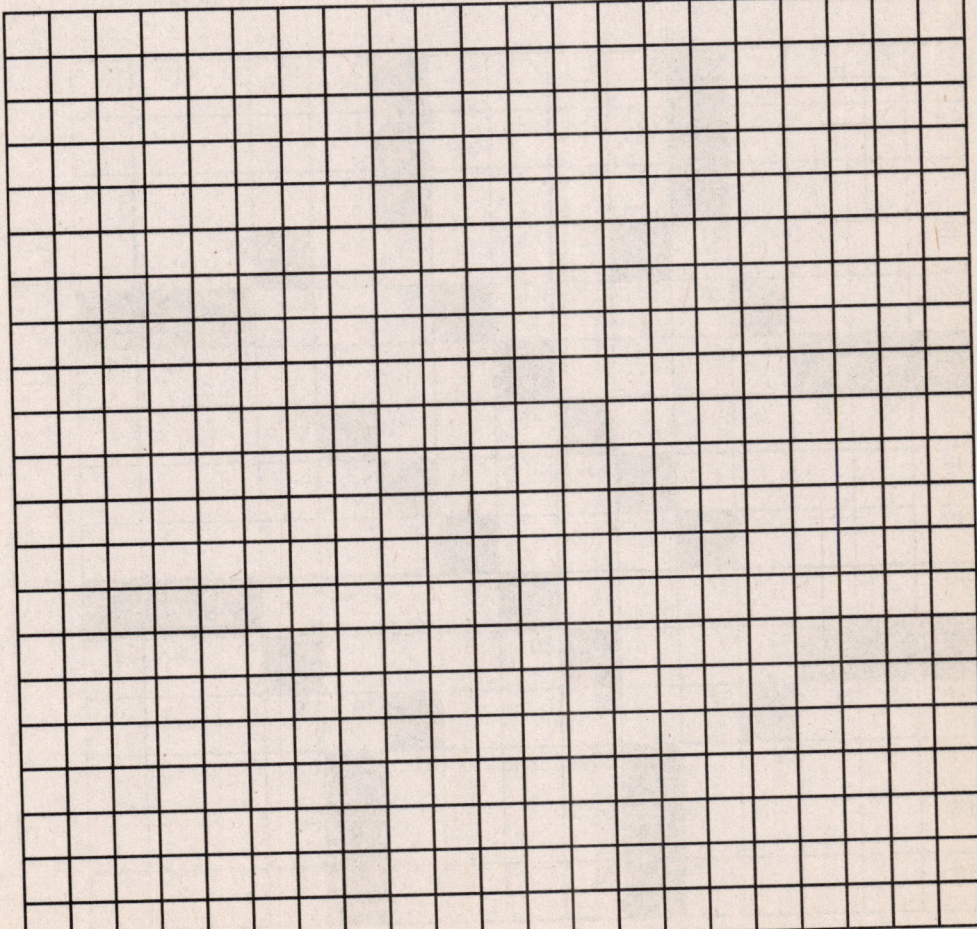

PUZZLE 109

ACROSS

1. ___ diver
6. ___ chowder
10. Josh
13. Issue
14. Flashy
15. RBI's kin
16. Arizona brick
17. Expand
18. Modeled
19. Finger count
20. Layered rock
22. Slow down
24. Imitating
26. Is in debt
27. Blurs
32. Horned snake
34. Spotted mount
35. Chapel song
38. Chair part
41. Extra
42. Flee
43. TV host
45. Bro's sibling
46. Black
48. Baby insect
49. Heckle
50. Most aged
51. Skillful
54. Old saw
58. Sorrow
60. Regretful people
62. Bawl
65. Push firmly
66. Go-between
68. Suit of mail
70. View
71. Jackets
72. Sheer fabric
73. Road bend
74. Male turkeys
75. Urged (on)

DOWN

1. RBI, e.g.
2. ZIP ___
3. Aware of
4. Baby apron
5. High cards
6. Texas dish
7. Wool fabric
8. Dazzle
9. Wordy bird
10. Cut wood again
11. Outraged
12. ___ Motel
14. Switch
21. Holds
23. Hit hard
25. Miss
27. Hot springs
28. Skirt type
29. Closes
30. Supped
31. Cowboy event
33. Odor
35. For
36. Daystar
37. Whichever
38. Ranch unit
39. Vrooms
40. Menu item
44. Enraged
47. Large snake
49. Hive dweller
50. Bard's always
51. Consent
52. Heehaws
53. Green fruits
55. Imagine
56. Uncles' wives
57. Receives
59. Truth
61. Wise
62. Arrogant
63. Dribble
64. Produced
67. Icky stuff
69. Tatter

PUZZLE 101

ACROSS
1. Extend
5. Machine cylinders
9. Masts
14. Mexican snack
15. Our Father closer
16. Noel
17. Particle
18. Deli choice
19. Bouquet
20. Klaxon
22. Glucose
24. Screen
25. Sweetie
26. Is obliged
28. Cold
30. Fibbed
31. Liberation
35. Hinder
38. Crucial
39. Queue
40. Breathing
41. Offer
42. Gap
43. Haul
44. Sizzling
45. Brunch dish
46. Gulp
48. Tethered
49. Second person
50. Celebration
51. Clever
54. More, to Juan
57. Fiery felony
59. Speed detector
61. Scallion's kin
63. Roused
65. Encrypt
66. Riot
67. Confused
68. Misjudges
69. Saber
70. Brash
71. Just-passing marks

DOWN
1. Stow
2. Terrace
3. Oak's nut
4. Alaska city
5. Meower
6. Tickled
7. Option lists
8. Glitch
9. Scanty
10. Average
11. Actor Kincaid
12. The Eternal City
13. Blind part
21. Din
23. Breezy
27. Tiny
29. Barked
30. Beautiful
31. Nourished
32. Indicator
33. Earlier
34. Converge
35. Horse food
36. Snow clearer
37. Pocket bread
38. Toolbox
41. Curtsy
42. Blur
44. Clock cycle
45. Grease
47. Lent
48. Crude carrier
50. Silly one
51. Worship
52. Army chaplain
53. Ringlet
54. Mothers
55. Again
56. Grain tower
58. Trade
60. Scored on serve
62. Above, in poems
64. Sup

PUZZLE 102

ACROSS
1. Vamoose!
6. Disagreement
10. Commotion
14. Eucalyptus eater
15. Hole
16. Drag
17. Fool
18. Furrows
19. Just got by
20. Erasure
22. Glasgow lid
24. Wet soil
25. Optimal
28. Screenplay
32. Conditions
33. Succeeded
35. Backless seats
36. Meddle
37. Footwear
38. Of ships
39. Bible boat
40. Lingers
41. Element
42. To's partner
43. Billfold
44. Place
45. Block
46. Joked
47. Road curves
49. Floor cleaner
50. Dog, e.g.
51. Affixed
57. Ember
60. Direction
62. Leek's cousin
63. Opposer
64. Blackthorn fruit
65. Sign
66. Red root
67. Incline
68. Depleted

DOWN
1. Slip
2. Cryptogram
3. Track
4. African shrub
5. TV's Lauer
6. Bud
7. Beat
8. Skill
9. Take the stand
10. Subject
11. Sturdy tree
12. Outstanding
13. Dated
21. Gremlins
23. Radio spots
26. For a time
27. Plundered
28. Bust
29. Begrudges
30. Rove
31. Queasy
32. Bug
34. Avian abode
35. Clip
36. Maven
37. Sailor
39. Offshoot
40. Had been
42. Swiftest
43. Cried
45. Low grade
46. Wrote quickly
48. Schism
49. Stoneworker
52. Feats
53. Cleave
54. Backpack
55. Balanced
56. Hollow
57. Hack
58. U2 song
59. Nibbled
61. Bitter drink

PUZZLE 103

ACROSS
1. Flees
5. Cigar remnant
9. Vamoose!
14. Eliminate
15. Smoking tool
16. Ring
17. ___ pop
18. Presser's need
19. Full of dandelions
20. Peel
21. Ninth follower
23. Besides
24. Final letter
26. Make a choice
28. Streetcar
30. Accept
34. "Doctor ___"
35. Improvement
38. Climbing plant
40. Sculpture, e.g.
41. Wake
42. Connecting link
43. Sticky glop
44. Badgers
46. Play part
47. Inhale and exhale
49. Hit repeatedly
51. Fire insect
52. Jazz instrument
53. "Body ___"
56. Brewing need
60. Spoken
64. Pungent
66. Pimples
67. Brass horn
68. African mammal
69. Leg bone
70. Lazily
71. Avoid
72. Mistake in print
73. Third letters

DOWN
1. Deficit
2. Berserk
3. Type of skirt
4. Poem division
5. Ill will
6. Trunk spare
7. Atop
8. Bowed
9. Carpenter's blade
10. Invent
11. Film segment
12. No ifs, ___, or buts
13. BLT dressing
22. Container
25. Grounded bird
27. Fruit dessert
28. Pulsate
29. Engine part
30. Cruel person
31. Leisure
32. Essential
33. Kick out
34. Tail motion
36. Attractive
37. Gee whiz!
39. To date
44. Cooking utensil
45. Health farm
48. Snacking
50. Strange
52. Office writer
53. Difficult
54. Cave sound
55. Extremely dry
57. Not west
58. Painful
59. Cut
61. Impudent
62. Adept
63. Situates
65. Mother deer

PUZZLE 104

ACROSS
1. Waste metal
6. Pea shells
10. Motor disk
13. Australian marsupials
15. Help a crook
16. Be in debt
17. Bring in
18. Settee
19. Saloon
20. Mexican coin
21. Restaurant
23. Oil derrick
24. Henry or Jane
26. Ventilate
28. Santa's aide
31. Host Serling
32. Naked
33. Main arteries
35. Blossom
36. Horn sound
40. Reel
41. Outlaw
42. Bicycle part
43. Sub
44. In shape
45. Mottled cat
46. Parched
48. Badger
49. Friend's pronoun
50. Shameless
53. Filleted
55. Ditch
56. Bob, e.g.
58. Pagan god
62. TV notices
63. Voice range
64. Once more
66. Okay grade
67. Whole bunch
68. Intensify
69. Historic time
70. Church song
71. Long curl

DOWN
1. Prance
2. Draw near
3. Chats
4. Distant
5. Bogey beater
6. Ziti, e.g.
7. Woodwind
8. Swindle
9. Remained
10. Hooded viper
11. Expect
12. Join
14. Shorthand pros
22. Include
25. Verbal
27. Mutiny
28. Toward sunrise
29. Run easily
30. Out of
32. Sister
34. November gem
35. Cave flier
37. Rework text
38. Per
39. Scheme
41. Bridge move
42. Book part
44. Ultimately
45. Paddled
47. Discuss again
48. Drift (off)
50. Strengthen
51. More impudent
52. Cruising
53. Tanned
54. Chopper
57. Gossip bit
59. Dunce
60. Lode loads
61. Camera eye
65. Catch

PUZZLE 105

ACROSS
1. Nile reptile
5. Shell food?
9. Current measures
13. Strong emotion
14. Pranks
16. Ham or bacon
17. Milky gem
18. Destroyed
19. Accurate
20. Cancel
21. Liquid measure
23. Citrus drink
24. German title
27. Sneaker feature
29. "___ Tide"
32. Immerse
33. Brood
34. Saturn safety device
36. Clear tables
37. Legwear
41. Iron output
42. Receptacle
43. Wild cat
44. Flat-needled shrubs
45. Bill
46. Spokesman?
47. Deuce topper
49. Slangy yes
50. Swimming center?
51. Made an entrance
54. The Plaza, e.g.
56. Frenzy
57. Approached
59. Truant
63. Fish organ
65. Caught congers
67. Bygone time
68. At a loss
69. Rebound
70. Nastiness
71. Clarinet's need
72. Wine choice
73. ___ estate

DOWN
1. Dolt
2. Hemp product
3. Ellipse
4. Star, briefly
5. Raised trains
6. Horse's gait
7. Wheat seed
8. Brief play
9. Capable
10. Upstanding
11. Modest one
12. Trapshooting
15. Grinchlike smirks
22. Whiskey blend
25. Eve's fellow
26. Buggy
28. Rule of conduct
29. Simple
30. Sting
31. Mixture
33. Enjoyable
35. Tack
36. Apron section
38. Peer
39. Appear evident
40. Misjudges
42. Howl
43. Use a keyboard
45. Not tough
46. Carve
48. Beluga delicacy
49. Calls for Heidi?
51. New dad's handout
52. Develop
53. Riot
54. Greetings!
55. Coat of paint
58. Equipment
60. Intertwined
61. "Tosca" song
62. Cry out
64. Fellow
66. Go auburn

PUZZLE 106

ACROSS
1. Pinnacle
5. Sales condition
9. Not hard
13. Miss Muffet's fare
14. Memento
16. Say yes to
17. Surrender
18. Violin's big brother
19. Hold firmly
20. Austere
22. Male heir
23. Heavy wind
24. Unpaired
26. Jolly
28. Red gem
31. Gray
34. Before music or session
37. Wee
38. Clipped
39. Outback bird
40. Fifi's adios
42. That boy
43. Cook's garment
45. Greeted
46. Vista
48. Litter's littlest
49. Previously, in verse
50. Senior
51. Bell
52. Dynasty
53. Boar's abode
55. Mother
58. Weep
61. Breakfast fare
66. Help a crook
67. Curse
69. Highway measure
70. Kind of gin
71. It also rises
72. Angers
73. Rough-cut
74. Single fist
75. Take five

DOWN
1. Hole punches
2. Karate blow
3. Butte's kin
4. Rubbernecker
5. Curved
6. Behold
7. Afflictions
8. Farm building
9. Drenched
10. Southern veggie
11. Flunk
12. Do data entry
15. Eel
21. Asian sauce
25. Smashed
27. Ms. Chlumsky
28. "Knight ___"
29. Combine
30. Brief farewell
32. Glimmer
33. Four-base hits
34. TV repeat
35. Amid
36. Football play
37. No longer wild
41. Customer
44. Paid athlete
47. Elegant
51. Exercise place
52. Supped
54. Pastry
55. Pulverize
56. Qualified
57. Cat's sound
59. Had a debt
60. Mr. Bridges
62. Arab ruler
63. Old Italian dough
64. Fraternal members
65. Assay
68. Invite

PUZZLE 107

CODEWORD

Codeword is a special crossword puzzle in which conventional clues are omitted. Instead, answer words in the diagram are represented by numbers. Each number represents a different letter of the alphabet, and all of the letters of the alphabet are used. When you are sure of a letter, put it in the code key chart and cross it off in the Alphabet Box. A group of letters has been inserted to start you off.

Code Key Chart:

1	2	3	4	5 A	6	7	8 O	9	10	11	12	13
14	15	16	17	18	19	20	21	22	23 T	24	25	26

Alphabet Box

~~A~~ B C D E F G H I J K L M N ~~O~~ P Q R S ~~T~~ U V W X Y Z

PUZZLE 108

ACROSS
1. Atlas items
5. Signs
9. Hunt
14. Oodles
15. Grandma
16. The press
17. Hubbub
18. Lower leg front
19. Lifeless
20. Gin and ___
22. Sense
24. Poker term
25. Place to work out
26. Waiter
28. Costly appetizer
30. Maple fluid
32. Grown-up
35. Gallery exhibit
36. Crowns' cousins
39. Ripped
41. Perched
42. Inconsistent
44. Be competitive
45. Ballet move
47. Take off
48. Barely earn
49. Mexican sauce
51. Conveyed
52. Carmine, e.g.
53. Staircase shape
56. TV spots
58. Meaty
61. Skunk's weapon
62. Was king
65. Frostier
67. Slithery biters
70. Hoard
71. Linen-closet item
72. Plus
73. Leg joint
74. Towel material
75. January forecast
76. Cravings

DOWN
1. Sail support
2. Choir member
3. Christmas plant
4. Long piece
5. Not outs
6. Slangy no
7. Blade
8. Less whacky
9. Grinned
10. Perfect score
11. Summer quenchers
12. Italian money, once
13. Singer Bush
21. Class
23. Elusive
26. Kind of tire
27. Wheel track
28. Grate
29. Verbal tests
31. Attack from above
33. Parking spot
34. Tot rod?
37. Hit head-on
38. Island chain
40. Poverty
43. Chest wood
46. Raised railways
50. Flashy
54. Wanders
55. Fiery crime
57. Dark
58. Clenched hand
59. Muscle strain
60. Stadium part
63. Tie
64. Dead ends?
66. Poetic contraction
68. Paid player
69. Make a quilt

PUZZLE 110

ACROSS
1. Stable bedding
6. Electric unit
9. Chronicles
14. Appraise
15. Tropical constrictor
16. Outline
17. Like many roofs
18. Where ___ at
19. Major vessel
20. Grape drink
21. Charm
23. Bandanna
27. Arts and ___
31. Detained
32. How come?
33. Baby's seat
34. Elegant
36. Dull
37. Skin opening
38. Prognosticators
39. Tiny poodle
40. Got wind of
41. Prepare to publish
42. Tone
43. Rushed
44. Scratch
45. Network
46. Pillar
47. Form of soccer
49. Assumed
53. Thread holder
55. Average degree
56. Tapered off
59. Hilo handout
60. Unimpressed
62. Stinker
63. 18 or 30
64. Assistants
65. Wool fabric
66. Pronoun
67. Whirls

DOWN
1. Utter words
2. Commerce
3. Large stream
4. Smashing serve
5. Unite
6. Remained
7. Theme
8. Leave behind
9. Sparkling
10. Smell
11. Needlefish
12. Opera division
13. Caribbean, e.g.
22. Sore
24. Visual aid
25. Cacklers
26. Class
28. Drift
29. Delay
30. Rushed
32. Ironic
34. Certain car
35. Bizarre
36. Anonymous John
37. Pasta topping
38. Teamster's rig
39. Bathroom item
40. Hinged fastener
42. Thyme, e.g.
43. Quick trip
45. Made of oak
46. Weaker
48. Portly
49. Blockade
50. Garden tool
51. Canvas prop
52. Frock
54. Boring
56. Pipe type
57. Ghostly greeting
58. Bloom-to-be
60. Pub counter
61. Prevaricate

PUZZLE 111

ACROSS
1. Dalai ___
5. Raised
9. Flood boat
12. Showy spring flower
13. Not singular
15. Hopper
16. Forwarded
17. Deli sausage
18. Lyric verse
19. Duet
20. "Chances ___"
21. Even
23. Wight, e.g.
25. Cloudiest
27. Arbitrary
30. Mr. Dern
31. Spaceman
32. Young adult
33. Dewy
37. Hustle
38. Bread grain
39. Podded veggie
40. Ship bottom
42. Injure
43. Beg
45. Etching fluids
47. Longs
48. Traditions
51. Paddles
52. Go in
53. Buddy
54. Adept
58. Noshed
59. Assault
62. Ambition
63. Slurp
64. Departs
65. Standard
66. Subways' kin
67. Matured
68. Probes

DOWN
1. Speech impediment
2. Place
3. Skirt type
4. Straddling
5. Shriek
6. Govern
7. Historic period
8. Pond barrier
9. Over
10. Goes by horse
11. Rested on one's knees
13. Sunday song
14. Flowering bush
22. Black-___ Susan
24. Junior
25. "The ___ Gatsby"
26. Undersized one
27. ___ of lamb
28. Soothing plant
29. Four plus five
30. Malt beverages
32. Sounds of heavy impacts
34. Copycat
35. Wicked
36. Mats
38. Impulse
41. Delayed
43. Church bench
44. Baked pasta dish
46. Reef material
47. Egg yellows
48. Suspend
49. Before
50. Dance movements
51. Rushed
53. Prepare for traffic
55. Expresses disapproval
56. Songbird
57. Graceful trees
60. Afternoon affair
61. Kind of sale

PUZZLE 112

ACROSS
1. Mend
6. Across, to Keats
9. Rowing items
13. Slanted type
15. Wood cutter
16. Ebb and ___
17. Red soup
18. Small drink
19. Cinco
20. Right on!
21. Snowy
23. Gravity center?
24. As well
25. Proclaim
28. Bother
31. Intent
32. Pull behind
33. Holiday treat
37. Poets
41. In any way
42. Makes mittens
44. Load a hook
45. Recover one's losses
47. Restricted
49. Family feline
51. That lady
52. Child's seat
53. Cavern
56. Mall habitue
57. Chased
58. Drink noisily
60. Trickle
64. Performs
66. Sunday topic
67. Develop
69. Mountaintop
70. Guitar's kin
71. Washes lightly
72. See
73. Through
74. Realtor

DOWN
1. Bread for hummus
2. Cartoon ant
3. Dull
4. Tribe
5. Triple, e.g.
6. Caravan stop
7. Leave
8. Utter again
9. Switch position
10. Existing
11. Fido's pal
12. Sugary
14. Unruly tuft of hair
22. Kind
24. Income
26. Cry
27. Mops
28. Frosting user
29. Babble wildly
30. Had memorized
34. Dribbled
35. Veto
36. Engraver
38. Baluster
39. Aria singer
40. Stride
43. Unexpected hit
46. Yield
48. Coffeepot
50. Throw into the air
53. Vine fruit
54. Hurries
55. Drawn from a keg
56. Radio part
59. Kindred
60. Ditty
61. Further
62. Divisible by two
63. Gnat, e.g.
65. Heavens
68. Latin way

PUZZLE 113

FLOWER POWER

The answers to this petaled puzzle will go in a curve from the number on the outside to the center of the flower. Each number in the flower will have two 5-letter answers. One goes in a clockwise direction and the second in a counterclockwise direction. We have entered two answers to help you begin.

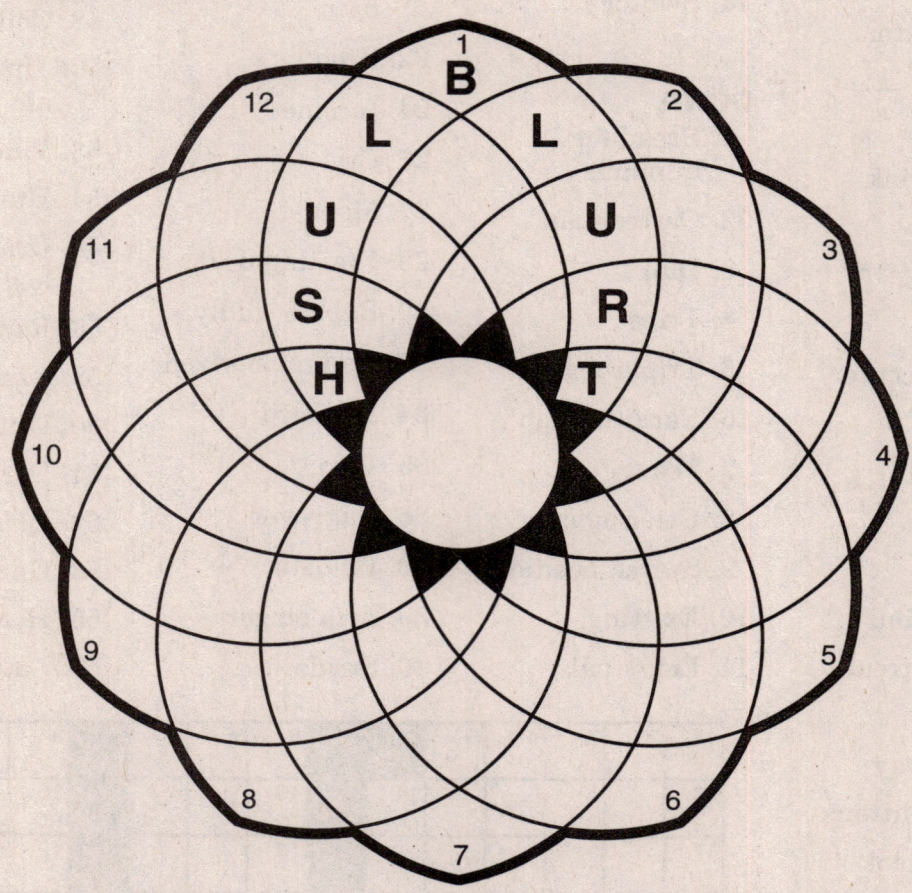

CLOCKWISE

1. Babble
2. Crouch
3. Period of history
4. Clean ___
5. Barrier
6. Highway
7. Bluish purple
8. Long cut
9. Foam
10. Phantom
11. Merciless
12. Sheep's comment

COUNTERCLOCKWISE

1. Redden
2. Frozen rain
3. Match
4. Burst of energy
5. Drift
6. Acknowledge
7. Year segment
8. Hollandaise, e.g.
9. Wind instrument
10. Somber
11. Picked
12. Consomme

FLOWER POWER FANS! *Fun is always in full bloom with every volume of Selected Flower Power. To order, see page 159.*

PUZZLE 114

ACROSS
1. Gore
5. Miss America's garb
9. Small particles
14. For takeout
15. Choir part
16. Wooden pin
17. Selves
18. Bungle
19. Laughing ___
20. Chinese temple
22. Foolish person
24. Dine
25. Festive
27. Coat sleeve
29. Not sold
32. Life story
33. Horse sound
36. Overhead
38. Gamblers' numbers
41. Farm yield
43. Journey
44. ___ board
45. Judge
46. Legend
47. Talking bird
48. Memo taker
49. Mitten part
51. Court
53. Large tree
54. "___ Hard"
55. Church area
57. Switch word
60. Harsh
62. Defrosted
66. Dry
68. Title
70. Pontiff
71. Goody
72. Russian emperor
73. Spring bloom
74. Dingy
75. That woman's
76. Boat floor

DOWN
1. Gait
2. Caesar's garb
3. Fascinated
4. Chest
5. Jungle trip
6. Entirely
7. Do homework
8. Tramp
9. Bond
10. Nursery item
11. Has a mortgage
12. Predinner reading
13. Spank
21. Obligation
23. Purple flower
26. Spacious
28. Very small
29. Feeling your ___
30. Be buoyant
31. Difficult
34. Bother
35. Lodging house
37. Impostor
39. Burrow
40. Utter slowly
42. Make curly
44. Fire's remnant
48. Ark skipper
50. Powerful
52. Aquatic mammals
55. Astound
56. Hasty
57. Chooses
58. Cost
59. Unattached
61. Foot part
63. Donned
64. Heroic story
65. Cubicle item
67. Boor
69. Disfigure

PUZZLE 115

ACROSS
1. Call at sea
5. Wane
9. Seeds
13. Bait
14. Reason
15. Bad
16. Jackanapes
17. Correct
18. Only
19. Large vase
20. Birthmark
21. Penalized
22. ___ wheel
23. Frost
24. Flower wreath
26. Flock
28. Tom-toms, e.g.
30. Scarf
33. Target
35. Apiece
36. Possess
37. Flavor
40. Edition
42. Grotesque
43. Incur debts
44. Pang
45. Scary street
47. Evergreen tree
48. Sober
50. Milky jewel
53. Years and years
54. Wiggly swimmer
56. Blushing
58. Transports
62. Osso bucco meat
63. Jalopy
64. Vigorous
65. Praises
67. Built
68. Wings
69. Topple
70. Some poems
71. Unspectacular
72. Bauble
73. Lairs

DOWN
1. Record
2. Cheer
3. Juice fruit
4. Until now
5. Flunked
6. Olympic event
7. Cigar remnant
8. Capture
9. Big truck
10. Kiln
11. Cable
12. Toboggan
14. Gator's kin
20. Skirt length
21. Cod, e.g.
24. Oahu bash
25. Host
27. Scrap
29. Watch again
30. Marsh
31. Hooter
32. Whichever
34. Minute
37. Trifle
38. Wonderment
39. Novel
41. Hebrew letter
42. One at home
44. Experts
46. Lounge
49. Spun
51. Gallery
52. Heavy
55. Orient
57. Gown
58. Ladies
59. Nimbus
60. Woes
61. Cancun coin
62. Travel permit
65. Center
66. Copy
67. Stylish

PUZZLE 116

ACROSS
1. Bawls
6. Bow
9. Compulsion
13. Comfort
15. Pair
16. Name word
17. More angry
18. Bear cave
19. Nippy
20. Louse spawn
21. Survey statistic
23. Clusters
25. Word for Beaver
26. Kitten sound
27. Musical ability
28. Extinct bird
29. Swift and graceful
33. Blemish
36. Undivided
38. Prepare to drag
39. Bee's output
40. Regulation
41. Pebble
43. In the back, matey
44. Bicuspids
46. Suggestions
47. Wife's mate
49. Self-images
51. Set ablaze
52. Ship's front
53. Cavity
56. Antelope
59. Uneven
60. Mate for mama
61. Hind part
62. Printer's need
64. Alpacas' kin
66. Leafy veggie
67. Be situated
68. Dieter's food
69. Husky's burden
70. Cunning
71. Trivial

DOWN
1. Twist
2. Scary
3. Please greatly
4. Peach leftovers
5. Use the eyes
6. Common viper
7. Regret
8. Hide
9. Straighten out
10. Hotel rental
11. Swallow eagerly
12. Tips
14. Fake
22. Snarled
24. Midnight movie
26. '50s hairstyle
28. Craps cube
29. Cattle tender
30. Press pleats
31. English county
32. Arden et al.
33. Former Iranian ruler
34. Soy product
35. Picnic crashers
37. Ten-gallon item
42. Not 'tain't
45. Requires
48. Bellowed
50. Devout
52. Slammer
53. Range
54. Detached
55. Ashen
56. Bothers
57. Buffet
58. Fair-skinned
60. Errand boy
63. Not a one
65. Crop

97

PUZZLE 117

ACROSS
1. Medics
5. Luxurious
9. Top-billed
13. Pinnacle
17. Declare frankly
18. Assess
19. Middle Eastern bread
20. Water bird
21. Office brief
22. Unwritten
23. Served perfectly
24. Takes to court
25. Surround
27. Mr. Cariou
29. Pumping ___
31. Newspaper page
32. Crate
33. Poi party
35. Alpine slider
38. Always, poetically
40. Remove print
42. Folks
44. Snaky swimmer
45. Coupe, e.g.
47. Stain
49. Pickle herbs
51. Inch along
53. Boston ___ Party
54. Polluted air
56. Fizzy drink
57. Dreadful
59. Attempt
61. Witchcraft
63. Animation unit
65. Society gal
67. Pave
68. Mortified
72. Highland hat
74. Province
79. Independent
80. Grimm brute
82. Relieve (of)
84. Co-op's kin
85. Resupply with weapons
87. Attractive
90. Bruise
91. Picnic spoiler
92. Florida fruit
94. Squad
96. Average grade
97. Bar bill
98. Thin
99. Curvy turn
101. Warty amphibian
103. Water pitcher
105. Fruity drink
106. Raised printing
109. Leer at
111. Atomic particles
114. Hum
117. On the peak
118. Soaks
119. Long journey
120. Icicle locale
121. Slit
122. In case
123. Evergreen plants
124. Tinter
125. Peek at

DOWN
1. Titled lady
2. Baking site
3. Quilt
4. Plunge
5. Poked
6. Boat rower
7. RR depot
8. Howdy!
9. Extend
10. ___-tac-toe
11. Gobbled
12. ___ tire
13. In addition
14. Advisor
15. Famous Stooge
16. Print measures
26. Supervised
28. World's fair, e.g.
30. Lamented
32. Attack
33. Weavers
34. Pull out
36. Gene or Grace
37. Bergman role
38. Every
39. Lira replacement
41. Set ablaze
43. High railways
46. Above, in verse
48. Credit ___
50. Bartender's rocks
52. Type type
55. Alum
58. Sample tape
60. Still
62. Gator's kin
64. Gofer

PUZZLE 117

66. Stark
68. Sports field
69. Safety straps
70. That woman
71. Guzzled
73. Kitchen gloves
75. Cut the grass
76. Stories
77. Still
78. Comment
79. Campus gp.
81. Coop item
83. Gambling cube
86. Lawn tunneler
88. Require
89. Food provider
93. Uncommon thing
95. Mother
100. Stitched
102. Diminish
104. Cowboy country
105. Invites
107. Sudsy cleaner
108. Chipper
109. It gives a hoot
110. Go right!
112. Mine yield
113. Recent
115. Straw's kin
116. Destruct ender

PUZZLE 118

ACROSS
1. Within
5. Best
8. Mr. Flynn
13. Crafted
14. Gorilla, e.g.
15. Underling
16. Shopping spot
17. Darn
18. Sell
19. Egg dish
21. Pelt
22. Always, in verse
23. Decade count
25. Vases
27. Huge
30. Pure
32. Tons
35. Above
37. Singular's opposite
39. Unearth
40. Flight part
42. Type of shark
43. French lids
45. Speaker's aid
47. Strike out
48. Office worker
49. Before, before
50. Rani's wrap
52. Cry
53. Frequently, in poems
56. Tease
57. Practical
62. Cockatoo
64. Hold the deed
66. Hard follower
67. Awaken
68. Sleepy's pal
69. Keenness
70. Mantel
71. Fawn's ma
72. Stench

DOWN
1. Rounds
2. Polite address
3. Lazy
4. Hollow
5. Tacky
6. Cracked, in poems
7. Sunday seat
8. Perpetual
9. Baton
10. Took a cab
11. Flirty look
12. Sly glance
15. Egg on
20. Write with acid
21. Amusement
24. Orderly
26. Sag
27. Explosive
28. Covered in creepers
29. Category
31. Adjust
33. Speak publicly
34. Thief
36. Whirls
37. Say
38. Folk wisdom
41. Antagonizes
44. Florist's product
46. Hordes
48. Bro or sis
51. Observance
53. White gemstone
54. Passenger
55. Stomped
58. Water jug
59. Decrease
60. Yen
61. Onion's kin
63. Bearskin ___
64. Unmatched
65. Seek to wed

PUZZLE 119

ACROSS
1. Large amount
5. Some vipers
9. Mimics
13. Control
14. Whisk
16. Smell
17. Mellowed
18. Planter
19. Exclusively
20. In favor of
21. Sea, in Paris
22. Sonnet, e.g.
24. Dense mist
25. Previously owned
27. Door fastener
31. ___ Gingrich
33. Legitimate
36. Fish eggs
37. Stags and bucks
39. Kind of bran
40. Baby's father
41. Burglar's target
44. Picture
46. Black-___ Susan
47. Songbird
48. Slit
49. Silent
51. Diver's tank
52. Class
53. Chess piece
56. Craze
58. Pull
61. Gave a meal to
63. Stuck-up one
66. Astonishment
67. Cook in oil
68. Face shape
71. Immature insect
73. Soft wood
74. Take out, as text
75. Washer's mate
76. Froster
77. 24th letters
78. Stoop
79. Hair goops

DOWN
1. Employees
2. Seaside pool
3. Come into view
4. Married
5. Burros
6. Vowed
7. Church seat
8. Dribble
9. Bouquet
10. Fountain ___
11. Snaky fish
12. Heaven
15. Con's opposite
21. Speechless
23. Building shape
26. Sagged
28. Server
29. Secret language
30. Principal
32. What time?
34. Go to dinner
35. Source of energy
38. Agile
40. Showroom model
41. Dog-paddled
42. Opera feature
43. Boston ___
45. Trendy
50. Insist upon
52. Basker's desire
54. Position
55. Grain of corn
57. Bits of land
59. Deep black
60. Medal
62. Fabric colorers
64. Not young
65. Prong
68. Poet's output
69. Disturb
70. Beer's kin
72. Dark bread
73. Glutton

PUZZLE 120

ACROSS
1. Head supports
6. Heidi's peak
9. Fell (in)
14. Once more
15. Sci. class
16. Deport
17. Female deities
19. Charter
20. Drift off
21. Dispense
23. Conducted
24. Boundary post
26. Dad's boy
28. Fastener
29. Bends
33. Elect
36. Ginger ___
37. Played part
38. Wander
40. Tiny bit
42. Roman wear
43. Reminder note
44. Mr. Perot
45. Harbinger
46. Iced ___
47. Once called
48. Scarcer
50. Essence
51. Target
53. Upright
55. Possessed
58. Market
61. Garland
62. Court excuse
64. No sweat
69. Flick
70. Ostrich's kin
71. Butter maker
72. Endure
73. Confed.
74. Vats

DOWN
1. Annoy
2. Bruised ___
3. Heel
4. Abduct
5. Prowl
6. Sit-ups target
7. Told a fib
8. Model
9. Bass's kin
10. Hewing tool
11. Glass tube
12. Threat word
13. Title ___
18. Gush
22. Donkeys
24. Tavern
25. African fly
27. Standard
28. Bristle
30. Smell
31. Actor Moore
32. Aircraft
34. ___ license
35. Most gentle
39. Castle ditch
41. Adrift
42. Singer Mel ___
49. Count (on)
50. Kimono wearer
52. With vines
54. Respond
55. Bad actors
56. Oodles
57. Opera singer
59. ___-do-well
60. Noblewoman
63. Coal box
65. Temp
66. Groaner
67. Bug
68. Naval off.

PUZZLE 121

ACROSS
1. Cows and hens
5. Intimidates
9. View
14. Gasp
15. Closed hand
16. Rhea's role
17. Higher than tenor
18. Furthermore
19. Pot fillers
20. Cookery method
22. Duffer's dream
24. Held session
25. Cartoonist's unit
26. ___ cube
28. Woolly female
30. Leaders
33. Warns
36. Boundary
37. Rice dish
39. Has lunch
41. Kong, e.g.
42. Pesto herb
44. Verve
45. Broadcast
47. Bush
49. Always, in poems
50. Smell
53. Self-regard
54. CIA agent
55. Short farewell
56. Many times, to bards
58. Subway posters
61. Relay section
63. Freedom
67. Horned animal
69. Battery liquid
71. Italian money, once
72. Tear jerker?
73. Bakery item
74. Bulb plant
75. Hairy beings
76. Group of computer bits
77. Questions

DOWN
1. Health havens
2. Pause
3. Attraction
4. PX, e.g.
5. Remotely
6. Tricky
7. Twisting turn
8. Cease to go
9. Uncommon
10. Pantry item
11. Music and dance
12. Guilty, e.g.
13. New York side
21. Somersault
23. Feel queasy
27. Previously, in poetry
28. Generations
29. Rubs
31. Pen part
32. Slit
33. Burning
34. Wall hangings
35. Prepare tea
38. Fireplace dust
40. Chipper
43. Drag
46. Society gal
48. Dunce
51. Hose
52. Passing grade
57. Gal's guy
58. "Ship ___"
59. Sup
60. Roasting bar
62. Attire
63. Happy song
64. Tarry
65. Voyage
66. Tibetan oxen
68. Luau offering
70. Shy

PUZZLE 122

ACROSS
1. Stockpile
6. Louses
10. Light tap
13. Occur
15. Take out
16. Guitar's kin
17. Intact
18. Diamond team
19. Blend
20. Avenue
22. Domestic
24. Pod dweller
26. Board member
28. Factual
29. Stetson, e.g.
30. Language
34. Botch
35. Broad
37. Coffeepots
38. Mr. Crosby
40. Strikes out
41. Gobbles up
42. Purchaser
43. Eye part
44. Hitch
45. Pulsates
47. Vigor
49. Buzzers
50. Rigid
52. Bizarre
53. Benefactor
56. Neutral color
58. Center
59. Sharp hit
61. Ignite
65. Wrath
66. Sinful
67. ___ worker
68. Meddle
69. Turn down
70. Swarms

DOWN
1. That girl
2. Cure hides
3. Liable
4. Helix
5. Good guy
6. Hoodwink
7. Off-kilter
8. Kitchen nooks
9. Music system
10. Mountain cat
11. Matching
12. Printed words
14. Bard's below
21. Bureau part
23. Place
24. Expire
25. Moneymaker
27. Employ
28. Counter
31. Rasped
32. Freed
33. Snaky turns
36. Wish
39. Creak
40. Melt
46. Cleared tables
48. Kisses
49. Rebound
51. Locomotive
53. Freighter
54. Feline sigh
55. Submit to
57. Uprising
60. Wield
62. Gaming cube
63. Flight
64. Raised rails

PUZZLE 123

ACROSS
1. Carryalls
6. Garment edges
10. Drop
14. Onto
15. Burn reliever
16. Give approval to
17. Mutiny
18. Land amid water
19. Come up
20. Botched
22. Hollows
23. Tinge
26. Flower part
28. Spanish galas
30. Weighty
33. Per
34. Respond
37. Arrest
39. Age
40. Itty-bitty
41. Icy center?
42. Powder
44. Penetrate
46. Stop
47. Messy people
49. Jogs the memory
51. Not quite all
53. Cozy abodes
54. Morsel
57. Choice group
60. Water tube
61. Rotate
62. Australian animal
67. Frank
68. MTV watcher
69. Completed
70. Nuisance
71. Yearns
72. Marsh stalks

DOWN
1. ___ and feather
2. Be in hock
3. Cafe check
4. Before, poetically
5. Pick
6. Narrow margin
7. Besides
8. Sculpts
9. Notice
10. Boss
11. Related
12. Survive
13. Caustic liquids
21. Behind
22. Fourth letter
23. Crowns
24. Remember
25. Volcanic dust
27. Old pronoun
28. Stompers
29. Stitched
31. Unoccupied
32. Produces
35. Favorite beast
36. Evil look
38. Hires
43. Remark
44. Slow start?
45. Monthly expense
46. Towel pronoun
48. Dangle
50. Tamer
52. Plains dwelling
54. Dice
55. Cowboy's gear
56. Puts to work
58. Debtor's burden
59. Rustic hotels
61. Pig's digs
63. Dollar
64. Orange cooler
65. Showed the way
66. TV breaks

105

PUZZLE 124

ACROSS
1. Picnic pests
5. Doll's cry
9. Random try
13. Harvest
14. Flies alone
15. Corn cake
16. Leisurely
17. Ships' frames
18. Overdue
19. Implore
20. Mas' guys
21. Partition
23. Slaved
26. ___ rummy
27. Dark haired
29. Good ___
33. Tempted
34. Grade
36. Winter flakes
37. Class
38. Stripped
39. Detect ender
40. Must-have
42. Copycat
43. Keeper
45. Dehydrating
47. Burns slowly
49. Doozie
50. Neater
51. Arbor
55. Beckon
56. Resort hotel
59. Child's toy
60. ___ bear
62. Young lady
63. Verse
64. Revises
65. On the peak
66. Gumbo must
67. Garage ___
68. Workout places

DOWN
1. Opera tune
2. Beatty and Sparks
3. Speak frankly
4. Enemy agent
5. Rodent snare
6. Bar none
7. Form
8. Appointed
9. Braces
10. Pond dweller
11. Poker word
12. Root ___
14. Bible word
20. ___ Piper
22. Through
24. Single
25. Beloved
27. Shade
28. Leader
30. College
31. Nomad
32. Pitchers
35. Cancel
38. Scot's instrument
41. Graduate's reward
43. Glided
44. Grape drink
46. Nothing
48. Perfumes
51. Memo error
52. Chess castle
53. Watcher
54. ___ pop
57. School dance
58. Swiss peaks
61. "___ Abner"
62. Joke

PUZZLE 125

ACROSS
1. Soprano's solo
5. Pouch
8. Strip
12. Fellow
13. Mr. Woods
15. Lessen
16. Touch
17. Zinc ___
18. Ingredient
19. Procession
21. British brew
22. Tide type
23. Poet's before
24. Broadway acronym
26. Caustic liquid
28. Recess
30. Morsel
33. Portico
36. Image
37. Beer
39. Hybrid fruit
41. Exhaust
43. Crude ship?
44. Eliminate
46. Scallion's kin
47. Thickness
48. Hygienic
51. DEA agent
52. Lily variety
53. Newt
56. Archaic pronoun
59. Odd
61. Consumable
63. Brawl
64. Thorny twig
66. Exit
67. Ricelike pasta
68. Weird
69. Load
70. Bubblegummer
71. Long fish
72. Old harp

DOWN
1. Open-mouthed
2. Concrete reinforcement
3. Toughen
4. Tropical ant
5. "___ Feet Under"
6. Hurried, in music
7. Give up
8. Net
9. Tardy
10. Lost
11. Sub
13. Pedicure subject
14. Kingdom
20. Indian sauce
25. Magnate
27. Squeal
28. Messenger
29. Write
30. Molding
31. Neural network
32. Journey
33. Finish
34. Chase
35. Mere
38. Confederate
40. Gaelic
42. Knickknack stand
45. Fizzle
49. Clay brick
50. Staff
51. Sofa style
53. Black
54. Pantry staple
55. Concise
56. Gait
57. Charter
58. Leak
60. Liberate
62. Emulated one
65. Feel lousy

PUZZLE 126

ACROSS
1. Matched groups
5. Loud noise
9. Ref
12. Box in
13. Differently
14. Paving liquid
15. Pretentious
16. Fruit stones
17. Mine output
18. Spoil
19. Gin source
20. Nose around
21. Thespian group
23. Proportional relations
26. Beethoven's "Moonlight ___"
28. Spring occurrence
29. Church dignitary
31. Homey desserts
33. Staircase shape
36. Collided
38. Compensate in advance
40. Psychology subject
41. Infuriate
43. Polar sight
44. Coal weight
45. Dry stream
46. Flowery wreaths
47. Orange beverage
48. Foil's alternative
49. Teen's problem
50. Heartbreaking
51. Rosary sphere
52. Entreats

DOWN
1. Jump from shock
2. Bloopers
3. Biceps decor
4. Enemy agent
5. Filled up
6. Medley
7. Daisylike bloom
8. Legal thing
9. Ideal place
10. Essential part
11. Victimizes others
19. Scanty
22. Remove pins from
24. Clothing
25. Yonder
27. Capone and Jolson
30. Utilized
31. Chinese temple
32. Pressed smooth
34. Per
35. Corset fastener
36. Greek letters
37. Fall in folds
39. Affirmatives
42. Thought
45. Net
46. Chemist's room

PUZZLE 127

ACROSS
1. Coarse file
5. Jazz style
8. Physicians, for short
12. Seed cover
13. Iron or Stone
14. Of an epoch
15. Deuce topper
16. Indeed!
17. Current carrier
18. Poetic sunset
19. Adversaries
20. Prior to, in verse
21. Actor Martin ___
23. Spotted wildcat
26. ___ forest
27. Most certain
28. Plug
30. Buzzing insect
32. Theater
35. Marzipan nut
36. TV pub
38. Talk
39. Dull fellow
41. Obtained
42. Met melody
44. Tavern treat
45. Decrease
46. Yankees' opponents
47. Went ahead
48. News flash
49. Dance move
50. Old card game
51. River bottoms

DOWN
1. Honey badger
2. Unpaid debt
3. Earthy pigment
4. Layer
5. Louisiana marsh
6. Arch type
7. Thick fog
8. Morning droplets
9. Medieval windows
10. Bugs's snack
11. Winter forecast
19. Chinese game
22. Seventies music
24. Christmas decoration
25. Supernatural
27. Luxury hotel
29. Crackpot
30. Wine
31. Drink
33. Cancel
34. Washed away
35. Culture mediums
36. System of belief
37. Goblet parts
40. Tub in the fridge
43. Deadly reptile
45. Untruth

MOVIES & TELEVISION

PUZZLE 128

ACROSS
1. Grotto
5. "____ of the Century"
9. Actress Macpherson of "Sirens"
13. Ms. Oyl of "Popeye"
15. Escape
17. "The ____ of New Orleans"
19. "Bates ____"
20. John Kelly of "NYPD Blue"
22. Ms. Munson of "Gone With the Wind"
23. "East of ____"
25. Actress Carrere
26. "____ Deal"
27. Ms. Donahue of "Get a Life"
29. Director Coward
30. Author Rand
31. "The Dick ____ Dyke Show"
32. And not
33. Research room
36. "____ and Gladys"
39. "The ____ of Navarone"
40. Actress Marie
43. Actor John ____ of "704 Hauser Street"
44. Der ____ (Adenauer)
45. "____ in the Attic"
48. "The Snake ____"
49. Actor Ed ____ of "Daniel Boone"
50. Actress Drescher
51. "Flying Down to ____"
52. Disney film
54. Sullen
55. "Getting ____ With Dad"
56. Director Kazan
57. Rosebud, e.g.
58. Eliot ____
59. Ruler: abbr.
61. "____ Sera, Sera" (Doris Day hit)
62. 1,002, to Nero
64. "____ Titanic"
67. Astringent
69. Wood smoother
72. Merkel or O'Connor
73. Actress Farrow
74. Loren film
75. "The ____ Vegas Story"
77. Andy Sipowicz of "NYPD Blue"
81. Olympic medalist Comaneci
83. Shankar's instrument
84. Concise
85. "Dallas" family name
86. Lois ____
87. "____ Trek"
88. Massachusetts motto's first word

DOWN
1. Singer Perry ____
2. "Home ____"
3. "____ Signs"
4. "All About ____"
5. Passover feast
6. Actor Young of "Mr. Ed"
7. Lemmon/Falk film
8. Magazine employees
9. Heathrow abbr.
10. Denise ____ of "The Garry Moore Show"
11. Tierney film
12. Literary work
14. Ms. Verdugo of "Meet Millie"
16. McClurg or Sedgwick
18. "Hell ____"
21. "____ Northside 777"
24. Knotts or Rickles
28. Singer Burl ____
29. "____ But the Lonely Heart"
32. Streisand film
34. "East of Eden" actor
35. Actress Clara ____
36. Mama's mate
37. ____ de Becque of "South Pacific"
38. "____ Recall"
39. Singer Campbell
41. "In Which We ____"
42. Indians
44. ____ Foster of "Punky Brewster"
45. Jonathan ____ of "Dark Shadows"
46. On the ____ (escaping)
47. "The ____ of Katie Elder"
49. Actor West of "Batman"
50. "Born ____"
53. "____ Hard"
54. Blue
55. Ms. Markey
57. "The Hollywood ____"
60. Shriver and Dawber
62. "____ About You"
63. Silly
64. Pickford film
65. Actress Barbara ____
66. "____ Barbara"
68. "The Big ____"
69. Measuring device
70. "Murphy Brown" painter
71. "The ____ Came"
74. Handle
76. "Riders of the Purple ____"
78. Actress Grey of "Three Smart Girls"
79. Rage
80. Carney or Linkletter
82. Wonder

109

PUZZLE 129

ACROSS
1. List of options
5. Woeful word
9. Engrave on glass
13. Forewarning
14. Fits
16. Bruised
17. Wharf
18. Creep
19. Hearty soup
20. Sharpener
22. Eyeshade
24. Gorilla
25. Initiated
27. Hauled
29. Expose
32. Play division
34. Unclose, poetically
35. "Render therefore ___ Caesar . . ."
37. Inclines
41. Above, to Byron
42. Had pizza
43. Cold
45. It gives a hoot
46. Shish ___
48. Humpty Dumpty's seat
50. Bill and ___
51. Spiny plants
53. Disagree
56. Anew
59. Wireless
61. Tropical snake
62. Head over ___
64. Conflict
68. Ship's prison
70. Meet the day
72. Polynesian feast
73. Stare at
74. Committee
75. Formerly, formerly
76. School exam
77. Arranges
78. Slangy refusals

DOWN
1. Floor washers
2. Throw off
3. ___-do-well
4. Make bare
5. Bend
6. Immature insect
7. Anti
8. Uses a needle and thread
9. 19th letter
10. Entire
11. Delicate pancake
12. Chopped
15. Skier's hillside
21. "The Princess and the ___"
23. Small
26. Excess
28. Hawaiian necklace
29. Certain chess piece
30. Duel tool
31. Action word
33. Spiral
36. Colorful salamander
38. Crazy
39. Couples
40. Type of gin
42. Embarrass
44. Lump of dirt
47. King's superior
49. Plane-transport system
52. Inexpensive
54. Snapshot
55. What bees spread
56. Monastery leader
57. Smithy
58. Locomotive tracks
60. Valuable possession
63. Periods of history
65. Atmosphere
66. Cummerbund
67. Shacks
69. Acquire
71. Chicago trains

PUZZLE 130 — A Few Choice Words

Find the 8-letter answers by choosing one letter from each of the letter groups to the right of each clue. For example, the answer to number 1 is AROMATIC.

1. Fragrant	<u>a</u>se	pq<u>r</u>	n<u>o</u>p	<u>m</u>rg	<u>a</u>fg	mi<u>t</u>	a<u>i</u>t	<u>c</u>eh
2. Funny guy	sce	olh	ame	ine	dul	igh	ano	gpn
3. Female child	qrd	uam	aou	lgr	iph	stw	yce	drl
4. Dainty	bsd	erp	ole	ria	clk	oea	otb	lex
5. Handkerchief	lbi	mia	npa	dti	ena	nto	nol	tya
6. Motionless	iml	run	ora	tic	tla	tim	ivo	edn

DOUBLE TROUBLE

PUZZLE 131

Not really double trouble, but double fun! Solve this puzzle as you would a regular crossword, except place one, two, or three letters in each box. The number of letters in each answer is shown in parentheses after its clue.

ACROSS
1. Overthrow (6)
4. Sudden burst (5)
6. Hat's edge (4)
8. Drink mixer (9)
10. Thick wool (4)
11. Formally appoint (6)
12. Easter stamp (4)
13. Author Dave ___ (6)
15. Single male (8)
16. Non-religious (7)
17. In order to avoid (4)
18. Environment (7)
20. Swiftness (5)
22. Coarse file (4)
24. Plus one (5)
25. Of the same size (10)
28. Tiny particle (4)
30. Boxing interval (5)
32. Wyatt's pal (3)
33. Prized fur (6)
35. Hence (4)
37. Think well (of) (7)
38. Statue's stand (8)
40. Praying ___ (6)
41. Swab the deck (3)
43. Shipwreck (6)
44. Social group (4)
45. Endear oneself to someone (10)
47. Put to sea (4)
48. French river (4)
49. Create (6)

DOWN
1. Belittle (6)
2. Doorway (6)
3. Viewed (4)
4. Wave riders (7)
5. Moolah (4)
6. Nuptial (6)
7. Trivial (5)
9. Remove government controls (10)
11. Symphony group (9)
14. Outfit (4)
15. Bundle cotton (4)
16. Denomination (4)
18. Dutch city, with "The" (5)
19. Sidewalk cafe (6)
20. Mayhem (5)
21. Thieve (5)
23. Seville's nation (5)
26. ___ pro quo (4)
27. Showing initiative (12)
29. Large volume (4)
31. Comprehend (10)
34. Relocate (4)
36. Target (4)
37. Liable (3)
38. Irritants (5)
39. Leave the track (6)
40. Fashion (6)
41. Reason (6)
42. ___ leather (6)
44. Brick materials (5)
46. Cloud juice (4)

Alpha Quotes

PUZZLE 132

Reveal the quotes by eliminating the letters of the alphabet that are not part of the quotes. The unused letters go in alphabetical order from A to Z.

1. A T H B I C S W D O E R L F D I G S B H U I T A C J A N K V L A S M T O N O U O P R Q I R M A S G T I N U V A T W I O X N Y S Z.

2. F R A I E B C D N D S E A R F E G H T I H E J F K L A M I M L Y N W E O C H P O Q O S R E S F T O R U O U V W R S X E L V Y E Z S.

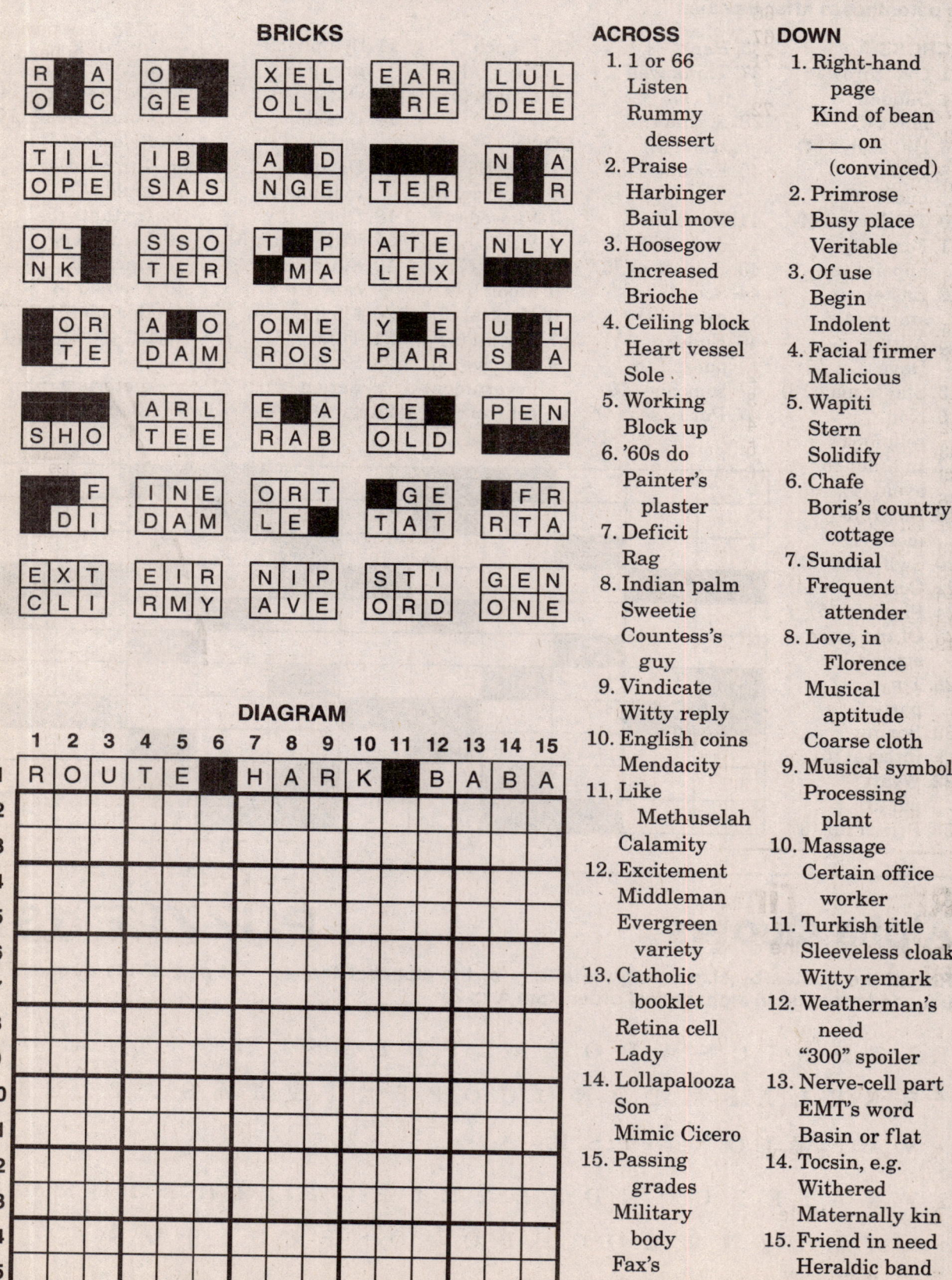

PUZZLE 134

ACROSS
1. Player's part
5. Snatches
10. Alda's series
14. On vacation
15. "____ and Juliet"
16. She went to Siam
17. Curious
19. Winter school closer
20. Glimpse
21. Be in the red
22. Baby deliverer
23. Swashbuckler Flynn
25. Tennis stroke
29. Affirmative word
30. High peak
32. 11th grader
33. Release
36. Treasures
38. In support of
41. Intersected
43. Put up
45. Inexperienced
46. Blazing
48. Overhang
49. Soup vegetable
50. Bear's pad
52. Opposite of ques.
55. Arrangement
57. Potent particles
61. Was overly fond
63. To the stern
65. Negative word
66. Baking need
67. Burdensome
71. Finished a book
72. Actor Michael ____
73. Work in rhyme
74. Stately trees
75. Lock of hair
76. No ifs, ____, or buts

DOWN
1. Increase
2. Deed holder
3. After
4. Ogle
5. Flourished
6. Trellis creepers
7. Qty.
8. Quilter's session
9. Lay lawn upon
10. Schooner part
11. Pester
12. Night noise
13. Birds of prey
18. Hot-dog holder
22. Have a hunch
24. Mare's meal
26. Catchall abbr.
27. Shorten again
28. Swerved
31. Like better
33. Film renter's need: abbr.
34. Historic period
35. Pronto!
37. Lazy person
38. School org.
39. Vroom
40. "____ to a Nightingale"
42. Greens mixture
44. Small coin
47. Alias letters
51. Devours
52. Love greatly
53. "The Great Gatsby," e.g.
54. Hot vapor
56. Tales
58. Hamburger extra
59. Budged
60. Wineglass parts
62. They may be split
64. Service charges
67. Halloween's mo.
68. Golf term
69. Dessert item
70. Fitness facility

PUZZLE 135

Rhyme Time

The answers to the clues below are pairs of rhyming words. For example: "Plump feline" would be FAT CAT.

1. Chilly metal
2. Fake friend
3. Cranky supervisor
4. Mired vehicle
5. Parisian pew

PUZZLE 136 — CODEWORD

Codeword is a special crossword puzzle in which conventional clues are omitted. Instead, answer words in the diagram are represented by numbers. Each number represents a different letter of the alphabet, and all of the letters of the alphabet are used. When you are sure of a letter, put it in the code key chart and cross it off in the alphabet box. A group of letters has been inserted to start you off.

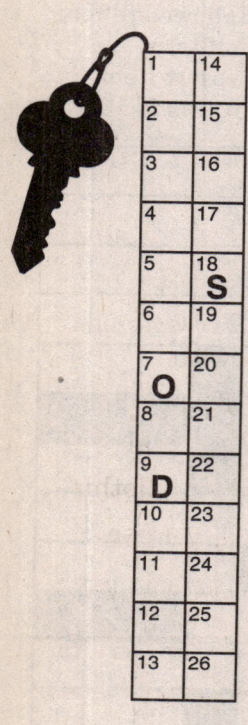

A	N
B	Ø
C	P
Ø	Q
E	R
F	S̸
G	T
H	U
I	V
J	W
K	X
L	Y
M	Z

PUZZLE 137 — Trade-Off

The answers to the two clues in each line below are 6-letter words that differ by only one letter, which we have given you. In the example, if you trade off the P from STRIPE with the letter K in the same position, you get STRIKE. The order of the letters will not change.

Example: Chevron S T R I P E   S T R I K E Hit

1. ___ cloud   F _ _ _ _ _   T _ _ _ _ _   Burrow
2. Argument   _ _ _ T _ _   _ _ _ _ S _   Belittle
3. Actor Beatty   _ _ R _ _ _   _ _ _ _ D _   Prison VIP
4. Walked   _ _ _ D _ _   _ _ _ _ K _   Pet
5. Creak   _ _ _ _ K _   _ _ _ _ L _   Tattle
6. Trouser part   P _ _ _ _ _   S _ _ _ _ _   Eye's site
7. Mare's abode   _ _ B _ _ _   _ _ _ _ P _   Fasten
8. Glen   _ A _ _ _ _   _ _ _ O _ _   Tennis shot

PUZZLE 138

ACROSS

1. KO caller
4. Consumes
8. School dances
13. Hole punch
14. Planetary path
15. High home
16. Pollinator
17. More loyal
18. Trite
19. Impetuous
21. Jog
23. Sorts
24. Published
26. Slant
28. Formal
30. Luau garland
31. Car-radio enhancer
34. Information
37. Seasonal beverage
39. Gazer
41. Imitators
43. Custom
45. Spry
46. Some engines
48. Happy
50. Whirling current
51. Implore
52. Celeb's resort
54. Sharp-edged
56. Was willing to
58. Broadest
62. Pond scum
65. Soil
67. Xbox user
68. Dispositions
70. Tollhouse
72. Have being
73. White heron
74. Gold bar
75. "___ Got a Secret"
76. Strapped
77. Union
78. Commanded

DOWN

1. Synagogue figure
2. Water jugs
3. Bugs
4. Miscalculate
5. Adjoin
6. Levels
7. Amble
8. ___ d'ane
9. Fasten again
10. Unwritten
11. Exploit
12. Spots
14. Alternate
20. Terrific
22. Piggies
25. Clangor
27. It's pocketed
29. Crop
31. Droughty
32. Blend
33. Victim
34. Statistics
35. Composition
36. Make coffee
38. Prank
40. Meeting plan
42. Just fair
44. Gab
47. Potato
49. Evergreen shrub
53. Legal excuses
55. VIII
56. Crossed a creek
57. Monotone
59. PC post
60. Wait on
61. Caught
62. Prayer's last word
63. Theater box
64. Mr. Vidal
66. Cato's clothing
69. Hog house
71. Cartoon cat

PUZZLE 139

ACROSS
1. Similar
5. Attack term
8. Vegetarian staple
12. Bro or sis
15. Server
16. Per ___
18. Paper amount
19. Tennis term
20. Grimm monster
21. Civilian clothes
22. Put in place
24. Withdraw from
25. Honest ___
26. Snow slat
28. Boat blades
29. Play part
31. Bow freshener
33. Capture
35. Slit
38. Bridge makers
40. Owl's question
43. Tow
44. Join
46. Bread grains
47. Hem's partner
48. Pub drink
49. Fighting
50. Wide-shoe width
52. Lamb's mom
53. "___ Got No Strings"
54. Loni's ex
56. Horde
58. Sticky glop
60. Put into print
62. Met offerings
65. Contradict
67. Taped movie
70. Caustic liquid
71. Knockout count
72. Naked
76. Solemn lyric poem
77. Distress
79. Generation
82. Born
84. Seed coat
85. Microscopic
86. Once, once
88. Firstborn
90. Canine
91. Depressed
92. Water storage
94. Odd job
96. Curvy shape
97. Songs for two
98. Motive
99. City haze
102. Motel
103. View starter
105. ___ school
109. Australian leaper
113. Thin cereal
115. House
116. Infirm
117. Maui feast
118. Inward
119. Fix copy
120. Wield
121. Permits
122. Sun. speech
123. Profits

DOWN
1. Store away
2. Compulsion
3. "Fame" star
4. Zoo gigglers
5. Rebuff
6. Raging fire
7. Snip
8. Boxer's coach
9. Bardic above
10. Removed
11. Ms. Thurman
12. Long legend
13. Cake decorator
14. Bunks
16. Amo, amas, ___
17. Rocket
23. Festive drink
27. Family
30. Nibble
32. Stare rudely
33. Beer
34. Resources
35. Hunk
36. Humdinger
37. Golden ___
38. Perfect
39. Big surprise
40. Defeat
41. Hold title to
42. Had IOUs
45. Reputation
51. Self
55. Foot part
57. Small gulf
59. Elect
61. Desire
63. Strengths

PUZZLE 139

64. Recognize
66. Till bills
67. Promises
68. Notion
69. Legal paper
73. Coiffure
74. Entrance
75. Frontier
78. Lode loads
80. Retribution
81. Oodles
83. Carve
87. Boring
89. Argument
93. Sprint
95. Dash
96. Omelet need
98. Fuse metal
99. Bypass
100. Shopping place
101. Merely
104. Nurture
106. Motored
107. Fume
108. Furry friends
110. 100%
111. French street
112. Meal starter
114. Hosp. workers

117

PUZZLE 140

ACROSS
1. Expel
4. Pismire
7. Overflowing
12. Topnotch
13. Dodge
15. Recess
16. Family
17. Bisque scoop
18. Object
19. Yalie
20. Directories
21. Impart
22. & or #
24. Went downhill
27. Leered
29. Soak (up)
30. Grain
33. Southwestern sight
36. Dark
38. Agile
40. Oak seed
42. Mass
44. Henhouses
45. Trail
47. Ruth's club
49. Sleep
50. Leap
51. Maple fluid
53. Eastern discipline
55. Shoulder gesture
57. Twist
61. Cushy
64. Starbucks offering
66. Big vase
67. Atmospheres
69. Astir
70. Flit
71. Noodle skin?
72. Retails
73. Actress Arden
74. Meekly
75. Sweet!
76. Mr. Buttons

DOWN
1. Roues
2. Coldly
3. Durable fabric
4. Helped
5. Drowses
6. Slants
7. Conjunction
8. Manipulate
9. Summit
10. Blackball
11. Drove
13. Standard
14. Office tables
23. Whiskers
25. Charged atom
26. Legendary
28. Get
30. Woodwind
31. Heidi's peaks
32. Dry run
33. Crush
34. Repeat
35. Cleanser
37. Throng
39. Honorable
41. Eat
43. Howl
46. Card game
48. Footing
52. Cougars
54. Biting bugs
55. Delay
56. Flunky
58. Gimlet type
59. Desire
60. Culminated
61. Lip
62. Hurt sound
63. Ravel
65. Soda
68. Snoop

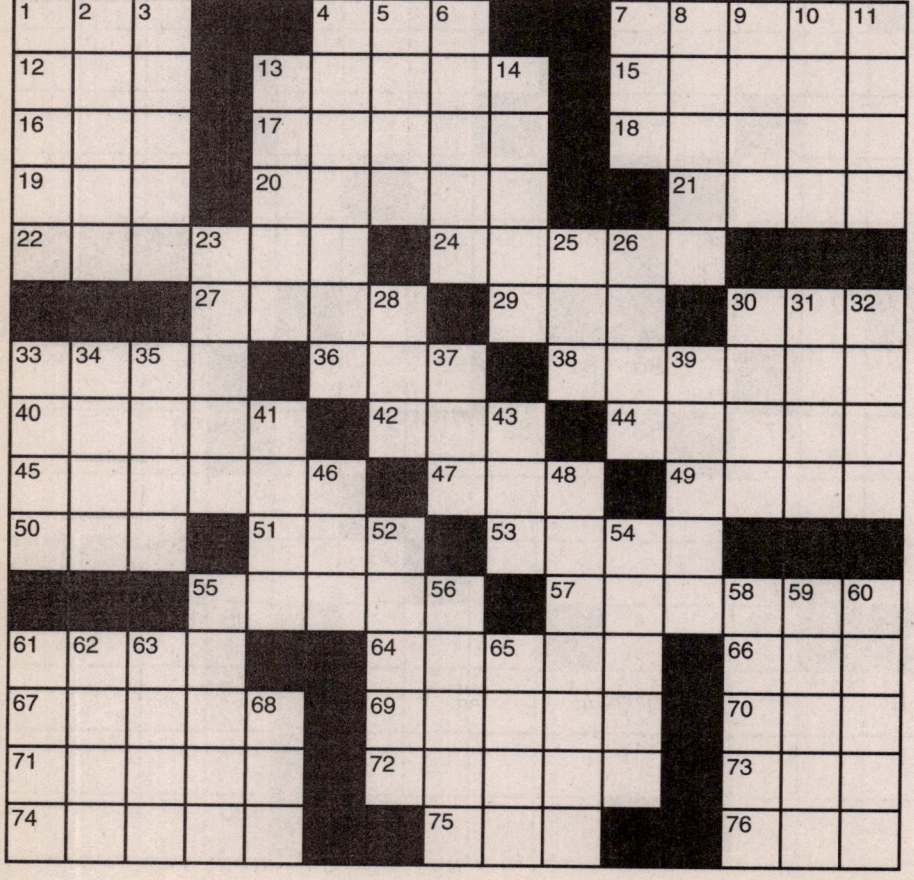

PUZZLE 141

ACROSS
1. Lump
6. Prowl
10. Prominence
14. Pointer
15. Opposed to
16. Computer symbol
17. Happy face
18. Has-___
19. Booted
20. Popular
21. Mass
23. Grooms' friends
25. Secure
27. Date
28. Health center
31. Storage place
33. Crest
36. White fur
38. Pull
40. Injure
42. Homeland
44. Olive stuffer
46. Cast
47. Make a dress
49. Good-natured
50. Quarrel
52. Pie piece
54. Talent
55. Great, man!
57. Numskull
58. Deli slice
61. Dawn moisture
62. '60s do
65. Heated tool
66. Thin branch
69. Vine-covered
71. Metal
72. Inlet
73. Exhausted
74. Fringe
75. Did garden work
76. Jerks

DOWN
1. Bread
2. Star's car
3. Neglect
4. Mr. Brooks
5. Awaiting the stork
6. Hare's kin
7. Billfold item
8. Gulped down
9. Less
10. Anglers
11. Throb
12. Anchor
13. Finalizes
22. Westerns
24. Mermaid's milieu
26. Aglow
28. Faction
29. Evidence
30. Divert
32. Trophy
34. Obsession
35. Ravi's strings
37. Warranty
39. Laugh
41. Shed
43. Bow wood
45. Encounter
48. Join
51. Boulder, e.g.
53. Sidestepped
56. Moat
58. Dimensions
59. Saharan
60. Hanker
62. Discharge
63. Stagger
64. Preakness postings
67. Pursue
68. "___ Gotta Crow"
70. Contest

PUZZLE 142

ACROSS
1. Donations
5. Impostor
9. Jittery
14. Appear
15. Skin woe
16. Love, in France
17. Fishing aid
18. Appeals urgently
19. Pennypincher
20. Fiery stone
21. Maui garland
23. Yields
24. Screams
26. Simmer
28. Foremost
30. Summer shoe
34. Jot down
37. Still-life jugs
40. Poker wager
41. Lodging house
42. Pitches a tent
44. Clangor
45. Rascal
47. Little
48. Plus
49. Flower girls' toss
51. Catcher's site?
52. Warm again
55. Thick
60. Talent
63. Swerve, at sea
64. Decrees
65. Wing it
67. Lounge
70. Applies
71. Leveling tool
72. Scrapes by
73. Chip's pal
74. Have a hunch
75. Strongly felt
76. Pipe joints

DOWN
1. Metal mix
2. Jeweler's glass
3. Honorable
4. Scent
5. Chemist's lair
6. Drink cubes
7. Sharp corner
8. Observe again
9. Lid for a lad
10. Distinguished
11. News finder
12. Bird-feeder treat
13. Strays
22. Possessive pronoun
25. Church spire
26. Glasses
27. Bothered
29. ___ up to (admit)
31. Tot's pa
32. Equivalent
33. Let borrow
34. Speak imperfectly
35. Before
36. Midge
38. Flock leader
39. Intelligent
43. Tissue layer
46. Sheen et al.
50. Wary
53. Loosened
54. Roused
56. Slip away from
57. Of the schnoz
58. Wonderful
59. Curved letters
60. Holes
61. Inactive
62. Custard dessert
66. Pollinator
68. Price
69. Cleo's snake

PUZZLE 143

ACROSS
1. Prima donna
5. Present!
9. Incision
13. Spent
14. Roof edges
15. Current
16. Foal's mom
17. Trickles
18. Sign
19. Fathers
20. Dorothy, to Em
21. Shipshape
22. Picturesque
24. Score
27. Choir singer
29. Additionally
30. Decline
33. Ship's wheel
36. Dejected
38. Grating
40. Like Yale's walls
42. Ditch
44. Result
45. Cowcatcher, e.g.
47. Hardwood
49. Pullovers
50. Bother
51. Vogue
53. Suds
55. Kinds
57. Narcissist
61. Art movement
64. Serving perfectly
66. Muck
67. Astounds
68. Reinforce
69. Landed
70. Brisk
71. Tanker
72. Part
73. Tot
74. Stag
75. Peat ___

DOWN
1. Unloads
2. Jacob's dad
3. Song component
4. Cool drink
5. Fabled race loser
6. Dispossess
7. Restate
8. Superman's logo
9. Callous
10. Bar fruit
11. Thought
12. Hiker's shelter
14. Commands
20. Zilch
23. Called
25. Journal
26. Knowledge
28. Paddle
30. Differently
31. Sad
32. Sewing groups
33. Stereo
34. Constantly
35. Connect
37. Pair
39. Opening
41. Resist
43. Bar bill
46. Talk
48. Sharper
52. Sweetie
54. Ovum
55. Flavor
56. Climb
58. Snow building
59. Dirties
60. Lugs
61. Dizzy
62. Gone
63. Roll-top, e.g.
65. Froster
68. Physique
69. Limb

PUZZLE 144

FLOWER POWER

Instructions for solving Flower Power puzzles are given on page 94.

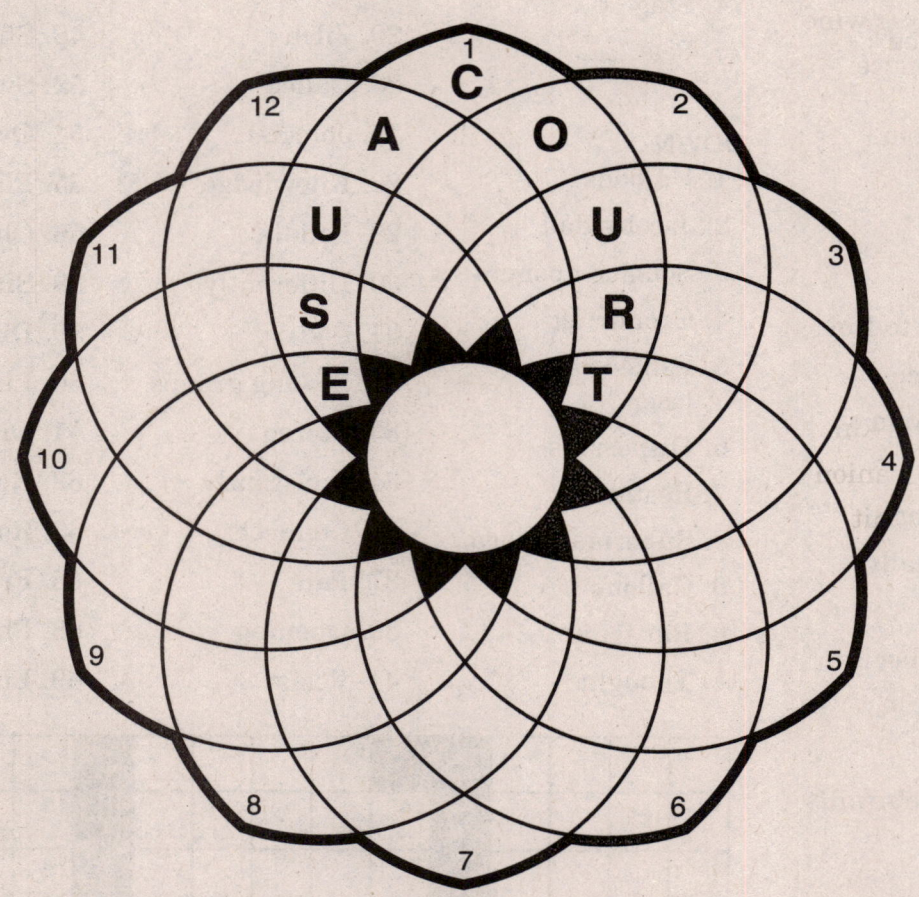

CLOCKWISE

1. Place for tennis
2. Body section
3. Embroidered mat
4. Powered by the sun
5. Free-for-all
6. Holdup
7. Arrange in folds
8. Tree with gray bark
9. Follow evidence
10. Like Oscar the Grouch
11. Chisel out
12. Violet's kin

COUNTERCLOCKWISE

1. ___-and-effect
2. Canning tool
3. Pour water over
4. "___, Wrong Number"
5. Slightly wet
6. "You Had Me From ___"
7. Airport problem
8. Prickly bush
9. Poke fun at
10. Inched along
11. Prayer before a meal
12. Pound stray

PUZZLE 145

ACROSS
1. Macaroni
6. Like a beet
9. Boring tools
13. Role players
15. Mature, as wine
16. Watch's face
17. Ditch
18. Broth
20. Cut down
21. Biblical boat
23. Tasted
24. Margin
26. Tease
27. Machete's kin
29. To's companion
31. Electric unit
34. Legal
36. Got down
39. Pigeon's cry
40. Footed vase
41. Enchant
43. Roadside hotel
44. Wow!
45. Makes a knot
46. Deteriorated
48. Blunder
49. Part of mph
51. No problem!
52. ERA or RBI
55. Computer operator
57. Go astray
60. Pen filler
61. City guide
64. Inflexible
66. Neglect
69. Extensive
70. Unpurified metal
71. More profound
72. Cruising
73. London brew
74. Pinch

DOWN
1. Trail
2. Land tract
3. Mulligan ___
4. Coal weight
5. Rainbow shape
6. Drying frame
7. Kind of maniac
8. Thick
9. Embrace
10. Chicken (out)
11. Gold fabric
12. Winter snow slider
14. Rug type
19. Bro's sib
22. Ump's kin
24. Sprite
25. Uncertainty
26. Shock
27. Less covered
28. Deed holder
30. Rear
31. Citric and amino
32. Dinero
33. Small lake
34. Toboggan
35. Luau wreath
37. Sleet or hail
38. Strikeout number
42. Cried
47. Rower's necessity
50. Hosiery mishap
52. Cupid's master?
53. ___-tac-toe
54. Deal out
56. Slip
57. Opera star
58. Generations
59. Pink wine
60. Thought
61. Pine
62. Site
63. Brew coffee
65. "We ___ Not Alone"
67. Fetch
68. Fresh

PUZZLE 146

ACROSS
1. Lived
6. Photo
9. Boys
13. Comment
15. Sooner than, in verse
16. Reed instrument
17. Beginning
18. Flexible fish
19. Seethe
20. Miles ___ hour
21. Saloon brew
23. Hoister
25. Venison source
26. Type of china
27. Crest
30. Good sign?
32. Precious
35. Wild horse
37. Other than
39. Zilch
41. Glowed
42. Raise up
44. Large antelope
45. However
46. Flat hill
47. Most bizarre
49. Medicine portion
51. Make ready
53. Main course?
54. Just
56. Emptiness
58. Fancy
61. Prepares to drag
62. Long lunch?
65. Not strong
66. Fear
68. Pass, as time
70. Like a bad excuse
71. Bawl
72. Fastened again
73. Santa's ride
74. Not shes
75. Watches

DOWN
1. Discontinue
2. "You ___ Meant for Me"
3. Asian official
4. Jet ___
5. Indian group
6. Jury member
7. Animosity
8. Yo-Yo's strings?
9. Chewy candy
10. Adjoin
11. Rounded roof
12. Vision expert?
14. Desk's leg space
22. Historical epoch
24. Surely
25. Reader's retreat
26. Gaucho's tool
27. Efficiently
28. Wept
29. Slogan
31. Actor Burton
33. Kind person
34. Laundry cycle
36. Mortar
38. Short visit
40. Troubadour's instrument
43. Peek at
48. Old man
50. Saturated
52. Holiday's precursor
55. Dog's lead
57. Small body of land
58. Nighttime hooters
59. True
60. Moniker
61. Confed. soldiers
62. Twirl
63. Applied
64. Flower plots
67. Deep sorrow
69. Had a knish

PUZZLE 147

ACROSS

1. Side dish
5. Insects
9. Host Leno
12. Italian money, once
13. Small fish
15. Lunched
16. Within
17. Harmonize
18. Paddle
19. Foreshadow
20. Coral, e.g.
21. Clutches
23. VCR button
25. Skinflint
27. Mas' mates
30. Hurried
32. Lawman
35. Scamper
36. Wear away
37. Flung
39. Unit
40. Dismiss
41. Ripen
43. Pub
44. Beginning
46. Rings up
48. Cold cubes
49. ___ pole
50. Overturn
51. Bo's number
52. Pointy
55. Beg
57. Peril
60. Island drink
62. Deaden
66. Tart's kin
67. Gloomy
69. Mime
70. Picnic drink
71. Sheared
72. Advance
73. Ushered
74. Impresses
75. Realize

DOWN

1. Block
2. Exec's auto
3. Saharan
4. Fishing boot
5. Nibble
6. Wild
7. Ox's kin
8. Tunes
9. Pickle holders
10. At the summit
11. Evergreen shrubs
13. Eye makeup
14. Had been
22. Bend
24. Assemble
26. Principles
27. Masters
28. Em and Bee
29. Slink
31. Agree
33. Planet's path
34. Calmness
37. Exams
38. Little bird
42. Shone
45. Climb
47. Authorize
53. Stage hogs
54. Oahu hello
56. Talent
57. October gem
58. Motor
59. Exploit
61. Avails
63. At the peak
64. Note
65. Make tea
68. Natural

PUZZLE 148

ACROSS
1. Circulars
4. Broomed
9. Sherpa's sighting?
13. However
14. Thin crowns
16. Uniform
17. Mine find
18. Register
19. Eyepiece
20. Solid
22. Gregarious
24. Accompany
26. Cartoon hunter
27. Hot spring
30. Keen
32. Interfered
34. Company
36. Increase
37. Fixed stake
40. Head skin
43. Picks
44. Cat sound
45. Trunk
47. Flexible
51. Disposition
54. Sneaky
55. Voiced
57. Kitchen tool
59. Sleeps loudly
61. Brick house
62. Folder
65. Tidier
67. Wordplay
68. Formal solo
69. Draconian
70. Barely manage
71. Whirl
72. Fresher
73. Date

DOWN
1. Domicile
2. Pressure
3. Funk
4. Driver
5. Victory
6. Auricles
7. Evidence
8. Perfumed powder
9. Scream
10. First female
11. Toe count
12. Those elected
15. Skid
21. Organizers
23. Total
25. Duos
27. Blooper
28. Bother
29. Sweet drinks
31. Wyatt cohort
33. Sagged
35. Tap
37. Mimics
38. Invalid
39. Platter
41. Parcel
42. Ready
46. Slanderer
48. 2,000 pounds
49. Presses
50. List
52. Weds secretly
53. Criticism
56. Exit
58. Roxie in "Chicago"
59. Emblem
60. Fuss
62. Remote
63. Great rage
64. Untruth
66. Before, to Keats

PUZZLE 149

ACROSS
1. Pant
5. Seed jackets
9. BLT topping
13. Soothing plant
14. Maui howdy
16. Church picture
17. Cogwheel
18. Sheets
19. Simple
20. Savory jelly
22. Shocking measurement?
23. Some poems
24. Hospital workers
27. Andean vulture
30. Track loops
33. Guitar's kin
34. Beach houses
39. Hooter
41. Two-piece piece
42. Wall art
43. Green soup
44. Wear away
45. Batter's goal
47. Rabbit, e.g.
48. Get lost!
50. Short respite
52. Gripe
57. Alum
60. Fragrance
61. Small pies
65. Train's need
66. Taunts
68. Honk
69. Orchard measure
70. Remnant
71. Stare
72. Eyesore
73. Cheerio
74. Duane ___

DOWN
1. Nuts
2. Kegs' contents
3. Sudsy cleaner
4. Interval
5. Close friend
6. ___ Oyl
7. Benefactor
8. Pecan hull
9. Brunch libation
10. Mastered
11. Long ago
12. Bucks
15. Opponent
21. Gator's kin
25. Stage work
26. Duelling pair?
27. Ice shape
28. Gumbo veggies
29. Below, to a poet
31. Momma's partner
32. Pleasing
35. ___ stop
36. Common verb
37. Nope
38. An out
40. Slat
45. Clip
46. Easy gait
49. Lots
51. Empower
53. Nudges
54. Decree
55. Hooded snake
56. Pay the tab
57. Small weight
58. Derby
59. Assumed manners
62. Cattail
63. Prepared to drive
64. Nimble
67. Health spring

PUZZLE 150

ACROSS
1. Smear
4. Acapulco coin
8. Leafy lunch
13. Wide rd.
14. "The Little Engine that ___"
15. Author Zola
16. ___ Dolorosa
17. Awful
18. Lap pups
19. Schooled
21. Collar site
22. Take a chance
23. In the sack
26. Jack Horner's fruit
28. Certain convent
30. Grocery tote
33. Rosary sphere
34. Not windward
35. Beer's bitter kin
36. Zodiac sign
38. Dander
39. Soft fabric
41. Tend a baby
42. Alpine lake
44. Ice-cream holder
45. Slick
46. Flavoring seed
48. Hooligan
49. ___ and sciences
50. Venetian dough, once
52. Carpet type
55. Penalizes
59. Commodities
61. "Call Me ___"
62. Ostrichlike animal
63. Dress shape
64. Premieres
65. Point a gun
66. Dish
67. Commanded
68. Major-leaguer

DOWN
1. Kevin Kline flick
2. Anxious
3. Wooer
4. Looks sullen
5. Cry of discovery
6. Lost control
7. Puzzling
8. Fall mo.
9. Rectify
10. Enjoy
11. Film's Guinness
12. Writing table
14. Assert as fact
20. Crass
23. Gifted
24. Hive dweller
25. Ogler
26. Hazard
27. Parishioners
29. Stables
30. Marshy inlet
31. "___ Comes Mary"
32. Hereditary unit
33. Big fiddle
37. Sun, e.g.
38. Garden flower
40. Is painful
43. Aardvark's quarry
47. Dodged
48. Adorns
49. FBI member
51. Ridiculous
52. Trade
53. Monty or Arsenio
54. Intricate solo
55. Dad
56. Stack
57. Arabian bigwig
58. Japanese wrestling
60. Regard
61. Gang

PUZZLE 151

ACROSS
1. Thought
5. Rub hard
10. That gal
13. Cash register
14. Irritated
16. 007-creator Fleming
17. Teamster's truck
18. Locomotive
19. Expel
20. Crescent
22. Some clams
24. Tile picture
27. Virus variety
28. Strife
29. Spiced sausage
32. Guitarist Paul
35. Stopping place
36. Mars, e.g.
37. Garbed
39. Flag feature
41. Camelot title
42. Stereo
43. Pocket bread
44. Rate
47. Lincoln center?
48. Make a seam
49. Lace hole
50. Gomez's cousin
51. Stray
53. Frothy
55. Auto extras
60. Canadian whiskey
61. Begin, in poetry
62. Accommodate
64. Castoff clothing
68. Terrier type
69. Blockades
70. Test tube
71. Picnic crasher
72. Small change
73. Jumpy

DOWN
1. "___ alive!"
2. Numbered cube
3. Tall tree
4. Phony moniker
5. Extraordinary
6. Preserve
7. Equips
8. Platoon
9. Fund-raiser
10. Parent
11. Kojak's lack
12. Quits
15. Bargain
21. Rough file
23. Gardener's material
24. Pious insect?
25. Elaborate
26. Elegant
28. Thin tuft
30. Licorice root
31. Only
33. Extract
34. Protection
38. Daily fare
40. Greener
44. ___ exercise
45. Female prophet
46. Stick around
52. Kanga's kid, et al.
54. Dish out
55. Parlor piece
56. Informed about
57. Following
58. Take flight
59. Placard
63. "___ Smart"
65. Relief
66. Muzzle
67. Cagey

PUZZLE 152

ACROSS

1. Lots
5. Engrave
9. Bible book
13. Curved lines
17. Spare ___
18. Cooking order
19. Mail drop
20. Heavenly body
21. Steady
22. Milky gem
23. Colossal
24. Cellist Ma
25. Kind of skirt
26. Round before the final
27. Stadium
29. Suture
30. Shrimp dish
32. Feline sounds
35. Vestibule
37. Atom with a charge
39. BLT spread
40. Make haste
41. Luau offering
44. Understood
46. TV, newspaper, et al.
48. Halt!
52. Actress Potts
54. Paintings, e.g.
56. Campaign in small towns
58. Let use
59. Before a conflict
61. Conceit
62. Vigor
63. Petal-puller's word
65. Short letters
67. Sit-ups target
69. Agape, to a bard
72. Above, to Keats
74. Certain basecoat
76. Prune
80. Outlaw
83. Obscure
84. Georgia city
85. Allay
86. Adversary
88. Corncob, e.g.
90. Both Begleys
91. Comfort
93. Eye water
95. Boxing count
96. "I ___ return"
99. Inquired
101. Prodded
106. Monkey suit
107. New Zealand bird
110. Fat-free
112. Salvation ___
113. In the center of
115. Cinema drink
117. Seaweed
118. Chantilly
119. Prong
120. ___ out (barely earned)
121. Piece of gossip
122. By any possibility
123. Boundary
124. Roulette bets
125. Defy
126. Observes

DOWN

1. Restrains
2. Public
3. Sports complex
4. Blue fabric
5. Coastal breakdown
6. Recording
7. Confine
8. Balloon gas
9. Fire remains
10. Bar mixer
11. Fast-food order
12. Goulash
13. Singer Grant
14. Rule the ___
15. More shy
16. Certain owl
28. "Hawaii" prop
31. Spear
33. Ewe's guy
34. Part of a Reuben
36. Colorful salamander
38. Imminent
40. Pilot's garage
41. Buddy
42. Unmatched
43. Wayside hotel
45. Small songbird
47. Bad temper
49. Bunny jump
50. Valuable dirt
51. Roadie's equipment
53. "___ Magic"
55. Couples
57. Have a bawl
59. Gazed
60. Corroded
64. Shed tool
66. Blooper

PUZZLE 152

68. Health spot
69. Poem
70. Pod vegetable
71. Superman's logo
73. Zoomed
75. Give forth
77. Sleuth Ventura
78. Wand
79. Type spaces
81. Ring
82. Complicated
84. Restaurant listing
87. Tibetan beast
89. Nom de plume
92. Sort
94. Put down tile again
96. Declare
97. Muggy
98. Chopping
100. Gamma follower
102. Glens
103. Serious
104. Roast host
105. Tinters
108. Froster
109. Roused
111. Ripening agent
114. "Gidget" star
116. Magazine spots

PUZZLE 153

ACROSS
1. Pricked
6. Screen
10. Blind section
14. Kayak's cousin
15. Harness part
16. Car
17. Straighten
18. Scissors stroke
19. Gradual
20. Wager
21. Agape, poetically
23. Has dinner
24. "___ That Jazz"
25. Hopeful
28. Become sick
31. Drifting
33. Archaic
36. High-seas robbery
38. Tad
39. Split ___ soup
40. Scent
41. Awry
42. Pave again
44. Stimpy's pal
45. Hint
47. Compete
48. Magazine fillers
49. Cheer
51. Expert
52. Lower limbs
53. Shad ___
55. Vatican figure
58. Huck's friend
59. Away
62. Futile
63. Poker stake
66. Weeper
68. Journey
69. Serve wine
70. Creepy
71. Military body
72. Uneasy
73. Balances

DOWN
1. Incrustation
2. Fairy ___
3. Division
4. Eggy drink
5. Italian port
6. Personally
7. Eternity
8. Emulate Picabo
9. In the know
10. Forward
11. Humdinger
12. Above
13. Hauls
22. Frolic
25. Santa's perch?
26. Cookie grain
27. Commence
28. Televised
29. Golf clubs
30. Felon's flight
32. Type of prisoner
33. Of sight
34. Depart
35. "Truth or ___"
36. Medic beginning
37. Hidden supply
41. Not theirs
43. Timespan
46. Tote
47. Begone!
50. Blood vessel
52. Cautious
54. Roast host
55. Flat bread
56. Fragrance
57. Purple fruit
59. ___ hydrant
60. Constraint
61. Unrefined metals
63. Chimpanzee
64. Indicate yes
65. ___ of war
67. Gun a motor

PUZZLE 154

ACROSS

1. Dominated
4. Breaches
8. Altar area
12. Part of IOU
13. Heating unit
15. Grandmother
16. Cartoon frame
17. Blazing
18. Cluster
19. Baltimore ___
21. Fasten
22. Chops
23. Brink
25. To's pal
27. Elderly
29. Cup handle
31. Crescents
34. Duplicate
35. Vinegar vessels
37. Rascal
39. Paddle's kin
40. Temp
41. Tiny drink
42. By means of
43. Cleverness
44. Clans
46. Slick
47. "Of ___ I Sing"
49. Diamond girl
50. Not busy
51. Sauna locale
53. Body organ
55. EMT's word
58. Periodical, briefly
60. Endured
64. Control
65. Polar cover
67. Chop
68. Apogee
69. Mojave, e.g.
70. Crib
71. Loud noise
72. Trunk
73. Messy abode

DOWN

1. Crazy
2. Water server
3. Hero store
4. Errand boy
5. Feel ill
6. Level off
7. Trailer truck
8. Hold down
9. Colorless
10. Winter fall
11. Chow
13. Bundled
14. Coral ridge
20. Hot box
24. Furry pet
26. Grind
27. Bide time
28. Circumference
30. Vend again
32. Courteous
33. Grin
34. Draw along
35. Mutt
36. Song syllables
38. Remit
40. Degree
45. Largest
46. Not evens
48. Value
50. Unsuitable
52. Betwixt
54. Startle
55. Random try
56. Mexican food
57. GI's bullets
59. Experts
61. Labels
62. Depart
63. Disavow
66. Passing grade

PUZZLE 155

HOLD IT!

ACROSS
1. Chocolate piece
5. Butts into
9. Every
13. Saga
17. Andean Indian
18. Press
19. Qualified
20. Ibsen's doll
21. Mild oath
22. Container for valuables
24. Jenna, to Barbara
25. Discredit
27. Drove (a vehicle)
28. Thick of things
29. Donkey serenades?
31. Victim
32. Soft or flat follower
33. Toll loudly
35. A Mama
37. Coal, e.g.
40. Bard's atop
41. Confound
43. Atelier props
46. Scoot
47. Unites
49. Tacks on
51. Crescent
52. Kind of model
53. Stir-fry sites
55. Loathed
57. Slugger Jeter
58. Very enthusiastic
61. Competed at Daytona
62. Demons
63. American patriot
64. Blacktop worker
65. Riverside
66. Scrabble square
67. Engagement
68. Moratorium
70. Burn slightly
74. Holiday lead-in
75. Pretenders
77. Fish sauce
79. Woolworth Bldg. site
80. Rebellious
82. Nickname on "JAG"
84. Rambled
86. Betting ratio
87. Stoke
89. Vowed
91. Etui contents, sometimes
93. Combined amounts
95. Wild feline
98. Stone or star
99. Container for landscapes
101. Skirt panel
102. A deadbeat does it
103. Previously
104. Abate
105. Silica gem
106. Witch feature
107. House of Lords member
108. Box lightly
109. Dickens character

DOWN
1. Pirate Captain ___
2. As to
3. Container for a sword
4. Consort of Ops
5. Precarious
6. Paul's partner
7. Cartoonist Walker
8. Wiretaps
9. Philadelphia player
10. "Northanger ___"
11. Loam lump
12. Spell
13. Whole
14. Container for explosives
15. Judi Dench film
16. Pious platitudes
23. North Germanic
26. Carps
28. Fortifies
30. Gusts of wind
32. Cunning
33. Moon jumper
34. Virginia family
36. Too
37. Set right
38. Suffered
39. Soup veggies
42. Grab
44. Converts
45. Brought to court
48. Babe and Wilbur
50. Stripling
52. Is malodorous
54. Cinnabar, e.g.
56. Topnotch
57. Cacophony
58. Elected

PUZZLE 155

- 59. Ingenuous
- 60. Container for documents
- 61. Judge
- 62. Tammy ___ Bakker
- 64. Bygone
- 65. Soothes
- 67. Henley and Ho
- 69. Asphalt
- 71. Container for epistle
- 72. Pro vote
- 73. Bookkeeper's abbr.
- 75. Thickens
- 76. Bundle
- 78. Everglades denizen, for short
- 81. Least occupied
- 83. Concedes
- 85. Pioneers' trail
- 87. Part of USAF
- 88. Absolute
- 90. Courtship participant
- 91. Till
- 92. Corn Belt state
- 93. Inflection
- 94. Insult
- 96. Doctoral hurdle
- 97. Inform
- 99. Certain tune
- 100. ___ nutshell

PUZZLE 156

ACROSS
1. Holy table
6. Movie auntie
10. Toothed tools
14. Bullwinkle, e.g.
15. Touched ground
16. Scratch
17. Monastery brothers
18. Radial, e.g.
19. Teen trouble
20. United
21. Wedding member
23. Gnaw away
24. Ostrichlike bird
25. Standard
27. Fluffy's doc
28. Amok
32. Spare material
34. Dazzles
35. Small fruit
37. Hair cream
38. Sum up
40. Label
42. Prince of India
46. Swerve, at sea
48. Child's seat
50. Long skirt
51. Panted
54. Forced
56. Curvature
57. Slumbering
59. Pot's cover
60. Shaving cuts
62. Narrates
64. Soft toss
67. Epoxy
68. Fossil
69. Avoid
71. Choice word
72. Wreck
73. Energize
74. Totter
75. Tentacles
76. Baker's need

DOWN
1. Caisson contents
2. Waterfowl
3. Manner
4. Solicit
5. Continue
6. Trig, e.g.
7. Foreign
8. Reflect
9. Parisian season
10. Injury trace
11. Dining nook
12. Roam
13. Pleasing
22. Breakers
23. Cinder
24. School themes
26. Shag, e.g.
28. Legal exam
29. She-sheep
30. ___ room (den)
31. Equipment
33. Held responsible
36. Four qts.
39. Fathers
41. Empty space
43. Crock
44. Tomahawk
45. Masked
47. "Charlotte's ___"
49. Opinion sample
51. Grating
52. Arraign
53. Bypass
55. Prudently
56. Enrage
58. Sturdy cloth
61. Ship's bottom
63. Eyepiece
64. Volcanic fluid
65. Sonnets' kin
66. Inclination
68. Swimsuit piece
70. Struggle (for)

PUZZLE 157

ACROSS

1. Dangle
5. Floor model
9. Beyond
13. Health balm
14. Ade fruit
15. Alpine reply
16. Speed
17. Dodge
18. Met solo
19. Naval off.
20. Humor
21. Combine
22. Sponge
24. Coliseum
28. Canola ___
30. Hateful
31. Quarrel
34. Poem verse
37. Provide
38. Develop
39. Not loud
40. What place?
42. Unwell
43. Publicize
44. Yonder
45. Swapped
48. Tissue layer
49. Treatment
50. Edible root
51. Deacon
53. Horse
57. Extra pay
61. Dance
63. Paris summer
64. Patron
65. Pungent
68. Dry wine
69. Pennant
70. Circular
71. Man Friday
72. Front
73. Deli request
74. Buck

DOWN

1. Greenish brown
2. Solo
3. Looped rope
4. Jewel
5. Silt deposit
6. Outback bird
7. Stylish
8. Small bill
9. Chime
10. Land parcel
11. Leg part
12. Frog's kin
14. Oahu wreath
20. Smart kid
21. ___ eagle
23. Deceive
25. Game official
26. At all
27. XC
29. Legal
31. Assault
32. Gape
33. Solder
34. Whack
35. Drudge
36. Crooked
41. Tough
44. Pros
46. Grate
47. Qty.
52. Horned mammal, shortly
54. Bizarre
55. Piano piece
56. Thwart
57. Polish
58. Norwegian city
59. Advance
60. Coax
62. Uneven
65. Handiwork
66. Talk fondly
67. Carpet
68. Wicked

PUZZLE 158

ACROSS
1. Night crawlers
6. Read a bar code
10. Aching
14. Model
15. Neck section
16. Lengthens
17. ___ Carlo
18. Vicinity
19. Golf hazard
20. Hardly an amateur
21. Telegraph
23. Traffic circle
25. ___ Jersey
26. Ram's mate
27. Garrets
31. Dozing
34. Fortify
35. Caboodle's partner
36. State falsely
38. Intense suffering
39. Frying liquid
40. Brownish gray
42. Prepare to drag
43. Habit wearer
44. Papa goose
45. Mend
48. Amazement
49. Gnome
50. What Horton heard
51. Receive
54. Go by mule
56. Mil. address
59. Beckon
60. List member
62. Braved
64. Authentic
65. Ages
66. Freeze-___
67. Tree beginning
68. Bright
69. "The Impossible ___"

DOWN
1. Weak person
2. Stench
3. Casino city
4. Porch rug
5. Droves
6. Catches
7. Twins' slugger Rod ___
8. Zoo attraction
9. Least distant
10. Love seat
11. Gumbo vegetable
12. Type of admiral
13. Notice
22. Foot component
24. It gives a hoot
27. Hostility
28. Treasure stash
29. ___ Pan Alley
30. Frigid
31. Have a cold
32. Escape
33. "The Pied ___"
34. Attention
35. Relations
37. At any time, to Keats
39. "___ House" (song)
40. Sunbathe
41. Connecting word
43. Keener
44. Unspoiled
46. Stripped
47. Mont Blanc, e.g.
48. Capricious humor
50. Small birds
51. Plays a role
52. Feel concern
53. Tip
55. Crosscurrent
56. Diva's solo
57. Social equal
58. Betting numbers
61. Overly
63. "You ___ Sixteen"

PUZZLE 159

ACROSS
1. Sermon response
5. Dewy
9. Narrow strip
13. Explorer Marco ___
14. Consumers
16. Fairy-tale beast
17. Absorbed
18. Kind of nerve
19. Designated space
20. Stanley or Davis
21. Quickest
23. Put into office
26. Devilish spirit
28. Snaky shape
29. The sky's the ___
31. Oolong, e.g.
33. Rescuer
37. Thrash
41. Concluded
42. Gypsy's card
44. Sharpen
45. Eccentric person
46. Most snobbish
48. Tiny drink
51. Love, in Paris
52. Talented
55. Answer
57. Tells all
61. Doer's counterpart
63. Feather stole
64. Cato's cloak
65. Essential
69. Troubadour
70. Agenda part
71. Show feeling
72. Adrift
73. Apple middle
74. Leered
75. Evaluate

DOWN
1. With speed
2. Big shot
3. Flee to wed
4. Seasonal quaff
5. The Dynamic ___
6. Egyptian serpent
7. Came across
8. Light bender
9. Mortgage
10. Approve
11. Lock
12. Warms
15. Scamper
22. Count starter
24. Salespeople
25. Song syllables
26. Stellar sopranos
27. Infinite
30. Floor pad
32. Spinning
33. Cabin material
34. "___ Waited So Long"
35. Commission
36. Spacious
38. Garden tool
39. Outs' opposites
40. Hamster, e.g.
43. Furthermore
47. Bath site
49. Provoke
50. Aggravate
52. Top story
53. Picture
54. Detroit athlete
56. Best quality
58. Degrade
59. Drills
60. Nasser's successor
62. Identify
66. Doll, e.g.
67. Supped
68. Guided
69. Dracula, often

PUZZLE 160

ACROSS
1. Bar bill
4. March date
8. Peruses
13. Bravo preceder
14. Void's partner
15. Sweetie
16. Commotion
17. Crater
18. Choice
19. Black brew
21. Walk through water
23. Crawling insect
24. Trickle
27. Soccer score
29. Split again
32. Index
35. Half dozen
36. Toddler
37. Stain
39. Sour compounds
41. Brownie
43. Sleuth Sam ___
44. Lunchtime stop
45. Fruit pastry
47. Tin
48. Sit a spell
50. Nonsense
52. Pop flavor
54. Chills and fever
55. Plant juice
58. Diner spread
60. Folk tales
64. Pack animals
66. Small bit
69. Joint
70. Valued things
71. Went fast
72. St. crosser
73. Slogan
74. Cultivated
75. Unfamiliar

DOWN
1. Capture
2. Nurse's ___
3. Novel, e.g.
4. Acquires
5. Pair
6. Pipe type
7. Scads
8. Revoke formally
9. Chow down
10. Opera tune
11. Celine ___
12. Dispatched
15. Dummy
20. Uncanny
22. Iron or Stone
25. Poison ___
26. Toll road
28. Speech impediment
29. Kitchen gizmo
30. Outcast
31. Ms. Burke
33. Part of NASA
34. Presently
35. Dispirited
38. Twice five
40. Compact ___
42. FDR's Scottie
43. Played a harp
46. Remnant
49. Popular soup
50. Come what ___
51. Florida island
53. Gal
55. Bridge term
56. To boot
57. Former
59. Sworn promise
61. "Less ___ Zero"
62. Busy place
63. Erupt
65. Encountered
67. As well
68. Crude copper

PUZZLE 161

ACROSS
1. Charter
6. Crumple
9. Actor Pitt
13. Sunday pipes
15. "You ___ Sixteen"
16. Slippery
17. Enlargement
18. Stick up
19. Grade
20. Positive particle
21. Scrapes
23. Stomped
24. Bawl
25. Appropriate
26. Imprint firmly
29. Copycat
30. Hurry
34. Pointers
37. Develop
40. Car coating
41. Castle piece
42. Pares
43. Clock
44. Chowed down
45. Peppermint ___
46. Singles
47. ___ of honor
49. Not odd
52. Shop sign
54. Gender
55. Cut a lawn
58. Milk drink
61. Of sight
63. First woman
64. ___ Minor
65. Med course
66. Vital
68. ___ belt
69. Viper
70. Watching secretly
71. Rabbit's kin
72. Golly!
73. Taunt

DOWN
1. Reasoning
2. Blooper
3. Torment
4. Noticed
5. Snare
6. Distort
7. Stood up
8. Society girl
9. Train beds
10. Posterior
11. Choir member
12. Stained
14. Outline
22. Avenue
27. In this way
28. Hint
29. Consult
31. Double
32. Ornate fabric
33. 24th letters
34. Mine cart
35. Small bit
36. Bard
38. Mesh
39. Craftiest
42. Window unit
43. Cargo weight
45. Father
48. Spin
50. Leaf ribs
51. Excluding
53. Roar
55. TV, radio, etc.
56. Bread bakers
57. Cram
58. Alda's series
59. Voyaging
60. Fraud
62. Vatican head
65. Sack
67. Observe

PUZZLE 162

ACROSS
1. Break
6. Somersault
10. Bikini part
13. Oil ship
15. Loony
16. Topper
17. Total
18. Lemon drinks
19. Finale
20. Little
21. Worry
23. Edgy
25. Which person's?
27. Cushioned
28. Cleaners
31. Dilly
32. Rise
33. Burrowed
34. Coffee shop
38. Deceivers
39. ___ of war
40. More exposed
41. Pathway
42. Animal park
43. ___-of-fact
44. Witness
46. Woodlands
47. Design
50. Fair
51. Enchant
52. Tart
53. Distant
56. Hurried
57. At the top
59. Realm
62. Rescue
63. Title
64. Jousted
65. Jimmy
66. Female sheep
67. "___ Family"

DOWN
1. Mulligan ___
2. Tresses
3. Poker play
4. Snow runner
5. Not him
6. Signal
7. Ore vein
8. Rink surface
9. ___ service
10. Mix
11. Cleanse
12. Extra
14. Tape
22. Mule's kin
24. Schooled
25. Anyplace
26. Layers
27. Dog breed
28. Barricade
29. Large continent
30. Skim
31. Tote
33. Twosome
35. Skills
36. Yard units
37. Misjudges
39. Drag
40. Stable
42. Last letter
43. Anchored
45. Protected
46. Winter ailment
47. Fragment
48. Seat
49. Convenient
50. Skeleton
52. Few
53. Movie
54. Region
55. Roulette bets
58. Dog's foot
60. Silent
61. Jacket type

CODEWORD

PUZZLE 163

Codeword is a special crossword puzzle in which conventional clues are omitted. Instead, answer words in the diagram are represented by numbers. Each number represents a different letter of the alphabet, and all of the letters of the alphabet are used. When you are sure of a letter, put it in the code key chart and cross it off in the Alphabet Box. A group of letters has been inserted to start you off.

1	2	3	4	5	6	7	8	9	10	11 A	12	13
14	15	16	17	18	19	20	21	22	23	24 E	25 R	26

Alphabet Box

A̸ B C D E̸ F G H I J K L M N O P Q R̸ S T U V W X Y Z

143

PUZZLE 164

ACROSS
1. Cathedral part
5. Dancer Moreno
9. Cattail, e.g.
13. ___ Raton
17. Lack
18. Wide-spouted jug
19. Fiend
20. War deity
21. Seal hunter
22. Departed
23. Fly high
24. Egg center
25. Aromatic spice
27. Strongbox
29. Luxury auto
31. Comrade
33. Ginza belt
35. Extinguishes
39. Kidder
42. Plodded
44. Outline
45. Defier
46. Tavern drink
48. Slip
49. Future chicks
50. Dark wood
51. Ostrichlike bird
52. Fox's prey
53. Wrathful person
55. Corncrib
56. Disagree
59. Fellow
61. Color fabric
63. Housewife
66. Young salamander
69. Empty of water
71. Monster in the closet, e.g.
73. Annoy
75. Marble slices
78. Doctrine
81. Nanny has three
82. Ghostly
84. Pea packet
85. Outrigger
87. Stimpy's buddy
88. Tree snake
89. "We ___ the World"
90. Insert an audio track
92. Unwilling
94. Midday nap
96. Sullivan and Begley
97. Newspaper page
98. Sale caveat
100. Bear's place
102. & or #
107. Moneyless
110. Mine find
112. Appends
114. Longing
115. Vibes
116. Mideast title
117. Trait carrier
118. Festive party
119. Brown songbird
120. Family rooms
121. Said aloud
122. Anna ___ of "Nana"

DOWN
1. Unknown auth.
2. Inca country
3. Faction
4. Dutch cheese
5. Marley's music
6. ___ Jima
7. Fidgety
8. Region
9. Prickly shrub
10. Psyche part
11. Of a notable period
12. Ridiculed
13. Louisiana marsh
14. Cancun gold
15. Cartoon unit
16. Solicit
26. Rudimentary stage
28. Supporting
30. Up-to-date
32. Gymnast's prop
34. Baseless
36. Polluted air
37. Chalet feature
38. Shadowbox
39. Madly zealous
40. Satire
41. "___-Hur"
42. Taunt
43. Crisp cookie
45. Society miss
47. Weaving frame
54. Feasted
57. Greek letter
58. Printing measures
60. Before, in poems
62. Decrease
64. Sour-tasting
65. "Citizen ___"
67. Companies
68. Clan
70. Scarves
72. Cure
74. New Zealand parrot
75. Hot springs
76. TV's Loughlin
77. "Zip-___-Doo-Dah"
79. Angry
80. Busybodies
83. Corn piece
86. Helped
91. "Surfin' ___"
93. Watercraft
95. It's a wrap
97. Sequence
99. Several
101. "Othello" villain
103. Large cups
104. Unruly kid
105. Stare rudely
106. Low in fat
107. Animal's foot
108. "___ Miss Brooks"
109. Valuable dirt
111. Commotion
113. Heredity inits.

PUZZLE 165

ACROSS
1. Support
5. Developer's interest
9. Blazing
14. Bouncing sound
15. Draws along
16. Semiconductor, e.g.
17. West Indian shrub
18. Like some laws
20. Returned the favor
22. Eternally, in poetry
23. Makeshift bed
24. Hold on property
26. Cheer for a matador
28. Ski race
31. Gathered, as bees
35. Graceful swimmer
36. Satire
38. "___ Fine Day"
39. Furor
41. Toothpaste form
42. Grudge
44. Greek vowel
45. Guts
47. Infuriated
48. Carve (wood)
50. Complainer
53. Game official, for short
54. Stained with pen fluid
55. Nude
58. Doctrine
60. Ventilate
65. Simple
68. High scorer
69. Work
70. Flu symptom
71. "___ So Cold"
72. Jeweled crown
73. Care for
74. Nuisance

DOWN
1. Smokey, e.g.
2. Skin woe
3. Break off
4. Soda-flavoring nut
5. Artist's lair
6. Charged particle
7. 'Twixt's partner
8. Medieval peasant
9. Commotion
10. Construction beam
11. Loony
12. Sonnets' kin
13. Unites
19. Upside-down smile
21. ___-advised
25. Expatriate
27. Sets down
28. Cut a wide ___
29. Hawaiian porch
30. Cuckoo
31. Serious
32. Watered silk
33. Infiltrate
34. Feat
35. Diving duck
37. Gun (a motor)
40. Feed the kitty
43. Brooch
46. Small and sprightly
49. Shaking
51. Approved
52. Pirate's yes
54. Effigy
55. Karate award
56. Jai ___
57. Country's McEntire
59. Immediately, on "ER"
61. Scrape
62. Feel great pity
63. Kickoff props
64. Hitherto
66. Gay Nineties, e.g.
67. Stand for office

PUZZLE 166

Theme Words

Four related words plus a fifth word describing their category are concealed in each diagram. Choose one square from each column, moving from left to right in order, to form a word. In the example the category is TOOL, and the related words are SAW and LATHE.

Example:

S	OO	HE	SAW
L	AT	W	LATHE
T	A	L	TOOL

1.

HE	VE	U	OO	EN
SP	E	PR	C	K
R	Y	L	RE	S
E	R	DW	OC	E
C	M	RG	ES	D

2.

D	A	PI	N	E
F	L	NA	S	ND
BA	TE	I	TA	T
C	I	AN	DE	CE
IN	IV	RE	C	L

PUZZLE 167

ACROSS
1. Narrow strip
5. Succor a scofflaw
9. Sweetie
13. Inclination
17. Robin Cook novel
18. Type of bean
19. ___ podrida
20. Egg cell
21. Kiln, e.g.
22. Becloud
23. Holy ___!
24. Scale
25. Curl
27. Pod inhabitant
29. Tiny fish
31. Dusk, to poets
32. Singer DiFranco
33. Max ___ Sydow
34. Hotel freebie
38. Spicy
40. Star's resort
43. Pointers
44. Musical symbol
46. Military clerk
47. Tennis shot
48. Ho's instrument
49. Cut
51. Relatives
52. Andean climber
54. Mattress frame
56. Encountered
57. Realms
58. Little songbird
59. Second swerve
60. Not us
61. Pampered
64. Family room
65. Garment ticket
69. Grads
70. Hive builder
71. Respond
72. Wish otherwise
73. Plus
74. Evening, in Rome
76. Fresh
77. Absolute
78. "___ Jude"
79. Panicked
81. Fool
84. Decorative vase
85. Juice drink
86. Bear hair
87. Calf bone
91. Miss Piggy's "me"
92. With quick beats
96. Wedded words
97. Lowest tide
100. Ballet bend
102. Similar
103. Oh, woe!
104. Glen
105. Explain
106. Fencer's weapon
107. Dist.
108. Took to court
109. Finch food
110. Pedestal part

DOWN
1. Highlander
2. Passion
3. Pulpit word
4. Bicycles for pairs
5. Lacking pigment
6. Beak
7. Ostrichlike bird
8. Roofing material
9. Province
10. Brit. rock group
11. Totally
12. Mr. Burr
13. "___ Free"
14. Lendl of tennis
15. Limo, e.g.
16. Diving duck
26. Corded fabric
28. Slangy sufficiency
30. Brainpower
33. Lode
34. Ticket part
35. Trek
36. Imitated
37. Pacific or Indian
39. Walking rhythm
40. Bridge feat
41. Apple or pear
42. Syrian fabrics
45. Child
49. Nerve-racking
50. Pay attention
51. Barrel
53. Citrus fruit
55. Dog-paddle
56. Chap
57. Snazzy
59. Final letter
60. Platters
61. Basin
62. Healing herb
63. Floating marker
64. College bigwig
65. Sunday bench
66. Genuine
67. Distinctive atmosphere
68. Went right
70. Wheat husk
71. Vouchers
75. Short trips
76. Bauble
77. Worded
80. Packed down
82. Abroad
83. Place
87. Decree
88. Out of service
89. Wild hog
90. WWII ally
92. Mound
93. Bug stage
94. Did perfectly
95. Malcolm Jamal Warner role
98. ___ de Cologne
99. Tavern brew
101. Majors or Marvin

DOUBLE TROUBLE

PUZZLE 168

Not really double trouble, but double fun! Solve this puzzle as you would a regular crossword, except place one, two, or three letters in each box. The number of letters in each answer is shown in parentheses after its clue.

ACROSS
1. Grow together (7)
4. Intone (5)
7. Existed (3)
9. ___ room (3)
11. German river (4)
12. Fly high (4)
13. Trendy (3)
14. Writer Bagnold (4)
15. Literary audience (10)
17. Prom attendee (8)
19. Jury group (5)
21. Des Moines's site (4)
22. Backbone (5)
23. Haul (3)
24. Wire-haired dog breed (15)
29. Japanese commander, once (6)
31. ___ weevil (4)
32. Lectured (6)
33. Whittle (4)
35. Faction (4)
37. Skater Babilonia (3)
38. Back end (4)
39. Sierra ___ (5)
41. Beginning (5)
44. Negotiation process (20)
48. Envelope addition (5)
49. Actor Gibson (3)
50. Sphere (3)
51. Rosie's forte? (8)
53. One-humped camel (9)
55. Critical attack (9)
58. Tennis event (4)
59. Art ___ (4)
60. Dictionary entry (4)
61. Maroon (6)
64. Actor Byrnes (3)
65. Tweed's foe (4)
66. Planting crops (7)
67. Fathered (5)

DOWN
1. Scored on a serve (4)
2. Canadian Indian (4)
3. Earthly (7)
4. Bar offerings (7)
5. Ark builder (4)
6. Journey (4)
7. Kind of rafting (10)
8. Colorado ski town (5)
9. Designed anew (12)
10. Apple drink (5)
16. Politician Stevenson (5)
18. Ambition (10)
19. Luxurious (5)
20. Eager (4)
21. Hercules's captive (4)
25. Yank's foe (3)
26. Apothecary measure (4)
27. Danger-is-over signal (8)
28. Round of duties (4)
30. Without equal (12)
34. Put up (5)
36. Polynesian kingdom (5)
38. Endorse (9)
40. One, in Berlin (3)
42. Sonnet section (6)
43. Packing down (7)
45. West African country (10)
46. Fade (3)
47. Actress Bergman (6)
52. Sleeveless garments (5)
53. Sagged (7)
54. Last name in cosmetics (5)
55. Window-shop (6)
56. Revered (6)
57. Shingles, e.g. (6)
62. Rajah's wife (4)
63. Famed Scott (4)

LOOKING FOR DOUBLE TROUBLE? You've found it! Treat yourself to special collections of your favorite puzzles—over 50 in each! To order, see page 159.

PUZZLE 169

BRICK BY BRICK

Rearrange this stack of bricks to form a crossword puzzle. The clues will help you fit the bricks into their correct places. Row 1 has been filled in for you. Use the bricks to fill in the remaining spaces.

ACROSS
1. Helpful
   Editor's direction
   Power tool
2. World's fair, e.g.
   Military branch
   Bow's partner
3. Broad comedy
   Break, of yore
4. Fire truck's sound
   Northern thrush
   Sea: Fr.
5. Pick
   S-shaped curve
   And: Ger.
6. Wagon track
   Distress
7. Swiss cottage
   Share
   Singing group
8. Gruesome
   Furniture wood
   Barren
9. Opposed to, for Li'l Abner
   Doggy-bag bit
   Infant's knitted sock
10. Be worthy of
    Dry, as wine
11. Previously known as
    Small monkey
    Dance step
12. Finback whale
    Distort
    Concerning
13. Wrist bones
    Long short story
14. Dispatch boat
    At all
    Neapolitan night
15. Plastic ingredient
    Gull's cousin
    Expedition

DOWN
1. Painter's plaster
   Bedecked
   Wound reminder
2. Primrose
   Enormous
   Gutter holder
3. Victor Vasarely's genre
   Molding edge
   Showy bloomer
4. Fool
   Towels, e.g.
   Fraternity letter
5. Sawed logs
   Territory
6. Convened
   Belly
   Microwave appliance
7. Hot-plate stand
   Pitchblende, e.g.
   Dill, of old
8. Roast host
   Dr. Seuss hat-wearer
   Cache
9. Youngster
   Puffin's kin
   Cloud lining?
10. Littlest of a litter
    Ante
    Coastal eagle
11. Vocal cord's locale
    ____ worker
12. Metric measure
    The same
    TV's "Empty ____"
13. Streetcar
    It was: Lat.
    Diminish slowly
14. Flung
    Weary
    Cavern
15. Liquid container
    Oxen harness
    Cube or flank

PUZZLE 170

• PERIODICAL PLEASURE •

ACROSS
1. Complaint
5. Flat-bottomed boat
9. Netman Wilander
13. Lori Singer series
17. Menlo Park middle name
18. Exile isle
19. Assam silkworm
20. Seed coat
21. Caliph's kin
22. Film ___
23. Mulligan, e.g.
24. Actor Hamill
25. Magazine
28. Indian clans
30. Cenozoic, e.g.
31. Outrage
32. Simpleton
33. Skater Harding
36. Pyramid, for some
38. Blimp sponsor
42. "___ Got a Secret"
43. Chutzpah
45. Expense
46. Actor Nicolas ___
47. Crew
49. Actress Sara
50. Bog
51. American composer Charles ___
52. Windsor's province
54. Actress Blakley
55. Say hello to
56. Hi and Lois's daughter
57. Athenian statesman
58. Yule month: abbr.
59. Free-for-all
62. Cordelia's sister
63. Matrimony
67. Waxed cheese
68. Prank
69. Red or Dead, e.g.
70. North Carolina college
71. Grain-storage tower
72. Skunk's defense
73. Extra
75. Hole in ___
76. "___ to Heaven"
78. Luminary
79. Clothing size
81. Villain of "The Lion King"
82. Singer Reed
83. Play on words
84. Show up
87. Magazine
93. Lively dance
94. Actor Stockwell
96. "The ___ Lagoon"
97. Relocate
98. And others: abbr.
99. Wisdom
100. Cowboy player Leon ___
101. Nuclear particle
102. Desiccated
103. Belgian river
104. Grub
105. Carson's heir

DOWN
1. Boxer Buddy ___
2. Pollster Roper
3. Depravity
4. Chris ___ of "Saturday Night Live"
5. Medicinal plant
6. Choke up
7. Japanese sashes
8. Period of hostilities
9. Intermediate, in law
10. Commedia dell'___
11. Ascot, e.g.
12. Serrate
13. Magazine
14. Syrian, e.g.
15. Bog
16. Wapitis
26. Modern Persia
27. Sphere
29. Singer Stewart
32. Choreographer Bob ___
33. A Jackson
34. Microwave, e.g.
35. Groovy!
36. Musical group
37. Eggs, to Ovid
38. Bridge expert
39. Chalet feature
40. Author James ___
41. Breather
44. Radiate
45. Church law
48. Magazine
50. Back tooth
53. Caviar
54. Actor Moore
55. Secondary-level degree: abbr.
57. Colonial Indian soldier
58. Expensive
59. Clutter
60. Prepare copy
61. Refrain syllables
62. Speeder's nemesis
63. Erode
64. Swan genus
65. Capitol Hill group: abbr.
66. Leg hinge
68. Lily-livered
69. Fitness spot
73. Trip
74. Twelfth Jewish month
77. Communications corp.
78. Mayday signal
80. Critter
82. Introvert
83. Sonnet writers
84. Metric land measures
85. Guitarist Townshend
86. Anjou, e.g.
87. Worry
88. Olive genus
89. Golf stroke
90. Carryall
91. Shakespeare's river
92. Verne hero
95. Greek Aurora

PUZZLE 171

FULL CIRCLE

To complete this circular puzzle fill in the answers to the AROUND clues in a clockwise direction. For the RADIAL clues move from the outside to the inside.

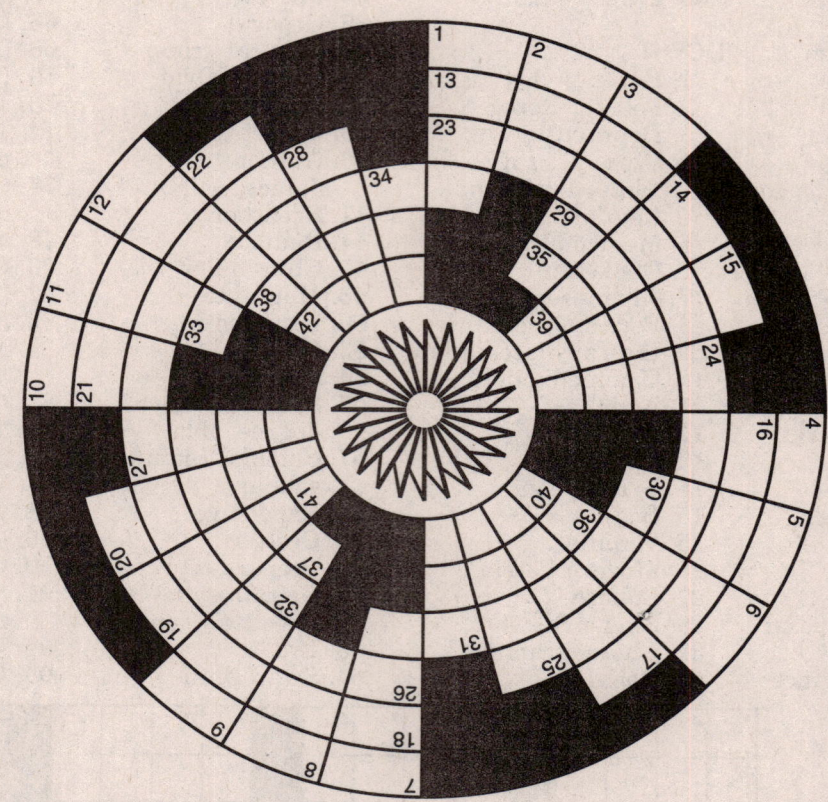

AROUND (Clockwise)
1. Foot digit
4. Pitching stat
7. Pad
10. Flying mammal
13. Actor Flynn
16. Singer Jenny ___
18. Vote into office
21. Subtle air
23. Customary
26. Aligns
29. Large volume
30. Actress Graves
32. Frost
33. Dense
35. Spheres
36. Seaweed
37. Greek god of war
38. Allowed the use of
39. Tippler
40. Endure
41. Table scrap
42. Nervous

RADIAL (Out to in)
1. Head, in Paris
2. Hockey's Bobby ___
3. Muse of poetry
4. Inventor Whitney
5. Civil disturbance
6. Temper, as steel
7. Flat-topped hill
8. Model Carol ___
9. ___ firma
10. Word for Scrooge
11. Car
12. Three times
14. Aromas
15. West Indies dance
17. "The Little Rascals" character
19. Egyptian city
20. Track official
22. Made an initial bet
24. Experiment
25. Table supports
27. Poetic romance
28. Warbled
31. Used a chair
34. Pig's home

PUZZLE 172

• FANCY FOOTWORK •

ACROSS
1. Who knows how long
5. Brownish gray
10. Unctuous mineral
14. Actor's reward
19. Yokel
20. Ore analysis
21. Chinese gelatin
22. Coat cut
23. Basement alternative
25. Toodle-oo!
26. Mountain chain
27. It's on the horizon
28. Prideful bunch
31. Something to do
32. Attain a maximum
35. Delightful region
36. With enthusiasm
38. Cheers, e.g.
42. Gat
44. Fervor
45. Easy wins
47. Bear's advice
49. Puts out
53. Acceptable
54. Primes a crime
56. Electronic device
58. Singer Horne
59. Harmonized
61. Condemn
63. Sediment
64. Incessantly
65. Nice parting word
67. Simpson sibling
69. Somme time
71. Victorian, e.g.
72. Sweeping blow
75. Mid-size racer
78. Gas found in tubes
80. Suffer
81. Literary letters
83. Music halls
84. Gave over
86. Nautical slammer
88. Dynamic leader
90. Urgent
92. Eavesdropper?
96. Concrete
97. Bugging bugs
99. Church courts
101. Comparative word
102. Attaching
104. North Sea feeder
106. Instrument panel
108. Does and roes
110. Facetious tributes
112. Wall hanging
113. Brisk in tempo
116. Diner's intake
117. Sta. postings
119. Hen pen
120. Brilliance
123. Lady of the house
128. Qatar coin
130. Jot
131. Kin of burlap
134. Quite peeved
135. Enlarged
136. Fake handle
137. Came down
138. Indian territory
139. Court order
140. Multitudes
141. Sandbox denizens

DOWN
1. Goes around in circles
2. Mentor
3. Israeli statesman
4. Needles a bit?
5. Slight experience
6. Horned viper
7. Dos Passos trilogy
8. Show anxiety
9. Grommet
10. Ragged
11. Anew
12. Back muscles, briefly
13. Meteorite's evidence
14. Row
15. Pocket calculator
16. Vinegar source
17. Guardian spirit
18. Marshlike
24. Change for a drachma
29. Roman date
30. Most down
33. Starbuck's captain
34. Nervous
37. Sentimentality
38. Terrible time?
39. Like some wines
40. King of comedy
41. Airport porter
43. Concerning
44. Cream component
46. Dry watercourse
48. Purple shade
50. Heptad
51. Ano starter
52. Wrapping film
55. Cavity-free
57. Plow innovator
60. German river
62. Got the lead out?
66. Ruhr Valley city
68. Step
70. Suit
72. Haifa native
73. Edgy
74. Troy story
76. Origins
77. Artwork overlay
79. Crossword pro
82. Loiterers
85. Plate
87. Course before landing
89. Skates
91. Curtain holders
93. Scorch
94. Zhivago's love
95. Extremities
98. Woo with song
100. Sec., e.g.
103. Pic maker
105. Highway
107. Fundamental
109. More stringy
111. Island greetings
113. Bitterly pungent
114. French department
115. True
116. Doles
118. Stockpile
121. Norse trickster
122. Drummer's staple
124. Card game of yore
125. Cylindrical structure
126. Army outfit
127. Certain NCOs
129. Floral wear
132. Bakery buy
133. Maxim

PUZZLE 173

• COLLECTIVELY SPEAKING •

ACROSS
1. Greek letter
4. Once again
8. Behaves
12. Leg
13. Broad valley
14. Female horse
15. A pride of ___
17. Suit to ___
18. Beerlike brew
19. Heavens
20. Search party
23. Barbecue site
25. Adjoin
26. Spiked club
27. Wt. units
30. Broadcast
31. Carnivals
32. Author Levin
33. Padre's abbr.
34. Fishing cord
35. Read quickly
36. Goodnight girl
38. Thick adhesive
39. Embankment
41. Sunbather's quest
42. Wedding phrases
43. A drove of ___
48. Beget
49. Topnotch
50. Tiny bite
51. Exam
52. Juicy fruit
53. Dawn to dusk

DOWN
1. Omelet need
2. Old sailor
3. Physicians' gp.
4. Confuse
5. Moniker
6. Highest note
7. Director Craven
8. Italian violinmaker
9. A host of ___
10. Coatrack
11. Psychic
16. Political cartoonist
19. Summers, in Paris
20. Carson's predecessor
21. Theater award
22. A raft of ___
23. "Common Sense" author
24. Farm measure
26. Primary
28. Unruly child
29. Rational
31. Run away
35. Went under
37. Bowler's button
38. Indiana player
39. Roster
40. Singer Adams
41. Albacore
43. Strike lightly
44. Caviar
45. Finale
46. Narrow inlet
47. Secret agent

PUZZLE 174

• GRAND SLAM •

ACROSS
1. Receive
4. Blanches
9. Pekoe, e.g.
12. Ms. Gardner
13. Actress Bow
14. Witch
15. Eldest
17. "___ Got a Secret"
18. Dog's bane
19. Gawked
21. Swab
24. Append
25. Practice
30. Warning sign
33. "Sands of ___ Jima"
34. Labors
36. Tankard's fill
37. Jewels
39. Charade
41. Shoebox letters
43. Might
44. Pushes forward
47. Notable times
51. Classic starter?
52. Play part
56. Limo
57. Came up
58. Golly!
59. Army or red
60. Satisfied
61. Psychic letters

DOWN
1. Fisherman's tool
2. Wicked
3. Vetch
4. One-hundredth pt.
5. Father's robe?
6. ___-tzu
7. Goofs
8. Kriss Kringle
9. Welles film, with "The"
10. Hangover?
11. Elderly
16. Identical
20. Fuss
22. Cereal grain
23. Stage item
25. Tractor-trailer
26. Ram's mate
27. Ship's place of registry
28. Knight's title
29. Sch. before JH
31. Chicago trains
32. Named at birth
35. RR depot
38. Behold
40. Watched closely
42. Lanchester et al.
44. Early Peruvian
45. Unkind
46. Evening, in Roma
48. Current fad
49. High cards
50. Dance move
53. Foldable bed
54. Verb ending?
55. Beatty of film

CODEWORD

PUZZLE 175

Instructions for solving Codeword puzzles are given on page 11.

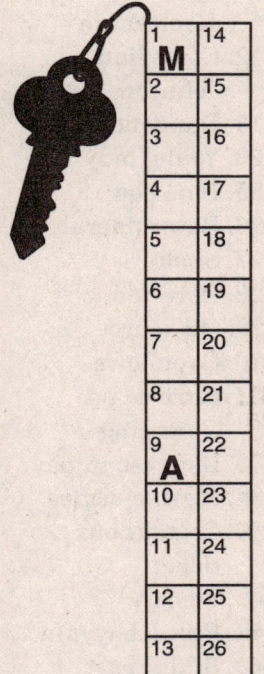

CODEWORD

PUZZLE 176

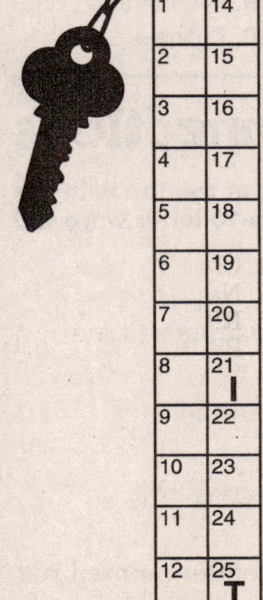

PUZZLE 177

• ANTE UP •

ACROSS
1. Walk to and fro
5. Sum
10. Lobster appendage
14. Prevaricator
15. Incensed
16. At this place
17. "Born Free" lioness
18. Challenges
19. Feminine suffix
20. ___ Wednesday
21. Pub drink
22. Scheduled
24. False god
27. 1970-74 British prime minister
28. Esteem
30. Looks over
32. Before, to Keats
35. "Home ___"
36. Lays macadam
37. Part of a train
38. Fork part
39. Weary
40. Leg part
41. First lady
42. Synthetic fabric
43. Capital of Idaho
44. French preposition
45. Shopping areas
46. Lassoes
47. Families
49. Cooking utensils
50. "Do unto ___..."
52. In favor of
54. Obese
57. Song for Sills
58. Rasps
60. Dress for a rani
61. Gratuities
62. Wipe off
63. Ardor
64. Party giver
65. Raves
66. Annexes

DOWN
1. Cop a ___
2. Suffers
3. Kick the bucket
4. Historic period
5. ___ basin
6. Type of exam
7. Weight allowance
8. Munched
9. Diminished
10. Swindle
11. Ignore displeasure
12. Comedian Johnson
13. Dandelion, e.g.
23. Young lady
25. Finished
26. Raw mineral
27. Shelters
28. Detested
29. Oil source
30. Overflows
31. Burnett or Channing
33. Increase in pay
34. Marine eagles
39. Certain bus ticket
40. Shortly
42. Poet Khayyam
43. Bikini part
48. Smallest amount
49. Sits for a portrait
50. Vow
51. Musical group
52. Outline
53. Take five
55. Inland sea
56. Metal containers
59. Pensioner's acct.
60. Witness

PUZZLE 178

Connections

Place the 7-letter answers to the clues into the diagram, each answer starting at the top with the letter S and ending at the bottom with the letter E. When the diagram is filled, a 10-letter word will read across the center of the diagram.

1. Reused space vehicle
2. Shine
3. Unfamiliar
4. Roofing piece
5. Abate
6. Assume as true
7. Exalted
8. Fairly large
9. Slender pointed rod
10. Prestige

PUZZLE 179

• BEFOREHAND •

ACROSS
1. Scrape
5. Roe source
9. Mall occupant
13. Garage event
17. Concluded
18. Nucleus
19. ___ of duty
20. Berserk
21. Simple
22. By ___ (from memory)
23. Stake
24. Terminate
25. Bake beforehand
27. Prune
29. Bartered
31. Conjunction
32. Traveled
33. Tolerate
34. Leverage
37. Teasing taunt
38. Watches beforehand
42. Rank below prof.
43. Brusque
44. Classic western
45. CEO, e.g.
46. Lyric poem
47. Drill
48. Signals
49. Composer Bartok
50. Ruin
52. Ecstasy
53. Visorless cap
54. Type of session
55. "Will & ___"
56. John or Jane
57. Divided
60. Bowling division
61. ___ point
65. Patriots, e.g.
66. Shalom!
67. Eroded
68. Not loud
69. Scarf
70. Bandleader Shaw
71. Gnash
72. Conifer
73. Tidy up beforehand
75. Secret writing
76. Command
77. Expressions of surprise
78. Frenzy
79. Exist
80. "... my kingdom for ___"
83. French noggin
84. Remitted beforehand
88. Droop
89. English river
91. Time measure
93. Utah ski resort
94. Margin
95. Container weight
96. Hence
97. Musical symbol
98. Sweetie
99. Stash away
100. Selected a card
101. Burmese currency

DOWN
1. Frolic
2. Declare
3. Moistureless
4. Mold beforehand
5. Atlantic haddock
6. Eye's partner
7. Still life, e.g.
8. Most profound
9. Put in motion
10. Whet
11. Umpire's call
12. Adolescents, beforehand
13. African trip
14. Within
15. Folk knowledge
16. Supplemented
26. Unit
28. Picnic crasher
30. Great review
32. Used to be
33. Boasts
34. Proceed slowly
35. Counsel
36. Sorbets
37. Panel of peers
38. Stage
39. At any time
40. Ruse
41. Tiff
43. Fly the ___
44. Duffer's shot
47. Little pest
48. Blaze
49. Borscht veggie
51. In shape
52. Reinforce
53. Skeletal part
55. Wheat or rice
56. Challenge
57. Tread
58. Partridge's tree?
59. Tardy
60. Greek cheeses
61. Ballot
62. Put ___ on it
63. Part of GWTW
64. Jug
66. Warms beforehand
67. Broad
70. Alack!
71. Shot beyond par
72. Bundle beforehand
74. 39th president
75. Grimalkin
76. Pay dirt
78. Modernize
79. Direction marker
80. Astonished
81. Secrete
82. Bond's guinea pig ___ de Polga
83. Barcelona bull
84. Knight's aide
85. Confederate
86. Willow genus
87. Dotty
90. Cauldron
92. Go wrong

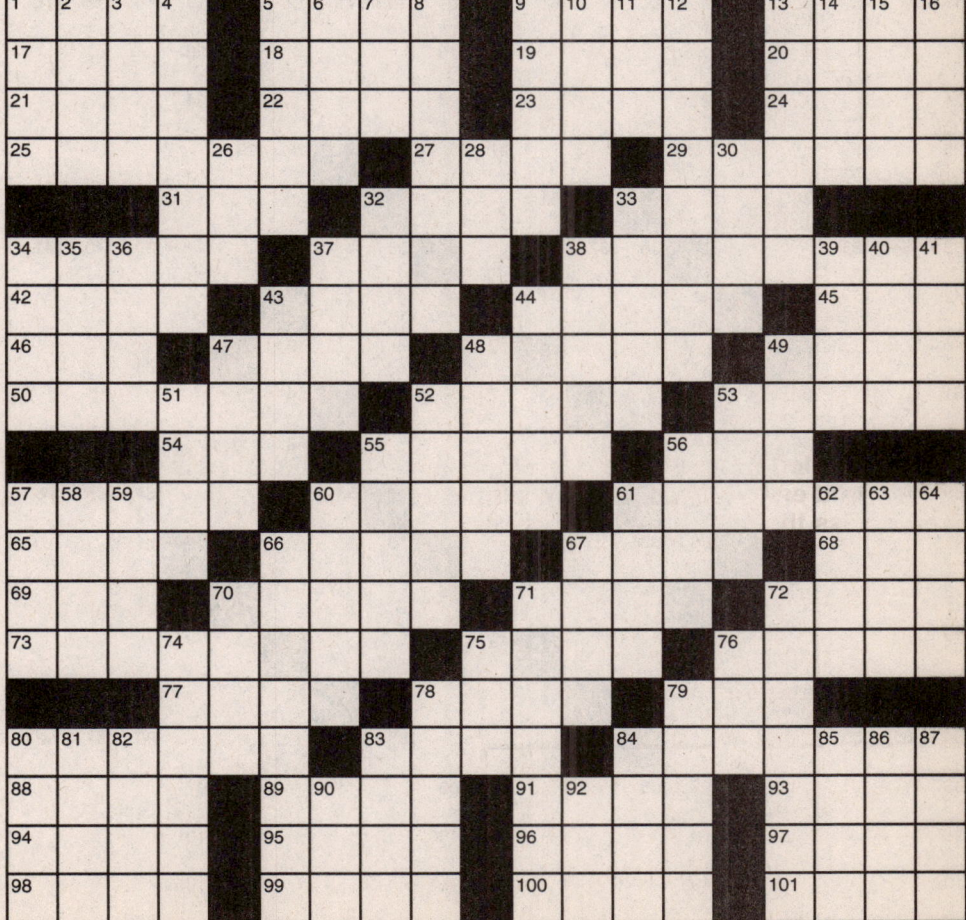

PUZZLE 180
• TITLE CHARACTERS •

ACROSS
1. Table spread
5. Nick and Nora's dog
9. Attempt
13. "Can't ___ Lovin' Dat Man"
17. Juicy part of a fruit
18. Mince
19. Scarlett's home
20. Daredevil Knievel
21. Being
22. Frolic
23. Algerian port
24. Dwell
25. 1959 Coasters song
28. Aviator Earhart
30. Assist
31. Song of praise
32. Immediately
33. Mucilage
36. Edison's middle name
38. Harrison Ford film
42. English composer
43. Cedar, e.g.
44. Race car
45. "___ Amigos!"
46. Double helix molecule
47. Rock's Blue Oyster ___
48. Fragrance
50. "___ kleine Nachtmusik"
51. Callas, for one
53. Permanent mark
54. Scandinavian country
56. Vase
57. Singer Midler
58. Diamond ___
59. Risk
62. Agave plant
63. Lectures
67. Heed
68. Beam of light
70. Chick's cry
71. Tank
72. Poetic muse
74. Fleur-de-___
75. Stack
76. Plateau
77. Drench
79. Ark builder
80. "Goodbye, Mr. Chips" star
81. Sicilian city
82. Neither's companion
83. Sculler's need
84. Storage area
87. 1958 Chuck Berry song
93. Keep
94. Cafe au ___
96. Leisure
97. Bird's crop
98. Solo for Domingo
99. She: Fr.
100. Very, in Nice
101. Be concerned
102. Refute
103. Darn!
104. Withered
105. Bullring cries

DOWN
1. Cartel abbreviation
2. Luxurious
3. "Born Free" lioness
4. Manage
5. Bitter
6. Pump or oxford
7. Mausoleum
8. Authorize
9. "Uncle Tom's Cabin" author
10. Mountain lake
11. Coach Parseghian
12. Tropical fruit
13. 1973 Paul McCartney & Wings song
14. Wrong
15. Anthropologist Claude ___-Strauss
16. Entreaty
26. Falsehood
27. Room within a harem
29. Comedian Sahl
32. Minute particle
33. Cushions
34. Florence's river
35. Breeze
36. Singer Guthrie
37. Wimbledon call
38. Reservoir
39. Dry
40. Artist Magritte
41. Viewed
43. Underground passage
44. Rub roughly
47. Astronomer Sagan
48. Stage performer
49. Napping
52. 1967 Rolling Stones song
53. Tennis's Monica ___
55. Thin puff
57. "One O'Clock Jump" bandleader
59. "Anything ___"
60. "East of Eden" character
61. Veal, e.g.
63. Jacob's wife
64. Kitchen appliance
65. Astronaut org.
66. RBI or ERA
69. Canadian prov.
70. Tiny veggie
73. Author Sarah ___ Jewett
75. Charlotte team
76. Tangier's location
78. Horn
79. Japanese drama
80. U.N.'s Hammarskjold
82. Remarks
83. Overweight
84. Jeremy's singing partner
85. Traditional knowledge
86. Ken ___ of "thirtysomething"
87. Spurn
88. Son of Loki
89. French-Belgian river
90. Word-of-mouth
91. Hazard
92. Lambs' mothers
95. In the style of

PUZZLE 181

• TOP O' THE MORNING •

ACROSS
1. Slovenly person
5. Incision
9. Guy
13. City haze
17. Calcium oxide
18. Korean statesman
19. Modernize
20. Stoma
21. Abu Dhabi native
22. Rank above viscount
23. Caspian Sea feeder
24. Long-tailed moth
25. Colorado peak
28. Seafarer
30. Palmer's org.
31. Mare's meal
33. Flat fee
34. It has a blade
37. Clare and Huxtable
40. Soccer star
42. Significant ___
45. Restorative resort
46. Valletta's land
48. Aria singer
50. Exclusive
51. Nuts
53. Director Fritz ___
55. Shopper's mecca
57. Violinist Bull
58. Kind of glasses
60. Well-coordinated
62. Summer shoe
64. Tennessee peak
68. Kilt features
71. Moving about
72. Tripod
76. Crude ___
77. Bogus butter
80. Nineteenth dynasty pharaoh
81. Tortilla treat
82. Grimm beginning
84. Chow
86. "Bolero" composer
89. Hit-show letters
90. Bailiwick
92. Donnybrook
94. Dijon dream
95. Monotonous sound
96. Drudge
98. Quarry quantity
100. "Ligeia" poet's monogram
102. Twinkle
105. Hawaiian peak
111. Size up
112. Mongolian desert
114. In ___ (entirely)
115. Eye lasciviously
116. Media, today
117. Dirk's kin
118. Caesar's cry
119. Byline find
120. Huff and puff
121. Go off course
122. Combustion product
123. Holland export

DOWN
1. Harsh criticism
2. Old Milano moola
3. Persian Khayyam
4. Jazz style
5. West Indies country
6. Starbuck's captain
7. Desiccated
8. Howdy!
9. Like a pie
10. White House beagle
11. Bede of fiction
12. Electrolytic
13. Supports
14. Oregon peak
15. Caen's river
16. Rotary Club symbol
26. Irish script
27. ___ robe
29. Auto, of old
32. Small
34. Frogner Park's locale
35. Each
36. 10k, for one
38. Detective Pinkerton
39. Coach Amos Alonzo
41. Model Herzigova
43. She, in Seville
44. Scottish dance
47. Inner personality
49. Part of AKA
52. Humpback's cousin
54. Tumbler
56. Weak, as an excuse
59. Countertenor
61. Computer key
63. Peachy-keen
65. Guernsey, e.g.
66. Shankar's instrument
67. Disk ___
68. Impecunious
69. Piece of dialogue
70. California peak
73. Miss America's attire
74. Hosiery shade
75. "Norma Rae" machine
78. Musical aptitude
79. "Taxation without representation" writer
83. Periodic table listing
85. Type of ant
87. Smooth
88. Pb
91. Family female
93. Japanese food fish
97. Beersheba's neighbor
99. Lewiston, Maine, college
101. "E.T. ___ home"
102. Traveling bag
103. Actress Flynn Boyle
104. Wield a reata
106. Marquand's Mr. ___
107. Quarterback Graham
108. Yikes!
109. Gustav Mahler's wife
110. Judge
113. Hymenopteran

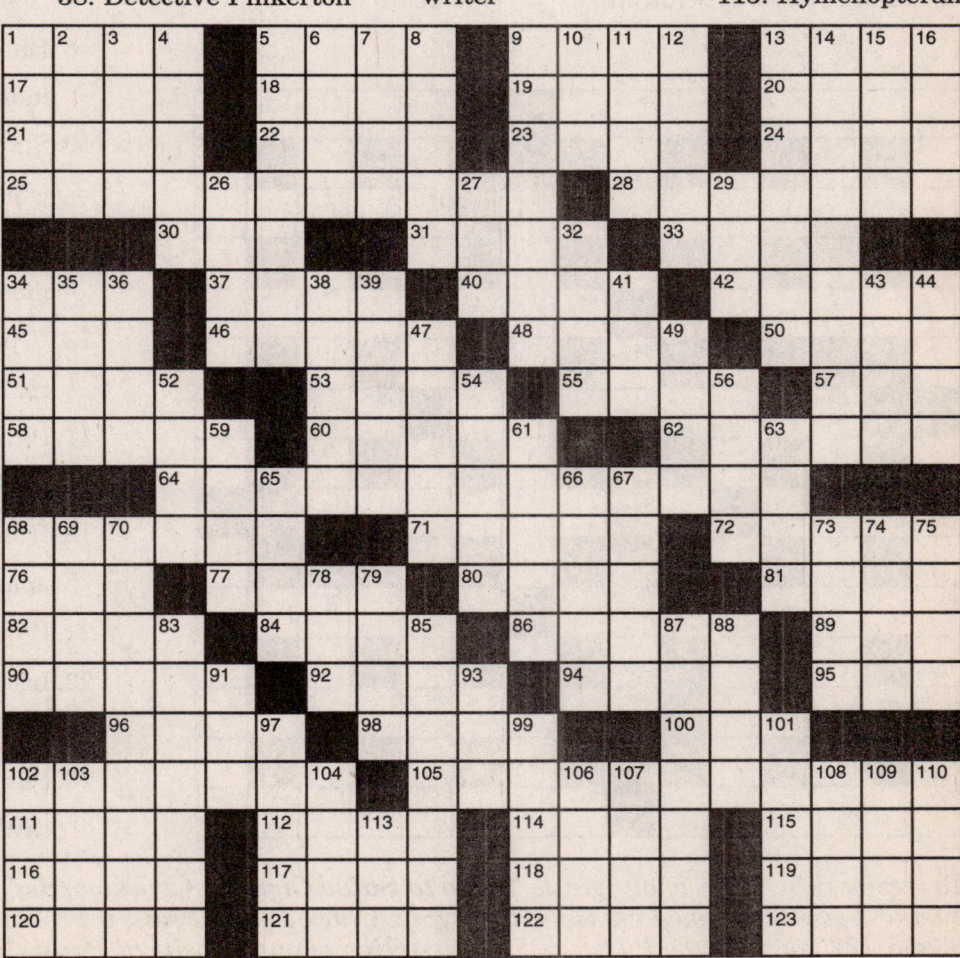

PUZZLE 182 — CRYPTIC CROSSWORD

British-style or Cryptic Crosswords are a great challenge for crossword fans. Each clue contains either a definition or direct reference to the answer as well as a play on words. The numbers in parentheses indicate the number of letters in the answer word or words.

ACROSS

1. In fact play part of university associate (8)
5. Shook container crimson on the right (6)
9. Money-crazed food rings (9)
11. Land area covered with footprints we hear (5)
12. Gets rid of former spouse quietly in front of some trains (6)
13. Nice people protect restricted advocates (8)
15. Business cost at zenith (8)
16. Instrument initially owned by old Egyptian (4)
19. Copied part of tape diary (4)
20. Sophomore hears Exeter is holding a tryout (8)
23. Lives in horsy clothes (8)
24. Place in unfinished horsy accommodation (6)
27. Avoid certain train badly scheduled (5)
28. Fox in Kent mistaken for a relative (4,2,3)
29. Tight skirt from southern moors (6)
30. Example isn't cane construction (8)

DOWN

1. Prince warned: Change! (6)
2. Behind, but after time, surpass (5)
3. Greek hero is unwell amid pines (8)
4. Oaf not at home after last fall (4)
6. Lost in last rays (6)
7. Right! Everyone qualified is subject to contact (9)
8. Hated taking exam indeed (8)
10. Shows up wave-riding experts? (8)
14. Reveal, then rate menace (8)
15. "Opus One" he played at realty show (4,5)
17. Pitmen have a right to become sailors (8)
18. "Hard Copy" to rip nut apart (8)
21. Protest goal (6)
22. Look at brush (6)
25. Memento to Follett (5)
26. Box enclosure hides cattle (4)

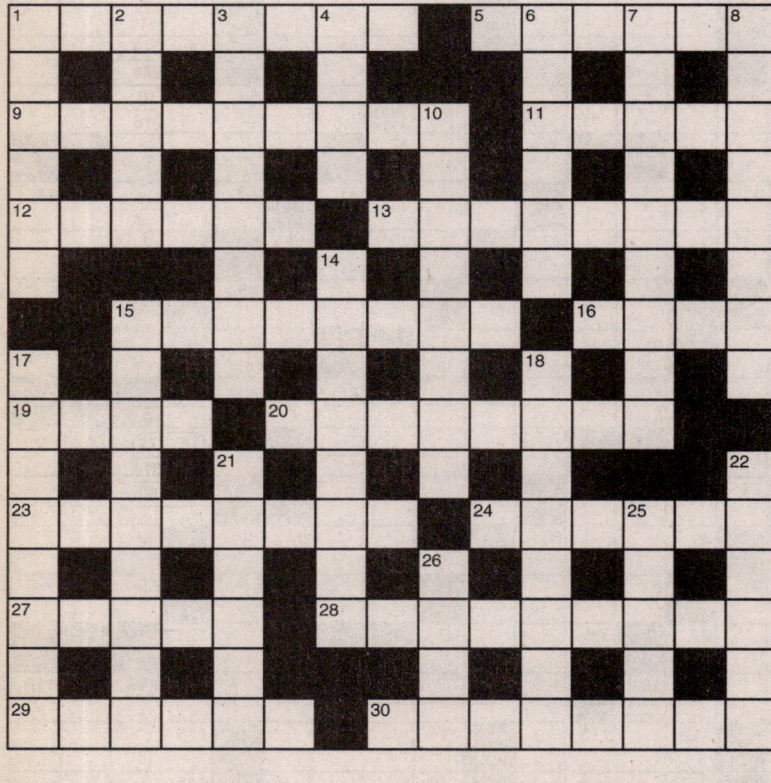

A Whole Book of Your Favorite Puzzle!

Our puzzle collections deliver dozens of your favorite puzzle type, all in one place!

3 EASY WAYS TO ORDER!

Mail coupon below | Call 1-800-220-7443 M-F 8AM-7PM EST | Visit PennyDellPuzzles.com Penny Selected Puzzles

---

PennyDellPuzzles™

DEPT. G • 6 PROWITT STREET
NORWALK, CT 06855-1220

☑ **YES!** Send me the volumes I've circled.

Name _____
(Please Print)

Address _____

City _____

State _____ ZIP _____

Payment method:
❏ My payment of $_____ (U.S. funds) is enclosed.
❏ Charge my: Visa / MC / AMEX / Discover

_____
Account number

_____ _____
Card expires   Cardholder's signature

88-UVG3L8

PUZZLE TYPE	VOLUMES (Circle your choices)						
Alphabet Soup (APH)	5	6	7	8	9	10	
Anagram Magic Square (ANG)	55	56	58	60	61	62	63
Brick by Brick (BRK)	275	276	277	278	279	280	281
Codewords (CDW)	370	371	372	373	374	375	376
Cross Pairs Word Seek (CPW)	6	7	8	9	10	11	12
Crostics (CST)	212	213	214	215	216	217	218
Crypto-Families (CFY)	69	70	71	72	73	74	75
Cryptograms (CGR)	135	136	137	138	139	140	141
Diagramless (DGR)	59	60	61	62	63	64	65
Double Trouble (DBL)	31	32	33	34	35	36	37
Flower Power (FLW)	40	41	42	43	44	45	46
Frameworks (FRM)	53	54	55	56	57	58	59
Letterboxes (LTB)	134	135	136	137	138	139	140
Match-Up (MTU)	1	4	6	9	10		
Missing List Word Seeks (MLW)	43	44	45	46	47	48	49
Missing Vowels (MSV)	357	358	359	360	361	362	363
Number Fill-In (GNF)	21	22	23	24	25	26	27
Number Seek (GNS)	2	3	4	5	6	7	
Patchwords (PAT)	68	69	70	71	72	73	74
Places, Please (PLP)	310	311	312	313	314	315	316
Quotefalls (QTF)	56	57	58	59	60	61	62
Share-A-Letter (SAL)	4						
Simon Says (SMS)	1	2	3	4	5		
Stretch Letters (STL)	5	6	7				
Syllacrostics (SYL)	114	115	116	117	118	119	120
The Shadow (SHD)	2	5	6				
Three's Company (TCG)	2	4					
What's Left? (WTL)	9	10	11	12	13	14	15
Word Games Puzzles (WGP)	32	33	34	35	36	37	38
Zigzag (ZGZ)	17	18	19	20	21	22	23

Allow 4 to 6 weeks for delivery. **CT & NY residents:** Add applicable sales tax to your total. **Outside USA:** Add $5 shipping & handling and add applicable GST and PST (U.S. funds). Offer expires 8/31/19.

_____ books at $5.25 each: _____

Shipping & handling: _____
Add $1.50 per volume or $4.50 total for 3 or more volumes

Total amount enclosed (U.S. Funds): _____

PUZZLE 183

• THE OTHER HALF •

ACROSS
1. Glossy fabric
6. Ship's mast
10. Slant
15. Bridge
19. Leave out
20. Common contraction
21. Chef's gadget
22. Otherwise
23. School chums
25. Blend
27. Black goo
28. Sound quality
29. Precursor
31. Ruled
32. Used in common
34. Opposite of hooked
36. Bishop's caps
37. Fateful date
39. Like the Gobi
40. Clog
42. Stylish
45. Surveyed
47. Timid one
48. Passing fancy
51. Unaccompanied
52. Exercise suffrage
53. Insert symbol
54. Eight furlongs
55. Kind of bran
56. Play tenpins
57. Paddles
59. Whittle
60. Original
62. Toward the rear
64. College treasurer
65. Liquefy
66. Scrimped
68. Small amount
69. Hopeful lists?
71. Give in
72. Joined by sewing
75. Subsequently
76. Carny
78. Within
80. Actress Gardner
81. State as fact
82. Requirements
83. Slugger Slaughter
84. TV headliner
85. Berth
86. Grades
87. Copper alloy
89. Voluminous dress
90. Flowerless plants
91. Ovine cries
92. Not all
95. Actively
98. Hunting dog
100. Highway inns
104. Foot-leg joint
105. Poetic form
107. Give off
109. Bigwig's letters
110. Deadlocked
112. Licit
115. High flier
116. Bizarre
117. Actor Aeryk ___
118. Carrying cargo
119. Visionary
120. Walks heavily
121. Shoe part
122. Put forth (effort)

DOWN
1. Denominations
2. Islamic god
3. Crownlike headpiece
4. Dog tags, e.g.
5. Settled, avian style
6. Graceful bird
7. Fountain and Rose
8. Cato's welcome
9. Breathe
10. Rubbernecked
11. Treated with calcium
12. Muscat's nation
13. Animal hide
14. Unit of work
15. Arab, for one
16. Carpenter's aid
17. Fall bloomer
18. Requires
24. Manner
26. Similar
30. Caustic
33. Jambalaya grain
35. Give off a powerful light
36. Part of MVP
38. Barge, e.g.
40. Stopper
41. Tints
42. Hoofbeat sound
43. Rime
44. Hinted
46. Book of maps
47. Supplied with workers
48. Captain's subordinate
49. Edison's middle name
50. Adult stag
52. Electrical units
53. 39th president
54. Soprano Callas
56. Hay-bundler
57. Rods
58. British cents
59. Diced
61. Measuring device
63. Begins
64. Groundwork
67. College bigwigs
69. Thick piece
70. Wash
73. Actor Hunter
74. Flit
76. Singe
77. Queries
79. Peat or Spanish
82. Actress Martin
83. Soothe
84. Don't strike!
86. Fracas
87. Restrain
88. Baby toys
90. Secondary news item
91. Pianist Sergio ___
93. Overlook
94. Capable of moving
95. Luxuriates
96. Let loose
97. Glide smoothly
98. Bergen's Mortimer ___
99. Kingly
101. Dodge
102. Volume unit
103. Tired out
105. Author Bellow
106. Director Preminger
108. Mineral source
111. Swab
113. Self-esteem
114. "Mad ___" (Gibson film)

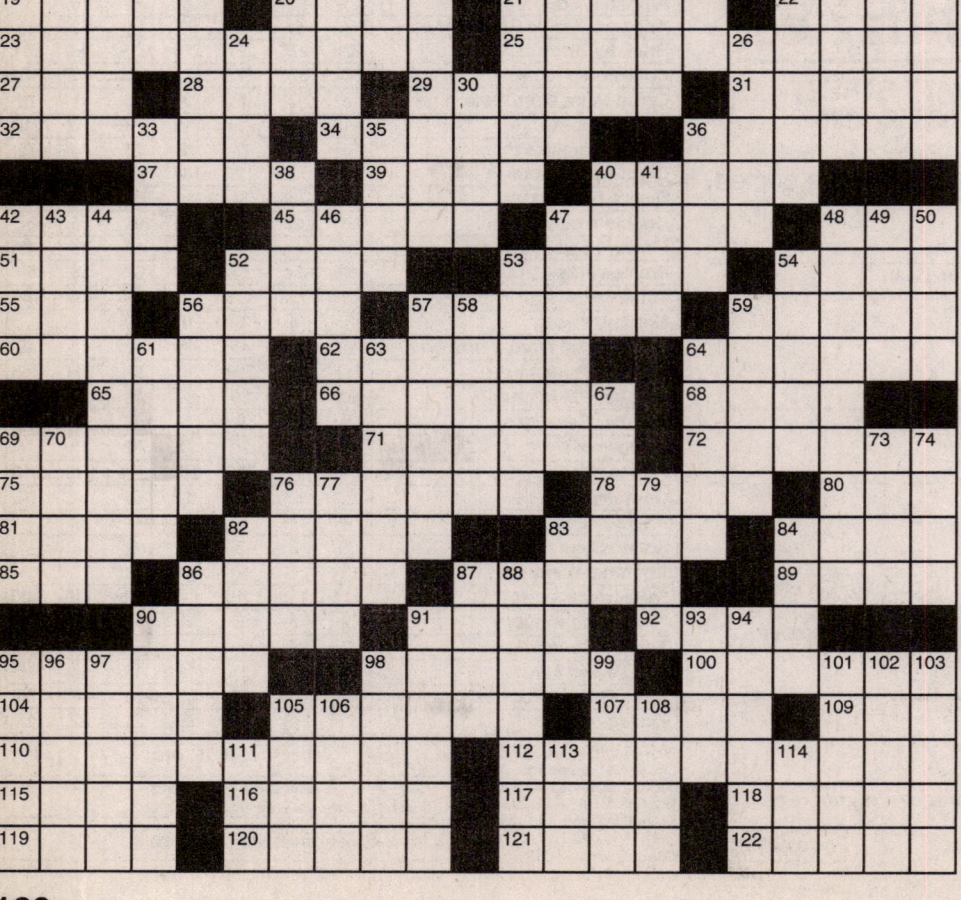

PUZZLE 184
• ANIMAL MOVIE HOUSE •

ACROSS
1. Hired vehicles
5. Shoelace end
10. Sail support
14. Joyous
18. Mental flash
19. Herman's Hermits singer
20. Up to it
21. Lying facedown
22. Al Pacino film
25. Jumbo
26. Prior to, in poetry
27. Numbers game
28. Folklore giant
29. Like some tuna
30. Keeps
32. Debatable
33. Easy gallop
34. So-so grade
35. Pound sterling
37. Holds (off)
39. Crow's cousin
42. Miss Muffet's morsel
43. Mingo in "Daniel Boone"
44. Hang low
47. Client
48. Wails
49. Prank
51. "J'Accuse" author
52. Mickey Rooney film
55. Dutch cheese
56. Reverend's speech: abbr.
57. Lily plant
58. Grandpa Walton actor
59. Band section
60. ___ monster (lizard)
61. High-school dances
63. Spanish surrealist Joan ___
65. Al or Bobby
68. Glide high
69. Spanish parlor
70. Dallas coll.
73. Poetic contraction
74. Elizabeth Taylor film
79. Actress Skye
80. Tennis's Chris ___
81. Speak formally
82. Florence river
83. Explosive letters
84. Forewarning
85. Remove a rind
86. Ship timbers
87. Disinclined
89. Rawhide
90. Pump purchase
91. Acting ruler
93. Mr. Astaire
95. Restoration
99. Secret
100. Way off
101. Tuckered out
103. French soul
104. Fix
105. Paul Hogan film
108. Slow, in music
109. Scorched
110. Breathing
111. Road curve
112. Witty remarks
113. Makes doilies
114. Guide a car
115. Martial ___

DOWN
1. Autumn drink
2. Cherish
3. Father
4. Melancholy
5. Somebody
6. Nannies, e.g.
7. Hay place
8. Within: pref.
9. Ess follower
10. Tropical fruit
11. Stops a mission
12. Gin flavoring
13. Finger count
14. Cary and Lee
15. Greene of "Bonanza"
16. Ire
17. Feat
21. Aircraft
23. Outer-space man
24. Church symbol
29. Grotto
31. Bitter
32. Core
33. Coral brooch
35. Tremor
36. Jars
38. Hoglike mammal
39. Tire tracks
40. Netman Arthur ___
41. Swerve
42. January quaff
44. Seltzer
45. Too bad!
46. Herds of whales
48. Shopper's paradise
49. TV's Kadiddlehopper
50. Porters
51. Goose egg
53. Lion's den
54. Plato's market
59. Fiber source
60. "Pretty Woman" star
61. Destitute
62. Violent talk
63. Paint finish
64. Nastase of tennis
65. Fixed quantity
66. Bright sign
67. Dispatched
68. British guns
69. Commence
70. Classify
71. ___ Blanc
72. Space saucers
74. Sidewalk material
75. Thwart
76. Longed for
77. Said aloud
78. Pay hike
84. Go to extremes
86. African language
87. Go-betweens
88. Earnest attempt
89. But, to Pedro
90. Sex
91. Juliet's love
92. Milestone
94. Marathons
95. "Superman" actor
96. Waterproof boot
97. Willow flowers
98. Yorkshire city
99. Peaceful
100. Sector
101. Fine sand
102. Ballet move
105. Chicago time: abbr.
106. "___ Boot"
107. Hoop group: abbr.

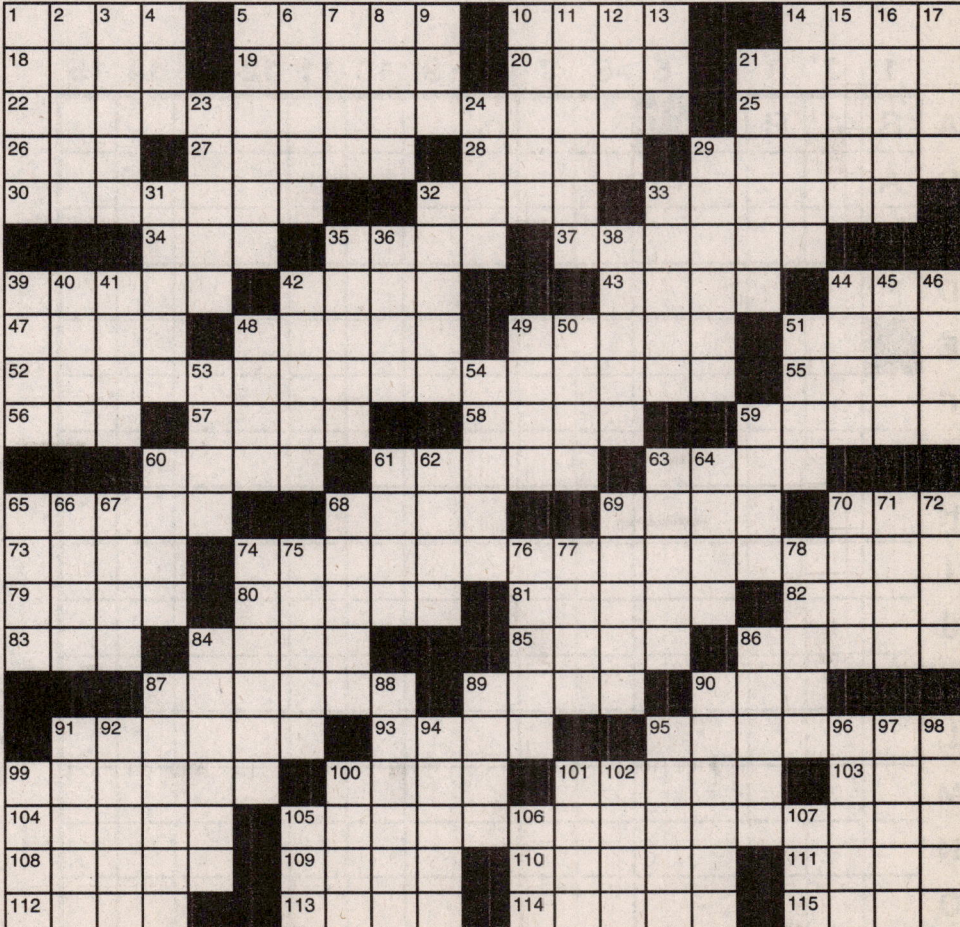

PUZZLE 185 — BATTLESHIPS

The diagram represents the sea, which contains a crossword puzzle; the answer words are Battleships. The letter-number combination to the left of each clue indicates the location in the diagram where a Battleship has been hit (for example, A2 is in the first row, second column). A hit is any one of the letters in the answer word. Using this clue, you must determine the exact location of each answer and whether it is an across or a down word. Fill in black squares to separate words as in a regular crossword. We have filled in the answers to clues A2 and C1.

- A2 Cutting remark
- A3 Bring up
- A4 Cookout
- A7 Buzz off!
- A14 Abyss
- B2 At a loss
- B6 Do the slalom
- B9 Leafy vegetable
- B13 It comes from the heart
- C1 Fugue master
- C2 Wimbledon champ
- C3 Blacken
- C7 Land in the water
- C8 Amalgam
- C12 Spruce up
- C13 Realm
- D2 Basil, for one
- D7 Charged atom
- D9 Minor
- D11 Jailor
- D13 Trees
- D14 Dance move
- D15 Le ___, France
- E5 Dark wood
- E7 Vegas venue
- E10 Muck
- E12 Movie genre
- F2 Rye fungus
- F4 Former Portuguese coin
- F6 Curious
- F11 Tell
- F14 Score
- G1 Approximately
- G3 Decipher
- G5 Rolls
- G9 Back talk
- G10 Break
- G13 Lived
- G15 Sports award
- H1 Top-drawer
- H2 Stares at
- H7 Fossil fuel
- H9 Zilch
- H12 Head part
- H13 Cool one's heels
- I1 Election mo.
- I6 Have bills
- I7 Night bird
- I8 Whopper
- I11 Shakespearean adverb
- J2 Boundless
- J6 Former acorn
- J10 Highway sight
- J11 Faxed
- J14 Reason
- K4 Puffin's kin
- K5 ___ State (Connecticut)
- K9 Coins
- L3 Ticket word
- L4 Cereal fruit
- L7 Sewer line
- L9 Good as gold, e.g.
- L14 Undiluted
- M1 Belief in God
- M2 Farmer's place
- M7 Tough fiber
- M9 Copyread
- M12 More crunchy
- M13 Compulsion
- M15 Strong metal
- N4 '50s ditty
- N7 Tom, Dick, or Harry
- N8 Olympic goal
- N10 Oolong, e.g.
- N12 By Jove!
- N14 Main drag
- N15 Calls it quits
- O1 Stirs
- O3 Skirt length
- O5 Primitive weapon
- O7 Request
- O13 Beatty film

	1	2	3	4	5	6	7	8	9	10	11	12	13	14	15
A	B	A	R	B	■										
B	A														
C	C														
D	H														
E	■														
F															
G															
H															
I															
J															
K															
L															
M															
N															
O															

PUZZLE 186
• ANAGRAM NAMES •

ACROSS
1. It may be grand
5. Days of yore
9. Not fem.
13. Red table wine
19. ____ sapiens
20. Greek prefecture
21. Winglike
22. Refer
23. Priestly vestments
24. Inca country
25. "Le Roi d'Ys" composer
26. Talmud scholars
27. NO ALIENS, DARLING
31. Track events
32. Iron alloy
33. A Jackson brother
34. Seabiscuit's grandpa
36. Fess up
38. Sawbucks
40. Withered
41. Low blow?
45. "Exodus" hero
47. Mrs. Copperfield
49. Gave a bum wrap?
51. Winter activity
56. Tease
58. Helped
59. Israeli dance
60. Estate measures
62. Ltd.'s kin
64. Coastal eagle
65. Tel ____
66. Jungle king
67. Ancient Lebanese tree
69. Emanate
73. Pierre Corneille tragedy
75. SO? I'M CUTER!
77. Sports figures
78. Occupation
79. All
80. "____ Zapata!"
82. Composer Satie
83. Circuit
85. Language suffix
86. Man of La Mancha
87. Heracles' beloved
88. Saintly
92. Zeus's queen
94. Ornamental shrub
96. Fried cakes
98. Ninny
100. Blasting letters
101. Insincere talk
102. Tailless amphibian
104. Thole inserts
106. Professor Dumbledore
110. Goes by
113. Ground grain
115. Em and Eller
117. Hold dear
120. I SELL THIN VERSES
123. William the Conqueror, e.g.
125. Mosque priest
126. Burden
127. Legend
128. Sheathe
129. Apportion
130. Swenson of "Benson"
131. This, in Toledo
132. Detached
133. ____ fixe
134. Footfall
135. Escritoire

DOWN
1. Some rugs
2. Nabokov novel
3. Sauntered
4. Mohammedan
5. Haydn's sobriquet
6. "____ We All"
7. ____ of Gibraltar
8. Mocked
9. Maldivian capital
10. Tocsin
11. Chip dips
12. Warbled
13. Elevator chamber
14. Andean ruminant
15. TEN ELITE BRAINS
16. Yokel
17. Blue-pencil
18. Hardy girl
28. Troy story
29. Contributors
30. Waterwheel
35. Twill or satin
37. Error's partner
39. Madras mister
42. Internet abbr.
43. It makes oil boil
44. Append
46. Stir up
48. Toulouse ta ta
50. Helen's abductor
51. Decalogue verb
52. Enthusiast
53. Type of heath
54. NERD AMID LATE TV
55. LP feature
57. Salad green
61. Tangle
63. Monte Carlo sight
67. Have a bawl
68. Uprising
70. Indian lute
71. Practical
72. Glacial ridge
74. Did business
76. Religious doctrine
81. Fight site
84. Michelangelo piece
86. Sub sausage
88. Half the NFL
89. New Deal org.
90. Hoisting machine
91. Cuts short
93. Kanga's kid
95. Map tome
97. Tuna au naturel
99. Vine ladder
103. Considered
105. Wise guy?
107. Rammed
108. Disquietude
109. Circus heighteners
111. Rental agreement
112. Party list
114. Shelf
116. Skulker
117. From square one
118. Finished
119. Killer whale
121. Hook's sidekick
122. Cut the mustard?
124. Sparks on the screen

PUZZLE 187

ROBIN HOODS

ACROSS
1. Small tack
5. Potent particle
9. Leafy vegetable
13. Inferno
17. Chalet feature
18. "Dies ___"
19. Teen suffix
20. Matinee hero
21. Comparable
22. Ceremony
23. Drizzle
24. ___ gin fizz
25. 1991
28. Design
30. Sea, to Jacques
31. Look
32. Hosiery shade
33. Duffel ___
36. Maiden
39. Egyptian Sharif
42. Summarize
46. 1938
49. Labyrinth monster
51. Placed
52. Ancient Phoenician port
53. Med. course
54. Fury
55. Female voices
57. Romanian city
60. Sault ___ Marie
61. Anti's answer
62. 1955-60
67. Felix, e.g.
70. Gentle animal
71. Fodder storage
72. Blooper
76. "Surfin' ___"
77. Lively spirit
79. Dominican Republic river
82. Snout
83. Fortification
85. 1981
87. Used money
88. Utah lily
90. Arthur ___ of tennis
91. Somber
92. Dog doc
94. Social insect
96. Bull ___ china shop
98. Getaway
101. 1973
107. Utensil
108. Pitcher Nolan ___
110. Ukraine capital
111. Sandwich cookie
112. Foreign car
113. Clearance
114. Fashion magazine
115. Phooey!
116. Husky's load
117. Radiate
118. Captures
119. Ultimatum term

DOWN
1. Crow's bill
2. Gather leaves
3. Tel ___
4. Jeans fabric
5. Planes
6. Threesome
7. Mare's meal
8. Track events
9. ___ Abdul-Jabbar
10. Ice-cream thickener
11. Orchid necklace
12. Bond villain ___ Stavro Blofeld
13. Stocking type
14. Jobless
15. Chamber
16. General Robert ___
26. Carter of "Swing"
27. Broadway blinker
29. Beta ___
33. Mr. Lugosi
34. Caspian's neighbor
35. Coarse sand
37. Foxy
38. Mediterranean country
40. "I ___ Camera"
41. Wash cycle
43. Abel's sibling
44. Halo
45. Target
47. Bloodhound's clue
48. Approaches
50. Cager Archibald
56. Bypass
58. Reagan's Star Wars
59. Snow building
63. Caffeinated soda
64. Coin-toss option
65. Director Glauber ___

PUZZLE 187

66. Coastal eagle
67. Mugs
68. Hurry-up abbr.
69. Myth
73. Some deer
74. Greek peak
75. Hollow stalk
78. Bridal-page word
80. Switch positions
81. Is successful
84. Null and void
85. "Clouds" singer Mitchell
86. Extend credit
89. Deep-red gem
93. Brief
95. Confiscated
97. Prior to, once
98. Athenian vowels
99. "Heart and ___"
100. Secret writing
101. Indonesian island
102. Cairo's waterway
103. Sash
104. Kind of exam
105. Soaks flax
106. Patient's portion
109. Sweet potato

PUZZLE 188

ACROSS
1. Gremlin
4. Used to be
7. Proves
12. Inverted caret
13. Raised beds
15. Dark tea
16. Former
17. Caper
18. In the know
19. Respond
21. Rapid
23. Itch
24. Screamed
26. Pantry staple
28. Checkup
30. Skunk
34. Tibetan monk
37. Exclude
39. Mexican dish
40. Serving perfectly
42. Tyke
44. Epics
45. Trainee
47. Summit
49. Take five
50. Draw back
52. Frail
54. Big rigs
56. Styles
60. Slangy film
63. Spiffy
64. Fool
65. Delete
67. Housetops
70. Fleecy mom
71. Metric unit
72. Adam's fruit
73. So-so grade
74. School theme
75. Pig's pad
76. House wing

DOWN
1. Off-white
2. Brawl
3. Move a bike
4. Conquered
5. Ship's back
6. Rigid
7. Kitchen tools
8. Fell
9. Approve
10. Sported
11. Observed
13. Paint type
14. Head part
20. Launderers
22. Chimney dust
25. Blot
27. Said
29. Doily
31. Confine
32. Woe!
33. Experiment
34. Den
35. Skin issue
36. Catcher's glove
38. Spoil
41. Foliage
43. Pull
46. Dub
48. ___ peeve
51. Royal headwear
53. Wake up
55. Curbs
57. Brother's girl
58. Wooden peg
59. Strong metal
60. Soccer great
61. Eye part
62. Felines
66. ___ horse
68. Take a side
69. Insect pest

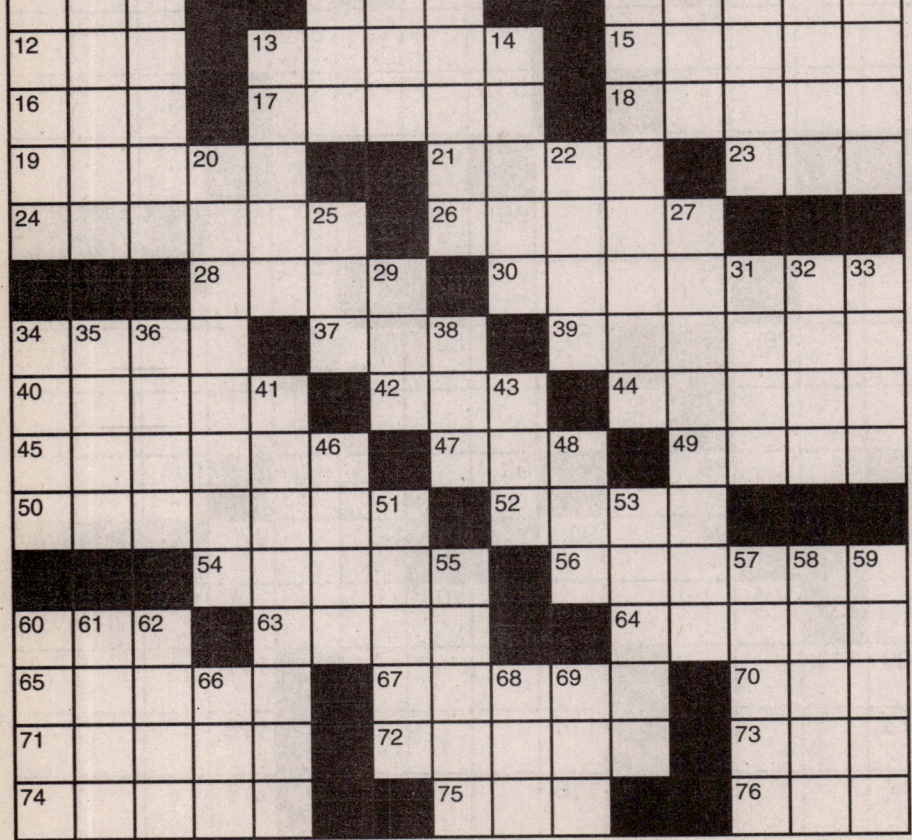

PUZZLE 189

ACROSS
1. Risks money
5. Puncture
9. Essential
13. Similar
14. Corner
15. Emerald ___
16. Art ___
17. Exposes
18. Land title
19. Ran wild
21. Telecast
22. Capsize
24. Ids' kin
26. Star's locale
27. ___ and con
28. Novel
30. Lessen
32. Very eager
34. Lady's mate
36. Flu symptom
39. Summarize
41. Grab
43. Male voice
45. Indifferent move
47. "I Got ___ Babe"
49. Scholar
50. Inform
52. Colony insect
54. Cow chow
55. Fire residue
58. Block
60. Sample
62. Not fresh
64. Brief swimsuit
66. Small bay
67. Dwindled
68. Trim
72. Bakery need
73. Lane
74. Movers' trucks
75. Sawbucks
76. Promgoer
77. Big birds

DOWN
1. Evil
2. Make do
3. Muscle twitch
4. Sleep noise
5. Pesky bug
6. Consent
7. Heavy hammer
8. "___ So Shy"
9. Type of skirt
10. Employers
11. Glossy
12. Lingerie item
14. Homes
20. Rustic hotel
21. Credit
22. Eggs (on)
23. Dog
25. Fool
27. Golf score
29. Prevail
31. Special nights
33. Clothes
35. Mr. Liotta
37. Make into law
38. Scoundrel
40. Throb
42. Feather wrap
44. Rosy
46. Lassie
48. Disheveled
51. Chatter
53. Summer hue
55. Broad tie
56. Range
57. Safe port
59. Holy book
61. Strainer
63. Camera eye
65. Alert
67. Nosh
69. Hoover ___
70. Large antelope
71. Tee preceder

PUZZLE 190

ACROSS
1. Phone
5. Part of rpm
8. Lengthy tale
12. Not home
13. Joke teller
15. Fired
16. Barely cooked
17. River horse
18. Cable
19. Biblical craft
20. Picnic pest
21. Bakes
23. Big quiz
25. Pig's place
26. Push firmly
27. Curds and ___
29. Boat basins
33. Widely
36. Good buddy
37. ___-advised
38. Minimal
39. Soda
40. Snowhouse
42. Summer skin hue
43. Angler's dipper
44. Boulevard
45. Got too large
48. Just fair
49. Thump
50. Emerald, e.g.
51. Actor Busey
55. "Anchors ___"
58. Retriever, shortly
59. Oahu keepsake
60. Guy
61. Nobility
63. Procreate
64. Nylons
65. Waterproof boot
66. Arena shape
67. Gobbles
68. Elope
69. Loop

DOWN
1. Jewel weight
2. Conscious
3. Pranks
4. Corrosive stuff
5. Sharp
6. Unoccupied
7. Mr. Van Winkle
8. Sandwich meat
9. Center of rotation
10. Fellow
11. Lime drinks
13. Pursued
14. Stockade
22. Canoe accessory
24. Couples
28. Headgear
29. Driver's aid
30. Shade of green
31. Burn soother
32. Mail drop
33. Palo ___
34. Boyfriend
35. Holler
36. Saucepan
39. Faithful's bench
40. That thing's
41. Rum mixture
43. Brother's son
44. Gloomy
46. Complaints
47. Cloth shred
48. Ushered
50. Skate
52. Breathing
53. Operated anew
54. Give way
55. Throb
56. Rider's command
57. Middle or Far
62. Legislation
63. Have a bawl

PUZZLE 191

ACROSS

1. Speed detector
6. Dill or thyme
10. Talon
14. Ooze
15. Mime
16. Patriot Nathan ___
17. Jazz form
18. Small prefix?
19. Release
20. Dowel
22. Bamboozle
23. Munches
24. Migratory fowl
26. Mourned
28. Triumphed
29. Pixieish
32. Side of Manhattan
35. Regularly, in poems
36. Coal product
37. Fragment
39. "___ the ramparts..."
40. Nightclub
43. Burr, to Hamilton
44. Serious theater
46. Country's Ritter
47. Deep respect
48. Sail pole
49. Trait carriers
51. Scarlet
52. Unemployed
54. Relubricate
56. Bush's office shape
59. CD collection?
61. Spigot
62. Thin coating
63. Aptly
65. Brief review
69. Berg
70. Baptism, e.g.
71. Deteriorate
72. Visualized
73. Coin opening
74. Postal machine

DOWN

1. Johnny ___
2. Chopper
3. Name a knight
4. Love greatly
5. Rest
6. Breakfast meat
7. "Ben-Hur," e.g.
8. Fame
9. Sea water
10. Spotted cat
11. Lhasa leader
12. Descended
13. Soaks
21. Silt deposit
24. Errand runners
25. Beguile
27. Nudnik
28. Kindling
30. Slangy "marvelous"
31. Peeved
33. African tour
34. Mason's tool
38. Feat
40. Jack or deuce
41. "The ___ & Stimpy Show"
42. Put forth
45. Letter bringers
49. Pet rodent
50. Burnt
53. Deceivers
55. Met musical
56. Switch positions
57. Nasty
58. Lily plant
60. Choir member
64. Until now
66. Portable bunk
67. Tangy beverage
68. Through

PUZZLE 192

ACROSS
1. Among
5. London trolley
9. Missing
13. Adult nits
14. Merrily
15. Hunch
16. Yoke of ___
17. Metropolitan
18. Adjacent
19. Skirt bottom
20. Ref's cousin
21. Mentally sound
23. Kuwaitis, e.g.
25. Enroll
29. Ahchoo!
32. Unrefined
34. Sunbeam
35. Best
37. Enmity
38. Appetites
41. Clear soup
42. Puts on
43. Adam's mate
44. First showing
46. Herbal drink
47. Young fellow
48. Make possible
51. Prelim
53. Harsh
55. False god
58. Liveliness
60. "You ___ My Love"
61. Lend
64. Celebrations
66. Box lightly
67. Boring implements
68. Detroit eleven
69. Await judgment
70. High spirits
71. On ___ (tense)
72. Inserts

DOWN
1. Hilo howdy
2. College dances
3. "The ___ Cometh"
4. Library
5. Canvas cover
6. Tease
7. Sorrowful cry
8. Mimicking bird
9. Flax fabric
10. "___ to Joy"
11. Mermaid's home
12. Roofing goo
14. Chewing ___
20. Client
22. Mr. Gingrich
24. Asks for alms
26. Three voices
27. Attain
28. Dark breads
30. Striped animal
31. Having handles
32. Bind again
33. Pallid
36. Male turkey
38. Sasquatch's kin
39. ___-steven
40. Cool!
42. Obligation
44. Trudge
45. Scrape
49. Jumped
50. Task
52. Shower off
54. Dweebs
56. Eyeball
57. Settled
58. Window ache?
59. Double curve
61. Dally
62. Wise bird
63. Hops beverage
65. Campfire item
66. Luxury hotel

FLOWER POWER

PUZZLE 193

Instructions for solving Flower Power puzzles are given on page 94.

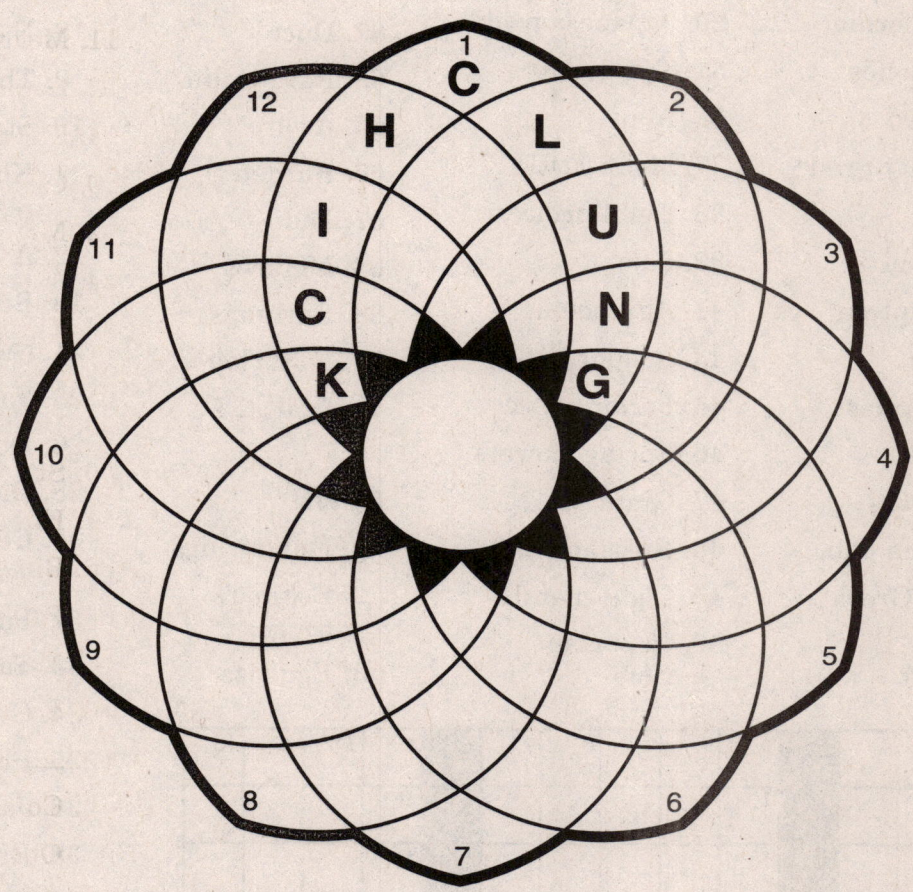

CLOCKWISE

1. Adhered
2. Model T starter
3. Boldness
4. Tuck, e.g.
5. Early invention
6. Walk
7. In what place?
8. Cooker
9. Cabin
10. Snapping sound
11. Sty animal
12. Show gratitude

COUNTERCLOCKWISE

1. Hen's baby
2. Metallic sound
3. Trim
4. Side
5. Twisted
6. Dense
7. ___ havoc
8. Transparent
9. Swipe
10. Note combination
11. Work hard
12. Not once

PUZZLE 194

J-WALKING

ACROSS

1. ___ California
5. Green stones
10. Unlatched
14. University grad
15. Divert
16. Casa room
17. Verne captain
18. ___ Rica
19. Mosque priest
20. Exultant
22. Family cars
24. Oklahoma tribe
25. Ancient Greek city
27. Maui gift
28. New Deal agcy.
29. Japanese peak
31. Tam
34. Abut
37. Monk's title
38. Delhi princess
39. Pals
41. Agreement
43. Rodents
44. Performance
46. Spring flowers
47. Giant Mel ___
48. Russian despot
49. Light metal
50. Important time
52. Nonmetallic element
54. Airplane
57. Scatters
60. Bible book
62. Duct
63. Rare violin
65. Aware
66. Burden
67. Fad
68. Mellows
69. Earnings
70. Ford flop
71. Dial ___

DOWN

1. Folk strings
2. Eskimo's cousin
3. Egg size
4. Mine, in Paris
5. American shrubs
6. In with
7. Clean
8. N.J. setting
9. The seven ___
10. Stage line
11. Kingston residents
12. A Ladd
13. Butts
21. "Alice" star
23. Yale man
26. Doubtless
28. Digits
30. Certain service
32. Pay (up)
33. Tarts
34. Curly coif
35. Phooey!
36. Jazz dance
38. Bit strap
40. Strikebreaker
42. Threesome
45. USC athletes
48. Game marble
51. Pee Wee or Della
53. Lace again
54. Extreme nationalist
55. Consumed
56. The ones there
57. Store
58. Albacore
59. Likewise
61. Ditch
64. Vexed

PUZZLE 195

UNLIKELY MATERIALS

ACROSS

1. High points
6. Mine entry
10. Ms. Parks
14. Baggy
15. Norse poem
16. Monumental
17. Viper vial?
19. Missile
20. Declared
21. Sprints
23. Sharp curve
24. Tax org.
25. Extra
26. Plastic pad?
31. Show off
34. TV E.T.
35. Debt note
36. Cadences
37. Giant great
38. Lassoed
40. Type measures
41. That girl
42. Cringes
43. Cedar Cherokee?
47. Hodgepodge
48. Bizarre
49. Cable-TV service
52. Small computer
55. Shrimp part
57. Leave
58. Parchment predator?
60. Not aweather
61. Fair
62. Ms. Verdugo
63. Geek
64. Low grades
65. Tears apart

DOWN

1. Pond plants
2. Young horses
3. Castle ditches
4. Latin verb
5. Meetings
6. "Gunsmoke" star
7. Pair
8. Pen filler
9. Drove
10. Moses parted it
11. Colorful fish
12. Father
13. Statutes
18. Swagger
22. Parabola
25. Shed
26. Shack
27. Dined
28. Full-grown
29. Go-getter
30. Foam
31. Went by jet
32. Exec's auto
33. As well
37. Buckeye State
38. Car style
39. Possess
41. Clipped
42. Apple drink
44. ___ line
45. British rock gp.
46. Seniors
49. Tom or Uta
50. Mix
51. Gumbo musts
52. Slant
53. Shaft
54. Wharf
55. Fencing blade
56. Clay square
59. Rd.

PUZZLE 196

RHYME TIME

ACROSS

1. Wild donkey
4. Litigate
7. Type of bean
10. D.C. figure
13. Glowed
14. Penn end?
15. Legalese
17. Self-aggrandizement
19. Price limit
20. Thrift gift
22. Half a pair
23. Part of REM
24. Dernier ___
27. Some
29. TV promos
30. Large fruit
32. Celeb's resort
33. Insect feeler
35. Messenger
36. Gory story
39. Surplus
40. Staff symbol
41. Bagel topper
42. Vivien or Janet
43. Biol. or chem.
44. Farm biddy
45. Pothook shape
46. Mr. Baba
47. Glide over snow
49. Shoe stew
56. Salmon variety
58. Amount of wood
59. Rigid
60. Literary olio
61. Midmorning
62. Pro ___
63. Ushered
64. Lay odds
65. Summate

DOWN

1. Kim's ex
2. Lament audibly
3. Greek covered walk
4. Finch
5. Join
6. Spot
7. Digresses
8. Chicago hub
9. Bigfoot's kin
10. Of use again
11. Letter from Athens
12. Soda
16. Soak hemp
18. Mr. Donahue
21. Editor's lead?
25. Deodorant type
26. List
27. Peaks
28. Self-love
29. Completely
30. Scant
31. Time piece?
32. Stone monument
33. Fie!
34. Sit-ups target
35. Tam, e.g.
37. Std.
38. Maui meal
43. Quenched
44. Back
46. Treasure
47. Quick bread
48. Gold measure
50. Aardvark's snack
51. December air
52. He's not striking
53. Details
54. Ancient
55. Give an advance
56. Tabby
57. Shade

174

PUZZLE 197

FLUNKIES

ACROSS

1. Reggae style
4. Singer Davis
7. Negative
10. Health resort
13. Lily ___
14. House shape
15. Honest ___
16. Keystone officer
17. Clean-air gp.
18. Foot part
19. Convert from code
21. Lackey
24. Proportion
25. Before, before
26. Journal
28. English river
31. Arm muscle
33. Eatery
36. Toady
39. Reporter's abbr.
40. Coal weight
41. Pig
42. Compass dir.
43. Sycophant
46. Stair
47. Buffalo
48. Verse, once
50. 24 hr. banker
51. View
53. ___-Saxon
57. Yes-man
61. Brutal
63. Operate
64. Eggs
65. Cereal type
66. Pay suffix
67. Hurry
68. Array
69. Payable now
70. Crafty
71. Jogged
72. Golf gadget

DOWN

1. Lance
2. Greek letter
3. Conform
4. Space rock
5. Askew
6. Nile queen
7. Low point
8. Portly
9. High-___
10. Rise dramatically
11. Father
12. Liable
20. Artifact
22. Lo-cal word
23. Actor Jared ___
27. Honkers
29. Black hue
30. Improper thing
31. Huge
32. Trial run
33. Salad name
34. Roman rooms
35. Cold condition
37. Huxtable son
38. Folk wisdom
40. Spike, once
44. Lady
45. Line of wk.
46. Harmony
49. Shiny fabric
51. Brain box
52. School paper
54. Phantom
55. Flood wall
56. Proclaim
58. Dove's cries
59. Rhine feeder
60. Large continent
61. Coal carrier
62. ___ Claire

PUZZLE 198

ON THE MOVE

ACROSS

1. Voucher
5. Squad
9. Harbinger
13. Pit vipers
17. Attache
18. Bitter herb
19. Roman attire
20. Former Korean ruler
21. It drives a ship
23. Nail topper
24. ___ model
25. Conger catcher
26. Ontario, e.g.
28. Deduced
30. Remnants
33. Tiller
35. Kind of review
36. Type of sale
40. Baldwin brother
42. Toast variety
45. Torrid
46. Spruce
48. Hodgepodge
50. Program
51. Skater Heiden
53. Attend
55. Romanov leader
57. "Many ___ called…"
58. Synopsize
60. Improve
62. Conned
64. Bullying
68. Support, politically
71. Beret's perch
72. Lost oomph
76. June bug
77. Sicily's volcano
79. Proofreader's marks
82. Ankle bones
83. TV's Moran
85. Porgy
87. Matured
88. Enjoin
89. Lint trap?
91. Adam's grandson
93. Persuading
96. Coup d'___
98. Adhesive strip
100. Train for a bout
101. College student, at times?
104. Sedate
106. Pageant prize
110. By mouth
111. Ham's father
113. Baseball term
116. Underscore
117. Flounder
118. "Dies ___"
119. Salinger girl
120. Beanery sign
121. Scrapes by
122. Hawaiian goose
123. Saturates

DOWN

1. Batman's wrap
2. Engage
3. Baal
4. Conical abodes
5. Sal, e.g.
6. Wholly
7. December air
8. Hebrew weight unit
9. Dramatic Moor
10. A stooge
11. Zounds!
12. Consumer advocate
13. Comes
14. Clergyman's headwear
15. Soccer great
16. Bird's food
22. Sea flier
27. New Zealand parrot
29. Bighorn
31. Periods
32. Convinced
34. Liquefy
36. "Mask" actress
37. Legends
38. Of the ear
39. Country music's Gibbs
41. Whitefish kin
43. Yielded
44. Dazzled
47. Incident
49. Honolulu's site
52. Guitarist's item
54. Hemmed
56. Charter
59. Full-strength
61. Western film
63. Mine opening
65. JFK sights, once

PUZZLE 198

66. Thus
67. Antique
68. Bliss
69. Comic Dunn
70. Swarming insect
73. Islamic month
74. Verve
75. Auto woe
78. Em or Clara
80. Heroic verse
81. Percolate
84. Stinging plants
86. Hunts illegally
90. Place
92. Whirlpool bath
94. Percentage
95. Mild oath
97. Uptight
99. Like a sprite
101. ___ vault
102. Italian song
103. Chess piece
105. Oliver's request
107. Part of a.k.a.
108. Incline
109. Affirmatives
112. Porter
114. Dripped
115. It's fourth before gee

PUZZLE 199

PARTY TIME

ACROSS

1. Indian chieftain
6. Minded
12. Maxims
18. Ms. Verdugo
19. Marine clinger
20. Take heed!
21. Bare skin
23. Appear
24. Buffalo
25. Great Barrier ___
27. Kooky
28. Ancient Tokyo
30. Sponsorship
33. To each his ___
35. Snaky letter
38. Slightest
41. Heaven on earth
43. Lion sign
44. Just
45. Ethereal
47. Diary item
49. Ends of series
51. Hawaiian attire
54. 007-nemesis Blofeld
55. Skillfully
58. Bull or buck
59. Baseball's Yogi ___
61. Cry of triumph
62. Pension-plan abbr.
63. Spider's trap
64. Charged atom
65. Harris of "K-9"
66. Uncooked
67. Seed coverings
70. Become tiresome
72. Relinquish
73. Trivial
75. Pekoe cart
78. LPs
80. Rug site
81. Social position
85. Notch
86. Host Linkletter
88. College mil. training
90. Accustom
91. Baste
92. Farm pen
93. Gambling game
95. Veto
96. Regulation
98. Engrave
102. Slackened
105. Popeye, e.g.
108. Insecure structure
113. Disregard
114. Fictitious
115. Be of use
116. Surrogate ruler
117. Calm
118. Grouchy

DOWN

1. Yank's rival
2. Muhammad ___
3. Jumping rodents
4. Con
5. Surprised interjections
6. Citrus fruit
7. Former Turkish title
8. Mammoth has three
9. "Paint ___ Wagon"
10. Well-known canal
11. Engagement
12. Japan's Shinzo ___
13. Villain
14. Dumbstruck
15. Backyard ornament
16. Joule's kin
17. Understand
22. Anonymous John
26. Combatant
28. Kind of wood
29. Actress Susan ___
31. Flawless
32. Common ___
34. Romance
36. Cut, as prices
37. Heartbeat
39. Linger
40. Sesame plant
42. Utmost
43. Harp's cousin
44. Done, to Donne
46. Promising person
48. Ridicule
50. Nasty
52. Nun's garment
53. Warble
55. Widespread atmosphere
56. Read-by-touch system
57. Boccie

PUZZLE 199

60. Buns
63. Somewhat hot
68. Departed
69. Song gal
70. Evidence
71. Main artery
72. Bluish color
74. Absent
76. Craggy peak
77. Somme summer
79. Fri. follower
82. Treeless plains
83. Psychic Geller
84. License info
87. Deli loaf
89. Louisiana cookery
92. Affirmed
94. Klutz
97. Bitter herb
99. Therefore
100. Pine product
101. Paige ___ of "Virginia"
103. Shoo!
104. Overhang
105. ___ Walter Scott
106. Candle count
107. Steep (hemp)
109. Pirate's domain
110. Corrode
111. Morse click
112. Crafty

PUZZLE 200

FICTIONAL PAIRS

ACROSS
1. Little songbird
5. Taunting cries
9. Musical pause
13. ___-Pei
17. Something about Mary?
18. Beach bouncer
19. Without end
20. Stylet
21. Muslim leader
22. Cameroon industrial center
23. Physical opening?
24. Spanish pot
25. "Super Friends" twins
28. Ribbed bivalve
30. M - CDXCVIII
31. Beach dollar
33. Room extension
34. East of Berlin
37. Actor McDonough
40. Fateful March date
42. Pouf the coif
46. "Rugrats' twins
49. Showed up
51. Cast opening?
52. Gov. worker
53. Poetic contraction
54. Exist
55. Greens
57. Wilson of "Mrs. Doubtfire"
60. Scottish dissent
61. Bled
62. "Harry Potter" twins
67. Male delivery?
70. System prefix
71. Make money
72. Vidalia, e.g.
76. Mr. Geller
77. Teen trouble
79. Reel shockers?
82. As to
83. Relief
85. Bobbsey twins
87. Cad
88. Wild ox
90. Garfield's pal
91. Compass dir.
92. Slip up
94. Mass robes
96. End of everything?
98. More meager
102. "Star Trek" twins
108. Castor's mom
109. Food
111. Raven of "Amen"
112. Pitt, to some
113. German auto
114. Amor
115. Bridle control
116. Hit
117. Baby-sit
118. Get a flat
119. Uncluttered
120. Periods in history

DOWN
1. Smart kid
2. Thai king
3. Spunk
4. Itinerant
5. Submissive
6. Pilgrim's journey
7. Olive genus
8. Does in
9. Send back
10. Garden party?
11. Puts in curlers
12. Vestige
13. Puffy
14. Road incline
15. A Guthrie
16. Glean
26. Granada girl
27. Brad
29. Second self
32. College official
34. Chooses
35. Diamond of Queens, once
36. Cultivate
38. Halsey's mil. rank
39. Incan transport
41. Gregg expert
43. Hebrew month
44. Evening, in Roma
45. Ancient garden
47. Page
48. Silly
50. Rip
56. Visionaries
58. Vitamin bottle abbr.
59. Correspond
63. ___ homo
64. Ms. Dixon
65. First page of a calendario

PUZZLE 200

66. Hollywood's Markey
67. Litigates
68. Viva voce
69. Finalizing legal word
73. Lodging places
74. Domesday Book money
75. English river
78. Spirit lamp
80. Inc., in London
81. Steak order, in Rouen
84. May stone
85. Rum-soaked cake
86. Exigency
89. Most aged
93. Bring up
95. Rudder's place
97. "Fur ___"
98. Job opening
99. LePew of cartoons
100. Yemen port
101. Like hens' teeth
103. Main course?
104. China site
105. Air freshener target
106. Portugal's Cabo da ___
107. Fraternal society
110. Perlman of films

PUZZLE 201

WHO LIVES HERE?

ACROSS

1. Large tart
4. Stretch
7. Pentateuch
12. Halt
16. Large vase
17. Loud noise
18. Altruistic
19. Scorch
20. 32 Windsor Gardens
23. Dynamic prefix
24. Inning ender
25. Slip into
26. Prehistoric megaliths
28. Generosity
32. Pitching stat
35. Sidestep
36. "___ My Party"
37. Museum guide
40. Fairy king
42. Whitetail
44. Boom box
45. Government org.
46. LA clock zone
48. 4 Privet Drive
51. Raison d'___
53. Boutique
55. Hold on property
56. Hunches
57. Cheer
58. Choice group
62. Playwright Joe ___
64. Sts.
65. "La Boheme," e.g.
67. Wire measures
69. Sheriff's gang
71. Sniffer
72. 17 Cherry Tree Lane
76. Free (of)
77. Muslim leader
78. Credit ___
79. Shack
83. Fountain treat
85. Rope loops
87. Bardic before
88. Plentiful
90. Make a blouse
92. Reserve funds
94. 100 centimos
96. Sweet tangelo
99. Spanish cry
100. Stink
101. 221B Baker Street
108. Sublet
109. Throbs
110. Feel unwell
111. Be in hock
112. Soviet news agcy.
113. Maine, e.g.
114. Correct!
115. Formerly named

DOWN

1. Little dog
2. Gershwin brother
3. Support
4. Amended
5. Relations
6. School subj.
7. Edible fish
8. Old card game
9. ___ Dawn Chong
10. Santa ___
11. Cow crowd
12. Baked in a sauce
13. 1313 Mockingbird Lane
14. Rowed
15. Likely
18. Weeder
21. Spaded
22. Like some wool
27. Above, to poets
28. Can top
29. Lunched
30. Light brown
31. Wound remnant
33. Name list
34. Missing
38. Quick drink
39. Implement
41. Listening organ
43. Greek letter
47. Business
49. Vicinity
50. Nino's uncle
52. Highway curve
53. Flavor
54. 742 Evergreen Terrace
56. Privy to
57. Mr. Howard
59. Visions

PUZZLE 201

60. Harangue
61. Tarzan player
63. Expresses a view
66. Urgent alarms
68. Whirled
70. Snaky sound
72. Welcome ___
73. Yoko ___
74. Of a meson group
75. Stance
80. Leading power
81. Work measure
82. ___ Moines
84. Permitted
86. Bar chairs
88. To the left, matey
89. Jason's wife
91. German sausage
93. House addition
95. Deadly vipers
97. Delight
98. ___ Alamos
102. Cabin
103. High note
104. Actress Lenz
105. Hasten
106. Meadow mom
107. Witness

PUZZLE 202

VISITING COLORADO

ACROSS
1. Coffee
5. Master
8. Author Angelou
12. Tennis legend
16. Make amends for
18. Paid a kidnapper
20. Clang
21. Colorado attraction
24. Riots
25. Lamb owner
26. Refuge
27. Baseball stat
28. Speck
29. Lower
31. Red roots
34. Not there
35. Cut
36. Saloon
39. Guns an engine
40. Hardy heroine
41. Transactions
42. One ___ million
43. "We ___ the Champions"
44. Israeli dance
45. Indian wraps
46. Snow runners
47. Troop movement
49. Gaucho's weapons
50. Versifiers
51. Colorado sandstone region
55. Spar
57. Plunders
58. Go by
61. Rind
62. Trivial
63. Chaise
65. Extremely long time
66. Sooner than, to Byron
67. Lairs
68. Listen
69. Missile
70. Demand payment
71. Through
72. Pork, e.g.
73. Chin. pets
74. Agts.
75. Skiff
76. Rails on high
77. Harmonize
80. Shipped
81. "Seinfeld" character
84. Colorado high point
89. Agatha's peer
90. Reporters, e.g.
91. Bizarre
92. Glimpses
93. Stink
94. Former name indicator
95. Sunrise direction

DOWN
1. Startle
2. Mr. Egoyan
3. Sotto ___
4. Short socks
5. Martial ___
6. Pantry item
7. Captivates
8. Watered silk
9. Asian island
10. Crave
11. Periodontists' gp.
12. Horrify
13. Coral and Yellow
14. Mata ___
15. Part of BPOE
17. Observers
19. Declare
22. Give ___ break!
23. Beef cuts
28. City in Arizona
29. Luggage piece
30. Astonishes
31. Lingerie items
32. Architect Saarinen
33. Colorado lake
34. Not him
35. ___ Jessica Parker
36. Colorado high point
37. Group
38. Deep voice
40. Pigeon-___
41. Seasons
44. Trumpeter Al ___
45. Sentimental one
46. Pop
48. Pursue
49. Waders

184

PUZZLE 202

50. Many pref.
52. Dice payoff
53. Recorder
54. Apparatus
55. Ran
56. Lima's land
59. Irritated
60. Tolkien creatures
62. Lay asphalt
63. Throne
64. Stetson, e.g.
67. Halley's discovery
68. Pagan
69. Brando film
72. French painter
73. Locale
74. Trait carriers
75. Comic Joy ___
76. English town
77. Iowa city
78. Pierce
79. Law
80. Fr. town
81. Besides
82. Mrs. Charles
83. Noun suffix
85. Galleon cargo
86. Nursed a baby
87. Valuable dirt
88. Backdrop

PUZZLE 203

IMAGINE THAT!

ACROSS
1. Persist
5. Tub soakings
10. Pluck
15. "Cat on ___ Tin Roof"
19. Same: pref.
20. Pianist Blake
21. Narrative writing
22. Harmony
23. Glitch
24. Redolence
25. Mansard features
26. Norse mariner
27. Imaginary opponent
29. Imaginary, fierce creature
32. Retained
33. Senior
34. Tennessee has two
35. Drank quickly
39. Drums
40. Johnnycake
42. WWII craft
43. Pursue
45. Trombone part
47. Ranch sound
50. Blanc or Cervin
51. Satellite
52. Sitcom star
54. Lunchtime stop
55. Hideaway, e.g.
56. Drew (off)
58. Provide
59. Encompassed by
60. Overplays
62. Staggered
64. Four-burner
65. Abandons
67. Foe
68. Swerved
69. Auditoriums
70. Timorous
72. Distilled wine
74. Girasol
75. Touch lightly
76. Shipwreck
78. Sportscaster Berman
81. Ospreys' cousins
82. Green and Yellow
84. Cloches
85. A Brubeck
86. Puppeteer Krofft
87. Emulated Marceau
88. Pitcher Satchel ___
90. Dog treats
91. Subdue
92. Hulls
93. Mighty
94. Riser
97. Sedate
99. Poetic lowland
101. Imaginary, tiny beings
104. Imaginary, eternal flower
109. Some
110. Singer Cleo ___
111. Hosiery fiber
113. Mrs. Dithers
114. Factory
115. ___ sanctum
116. Plow pioneer
117. Appendage
118. Gorge
119. Shabby
120. Wagered
121. Scram!

DOWN
1. Damsel
2. Eller, to Laurey
3. Asterisk
4. Freeborn's wear
5. Smiled
6. Of hearing
7. Govt. security
8. That guy
9. Navy builders
10. Disburses
11. Wind or union
12. Red ___ (game)
13. Moocher
14. Jumble
15. Drill command
16. William and Mary Beth
17. Reserved
18. Mechanics, e.g.
28. Hone
30. "Ragged Dick" author
31. Island bird
35. Unable to speak
36. English horn
37. Imaginary place
38. Rebel Turner
39. Welles role
40. Ached
41. Stench
43. Manage
44. Leaps
45. Slight
46. After the bell
47. Imaginary path
48. Dynamic
49. Supported
51. Welcome items
53. Scads
54. Obsolete
56. Outdoes
57. Tee club
61. Food-court havens
63. December 31, e.g.
64. Export
65. Certain platforms
66. Bay of Naples isle

PUZZLE 203

67. Dismantled
68. Moving trucks
70. Offense
71. Babble
72. Crow
73. Estimate
75. Sinister
77. "___ Diamond Ring"
79. Balanced
80. Snake's home
83. Ruin
85. Ellipsis part
87. Crumbly soil
89. Book supplement
90. Afrikaner
91. Football's Y.A. ___
92. Flimsy
93. Smoothed
94. Bridge triumphs
95. Fibula's companion
96. Skewed
97. English Channel feeder
98. Modified
99. Manservant
100. Passion, in Pisa
102. Crimsons' foes
103. Glass unit
105. Pretends
106. Ancient mariner
107. Ensemble
108. Heavenly glow
112. Desire

PUZZLE 204

SHORT MONTHS

ACROSS

1. Avoid doing
6. Gaucho's tool
10. Crinkly fabric
15. A Diamond
19. French composer
20. Does well on
21. Wanders
22. Free
23. Family member
24. Store
25. Lifeless
26. Young horse
27. Set up tents
29. Ebony cuckoo
30. French seaport
32. Phooey!
33. Nose parts
35. Succinct
36. Inner man
39. Dress finely
41. City on the Rhone
43. Ski event
47. Ontario Indian
48. Comfy
50. Mother's kin
53. Molder
54. Walking ___ (elated)
56. Norway's saint
58. Extras
60. ___ voyage!
61. Separate
63. Touched down
65. Dumbfound
66. Pantry fillers
67. Bagel seed
68. Vestige
70. Liable
71. ___ Major
72. Wear's partner
74. Clairvoyants
76. Gull's kin
78. Way
81. Place
83. Some songs
85. Lifts up
89. Ardent
90. Certain exam
92. Dijon dad
93. Bar bottle
94. ___ Juan
95. Traps
97. Held onto
99. Fielder's blunder
100. Alaskan native
102. Forfeits
104. Loom threading
106. Glen
107. ___ and pestle
109. Finish-line line
111. Auto, of old
112. Bedazzled
113. Curl
116. Cupid's master
118. Rowboat paddle
120. "Psycho" star
124. Be suitable for
125. Snake sounds
129. Borodin's prince
130. Icy abode
131. Theater award
133. Electron tube
134. Ground grain
135. Swiss mathematician
136. Celebrity
137. Piano exercise
138. Pale
139. Heraldic bar
140. Rats!
141. Poet Thomas

DOWN

1. Sea eagle
2. Prideful
3. With, to Henri
4. Joltless joe
5. Fragrant resin
6. Coll. degrees
7. Having eight angles
8. Ms. Helmsley
9. Going in circles
10. Some reds
11. A Barrett
12. Turn inside out
13. Intrinsically
14. Chemical compounds
15. Type of energy
16. Organic compound
17. Inactive
18. Builders' buys
28. Vets' patients
31. Capri and Wight
34. Watch carefully
36. Barges
37. Bert's friend
38. Inclines
40. Yoko ___
42. Piles
44. Of the lungs
45. Aromas
46. The brainy bunch
49. Squalls
51. Soho so long
52. Burst forth
55. Famous Colosseum location
57. Rasped
59. Breaks in
62. Crossbow, e.g.
64. Traffic jam
66. College sports team

PUZZLE 204

69. Up a ___
73. Countrified
75. Spread
77. Regatta
78. Female title of respect
79. Convex molding
80. Beanery
82. Edible root
84. Gap
86. Cereal stalk
87. Pierre's school
88. Rip
91. In case
95. Maze word
96. Beach
98. It's past due?
101. Absolutely
103. Mineral springs
105. Nonsense!
108. Comfort
110. Surround
114. Smooth transition
115. Window parts
117. Leg bone
119. Supported
120. Iwo ___
121. Many years
122. Pair picker
123. Exits
126. Record-shop category
127. Norse poetry
128. Detected
132. Chang's twin

PUZZLE 205

SOUNDS LIKE...

ACROSS
1. Glitzy party
5. Pueblo Indian
9. Minor quarrel
13. Baseball ___
16. Racetrack shape
17. Giant
18. British composer
19. Malarial fevers
22. Reindeer herder
23. Squadrons
24. Tidbit
25. Care for
26. Brit bird's dish?
29. Hindu term
30. Meadows
31. Vamoose!
32. Gov. edible agency
34. Marsh
35. Bakery treat
39. Commandment number
40. Magician's word
42. Apron part
45. Arctic, e.g.
47. Harpoon
49. Slips up
52. "The Piano" role
53. Sallow
54. Teenage problem
55. Amo, amas, ___
56. Bering, e.g.
57. Dove's timepiece?
61. Small, e.g.
62. Cul-de-___
63. Dismiss
64. Prunes' start
65. Modernize
66. Gold measure
68. Towel off again
69. Market town
71. Lariat
73. Fruit pulp
74. Cartoonist Goldberg
75. Commotion
78. King beaters
79. Boa's towel words?
82. Scamper
83. Asian language
84. Sorrowful cry
85. Fencer's blade
86. ___ Aviv
87. Movie locales
88. Convict
90. Baker's need
92. Hog's haven
93. Declaration
95. Actress Mendes
98. Green and abundant
99. Spring mo.
101. Tenet
102. Give a view
104. Every one
108. Bring into position
110. Mr. Ed's favorite book?
115. Le ___ (port city)
116. Inactive
118. Harden
119. Mice, to cats
120. Iron output
121. Understood
122. Gold, to chemists
123. Hog fat
124. Swedish rug
125. Devours
126. Lo-cal
127. Besides

DOWN
1. Palmer's sport
2. Serve
3. Backslide
4. Greek letter
5. Female deer
6. Of the ear
7. Walkways
8. Bug
9. Asian boats
10. Light refractor
11. Colony bug
12. Shirt style
13. Tent material
14. Spanish water
15. "Cats" presentation?
17. Large cask
20. Medieval laborer
21. Actor Connery
27. Concerning
28. Poetic before
32. Former French coin
33. Bo or John
36. Locust shrub
37. Vacation spot
38. Nevada lake
40. ___ Bill
41. Short trailer
42. Deep voice
43. Proposal
44. Second-guessing sheep?
46. UN HQ locale
48. Booming
50. Knock down
51. Mulligan ___
58. Met event
59. Of the past
60. Made well
63. To's partner
65. Bemoan
67. St. Francis of ___
68. Ms. Rene ___

PUZZLE 205

69. Part of FBI
70. Fixate
71. Back muscles, for short
72. Dull pain
73. Church song
74. Resist
76. Piece for two
77. Lone
79. Knife handles
80. Small intestine part
81. Yo!
89. Huey and Dewey, to Donald
91. Biblical word
94. Movie theater
96. Roman seven
97. Temper, as steel
99. Oohs and ___
100. City map
102. Small hooter
103. Boredom
105. Eve's fruit
106. Reef stuff
107. Weed removers
109. Dreary
111. Mongolian dwelling
112. Bona fide
113. Dress bottom
114. Jekyll's other self
116. DDE, to friends
117. Genetic letters

PUZZLE 206

KIDS' CHARACTERS

ACROSS

1. Postpone
6. Fertile soil
11. Goose comment
15. Louse
18. House of Congress
19. Past
20. Section
21. Color tone
22. Kids' boy detective
25. "We ___ the World"
26. Stockpiled
27. Inquired
28. Discard
30. Yank
31. Outdoes
34. Russian jet
35. PC post
37. Assemble
40. Spring back
42. Twilight
45. Flux density units
47. Kids' girl detective
49. Long time
50. Magazine piece
52. Pallid
53. Subsided
54. Kids' aspiring writer
57. Adventurous search
59. Slanders
60. Cavort
61. Wire thickness
62. Brass instrument
63. Line of wk.
64. Italian three
65. Bucks
66. Barbecue
67. Take wing
68. "Star Trek: Voyager" role
71. Meat cut
73. Hepburn costar
74. Former French coin
75. Pre-Easter season
76. Of bees
78. Playful trick
79. Kids' literate spider
81. Protect
82. Kept secret
83. Mom and Dad's dads
84. Spheres
85. Kids' mischievous redhead
88. Scoffs
92. Imps
94. Like freeway entrances
96. Therefore, to Shakespeare
97. Lady duck
98. Thin fish
99. Math course
101. Cato's eggs
102. Adolescents
104. Wed in secret
106. Fibrous protein
109. Fully
110. Kids' braided Swede
115. Greek letter
116. Border lake
117. Dress cut
118. Emerges
119. Shark's home
120. Escort
121. Brought back
122. Canvas homes

DOWN

1. False tooth
2. Coops up
3. Wray and Masterson
4. Clearly outline
5. Rent again
6. Cut off
7. Bullring bravo
8. Icelandic work
9. Of an earthquake
10. Deceitfully
11. Firm
12. Spanish gold
13. ___ Jersey
14. Wichita native
15. Kids' golden ticket owner
16. General mood
17. Low in pitch
18. Six-line stanza
23. Fragrance
24. Implore
29. Worth summoning
32. Writing tool
33. Milan's La ___
35. Happening
36. Kitten sound
38. Fasten
39. Bakery item
41. Dollar
42. Scratch out
43. Activist
44. Terminates
46. Flower part
48. Live
51. Osiris's wife
53. Glimpse
54. Van Gogh's forte
55. Likewise not
56. Kids' literal maid
57. Fast
58. Unsightly
62. Cereal grain
63. Drinks noisily
65. Red deer

PUZZLE 206

66. Alums
67. Froth
69. Treebeard, e.g.
70. Sault ___ Marie
72. Rower
73. Adorns
74. Contributor
75. Also-ran
76. Highly curious
77. Feline sigh
78. Fake
79. Prowled
80. Actress Wood
83. Sports facility
85. Scale notes
86. Divided into small pieces
87. First British prime minister
89. Swellhead
90. Chasms
91. Vernaculars
93. Spoke imperfectly
95. Food plan
98. Yale attendee
100. Crow
102. Faucets
103. Otherwise
104. Duel tool
105. Camelot woman
107. Property unit
108. Outer layer
111. Author Levin
112. Peach center
113. African antelope
114. Gender

PUZZLE 207

Diagramless crosswords are solved by using the clues and their numbers to fill in the answer words and the arrangement of black squares. Insert the number of each clue with the first letter of its answer, across and down. Fill in a black square at the end of each answer. Every black square must have a corresponding black square on the opposite side of the diagram to form a diagonally symmetrical pattern. Puzzles 207 and 208 have been started for you.

ACROSS
1. Historic age
4. Get it?
7. Subways' cousins
10. Voyage part
11. Flood boat
12. Used a bench
13. Fury
14. Victory sign
15. Sauna locale
16. Dance for two
18. No problem!
19. Goes in
21. Not nays
22. Watching
24. Super serves
27. Tropical trees
31. Great review
32. Edit a film again
33. Lode yield
34. Lobe's place
36. Lyric verse
37. Chess pieces
38. ___ trip
39. Neckwear item
40. TV promos
41. Unworthy
42. Lay turf

DOWN
1. Upper crust
2. Telecast again
3. 007, e.g.
4. Tasty
5. Sooner than, in poems
6. ___ out a living
7. School paper
8. Blunder
9. Sticks around
17. Ganders' mates
18. National bird
20. Bro or sis
23. Limited
24. Fragrance
25. Minded
26. Not odds
28. Glasgow natives
29. Video's partner
30. Mount
34. Wiggly fish
35. In the past

PUZZLE 208

ACROSS
1. Drama part
4. Insulting remark
6. Lady, in Madrid
10. Window ache?
11. Wicked
12. Wild donkey
15. Small plateau
17. Thaw
18. Bigwig's initials
19. Marcia, to Jan
21. Showy bloom
23. Equipment
24. Dog doctors
30. Sofer of Hollywood
31. Honest
32. New York team
34. Summer, to Bardot
35. Exchange premium
37. Location
39. Inquire
40. Hindu mentor
41. Slime
43. Finishes
44. Asta's owner
45. Butter serving

DOWN
1. Nile biter
2. Silent type
3. Melodies
5. Acquiescence
6. Misconduct mark
7. Above
8. Nothing
9. Computer key
12. Tel ___
13. Kingly address
14. Skewer
16. On a cruise
20. Roofing liquid
22. Solemn
25. "The Crying Game" star
26. Rustic hotels
27. Kind of code
28. Cashew and almond
29. Hide's partner
32. Encircle
33. Crouch
35. 18 or 21
36. Western's prop
38. Pound of poetry
42. Nibble

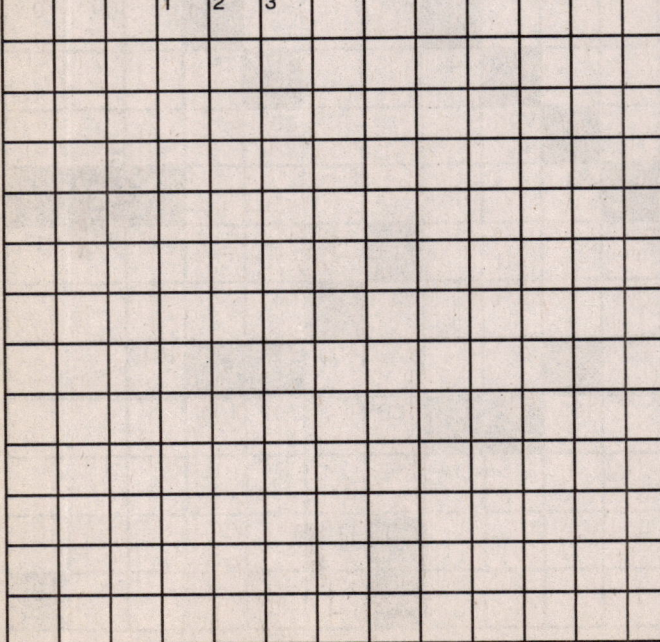

PUZZLE 209

ACROSS
1. Mop
5. Follow
6. Rambles
9. Pine tree
10. "A Boy Named ___"
11. Secreted
12. Moral lapse
13. Misplace
14. Repair
15. Rapid
16. Highway
18. Make the scene
19. Tomato or pea
20. Control
21. Quarrel
22. Above
24. Mix
25. Writing tool
26. Preserve
27. Conclude
28. Montego ___
29. Perplexed
32. String
33. Playthings

DOWN
1. Top-billed player
2. Pallid
3. Help
4. Hallowed
6. Broad
7. Spoil
8. Transmit
9. Fighting hand
11. Nylons
13. Mary's pet
14. Chart
15. "___ Your Eyes Only"
16. Bellow
17. Three strikes
18. Eight ounces
19. Twirl
20. Behavior
21. Command to Fido
22. Mimics
23. Portable shelter
24. Many
28. Cots
30. Cow cry
31. Snoop

Starting box on page 562

Carry-Overs
PUZZLE 210

Add and subtract letters from the ROOT WORDS to form answers to the CLUES. Start with the first ROOT WORD, subtract one letter, and rearrange the remaining letters to form the answer to the first CLUE. Carry over the letter you subtracted to the next line, add it to the second ROOT WORD, subtract the number of letters indicated, and rearrange the remaining letters to form the second answer. Continue solving in this way.

	ROOT WORDS			CLUES
1.	CASTLE	− 1 =	_____	Slightest
2. ☐ +	ALLURE	− 2 =	_____	Transparent
3. ☐☐ +	FATE	− 2 =	_____	Energy source
4. ☐☐ +	DELIVER	− 3 =	_____	Take a trip
5. ☐☐☐ +	TEAM	− 0 =	_____	Referee

PUZZLE 211

ACROSS
1. Sounds of pain
4. Kiwi's relative
7. Centers
9. Damages
10. Deeds
12. Fragments
13. Bring up
15. Chip in a chip
16. Complain
18. Music system
21. Fly catcher
22. Life story, for short
23. Fiery
24. Kumquat, e.g.
26. Aardvark's morsel
27. Taking care of
30. Greek vowel
33. Warrant officer
34. Eggs
37. Scale tone
38. Chilly
39. Sackcloth
41. Pipe puffer
43. Amend, as copy
44. Leg part
45. Church dish
47. Rose essence
50. Seaweed product
51. Actress Lamarr
52. Gas guzzler
53. Female ruff

DOWN
1. Switch position
2. Trouble
3. Sacred beetle
4. London parent
5. Mouths, to Pliny
6. Donkey
8. Thing
9. Choral work
11. Brazilian dance
12. Excited by
14. Bridle control
15. Light gray
16. Sasquatch cousins
17. Decompose
19. Small newt
20. Miner's quest
21. Black _____ (spider)
25. Open, as a gate
28. Knob
29. Oxlike beast
30. Pluralizer
31. Male cats
32. Hilo hello
34. More senior
35. Narcissistic
36. Liable
38. Lessee
40. Pave again
42. Kin's partner
45. Inner shoe
46. Turkish general
48. Citrus refresher
49. Sandwich bread

Starting box on page 562

PUZZLE 212 Pencil Pusher

Can you draw the figure below without lifting your pencil from the paper, without crossing a line, and without retracing any lines?

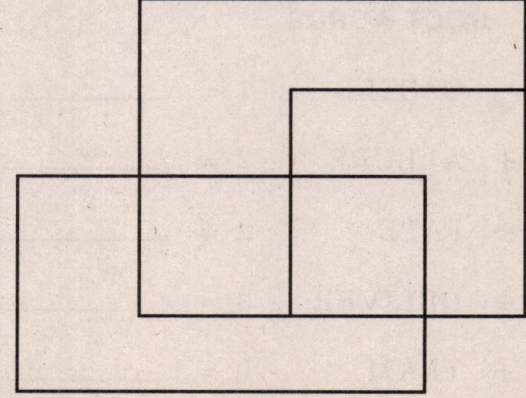

PUZZLE 213

ACROSS
1. Food fish
5. Tease
8. Brace
9. Single
10. Take long steps
12. Glass unit
13. Panache
14. Not up yet
16. Hold fast
17. Kisser
18. Deficiency
19. Barnyard bird
20. Pipe type
23. Came up
25. Nasty mutt
26. Make something up
27. Aspiration
28. Convened
29. Ditty
30. Gibbon, e.g.
31. Chasm
32. Records
33. Absolutely!
34. Bit of advice
35. Donated
36. Cone producer
37. Amusements
38. Pet peeve?
39. Attempts
40. Nautical greeting
42. Pal
44. Coal product
45. Folder holder
46. Cyclops's singleton
47. Blissful abode

DOWN
1. Parsley portion
2. Tresses
3. Assistance
4. Idealist
5. Highway
6. Tavern
7. Busy buzzer
10. Bread piece
11. Cistern
12. Pin
13. Glimmer
15. Hot-dog roll
16. Shuts
19. Shanty
20. Marries on the run
21. Row
22. Lower limbs
23. Gone
24. Ready to eat
25. Bottle top
28. Juniper juice
29. Rescues
31. Tall animal
32. Made gentle
34. Dead heat
35. Benefit
36. Take wing
37. Unseasoned
38. Links cry
39. Floor square
40. Noshed
41. Dried grass
43. Get ___ of

Starting box on page 562

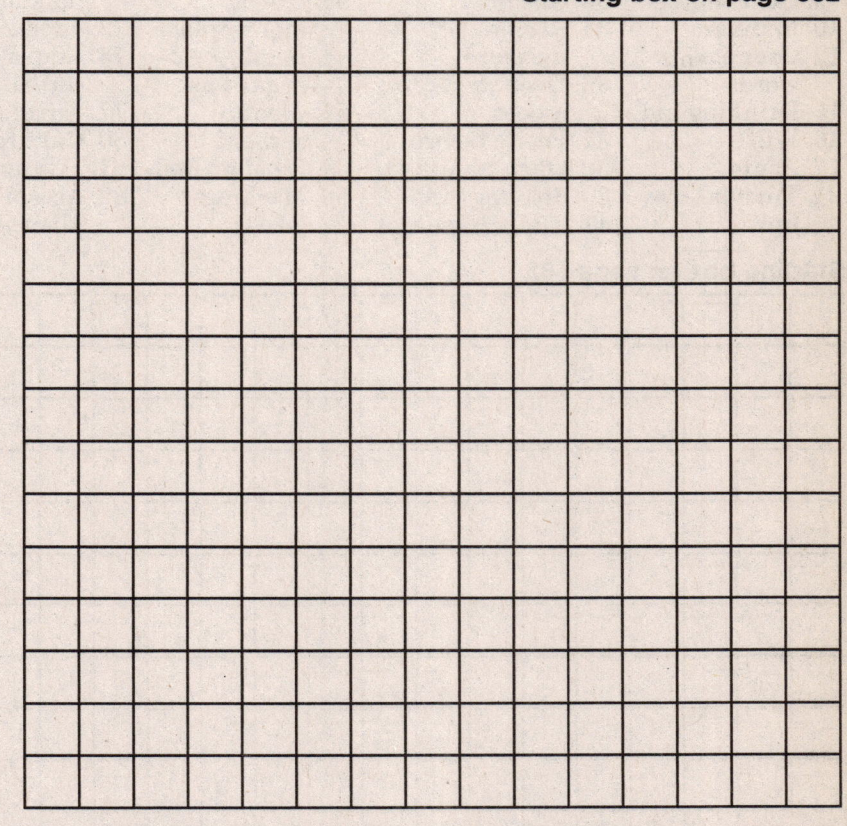

Hexagon Match

PUZZLE 214

Place the seven words into the hexagons so that each letter will match the letter in the adjacent hexagon. All the words will read in a clockwise direction. One letter has been entered to get you started.

ENGINE   SUDDEN

HINDER   TUNNEL

INSULT   UNIQUE

NAPPED

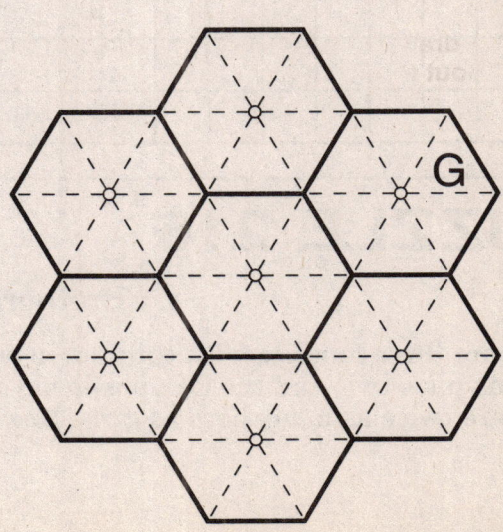

PUZZLE 215

ACROSS
1. Stereo component
4. Whimsical
7. Oaf
9. Gold source
10. Manners
12. Group of words
15. Drinking aid
16. Wilt
17. Acute
21. Turn bottom up
24. Probe
25. Dry, as wine
28. Help a crook
29. Coastal eagle
31. Malaysian coin
32. Swindler
34. Recipe measure
36. Over there, to a poet
37. Poetic before
38. Open-mouthed
39. Solo for Sills
41. Apply henna to
43. Church tribunal
44. Sign, as a check
46. Tied contest
50. That woman's
52. Mongolian dwelling
53. Greek marketplace
54. Maple-sugar base
57. Cleo's serpent
59. Dead or Red
60. Marking post
61. Snout stretcher
62. Sun, e.g.
64. Happy start
66. Lamb's ma
67. Hacienda material
69. Polished
71. Waiter's handout
72. Erode
73. Like a hot cereal
77. Angel
80. Care for
81. Five-and-___
82. Accomplished
83. Go onstage
84. Williams of baseball

DOWN
1. Charity gifts
2. Questionable
3. Kitten's sound
4. Fake document
5. Notable age
6. Pro vote
8. Scone
11. Large mop
12. 23rd Greek letter
13. Mist
14. Add to
18. Other
19. "___ in My Heart"
20. Hawaiian bird
22. Thin-shelled nut
23. Hardy
24. Refuse to accept
25. Wound remainder
26. Hence
27. Joseph's was multicolored
30. Bump
33. Brilliant fish
35. Reverent
40. Catch
42. Anxious
44. Formerly
45. Banal
47. Assigned part
48. Lined up
49. Subside
51. Relieve
53. Clap
54. Bridge coup
55. Camp helper, e.g.
56. Peasant
58. Beauty contest
63. Sow's opposite
65. One billion years
68. Public conveyance
70. Greatest
74. Harness-racing gait
75. Laborer
76. Exigency
78. Greek vowel
79. ___ room (family room)

Starting box on page 562

PUZZLE 216 — Deduction Problem

Brothers and Sisters

There are three families with children in our neighborhood. The Archers have one child, the Bensons have two, and the Campbells have three. Among the children who have no brother, there are twice as many boys as girls. How many boys and girls does each family have?

PUZZLE 217

ACROSS

1. Atlantic coast
5. Dove's abode
9. Aggressively manly
10. Underground conduit
11. Loftier
12. Hawker, to some
13. Placed on a cay
14. Patterned fabric
15. Enough
17. Scarcer
18. Ready to pick
19. Age of note
20. Furniture wood
22. Travel stamp
24. Butter squares
25. Physicians, briefly
28. Uppity one
29. Dogma
30. Legal hold
32. Delighted
34. Fabled birds
35. Not pizzicato
36. Angel
38. Angler's catch
39. Kite feature
40. Dried fruit
42. Costly fur
43. Like parquetry
45. Hindu title
47. Padre
48. Acid neutralizer
49. Go over again
50. Stirs up
51. Lyric verses
52. Dollar component

DOWN

1. Golfing coup
2. Head woe
3. Farm building
4. Craggy hill
5. Moth repellent
6. Night flyers
7. Tree of India
8. Go wrong
9. Deceive
10. Dotted, in heraldry
11. Nile animal
12. Small umbrella
14. Adventurous
15. Mountain ridges
16. Among
17. Sun. speakers
20. Cowboy's home
21. Tropical nut
23. Desert garments
24. Folks
26. Current path
27. Minute segment
29. Follow
31. Central point
33. Particulars
37. Jewish cleric
40. Earnest requests
41. File
42. "Thou ____ not kill"
43. Angered
44. Kind
45. Blackthorn
46. Allied by nature
47. Compensated player
48. Bow

Starting box on page 562

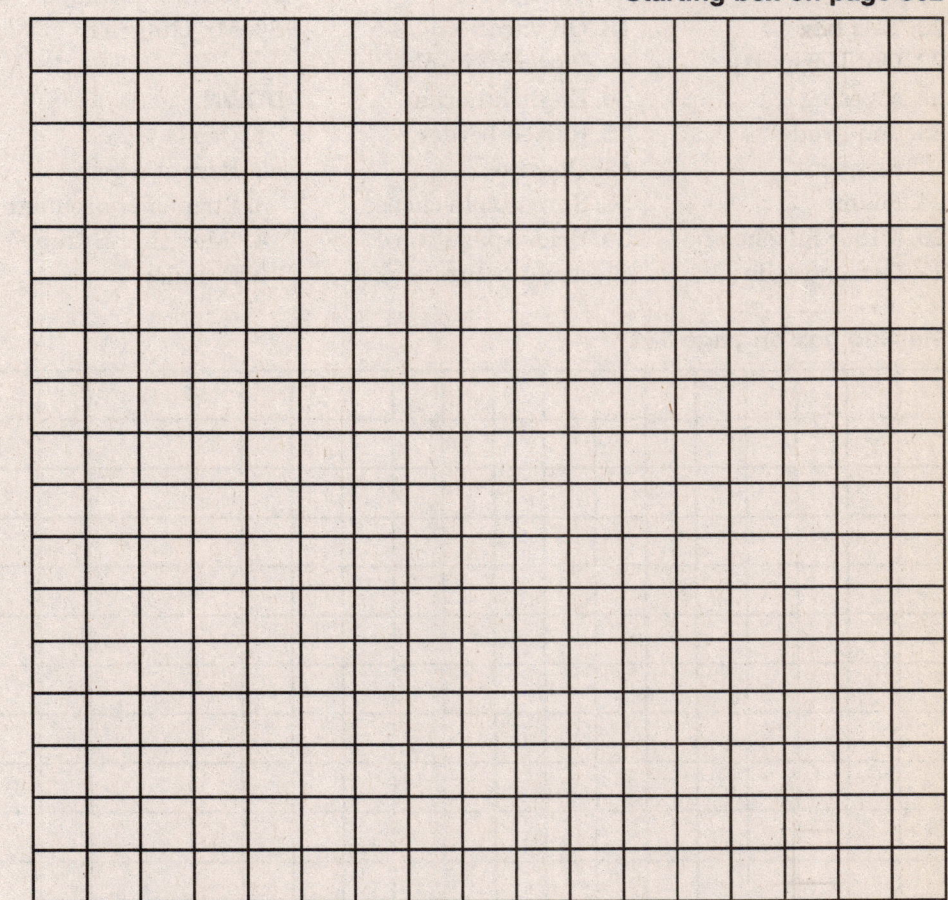

Block Letters   PUZZLE 218

A single letter is on each of the six sides of four toy blocks. No letter is repeated. Any side of a block can be faceup, and the blocks can be in any order. The twelve words listed can be spelled faceup using the four blocks. What are the six letters on each block?

| BAYS | FLAP | HIES | MOLD | QUIP | WARN |
| CRIB | GAME | JURY | OXEN | SUNK | ZING |

PUZZLE 219

ACROSS
1. Astringent ingredient
5. Rabbit fur
6. Sheep's stomach, to a chef
11. Rocky peaks
12. Pinker, as steak
13. Salesman's pitch
15. Oxygen form
16. Solder
20. Talkative
22. Outdoor party covering
23. Top-grade recipient
24. Foam
26. Minor falsehood
29. German wife
30. New World cuckoo
31. Likewise
32. Certain engines
35. Carpentry tool
37. "Lady and the ___" (Disney film)
38. Scraps
41. Hindu dress
42. Spell
43. Per se
46. Shed tears
48. On vacation
49. Powerful dunk
50. English horns
52. Raised border
53. Observe
58. Spreadable cheese
59. Bridal-page word
61. Architectural curve
62. Electrified particle
63. Everglades bird
65. Cabbage salad
66. Con game
69. Step on a peel
71. TV's Danson and Knight
72. Wagner composition
73. Shrill barks
76. Ulnae neighbors
77. Trim excess from
78. Odor
79. Religious image
80. Mr. Gingrich

DOWN
1. Deeds
2. Part of a bow
3. Strip of equipment
4. "Me, ___ & Irene"
6. Promise
7. Demolish
8. Branding ___
9. Confined
10. Sooner than, to a bard
14. Italian money, once
16. Blow gently
17. Neutral color
18. Shakespeare's "King ___"
19. Defeat decisively
21. Dwarfed tree
25. Coronets
26. Linen source
27. Dogma
28. Charlie Parker's style
31. "Where the Boys ___"
33. Heeds
34. Sibling, for short
36. Determination
37. Stuffing seasoning
39. Romanov title
40. Stitching
41. Pigpen
44. Dubbers
45. Jekyll's lair
46. Dime or nickel
47. Female ruff
50. Kimono sash
51. Slangy chum
54. Gala giver
55. Leer at
56. Spearhead
57. Moistens, poetically
60. Squirmy
63. Paperless letter
64. Cravat jewelry
66. Unwanted computer message
67. Relinquish
68. Seed shell
70. Come in second
72. Conjunctions
74. Front of a boat
75. Forwarded

Starting box on page 562

PUZZLE 220
• GAMBOLING •

ACROSS
1. Sty dweller
4. Bauxite, e.g.
5. Notable periods
9. Groups of seven
13. Ancient ascetic
15. Sponges
16. Speck
17. Give new energy to
20. Monumental story
21. Elicit
25. Kind of code
26. Lima ___
28. Related
31. Chum
32. Diversify
33. Exec. ability
34. Oolong or pekoe
35. Biological unit
36. Clay became him
37. GI's address
38. Type of shaft
39. Weekend TV institution
40. Schoolyard game
45. Dit's opposite
47. Lend a hand
48. Velocity
49. Skirt edge
50. Ticked off
52. Ripped
53. Seize
55. Mayberry lad
57. Hi-___
58. Born as
59. Concentrated beam
60. Dallas hrs.
62. Fiddle stick
63. Frozen in
66. Pi follower
67. Speller's event
69. Dust cloth
70. UFO riders
73. Unite
74. Shopworn
75. Paving goo
76. State firmly
77. NL city
78. Essence
80. Arrogant sort
82. Dancer Falana
83. Belt spot
86. Italian tower locale
88. Money holder
92. Tax gp.
94. Back
95. More optimistic
96. A good seat to have
98. Actual
99. Infinite time
100. Move a tail

DOWN
1. Matthau film
2. Crumb
3. Turned right
5. Curved letter
6. Steep flax
7. Santa ___ winds
8. Balkan native
9. Dine late
10. Give off
11. Low digit
12. Norm abbreviation
13. Chef Lagasse
14. Neuter
15. Crooked
17. Indonesian island
18. Eurasian mountains
19. Cadence
22. Capsize
23. Dial up
24. Building wing
27. Enraptured
29. Salonga or Thompson
30. Beaver's construct
35. "___: Miami"
37. Dull finisher
41. Approx.
42. To the left, at sea
43. Parisian pop
44. Swamps
45. Munich article
46. Sound blaster
47. Farewell
49. Tint
50. Ancient Jordanian kingdom
51. Lhasa ___
53. Dos preceder
54. Mend clothing
56. Coastal eagle
59. Relay division
60. Spicy dish
61. Ho or Shula
62. Mattress piece
63. Modern Persia
64. Chocolate substitute
65. Consume
66. Roster
67. Quagmire
68. Yale grad
71. Highway fee
72. Swipe
73. Head bone
75. Romanov ruler
76. Wings
79. Level
81. "The Simpsons" son
84. Attack!
85. La-la lead-in
87. Dejected
89. Negative connector
90. Big-12 sch.
91. Contest
93. Cook slowly
97. ___ constrictor

Starting box on page 562

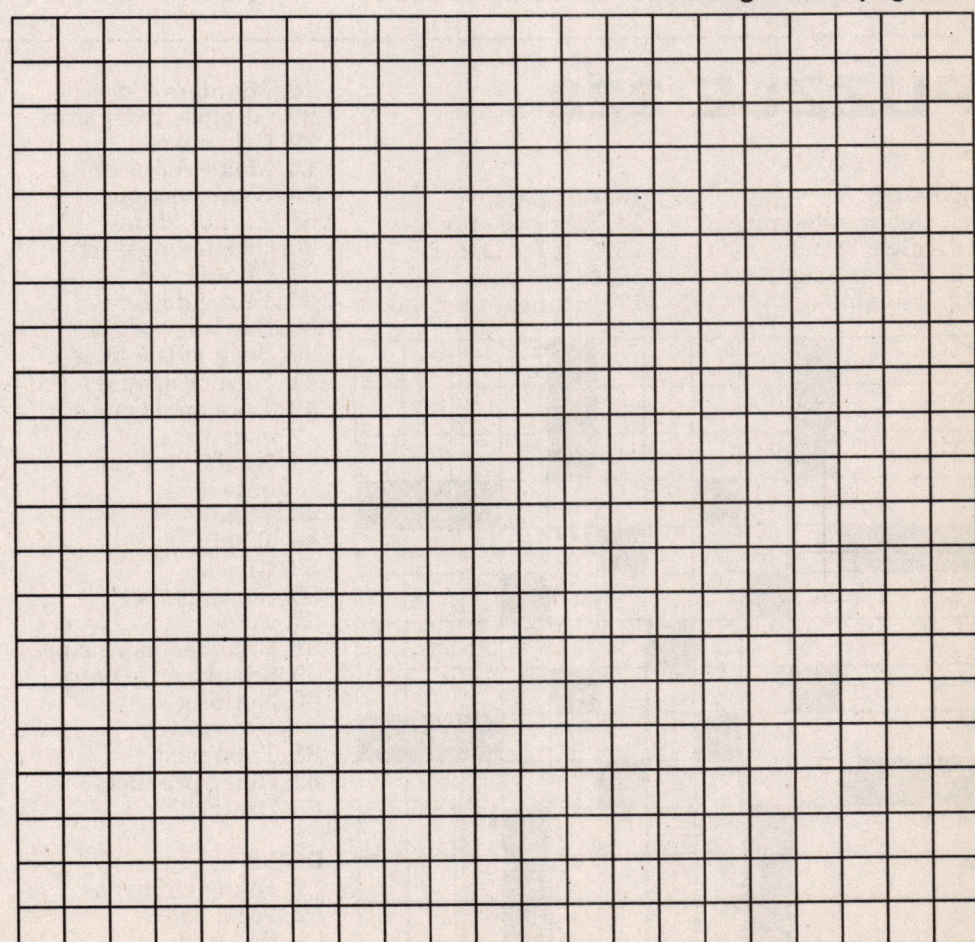

PUZZLE 221

ACROSS
1. Concept
5. Drag
9. Downs' partners
12. Hawaiian cookout
13. Actress Sommer
14. Baltic or Bering
15. British nobleman
16. Was sorry for
17. Tee preceder
18. Article
20. Circumference
22. Forbidden
25. Shortcoming
27. Historic time period
28. Bland
30. Oral history
34. Come to one's aid
36. Munched
38. Shark variety
39. Pale
41. Zone or table
42. "___ It Romantic?"
44. Stale
46. Magic formula
49. Rave
51. Stable food
52. Spectacular
54. Large weight units
58. Had lunch
59. Chalet feature
60. Prepare copy
61. That girl
62. Asked urgently
63. Put trust (in)

DOWN
1. In the infirmary
2. Twins
3. Sound organ
4. Television sound
5. In this place
6. Female college grad
7. Guitar's kin
8. Mantel
9. Patron
10. Bothersome person
11. Soft belt
19. Health food
21. Do nothing
22. Length
23. Region
24. Sun
26. Imprint with acid
29. Not fatty
31. Is obligated to
32. Tenant's fee
33. Crosscurrent
35. Spiral
37. Religious song
40. Compete
43. Shuteye
45. Say
46. Iranian ruler, once
47. Liver spread
48. Watcher
50. Scored on serve
53. Chum
55. "___ to a Nightingale"
56. Naught
57. Enclosure for swine

PUZZLE 222

ACROSS
1. Gooey substance
4. Silent type
8. Flower urn
12. Valuable dirt
13. Ear part
14. Favorite star
15. Gift for Dad
16. Flows back
17. Inclines the head
18. Mambo's kin
20. Glimpse from afar
22. Green with ___
24. Make very happy
28. Glass section
31. ___ of Man
33. Crusted dessert
34. Odors
36. Young doctor
38. Bowling target
39. Back of the neck
41. Former spouses
42. Take on as one's own
44. No ifs, ___, or buts
46. Windy
48. Tingly
52. Knocks
55. Camp helper
57. Color
58. Becomes more ripe
59. Square or granny
60. Nothing's alternative
61. Time past
62. Hens' products
63. Draw off

DOWN
1. Young children
2. Vocal solo
3. Rod and ___
4. Tidy
5. Tennis stroke
6. Monasteries
7. Military meal
8. Floor covering
9. Stir
10. Grassy layer
11. Chicago Loop trains
19. Appear to be
21. Hammer end
23. Traveler's permit
25. Highest point
26. Whitewall, e.g.
27. Bards' sunsets
28. Mama's mate
29. Like the Sahara
30. "___, Nanette"
32. Property right
35. Opposed to
37. Examination
40. Remitting funds
43. Old-fashioned
45. Says no to seconds
47. Garden tool
49. Chew the fat
50. Grass-skirt dance
51. Holler
52. Actor Bolger
53. Gone by
54. Part of mph
56. Beagle or collie

PUZZLE 223

• CRAYON BOX •

ACROSS

1. Track numbers
5. Heavy club
9. Cattle roundup
11. Push over the edge
14. Maryland's state flower
18. Messy room
19. Lost traction
20. Brandish
21. Absorbed
25. Cutlery items
27. Great Lake
28. Hack
31. Flat top
33. Sup
34. Breeze
35. Stop right there!
37. Type of jockey
40. Bowler, e.g.
41. Flurry
42. "Chances ___"
43. Wrap
45. Jersey hub
47. Remotely
48. Lump
49. Pine
50. Forehead
52. Soap opera, e.g.
55. Home run king
57. Prohibit
58. New Deal org.
59. Label
61. Waters
63. Limbs
64. Stone
65. Tune
66. Hatfield's foe
68. Drain
69. Ocean bird
70. Snappy comeback
73. Dandelion, e.g.
74. Music maker
77. Roman ruler
79. Corn core
82. Gershwin classical piece
85. Lethargy
86. Clean the slate
87. Bonfire
88. Army insects

DOWN

1. Sun and moon
2. Blockhead
3. Significant time
4. Not sweet
5. Certain sch.
6. Fill in the blank
7. Set sail
8. Abate
10. Approves
12. Maiden
13. Discontinue
15. Deer
16. Yang's partner
17. Safe to eat
21. Sleuth's dish?
22. Met solo
23. Pub order
24. Links peg
26. Dog's doc
28. "The Godfather" actor
29. Deputy
30. Was economical at lunchtime
32. McCourt memoir
35. Ports
36. Roomy boat
38. RR depot
39. Treasury
44. Animal home
46. Spirit
51. Sorrow
52. Hang low
53. Code or rug
54. Light source
56. Viet ___
57. Over and above
59. Rushed
60. British princess
62. Argumentative
63. Parking site
65. Embroider
67. Suppress
71. Spanish king
72. Numerical prefix
74. Scrap
75. Pi follower
76. Williams role
78. Dollar
79. Faction
80. Drive out
81. Buzzers
83. Lode-bearer
84. Bikini top

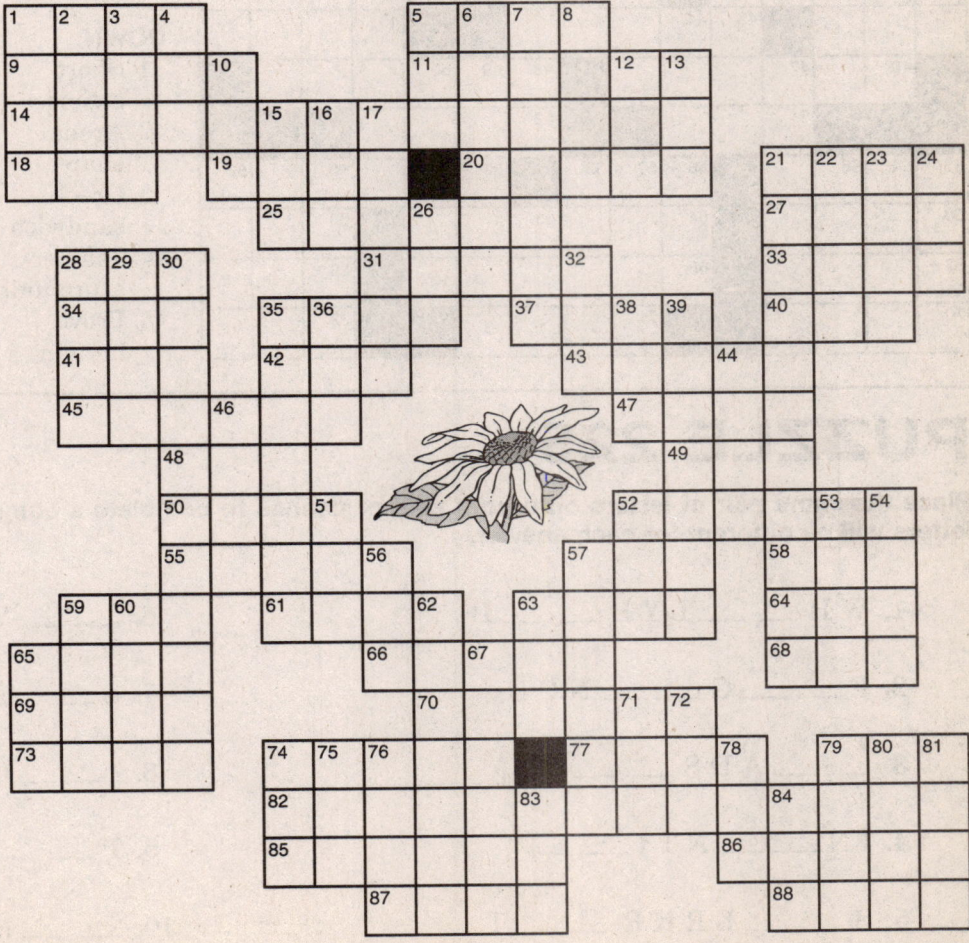

203

PUZZLE 224

ACROSS
1. Beagle or collie
4. College official
8. Caffeinated soda
12. Clinging vine
13. Black-footed ___
15. Skating jump
16. Accepted standard
17. Wading birds
18. Baltic and Caspian
19. Less speedy
21. Fire remnant
22. Knowledge, briefly
23. Porters, e.g.
25. Atom with a charge
27. Potato type
29. Munitions storehouse
32. Hair divider
33. Important vessel
35. Give assistance to
37. Boundaries
39. Retrieve
40. "A ___ Runs Through It"
42. Key lime dessert
43. Yonder
45. Depend
46. Printed
48. Marketed again
51. Curious
52. Show fatigue
53. Pond-scum ingredient
56. Jewel
59. Even chance
63. You ___ what you sow
64. Dodger
66. Personality facet
67. Zoo enclosure
68. Free from harm
69. 100 percent
70. Shadowbox
71. Spots
72. Caustic liquid

DOWN
1. Short swims
2. Arena shape
3. Greek sandwich
4. Temperature unit
5. Prove human
6. Neighborhood
7. Tuna catchers
8. Gambling establishment
9. Yoked animals
10. Page
11. Furthermore
13. Senses
14. Jeans partner
20. Garbage
24. Organized
26. Poet Khayyam
27. Semidiameters
28. Moves to action
29. Thoroughfare
30. Untangle
31. Triangular sign
32. Liveliness
34. "___ the ramparts..."
36. Desertlike
38. Wall component
41. Clubs for Woods
44. Rows of bushes
47. Serial drama
49. Food consumers
50. Cursed
53. Crescents
54. Pounce
55. Ardently fond
57. Nights before celebrations
58. Kitchen spice
60. Flippered mammal
61. Homely
62. Column
65. Now payable

PUZZLE 225   Pairs

Place the same pair of letters onto both sets of dashes to complete a common word. The pair of letters will be different for each answer.

1. W H ___ ___ L Y B ___ ___ D

2. F ___ ___ G ___ ___ N C E

3. ___ ___ A D S ___ ___ O L

4. I N ___ ___ N T I ___ ___

5. S ___ ___ E R K R ___ ___ T

6. ___ ___ V E ___ ___ R N

7. S ___ ___ D B ___ ___ K

8. ___ ___ U R ___ ___ N

9. P ___ ___ A T I ___ ___

10. ___ ___ M ___ ___ U S

PUZZLE 226

ACROSS
1. Box lightly
5. Hitherto
9. Invited
14. Spelling mistake
15. Cold-cuts shop
16. Boutique
17. Metallic deposits
18. Like some cars
19. Inclined
20. "___ No Angels"
21. Collections of laws
23. Just managed to earn
24. Root ___ (soda)
26. Farm animal
28. Hazy image
30. Reminds (oneself)
35. River span
37. Dramatist Coward
38. Relief exclamations
40. Deep grooves
41. Multitude
43. The Kingston ___
44. Cigar residue
45. Dirt stain
46. Shrewdness
48. Main female characters
51. Turkish notables
52. Fruit cooler
53. Timber wolf
55. Applicant's blank
58. Rub hard
61. Brine-cured cheese
65. Accustom
67. Pelt
68. Voter's district
69. Offspring
70. Tense
71. Enthusiastic
72. Cares for
73. Fixed charges
74. Weightlifting term

DOWN
1. Stash
2. Bonfire
3. Mocker
4. Baby blossoms
5. Elicit
6. Soak up again
7. Musher's vehicle
8. Neap or spring ___
9. Cleopatra's snake
10. Scattered
11. Strange person
12. Ocean bird
13. Accomplishment
22. Diagram
25. Unit of work
27. Petroleum product
28. Painter's need
29. Pliant
31. Descended maternally
32. Rocky peak
33. Destiny
34. Recoils
35. Swimsuit top
36. Catches sight of
39. Heir
42. Prevailed
43. Power struggle
45. Grass
47. Taxi
49. Rifle cleaner
50. Ooze
54. Minds
55. Clenched hand
56. Formerly
57. Devastate
59. Skilled cook
60. Carnival feature
62. Roofline detail
63. Journey
64. Attaches
66. Nanny has three

Split Personalities

PUZZLE 227

The names of eight male musicians of the '60s have been split into 2-letter segments. The letters in each segment are in order, but the segments have been scrambled. For each group, can you put the pieces together to identify the musician?

1. RE EY VI SL EL SP _____
2. RC TH AI YF PE _____
3. CH NE DL GE AN ER _____
4. UC RY KB CH ER _____
5. YG BO DS RO BB OL BO _____
6. IN RV YE MA GA _____
7. ED ON FR CA DY NN _____
8. RL HA RA ES YC _____

205

PUZZLE 228

ACROSS
1. Aural rebound
5. Intimidates
9. Movie award
14. Hit
15. Iridescent gem
16. Stringed instrument
17. Zero
18. Flora
20. Deviled item
21. Unruffled
22. Flexible Flyer, e.g.
23. Greek market
25. Grand Coulee ___
27. Amble
29. Blood parts
30. Twice
33. Small ensemble
34. Wide-mouthed jug
36. Mane
38. Carpets
39. Skinny candle
41. In addition
42. Despaired
44. Tree swing, often
45. Depressed
46. Awfully moist
47. Sneaking suspicion
49. Witness
51. Screw up
52. Lawn barrier
53. Mining car
57. Improvement
59. Playing marble
62. Newlywed getaways
64. Send away
65. Plant swelling
66. Theater section
67. Bingo's kin
68. Bar legally
69. Elevator man
70. Infuriated

DOWN
1. Anglo-Saxon peon
2. Congest
3. Slangy direction
4. Unlock, in poems
5. Bedspread
6. "Don Giovanni," e.g.
7. Engage in
8. Slimmer
9. An avis lays them
10. Takes a load off
11. Helix
12. Burn reliever
13. "The Fountainhead" author
19. Salty droplet
21. Fa's follower
24. Gander's mate
26. Raincoat, in London
27. Dried wheat stalks
28. Cease-fire
29. Dark brown
30. Flock leader
31. Magazine edition
32. Guide
35. Swimmer's sport
37. Renaissance fiddle
40. Turns around
43. Game cube
48. Oil barrel
50. Roadside stop
52. Mushrooms
53. Quaker pronoun
54. Fishing poles
55. Dill, formerly
56. Office communique
58. Whistle sound
60. First-rate
61. Grove
63. Bark sharply
64. Glide downhill

PUZZLE 229 — Number Sleuth

One of the numbers in the hexagons has been circled because it and the numbers in the six surrounding hexagons are all different. There are 12 others like this. Are you a sharp-eyed sleuth who can find them all?

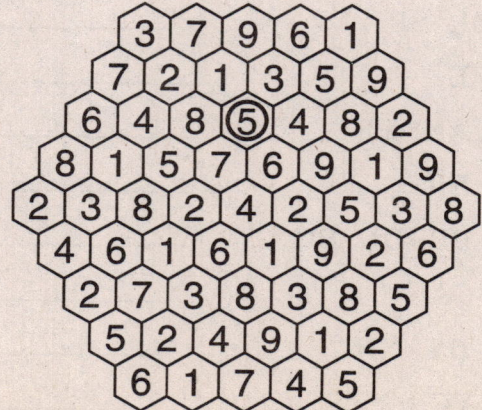

BRICK BY BRICK

PUZZLE 230

Rearrange this stack of bricks to form a crossword puzzle. The clues will help you fit the bricks into their correct places. Row 1 has been filled in for you. Use the bricks to fill in the remaining spaces.

ACROSS

1. Running bill
   Corrode
   Opposite of hawed
2. Beauty preceder
   Lively dances
   Property measure
3. Corn core
   Adjust
   Entreat
4. Sarcasm
   Insurance figure
   Point
5. Pudding thickener
   Indian nanny
6. Nearer
   Biblical verb
7. Emerge
   "All That ___"
   Greek letter
8. Python's relative
   Birds in a gaggle
   Cry noisily
9. Chop off
   Galvanizing metal
   Small restaurant
10. Overjoy
    Sparkling
11. Legitimate
    Righteous
12. Snack shop
    Young women
    Unnerve
13. Auricular
    Fly
    Dashed
14. Conceal
    Weekly TV show
    Superman's emblem
15. Spot
    Ms. Evans
    Meet the bet

DOWN

1. Implied
   Proficient
   Circular vault
2. Plato's market
   Join together
   Airport initials
3. Scat-singer's syllables
   Mama's mate
   Speak imperfectly
4. French resort
   Difficult
5. Bribe
   Zorro's mark
6. Bilge
   Welsh dog
   Turkish officials
7. Extremes
   Placed in bondage
8. Ocean bird
   Kick out
   Italian dough, once
9. Trumpet blasts
   Attack verbally
10. Look to be
    Horselike mammal
    Shirt type
11. Shaping tool
    Showy blooms
12. South American cowboy
    Out of ___
13. Light color
    Hitherto
    Counter-weights
14. Units in physics
    God of thunder
    Wipe off
15. ___-dish pie
    Vagrant
    Heavily populated

BRICKS

| S O B | D E L | E T H | ■ D O | B O A |
| T R O | O T I | R H O | Z Z ■ | L O P |

| L K A | E L A | ■ S C | E R I | S T A |
| T U N | ■ ■ ■ | ■ T E | D A L | L ■ S |

| A R E | C L O | R A T | K ■ S | S E R |
| R A N | E A R | A ■ A | K Y ■ | ■ J A |

| ■ ■ ■ | M A S | N Y ■ | I ■ G | S ■ A |
| A P P | E S P | I O C | C A ■ | E ■ U |

| R R Y | A G E | A L S | E ■ C | E E S |
| A I N | C O B | V I A | M A H | N C ■ |

| T E ■ | U S P | P O ■ | E ■ ■ | ■ ■ G |
| R E A | ■ ■ ■ | A T ■ | B I S | Z ■ I |

| E S S | ■ ■ ■ | I R O | C R E | E S ■ |
| S E E | T E D | T A P | R G E | E ■ ■ |

DIAGRAM

	1	2	3	4	5	6	7	8	9	10	11	12	13	14	15
1	T	A	B	■	■	■	R	U	S	T	■	G	E	E	D
2															
3															
4															
5															
6															
7															
8															
9															
10															
11															
12															
13															
14															
15															

PUZZLE 231

ACROSS
1. Fellow
5. Outguess
10. Door clasp
14. Arab chief
15. Island hello
16. Fragrance
17. Skirt type
18. Finger
19. Law
20. Walk
21. Paving stuff
22. Stopcock
23. Dollars
26. Maui meal
28. Finger count
29. Light casts it
32. Block up
34. Long period
35. Oozed
39. Army insects
43. Capture
45. Position
46. Love greatly
47. Cedar, e.g.
48. Praise
50. Pistol
51. Wise hunter
53. Awakened
55. Cerise, e.g.
58. Brat
60. Clumsy boats
61. Put forth
63. Dashed
65. Results
69. Old instrument
70. Scout
72. Bus fee
73. Intention
74. Serpent
75. Module
76. Session
77. Silly birds
78. Circuits

DOWN
1. Jewels
2. Radiate
3. IX
4. Camera holder
5. Cushion
6. Gashes
7. Hindu philosophy
8. Peep
9. Stetson, e.g.
10. Round dance
11. Grown-up
12. Deduce
13. Groom
22. By route of
24. Snack
25. Mama sheep
27. Not even
29. Faction
30. Frost
31. Initial bet
33. Irate
36. Raised RRs
37. Caress
38. Look at
40. Egg drinks
41. Valid
42. Dispatch
44. Office VIP
46. Berserk
48. Horror street
49. Botch
52. Wag
54. Practical
55. Ignited again
56. Secrete
57. Dissuade
59. Priss
60. Llamas' home
62. Paper amount
64. Helper
66. Granny
67. Leak
68. Adjusts
70. Quip
71. Poet's before

PUZZLE 232

ACROSS
1. Band
5. With speed
10. "We ___ Family"
13. Healing herb
14. Ivory keyboards
15. Commanded
16. Diviner
17. Adjusts
18. Launch ___
19. Hard hat
21. Ump's kin
22. Peek at
23. Cold comment
25. Paper measure
27. Cane source
30. Punches
33. Narrative
34. Most tardy
37. Fate
39. Not fitting
41. Plant juice
42. Sung drama
44. Fido, e.g.
45. Dragster
48. Deserve
49. Cut
51. Smooth
53. Move slowly
55. By what method?
56. Teen dance
59. Adult swine
61. Sneak
66. Tear
67. Greens dishes
69. Ripple
70. Jungle beast
71. Remit early
72. Nights before
73. Japanese coin
74. Appended
75. Imprint

DOWN
1. Incision
2. Nautical term
3. Christmas
4. Seed
5. Feel queasy
6. Couple
7. Hostility
8. Admit to
9. Snaky curve
10. Swiss peaks
11. Harvest
12. Ocean motion
14. Police unit
20. Decrease
22. Outback bird
24. Bake
26. Palo ___
27. Evils
28. Playing marble
29. Atlas chart
31. Glimmer
32. Regretful
33. Drink slowly
35. Roofing goo
36. Era
38. Beige
40. At the time
43. Green soup
46. Grove
47. Sleepy
50. Vitality
52. Flock mama
54. Punctured
56. Say grace
57. Mature
58. "___ Sesame!"
60. Stare
62. Astounded
63. Keep
64. Balanced
65. In case
67. Resort hotel
68. "Major ___"

PUZZLE 233

ACROSS
1. State further
4. Two-door car
9. Winter outerwear
13. Pod content
14. Come into view
16. Massive
17. Pixie
18. Dispute
19. Presser's need
20. Particular place
22. Fish snare
23. Mom's boy
25. Travel endorsement
27. Refund
30. Long heroic poem
32. "___ Goes My Baby"
34. Miner's goal
36. Stomach
37. Jealousy
38. To and ___
39. "Roses ___ Red"
40. Outrigger
42. Devotee
43. Stamp out
44. Leg bone
45. Church responses
47. Ask humbly
48. Propel a bike
50. Canary food
51. Cheapen
53. Canyon sound
55. Bother
56. Good buddy
57. Flying stinger
61. Pang
64. Avoids
67. Strife
68. Pivot
69. Expose
70. ___ of Reason
71. Solder
72. Robe fabric
73. Shrill bark

DOWN
1. Mimics
2. Lunchtime stop
3. Foolish
4. Rogue
5. Unzips
6. Cheerful
7. ___ moss
8. Feast
9. Great Wall locale
10. "___ Gang"
11. Gone by
12. Five plus five
15. Store up
21. Diabolic
24. Heed
26. Frozen
27. Gambling city
28. Chewy candy
29. Chore trip
30. Spookier
31. Vow
33. Red hair-dye
35. Eternities
36. Fishhook point
40. Cashier
41. General's helper
44. ___ of the moment
45. Fire remnant
46. Cat's call
49. Person in charge
52. Banqueted
54. Transparent
56. Lay asphalt
58. Not at home
59. Heroic narrative
60. Kind of school, for short
61. Dog's foot
62. Hatchet
63. Ailing
65. Horse doc
66. Like a fox

PUZZLE 234

ACROSS
1. Sci-fi doctor
4. Descended
8. Indian lute
13. Operate
14. Reward
16. Got up
17. Circle part
18. Shorthand pro
19. Slalomed
20. Request
22. Deep ditch
24. Scale notes
25. Ink stains
27. Acorn source
29. Breach
31. Placing
34. Worries
35. Brief life stories
37. Shredded
39. Mass robe
40. "___ Night"
43. Pollinator
44. Radar spot
46. Interrupt
47. Baby hooter
49. Organized
51. Discard
52. Lopsided
53. Glide
56. Pirate drink
59. Rhode ___
61. Dull sound
65. Coral reef
67. Precincts
69. Slip up
70. Part of USNA
71. Hull part
72. Mature
73. Subject
74. Fume
75. Morning drops

DOWN
1. Package
2. Fling
3. In the past
4. Sit-up targets
5. Sweepstakes
6. Inactive
7. Melodies
8. Strut
9. Annoy
10. Hard work
11. On a cruise
12. Crimson hues
15. Dad's boy
21. Talented
23. Glide
26. For fear that
28. Young fox
29. Corridors
30. Flight path
31. Attic
32. Grand
33. Avarice
34. Hired car
35. Droplet
36. Unhealthy
38. Gain
41. Curds' mates
42. Emcee
45. Furry foot
48. Hone
50. Grating
53. Delhi dresses
54. Genuflected
55. Proverb
56. Holler
57. Mormon's state
58. Chess play
60. Testing place
62. Noodle
63. Impulse
64. Sketched
66. Flight
68. Make a dress

PUZZLE 235

ACROSS
1. Gels
5. Overhead rails
8. Apartment
12. Fiery stone
13. Aptitude
15. Roman money, formerly
16. Dossier
17. Promo producers
18. Square
19. Takes
21. Requiring
23. Meddle
24. Highland hat
25. Dawn to dawn
26. Occurrence
30. Clangor
32. Cauldron
33. Heart
36. Carries on
40. Froze
42. Bus station
44. Leaf opening
45. Sour fruit
47. Dubbed
49. Repent of
50. Cartoon frame
52. Flowering plant
54. Fire leftover
57. Attack command
59. Toss easily
60. Spotted cat
62. Emergency transport
66. Wee
67. Pine product
69. Inspiration
70. In the past
71. Oscillated
72. Attendee
73. Oboe insert
74. Thus far
75. Angled pieces

DOWN
1. Love seat
2. Heroic tale
3. Soft mineral
4. Slumbers
5. Ceases
6. Robber's run
7. Aroma
8. Bolted
9. Enraged
10. Bout spot
11. Spicy
13. Grasshopper
14. Massage
20. Senior dance
22. Arab chief
26. Heinous
27. Tempo
28. Newsy bit
29. Paradise
31. Carpet pile
34. Fitness club
35. Tut's place
37. Average
38. Devoted
39. Foreteller
41. Sneezy's pal
43. Relating
46. Wren's home
48. Way out
51. Deceivers
53. Require
54. Role player
55. Glisten
56. Therefore
58. Tough
61. Leered at
62. Slangy negative
63. Admired one
64. Sense
65. Old salts
68. Lyon of film

PUZZLE 236

ACROSS

1. Fades
5. Applaud
9. Parrot
13. Capture
14. Pointed
16. Crazy bird
17. Pious
18. Campfire treat
19. Spirit
20. That thing's
21. Deary
22. Verse
24. Pure
27. Grand party
29. Heifer
30. Beet soup
35. Bermuda ___
38. Thickness
39. Couple
40. Escorts
41. Horse feed
42. Co-op's kin
43. Ambience
44. Egg warmer
45. Firmly planted
46. Beauty
48. Santa's aide
49. Small drop
51. Largely
55. Team list
59. Pub drink
61. Bread type
62. Toward
63. Coat of mail
65. Milan money, once
66. Tinted
67. Tramps
68. Makes do
69. World's fair, e.g.
70. Oxen team
71. Experiment

DOWN

1. Morality
2. Soup base
3. Light wood
4. Eavesdrop
5. Curved nuts
6. Exec's car
7. Amid
8. For each
9. Further
10. Codger
11. Clock cycle
12. Mere
15. Arrange troops
23. Rower's tool
25. Yell
26. Tykes
28. Efficiently
31. Lampoons
32. Is unable
33. Conceal
34. Tramped
35. Buck
36. Tow behind
37. Gumbo must
38. Criticize
41. Zeus's wife
42. Pop flavor
44. Cheer
45. Car gear
47. Solemn work
50. Rumba's kin
52. Kid's wheels
53. Old strings
54. Leavening
55. Gallop
56. Black gem
57. Stair
58. Commotion
60. Glance
64. "Rob ___"
65. Authorize

PUZZLE 237

ACROSS
1. Selects, with "for"
5. Trades
10. Bro's pal
13. Enticement
14. Indian village
15. Chef's item
16. More than
17. Lemon hue
18. Enjoyed dinner
19. Creepier
21. Dawn droplets
22. Cinch
23. Faded
25. Take five
27. Freighter
30. Fights
33. Gotcha!
34. Fathered
36. Multiply
38. Mama's guy
40. Furnishing style
42. Title
43. Portents
45. Albacores
47. Bakery offering
48. Bordered
50. Mice, e.g.
52. Checkup
54. Enrage
55. Type of duck
58. Pronto!
60. Excuses
64. Witch
65. Floating
67. Golly!
68. Before, in verse
69. Sweetie
70. Saint's headgear
71. Subways' kin
72. Laundry machine
73. Cook slowly

DOWN
1. Band instrument
2. Do roadwork
3. Layer
4. Long pace
5. Prosecute
6. Fuse
7. Fitter
8. Turned the soil
9. Plant
10. Bridge
11. Tiny bit
12. Gait
14. Pharaoh's tomb
20. Significant periods
22. Rigid
24. Flat hat
26. Stand-in
27. Embarrass
28. Not live
29. Repeat
31. Hurdled
32. Big trailers
33. Mil. address
35. Contributor
37. Kiki or Ruby
39. Cherub
41. Glow
44. Male or female
46. Vend
49. Temper
51. Stable sounds
53. Kind of eel
55. Old pronoun
56. British noble
57. Many moons
59. Telegraph
61. Dinghy, e.g.
62. Florida Key
63. Demonstrate
65. Do sums
66. Pine tree

PUZZLE 238

ACROSS
1. Location
5. Refs' kin
9. Leather band
14. Berserk
15. Shredded
16. Egyptian city
17. Delayed
18. Not fat
19. Assisted
20. Mature
21. Asian
23. Sample tape
25. Glass edge
26. Presidential noes
30. Imitator
32. Can top
33. Quick blow
34. Medicated
36. Zero
37. Despot
38. Ledger entry
39. Place
40. Rancher's mark
41. Porter et al.
42. Soaking
43. Whines
44. Barnyard pen
45. Briny deep
46. Mend
47. Annoy
49. Bear hair
50. Active
54. Joking
56. Fish eggs
57. Swift
60. Feed the pot
61. Soda choice
62. Mindful
63. ____-do-well
64. Functions
65. Small amphibians
66. Tacks on
67. Nuisance

DOWN
1. Cold dish
2. Impression
3. Clan symbol
4. ____ out (just make)
5. Spoke
6. Angora fabric
7. Rainbow maker
8. Posted
9. Frightened
10. Pollute
11. Disburden
12. Exist
13. Seed envelope
22. Vice
24. Haven
27. Church item
28. Merits
29. Went fast
31. Fido, e.g.
32. Fired up
34. Actress Burke
35. Heeds
36. Fanatic
37. Some exams
38. Short race
39. Tiny veggie
40. Tropical snake
42. Garden growth
43. Business unions
45. Slips
46. Pursued
48. Mini or maxi
49. Penalized
51. Novel text
52. Movie parts
53. Brewing need
55. Comic Carvey
57. Bolted
58. Wonderment
59. Kitten's foot
61. Mug

215

PUZZLE 239

ACROSS
1. Stomach muscles
4. Murky
7. Naples staple
12. Long scarf
13. Canned fish
15. Enjoyed
16. Over there
17. Drum type
18. False name
19. Office pro
21. Smooth
23. Got smaller
25. Street sign
29. Defrost
32. Worn away
34. Meadow mama
36. Hurl
38. Wine's aroma
39. Nope
40. Biblical boat
41. Church bench
42. Sale caveat
44. Ship's rear
46. ___ a living
47. Friendly
49. Frustrate
51. Epistle
53. Fruit juice
57. Fragrances
60. Form
61. Another time
65. Be skeptical
67. Undies item
68. Angler's net
69. Beige shades
70. Prune
71. Job benefits
72. Beer barrel
73. Type spaces

DOWN
1. Chasm
2. Stall
3. More sensible
4. Set of two
5. Travel stops
6. Creche figures
7. Participant
8. Become sick
9. Descend a slope
10. Pekoe, e.g.
11. Infomercials
13. Loin steak
14. Fly alone
20. Naked
22. Understood
24. Scout Carson
26. Conquered
27. Borrow
28. Si and oui
30. Talk
31. Messed up
33. Lawn drops
34. Studio stand
35. Complain
37. Gumbo veggie
39. Carp at
43. Park it
44. Husky's load
45. Convent woman
46. Desire
48. Makes up
50. Lofty homes
52. Galloped
54. Postpone
55. Cook's wear
56. Gains
58. Boulder
59. Confident
61. Cobra's kin
62. Gosh!
63. Tune
64. Pen filler
66. Pester

CAMOUFLAGE

PUZZLE 240

The answers to the clues can be found in the diagram, but they have been camouflaged. Their letters are in correct order, but sometimes they are separated by extra letters that have been inserted throughout the diagram. You must black out all the extra Camouflage letters. Each of the remaining letters will be used in a word reading across and a word reading down. Solve ACROSS and DOWN together to determine the correct letters where there is a choice. The number of answer words in a row or column is indicated by the number of clues.

	1	2	3	4	5	6	7	8	9	10	11	12	13
1	S	T	A	A	T	E	B	T	L	A	S	N	T
2	T	H	R	E	O	N	E	T	E	N	M	O	R
3	R	I	G	H	H	T	H	R	A	I	M	P	N
4	U	B	U	A	N	I	T	E	L	T	E	R	A
5	I	N	V	E	L	R	T	A	S	L	A	D	M
6	C	O	M	M	E	T	E	N	T	E	R	A	P
7	T	H	E	R	M	E	F	D	A	R	O	L	P
8	G	I	N	G	O	H	A	M	D	R	U	L	L
9	R	O	T	A	U	R	T	E	U	N	T	S	O
10	A	G	R	V	E	E	T	A	L	L	P	E	R
11	B	A	K	V	A	I	L	N	E	A	U	R	N
12	S	T	E	E	R	R	C	O	P	P	U	R	E
13	P	E	P	N	T	D	E	T	L	E	T	S	O

ACROSS
1. Utter • Explode
2. King's chair • Choir member
3. Correct • Incline
4. Bring together • Oolong or pekoe
5. Motionless • Shut loudly
6. Remark • Time period
7. Topic • Let fall
8. Checkered cloth • Boring
9. Spin • Do ___ others
10. See eye to eye • Candle
11. Help • Close by
12. Cattle • Untainted
13. Energy • Asian observance • Allows

DOWN
1. Stern • Grab hold of
2. Slim • Cleveland's state • Fence opening
3. Debate • Ribbed fabric
4. Skirt edge • Donated
5. Musical pitch • Beef
6. Whole • Beneficiary
7. Wager • Tell
8. Tendency • Intended
9. Smallest • Swordplay
10. Animal horn • Neck back
11. Smudge • Production
12. Milky gem • Makes mistakes
13. Hobo • Folk knowledge

217

PUZZLE 241

ACROSS
1. Pretend
4. "____ the night before . . ."
8. In the sack
12. Batman and Robin, e.g.
13. Musical symbol
14. South American lasso
15. Wisely
17. Dawn's direction
18. Model's stance
19. Forest filler
20. Bullets, to a GI
23. Memorable periods
26. Grandpa Walton portrayer
27. At the top
28. Sounds of hesitation
31. Hams it up
33. Channel
35. Dispute
36. Slippery
38. Killer whale
39. Take apart
40. Pale
41. Wedding attire
44. Current events
47. Declare frankly
48. Sent payment
52. Play possum
53. Settled
54. Naval agreement
55. Bolted
56. Legend
57. Inky implement

DOWN
1. Magazine spots
2. Billiard stick
3. Coal measurement
4. Singing group
5. Meshes
6. Snoozing
7. Porky's pad
8. Helps a felon
9. Swine
10. Besides
11. Social appointment
16. Baseball or soccer
20. Golden ____ (retiree)
21. Notation
22. Cat's call
24. Bright
25. Aardvark's prey
27. Employed
28. Jug handles
29. Prosperous
30. Linger
32. Still, in poems
34. Swelter
37. "Only the ____"
39. Single
41. Fisherman's hook
42. Egg shape
43. Got up
45. Give off
46. "Gone ____ the Wind"
48. Thrust
49. Faucet
50. View
51. TV room

PUZZLE 242

ACROSS
1. Flower stalk
5. Certain vipers
9. Astern
12. Possess
13. Easy job
14. Podded vegetable
15. Yaks
16. Evil
18. GI's poster
20. Heat outlet
21. Grabbed lunch
23. Hymn finale
27. That woman
30. Guzzle
32. Not yup
33. Spider's lacework
35. Heaps
37. Singer Lane
38. Particle
40. Permit
41. American Beauty, e.g.
42. British brew
43. Farmer's locale?
46. Wacky
51. Courteous
55. Majestic address
56. Make public
57. Boat bottom
58. Amend copy
59. Layer
60. Waves
61. Highway vehicle

DOWN
1. Market
2. Car for hire
3. Tie
4. Restaurant listing
5. Wild donkey
6. Cry
7. Window part
8. Go round and round
9. Fitting
10. Service charge
11. Road stuff
17. "____ by Me"
19. Sheet of paper
22. Band instrument
24. "____ Flanders"
25. Fencer's weapon
26. Cozy spot
27. Cut remnant
28. Tramp
29. Loses intensity
31. Swimming site
34. Overgrown
36. Sign
39. Chatterbox
44. Fraternal group
45. In ____ of (instead of)
47. Applies
48. Ocean surge
49. Take the edge off
50. Sasquatch's cousin
51. Drink like a cat
52. Need aspirin
53. Parched
54. Sprite

DOUBLE TROUBLE

PUZZLE 243

Not really double trouble, but double fun! Solve this puzzle as you would a regular crossword, except place one, two, or three letters in each box. The number of letters in each answer is shown in parentheses after its clue.

ACROSS
1. Peaceful (6)
4. Cattle farmer (7)
7. Hindmost (4)
9. Given a title (5)
10. Very hot (7)
12. Ravine (5)
13. Overflow (4)
14. In one piece (6)
15. Glow with joy (7)
17. Frenzied (7)
19. Provide with food (5)
20. Mansard feature (4)
21. Barrel piece (5)
22. Financier (6)
25. Primary pipe (4)
27. Deal maker (10)
30. Depend (on) (4)
31. Work on a vintage auto (7)
33. MGM's symbol (4)
34. Eat elegantly (4)
36. "What Lies ___" (7)
38. Capable of being held (7)
40. Shirt feature (6)
41. Frost's forte (6)
42. Satiate (4)
44. Chip's buddy (4)
45. Spectator (9)
47. Bona fide (6)
48. Social grace (4)
49. Gave a sly look (6)
50. Just (6)

DOWN
1. Lawmaking body (6)
2. Know by heart (8)
3. Urgent want (4)
4. Turn upside down (7)
5. Play unfairly (5)
6. Drop the ball (3)
7. Oversee (8)
8. Coyly roguish (4)
11. Thankless person (7)
14. Come between (9)
16. Unclean (5)
18. Baltic or Red (3)
19. Admonition (6)
21. Depot (7)
23. Earth's center (4)
24. Exclusively (4)
25. Mustang mamas (5)
26. Keen on (4)
28. He was slain with a stone (7)
29. Run-of-the-mill (8)
32. Resist authority (5)
35. Wyo.'s neighbor (3)
37. In the neighborhood (6)
38. Moved unsteadily (8)
39. Professor's discourse (7)
40. Gather (7)
41. Mull over (6)
43. Solidly (7)
44. Facts and figures (4)
46. Like old bread (5)
47. Wile E. Coyote's brand (4)

Crackerjacks

PUZZLE 244

Find the answer to the riddle by filling in the center boxes with the letters needed to complete the words across and down. When you have correctly filled in the Crackerjacks, the letters reading across the center boxes from left to right will spell out the riddle answer.

RIDDLE: I can travel from there to here by disappearing, and from here to there by reappearing. What am I?

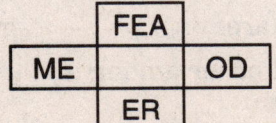
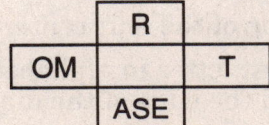

ANSWER: _____

PUZZLE 245

ACROSS
1. Farmer's harvest
5. Baby buggy
9. Pinnacles
14. Roster
15. Indian melody
16. Large deer
17. Frank
19. Flat surface
20. Had brunch
21. Overweight
22. Web surfer
23. Nutmeat
25. Coed's digs
28. Protozoan
31. Bounce on a knee
35. Grind to a halt
38. Mom
40. Pitcher handle
41. Made of a hard wood
43. "Where the Boys ___"
44. Plant swelling
46. Chestnut seedcase
47. Untethered
50. October's stone
51. Withhold food
53. Coral reef
55. Stared at
57. Write down
61. Fashion magazine
64. Vestige
67. Huge
68. Down-under animal
70. Dreaming
72. Wound up
73. Essence
74. Brim
75. Monopoly cards
76. Editor's mark
77. Garden nuisance

DOWN
1. Frog noise
2. Highway
3. Playful animal
4. Faux ___
5. Dilemma
6. Libertine
7. Generations
8. Like a horse
9. Gig gear
10. Pillar
11. Ostrichlike extinct birds
12. Laborer of yore
13. Soothsayer
18. Metered composition
24. Scruff
26. "___ to Joy"
27. Burger order
29. Wild hog
30. Heart chambers
32. Intense
33. Tibetan holy man
34. Epochal
35. Cries
36. Tightly drawn
37. Soup vegetable
39. Hoist
42. ___ blue
45. Fool
48. GPA spoiler
49. This evening
52. Spun
54. Places
56. Trickles
58. Wait
59. Hint
60. ___ on (encouraged)
61. Made do
62. Only
63. Fill the hull
65. Issue
66. After the bell
69. Magazine fillers
71. Brand-___

PUZZLE 246

Mystery Word

There is a six-letter Mystery Word hidden in the diagram. Can you find it in four minutes or less?

O	F	I	K	L	H
N	P	E	A	J	M
E	C	U	I	T	G
R	L	H	B	R	P
V	I	F	L	A	S
T	W	Y	I	X	U

My first letter is directly to the right of the 20th letter of the alphabet.

My second is the only vowel in the diagram to appear just once.

My third is diagonally adjacent to four vowels.

My fourth is in one of the four center squares.

My fifth is the first letter in alphabetical order among all the letters around the edge of the diagram.

My last letter is the only letter to be repeated in a row.

Mystery Word: ___ ___ ___ ___ ___ ___

PUZZLE 247

ACROSS
1. Point gainer
5. Go it alone
9. Vaults
14. Fit
15. Extremely dry
16. Iron block
17. Corporate emblem
18. Narrative
19. Purloined
20. Passenger restraint
22. To be paid
23. "Chances ___"
24. Blood fluid
28. High voice
32. Shuttle plane
35. Mimicked
36. Conductor's tool
38. Crooner Cole
40. "___ My Party"
41. Egg entrees
43. Consumer-protection gp.
44. Set ablaze
45. Merrier
46. Arizona river
47. Shepherd's aide
49. Trooper's prey
52. Advances
54. Wayside hotel
55. Farewell
58. Tape holder
63. Fragrance
65. Posted
66. Track part
67. Initiated
68. Division term
69. Wood splitters
70. Impudent
71. Movie segment
72. Italian money, once
26. Public melee
27. Coffee servers
28. Spinnaker, e.g.
29. Sight-related
30. Pasta sauce
31. Minded
33. Not summoned
34. Black fur
37. Beer kin
39. Skier's lift
41. Stare rudely at
42. Principal
46. Military mogul
48. Andean haulers
50. Revolver, e.g.
51. Type spaces
53. Incident
55. Pub bills
56. Territory
57. Clothes
59. Pot contribution
60. Hired vehicle
61. Bleacher feature
62. Threat word
64. Random choice
65. Polite address

DOWN
1. Guys' dates
2. Wind instrument
3. Pond growth
4. Dancer's garment
5. Lustrous fabric
6. Spoken
7. Sings happily
8. Tribute in verse
9. Spanish article
10. Put in a sepulcher
11. Admit openly
12. Heap
13. Winter slider
21. Two-piece piece
25. Cafe patrons

Suspended Sentence
PUZZLE 248

The words in each vertical column go into the spaces directly below them, but not necessarily in the order they appear. When you have placed all the words in their correct spaces, you will be able to read a quotation across the diagram from left to right.

SAME	SPEECH	TALK	OLD	UNDER	AT
FIRST	ROOF	AND	MANY	FRIENDS	YET
NEVER	MAY	ARE	TWO	YEARS	THE
TWO	MEET	FOR	TOGETHER	OTHERS	

221

PUZZLE 249

CLAPBOARD

In this crossword puzzle all words in the same row or column overlap by one or two letters.

ACROSS
1. Bob Hope, e.g.
8. Cancel out
14. Ham it up
15. Colorful songbird
16. Badman Brown
17. Sherpa sighting
19. Courageous woman
22. "A Chorus Line" finale
24. Crosscurrent
25. Holler
27. Pass on the track
28. Cathedral nook
30. ___-ending
31. Netman Lacoste
33. Crazy ___
35. Good grief!
37. Letters from Greece
38. Bishop's jurisdiction
39. Chapter in history
40. Religious sayings
41. Pennsylvania sect
43. Noah's son
45. Tattoo word, often
47. Nor'easter
49. Relocate
50. O'Neill or Ionesco
51. Envision
53. Animated Chihuahua
54. Blow up
56. Cheerleader's cry
57. Sprayed
59. Be en garde?
61. Go on foot
63. Molecule components
65. ___ palm
66. Milky jewel
67. Golfer Trevino
68. Endangered goose
69. Cochlea site
70. Yank's foe
71. Give a little
72. German article
73. Practical joke
74. Fish features
75. Sailor's instrument

DOWN
1. Army officers
2. It's in your range
3. Simple
4. Wore down
5. Fantasize
6. Rocks
7. Thoughtful
8. Spike
9. School subject
10. Coupe coop
11. Mature
12. "Dick Tracy" girl
13. Highlands language
18. Give the once-over
20. Short-lived
21. Opening word?
23. Meet halfway
24. Zsa Zsa's sister
26. Apartment agreement
29. Potent
32. Grover's pal
34. Trinket
36. Back
37. Gossip
42. Encore!
44. Story-telling dance
46. Least aggressive
47. Pounced
48. ___ Rios, Jamaica
49. Rumple
50. Cover up
52. "My Cousin Vinny" Oscar winner
54. Tiptoes
55. Collect bit by bit
57. Novelist Maxine ___ Kingston
58. Inherited title
60. High point
61. Need
62. "Jake's Women" star
64. Lady Grey, e.g.
65. Erie Canal mule

CODEWORD PUZZLE 250

Instructions for solving Codeword puzzles are given on page 11.

CODEWORD PUZZLE 251

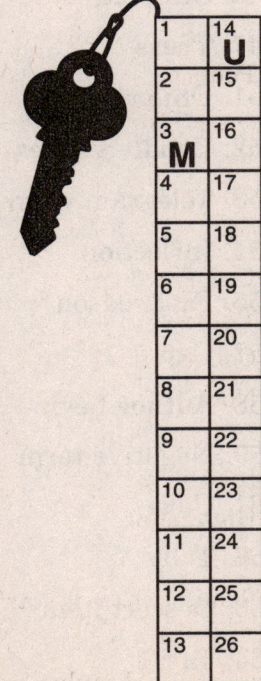

PUZZLE 252

ACROSS
1. Jogger
6. Bosc, e.g.
10. Fastener
14. Come to
15. Diva's song
16. Mama's fellow
17. Foxier
18. Mars
20. Beseech
22. Eradicate
23. Heavenly dish
26. Memorable times
28. Flag holder
29. Rovers
34. Oaf
35. Inaugurated
36. Boring tool
38. Chair part
39. Goes off the track
41. Caspian, e.g.
42. Longing
43. Path
44. Scram!
45. Iowa city
48. Vow
49. Orient
50. Hint at
52. Showy bloom
55. Hawaiian gift
56. Plot
60. Alter
65. Corn bread
66. Press
67. The press
68. Hied
69. Scurry
70. Directory

DOWN
1. Scale notes
2. Barn bird
3. Wages
4. ___ out (just earn)
5. Aired anew
6. Open space
7. Shelley's before
8. Help
9. Tap
10. Meager
11. Grandma
12. Gorillas
13. Party paste
19. Uncovers
21. Noticed
23. Anchored
24. Female grad
25. Court divider
26. Less at ease
27. Actual
28. VCR button
30. Sudden
31. Peachy keen!
32. Scamp
33. Perspiring
37. Wood strip
39. Dismal
40. Geologic ages
44. Drench
46. Swerved
47. Truss
51. Ohio river
52. Deadly snakes
53. Telegram word
54. Inflection
55. Fast season
57. Cap
58. Author Levin
59. Negative term
61. Cave
62. Tally
63. Dessert item
64. Tariff

PUZZLE 253

ACROSS
1. Swimsuit top
4. Ali ___
8. Expenses
13. Diamond ___
14. Drive off
15. Restrict
16. Sternward
17. Plumed wader
18. Evade
19. Whacks
21. Puccini work
23. Fitness area
24. Land
26. Boxing arena
28. Wise bird
29. Chirped
33. Research site
36. Depressions
40. Blur
41. Lode's yield
42. Blacktop
44. Adam's mate
45. "Under ___"
47. For takeout
48. Actor Ayres
49. African tour
51. Fall back
54. Master
56. Niches
60. Shoemaking tool
63. Slalom racer
65. WWII craft
66. Horned mammal
68. Flash
70. Snivel
71. Yule song
72. Put forth
73. Everybody
74. Male elks
75. High schooler
76. Corrosive stuff

DOWN
1. Explosion
2. Long gun
3. Church table
4. Beseech
5. Chef's attire
6. Honk
7. Modify
8. Least dirty
9. Lubricate
10. Arrogant
11. In order
12. Originate
14. Recut, as wood
20. Debate side
22. Tear
25. Ailments
27. Ruby, e.g.
30. Lemon skin
31. Roof extension
32. Sketched
33. Defeat
34. Concert solo
35. Complain
37. Make a choice
38. Which person?
39. Droop
42. Some cans
43. Loiter
46. Maiden
50. Annoy
52. Severe
53. Lump
55. Numeral
56. Stand up
57. Outspoken
58. Not late
59. Elegance
60. Circle sections
61. Huh?
62. Former Roman coin
64. Additionally
67. Yuletide drink
69. Priory female

PUZZLE 254

ACROSS
1. Crate
5. Throb
9. Load
13. Exact
14. ___ puff
15. Health herb
16. Lazy stride
17. Impulsive
19. Fired up
20. Sunbathes
21. Detests
22. Lyric verse
23. Experimental
26. Pricked
28. Candor
32. Eminent conductor
35. Tart's kin
36. Grate
39. Weeder
40. Breathe hard
41. Query
42. Animal trainer
45. Say softly
48. ___ Coast
51. Sky craft
54. Electric fish
56. Markets
59. Bar orders
60. Winter virus
61. Analogy
64. Suffers
65. Not windward
66. Jesse ___
67. Coin taker
68. Look after
69. Bjorn ___
70. Hems

DOWN
1. Bass's kin
2. Shuns
3. Group of seven
4. Compass dir.
5. Don't exist
6. Suspend
7. Held
8. Type measures
9. March
10. Gobs
11. Pine ___
12. Barrels
14. Alter
18. Formerly
20. Albacore, e.g.
24. Tatter
25. Overly
27. Baseball off.
29. Posh resort
30. ___ can
31. Nevertheless
33. Clever
34. Cargo unit
36. Immature
37. Bat wood
38. Slalom
40. Debate side
42. "___ Alibi"
43. Sheets
44. Dusks
46. Exhausted
47. Tower city
49. Grind again
50. Lemon hue
52. Light beam
53. Beside
55. Desires
56. Jazz style
57. Crater
58. Future sign
62. Swindle
63. ___ Jima
64. Wild donkey

PUZZLE 255

ACROSS
1. Rotates
6. Distinct periods
10. Killer whale
14. Dated ditty
15. Charge
16. Chilly
17. "The Most Happy ___"
18. Flushed
19. Furnace fuel
20. Summer quaff
21. Lucky stroke
23. Hearty
24. Me, to Gigi
25. Headliner
27. Filled pasta
31. VI
32. Move about
35. Revise
36. Designate
38. Naked
39. Drill
40. Despised
41. Forget
42. ___ Bunny
43. Public
44. Wake up
45. Fury
46. Stable bit
47. Kitchen item
49. Skirt length
50. Baby louse
51. Face part
54. Not live
57. Sink down
60. Volcano's flow
61. Beaut
62. Elicit
64. Kiln, e.g.
65. Scent
66. Pine product
67. Trial
68. Equal
69. Rock

DOWN
1. Love seat
2. Implored
3. Inactive
4. Nothing
5. Clams, e.g.
6. Hose hue
7. Chess piece
8. Appraisal
9. Pig's abode
10. Happen
11. Kanga's kid, et al.
12. Layer
13. Comrade
22. Diamond ___
23. Not strict
24. Ore pits
26. Secured
27. Jewish title
28. Romance
29. Brink
30. Lack of skill
32. Range
33. Get up
34. Hinder
37. Supped
38. Promote
40. Sham
44. Football team
46. Desk wood
48. Buck
49. Intended
51. Lump
52. Hold
53. Nights before
55. Burn balm
56. Cat sound
57. Average
58. Similar
59. Mr. Wilder
61. Trim
63. Pet doc

PUZZLE 256

ACROSS
1. Potato
5. Great weight
8. Tart
12. Sound
13. Vinegar bottle
15. Commotion
16. Destruction
17. Shabby
18. Tip slightly
19. Play part
20. Rant
21. Dried plums
23. Anyplace
25. Charged atom
26. A Knievel
27. Aerial
31. Consented
34. Sharp turn
35. Above, in poems
36. Bore
37. Clash
38. Bride's man
40. Have a bite
41. Verve
42. Crevice
43. Sniffed
46. Sis's sibs
47. Lend a hand
48. Dawdler
52. Chatted
55. Grassy area
56. Cured salmon
57. Withdraw
58. Catch on
60. Auto's spare
61. Female singer
62. Roof edges
63. By any chance
64. Big jump
65. Crimson
66. Tidy

DOWN
1. Soda sipper
2. Sack
3. Join
4. Bear's cave
5. Take a trip
6. Exterior
7. Fisherman's tool
8. Harmonize
9. Penny, e.g.
10. Resting
11. Specks
13. Yearned for
14. Emulating a secretary
20. Frolic
22. Decompose
24. Film spool
27. Telecast
28. Midnight's opposite
29. Broadway sign
30. Service branch
31. Summer drinks
32. Metric mass
33. Sacrament
34. Strike suddenly
37. Get hitched
38. Matured
39. Rough file
41. Sell
42. Tiaras
44. Compact computer
45. Invention
46. Bellowed
48. Work hard
49. Oily fruit
50. Asian land
51. Put forth
52. Legitimate
53. Shaft
54. Pocket bread
59. Cup handle
60. Boxing count

PUZZLE 257

ACROSS
1. Bygone
5. Fruit beverages
9. Avoids food
14. Voice range
15. Salad fish
16. WWII craft
17. Pack away
18. Fall faller
19. Cuban dance
20. Blacktop
21. Scoundrel
23. Exam
24. Stadiums
26. Stumbles
28. Parodied
30. Great rage
31. "The ___ Squad"
34. Out of
37. Piglet's mother
39. Show up
41. Defame in print
43. Foil metal
45. Award pin
46. Loves
48. Pester
50. Mound
51. Little
52. Kind of evergreen
54. Toll road
56. Purse handle
58. Distant
62. Otherwise
65. Constant
67. Habitual manner
68. Nutty birds
70. Dog's wagger
71. Poker term
72. ___ up (botch)
73. Skin condition
74. Look slyly
75. Buying frenzy
76. Court dividers
77. Slips up

DOWN
1. Manicotti, e.g.
2. Priest's platform
3. Market
4. Pull behind
5. Map books
6. Club fees
7. Pass, as a law
8. African adventure
9. Canine coat
10. Borders on
11. Any
12. Flaps
13. Immediately, in medicine
21. Hip-hop music
22. Italian money, once
25. Title giver
27. Salon treatment
29. Polka ___
31. Skirt type
32. Track shape
33. Small valley
34. Blemish
35. Carousel, e.g.
36. Reed instrument
38. Prevail
40. Alter slacks
42. Exited
44. Doze off
47. Noblemen
49. Corsets
53. Wicker material
55. Lock opener
56. Hunch
57. Calmness
59. Proprietor
60. Spud
61. Watchers
62. House wings
63. Noose
64. Sweet and ___
66. "___ No Sunshine"
69. Look at
71. Beer's kin

PUZZLE 258

CRISS-CROSSWORD

The answer words for Criss-Crossword are entered diagonally, reading downward, from upper left to lower right or from upper right to lower left. We have entered the words COOP and FOB as examples.

TO THE RIGHT

1. Chicken home
2. Grippe
3. Office machine
4. Male swan
5. Place
6. Australian mammal
7. Grassy expanse
9. Tulip start
11. Silt deposit
12. Pair
16. Piquancy
18. Smack
19. Canvas sheet
22. Offshore
23. Ilium
25. Tastier
27. Twilled cloth
29. Tartan
30. Drive out
34. Necessity
36. Deli side
37. Gym wing

TO THE LEFT

2. Watch chain
3. Cumulus
4. Unit of verse
5. Soak through
6. Chat
7. Fate
8. Boyfriend
10. Unfortunately
13. Sheep
14. World holder
15. Boring
17. Flushed
20. Allay
21. Journey
24. Fall fruit
26. Commotion
28. Endure
31. Hill
32. Shoelace tip
33. Hay bundle
35. Think
38. Sound receiver

PUZZLE 259

ACROSS

1. "___ So Cold"
5. Ladder step
9. Wails
13. Employ
14. Indian dwelling
15. Hunch
16. Distantly
17. Former Ford model
18. Sports group
19. Fired
21. Magazine edition
22. Frequently, to Keats
23. Look after
25. Felt
28. More boring
32. Jazz instrument, for short
33. Informant
35. Wept
37. Twining plants
40. Name
42. ___ shuttle
43. Secondhand
45. Picked up
47. Cut wood
48. Wanders away
50. Snoozing
53. Presidential refusal
55. Coop female
56. School mark
60. Swamp dweller
65. Cuckoo
66. Direct
67. Long skirt
68. Not shut
69. Arm joint
70. 24th letters
71. Cribs
72. Corrosive liquids
73. "A Chorus ___"

DOWN

1. Herringlike fish
2. Music system
3. Important ages
4. Sunday lecture
5. Stoplight colors
6. Angry
7. Required
8. Styling aid
9. Rests
10. Some poems
11. Boyfriend
12. Identical
14. Examiner
20. No ___, ands, or buts
21. Lazes
24. Cashew, e.g.
25. Goalies' goals
26. Live
27. Mom's mate
29. ___ dog
30. Clear a cassette
31. Brief review
32. ___ Lancelot
34. Yank
36. Lawn droplets
38. Corn piece
39. Unpaid toiler
41. Large snake
44. Gawk
46. Casual garment
49. Like the night sky
51. Drumstick
52. Tooth coating
54. Dated ditty
56. Small drop
57. Lasso cord
58. Served for a point
59. Wears
61. Smaller amount
62. City vehicle
63. Yoked beasts
64. Grow
66. Hooting bird

PUZZLE 260

ACROSS
1. Glory
5. Iranian ruler
9. Bound
13. False god
14. Winter drink
16. Spindle
17. Provoke
18. Regretting
19. Autograph
20. Coral, e.g.
21. More difficult
22. ASAP, on "ER"
23. Rutabaga, e.g.
25. Id's kin
27. Poetic works
29. Visit
30. Pig's place
33. Took a dip
36. Chamber
38. Blazing
40. Arctic
42. Dumbfound
43. Repeat
44. Weaken
45. Bank (on)
47. Neckline shapes
48. Damp
49. TV breaks
51. Loaf
53. Cool drink
54. Breakfast food
58. Small change
61. Dress
65. Named at birth
66. In the know
67. Check accounts
68. Coastal bird
69. Destiny
70. Soup server
71. Within
72. Linen source
73. PC operator
74. Farewells

DOWN
1. Foremost
2. Sayonara
3. Wisdom tooth
4. Actress Keats
5. Ice remover
6. Clock cycle
7. Lab fluid
8. Sharpen
9. Lariat
10. Way out
11. Pond growth
12. ___-up
15. Assent
21. Cached
24. Wanderer
26. Cogwheel
28. Flies high
29. Scent
30. Parent
31. Factual
32. Yearns
33. Erupt
34. Donned
35. Gobs
37. Have a debt
39. Cabin ___
41. Recite
46. Pleasure-boat man
50. Transfer
52. Zorro's mark
53. Ell
55. Adversary
56. Lofty abode
57. Advances
58. Sleeve part
59. Fiery gem
60. Mite
62. Oahu feast
63. Chances
64. Clay square
68. Pocket flap

PUZZLE 261

ACROSS
1. Redden
6. Long fish
9. Rage
12. Pound part
13. Epics
15. Mr. Gershwin
16. Caves
17. Queen's headgear
18. Negative
19. Ballet skirt
20. War god
21. Wipe out
23. Exposed
25. Antenna
26. Stereo component
29. Raven's call
30. Standard
31. Mink's cousin
33. Wooden nail
34. Skillful
38. Radiates
39. Viewed
40. Ponder
41. Dimwit
42. Relatives
43. Beach sight
44. Computer operator
46. Tool set
47. Rent
48. Ill-behaved
51. Apple drink
53. Ranch rope
54. Extensions
55. Canyon sound
59. Bible craft
60. Of yore
62. Paddled
63. Last letter
64. Equals
65. Cherish
66. Always, in verse
67. Pen's fluid
68. Input errors

DOWN
1. Take off
2. Poi party
3. Army group
4. Scour
5. Males
6. Like some seals
7. Selves
8. Statute
9. Ultimate
10. Got up
11. Library stamp
13. Fastener
14. Show scorn
20. Asia's ___ Sea
22. Comment
24. Crackerjacks
25. Heavy mist
26. Flabbergasted
27. Office note
28. Reimbursed
30. Unused
32. Pub brews
33. Shallow pot
35. Bubble
36. Only
37. Rework, as text
39. Guy's title
40. Morsel
42. Lock opener
43. Auction offers
45. Small porch
46. Pottery ovens
48. Fire
49. Street show
50. Inquirer
51. Salesperson
52. All set
54. Eve's abode
56. Farm yield
57. Leading man
58. Keats poems
61. Flower garland
62. Cookie grain

PUZZLE 262

ACROSS
1. Make raw
5. Bears' feet
9. Soda flavor
13. Audition aim
14. Go to see
15. Head ___ heels
16. Segment
17. Cello, e.g.
19. Rowdy crowd
20. Fri. follower
21. Alters
22. Lively
24. Dozed
26. ___ detector
28. Set (down)
29. Auction cry
33. Adrift
36. Turn aside
38. Dawn to dusk
39. Steamer, e.g.
40. Do well
42. "The Twilight ___"
43. Possesses
44. Fix up
45. Ticks off
46. "Bright ___"
48. Swimsuit top
49. Long time
51. Reef substance
53. Stage performer
57. Evade
60. Punch
62. Fish eggs
63. Uttered suddenly
66. Fog
67. Dull fellow
68. Ranch guests
69. Chilled
70. Went quickly
71. Installs turf
72. Chaos

DOWN
1. Bread bit
2. Esteem
3. Suspect's excuse
4. Fido, e.g.
5. Half a quart
6. Stubborn animal
7. Cleverness
8. Boulevard
9. Heavenly bodies with tails
10. Cake baker
11. ___ a hand (help)
12. Martial ___
14. Through
18. Ref's cousin
20. Use snow runners
23. ___ dunk
24. ___ delivery
25. Baited
27. Adam's mate
30. Perfume
31. Slender
32. Colors the hair
33. Tooth pain
34. Do in, as a dragon
35. Let up on
37. Spare
41. Drain-opener chemical
42. Metallic element
47. Fearful
48. Reproduces
50. Certain grain
52. Pick
54. Copy
55. Drips
56. Marsh stalks
57. Diminishes
58. Pig's lunch
59. Successful treatment
60. Tones
61. ___ in the bag!
64. Batman and Robin, e.g.
65. Bizarre
66. Not her

PUZZLE 263

ACROSS
1. Demean
6. Papa
9. Festoons
14. Sail supports
15. Personality part
16. Howdy!
17. Petitions
18. T-man
19. Ta ta
20. Fabric joint
21. Like a fence gate
23. Mover's ride
24. Put on a coat
26. Ward (off)
27. Mule's father
30. Poetic form
31. Ready to eat
33. Scribble
34. Embarrassed
35. Activator
39. Soaring
41. Troll
42. Mend, in a way
45. Which lady?
47. Zilch
48. Employer
49. Swindled
50. Boar's abode
51. Not up yet
54. Arms depot
57. ___ Juan
58. Overjoyed
59. Pond plant
63. Gang
65. Tiny amount
66. Bedeck
67. Leered
68. Ailing
69. Parade entry
70. Irritable
71. Third letter
72. Is inclined

DOWN
1. Hi-fi units
2. Bundle
3. Confused
4. Postal seal
5. Tee preceder
6. Described
7. FBI member
8. Los Angeles nine
9. Roe producer
10. Married
11. Vibrant
12. Gather
13. Utterance
21. Disguise
22. Censor
25. Main vessels
26. Forest growth
27. Cracked open
28. One and only
29. Load
32. Eastern temple
36. Coal measures
37. Give out
38. Bank (on)
40. Quarrel
43. Baby beef
44. Irregular
45. Cajole
46. Assistance
51. Tie type
52. Canal sight
53. Organic compounds
55. Trite
56. Soup scoop
58. Crosscurrent
60. Water bird
61. Alum
62. Army insects
64. Moist
66. Behind

PUZZLE 264

FLOWER POWER

Instructions for solving Flower Power puzzles are given on page 94.

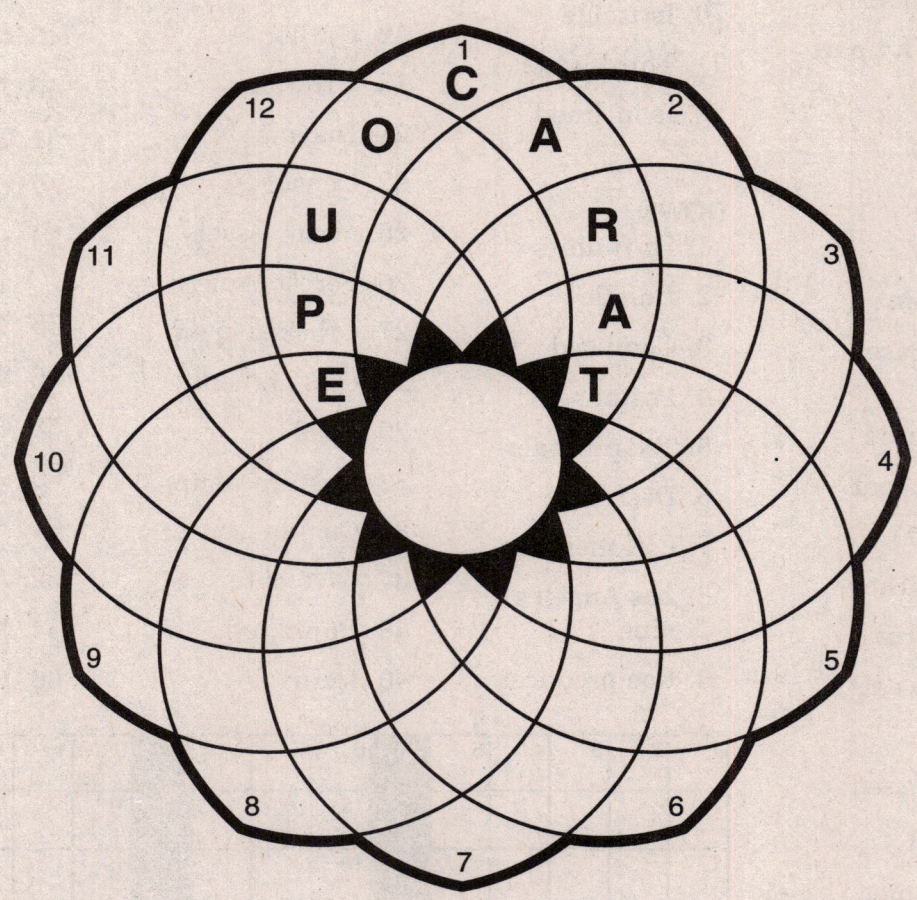

CLOCKWISE

1. Gem measure
2. The ones here
3. Drink noisily
4. Grouchy
5. Pursuit
6. Salesperson
7. Lifting device
8. "___ Suite"
9. Grumble
10. Energetic
11. Noise
12. Strength

COUNTERCLOCKWISE

1. Car style
2. Golden brown
3. Rip
4. Transparent
5. Loaf's outer surface
6. Small task
7. Fastening device
8. Push
9. Fierce look
10. Joke
11. Nab
12. Dad

PUZZLE 265

ACROSS
1. Chills
5. Snoozes
9. Rug type
13. Display
14. Adage
15. Yarn
16. Director Wertmuller
17. Ring
18. Peer
19. Rapture
21. Light tan
23. Twitch
24. Glided
27. Gazelle
32. Lace hole
34. Learned
35. Scheduled
37. Ramble
38. Motor disk
39. Pod legume
40. Card spot
41. Historical ages
43. Solid
45. ___ Arnaz
46. Cancel
48. Announced
50. Break
52. Flight
53. Comet part
54. Competent
58. Besides
61. Raw-fish dish
63. Tackle
64. Nasty look
65. More loyal
66. Jug handles
67. Chapel seats
68. Spout
69. Fellow

DOWN
1. Capri, e.g.
2. Fashionable
3. Geologic ages
4. Whacked
5. Never
6. Tree chopper
7. Longs for
8. Slapped
9. More sturdy
10. Old witch
11. Fully
12. Goodness!
14. Team's symbol
20. Hurt
22. Beam of light
25. Runaway groom
26. Contrive
27. Bent
28. Closer
29. Mexican food
30. Peace ___
31. Correct
33. Warm
36. Leisure
42. Zones
43. Ceases
44. Rich pastry
45. Marred
47. Pekoe, e.g.
49. Race unit
51. Drink noisily
54. Nibble
55. Suitor
56. Hog fat
57. Celtic
58. High peak
59. Bruce ___
60. Darn
62. Bring to court

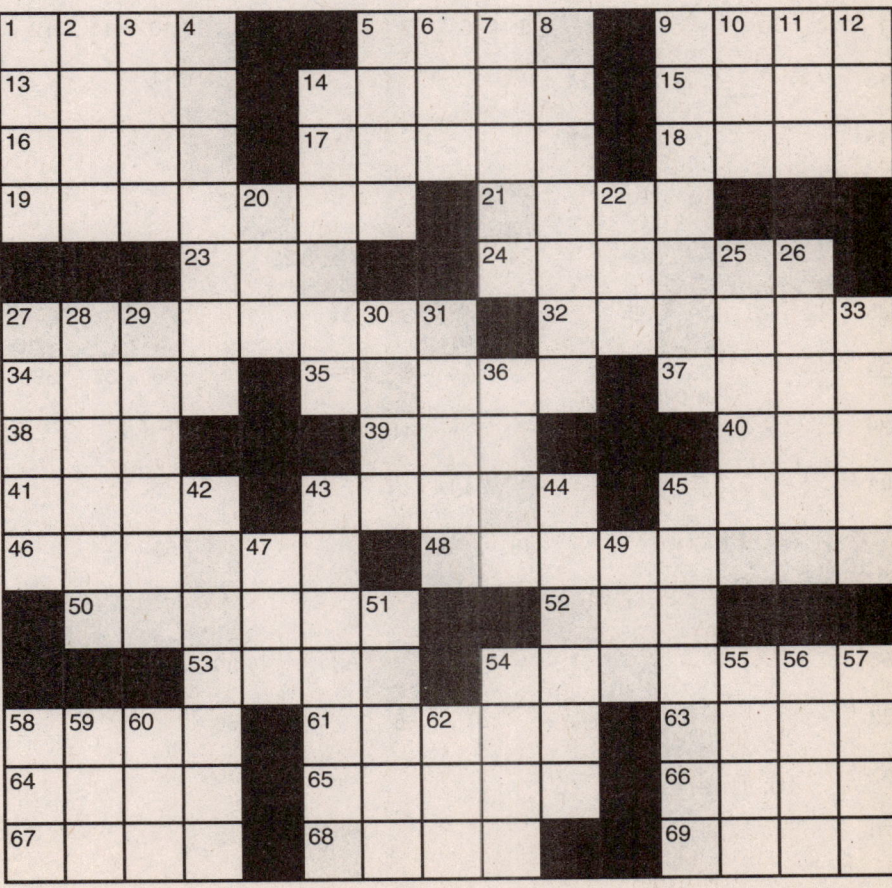

PUZZLE 266

ACROSS
1. Confused
5. Observe
10. Stipulations
13. Submit
14. Entertain
15. Stag's mate
16. Deck wood
17. Text reviser
18. Metal source
19. Emphasize
21. Drumstick
22. Snow toy
23. Thin cookie
25. Overgrown
26. Duffel ___
29. Pub order
30. Top-billed
32. Circus tumblers
35. Fasten
39. Beat
40. Makes cookies
42. Resonate
43. Soup bean
45. Inside
47. Thought
49. Aggravate
50. Poetic before
51. Choir voices
54. Vogue
56. Jan & ___
57. Sault ___ Marie
58. Accompany
63. Road guide
64. Wall paintings
66. Fine
67. Blvd.
68. Wipes off
69. Expedition
70. Mr. Flanders
71. "Scrubs" actress
72. Sensible

DOWN
1. Dabs
2. Aid
3. Phobia
4. Tot
5. Marry
6. Nimble
7. Spuds
8. Plug up
9. "___ Alibi"
10. Heroes
11. Golf cries
12. Filthy
14. Like some used cars
20. Popeye's mop
22. Classifier
24. Greek cheese
25. Gym pad
26. Sob
27. Dull pain
28. Wide smile
31. Bland
33. Choice
34. Snow blade
36. Teen trouble
37. Blacken
38. Gap
41. Jealousy
44. Psyche parts
46. Former mates
48. Off target
51. Promo writer
52. Exit
53. Recorded
55. Kid
57. Certain
59. Army beds
60. Gumbo veggie
61. Downpour
62. Kind
64. French sea
65. "___ Miserables"

PUZZLE 267

ACROSS
1. Radar spot
5. Game callers
9. Shore up
14. Bakery item
15. Egg-shaped
16. Halos
17. Car part
18. Subtractions
20. Orange drink
22. Pitching stat
23. Uncovered
24. Sew loosely
27. Pigpen
29. Bro's sib
30. Pipe type
31. Hornet
35. Had debts
37. Ticket end
39. Average grade
40. Unpaid
41. Roman garb
42. Thus
44. Persian title
48. Small gulf
50. Habit wearer
51. Current
52. Make ready
54. Bigfoot's cousin
56. Not near
57. Expense
58. Young lad
61. Scale
63. Ornate fabric
65. Triumphed
67. Victory sign
68. Glossy-coated plates
71. Mr. Egoyan
75. Of sound
76. Release
77. Bird or fruit
78. Strict
79. Limbs
80. Shout

DOWN
1. Undies top
2. Cured salmon
3. Unwell
4. Kilt fold
5. Motored
6. Seth's mom
7. Dissolve
8. Slanders
9. Cave flier
10. Demolish
11. Excite
12. "___ Camera"
13. Snaky curves
19. House pet
21. Lawn droplets
24. Optimum
25. Female voice
26. Punch
28. "___ Send Me"
32. Sore
33. Behold
34. Cent
36. Mae ___
38. Movie swine
40. Ding
43. Reminder
45. Music system
46. Early man
47. Thyme, e.g.
49. Capable
52. ___ butter
53. Built again
55. Solid water
57. Fido's bane
59. Hole punch
60. Peg
62. Holey
64. Arab bigwig
66. Label
67. Pet docs
69. Geologic age
70. Fit out
72. Secure
73. Night hunter
74. Acad. type

PUZZLE 268

AM I BLUE?

ACROSS
1. Kissers
5. Medium's card
10. Roaring-lion co.
13. Polite address
17. Field
18. Greek market
19. Tycoon Onassis
20. Pelvis portions
21. Blue shade
23. D.C. denizen
24. Toy figure
25. Involve
26. Crusader's foe
28. High home
29. Kindled
31. Cacophony
32. Reply to the Little Red Hen
34. Blue shade
39. Layer's output
41. Squirm
45. Writer Waugh
46. Axis
48. Fish group
49. Pares
51. Self-regard
52. Ostrich's kin
54. Caesar dressing?
55. Sub staple
57. Athenian vowel
59. Far-out!
62. Soissons salt
63. Blue shade
67. Catchall abbr.
70. Ref's call
71. In the manner of
72. Plebe's response
77. Fellow
79. Negative word
82. Part of Q and A
84. Lasso
85. Farm implement
88. Repeats from memory
91. Golf's Norman
92. Torrent
93. Rhine whine
94. Blue shade
96. Clothes line
98. The NRC replaced it
100. Refrain opener
101. Male cats
104. Quick-drying paint
107. Comes up
112. ___ B'rith
113. Dundee denial
114. Blue shade
116. Diva Gluck
117. Spanish cheer
118. Modern missive
119. Ceramic slab
120. Actor O'Neal
121. For shame!
122. Sandwich shops
123. Humdinger

DOWN
1. Fine net
2. Mangle
3. Saucy
4. Yemeni capital
5. Counts up
6. In the past
7. Tiffs
8. Companion of Artemis
9. Lingered
10. Not fem.
11. Raw
12. Small swimmers
13. Blue shade
14. Century plant
15. Is sick
16. Milk drink
22. Stuff
27. Perspective
30. Cassette
33. It's beyond your control
34. Bottle tops
35. Ancient Greek city
36. Stagger
37. USC rival
38. Niamey's country
40. Treasure
42. Sticky substances
43. Theater section
44. Mideast flier
47. ___ bene
50. Filth
53. Swiss canton
56. Sort
58. Medical org.
60. To some extent
61. A few bucks?
64. Cargo measure
65. Asia's ___ Mountains
66. Spouts off

PUZZLE 268

67. Lover of Narcissus
68. Comparison term
69. Singer Vicki ___
73. Show relief
74. Delhi wrap
75. Road to Rome
76. Tantrum
78. Blue shade
80. Mouths
81. Summary
83. Throne
86. Sugar suffix
87. Bric-a-brac stand
89. Chirped
90. Stretches out
95. Combining form for "equal"
97. Lunch and dinner
99. Thick liqueur
101. Stowe tow
102. Sole
103. Cradle cry
105. Gentle
106. Inland sea
108. Hooked on
109. Hide
110. Cherbourg she
111. Psychic
115. Three, to Cato

PUZZLE 269

12 INCHES

ACROSS

1. Mario Batali, e.g.
5. 1/8 of an ounce
9. Slant
13. Renovate
14. African antelope
15. Ms. Falco
16. Jason's ship
17. Concentrate
18. Fog
19. Convene
20. Hassock
22. Villain
24. Furious
25. Disdains
27. Consistent
28. Phoned
29. Escape
30. Gamble
33. In the thick of
34. Smash into
35. Blaze
36. D.C. figure
37. Equitable
39. Impassive
41. Saharan
42. Supplicate
43. Sequence
45. Jacket
46. Treadle
49. Dub
53. Pause
54. Precise
55. Gula
56. Termite, e.g.
57. "___ Marner"
58. Shred
59. Colony critters
60. Stride
61. Guitarist Duane ___

DOWN

1. Squeeze
2. In this place
3. Sharpness
4. Secure position
5. Salivates
6. Puerto ___
7. Border on
8. Letter
9. Wail
10. Dolt
11. Pathway
12. Pair
14. Insult
21. Aspen, e.g.
23. Before, to Shelley
25. Equal
26. Crop
27. Type of wood
28. Sedan, e.g.
29. Removed
30. Defraud
31. Canal of song
32. Mr. Knight
34. Disburden
35. Explanatory comment
37. Worry
38. Like a vacuum
39. Horse's noises
40. Power org.
41. Embraces
42. Polar mass
43. A lot
44. Perch
47. Leave
48. Singer Jerry ___
50. Ancient
51. Honey liquor
52. Weird
53. Health resort

PUZZLE 270

FORECASTS?

ACROSS

1. Rugged ridge
6. Voyaging
10. Health ___
13. Effusive
14. Bearing
15. Tory opponent
16. Come after
17. Wayside et al.
18. Bee home
19. Witnessed
20. Skittish
21. Temptress
22. ___ Lama
24. Shiny leather
25. Say again
28. Murphy costar
30. Warning
31. Soil sweetener
32. Bank holding
36. Dr. Evil's ___-Me
37. Actress Braga
38. Ames locale
39. Quaker leader
40. Southern senator
41. Endora portrayer
42. Chart
44. Bogart film
45. Game song
48. Tennis champ
50. Got along
51. Black bird
52. Wine valley
56. ___-the-counter
57. Ambition
58. Italian city
59. Oboe need
60. Mine entry
61. Ratify
62. "ER" trains
63. Forbids
64. Concur

DOWN

1. Mellows
2. Norse poem
3. Latin verb
4. Woody Herman band
5. Storm center
6. Buddha of paradise
7. 1952 musical
8. Counting word?
9. Reply to a ques.
10. English county
11. "Entourage" actor
12. Broker
15. Reynolds film
20. Annex
21. Posed (for)
23. High, in music
24. ___-bargain
25. Sloping walk
26. Laureate Wiesel
27. Neighbor of Ky.
29. Exclude
31. Encircle
33. Hebrides isle
34. Jug
35. Houston gp.
37. Bridge coup
41. Swiss river
43. Sunburned
44. Darn
45. Earlier, once
46. Orange type
47. Kilmer poem
49. Power units
51. Finale
53. Of wings
54. Cadence
55. Kitty food
57. Talk idly
58. ___ culpa

PUZZLE 271

• BEYOND •

ACROSS
1. Windy curve
4. Hockey great
7. Formerly
11. Road-map abbr.
12. Cheney, e.g.
14. Ten: pref.
15. Guile
16. Nobelist Wiesel
17. Rocker Ant ___
18. Wee one
19. Nevada city
20. Pack animal
21. Exceed
23. French pronoun
24. Lake or Canal
25. Minimum
28. ___ de deux
30. Night before
31. Affirm
34. Digests
37. Peg
38. Veto
42. Pup ___
44. Indicator
45. Cusp
46. Caesar's way
47. Certain dancer
48. Fruit drink
49. Network
50. Jazzy Fitzgerald
51. Born
52. Gaelic
53. Cato's "but"
54. Bitter vetch

DOWN
1. Byron's Muse
2. Tried
3. Irish ___
4. Out of the country
5. Rent again
6. French queen
7. Waxed cheese
8. Bring down
9. Climbs
10. Most docile
13. Folks
22. Primed
26. Glut
27. Erode
29. Cloy
31. Garb
32. Seesaw
33. Beliefs
35. New Orleans university
36. Baseball pitch
39. Stringed instruments
40. Bald bird
41. Dueling blades
43. Ash, e.g.

PUZZLE 272

• A DIFFERENT DRUMMER •

ACROSS
1. Jolt
5. Boys
9. Barrier
12. Israeli airline
13. Final notice
14. One ___ kind
15. Lab burner
16. Sleuth Wolfe
17. Siouan
18. Beatles drummer
21. Curtain raiser?
22. Ms. Tan
24. "Mona ___"
28. Highland denial
29. Genesis drummer
33. Stimpy's cohort
34. Dormant
35. Rowing blade
36. Witnesses
40. Latin jazz drummer
45. Cheer
47. Wyatt ___
48. Fees
50. Lode load
51. Wearing loafers
52. Probabilities
53. Burrow
54. Tokyo wrestler
55. "Batman" portrayer

DOWN
1. Drone
2. Extreme
3. Overly zealous
4. Factory
5. ___ avail
6. Vigoda et al.
7. Grime
8. Greek porch
9. Porter
10. Astern
11. ___ Tse-tung
19. Fish part
20. Madras queen
23. Surely
25. Henri's "here"
26. Turf
27. 100%
29. Expert
30. Idolater
31. Crucifix letters
32. ___ majesty
37. Grant
38. Musical piece
39. Kernels
41. Hardy girl
42. Honolulu's site
43. Senior event
44. Hairstyle
45. Reel's mate
46. "We ___ the World"
49. Boom-maker

FOUR-MOST

PUZZLE 273

All of the 4-letter entries in this crossword puzzle are listed separately and are in alphabetical order. Use the numbered clues as solving aids to help you determine where each 4-letter entry goes in the diagram.

4 LETTERS

AGON
AGUE
AIDE
ALEE
ALMS
AMMO
ARIL
ATLE
CART
EARN
EAST
EVOE
FILE
FRAT
HANG
IDLE
IRIS
LEER
MIND
MISS
MOAT
MUTE
NERD
OATH
OLEO
OVEN
PAIR
PEEN
RISK
SAFE
SAKE
SERE
SETA
SLED
SLOP
STOA
TEAR
TERN
TIDE
TOOL

ACROSS

9. Radio offering
16. Met offering
19. Moving about
20. "___ My Party"
21. Clearings
24. Grenadier
26. Tiny colonist
28. Funny Philips
29. Pastry vendor
37. Without gender
39. Pub beverage
40. French book
42. Be unwell
43. Gift recipient
45. Bard's work
46. Knave
50. Nib
52. Stetson or bowler
54. Ruby-colored
55. Make blonder
62. Erase
65. Literary collection
66. Jeweler's glass
70. Sailor's pal
73. Cordwood measure

DOWN

1. Part of a flight
2. Main artery
3. Impose fraudulently
4. Add-on shape
5. 1,000 squared
6. Standard of excellence
9. Ostrichlike bird
10. Overturns
21. Slangy leg
29. Made
48. Solidify
51. Appropriate
53. Birthday number
55. Intense beam
56. Eurasian forest
57. Boredom
58. Consumer advocate
67. Needle's hole
69. Atlas chart

PUZZLE 274

• CREATIVE TYPES •

ACROSS
1. Feels poorly
5. Gush
9. ___ in the bud
12. Sherbet portion
14. Exploding star
15. Morse, for one
16. Truce negotiator
18. Property attachment
19. Slangy negative
20. Travelers' needs
21. Changes
24. Long-billed sandpiper
26. Rector's house
27. It's in a blind
28. Quiet
31. Campus military gp.
32. Asian peninsula
34. ___ port in a storm
35. Rainbow
36. Make lace
37. Young fox
38. Cheer
39. Faith
42. Jo's sister
43. Shade tree
44. Verve
45. Dote on
47. ___ Ababa
49. From side to side
50. Carbon fuels
52. Pocket bread
53. Prophetic sign
54. Seamstress
60. Papa on "Mama"
61. Partner of void
62. Action place
63. Naval off.
64. Pot builder
65. Ogled

DOWN
1. Dangerous snake
2. Drink cube
3. Mauna ___
4. Coll. course
5. Breaks sharply
6. Jab
7. Night before
8. "The Winds of ___"
9. Party favors
10. Notion
11. Ink-users
13. Sean and William
15. Hockey infraction
17. Data converter
20. Resume
21. Without standards
22. Cupids
23. Letter abbr.
24. Blackboard
25. Vote against
27. Destroyed
29. Brings together
30. Fable
31. Cooking order
33. Map book
39. Floral sites
40. Yale man
41. Information
42. Halloween word
46. Stage offering
48. Lions' homes
49. Bride's walkway
50. Songwriter Porter
51. Muscat's land
52. Hide
54. Identity-clue inits.
55. Move fast
56. How ___ you?
57. Lock opener
58. Opposite of WSW
59. X-ray unit

PUZZLE 275

Crossroads

Fill in the squares of each diagram to form a compound word or phrase. One part of the answer reads across, and the other part reads down. The first part may be in either the across or the down boxes. Use only the letters given above the diagram. The letter shown in the diagram is shared by both parts of the answer.

1. A A E F I N N O R U W

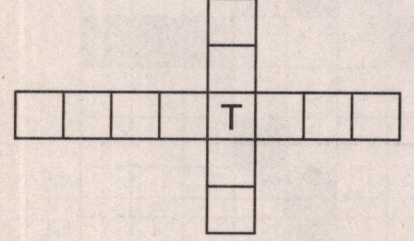

2. C C K N R W

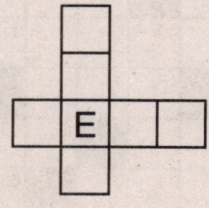

3. A A B D E I K L M N S U

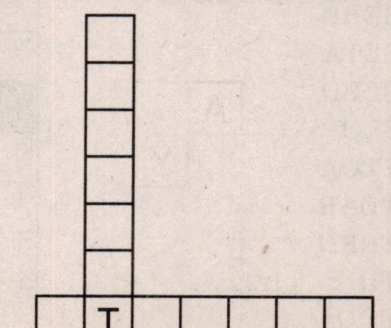

DOUBLE TROUBLE

PUZZLE 276

Not really double trouble, but double fun! Solve this puzzle as you would a regular crossword, except place one, two, or three letters in each box. The number of letters in each answer is shown in parentheses after its clue.

ACROSS
1. Cease (4)
3. Steel, e.g. (5)
5. Under (7)
8. Drawing (12)
10. Plain-spoken (10)
12. Swerve (4)
13. Steady gaze (5)
14. Mukluk (4)
15. Frankness (7)
17. Chat (8)
19. Must-have (4)
20. Bog fuel (4)
21. Ferocious (6)
22. Supper (4)
24. Doorway (8)
26. Halloween garb (7)
28. Thick carpet (4)
29. Golf club (6)
30. Seemingly (5)
32. Dream (4)
34. Influence (8)
36. Stark (7)
37. God of thunder (4)
38. Climb (4)
39. Butter square (3)
40. Strengthen (9)
43. Emerge (11)
46. Flower organ (6)
47. Fender flaw (4)
48. Ship's pole (4)

DOWN
1. Motionless (5)
2. Creative work (4)
3. Occupation (6)
4. Eagle's claw (5)
5. Train bunk (5)
6. Adjacent (4)
7. Femur (9)
9. Mockery (8)
10. Eternally (7)
11. Hauled (5)
13. Body position (6)
15. Famous diamond (4)
16. Make orderly (6)
17. Compel (6)
18. School term (8)
21. Get by trickery (7)
23. Styptic substance (4)
25. Rubbish (5)
26. Bungalow (7)
27. Liken (6)
29. Handbag (5)
31. Royal address (4)
32. Amid (6)
33. Stubbiest (8)
35. Confirm (6)
36. Italy neighbor (7)
39. ___ leather (6)
41. Appoint (4)
42. Moral crime (3)
43. Fashioned (4)
44. Flat bean (4)
45. Gusto (4)

Blockbuilders

PUZZLE 277

Fit the letter blocks into the diagram to spell out the name of a famous actress.

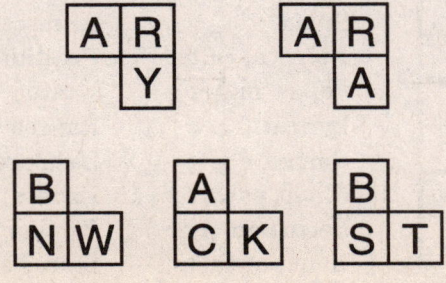
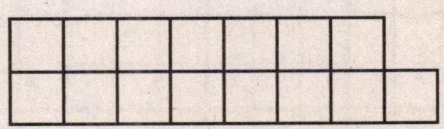

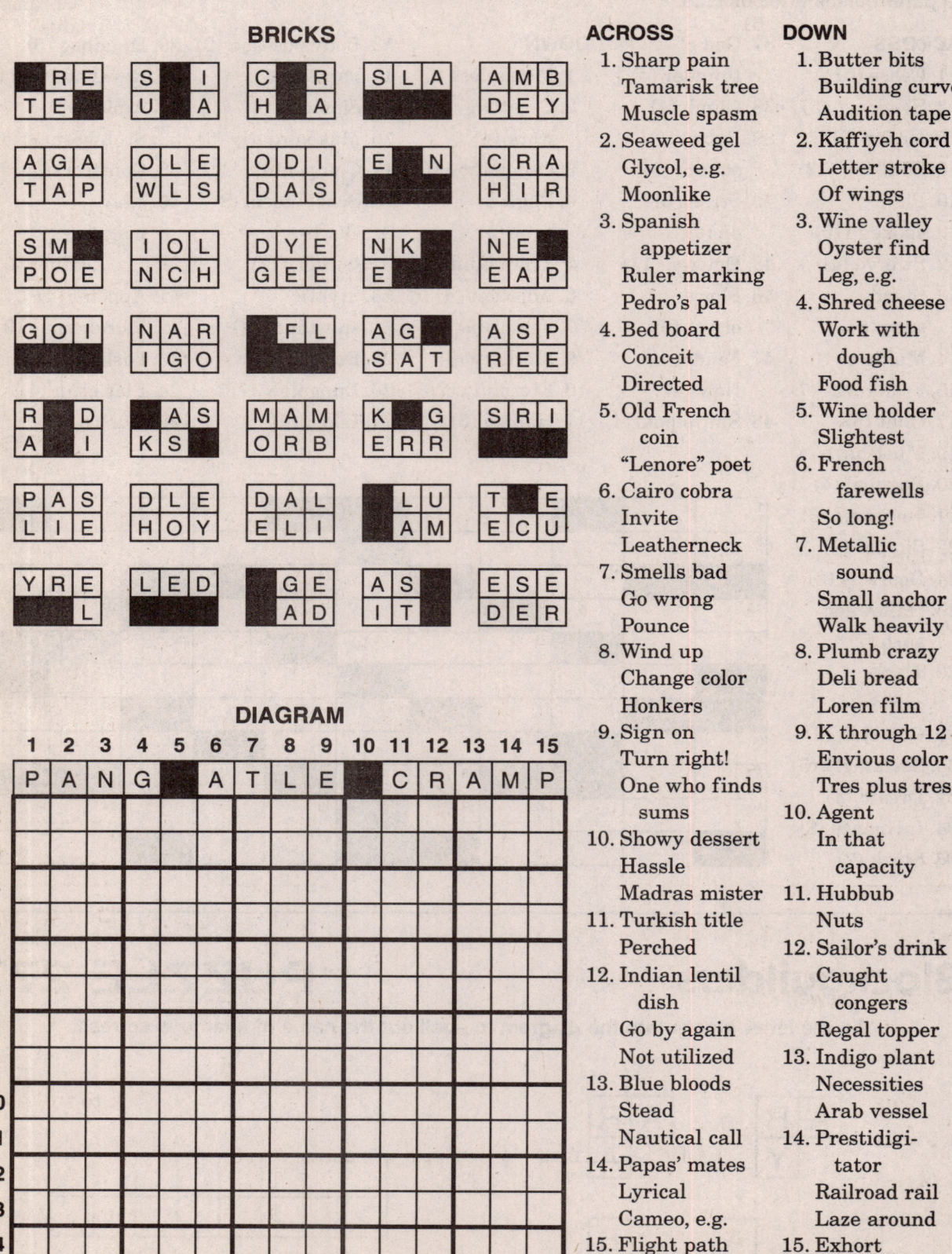

PUZZLE 279

• ROUGHHOUSING •

ACROSS
1. Terrain
5. Panza of "Don Quixote"
11. Line of fashion
14. Of wings
15. Muse of comedy
16. UK's neighbor
17. Explode angrily
19. Scale notes
20. Baseballer Reese
21. Regret
22. Italian spewer
23. Gave courage to
25. ___ Wednesday
26. Bar bills
29. Suffix for malt
30. Simmers
33. Color tone
34. Kitty's foot
36. Ousting
38. Pencil end
40. Sounding like a babbling brook
41. Digging pick
43. Fond du ___
44. Bravo!
45. Rocker John
46. Miss Gabor
48. Headliner
49. Loft contents
50. Envoy
53. Song for two
55. "___ of Me"
56. Bridge in Venice
60. Blunder
61. Good-luck gesture
63. Actress Zadora
64. Actor Rex ___
65. Legendary vessel
66. Recipe qty.
67. Honshu city
68. Annum

DOWN
1. Northern European
2. ___ vera
3. Scruff
4. Submerges
5. Navigate
6. Contented sounds
7. Oyster linings
8. Murky
9. Employ
10. Furniture wood
11. Satisfied a yen
12. Hibernia
13. Flat-topped hill
18. Maiden-named
22. Prohibit, legally
24. Oath
25. Meat jelly
26. Topic
27. Acoustic
28. Escape a jail sentence, slangily
31. Half of a Washington city
32. More foxy
34. Showy bloomer
35. Circle segment
37. Important age
39. Summer ermine
42. Cereal company
43. Be tardy
47. Popular fastening choice
48. Nautical route
51. Scent
52. Badge material
53. Govt. branch
54. "Exodus" author
55. Magnani or Sten
57. Mythology
58. Roman garb
59. Skunk feature
61. Relations
62. Bandleader Kyser

Cross Anagrams

PUZZLE 280

The answer words in diagram A will have the same letters, but in a different order, as the corresponding answer words in diagram B. Work from both sets of clues to solve the puzzle.

A. (LILACS shown on diagonal)

B. (SPRING shown on diagonal)

1. Women
2. Flyers
3. Meager
4. Bering, e.g.
5. Posture
6. Hog sounds

1. Took to the sea
2. Became rancid
3. To a degree
4. Warhol or Monet
5. Rise
6. Threaded beads

249

PUZZLE 281 CODEWORD

Instructions for solving Codeword puzzles are given on page 11.

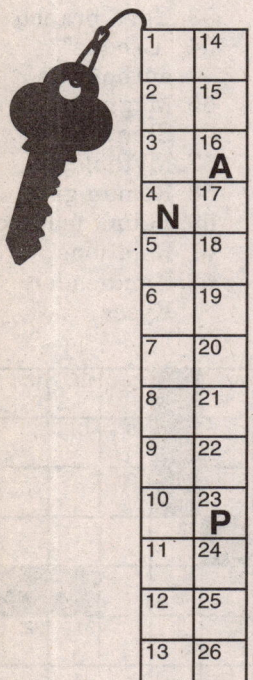

PUZZLE 282 CODEWORD

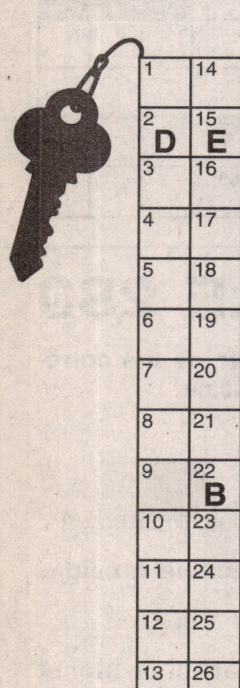

PUZZLE 283

ACROSS
1. Squeegee
6. Aroma
10. Stage hogs
14. Idolize
15. Catholic leader
16. Burn balm
17. Drink loudly
18. Altitude
20. ___ se
21. Moore costar
23. Merchandises
24. Excavation
25. Challenge
27. Observe
28. Kitchen cloth
32. Local star
33. Iterate
34. Heckler's word
36. Uproar
41. Plunders
43. Many times, in verse
45. Uncanny
46. Provides with funds
48. Yule tree
50. Ids' mates
51. Wear away
53. Satisfied
55. Appropriate
58. Midterm, e.g.
60. Tour vehicle
61. Minimal
63. Clan emblem
65. Big heart?
68. Bank patron
70. Beneath
72. Even once
73. Butte's kin
74. Pass over
75. Snooze
76. Hunted animal
77. Fixed routines

DOWN
1. Winged stinger
2. Inactive
3. Rain hard
4. Stray
5. Mend
6. Exposed
7. Dispersed
8. Music dramas
9. Ser. giver
10. Abhor
11. Skirt style
12. Temperamental
13. Logic
19. Thoroughfare
22. Thrust
24. Snapshot
26. Wagon track
28. Stet's opposite
29. Revered image
30. Not barefoot
31. Sticky mess
35. Amiss
37. Encounters
38. Compulsion
39. Maned creature
40. Sample
42. Sugary foods
44. Facial twitch
47. Jazz horn
49. Pajama topper
52. Shred
54. Digit
55. Birch tree
56. Annoy
57. Records
59. Large deer
62. Put in order
64. Platter
65. Dismounted
66. Morse ___
67. Fleecy moms
69. Brat
71. "Xanadu" gp.

PUZZLE 284

LEGENDS OF THE WEST

ACROSS

1. Hide
5. Attention getter
9. Church recess
13. Flings
18. Roof extension
19. Actress Perlman
20. Hogwash
22. Young hooter
23. OK Corral gunfighter
25. Leg bone
26. Not anybody
27. Cong. member
28. Rabbit's kin
29. Alamo defender
31. ___ and call
32. Error's pal
33. Bewail
34. In style
37. Foreground
38. Ski lift
40. Mule's kin
43. Subside
44. Leak
45. Plumed wader
47. Recognized
48. Optical glass
49. Official stamp
50. Had been
51. Peruvian native
52. Mai ___
53. Mighty lumberjack
57. Friendship
58. Iced desserts
61. In regard to
62. Loamy deposit
63. Unsteady gait
64. Brit. school term
65. Office writer
67. Jewish scholar
69. Burn with steam
71. Shore
74. Sun-dried brick
75. Outlaw queen
77. ___ West
78. Wrench, e.g.
79. Recital piece
80. Brink
81. Skid
82. Marine bird
83. Packs down
85. Fairy ___
86. Spectacle
87. Realize
88. Tiny amount
89. Crooner Como
91. Tinkered
92. Singer DiFranco
93. Metal mixture
94. Friend
95. The Sundance Kid's partner
100. Ripped
101. Shirt part
104. Spirit
105. Snowy
106. Lewis and Clark's guide
108. Stainless ___
109. Complication
110. Kinds
111. Hideaway
112. Equine
113. Sobbed
114. Ione or Azura
115. Wildcat

DOWN

1. Darns
2. Ms. Ballard
3. Actor Dixon
4. Capture
5. Sermonize
6. Hammerhead, e.g.
7. Dried up
8. Light knock
9. Reach
10. Personal
11. Classical prophet
12. Hero's story
13. Agree
14. Came to
15. ___ gin fizz
16. Camp shelter
17. Editor's comment
21. Spike of corn
24. Not those
29. Plunge
30. Make a speech
31. Scraps
32. Warble
34. Fountain drinks
35. Fetish
36. Wilderness Road clearer
37. German wives
38. Goody
39. Swiss city
40. Sharpshooting star
41. Factions
42. Influences
44. "___ Becomes Her"
46. Nell ___ (early English actress)
47. Japanese robe
49. Line of wk.
54. Intrinsic
55. Cry of defeat
56. Geeks
57. Actor Baldwin
59. Broken remains
60. Soft cheese
65. Suit fabric

PUZZLE 284

66. Container weight
67. Evaluates
68. Revere
69. Actress Blair
70. Hoof sound
71. Unhappily
72. Parisian river
73. Did data entry
75. Schooner
76. Weepy
79. Impassive
81. Ripoff
84. Divide
85. Helen of ___
86. Thrown
88. Take a breath
90. Firstborn
91. Word group
92. Zeniths
93. Stage whisper
94. Arrogant
95. Hit hard
96. Golden-rule word
97. Layer
98. Bristle
99. Movie
100. Speak
101. Not here
102. Leash
103. Groucho or Harpo
106. Brother's sib
107. Entire

PUZZLE 285

THE STATES

ACROSS
1. Bursts
5. Raccoon's kin
10. Forbids
14. Ambiance
15. Before
16. Heroic story
17. Remain
18. Slanting edge
19. Donated
20. Twice five
21. Band booking
22. Quick drink
24. Sprinted
25. The Natural State
28. Cuddle
30. Ditch
31. Tusk material
33. Corrodes
36. 62, to Cato
37. Scarce
41. Con
42. Partners
43. List unit
44. Posture
45. Once more
46. Poetic feet
47. Lark
49. Ms. Landers
50. Food closet
53. The Cornhusker State
58. Big fuss
59. Bullring cry
61. Falsehood
62. Check
63. Spiral
65. Fortified
67. Scant
68. Celtic
69. Sister's girl
70. Tidy
71. Exploit
72. Hollows
73. Selects

DOWN
1. Noodles
2. ___ space
3. Trick
4. Announce
5. Picasso, e.g.
6. European river
7. Sporty trans.
8. Secures
9. The Prairie State
10. Plead
11. Detached
12. Opponent
13. Locale
21. Wildebeests
23. For each
26. Most pretentious
27. "___ Candles"
29. Clooney film
32. Observe
33. Sharp blow
34. Numero ___
35. Rds.
36. Memory ___
38. 24-hr. banker
39. Yank's foe
40. Type concerns
42. The Old Line State
46. Regarding
48. In favor of
49. Remains
50. Went to and fro
51. Cherish
52. Ruckus
54. Choose by vote
55. Expensive
56. 24-___ gold
57. Aids a crook
60. Famous canal
64. Escorted
66. Fellows
67. 6, on phones

PUZZLE 286

COUNTRY LIVING

ACROSS

1. Blockade
6. Healthy place
9. Harmless
13. Feedback
14. Basic
16. Parisian annuals?
18. Palmer's pegs
19. End
20. Rebel
21. Civil wrong
23. Droop
25. Flee to wed
27. Young man
28. Hammett's Spade
31. Identical
32. Shropshire
34. Spy gp.
36. Ankara candies?
39. Annex
40. Loses heat
41. Small stream
42. Wind dir.
44. Ms. Meriwether
45. Rich soil
46. Certain mil. personnel
48. Habitual course
49. Betel palm
52. Fen
53. Christen
57. Insects from Honshu?
61. Plato's pupil
62. Bonds
63. Regatta
64. Took a load off
65. Adhesive

DOWN

1. Filter
2. With regard to
3. Dueling sword
4. Firearm part
5. Et al.'s kin
6. Bang
7. For each
8. Bardot's pal
9. Horses' sounds
10. King of the Huns
11. Fashion trends
12. Extra
14. Radiate
15. Same, to Simone
17. Hound's quarry
22. Eye's nerve
23. Burton's birthplace
24. Admired one
25. Ooze
26. Rendered fats
27. Tureen adjunct
29. Hurts
30. Chiggers
31. Kennedy abbr.
32. Boots
33. Edging loop
35. Request
37. Alone
38. Hyson
43. Wrap
45. Theater section
47. Jargon
48. Choir wear
49. Close to closed
50. ___ avis
51. Grandiose
52. Karate award
54. Word of regret
55. Go soft
56. Latin being
58. Aurora
59. RR stop
60. Clairvoyance, for short

PUZZLE 287

AGELESS

ACROSS
1. Distort
5. Mummy's bed
9. Cassette
13. ___ Minor
14. Diva's songs
16. Bone-dry
17. Ageless problem-solving?
19. Await
20. Quickness
21. Law org.
22. Simple
23. Borders
26. Pub pints
28. Ageless castaway's effort?
33. ___ Lancelot
34. Frog's kin
35. Spanish rattle
37. Norwegian king
39. State off.
41. Mongolian dwelling
42. ___ leather
45. Slant
48. Fitting
49. Ageless arctic route?
52. Norse god
53. Tiny bit
54. Delhi dress
57. Snare
59. Corpulent
63. Oil org.
64. Ageless trash haulers?
67. Voyaging
68. Rigid
69. Leg bone
70. ___-mell
71. Warmth
72. Abode

DOWN
1. Bankrolls
2. PDQ's kin
3. Hoar
4. Gait setters
5. Sunbathe
6. Food scrap
7. Ms. Sorvino
8. African plant
9. Wall hanging
10. Realm
11. Brooches
12. Whirl
15. Ski race
18. Shelley, e.g.
24. "O Sole ___"
25. Glitch
27. Timetable info
28. Italian city
29. Poetry muse
30. Clay brick
31. Praises
32. Off-whites
33. Soak up
36. Nibbled
38. Upright
40. Travel permit
43. Ultimate
44. Sandals
46. Court rep.
47. Track
50. Garland
51. Waylay
54. ___ opera
55. Church nook
56. Movie unit
58. Elm, e.g.
60. Resound
61. Scan
62. Serf
65. Bikini top
66. It's a blast!

PUZZLE 288

ARK PAIRS

ACROSS
1. Clique
6. Corrida cry
9. Defeats
14. Ms. Astaire
15. Bam!
16. The most
17. Pair of sheep
19. Sanitary
20. In the past
21. Man's title
22. Garden tool
24. Tropical wood
26. Faux ___
28. Touched down
32. Snoot
34. Discolor
36. Doctors' org.
37. Bungalow
39. Ripened
40. Young louse
41. Pair of horses
46. ___ Aviv
47. Indecent
48. ___-disant
49. Drama part
50. Improvise
52. Movie feline
55. Prickly
57. Negative word
59. Lingers
61. Picnic drinks
63. Once named
65. Mil. food
66. Doc
69. Pair of swans
72. Dispatch boat
73. Commotion
74. Glens
75. Modernize
76. Toe count
77. Bjorn Borg, e.g.

DOWN
1. Jewel weight
2. Proverbs
3. Regret
4. ___ carte
5. Contact ___
6. Sung dramas
7. Unworthy
8. Slender jug
9. Pair of deer
10. Ms. Burstyn
11. Feasted
12. ___-la-la
13. ___ Diego
18. Downturn
23. Strangers
25. Eye makeup
27. Substitute
29. Ms. Delany
30. Arab ruler
31. Court
33. Pair of cattle
35. Turkish ruler
38. Tint cloth
41. RBI, e.g.
42. High-___
43. Voice part
44. Night bird
45. Factory
51. Candy treat
53. Taste
54. Consented
56. Elevate
58. British brew
60. Hunch
62. Shoo!
64. Concludes
66. Deface
67. Adam's mate
68. Ruckus
70. Lyric verse
71. Small crow

257

PUZZLE 289

FLOWER POWER

Instructions for solving Flower Power puzzles are given on page 94.

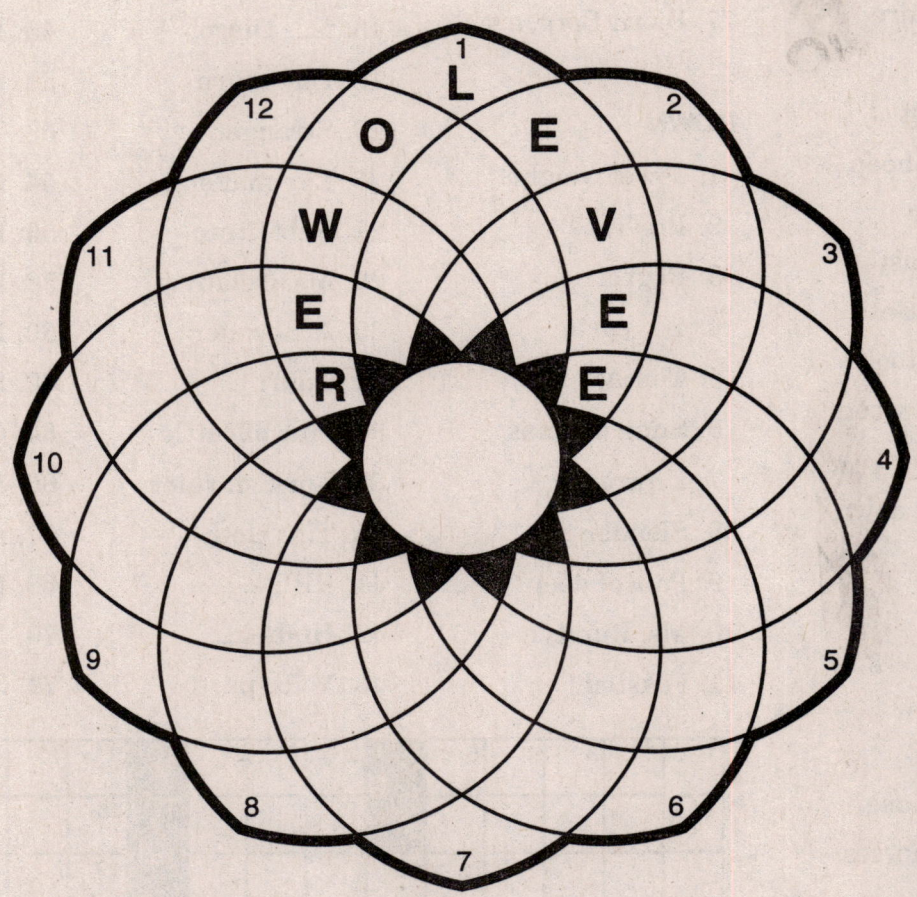

CLOCKWISE

1. Flood foiler
2. Mend
3. Spoof
4. Cuban line dance
5. Frenzy
6. Walnut's kin
7. Cash
8. Jazz group
9. Like a teetotaler
10. Fishing boot
11. Tall structure
12. Whirlybird blade

COUNTERCLOCKWISE

1. Quieter
2. Lose strength
3. Prefer
4. Provide service
5. Power
6. Jab
7. Join together
8. Bedtime drink
9. Submarine finder
10. Grown girls
11. Certain feline
12. Cowboy event

PUZZLE 290

• PERRY MASON, MANY WAYS •

ACROSS
1. Beame or Lincoln
4. Butter serving
7. 15th of March
11. Grouch
13. Quick-witted
16. Story
17. Tableland
18. Guide
19. A Great Lake
20. German river
21. Lawyer
23. Back end
26. First woman
27. Torments
29. Save
33. Beard of grain
34. Double curve
35. Sole
37. Ravioli, e.g.
38. Third letter
39. External
40. Scrabble piece
41. Pub pint
42. Certain medicines
43. Deduce
45. Beginning
46. Ocean
47. Scottish hillside
48. Lawyer
52. Young lady
56. Discharge
57. Scorches
59. Skip
60. Region
61. Blunder
62. Provoke
63. Swarm
64. Computer acronym
65. Gem cutter's cup

DOWN
1. Summit
2. Raised, as dogs
3. Facility
4. Mas' mates
5. Sacred table
6. Annoyed, with "off"
7. Willow genus
8. Flit
9. Author Wiesel
10. Look at
12. Lawyer
14. Car gear
15. Collections
22. Those, to Yves
24. Kett of comics
25. Busy ___ bee
27. Plait
28. Bridal path
30. Lawyer
31. Loosen
32. Choose by vote
33. Likely
34. Shoebox letters
36. Mos. and mos.
38. More sanitary
39. Mrs. Chaplin
41. Opposed
42. Rocky peak
44. Prefix for "equal"
47. English poet
48. Million ender
49. Maple, e.g.
50. Giants or Mets
51. Jug handles
53. Among
54. Farm tower
55. Walk
56. Lard
58. Mexican Mrs.

End of the Line

PUZZLE 291

For each of the categories listed, can you think of a word or phrase ending with each letter on the right? Count one point for each correct answer. A score of 15 is good, and 21 is excellent.

FABRICS	FEATHERED FRIENDS	WORLD CITIES	CLOTHING	MOUNTAINS	
					D
					A
					I
					S
					Y

PUZZLE 292

• FAULKNER NOVELS •

ACROSS
1. Rules
5. Street sign
9. Snatch
13. Refer ending
17. Theater award
18. Model's stance
19. Timber wolf
20. Weaving frame
21. She, to Juanita
22. 1936 Faulkner novel
25. ___ manner (doctor's attitude)
27. Snout
28. "Agnes of God" actress
29. Johnnycake
30. Jogs
31. "Good Earth" heroine
33. Pituitary or pineal
35. "Soap" family name
36. Type of heel
40. Certain paints
41. Rocky peaks
42. Fork's partner
43. Up in the ___
44. Give weapons to
45. River in Switzerland
46. Kind of beef
47. Opposite of aweather
48. Garfield's favorite meal
50. Feudal servant
51. Unique people
52. 1932 Faulkner novel
56. Movie effect, briefly
59. Envelope abbr.
60. "Invisible Man" author
64. Grasslands
65. Cords
67. Letterman's rival
68. Lager's kin
69. Exclamation
70. Pens
71. Actress Louise
72. Snick's partner
73. Having more undergrowth
75. Actor Carvey
76. Ornamentation
77. Orderly
78. Cheeky
79. Cartoonist Groening
80. "And all I ask is ___ ship..."
83. Asian river
84. Meadow
87. 1951 Faulkner novel
91. Set down
92. Tightly drawn
93. Mountain lake
94. Tatting
95. Painter Roman ___-de Tirtoff
96. Buffalo's lake
97. Skin-cream ingredient
98. Went very fast
99. Baseball's Nolan ___

DOWN
1. American physiologist
2. Equal to the task
3. 1939 Faulkner novel, with "The"
4. Vivaldi's "The Four ___"
5. Fictional detective Sam ___
6. Hamlet's soliloquy starter
7. WWII intelligence agency
8. Charles Schulz's strip
9. Luster
10. Eternal City
11. Camel's-hair fabric
12. Rocker Geldof
13. "Seinfeld" role
14. Steelers' coach Chuck ___
15. Indifferent
16. Grammy's cousin
23. "The ___ Ranger"
24. Old
26. Ill. neighbor
30. Not often seen
31. Milo's movie buddy
32. Hoist
33. Ambition
34. Milan money, once
35. Pentateuch
36. Confused situation
37. Story
38. Level
39. Mineral-bearing rocks
41. Flavor
42. Islamic holy book
45. Exchange fee
46. Has a landlord
47. Against
49. Gifts for the poor
50. Places
51. City in Norway
53. Small candle
54. Actress Davis
55. Forelimb bone
56. Chunk
57. Cordelia's father
58. Hawaiian island
61. 1931 Faulkner novel
62. Bread spread
63. ___-do-well
65. Sudden assault
66. Curved molding
67. Dryer leavings
70. Hot pepper
71. Foot bones
72. Colonist
74. Pentagon greeting
75. Darling
76. "___ Boot"
78. Supine's opposite
79. Like a lion
80. Comedian Johnson
81. Sign of crying
82. Watery prefix
83. Hairstyle
84. Brownish purple
85. Actress Moreno
86. Biblical location
88. Greek letter
89. ___ de mer
90. Brief sleep

PUZZLE 293
• BY ANY NAME •

ACROSS
1. Sawing wood?
5. Footfall
9. Med. course
13. British service acronym
17. Trim fabric
18. Whopper
19. Manage
20. Attendance call response
21. The Great Emancipator
24. At a standstill
25. French pointillist
26. Multinational currency
27. "Ragged Dick" author
28. Rebellious
32. Scrooge, for example
34. Big Mac
38. Car's front-end cover
39. Tailless primate
42. Succulent plants
43. Film composer Schifrin
44. Church key
46. Wimbledon winner Smith
47. Ms. Trueheart
48. Hawkeye portrayer
51. All excited
52. Sauce with capers
54. German lancer
55. Worker with a pad
56. The Greatest
61. Teed off
65. "At Wit's End" writer Bombeck
66. Respond
71. Bard
72. Catalpa, e.g.
73. Atop
76. Sleep time, to some
77. Cantankerous
79. Margin
80. Daybreak
81. Ike's initials
82. Assn.
84. Yankee Clipper
86. Autumn flower
88. Fan
89. Jeweler's help
91. "Bus Stop" playwright
93. Childbirth method
98. Opposed
99. Lady Bird
103. "Jurassic Park" actress
104. Radius's neighbor
105. Enrobed
106. Exclamation of dismay
107. Prohibitionists
108. Kodiak
109. Unearthly
110. Strip

DOWN
1. Word said with a sigh
2. Athlete Zaharias
3. Light beige
4. Honey
5. Unmoving
6. Round cap
7. Cloth measure
8. American architect
9. "J____" (Zola letter)
10. Jordanian queen
11. Poise
12. Agent's percentage
13. Although
14. The Galloping Ghost
15. First name in mystery
16. Not once, to a poet
22. Injures
23. Prefix for surgeon
27. Stat's kin
29. Gawk
30. "____ brillig and . . ."
31. Museum paintings
33. Mangle
34. Sail holder
35. Western ski resort
36. Leonine call
37. Superman's alter ego
40. Laborer
41. Therefore
45. Corrode
47. Play about Capote
48. In the style of
49. Stripling
50. Alicia of "Falcon Crest"
53. Jo's youngest sister
54. Thurman of "Pulp Fiction"
55. Misdeed
57. White House beagle
58. Metric unit
59. Sra., in Sevres
60. Deity of the hearth
61. Like a snake
62. Direction, in Dijon
63. The Singing Cowboy
64. AAA recommendation
67. Cozy
68. Pinion
69. Needle case
70. "____ Man"
72. Phoenician capital
73. Utah city
74. Word from Caesar
75. Desert ruler
78. Learning method
79. Predicted
80. Bernhardt or Churchill
83. Grating
84. Animal or car
85. Tune
87. Whirls
89. "Charlie's Angels" star
90. Eccentric
92. Role on "Suddenly Susan"
94. L-Q connectors
95. Tennis star from Richmond
96. Region
97. Chemical compound
99. Pup's cousin
100. Gems, to a yegg
101. Tavern request
102. Jostle

PUZZLE 294

• NIGHT SIGHTS •

ACROSS
1. Greek group
5. Rock's Steely ___
8. Swine fare
12. Sibilant sound
16. Reduce
17. Make new
18. Program instructions
19. Forget
20. West of Draco
22. East of Cassiopeia
24. Dead end?
25. Female gametes
26. Before
27. Professor Schickele
28. Nice time of year?
29. Tax
31. ABA member
33. Aquarium attraction
36. Repugnant
37. Jai ___
38. Addams family cousin
41. West of Orion
44. South of Norma
46. Wide rd.
47. Military helper
48. Baseball's Mel et al.
49. Lady of Spain
50. Hanoi holiday
51. Public disgrace
54. Photocopier liquid
55. Solicit
56. Sturm ___ Drang
57. Hole-making implement
58. Striped cat
61. Trattoria treat
64. Hundredth pt.
67. Clarinet's kin
68. Persuade
71. Presently
72. Barcelona cheer
73. South of Cetus
75. North of Aries
78. Fast plane, for short
79. Female ruffs
80. Cure
81. Trickle
82. Darkens
83. Poster
84. Vigoda or Lincoln
86. Calliope power
89. Recreation
90. Sharp ___ tack
91. Lennon's mate
94. South of Lupus
97. West of Pegasus
100. Lotion ingredient
101. Astronaut's agcy.
102. Miners' quests
103. Farmer's locale?
104. Blend
105. Available
106. Bird's instrument
107. Woody's boy

DOWN
1. Longtime squabble
2. Exceptional
3. Cape fox
4. 1773 jetsam
5. ___ vu
6. Hubbub
7. Negative connector
8. Frightening
9. Solitary
10. Unusual
11. ___ your request
12. Cozy
13. "___ a man..."
14. Faction
15. Headliner
17. Carry on
21. Word for word?
23. Pertaining to the eye
26. Constantly
28. Inventor Whitney
29. Flax fabric
30. Brit. band
31. Descended
32. Salts
33. Shoo!
34. Overhanging edge
35. Dill seed
36. Pitcher Blue
37. Opera division
38. Aware of
39. Harmony
40. Romanoff ruler
42. Impudent
43. Singer Jagger
45. Worshiper's statue
48. Auto pioneer
52. Properly
53. Santa ___
54. Nasal tone
55. Biblical sibling
57. Directly
58. Flip
59. Fundamentals
60. Boxing match
62. Japanese, e.g.
63. Soccer score
64. Battery terminal
65. Crossword unit
66. Substitute worker
68. Arise
69. Misfortunes
70. ___ Antiqua
74. ___ ballerina
75. Narrow
76. Std.
77. Put to work
82. Courted
83. Author Sontag
84. Egyptian snakes
85. Scrooge's exclamation
86. Ripoff
87. Phone starter
88. Chemical compound
89. Weld
90. Mr. Haley
91. Lulu
92. Nonexistent
93. Scandinavian seaport
95. Numero ___
96. Criminal charge
97. Positive guidelines
98. Important time
99. Violinist Kavafian

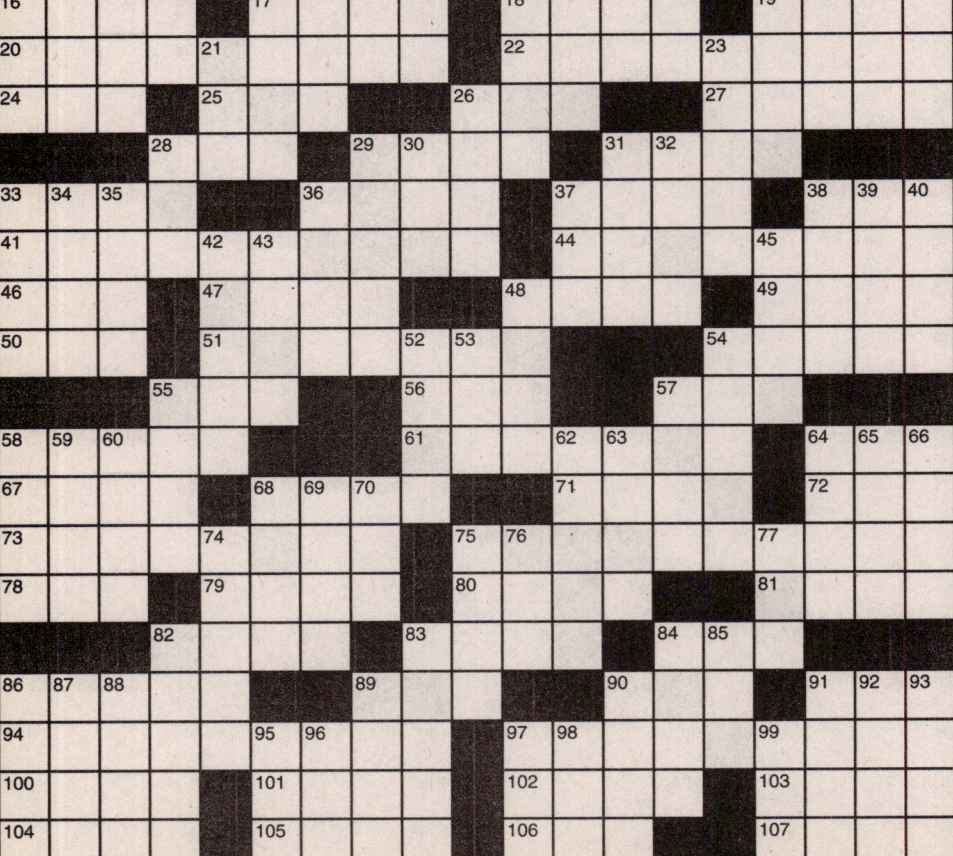

PUZZLE 295
• OPEN CARD GAME •

ACROSS
1. Craving
5. Glide on ice
10. Painted metalware
11. Employer
12. Teem
14. Oiler
15. Court
16. Small town
17. Fast plane
20. Heart-pumping exercises
24. Jim Carrey role
27. Let
30. Pigeon coops
31. Grow older
32. What there oughta be
33. Short socks
35. Bath, in Madrid
36. Patriotic org.
37. Persian rulers
39. Clean air gp.
40. Comparative ending
42. Monastery head
46. Cycle starter
47. Naked
48. Like old movies
52. Pakistan's neighbor
53. Box-office letters
56. Big slipknot
57. Spiciness
58. Canopied bed
60. Gentlemen
62. Owns
63. Onion's kin
64. Pole or lodge
67. Develop gradually
70. Weary
73. Western lake
74. Cunning
75. Rock
76. Man or Capri

DOWN
1. Part of TGIF
2. Pull behind
3. Hammer part
4. Brave sandwich?
5. Puppeteer Lewis
6. Alaskan crustaceans
7. Noah's craft
8. Casual shirt
9. Make a mistake
13. Complain
14. Brass horn
16. Tunnel (through)
17. Hare
18. Environmental sci.
19. Head, in Paris
21. JFK posting
22. Carpet
23. Psalm word
25. Dog's doc
26. Curvy letter
28. Grandma
29. Well-pitched games
33. Citrus drink
34. California city
38. Withered
41. Clear (of)
43. Silents star Theda ___
44. Borneo ape
45. ___ hat
48. Less than dos
49. Negatives
50. "Goodbye, Columbus" author
51. Confused
53. Drench
54. Seek office
55. Food scrap
58. Skedaddle
59. Secretive "Hey, you!"
61. Embankment
65. New Zealand bird
66. Spring flower
67. UFO's crewmen
68. Large container
69. Cry of discovery
71. Angled addition
72. Coloring agent

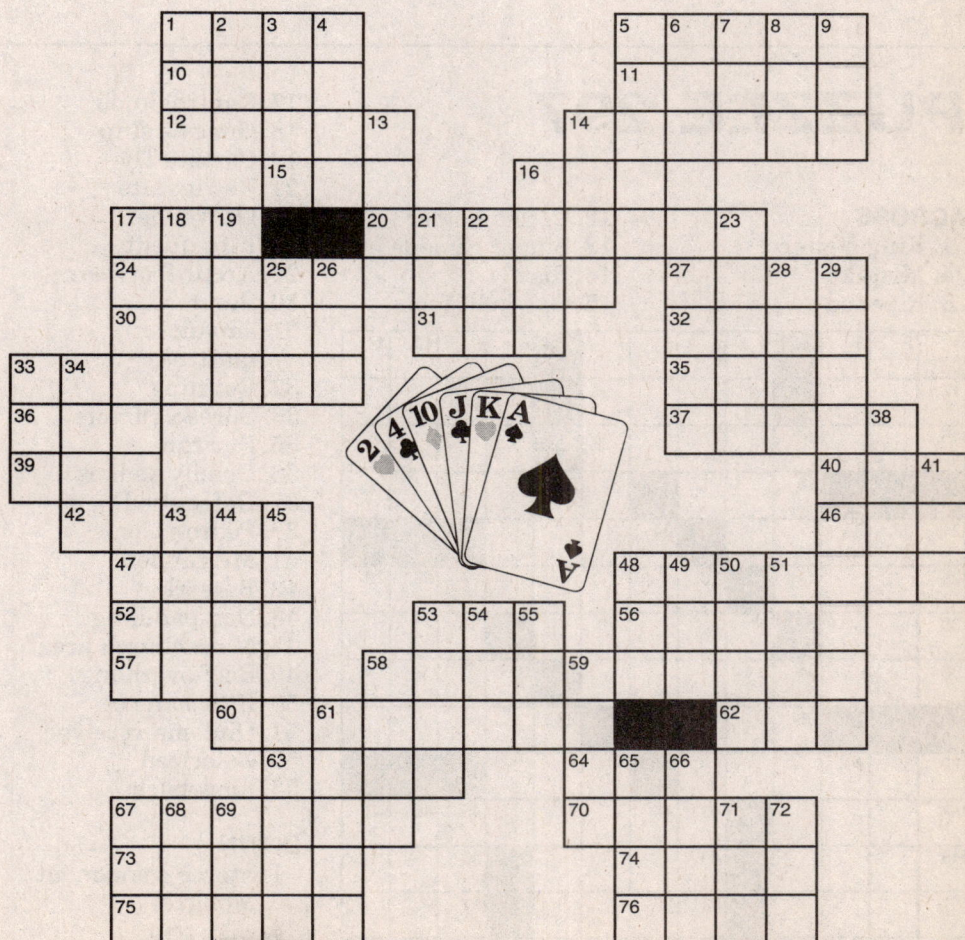

263

PUZZLE 296

ACROSS
1. Evergreens
5. Pickling ingredient
9. Bachelor
12. Painful
13. Down the dogie
14. Lemon cooler
15. Brown songbird
16. Vittles
17. Haul
18. Midday meal
20. Sandpiper, e.g.
22. King Kong, e.g.
24. Atmospheres
27. Berlin's lang.
30. Chimed
32. Asian staple
33. Warnings
35. Military wing
37. Ballet exercise
38. Earmarks
40. Orchid necklace
41. More sensible
43. Felon's flight
44. Bird herd
46. Blue-gray stone
51. Pekoe, e.g.
53. Skiff
55. Operator
56. Hooter
57. Not busy
58. Smaller amount
59. Crooner Torme
60. Finger tip
61. Survive

DOWN
1. Sailing vessel
2. Beige
3. What time?
4. Harmony
5. Woof
6. Ease
7. Informed about
8. Radio and TV
9. Substance
10. Hubbub
11. Just bought
19. Hurt
21. Cat's sound
23. Bygone
25. Property measure
26. Big rig
27. Spaces
28. Jazzy Fitzgerald
29. Precipitation
31. Dotty
34. Film spool
36. Doctrines
39. Acid's opposite
42. Comedian Williams
45. Musical conclusion
47. Storm break
48. On the Atlantic
49. Hardy heroine
50. Once, formerly
51. Mr. Hanks
52. Ram's mate
54. ___ Aviv, Israel

PUZZLE 297

ACROSS
1. King beater
4. Mistake
8. Ripened
12. Coffee holder
13. Singer Simone
14. Risk
15. Gas-grill fuels
17. Control knob
18. Genesis ship
19. Certain fly
21. Refrigerate
24. Off yonder
25. Infrequent
26. Arctic footwear
30. Stout
31. Japanese mattress
32. Puzzling
33. Spread rumors
35. Puritan
36. Deadly snakes
37. Detective Drew
38. Pedro's cloak
41. Mr. Linden
42. Berserk
43. Dog-paddling
48. Main church area
49. Roof overhang
50. By means of
51. Diploma receiver
52. Colorized
53. Flow back

DOWN
1. Stereo component
2. Mongrel
3. ___ trip
4. Snarl
5. Pigsty sound
6. ___ for the books
7. Burgers, fries, etc.
8. European vipers
9. Walking rhythm
10. Stats for Dodgers
11. Proofreading mark
16. Turn white
20. Severed, as an oak
21. Rugged rock
22. Crown of light
23. Enrages
24. Poker bets
26. Assumed
27. Antler
28. Lyrical
29. Fidgety
31. Trout, e.g.
34. Dismissed
35. Date tree
37. Christened
38. Sharp pain
39. General Bradley
40. ___ Scotia
41. Honey factory
44. Route
45. "___ Got a Secret"
46. Penpoint
47. Yak

PUZZLE 298

ACROSS
1. Spud
6. Extol
10. Belfry denizens
14. By oneself
15. Light beige
16. Oodles
17. Minimal
18. Peddle
19. Become bored
20. Was in front
21. Luau instrument
23. Cycle part
24. "Desire," e.g.
29. Grassy layer
30. Grading
32. Went by bike
33. Religious pictures
34. Abrasive material
39. Spring peeper
40. Swine enclosures
41. Boyfriend
42. Charity broadcasts
44. Cowboy's transport
45. Steakhouse request
46. Skilled
47. Division of time
50. Instant
52. Western show
54. Married
55. Enthusiasm
58. Vile
59. Cooking herb
62. Stockholm native
64. Mediocre grades
65. Fiery gem
66. British noblemen
67. Valid
68. Cheer
69. Shade providers

DOWN
1. Towering
2. Away from the wind
3. Kind of mushroom
4. Some dashes
5. Comes back
6. Flood wall
7. High card
8. Coffee server
9. Fireworks flop
10. Tub
11. Assumed name
12. Body section
13. Knight's charger
22. Beer barrel
23. Type of school
25. Trace of color
26. Novice
27. Roadway markers
28. Tallies
30. Break in friendship
31. Property measure
34. Tempest
35. End, NASA style
36. Stick to it
37. Leisure
38. Regretted
40. Fraud
43. Threesome
44. Earphones
46. Be in contention
47. Assemble
48. Wanderer
49. Fifi's farewell
51. Reside
53. Otherwise
56. Meaningless
57. Chow hall
59. Nutritious bean
60. Jungle animal
61. Young woman
63. Major conflict

Step by Step

PUZZLE 299

In five steps change each word one letter at a time into a new 5-letter word so that by the fifth step each letter has been changed. Do not rearrange the order of the letters. You do not have to change the letters in order.

Example: Rouge, Rough, Cough, Couch, Conch, Cinch

1. CREAK
2. MERRY
3. THANE
4. ALONG

PUZZLE 300

ACROSS
1. Intertwine
5. Flubs
9. Kolkata coin
14. Ersatz butter
15. Pew
16. Laura Bush, to Barbara
17. Backup
19. Mitt
20. High homes
22. Observer
23. Twerp
26. June and July
28. Oahu veranda
29. Brazen
32. Slanted type
34. Fill
35. Tiny legume
37. Adorable
38. Dribbling
40. Daytime show
41. Earlier, to Keats
42. Show surprise
43. Parody
45. Steep slope
47. Kewpies
48. Warnings
51. Elementary
52. Poet's daybreak
55. Pekoe vessel
57. Deteriorate
59. Doubtful
64. Narrow boat
65. Ship
66. Fizzy quaff
67. Swing band members
68. Cognizant of
69. Loses intensity

DOWN
1. Extinct New Zealand bird
2. Annex
3. Adjust
4. Gardening tool
5. Serf
6. Outfit again
7. Proportion
8. Small antelope
9. Surrey
10. Barring
11. Tactic
12. Chalet feature
13. Decorative pitcher
18. Spokes
21. Wanders
23. Disposition
24. Mother's family
25. Chest rattle
27. Scammed
28. Classroom parasites
30. Goes bad
31. Annually
33. Red wine
34. Circuit
36. Simians
39. Steamed coffee
40. Plato's porch
42. Miss
44. Capable
46. Votive, e.g.
49. Confiscated
50. Odor
52. Jumble
53. Predatory dolphin
54. Soup thickener
56. Hairstyle
58. City trains
60. Drink chiller
61. Male swan
62. Priest's robe
63. "Viva ___ Vegas"

PUZZLE 301 — Matchmaker

Fill in the missing first letter of each word in the column on the left. Next, look for a related word in the group at the right and put it in the blank in the second column. When the puzzle is completed, read the first letters of both columns in order, from top to bottom, to reveal a saying.

___ational   _____
___n   _____
___umber   _____
___asy   _____
___ater   _____
___olar   _____
___nscribe   _____
___even   _____

Difficult   Off
Eclipse   One
Guard   Seas
Nymph   Write

PUZZLE 302

ACROSS
1. Designer Perry ___
6. Part of TGIF
9. Marine predator
13. Reserved
15. Highest point
16. Blood vessel
17. Chest of drawers
18. Glazed
20. Sault ___ Marie
21. Picture taker
23. Rink material
24. Newts
26. Female sibling
28. Discolor
31. Relinquish
32. Fails to include
33. "A Bridge ___ Far"
35. Geek
39. TV's "Get ___"
40. Raised border
41. Harness-racing horse
42. Shoe bottom
43. Matterhorn, e.g.
44. Courtyards
45. Pretentious
48. Savings or checking ___
50. Marble figure
53. Scorch
54. Yet, poetically
55. Mistakes
58. Man/mouse link
61. Angel's tear?
63. Motto
66. Atoll
67. Bullfight cheer
68. Large game fish
69. A yard has three
70. Crimson
71. Banana skins
22. Smoker's need
24. Beseech
25. Clenched hand
27. Member of Congress
28. Fling gently
29. Bullets and bombs
30. Irani coin
31. ___ disc player
34. Sunflower product
36. Neutral hue
37. Restraint
38. Phooey's kin
41. Tropical rodent
46. Was sorry about
47. Intense fear
49. Ravine
50. Letter stroke
51. Tantalize
52. Doddering
56. Audition prize
57. Parodied
58. Rude look
59. Banister
60. Landers and Jillian
62. Ping-Pong divider
64. Once around the track
65. Gold source

DOWN
1. Subsides
2. Oaf
3. Folk wisdom
4. Eisenhower's nickname
5. Neptune's milieu
6. Detail
7. Dial sound
8. Thinly scattered
9. Preholiday night
10. Ignited again
11. Elizabeth II, to Edward VIII
12. Closer
14. Channels
19. Occupation on "Hazel"

Zip It
PUZZLE 303

The letters of six common words are listed below, but we've separated the odd letters (first, third, and fifth) from the even letters (second, fourth, and sixth). Without scrambling the order of the letters in the 3-letter groups, determine which two groups, when zipped together, form each of the answer words. For example, CRL and ICE zipped together form CIRCLE.

ABT   COI   EAE   IHR   ___ ___ ___ ___ ___ ___   ___ ___ ___ ___ ___ ___

ISD   MNC   MSE   OKE   ___ ___ ___ ___ ___ ___   ___ ___ ___ ___ ___ ___

RBI   SAK   WNY   WTE   ___ ___ ___ ___ ___ ___   ___ ___ ___ ___ ___ ___

PUZZLE 304

ACROSS
1. Fine powder
5. Distant
8. Molecule part
12. Vocal solo
13. Animosity
14. Indian palm
15. Treed
17. Lack
18. Make a minor adjustment to
19. Slangy refusal
21. Antitoxins
23. Glorify
27. Blind section
30. The Emerald ___
32. Fib
33. Fragrant shrubs
35. Unobserved
37. ___-advised
38. Actual
40. Penny
41. Nightclub
43. Repenter
45. Chilled
47. Billiards shot
51. Poet Khayyam
54. Denial
56. Nonclerical
57. Wildebeest
58. Bump
59. ___ Stanley Gardner
60. Swine's home
61. Witches

DOWN
1. Social grace
2. In line
3. Italian money, once
4. Card game
5. Pine
6. Coliseums
7. Update
8. Attach
9. Even score
10. Unlatch, in verse
11. Furious
16. Supplement
20. Hammer end
22. Ascend
24. On the sheltered side
25. Legal claim
26. Hiker's abode
27. Skidded
28. Leslie Caron film
29. "___ Fair in Love & War"
31. Doozie
34. Gator's kin
36. Relieve an itch
39. Eager
42. Mythical enchantress
44. Flightless bird
46. Work units
48. Greek porch
49. Warbled
50. BPOE members
51. Bullring bravo
52. Damage
53. Be troubled
55. Purchase

PUZZLE 305

ACROSS
1. Hair goo
4. Low-___ diet
8. Adorable
12. Big monkey
13. Skating jump
14. Similar
15. Fruity dessert
16. "___ Man" (Estevez film)
17. Heal
18. Waste metal
20. Twinge
22. Salami seller
24. Vitality
28. Rani's attire
31. Amor
33. Pro vote
34. Dishes
36. Sharper
38. Tire filler
39. Celebrity
41. Three feet
42. Prepare tea
44. Stare blankly
46. Use a keyboard
48. Strangely
52. Turkish ___
55. Humdinger
57. Pal of Pooh
58. Spiny houseplant
59. Sidle
60. Invite
61. Whitetail
62. Earmarks
63. Golf gadget

DOWN
1. Holes
2. "Iliad," e.g.
3. Evil look
4. ___ diem (seize the day)
5. Wood chopper
6. Fix
7. Alliance
8. Brief role
9. Luau instrument
10. Can material
11. Finish
19. Cave access
21. Fire-truck item
23. For fear that
25. Talking bird
26. Coworker
27. Difficult
28. Hot springs
29. Touched down
30. Uncommon
32. Southern vegetable
35. View
37. Black-___ pea
40. Meeting plan
43. Old anesthetic
45. Studies intently
47. Verse writer
49. Doggone it!
50. Come in last
51. Oxen team
52. Faulty
53. Foamy drink
54. Sock part
56. Hen product

CODEWORD

PUZZLE 306

Codeword is a special crossword puzzle in which conventional clues are omitted. Instead, answer words in the diagram are represented by numbers. Each number represents a different letter of the alphabet, and all of the letters of the alphabet are used. When you are sure of a letter, put it in the code key chart and cross it off in the alphabet box. A group of letters has been inserted to start you off.

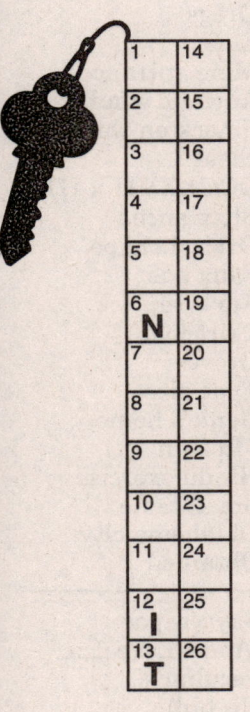

All Fours

PUZZLE 307

How many common 4-letter words can you find in the diagram by moving from letter to adjacent letter up, down, forward, backward, and diagonally? A letter may be used more than once in a word, but only after leaving it and coming back. Proper names, abbreviations, contractions, and foreign words are not allowed.

YOUR WORD LIST

PUZZLE 308

• ICE-CREAM CONE •

ACROSS
1. Brouhaha
4. Rani's wrap
8. Icy
12. Tex-___
13. Appearance
14. Ladd of films
15. Malt brew
16. Caesar's last day
17. Tableland
18. Checkout line, e.g.
21. Sunburned
22. Scribble
26. Swedish rock group
29. Actress Ryan
30. Poetic "above"
31. Betrayer
35. Gov. agency
36. Certain Ivy Leaguer
37. Minus
38. Fez ornament
40. Upsilon follower
42. Baseball feat
47. Palm starch
50. Wharf
51. Past
52. Matinee star
53. Marine fish
54. Face
55. Crown
56. Breaks bread
57. ___ green

DOWN
1. Latin I verb
2. Salami seller
3. Yoke mates
4. Beam
5. Fostered
6. Atoll
7. Confidant
8. Bit part
9. Corrida cry
10. ___ Cruces
11. Genetic-info carrier
19. Seize
20. MGM's lion, e.g.
23. Prescribed amount
24. Dregs
25. Sins
26. Mine entrance
27. Adriatic wind
28. Smack on the cheek?
29. CCCLXVII x III
32. Sly glance
33. Orbital shape
34. Faux pas
39. Fur wrap
40. Skirt fold
41. Droves
43. Type size
44. Genie's home
45. Flu sign
46. Hindu exercise
47. Small taste
48. Oklahoma city
49. Obtained

PUZZLE 309

• OOPS! •

ACROSS
1. Love taps
5. Small barracuda
9. Today: Sp.
12. Out of port
13. Part of SATB
14. Dutch commune
15. Cheat
16. Sends on
18. Wind-driven plant
20. Very, musically speaking
21. Capital of Morocco
25. Short skirt
29. Infatuated
30. Zipper
35. Retail event
36. Half: pref.
37. ___ Flow (bay)
39. Racket
44. Mechanical mallet
48. South Dakota's Mount ___
51. Pressure: pref.
52. Orangutan
53. Of the ear
54. Personalities
55. Seattle hours: abbr.
56. Standing
57. British poet

DOWN
1. Noodles
2. Truffle's spore sac
3. Sports groups
4. Brazilian dance
5. Secure
6. Cultivate
7. To be: Fr.
8. Skyscraper
9. "And I Love ___"
10. Peculiar
11. Uh-huh
17. Proverb
19. Citrus fruit
22. Forbid
23. Vital statistic
24. Tobacco residue
26. Uncertainties
27. Highland "no"
28. Particular practice
30. Draft letters
31. Varnish ingredient
32. Wharf group: abbr.
33. Complexity
34. Singer Turner
38. Metal suit
40. Old card game
41. Adult insect
42. Goat antelope
43. Notched
45. Particle
46. Borrowed sum: abbr.
47. Mild expletive
48. Music genre
49. FedEx's rival
50. Tennis-match unit

BRICK BY BRICK

PUZZLE 310

Rearrange this stack of bricks to form a crossword puzzle. The clues will help you fit the bricks into their correct places. Row 1 has been filled in for you. Use the bricks to fill in the remaining spaces.

ACROSS

1. Boundary post / Chow hall / Selects
2. Camp craft / Bad marks / Met rendering
3. Floral essence / Speak sloppily / Satisfy
4. Letters / Border on / Lab doctor
5. Dandy tie / Ailment
6. Band aid / Torah keeper / Mouse trap?
7. Barnyard alarms / Woods
8. Idle on screen / Document / Decline to sign
9. Upper house / Optimist
10. Foxy / Mouth margin / Baa maid?
11. Vast plain / Subsidiary statute
12. Louvre affair? / Grimm baddie / Weapons
13. Speck / Put on weight / Along the middle
14. Arrestee's concern / Therefore / Category
15. Early man? / Feat / Augmented

DOWN

1. Con game / Bellicose deity / Brazilian dance
2. "Cheerio!" / "Encore!" / Group of three
3. Opponent / Yuletide staple
4. It's not a bear / Resell for profit / Shade source
5. Auction finish / Held session / Data-entry error
6. Dessert pancake / Goaded
7. Barker and Rainey / Gumbo vegetable / Almost extinct
8. Brilliant success / Espionage expert / Pale brown
9. Deliberately ignore / Elusive / Affirmative action?
10. Blood component / Delicate
11. Mexican fare / Bad Ems, e.g. / Muslim official
12. Clod / Grub, e.g. / Shined, as a floor
13. Detective / Citrus peel
14. Made a mosaic / Simmer / Stable mate
15. Like tears / Sped / Arctic transport

BRICKS

| L E | A B | O E | I P | V E T |
| M D | O T | A R | L A W | A D Y |

| R I A | E R I | E T O | K | E W E |
| I L L | S E N | Y E R | R S | |

| R G O | R E | S | B A I | L |
| E E D | A I N | S T E | A D A | B Y |

| A R T | L Y | U T | A R | G E |
| M I T | P P E | M A L | S T E | A D |

| C | P | E | A | C A | A M P | M A I |
| A T E | R | F | F O R | R O O | |

| C A N | A | T | R V | N R E |
| A T T | A X | E S T | A S A | D E D |

| O G | A P E | A C N | R M S | L |
| E G | Y E | S L U | I A L | A S C |

DIAGRAM

	1	2	3	4	5	6	7	8	9	10	11	12	13	14	15
1	S	T	A	K	E		M	E	S	S		O	P	T	S
2															
3															
4															
5															
6															
7															
8															
9															
10															
11															
12															
13															
14															
15															

PUZZLE 311

ACROSS
1. Vintage
4. Lip
8. Umps' kin
12. Pelt
13. Liquid rock
14. Skip
15. Winter sickness
16. Black stone
17. Responsibility
18. Poison ___
20. Cold cube
22. Slalom
24. Sweetheart
28. End
31. Oz visitor
34. Adam's mate
35. Corn unit
36. Fragment
37. Suffer
38. Epoch
39. "That was close!"
40. Comrade
41. Louisiana marsh
43. VI
45. Cunning
47. Gossipy
51. Scent
54. Equal
57. Pro
58. Well
59. Mud
60. Small truck
61. Mounted on a peg
62. Gaze
63. Half ems

DOWN
1. Ons' opposites
2. Dilly
3. Snare, e.g.
4. Obstruct
5. Fled
6. ___ League
7. Skirt type
8. Bronc-riding event
9. Ostrichlike bird
10. Proper
11. Pen
19. Horned viper
21. Hoof sound
23. Craving
25. Meat choice
26. Hateful
27. Bank (on)
28. Nonunionist
29. Roman wrap
30. Heed
32. Pay dirt
33. Fancy marbles
36. Incite
40. Chop
42. Paddled
44. Private
46. Stand-in
48. Flutter
49. Browse
50. Desires
51. A lot, poetically
52. ___ cast
53. Unit
55. Compete
56. Bard's before

PUZZLE 312

ACROSS
1. Over
5. ___, crackle, pop
9. Skillful
12. Exec's auto
13. Painful cry
14. Gunk
15. Purple fruit
16. "Do ___ others..."
17. Omelet need
18. Shoemaker's device
20. Fusses
22. Great Wall site
25. Stir-fry pan
26. House locale
27. Hoard
30. Furthermore
34. Rich Little, e.g.
36. Downturn
37. Bored reaction
38. Floor model
39. Statistics
41. Struggle (for)
42. Motor coach
44. Shuts hard
46. Jerk
49. Cloud's place
50. Above, to a poet
51. Father
54. Creative spark
58. Golf norm
59. Meadow mowers
60. Electric-sign gas
61. Subways' kin
62. Salesmen
63. Fellow

DOWN
1. Swiss peak
2. Zero
3. Flightless bird
4. Lady
5. James Brown's music
6. Sister
7. Deed
8. Album entry
9. Ancient
10. ___ stick
11. Clothing
19. Lived
21. Authorize
22. Clothed
23. Crosby's pal
24. List component
25. Wailed
28. Tacks on
29. By way of
31. Molten flow
32. Enjoy a pool
33. Dollar bills
35. Toga
40. Pose a question
43. Higher
45. Fibbing
46. Contend (with)
47. Not imagined
48. Missteps
49. Back talk
52. Shock
53. Energy
55. Barely-passing grade
56. Geologic division
57. Picnic crasher

PUZZLE 313

ACROSS
1. Coarse sand
5. Large mop
9. Meal starter
12. Cry of pain
13. Italian money, once
14. Playing cube
15. Submit
16. Dark
17. Keats work
18. Muffle
20. Paddled
22. More timid
25. Cow's chew
26. Shade
27. Bossa ___
30. Long story
34. ___-advised
35. Zilch
36. Ewe's mate
37. Dad
39. Abandoned
41. Rascal
42. Porky's pen
44. Approves
46. Tingly
49. Big rig
51. Buck's mate
52. Pocket bread
54. Yuletide
58. Chemical
59. Done
60. Donate
61. Snaky shape
62. Stitched
63. Winter vehicle

DOWN
1. Glop
2. Polish
3. Sorbet
4. Herb
5. Skirt feature
6. Chablis, e.g.
7. Biblical boat
8. Marsh
9. Smell
10. Helper
11. ___ off (mad)
19. Container
21. Promos
22. Boat
23. Maui dance
24. Squeal
25. Young cow
28. Just
29. Compete
31. Opera solo
32. Strong, as meat
33. Current units
38. Cigar residue
40. Mr. Brokaw
43. Errors
45. Rulers
46. Not at work
47. Fiddles
48. So-so marks
49. Hearty soup
50. Deserve
53. "___ Got a Secret"
55. Grease
56. Ms. Arden
57. Guided

PUZZLE 314

ACROSS
1. Green
4. Suit item
8. Liquid measure
12. Service point
13. ___ code
14. Greasy
15. This woman
16. Daybreak
17. Incision
18. Tea type
20. Choppers
21. Appeal
25. Sail pole
28. Approach
29. Have title to
32. Matterhorn, e.g.
33. Trapped
34. Seek to marry
35. Tissue layer
36. Single
37. Finch food
38. Important
40. Twist
44. Watchers
48. Nylons
49. Side dish
52. Gloomy
53. Loiter
54. Furry feet
55. Large antelope
56. Coworker
57. Skillfully
58. Coop product

DOWN
1. Scrape
2. Long
3. Seven days
4. Darth ___
5. Notable time
6. Attach buttons
7. Turn brown
8. Medicine unit
9. Enrage
10. Disembarked
11. Fable
19. Pick
20. Excursion
22. Leading man
23. Adolescent
24. Host
25. Road diagram
26. Totally
27. Bond, e.g.
29. Be in the red
30. Sorrow
31. Head motion
33. Snail's kin
37. Sow's home
39. Gossipy
40. Flog
41. Took a bus
42. Capri, e.g.
43. ___-do-well
45. Margin
46. Boxing site
47. Cocky
49. Health resort
50. Testing place
51. Drill

PUZZLE 315

ACROSS
1. Clod
4. Stompers
8. Pout
12. To's mate
13. Furor
14. Mellowed
15. Less than many
16. Clothes presser
17. Lag behind
18. Spicy dip
20. Honkers
21. Grouchy
25. Thought
28. Chowder ingredient
29. Bumper ___
32. Action word
33. Check
34. Seconds
35. Woolly mom
36. Seep
37. In the sack
38. Fancy
40. Unpaid worker
44. Lawn cutter
48. Grape drink
49. Presidential "no"
52. Hole in one
53. Martial ___
54. Berserk
55. Ship's pronoun
56. Athletic event
57. Melody
58. Seed holder

DOWN
1. Not ons
2. Sector
3. Turkey or chicken
4. Tuck, for one
5. Bend an ___
6. Kind of maniac
7. Boxing count
8. Crafted
9. Monster
10. Round veggies
11. Border
19. Wound covering
20. Sports facility
22. Leading man
23. Fire
24. Infants
25. "___ Got Sixpence"
26. Mountain ___
27. Browning's before
29. Corn unit
30. Be
31. Checkers side
34. BLT topping
36. Song of praise
39. Puff away
40. Did the backstroke
41. Italian money, once
42. Contribute a chip
43. Suit part
45. Yellow jacket
46. Cave sound
47. Clarinet feature
49. Large vessel
50. Ostrich kin
51. Heavy weight

PUZZLE 316

ACROSS
1. Finn's vessel
5. Defeat
9. Moved with speed
12. Burn soother
13. Tiny bit
14. Past
15. Seed
16. Talk back
17. Electric atom
18. Docking place
20. Romantic dance
22. Ladle
25. Hoax
27. Long time
28. Dog's pest
30. Manhandle
34. Loony
36. Shirt
38. Cypress, e.g.
39. Just fair
41. British beverage
42. ___-do-well
44. Oak starter
46. Engine
49. Word from a crib
51. Mature
52. Lively dance
54. Mama's man
58. Great fury
59. Unwritten
60. Paradise
61. Headed
62. Depend
63. Pew

DOWN
1. Waste cloth
2. Ginger ___
3. Dedicated to
4. Musical pace
5. Knowledgeable
6. Throaty
7. ___ a living!
8. Ziti, e.g.
9. Drizzle
10. Very eager
11. Taboo
19. Data
21. Bullets and bombs
22. Faction
23. Serve wine
24. Formerly
26. Taxis
29. Mislay
31. Car
32. Operator
33. Slender
35. Game of chance
37. Burden
40. Trying time
43. Blunder
45. Some garments
46. Send a letter
47. Fiend
48. ___-off (mad)
50. Associate
53. Previous to
55. Lemon drink
56. Legume
57. Hill builder

PUZZLE 317

ACROSS
1. Pack animal
4. Poisonous snakes
8. Grub
12. Which person?
13. Cotton shirt
14. Island dance
15. Near the ground
16. Hound's trail
17. Comply with
18. Submarine locater
20. Corrode
22. Where ___ at
24. Parasite
28. Grace ender
31. Thin bit of smoke
34. "People ___ Funny"
35. Rampage
36. Electrical unit
37. Attract
38. Lodge
39. Memo error
40. Shade sources
41. Seventies music
43. Fasten
45. Exude
48. Backbone
52. Pepper type
55. Exam format
57. Newcomer to society
58. Arena shape
59. Dial sound
60. Soft toss
61. Dealer's car
62. Inserts
63. Printers' concerns

DOWN
1. Hole-making tools
2. Drive away
3. Planted
4. On a ship's left side
5. Patch of grass
6. Snow remover
7. Hurting
8. Job
9. Focal point
10. Flamenco cry
11. Direction
19. "___ She Sweet?"
21. European peak
23. Persuade
25. British title
26. Stuff full
27. Chops
28. Parched
29. Shortest skirt
30. Vast time periods
32. Naughty child
33. Blemish
37. Not shallow
39. Huck's friend
42. String instrument
44. Small landmasses
46. Pinch
47. Trampled
49. Loaf
50. Light-tube gas
51. Recedes
52. Figure, informally
53. Adam's mate
54. Take it on the ___
56. In addition

278

PUZZLE 318

ACROSS
1. Adventure story
5. Noah's number
8. Hoof sound
12. Urge on
13. Crude
14. Italian money, once
15. Particle of matter
16. First woman
17. Bakery employee
18. Very black
20. Disorder
21. Album entry
24. Wipe gently
26. Tear
27. Wearies
30. To's companion
33. Poetic work
34. Worshiped objects
35. High tennis shot
36. Animal's cage
37. Classic song
38. Astonish
39. "___ Day Now"
40. Full of gossip
42. Mast or boom
45. Mouthful
47. Ship's tiller
48. Sweetie
49. Control the realm
53. Atop
54. Clumsy person
55. Blue spring flower
56. Garlic feature
57. Authority
58. Finishes

DOWN
1. Health facility
2. Sculpture or dance
3. Thick stuff
4. Confess
5. Hard trip
6. Uneven
7. Have unpaid bills
8. Ascend
9. Parasitic insects
10. Metal deposits
11. Norms
19. Idea
21. Stage item
22. Skin
23. Unfold
24. Salami vendor
25. Agree
28. Lazily
29. Fishing gear
30. Fault
31. Paddles
32. Follow orders
39. Knight's suit
41. Mysterious
42. Go away!
43. Await judgment
44. Choir voice
45. Wild swine
46. Data
48. Bunny's movement
50. Coffee vessel
51. Jar's cover
52. Curvy letter

279

PUZZLE 319

ACROSS
1. Pony food
5. Blotch
9. Letters
13. Knitting stitch
14. November's gem
16. Land tract
17. Quartet less one
18. Puccini work
19. "___ You Tonight"
20. Asian boat
22. Hawaiian staple
24. Pounds
28. Shriek
31. Mr. Clinton
34. Blossom section
36. Touch-me-___
38. Aladdin's pal
39. British noble
40. Dove's cry
41. Exact
43. Inform
46. 21, e.g.
47. Orderly
49. Ranked
50. Bear's cave
51. Certain hot brew
52. Blessing ender
53. Blend
55. Bestow
57. Trendy
59. Remove shoestrings
64. Fastener
67. Broad tie
71. Miners' finds
72. Adored one
73. Heap
74. Profound
75. Damp
76. Mexican currency
77. Lenient

DOWN
1. Chooses
2. Allure
3. Lean
4. Spill liquid
5. Rock
6. Snap
7. Ajar, in poetry
8. Asphalt
9. Craziness
10. Master
11. Rage
12. Went before
15. Strike suddenly
21. More skilled
23. Wise bird
25. Resembling King Kong
26. Londoner's beverage
27. Wandered off
29. Provoke
30. Free
31. Light browns
32. Meaning
33. Whopper
35. Heidi's milieu
37. ___ the line
38. Elated
42. Had a meal
44. Crustacean
45. Male bighorn
48. Spanish title
51. NBA player, e.g.
54. Hint at
56. Excel
58. Water blockade
60. Gold source
61. Domain
62. Mediocre grades
63. View
64. Covered up
65. Lemony drink
66. Female pig
68. Soak in gravy
69. Prompt
70. Switch positions

PUZZLE 320

ACROSS
1. Comforts
6. Egyptian snakes
10. Assistance
14. Hurrah
15. Department
16. On a voyage
17. Commence
18. Caesar's garb
19. Wound's mark
20. Workers
23. Consult
24. Midday nap
27. Shredded
28. Green soup
29. Do arithmetic
30. Fire remains
32. Closer
34. Lode
36. Title
38. "To ___ For"
39. Diner customer
41. Light knock
43. Cowboy's tool
47. Take a spouse
49. Spider's work
51. Snow remover
52. Cut deeply
55. Vroom
57. Animosity
58. Cook's utensil
59. Eternally
61. Knocked
63. Genesis ship
64. Pie topping
66. Black-tie event
68. Phone wire
69. Buddhist priests
73. Like some wine
74. Gambler's concern
75. Quality
76. Hair holders
77. Annoying one
78. Sneakily

DOWN
1. Flow back
2. "Bells ___ Ringing"
3. Hang down
4. Sins
5. Piano piece
6. Limo, e.g.
7. Grunt
8. City bird
9. Played the lead
10. Contains
11. Flee
12. Renter
13. Winter coat
21. Low voice
22. Slowpoke
24. Collect
25. Notion
26. Correct text
31. Popular show
33. Harvest
35. Hot tip
37. Uncooked
40. Tailor again
42. For each
44. Mistake
45. Hurt
46. Had bills
48. Mature
50. Ice mass
52. Indoor parking
53. Sock type
54. Ridicule
56. Safes
58. Heathen
60. Peelings
62. Oyster's prize
65. Bird's dwelling
67. Subway posters
70. April's follower
71. Hurt
72. Pig's pad

PUZZLE 321

ACROSS
1. Tossed greens
6. Frost
10. Venomous snake
13. Love, in France
14. Momma's partner
15. Orchid necklace
16. Great!
17. Incapable
18. Below-average grade
19. Provide
20. Shade
21. Credit ___
22. Wound mark
24. Long, long ___
26. Antic
29. Tilts
32. Game of chance
33. Move slowly
36. Arose
38. Sorts
39. Kind of acid
41. Like an omelet
42. Ms. Burke
44. Printed mistake
45. Wise man
46. Round cap
48. Sucker
50. Fitness facility
51. BLT dressing
53. Defensive spray
56. Bucket
58. Flat boats
63. Hatchet
64. Squander
65. TV's "F ___"
66. Last letter
67. Privileged class
68. Serious
69. Certain railroads
70. Deep voice
71. Tatter

DOWN
1. Sensible
2. Prayer word
3. Pile on
4. Vehicle
5. Make sleepy
6. Deep respect
7. Not closed
8. Plea
9. Rodent pest
10. Robert or Alan
11. Oracle
12. ___ Piper
14. Mideastern bread
21. Competition
23. Nursery bed
25. Motorist's buy
26. Movie star, for short
27. Leg part
28. Letter's fee
29. Ocean vessel
30. Caesar's garments
31. Soaked
32. Youth
34. Jot down
35. Shed tears
37. Stain
40. Duplicate
43. At least one
47. Antelope
49. Heart arteries
51. Catchers' gloves
52. Opposed to aweather
53. Labyrinth
54. Skating feat
55. So-so grades
57. Sale condition
59. Curved doorway
60. Twice two
61. Carryall
62. Zoomed
64. Spider's trap

PUZZLE 322

ACROSS
1. Lifetimes
5. Hornet
9. Dowels
13. Grandma
14. Locations
16. Broth, e.g.
17. Happy
18. Meager
19. Stage gp.
20. Graceful tree
21. Not us
22. Wing
24. Fish delicacy
25. Rubies
26. Wanderers
30. Kilt fabric
32. Crowd
33. Heartache
34. Basis
37. Emit
39. Weather meas.
42. Baby grand, e.g.
44. Inquires
45. Ecstasy
47. Dull-witted
49. Mule's kin
50. Floating zoo
52. Skirt fold
55. Film again
57. Groovy!
59. Fawn's ma
61. Social drink
62. Snake sound
63. Silent
64. Mimic
67. Texas fare
69. Asian staple
70. Spar
71. Belief
72. Persia, now
73. Hits
74. Crafted
75. Await action

DOWN
1. Infuriate
2. Horse's speed
3. Tooth coating
4. Sorrowful
5. Done for
6. Bowed
7. Cloth joints
8. Criticize
9. Sacred hymn
10. Vast timespan
11. Belly
12. Health club
15. Exec's scribe
21. Three voices
23. Stud's spot
27. Intimidates
28. Pier
29. Places
31. Slithery biters
32. Food list
35. Jeopardy
36. Kitty
38. Green stone
39. Skier's lift
40. Other
41. Haze
43. Contrary
46. Benefit
48. Ailments
51. Answer
53. Praise
54. Colorful bird
56. Small bits
57. Dinnerware
58. Lubricated
60. Revise
64. Decline
65. Talk fondly
66. Jump
68. Shorten
69. Tear

PUZZLE 323

ACROSS

1. Crude
6. Youngsters
10. Insult
14. Immerse again
15. Fictional monster
16. Household
17. Covered with water
18. Food plan
19. Peepers
20. Swat
21. Separate
24. Small insect
25. Scope
27. Green gems
29. Skater's jump
31. Observes
32. Dolt
35. Soda ___
37. Principal's domain
41. Capsize
43. ___-tac-toe
45. Miss America's crown
46. Scatters
48. Sever
50. ___ out (barely managed)
51. Look like
53. Corduroy ridges
55. Anything
59. "___ Weapon"
63. In the know
64. Under
66. Ostrichlike animal
67. Pivot point
69. Fence bar
70. Passion
72. Religious season
73. Skin breakout
74. Fashionable
75. Tense
76. More or ___ (somewhat)
77. Large jugs

DOWN

1. Mania
2. Polish again
3. Modify
4. Bro's pal
5. Huge Egyptian statue
6. Commotion
7. Limber
8. Nightly visions
9. Love seats
10. This woman
11. Faithful
12. Improve
13. Annoyances
22. Dance instruction
23. Construct
26. Sincere
28. Palest
30. Parking field
32. Transit coach
33. Select
34. "___ the ramparts . . ."
36. Slangy film
38. Acorn bearer
39. Unrefined mineral
40. "___: A Dog"
42. Nerd
44. Nasty mutt
47. Some
49. Slant
52. "Dennis the ___"
54. Act properly
55. Moby Dick, e.g.
56. Jinxed
57. Imitating
58. Bridle straps
60. Shrub wall
61. Romance
62. Entices
65. Malty drinks
68. Swine's enclosure
71. Line of seats

PUZZLE 324

ACROSS
1. Form
5. Playful bite
8. Trig, e.g.
12. Imitator
13. Type of boom
15. Yearn
16. Don't leave!
17. Spotted horse
18. Stern
19. Scale notes
20. Thorny flower
21. Arm joints
23. Sailing vessel
25. Container
26. Shakes, as a tail
27. Pipe filling
31. Orb
34. Merry month
35. Lass's mate
36. Praises
37. Dunk
38. Grant
40. Need aspirin
41. Assist
42. Remains
43. Argue
46. Farm yield
47. Wiggly fish
48. Certain tires
52. Burger garnish
55. Forget
56. Jogged
57. More than
58. Walks through water
60. Fiddling emperor
61. Small duck
62. Paid out
63. Wise about
64. Just
65. Kid
66. Stinger

DOWN
1. Tall spars
2. Of the eye
3. Dog's rope
4. Like a desert
5. Sounds
6. Enclosed
7. Hole
8. Berth place
9. Poker holdings
10. "All ___ Jazz"
11. Not his
13. Sink item
14. Dallas player
20. Laughs loudly
22. Make fun of
24. Was obliged
27. Pub feature
28. Attired
29. Show concern
30. Evens' opposites
31. Deli side order
32. Duo
33. Hawaiian dance
34. Center
37. Playing cube
38. Cancel a liftoff
39. Rub lightly
41. Concedes
42. Painter, e.g.
44. Almost
45. Earn
46. Sidewalk material
48. Wild West show
49. Sports field
50. Dashes quickly
51. Pry
52. Dorothy's dog
53. Baking place
54. Diner offering
59. Fitting
60. Pronto!

PUZZLE 325

ACROSS
1. Naughty child
5. Drum's accompaniment
9. Lawful
14. Former Italian money
15. Broiler
16. Bouquet
17. Unwrap
18. Dark breads
19. Bears and Lions
20. Freshman's hat
22. Abundant
24. Preschooler
25. Pipe type
26. Basted
28. Young actress
32. Straight
35. Lump
36. Flit about
38. Equipped
40. Rapidly
43. Wipe
45. Curtain
46. Shoo!
48. Lubricant
50. Petite
51. Greek letters
53. Winter-sport vehicle
56. LPs' successors
58. Casper's call
59. Burro
62. Quantity of paper
63. Soundness
67. Heart rate
69. Feud
71. Dull pain
72. Computer letter
73. Frozen sheet
74. Promgoer
75. Like a baby chick
76. Psychic
77. Weapons

DOWN
1. Globule
2. Fully developed
3. Realm
4. Leather maker
5. Asta's front limb
6. Poison ___
7. Senses
8. Resulted
9. Ready for a shave
10. Prior to, in verse
11. Sheep's kin
12. Bullets, to a GI
13. Final
21. Sickly
23. Gulp
27. Sweetie
28. Mop
29. Recorded
30. Motto
31. Pave
33. Baby's creep
34. Wigwam's kin
37. Twosome
39. Land title
41. Nippy
42. Totally
44. Highchair attire
47. Comfort
49. Crab's cousin
52. Winter mufflers
54. ___ constrictor
55. Brahms piece
57. Happy face
59. Mimed
60. Japanese wrestling
61. Sandwich side
64. Froster
65. Those people
66. Cravings
68. Go wrong
70. Opponent

286

PUZZLE 326

ACROSS
1. Citric ___
5. Animation frame
8. Guess
12. Finished
13. Rustic
15. Extent
16. Part of CD
17. Proclaim
18. Ham or bacon
19. Foxiest
21. Boat
23. Fib
24. Zero
25. Tanker
27. ___ Circle
30. Luxury fabric
33. Average grade
34. Danish, e.g.
36. Comment
40. The woman's
41. Lump
42. Bikini piece
43. Adam's place
45. Trunks
47. Jelly holder
48. Merge
50. Pensive
52. Steak variety
55. ___ room
56. Untrained
57. Light-bulb word
61. Radio noise
64. Opera solo
66. Film
68. Pocket bread
69. Bronze coin
70. Bamboo eater
71. Eternally
72. Border
73. Golf peg
74. Deep-sleep times

DOWN
1. Attaches
2. Spiral
3. Dishonest
4. Fraud
5. Mutt
6. Important times
7. Strip of wood
8. Fool
9. Ogre
10. Lofty abode
11. Dough nut?
13. Disintegrate
14. Kauai gift
20. Blooper
22. Hawaiian food
26. Lodging
27. Pang
28. Bamboo, e.g.
29. Saguaros, e.g.
30. Shop
31. Crest
32. Print errors
35. Notch
37. Purpose
38. Streetcar
39. Qualify for
44. Sister
46. Group
49. Not old
51. Jumper
52. Tiny bit
53. Uncovered
54. Unpaid
58. Horned viper
59. Not this
60. Sound
61. RR depot
62. List member
63. Coupes
65. Dined
67. "___ to Joy"

PUZZLE 327

ACROSS
1. Lessens
5. Dad
8. Capri or Skye
12. Ensnare
13. Savory jelly
15. Milky gem
16. Devout
17. Assessor
18. Captures
19. Part of TGIF
20. "Diamond ___"
21. Wheel part
23. Average grade
24. Magnetism
27. Rani's attire
29. Ajar, in poems
30. Chide
34. Liquefy
37. Narration
39. Fashion periodical
40. Bunny jump
41. Wilder's "___ Town"
42. Paving material
43. Refs' kin
45. Rodeo rope
47. Workout places
48. Love song
50. Neckline shape
52. Eye test
53. ___ bee
58. Slangy negative
60. Tent stake
62. Coat sleeve
63. Miss
64. Operates
66. Slow-moving mollusk
68. Additionally
69. Pre-Easter time
70. Golden brown
71. Pans' kin
72. ___ Godiva
73. Soaked
74. Nursery items

DOWN
1. Principle
2. Soup liquid
3. Light wood
4. Secret agent
5. Sunday song
6. Select
7. Dock
8. Electric particle
9. Particular skill
10. Not punctual
11. What ___ is new?
13. Stands up
14. Brittle
20. Glass edge
22. Spoil
25. Employ oars
26. Stirs up
28. Fish beginnings
31. Proves human
32. Chowder type
33. That girl's
34. In this way
35. "___ Alone"
36. Nab
38. Frog's kin
44. Gender
45. Weakest, as an excuse
46. Excessively
47. Hair-care goo
49. Brief doze
51. Shade tree
54. Artist's need
55. Icy abode
56. Offensive
57. Shine
58. Invalid
59. On the water
61. Chew steadily
65. Hog enclosure
67. Fearful wonder
68. Prone

DOUBLE CROSSER

PUZZLE 328

Fill in the missing letters in the crossword diagram, making sure that no word is repeated. Then transfer those letters to the correspondingly numbered dashes below the diagram to reveal a quotation.

$\overline{1}\ \overline{2}\ \overline{3}\ \overline{4}\ \overline{5}\ \overline{6}\ \overline{7}\ \ \overline{8}\ \overline{9}\ \overline{10}\ \overline{11}\ \ \overline{12}\ \overline{13}\ \overline{14}\ \overline{15}$

$\overline{16}\ \overline{17}\ \ \overline{18}\ \overline{19}\ \overline{20}\ \overline{21}\ \ \overline{22}\ \overline{23}\ \overline{24}\ \ \overline{25}\ \overline{26}\ \overline{27}\ \ \overline{28}\ \overline{29}\ \overline{30}$

$\overline{31}\ \overline{32}\ \overline{33}\ \overline{34}\ \overline{35}\ \overline{36}\ \overline{37}\ \ \overline{38}\ \overline{39}\ \overline{40}\ \overline{41}\ \ \overline{42}\ \overline{43}\ \overline{44}$

$\overline{45}\ \overline{46}\ \overline{47}\ \overline{48}.$

289

PUZZLE 329

ACROSS
1. Ticket remnant
5. Shut loudly
9. ____-hop
12. Coloring
13. Fuss
14. Undivided
15. Banish
16. Scrape
17. Broke a fast
18. Unclose, in verse
19. Sweet tuber
20. Fragment
22. Dig further
24. Probes
25. Make angry
27. Jeans patch site
28. Pizza herb
30. Chapel song
32. Salad fixings
35. Drip
36. West Pointers
38. Annoyed
40. Cushion
41. Noah's boat
42. Neither's partner
43. Street
45. Diva's tune
46. Feel sick
47. Jobless
48. Polite chap
49. Slippery
50. So-so grades
51. Verge

DOWN
1. Got up
2. Wig
3. Invisible
4. Wager
5. Unfamiliar
6. Fertile soil
7. Classifieds
8. Floor cleaners
9. Husky, as a voice
10. Certain air duct
11. Chirps
19. Crave
21. Paddled
23. Punctual
26. Easter edible
27. Work dough
29. Game rooms
30. Noble
31. Every twelve months
33. Came closer
34. Kite cord
35. Biblical mount
37. Glide
39. ____ the Red
40. Ashy
44. Shelley poem
45. Ripen, as cheese

PUZZLE 330

ACROSS
1. Relaxation
5. Brief farewell
8. Pant
12. Protected, at sea
13. Lobster eggs
14. Surface
15. Actress Lockhart
16. Bird of prey
17. Employer
18. Calculate
19. Moreover
21. Tangle
22. Listened to
25. Andean animal
27. Compelled
29. Medicine measure
30. This evening
32. Shortcoming
34. Dishes
37. Woodworker's machine
38. Makes up (for)
40. Inclined
41. Daybreak
44. Dog doc
45. Blend
47. VCR button
48. Hour
49. Ripped
50. Crude metal
51. Bawl
52. Went quickly
53. Marry
54. Probability

DOWN
1. Prince of India
2. Dodged
3. Return to ____
4. Golf gadget
5. Enlarge
6. Cry in distress
7. Squiggly swimmers
8. Chatter
9. Scents
10. Bun seed
11. Spaghetti, e.g.
20. Dated
23. Gully
24. Brought to mind
26. Sweepstakes
28. Little bite
31. Peeked
32. Compact computer
33. Apparel
35. Was jealous of
36. Pretended to be
37. Perseveres
39. Stages
42. In a line
43. "____ No Angels"
46. Crimson
48. Duo

DOUBLE TROUBLE

PUZZLE 331

Not really double trouble, but double fun! Solve this puzzle as you would a regular crossword, except place one, two, or three letters in each box. The number of letters in each answer is shown in parentheses after its clue.

ACROSS
1. Do homework (5)
3. Newlywed (5)
5. Forgo, as a right (5)
7. Rouse (6)
9. Next to (6)
11. Curt (5)
13. What bit Cleopatra (3)
15. Profitable (12)
17. Dominant (12)
20. Coffee break (4)
21. Religious season (4)
22. Finale (3)
23. Fugitive (6)
25. Pry bar (5)
27. Hence (4)
29. Slate wiper (6)
31. Equipment (4)
33. Work by Shelley (3)
35. Venerates (7)
37. Beijing's site (5)
39. Jet hotshot (3)
41. Quibble (5)
43. Space shuttle name (9)
45. Consider (11)
48. Pave (3)
49. Discolors (6)
50. Species (5)
52. Dire (7)
55. Tempt (4)
56. Staked (5)
57. Saucy (4)

DOWN
1. Ticket part (4)
2. Pigments (4)
3. Corrupt with money (5)
4. Crave (6)
5. Restaurant worker (6)
6. Adaptable (9)
8. Harangue (6)
10. Bashful (6)
12. Incident (5)
14. Brussels ____ (6)
16. Snuggle (6)
17. Primp (5)
18. Think about (6)
19. Stag feature (6)
24. Mindful (5)
26. Brink (5)
28. Muck (3)
30. Aided (6)
32. Treasury (7)
34. Vamoose (6)
36. Oppose (6)
38. Not any (4)
39. Confront (6)
40. Involve (6)
42. Small town (7)
44. Rough (6)
46. Secure (6)
47. Resident (6)
51. Mouthpiece part (4)
53. More mature (5)
54. Unseat (4)

Say That Again?

PUZZLE 332

Four well-known quotations or phrases have been reworded below, but the original meanings have been kept. Can you identify the originals?

Example: *Lack of awareness brings elation.* (**Answer:** *Ignorance is bliss.*)

1. It isn't recommended to destroy all one's connections.

2. Distinguished intellects have similar reasoning skills.

3. Scoundrels abandon the failing venture.

4. Truthfulness represents a most advantageous course of action.

PUZZLE 333

ACROSS
1. Feel pain
5. Pick
8. Heavy mists
12. "High ___" (Cooper film)
13. Girl Scout group
15. Milky gem
16. Gumbo need
17. Single printing
18. Sitar music
19. Made a tree home
21. Timetable abbr.
22. Counterfeit
23. More uncanny
25. Close to the ground
27. ___ trip
29. Plus
30. Wooden pins
33. European mountain
34. Maui mementos
36. Carrier
38. College woman
40. Shorthand pro
42. Fully developed
43. Sultans' groups of wives
45. Advise of danger
47. None
48. Filled tortilla
49. UK's neighbor
50. 24-hour period
51. "___ to a Nightingale"
53. Conceals
55. Laugh loudly
58. Baden-Baden, e.g.
60. Author
63. Seaweed
64. Present occasion
66. Contend (with)
67. Blind section
68. Church officer
69. Reflex-test site
70. Peel, as fruit
71. Caustic material
72. Go in search of

DOWN
1. Promptly
2. Coal by-product
3. Western
4. Maternally kin
5. Surgery rms.
6. Puzzling question
7. Advertise
8. Deny vehemently
9. Colorful fish
10. Nuts
11. Way to dance or dunk
13. Cleanliness
14. Chime
20. Pertaining to an epoch
24. Revise
26. Agape, in verse
27. Every individual
28. Boast
31. Sharpening wheel
32. Dark brown
35. Embroider
36. Library patron
37. Count (on)
39. Honor with a medal
41. Tack
44. Trendy
46. Advance upon
52. Medieval slave
53. Bonbon, e.g.
54. Punts
55. Scrape
56. Stewpot
57. Food thickener
59. Sampling of voters
61. Sporting blade
62. Smell strongly
65. Middling mark

PUZZLE 334 — Classified Adds

Fill in the spaces with answers that begin and end with the given letters and fit the categories shown. Answers may be any length. For example, in number 1 below, you must think of an Asian capital beginning with the letter T and ending with the letter N, a metal object beginning with the letter N and ending with the letter L, and so on. There are many possible solutions.

	ASIAN CAPITALS	MADE FROM METAL	MAMMALS	COLLEGE OR UNIVERSITY	USED IN SPORTS
1.	T___N	N___L	L___A	A___T	T___T
2.	D___S	S___E	E___T	T___S	S___K
3.	S___L	L___R	R___S	S___H	H___T
4.	B___G	G___L	L___D	D___W	W___E
5.	B___K	K___Y	Y___K	K___E	E___G

PUZZLE 335

ACROSS
1. Equine
6. On a cruise
10. City map
14. Assists in crime
15. Norms
16. Highway section
17. Rich veins
18. ___ Benedict
19. Related
20. Celebration
21. Lingerie item
22. Abroad
24. Rations out
26. Vaselike vessel
27. Swamp
29. Flightless bird
30. Loamy deposit
33. Magazine fillers
34. Curt
37. Hosiery problem
39. Find out
41. French summer
42. Fair booth
43. Humdinger
44. African fly
46. 23rd Greek letter
47. ___ maid
49. Cup edge
50. Tiny amount
51. In the past
52. More stylish
54. Hollow reed
57. Lodge member
58. Tardy
61. District
62. Trim
64. Sweetener
65. Wedding band
66. Neutral shade
67. Decorate
68. Nothing, in Madrid
69. Paper quantity
70. Solid

DOWN
1. Fifty percent
2. Orchestra member
3. Clearance event
4. Hard metal
5. Shapely curve
6. Openings
7. Epics
8. Energy unit
9. Attack
10. Most obvious
11. Huron or Tahoe
12. Indigo plant
13. Baby-sit
21. Flop
23. To-and-___
25. Low in fat
27. Formal dance
28. Theater
31. Flower with showy spikes
32. Mexican condiment
35. Western tribesman
36. Oil
38. Fluent
40. Kind of turnip
42. 18-wheeler
44. Cavalry soldier
45. Go to the bottom
48. Personality
52. ___ firma
53. Sidestep
54. Cowshed
55. Solo for Sills
56. Repair
59. Old salts
60. Marine eagle
63. 1 or 11, in blackjack
64. Woebegone

Anagrams Plus
PUZZLE 336

Find the names of ten New England schools by adding one of the given letters to each word and rearranging the letters. Each letter will be used only once.

B B H I M S S S W Y

1. LEA + ? = _____
2. BORN + ? = _____
3. CLOY + ? = _____
4. THIS + ? = _____
5. BETA + ? = _____
6. NABOB + ? = _____
7. SARDINE + ? = _____
8. STREAM + ? = _____
9. SAWMILL + ? = _____
10. MONISM + ? = _____

293

PUZZLE 338

ACROSS
1. Tropical rodent
5. Superman's garment
9. Congregation responses
14. Jamaican citrus
15. Encourage a wrongdoer
16. Textile fiber
17. Bartlett or Bosc, e.g.
18. Grandma
19. Dinnerware
20. Fleets
22. List entry
23. Guideline
24. Enjoy a pool
27. S.W.A.T. need
29. Educational conferences
33. Individual
34. Midday gathering
36. Lend ____ (listen)
39. 18-wheeler
40. African animal, for short
41. Snickered
43. Decompose
44. Respected
46. Exit
48. Switch positions
49. Cajun soup thickener
51. Hideaway
54. Capable of being heard
58. Isolated
60. Attentive
62. Spread plaster over
63. Inn
64. Wide-spouted jug
65. Therefore
66. Collar stiffeners
67. Bone-dry
68. Observed

DOWN
1. Insect stage
2. Antiquing material
3. Chowder type
4. Military wing
5. Suez or Erie
6. Belittles
7. Fountain ____
8. Timetable info
9. Circle section
10. Dolphinfish
11. Send forth
12. Diamond team number
13. Row of stitches
21. Musical twosome
24. Arrogant
25. Gain victory
26. Small measure
27. Cowgirl Oakley
28. Encounters
30. Omit, as a vowel
31. Printer's proof
32. Lethargy
33. Stable morsel
35. Touch-me-____
37. Counselor
38. Coral shelf
39. Radiation units
42. Rink judge
45. Cloth dealer
46. Failure
47. Certain chemical compounds
50. Bizarre
51. Unlawful flights
52. Much
53. Smidgen
55. Exposed
56. Winter Olympics event
57. Dark, to a poet
59. Aboveground trains
60. Legal matter
61. Fill with wonder

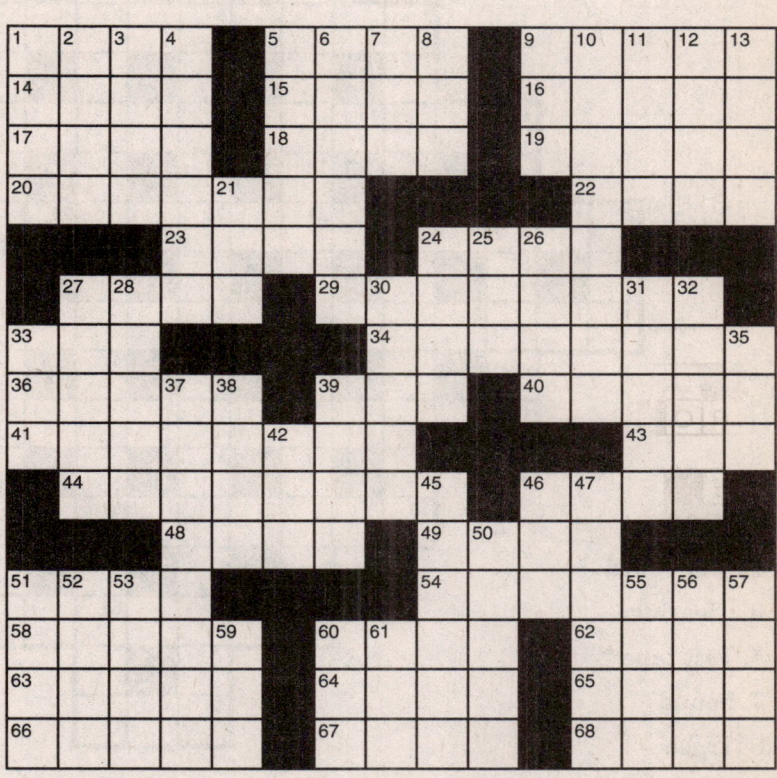

PUZZLE 339

Letter Tiles

Form four words reading across and five words reading down by placing the eight Letter Tiles into the diagram. Horizontal tiles go into horizontal spaces, vertical tiles into vertical spaces. In the example, three tiles fit together to form the words SAW, ONE, SO, AN, and WE.

Example:

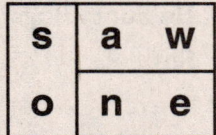

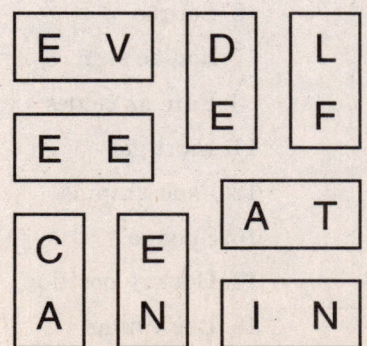

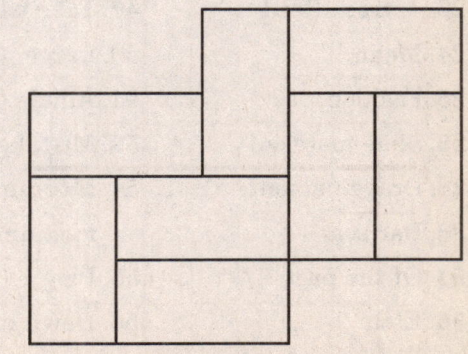

PUZZLE 340

OVERLAPS

Place the answer to each clue into the diagram beginning at the corresponding number. Words will overlap with other words.

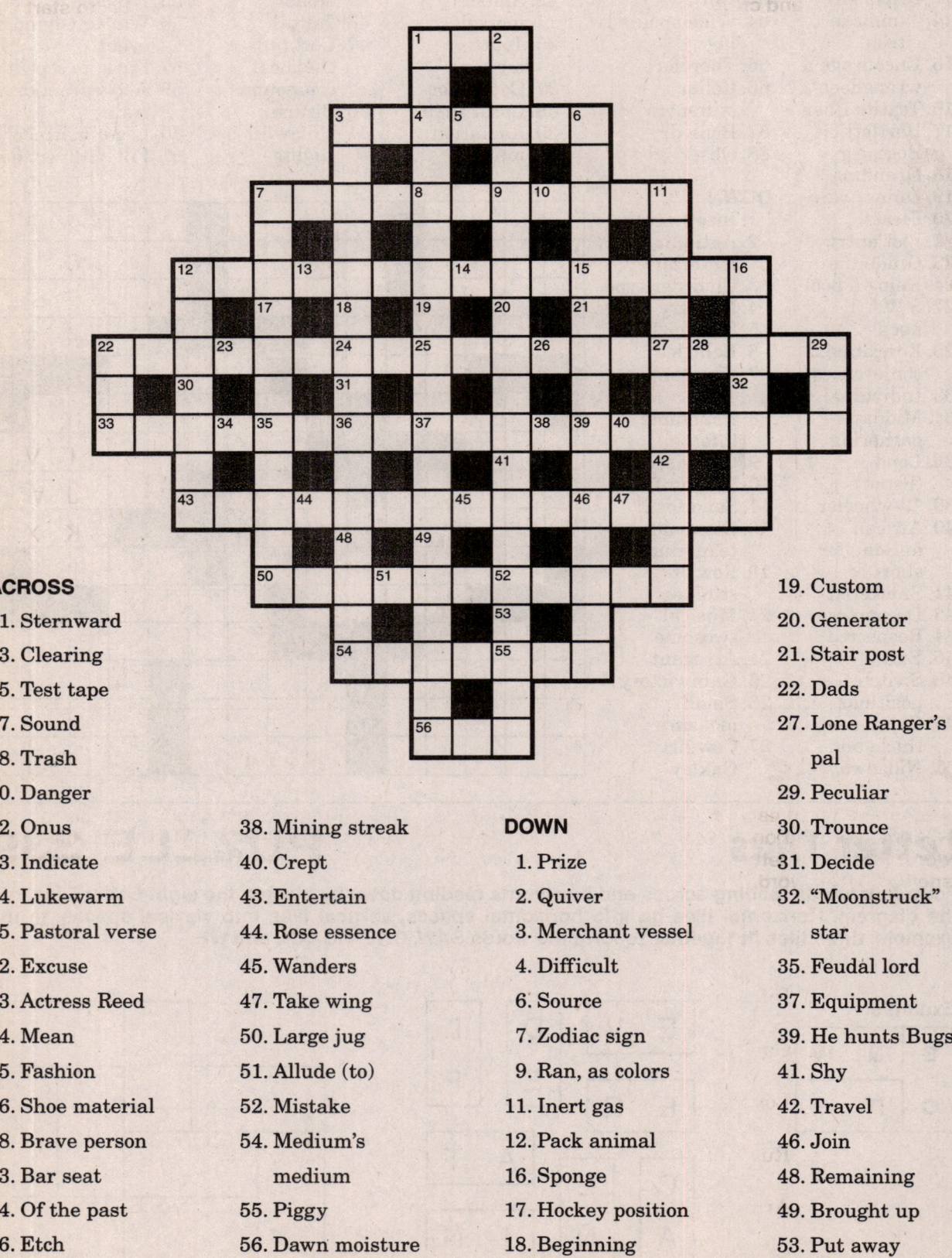

ACROSS

1. Sternward
3. Clearing
5. Test tape
7. Sound
8. Trash
10. Danger
12. Onus
13. Indicate
14. Lukewarm
15. Pastoral verse
22. Excuse
23. Actress Reed
24. Mean
25. Fashion
26. Shoe material
28. Brave person
33. Bar seat
34. Of the past
36. Etch
38. Mining streak
40. Crept
43. Entertain
44. Rose essence
45. Wanders
47. Take wing
50. Large jug
51. Allude (to)
52. Mistake
54. Medium's medium
55. Piggy
56. Dawn moisture

DOWN

1. Prize
2. Quiver
3. Merchant vessel
4. Difficult
6. Source
7. Zodiac sign
9. Ran, as colors
11. Inert gas
12. Pack animal
16. Sponge
17. Hockey position
18. Beginning
19. Custom
20. Generator
21. Stair post
22. Dads
27. Lone Ranger's pal
29. Peculiar
30. Trounce
31. Decide
32. "Moonstruck" star
35. Feudal lord
37. Equipment
39. He hunts Bugs
41. Shy
42. Travel
46. Join
48. Remaining
49. Brought up
53. Put away

CODEWORD

PUZZLE 341

Codeword is a special crossword puzzle in which conventional clues are omitted. Instead, answer words in the diagram are represented by numbers. Each number represents a different letter of the alphabet, and all of the letters of the alphabet are used. When you are sure of a letter, put it in the code key chart and cross it off in the alphabet box. A group of letters has been inserted to start you off.

Add One

PUZZLE 342

Add one letter to each of the given words to form the answer to one of the clues. Each given word will only be used once. The added letter may be at the beginning, the end, or in the middle of the word. Place that letter in the box next to its clue. The added letters, read from top to bottom, will spell a 6-letter word.

BACON CARET DETER DEUCE SALON SAUTE

1. Infer ☐ _____

2. Calorie counter ☐ _____

3. Lox fish ☐ _____

4. Rug's kin ☐ _____

5. Army greeting ☐ _____

6. Signal light ☐ _____

PUZZLE 343

ACROSS
1. Somber
4. Suggestive
8. Mr. Crosby
12. NFL player
13. Column
15. Toward shelter
16. Ham it up
17. Electrical unit
18. Joy
19. Transparent
21. Preoccupation
23. Telecast again
25. Awry
28. Donkey
30. Flower children
32. Magnifying glass
33. Started
36. Engrave with acid
37. Tall tree
38. Toupee
39. Furthermore
40. Woeful sigh
42. Restore
44. Vegas game
45. Snuggles
47. Stockpile
49. Form of trapshooting
50. Grimace
52. Worshiper
54. Below, to a poet
58. Edge line
61. Fix a text
63. "___-Baby"
64. Insist upon
65. Abounded
66. Knock
67. Saloon order
68. Was aware of
69. Needle hole

DOWN
1. Resorts
2. Curved support
3. Be overly fond
4. Hoop part
5. Greek letter
6. Unsoiled
7. Knitter's thread
8. Scottish instrument
9. ___-advised
10. Formerly named
11. Exclamation
13. Peeling device
14. Recoup
20. Missteps
22. Baseball official
24. Stick up
26. Child minder
27. Runner-up's place
28. Southern beauties
29. Expose
30. Mammoth
31. Scat!
32. Low in fat
34. She-sheep
35. Cotton machine
41. Ocean crosser
42. Reply
43. "___ Do You Love"
44. Cabbage's cousin
46. Governed
48. Possessed
50. ___ seas
51. Larceny, e.g.
53. Smell
55. Land unit
56. Waiter's burden
57. Hoopla
58. Hoagie
59. Earlier than, in poems
60. Mature, as wine
62. Make a blouse

PUZZLE 344

ACROSS
1. Sty fare
5. Thin tuft
9. Plate
13. Soda choice
14. "___ Attraction"
15. Acting gp.
16. TV's Griffith
17. Edition
18. Smooth
19. Loathe
21. Soup tin
23. Work unit
24. Provoke
25. Mata Hari, e.g.
27. Desert refuges
29. Hoover, e.g.
31. Craving
33. Toward
34. Employed
36. Galley blade
37. Painting, e.g.
38. Gumbo veggie
39. Knot
41. Droves
45. Pursue
47. Dunk
48. Long ago
49. Flirt
51. Not west
53. Cauldron
54. Flush
55. Bizarre
56. Oahu instrument
58. Wild donkey
59. Sack out
61. Lives
64. Inkling
66. Refresh
69. ___ tide
70. ___ Grey tea
71. Felony
72. Curly greens
73. Whiskeys
74. Derbies
75. Seethe

DOWN
1. Large amount
2. By oneself
3. Veteran
4. Bill settler
5. Had been
6. ___ a girl!
7. Audacious
8. Reason
9. Daniel ___ Kim
10. Take stock?
11. Music box
12. Suspends
14. Proper
20. Snow slat
22. Film ___
25. Glance at
26. Worded
28. Restless
29. Pair
30. Consult
32. Fast-food option
35. Sunrises
37. Swiss range
40. Main drag
42. Small sofa
43. RBI's kin
44. Moist
46. Cattle
49. Lose
50. Guarantee
52. Monkey suit
54. Speeder
55. Sung drama
57. Quirks
60. Foot part
61. Mother sheep
62. Narrative
63. Spit
65. Chicago rails
67. Young bug
68. Type measures

PUZZLE 345

ACROSS
1. Skid
5. Fawn's father
9. Sit-ups target
12. Musical pitch
13. Coil
15. Just out
16. Litter's littlest
17. Verse
18. Iced ___
19. Agape, to a bard
20. Lark, e.g.
21. Hoarse sounding
23. Flawless
25. Flower part
27. Adventure
29. Fishing rod
33. Spin
36. Draws off
38. Swear
39. Owned
40. Clothing
43. Thirst quencher
44. Ill will
45. Handle roughly
46. Lazy person
48. Wild attempt
50. Hand-thrown bomb
53. Operator
55. Corrected
59. Cubicle
62. "___ Trek"
63. Actor Milland
64. Keats's vessel
65. Computing device
68. Short letter
69. Guy's date
70. Reveres
71. At all times
72. Crafty
73. Computer unit
74. Decade numbers

DOWN
1. Barber's sharpener
2. Jeweler's glass
3. ___ tube
4. Teacher's ___
5. Athletics
6. Evened up
7. Renoir's forte
8. Needlefish
9. Tiny colonizers
10. Honk
11. Persuade
13. Hot
14. Old harp
20. Chaos
22. Electrical unit
24. Dedicated to
25. Singe
26. Variety
28. Not fresh
30. Oblong
31. Ore vein
32. Widemouthed pitcher
33. Now hear ___!
34. Toad bump
35. Brainchild
37. Patio door, perhaps
41. Book leaf
42. Cat sound
47. Rumpus room
49. However
51. Mother ___
52. Gather
54. Persian king
56. Went by car
57. Dined
58. Tinters
59. ___ Bunny
60. Verbal exam
61. Merely
62. Highlander
66. Host Barker
67. Whichever
68. Capture

300

PUZZLE 346

ACROSS
1. Offense
6. Horse feed
9. Linger
14. Homebody
15. Formerly
16. Used a drill
17. Vow site
18. Droop
19. Made cookies
20. City light
21. Platform
23. Secret agent
24. Shelve
27. Seeded bread
29. Maple juice
32. Payable
33. Corroded
36. Humiliates
38. British bar
39. Difficult
41. Standards
42. Title
43. Pave a road, again
44. Wayne's nickname
45. Headgear
46. Triumphant cry
47. Baby powder
49. Snow slat
50. Unprecedented
51. Fall behind
52. Teeny's partner
54. Fido's trick
57. Pitt film
59. Gumbo must
63. Halt, matey!
65. Egos' kin
66. Model
67. "___ Eagles"
68. Develop
69. Edgy
70. Furious
71. Commanded
72. Spills

DOWN
1. Tribe
2. Drama part
3. Towards
4. Intended
5. Mess up
6. Annoy
7. Marble
8. Hindu practice
9. Monasteries
10. Tropical snake
11. Bothers
12. Not shallow
13. Vortex
22. Chow
25. Lime drinks
26. City vehicle
28. Anesthetic
29. Dune material
30. Roughly
31. Hooded jacket
33. Polish
34. Gobbled up
35. Duck's mate
37. Sniff
38. Situate
40. Sketch
42. Pond barrier
43. Demolish
45. Titanic
46. Barely earn
48. King's home
49. Detected
52. Cheese chunk
53. Mountain call
54. "___ Ha'i"
55. Constantly
56. Dotty
58. Glass tube
60. Bingo's kin
61. Grate
62. Londoners' drinks
64. Rested
66. "___ De-lovely"

PUZZLE 347

ACROSS
1. Jab
5. Cancel a mission
10. Cabbage salad
14. Milky gemstone
15. Yard cleaner
16. Garden walk
17. Bonus
18. Yearn for
19. Comply with
20. Generation
21. Curds and ___
22. Consult
24. Small bags
26. Lecture
30. Windy
31. Tofu bean
32. Likewise
33. Knolls
35. Cargo unit
36. ___-a-lug
37. Ride a ten-speed
38. Baby's napkin
39. Large boats
40. Flowery wreaths
41. Spotted playing cube
42. Seasoning
43. Individual
44. Gamble
45. Cannon sound
46. Plaid
48. Sagging
52. Had been
53. Ice arena
54. Blemish
55. Strongbox
58. Sidestep
60. Tibetan monk
61. Eye rudely
62. Green fruits
63. Matured
64. Mope
65. Baker's need
66. Takes a spouse

DOWN
1. John Paul II et al.
2. "Carmen," e.g.
3. Unit of gold content
4. BPOE member
5. Bowmen
6. Hardly
7. Says yes
8. Gun, as an engine
9. State crime
10. Conversed
11. Testing area
12. Gobbled
13. How come?
21. During
23. Bond, e.g.
25. Rings up
27. Moral
28. Car style
29. Pigs
31. Cry noisily
33. Laughing ___
34. More frozen
35. Neckwear
36. Ape
37. Thicken
38. Iota
39. Ghost
41. Closely
42. Quickest
44. Lamb's lament
45. Grooms' ladies
47. Chirp
48. Tragedy
49. Reflection
50. "A Boy ___ Sue"
51. Diploma receivers
55. Dunk
56. In the past
57. Common ailment
59. Contend
60. Order's companion

PUZZLE 348

ACROSS

1. Ties the knot
5. Nasty remark
9. Inlet
13. State publicly
14. Indifferent
16. Comply with
17. Sasquatch's kin
18. Copter blade
19. Pine fruit
20. Kick
22. Hampers
24. Flax product
27. Imbibe
28. Raw rock
29. Twitch
32. Pinch pennies
35. Yelp
36. Not fitting
38. Legend
40. Pale gray
41. Make bigger
44. Caribbean export
45. Ogle
47. Bow down
48. Onassis, to chums
49. Sways
52. Microscopic
53. Railroad unit
54. Fruit pastry
55. Embers
57. Fast cat
61. VHS predecessor
63. Bank deal
64. Mend once more
66. Observance
70. Altar area
71. "___ John B"
72. Diabolic
73. Exploit
74. Mexican money
75. Writing surface

DOWN

1. Custom
2. Ms. Arden
3. Period
4. Steal
5. Cowshed
6. Oodles
7. Go bad
8. ___ tube
9. Pilot's place
10. English horn
11. Heat outlet
12. Peepers
15. Belgian coin
21. Let loose
23. Gielgud's title
24. Trustworthy
25. Showy blooms
26. Sister's son
30. Rural hotel
31. Seals
32. Spread
33. Spanish rattle
34. Multiple
37. Bad review
39. Muslim rulers
42. Wow!
43. Put into office
46. Matured
50. Young insect
51. Equips
56. Paddled
57. Clothed
58. Optimism
59. Convenience
60. Benefit
61. Life stories
62. World's fair, e.g.
65. Rival
67. "___ Waited So Long"
68. Song syllables
69. Moose's kin

PUZZLE 349

ACROSS
1. Gear teeth
5. Mama's fellow
9. Hang open
13. Ring of light
14. Put up
16. Portent
17. Detail
18. Calm
19. Morsel
20. Bird's noise
22. Bluish green
24. Faintly lit
25. ___ deco
28. Enjoy Mt. Snow
29. Porky's digs
30. Snoop
33. Campus people
35. Counterpart
37. Ill temper
38. Dial sound
39. Female pig
40. Lullaby, e.g.
42. Shift
44. Every
48. Young louse
50. ___ the line
52. Sticky glop
53. Border on
55. African giggler
56. Choose
57. Green veggie
58. Average mark
60. Not loud
61. Large vase
62. Rabbit's kin
64. Bellybutton
69. Near
71. Figure out
74. Abide
75. Fantasy
76. Votes in favor
77. Voyaging
78. Droves
79. Matched groups
80. Fax

DOWN
1. Stylish
2. Vow
3. Cheerfulness
4. Not all
5. Energy
6. ___ you kidding?
7. Soil enricher
8. Entry
9. Clump
10. Among
11. Small
12. Foe
15. Furniture wood
21. Deal
23. Chauffeured car
26. Hen's perch
27. Nomad's home
30. Sib
31. Not anti
32. Desire
34. Goddess, e.g.
36. Great respect
39. Office writer
41. Bearded antelope
43. Yuletide
45. Long, long ___
46. Lawman
47. Burning
49. Urge
51. Sunrise
53. Antenna
54. Bracelet
55. Valiant types
57. Football kicks
59. Effortless
63. Otherwise
65. Too bad!
66. Clamp
67. Parallel
68. Top spot
70. Chop
72. Former GI
73. Curvy turn

PUZZLE 350

ACROSS
1. Maple's fluid
4. "Rosemary's ___"
8. Thin pancake
13. Tin Woodman's request
14. ___ vera
15. Journey
16. Sweet drink
17. Dryer fuzz
18. Metal fasteners
19. Biked
21. Very small amount
22. Candy ___
23. Get even for
26. Grazing group
28. Discourage
30. Geological period
32. Yield to another
33. Legendary hairy creature
34. Curved line
35. Pay hike
37. Youngster
38. Mr. Spelling
40. Globe, e.g.
41. Midday
43. Had been
44. Cartoon frame
45. Pulls
47. Auction calls
48. Close again
50. Ready for business
52. Cheerio!
53. Delicate
57. Disregard
60. Mix
61. Yuletide drink
62. Tilted
63. Remain undecided
64. Thick mist
65. ___ up (tense)
66. Liberal ___
67. Light-switch positions

DOWN
1. Daytime TV
2. Nurse's helper
3. Appealed
4. Narrative poem
5. E.T., e.g.
6. Joined
7. Until now
8. Standards of judgment
9. Crow's cousin
10. Cain's mother
11. Family animal
12. High railways
15. Hot-dish holder
20. Land units
21. Paired
24. Furnished
25. Mistakes
26. Listener
27. Taste-worthy
29. Looking at
31. Teen bane
32. Gator's relative
36. Made beloved
37. Tree marsupial
39. Inspiring reverence
42. Spoke in public
46. More fluffy
47. Goatees, e.g.
49. Boulder
51. Patterned fabric
54. The lowdown
55. Crazy bird?
56. Hens' products
57. Kind
58. Golly's partner
59. No vote
60. Fitness club

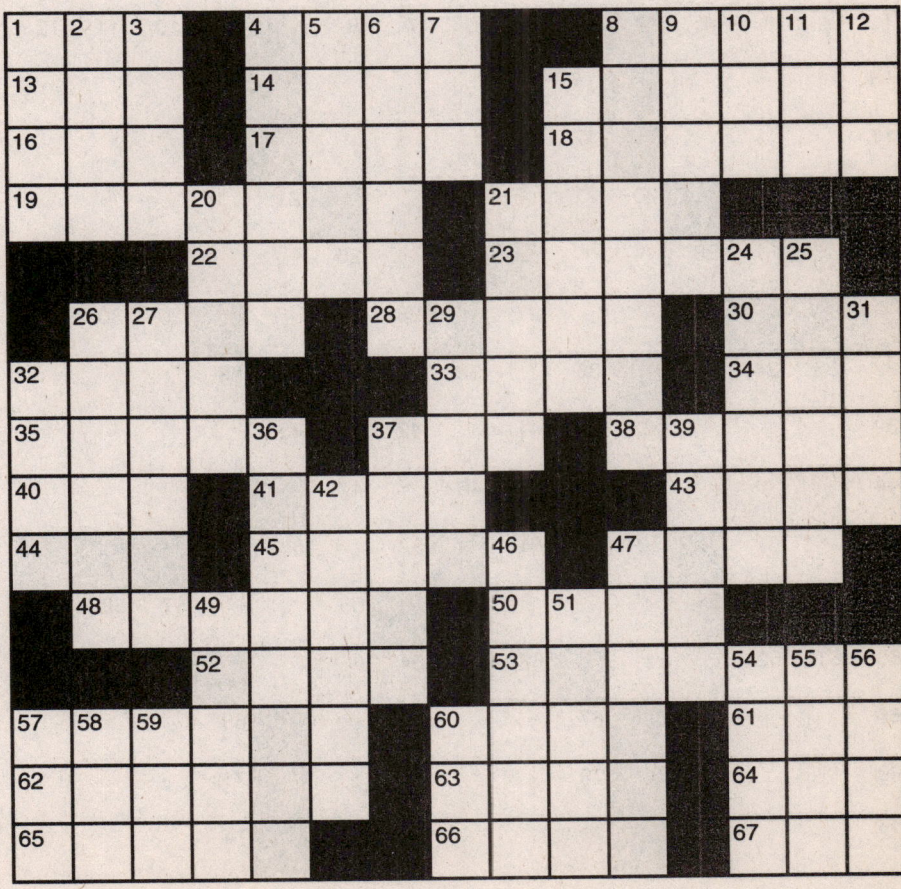

305

PUZZLE 351

ACROSS
1. Peat ___
5. Hammer part
9. Bands' gear
13. Poker chip-in
14. Small task
15. Not bogus
16. Muck's partner
17. Blew up
18. Flatfish
19. Feather wrap
20. Twirler's item
21. Promised
22. Advancing
24. Silky fabric
26. Fifty percent
28. Lancelot's title
29. Sort of resort
32. Aft's opposite
35. Distinctive time
37. Habit
39. WWII craft
41. Bird that hoots
43. Make a run
44. Rarely
46. Chop
48. Uncover
49. Needle part
50. Commotion
52. Sweetheart
54. Cabs
56. Scuff
60. Back street
63. Slide
65. Neon, e.g.
66. Motel offering
67. Rent
68. Rolls of cash
69. Capture
70. Senior
71. Charter
72. Shipped
73. Colors the hair
74. Dollar bills

DOWN
1. Caribbean dance
2. Leek's kin
3. Drinking tube
4. Observe
5. Converse
6. Trademarks
7. Stadiums
8. Got hitched
9. Fire-setting crime
10. Kitten sound
11. Light-hued
12. Toboggan's cousin
14. Baby's bed
20. Bikini top
21. Computer ill
23. In front
25. ___-tac-toe
27. To's opposite
29. Finish
30. Study steadily
31. Minister's word
32. Unite
33. Heed
34. Actor's goal
36. Cobbler's tool
38. Scrub
40. Lauer's show
42. Toss
45. Combine
47. Annoy
51. Pleasantly
53. Service point
54. Lure
55. Sun shield
57. Another time
58. Father, in Madrid
59. Double curves
60. Skills
61. Folk wisdom
62. Kind of shark
64. Purposes
67. Escorted
68. He's on first

PUZZLE 352

ACROSS
1. Hurry
5. Numbers game
10. Society newcomer
13. Aware of
14. Bellowed
15. Blvd.
16. Clock face
17. Lengthen
18. By birth
19. Accent
21. Fedora, e.g.
22. Make money
23. Hog meat
25. Seabird
27. Deadly snake
30. To be paid
32. Transfer
35. Locality
37. Soak up
39. Wisdom tooth
41. Twice four
42. Fancy resort
43. Ascended
44. Step
45. So far
46. Sublets
47. Show scorn
49. Unwell
51. Hartford hrs.
52. Yard parts
54. Mine output
55. Deeds
58. Good buddy
60. Fit to eat
65. Sunbeam
66. Movable
68. Advance
69. Anger
70. Gone to bed
71. Just
72. Low grade
73. Silly birds
74. Not theirs

DOWN
1. Poles
2. Component
3. Headliner
4. Crater
5. Bagels and ___
6. Pledge
7. Deal with
8. Camped
9. Different
10. Ms. Delany
11. At all times
12. Has-___
14. Cut again
20. Boot shaper
22. Theater cry
24. Unkempt
26. Commented
27. Chimpanzees
28. Narrow cuts
29. Heathen
31. Fools
33. Isolated
34. Endures
36. Tribe rulers
38. Outdoor area
40. Timeout
48. Calmness
50. Crawl
53. Postpone
55. Dry
56. Worry
57. Small child
59. Tall tales
61. Recon result
62. Wooer
63. Hideaway
64. Bungles
66. Periodical, shortly
67. Grant's foe

PUZZLE 353

MOVIES & TELEVISION

ACROSS
1. "Enemy at the ___"
6. "Babes in ___"
10. "___ Jim"
14. Funny Tracey ___
16. "___ and Main"
18. Direction for Sinbad
19. Actress Kidman
20. Ms. Knightley
21. Charlotte et al.
22. Bardot's head
24. Colbert film, with "The"
26. "___ Believer"
29. "The ___ Sack"
32. TV Tarzan
33. "Lou Grant" role
35. Surprise hit
37. Melmac native
40. Actress Begovic
41. Comic Sid ___
43. Dragon of puppetry
45. Lt. Worf portrayer
46. "A ___ White Season"
48. "Hot Spell" role
49. "___ and Old Lace"
52. "Wuthering Heights" star
55. "Diner" offering
56. Yikes!
59. "Christopher Columbus" ship
60. Gibbs of "227"
62. Movie pass
64. "To ___, With Love"
67. "Ghost" character
68. Ms. Portman
71. "___ Africa"
73. "Black ___ Affair"
74. Popeye, e.g.
75. Writer Ayn ___
76. "Shane," e.g.
80. Tools for Vila
83. "Monty Python" actor
84. Does film cutting
88. Actress Bacall
92. "Judge John ___"
93. "___ in a Blue Dress"
94. Ms. Francis
95. "Road ___"
96. Casino town
97. "___ by the Bell"

DOWN
1. "Miami Vice" prop
2. "___ Baba"
3. Cable channel
4. Hams it up
5. "___ of the Century"
6. "Go ___ Alice"
7. TV's 66: abbr.
8. ___ tai
9. "Doubt" star
10. "Doctor Zhivago" heroine
11. "The Good Earth" role
12. Rex or Donna
13. Actor Arnaz
15. "Big Top" safeguard
17. "Iron ___"
23. Emeril's mixture
25. Sandwich, to Zorba
26. Three, to Benigni
27. Mr. Perlman
28. "Invasion ___"
30. Bundy and others
31. "___ Again"
34. Elvis, e.g.
36. Make a blunder
37. "___ Need"
38. Rickey fruit
39. "Cape ___"
42. "Exodus" part
44. "Dante's Peak" flow
45. Charlie ___ of "Evening Shade"
47. "Lost in ___"
49. "Platoon" need
50. Actor James ___
51. "Two Mules for Sister ___"
53. "People's Court" no-no
54. "Long Day's Journey ___ Night"

PUZZLE 353

57. "Airport" abbr.
58. "Rob Roy" costume
61. "Atlantic City" action
63. Spy group: abbr.
64. TV channel: abbr.
65. "Weird Science" atom
66. "Mayberry ___"
69. Telecast
70. "___ Mercies"
72. Ms. Andress
76. "Eyes ___ Shut"
77. Hagman's costar
78. "Balto" vehicle
79. Danson et al.
81. Julia Child's phrase
82. "Star ___"
85. "___ Got a Secret"
86. "Pushing ___"
87. ___-mo
89. Prepare to race
90. Compass point: abbr.
91. Actor Beatty

PUZZLE 354

ACROSS
1. Quiz choice
6. Biblical verb
10. Kept secret
13. Melodies
14. Trinket
15. Earlier than, in poems
16. Vends
17. Foreign
18. Commotion
19. Cheerio
20. Sorrowful
21. Black
23. Closet pest
26. Needle hole
27. Winter vehicle
30. Dad's spouse
32. Healthy place
35. Income ___
36. Cookbook entry
38. Boys
40. Call a game
41. Pencil parts
43. Wrongdoing
44. Consider
46. Retaliate for
47. Dead or Red
48. Cagey
49. Part of mph
50. Relax
52. Quaker pronoun
54. Ocean oasis
55. Manly
58. Slangy film
60. Hit hard
64. Mine and yours
65. Vanna or Betty
67. Brownish gray
68. Dined
69. Not now
70. Fossil resin
71. Pull or haul
72. Took a dip
73. Ganders

DOWN
1. Quick
2. Locality
3. Bouncy tune
4. Deli sausage
5. Road bend
6. ___-Hoop
7. Withered
8. Ascot, e.g.
9. Hive product
10. Champion
11. Steam appliance
12. Moist
14. Moola
22. Most favorable
24. Grimm villain
25. Treatment
26. Develops
27. Upright beam
28. Rich fabrics
29. Banish
30. Skinflint
31. Ajar
33. Dated
34. Good-bye
37. Bear's home
39. Crisp cookie
42. Marine mammal
45. Fable
51. Bun seed
53. Wolf cries
54. Bakery worker
55. Castle feature
56. Wheels
57. Ship's staff
58. Pocket bread
59. Component
61. Grease job
62. Tarzan's friends
63. Insignificant
66. "Hee ___"
67. Ticket

PUZZLE 355

ACROSS
1. Head cook
5. Woe is me!
9. Initial bet
13. Desire
14. Spiral
15. Wicked
16. Came to rest
17. Greek vowel
18. Connection
19. Remember
21. Carries along
23. One-spots
26. Permit
27. Radio promos
30. Squidlike animal
34. Medic
35. Host
36. Uncover
38. Fixes text
40. Glazed ___
41. Small drum
42. Davenport
43. Effuse
45. Quarrel
46. ESP
49. USN rank
50. Pizza ___
51. Tinter
52. Shipwreck
55. Summer garment
60. Sailor's hail
61. Metric units
65. Drifting
66. Stare
67. Uneasy
68. Slender
69. Water server
70. Hurried
71. Cages

DOWN
1. Scorch
2. Breach
3. Heroic story
4. Greek cheese
5. Leather punch
6. Glass part
7. Fire residue
8. Stall
9. Drive
10. Electric sign
11. Flavor
12. Finales
14. Fine powder
20. Shoestrings
22. TKO caller
24. Engraves
25. Simmered
27. Picnic drinks
28. Silly people
29. Movie genre
31. Sour
32. Bowling term
33. Wading bird
37. TV staple
39. Wage earner
41. Oracles
44. Fly out of Africa
47. ___ can
48. Shrub fences
52. Wise herb?
53. Defrost
54. Heavy cord
56. Door clasp
57. Man, e.g.
58. Restraint
59. Scots' hats
62. D.C. fig.
63. "We ___ Not Alone"
64. Halfway

PUZZLE 356

ACROSS
1. Hindu garments
6. Ambush
10. Aloe ___
14. Wear away
15. Used to be
16. Choppers
17. Rent
18. Small bit
19. Intertwine
20. Trend
21. Theme
23. Shopping binge
24. Winter ill
25. Dilly
27. Hosiery shade
28. Examiner
32. Most unsophisticated
34. Theater balcony
35. Check
37. Hoover, e.g.
38. News medium
40. Failure
42. Seashore
46. Concealed
48. Canine command
50. Bee Gees, e.g.
51. Clothing trends
54. Appropriate
56. Type of antelope
57. Deuces
59. Sit-ups concerns
60. Bodies of knowledge
62. Scale
64. Probable
67. Holds
68. Fibs
69. Arctic house
71. Gore, for one
72. Sailboat
73. Cruel
74. Small whirlpool
75. If not
76. Sheen

DOWN
1. ___-control
2. Vicinity
3. Auto's path
4. Topics for Freud
5. Fitting
6. Tease
7. Lubricate again
8. Crafty
9. Green soup
10. Flirt
11. Strains
12. Guide to another chair
13. Gray
22. Banish
23. Poison ___
24. Meaty
26. "___: A Dog"
28. Mt. Blanc, e.g.
29. Neither
30. Stone or Bronze
31. Young boy
33. Hams it up
36. City vehicle
39. River sediments
41. Chip sauce
43. Limb
44. Short drink
45. Little one
47. Dawn drops
49. Stuff full
51. Flurried
52. Rotated
53. Friendly
55. Decreasing
56. Mitten's kin
58. Large numbers
61. Notice
63. Capri, e.g.
64. Part of a.k.a.
65. Kettles
66. Playthings
68. Caustic material
70. Lassie

PUZZLE 357

ACROSS
1. Energy source
5. Legend
9. More positive
14. Choir gown
15. Imitated
16. Covet
17. Lunar body
18. Adventurous
19. Feeds the pot
20. Type of clam
22. Interject
23. Comic strip
26. Taunt
28. Circle portions
30. French peak
33. Sable, e.g.
34. Fame
37. Cee's follower
38. Balloon input
39. Towel insignia
40. Australian bird
41. Porch welcomer
42. Finish a cake
43. Came in
45. Snaky curve
46. Maroon
47. Beef dish
48. Chap
50. Constructed
53. Grinned
58. Drastic
62. Engaged in
63. Grape drinks
65. Western tie
66. Amid
67. Fat
68. Burglar's goods
69. Late
70. Catholic leader
71. Enlarges

DOWN
1. Tentacles
2. Whistle sound
3. A woodwind
4. Peril
5. Cavalry sword
6. To the left, matey
7. Hair goo
8. Remark further
9. Skim
10. Coffee vessels
11. Evaluate
12. At all
13. Intermission
21. Wetlands
22. Earnings
24. Boat rower
25. Sequence
26. Fruit drink
27. Blundered
29. Smeared
30. Promo producers
31. Fewest
32. Strokes
33. Carnival
35. Colored
36. Fall flower
44. Woolly grazer
49. Good to munch
51. Slink
52. Flavor
53. Hit suddenly
54. Doll's cry
55. Frankenstein's aide
56. Advance
57. Uneasy
59. Prepare food
60. Burn soother
61. Much
63. Deadly snake
64. Twins

PUZZLE 358

ACROSS
1. Oy!
5. Curve
8. Gaucho's tool
12. Gambling game
17. Need
18. Mako's milieu
19. Soon after
20. Publicized
21. Menacing
23. Relaxation
24. Implore
25. Raw metal
26. Assistant
28. Position
30. Mule's pop
31. La Brea goo
32. Animator Burton
34. Hits
36. Cook-off dish
38. Sherpa sighting
39. Adopt
42. Indicators
43. Deteriorated
45. Pupil's site
46. Climax
47. Pottery oven
49. Maturity
52. Dig find
54. Lobster's "hand"
56. Inclined
57. Egg layer
58. Mellow
60. Fired up
62. Pen fluid
63. Seasonal virus
66. Buy off
68. Comparison word
70. Mumbai clothing
72. Organizer
75. Carpets
77. Sugar unit
78. Produced fiction
79. Logic
82. Singing groups
84. Shelter
87. Closed
88. Vital vessel
89. Fender ding
90. Old witch
91. Jog
92. Topnotch
94. Slim
97. Essay topic
100. Chow checker
103. Sword thrust
105. Crow's ___
107. More jovial
109. Lime hue
110. Neck back
111. For the chap
112. Emerald ___
113. Did sums
114. Polaris, e.g.
115. Take one side
116. False face

DOWN
1. To boot
2. Animal's home
3. Skin woe
4. Do the downhill
5. *
6. Stagger
7. Complain
8. Mexican roll-up
9. Ajar, in verse
10. Deficit
11. Poker move
12. Small computer
13. Clampett's strike
14. Fortune
15. Drinks in bags
16. Likeliness
22. Layered rock
27. Unending
29. Toning targets
31. Wild cat
33. At the center of
35. Aim
36. Hidden supply
37. Person
38. Shout
39. Revising copy
40. Marcia, to Greg
41. Heir ending
42. Deep cut
44. Distinct time
48. Former glacier part
50. Dowel
51. Large deer
53. Fix socks
55. Sense of humor
59. Musician's job
61. Done with
63. Kiwi or pear
64. Heavenly scales

PUZZLE 358

65. Avails oneself of
66. Emblem
67. ___ long (shortly)
69. Bee, to Andy
71. Oak's nut
72. Every one
73. Pedro's river
74. Flushed
76. Most frightening
80. Lenten Wednesday
81. Smash
83. Abode
85. Aspire to
86. Utmost
92. Pond organism
93. Miss Muffet's tidbit
95. Hotels
96. Prim
98. Bouncing sound
99. Steamer
100. Traveler's permit
101. Snakelike fish
102. Expedition
104. Center of light?
106. Mountain spring
108. Fringe

PUZZLE 359

ACROSS
1. Ballroom dance
6. Offer
9. Deadly snakes
13. Sum
15. Keats work
16. Which thing?
17. Fungal growth
18. Physician, briefly
19. Overdue
20. Fruity drinks
21. Spotted wildcat
24. Pinocchio's sin
25. Blond shade
26. Ower
28. Large primate
31. Stag's mate
32. Not imagined
33. School friend
36. Horses' colors
40. Aquatic bird
41. Heroic tales
43. Diva's number
44. Leafy dish
46. Joining the army
48. Aft
50. Previously
51. Ms. Sandra ___
52. Expensive furs
55. Motel
56. Color shade
57. Flat TV
60. All right
64. Dormant
66. Tavern order
67. Connected
69. Movie
70. Currently
71. Put away
72. Child's treasures
73. Toe count
74. Exchanges

DOWN
1. Papa's lady
2. Within
3. Beauty spot
4. Sprouts
5. "Still the ___"
6. Foreshadow
7. Religious statue
8. Break a cipher
9. Boring tool
10. Intend to, in verse
11. Terrace
12. Beef animal
14. Duo
22. Less costly
23. Slice
25. Paid notices
27. Swell
28. Works onstage
29. Petition
30. Nobleman
32. Recover
34. Growl
35. Metal can
37. Bone-dry
38. Four plus five
39. Stuffing herb
42. Cues
45. Bottomless
47. Male child
49. Tilted
52. Work period
53. TV sound
54. Abdomen
58. Natural balm
59. Patched
60. Winter flakes
61. Southern veggie
62. Ooze
63. ___ and ends
65. Type measures
68. ___ a girl!

PUZZLE 360

ACROSS
1. Purse band
6. Everybody
9. Gear teeth
13. Satiric
15. Jungle snake
16. Grimm heavy
17. Attorney
18. Hit
19. Apartment
20. Box top
21. Adequate
23. G-men
24. Hog's place
25. Bashful
26. Poet's ajar
28. Against
30. Gratify
34. Shorthand pro
37. Taco sauce
40. Soup veggie
41. Jackets
42. Self-esteem
43. Objects
45. Curvature
46. Cold abode
48. The South
49. Fix a shoe bottom
51. Model
53. '60s do
54. VCR button
55. Chatter
58. Univ. teacher
61. Eagerly
64. Down-under bird
65. Prom car
66. Gratuity
67. Breadwinner
69. Customer
70. Compass dir.
71. Burdensome
72. Fellow
73. Mr. Rather
74. Exploits

DOWN
1. Window ledges
2. Attribute
3. Disorderly
4. At least one
5. "The ___ Piper"
6. Convent
7. Water bird
8. Small computers
9. Java
10. Stare
11. Alum
12. Groups
14. Summit
22. Carve
27. Scottish fabrics
28. Hill builder
29. Snoopier
31. Peak
32. Large truck
33. Slacken
34. Old wound
35. Ripped
36. Per
38. In history
39. Curved around
44. Bind
47. Crowed
50. Attempt
52. Young hooter
54. Mellow
55. Lamp spirit
56. Alter
57. Small towns
58. Promote
59. Increase
60. Portent
62. Travel document
63. Lawn
68. Dark bread

317

PUZZLE 361

ACROSS
1. '60s do
4. Shopping spot
8. Lullaby, e.g.
12. Judge's field
13. Slender sword
15. Parcel
16. Bad temper
17. Pumpkin color
18. Humpback's kin
19. Sweat
21. Sealed
23. Coins
24. Not home
25. Ascend
28. Pavement pit
32. Ridge of coral
33. Baseball call
36. Fake hair
37. Fundamental
39. Cool, formerly
40. Navigation device
42. One who excels
43. Martini garnishes
46. Parisian mother
47. Dan Rather, e.g.
49. Crave water
51. Electric-guitarist's need
52. Astir
54. Sports venues
57. Word list
61. Cartoon's Elmer ___
62. Infuriate
64. Court romantically
65. Pond growth
66. Counted calories
67. Deer's kin
68. Rod and ___
69. Not as much
70. Take in

DOWN
1. Turn over quickly
2. Occasional
3. Debtor
4. Leathernecks
5. Separate
6. Actor's dialogue
7. Foot's limb
8. Not rough
9. Paddles
10. Friendly
11. Happy
13. Cords
14. Reheat
20. Futuristic story form
22. Stringed instruments
25. Like a city
26. ___ and quiet
27. Stitch again
28. Smoker's tool
29. Possessor
30. Deceivers
31. Wading bird
34. Slim
35. Gun (an engine)
38. Punctuation mark
41. Passes over
44. Expired
45. Larry, Curly, and Moe
48. Summer shoe
50. Watered
52. Be in accord
53. Soho pads
54. Yonder
55. Govern
56. Fringe
58. Impresses
59. Walk-on
60. Oxen team
63. Naught

PUZZLE 362

ACROSS
1. Swamp
6. Tub
10. So-so grade
13. Speak
14. Hurts
16. Upper-body part
17. Nail's kin
18. Firm
19. Pizazz
20. At that time
21. Look
22. Kick out
24. Held title to
27. Scrappy
28. Totally
31. Sweltering
32. Glacier piece
33. Applied shingles to
35. Take a spouse
36. Sad sound
40. Decorative filling
41. Pork source
42. Father
43. Salami seller
44. ___ peeve
45. Tenpins player
46. Behind
48. Heckler's word
49. Self-regard
50. Scale
53. Sugar tree
55. Brief film
56. Mink, e.g.
57. Exploding star
61. Tiny amount
62. Wake up
64. Questioned
65. "___ Got to Be Me"
66. Favorable votes
67. Fruit pulp
68. Blushing
69. Breather
70. Eye drops

DOWN
1. Greatest
2. Overhead curve
3. Hamburger order
4. Office writer
5. Chop down
6. Hunting hound
7. Portrayed
8. Biblical pronoun
9. That girl
10. Cloaks
11. Upright
12. Vacant
15. Scoff
23. Type of puzzle
25. Muffet's fare
26. Motion of assent
27. Gave lunch to
28. Desertlike
29. Sole
30. Lounge around
32. Panhandle
34. More equitable
35. Comedian
37. Loiter
38. Brady kid
39. Good guy
41. Part of mph
42. Place to swim
44. Sketch ___
45. Hit
47. Access
48. Least ornate
50. Out of bed
51. Remove whiskers
52. Translated a cipher
53. Ponders
54. Come about
56. Melt together
58. Gumbo ingredient
59. Zigzag
60. Citrus drinks
63. Poet's above
64. Competent

PUZZLE 363

ACROSS
1. Opposite of out?
5. ___ World
10. Mail
14. Greasy
15. Integrity
16. Feel bad
17. Azure
18. Bracelet locale
19. Pro votes
20. Cheap
22. Yearnings
24. Pretend
25. Smirk
27. Stocky
29. Eats away
31. Different
33. Escorted
34. Homely
36. Ceases
39. Witness
40. Poker-faced
42. Stun
44. Extinct bird
46. Impolite look
47. Microscopic
48. Church keys
50. Dog pound
53. Design
56. Not east
57. Golf mound
58. Glitch
61. Chop
62. Increases
64. Print
66. Alpine sound
70. Traveling trio
71. Yellow resin
72. Drip
73. Get ready
74. Is defeated
75. Copy

DOWN
1. Weep
2. Be ill
3. Winter virus
4. Shadow spot?
5. Defrost
6. Dearie
7. Very black
8. Part played
9. Saturate
10. Wages
11. Arctic, e.g.
12. Cabin
13. Irritable
21. United
23. Luster
25. Strong desire
26. Oakley's show
28. Coffee vessel
29. High trains
30. Prosecute
31. Of yore
32. Classify
35. Big event
37. Mornings
38. Sugary
40. Coeds' abodes
41. Bible craft
43. Moray, e.g.
45. Female deer
49. Kindly
51. Flock mama
52. Most recent
53. Imprint
54. ___ Rapids
55. Shrub border
59. Bullets, for short
60. Chats
61. His and ___
63. Tiny drink
65. Gosh!
67. Bee's follower
68. Curse
69. Pick

HEADHUNTING

PUZZLE 364

Don't lose your head as you fill in the diagram. The first letter of each answer word will go somewhere within the word itself; all the other letters appear in order. For example, CART might be aCrt, arCt, or artC. (NOTE: The second letter of the answer word is always first.) Look for the letters which are shared by across and down words.

ACROSS

1. Aid a criminal
5. Bus terminal
10. Gardner of mystery
14. Scottish family
15. Ranch animal
16. High cards
17. Sounds of laughter
18. Video's partner
19. British noble
20. Waver
22. Songbird
24. Made angry
27. Sense of self
28. Pink bird
31. Remorse
35. Guinness or Baldwin
36. Growl
38. Boat paddle
39. "My Gal ___"
40. City trains
42. ___ Lancelot
43. School subject: abbr.
44. Recline
45. Sheriff's gang
47. Ladder rung
48. Calm
50. Headway
53. "___ Miniver"
54. Wander off
55. Beg
59. Horse's home
63. Make ready
64. E.T., e.g.
67. Lulu
68. Slim
69. Stop
70. Grew older
71. "___ Girl"
72. Fe or Clara
73. Fewer

DOWN

1. Competent
2. Warmth
3. Engrave
4. Enthusiast
5. Go back
6. Mountain resort
7. Stag's mate
8. Thought
9. Mightier
10. Moon cavity
11. Delight
12. Dried up
13. Genuine
21. Waikiki wreath
23. Liverpool lockups
25. Hackman and Kelly
26. Hoopla
28. "Kate & ___"
29. Relieved
30. Tiny
32. Delete
33. Suit fabric
34. Crouch
37. Previous
40. Forms a mass
41. Congregate
46. Soak flax
47. Peculiar
49. Dad, e.g.
51. Playing marbles
52. Double agent
55. Not there
56. Cruising
57. Animal hide
58. Goatee's site
60. Cain's brother
61. Wild plum
62. Beatty film
65. Iced brew
66. Reply: abbr.

PUZZLE 365

ACROSS
1. Pick, with "for"
4. Fall mo.
7. Klutz
10. Cornfield unit
14. Pay suit to
15. Infrequent
17. Concluded
19. Jennifer or Joel
20. Graceful tree
21. Section
22. Cool!
23. Gutter locale
24. Ho-hum
26. Insults
28. Liver paste
30. Nasty mutt
31. Sleep
33. Drive out
35. Cooks pastries
37. Sun-dried brick
40. Destroyed
41. Babies' napkins
43. Elsie's chew
44. Broadcast medium
47. Prayer word
49. Hold it!
53. Bustle
55. Savings receptacle
57. Be competitive
58. Insect feeler
60. Optic ailment
62. Print measures
63. Russian drink
66. Piercing implement
68. Gold-purity measure
70. Mine output
71. In the buff
75. Nullified
79. Glacier material
80. Submarine equipment
82. Tip, as a hat
86. Feminine title
88. Rats!
89. Tire's surface
91. Melody
92. Ferocious feline
94. Chimney shaft
96. Preface, for short
98. Paperless letter
101. Lemony
102. Funnyman Jay ___
104. Plant holder
105. Seaweed
108. Jazz style
110. Channel
114. Presently
116. Eagle's home
118. Self-images
120. Line of seats
121. Heraldic border
122. Cake layers
123. Clock's noise
124. Glop
125. Merge
126. Behold
127. Phi's follower
128. Superman's emblem

DOWN
1. Has debtors
2. Equine sport
3. Selleck and Jones
4. Mouths, to Pliny
5. Food components, briefly
6. Foot the bill
7. Count starter
8. Make suitable
9. Greek cheese
10. Vital statistic
11. Split
12. Musical show
13. Watchers
16. Face flanker
17. Result
18. Decimal point
25. Sphere
27. Deli meat
29. Wane
32. At any time, in verse
34. Clean with a mop
36. Volcanic output
37. Accomplishment
38. Couple
39. Flaky
40. Endorse
41. Warped
42. Like pen fluid
45. Skillful
46. Stamping tool
48. Pas' partners
50. Affirm
51. Peruvian city
52. Analysis
54. Desk wood
56. Exhibits boredom
59. Bobbsey twin
61. ___ out (gain laboriously)
63. Emptiness
64. Predatory dolphin
65. Think
67. Sermon
69. Cipher, in a way

PUZZLE 365

72. Lofty coif
73. College official
74. Stray
76. Author Vidal
77. King Kong, e.g.
78. Chinese beverage
81. The lowdown
83. Cereal grain
84. Evergreen
85. Associate of to
87. Inventor Whitney
90. Ruckus
93. Kind
95. Greases
97. Drowse
98. ___ salts
99. 007 portrayer
100. Coral ring
101. Binge
102. Reason
103. Distinctive era
106. Have chips
107. Oahu wreaths
109. Play the ponies
111. Force along
112. Murmurs fondly
113. Pairs
115. Beatty of films
117. Outrage
119. Use snow runners

323

PUZZLE 366

CRISS-CROSSWORD

The answer words for Criss-Crossword are entered diagonally, reading downward, from upper left to lower right or from upper right to lower left. We have entered the words LODES and COW as examples.

TO THE RIGHT

1. Metal deposits
2. Docket item
3. Survey
4. Tale end?
5. Light carriages
6. Serenity
7. Briny deep
9. Sardonic
11. Spookiest
13. Part of OSU
14. Excavated
16. Shade tree
17. Babbling
19. Late bloomer?
20. German article
22. Small pickle
24. Attempted
26. Seer's card
28. Adversary
30. Wad
32. OR workers
34. Freezing

TO THE LEFT

2. Milk source
3. Priest
4. Ambled
5. Shoe bottoms
6. Sweater stitch
7. Napoli night
8. Oyster output
10. Maven
12. Monstrosity
13. Flirty look
15. Floor fabric
16. Skating figure
18. Thwart
19. Tune
21. Grab a chair
23. Overlook
25. Be wrong
27. Seizes
29. Labor group
31. Spacious
33. Clear (of)
35. Purchase

PUZZLE 367

Bubbles

In each of the circles is the name of something Irish minus one letter! Find that missing letter to complete the Irish term. Then arrange the missing letters to spell the bonus Irish term.

1.
2.
3.
4.
5.
6.

1. _____
2. _____
3. _____
4. _____
5. _____
6. _____

BONUS: _____

PUZZLE 368

ACROSS
1. Feathery wrap
4. Grade
8. Teheran money
12. Paddle
13. Mr. Alda
14. "Jagged ___"
15. In the wings
17. Adolescent
18. Feminine pronoun
19. On the ship
21. Indian cow
24. Artist's poser
26. Changed
28. Maxim
32. Fruit pastry
33. Dialect
35. June honoree
36. Prance
38. Rich
40. Rascal
42. Hymn closer
43. Mumbai princes
46. Sounds of surprise
48. Fascinated
49. Situation
54. "___ of Earl"
55. Maddened
56. Fitness club
57. Visualizes
58. Formally yield
59. A March sister

DOWN
1. Ghostly greeting
2. Klutz
3. Woof
4. Spouse
5. Terrified
6. Dustcloth
7. Work dough
8. Narrated again
9. Brainchild
10. Maturing agent
11. Let borrow
16. Avoid
20. Grins widely
21. Sudden jolts
22. Discharge
23. Foamy brew
25. Intense hatred
27. Gully
29. Abel's father
30. Tempest
31. Genesis home
34. Conflicting
37. Practices
39. Playbill listing
41. Tomato jelly
43. Angle measures
44. Chills and fever
45. Gag
47. Pelt
50. Crude metal
51. Creed
52. Ajar, to a bard
53. Henpeck

PUZZLE 369

ACROSS
1. Nitwit
5. Possesses
8. College residence
12. Turkish title
13. Stereo component
14. Rapier
15. "Titanic" foe
16. Adjective for Abner
17. Dryer fuzz
18. Tenn. neighbor
19. Musical closing
20. Once called
21. Repeat
23. Keen
26. Kind
27. Not ours
28. Tropical fruits
30. Fixed beforehand
32. Fewer
35. Layered
36. Maternally kin
38. 100%
39. Tinted
42. Smidgen
43. Chemise
45. Pool circuit
46. Shrill barks
47. Tex-Mex fare
48. Inventor Whitney
49. ___ Stanley Gardner
50. Previously, of old
51. ___ room (den)
52. Flake

DOWN
1. Exclude
2. Eggy dish
3. High-seas robbery
4. Energy unit
5. Angel's crown
6. Inside
7. Ostentatious
8. Shannon of song
9. View expresser
10. Subscribes again
11. Allotted
19. Pleat
22. Superior
24. Mended
25. Surfaced
27. Make a doily
29. Vendor
30. Column
31. Ruins
33. Irony
34. Fasten
35. Savor
37. Ford failure
40. Harvard's rival
41. Heroic tale
44. Poker prize
46. Slangy affirmative

325

PUZZLE 370 — CODEWORD

Codeword is a special crossword puzzle in which conventional clues are omitted. Instead, answer words in the diagram are represented by numbers. Each number represents a different letter of the alphabet, and all of the letters of the alphabet are used. When you are sure of a letter, put it in the code key chart and cross it off in the alphabet box. A group of letters has been inserted to start you off.

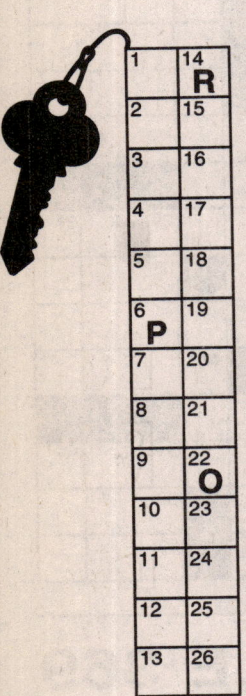

PUZZLE 371 — Fitting Description

Fill in the blanks to complete a Fitting Description of a famous person. Place the letters you have added into their corresponding boxes to form the name of that person.

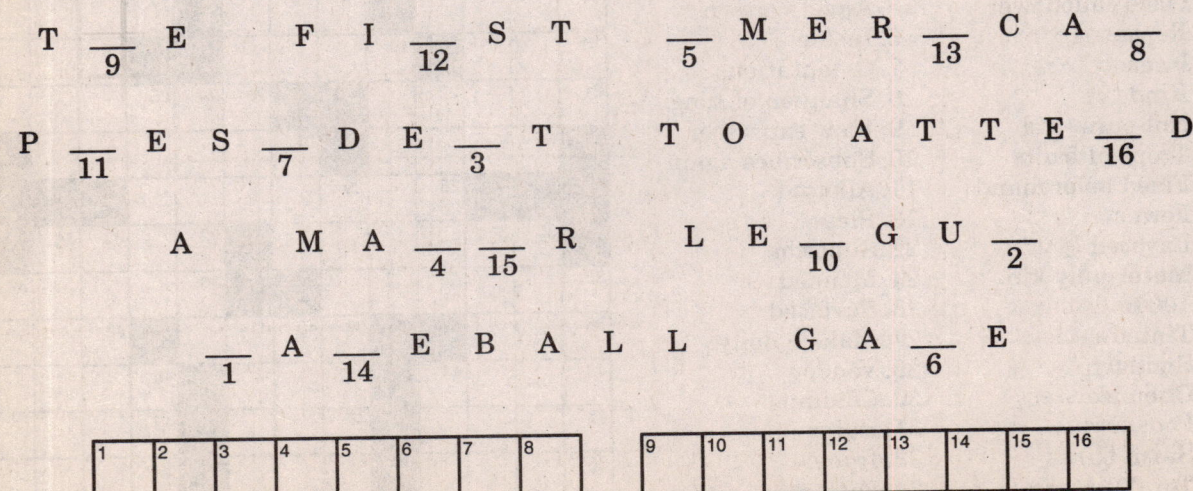

BRICK BY BRICK

PUZZLE 372

Rearrange this stack of bricks to form a crossword puzzle. The clues will help you fit the bricks into their correct places. Row 1 has been filled in for you. Use the bricks to fill in the remaining spaces.

ACROSS

1. Fibbed
   Soybean curd
   Annoy
2. Formerly
   Outpost
   Beatty of films
3. Wrap up
   Loosen, in a way
   Downcast
4. Obvious statement
   Like crazy
   Thickness
5. Positive answer
   Greek letters
   Clamp
6. Subtlety
   Teen's bane
7. Gave medicine to
   Enlistment specialist
8. Home
   Always, to Keats
   Farm implements
9. Short notes
   Faultiest
10. Looker
    Loss of hope
11. Heat up
    Go astray
    Rug cleaner, briefly
12. Cigarette residue
    Drei minus zwei
    Rather queer
13. Originally named
    Drive forward
    Additionally
14. Gooey substance
    Hero staple
    Cabbage dish
15. Poetic palindrome
    Back muscles, briefly
    Dried grasses

DOWN

1. Towering
   Sir's wife
   Gambler's wager
2. Accustom
   Heed
   Burn to a crisp
3. Eggshell tones
   Approximately
4. Appetizing store
   Felt topper
5. Web spinner
   Corded fabrics
6. Cook's spice
   Fleet commander
7. Freight weight
   Composed
   Big Easy acronym
8. Widemouthed jar
   Gardeners' packets
   Minor dispute
9. Young equine
   Fragments
   Printing measures
10. Expose
    Garlicky mayo
11. Legendary humanoid
    Toward the breeze
12. Billy Budd, e.g.
    Dart
13. Examiner
    Country house
14. Unaffected
    Current events
    Ore analysis
15. Rafter's peril
    Formerly, of old
    Eats heartily

BRICKS

| EI | TRU | ASH | ESS | PLY |
| PR | YES | NEE | REC | E |

| EER | CNE | ISH | LAM | R D |
| NDA | TER | LSO | ATS | ARM |

| ONC | I S | NY | TAR | ISM |
| FUR | H | CE | ERE | PI |

| EYE | NED | | FIN | SA |
| W | SAD | VAC | ED | L |

| OLO | ESP | E A | AL | ODD |
| NLA | S | RUI | S | LA |

| PL | AIR | | NS | OT |
| WO | IN | DOS | OPE | VIS |

| OWS | LAW | DE | ABO | E C |
| RST | AYS | ORA | MEM | L U |

DIAGRAM

	1	2	3	4	5	6	7	8	9	10	11	12	13	14	15
1	L	I	E	D	■	■	T	O	F	U	■	■	I	R	E
2															
3															
4															
5															
6															
7															
8															
9															
10															
11															
12															
13															
14															
15															

BRICK BY BRICK FANS! Get a ton of Brick by Bricks—over 50 fun puzzles in each of our special collections! To order, see page 159.

PUZZLE 373

ACROSS
1. For Pete's ___!
5. Long-legged wader
9. Real-estate map
13. Cattle
14. Songlike
16. "On ___ Toes"
17. Boxing site
18. Filtrate
19. Appraise
20. Vocally
22. Patrol or instructor
23. Frenzied
24. Fall faller
27. On the ___ (in hiding)
29. Come to pass
31. Under the weather
34. Natural resin
35. Smears
37. Venerated ones
39. Wise bird
40. Food fish
42. One-seventh of a semana
43. Furnish with glass
45. Colorless gas
46. Find a sum
47. Vapory
49. Isolate
51. Brouhaha
52. Dispatched
53. Oblong
56. Border
59. Raisin, formerly
63. Chianti, to Luigi
64. Jagged
67. Psychology topics
68. Component
69. Easy strider?
70. Attain
71. Clutter
72. Close at hand
73. Lumber source

DOWN
1. Marsh rail
2. Leaf-stem angle
3. Casino game
4. Consume
5. Bedridden
6. Ciao
7. Levin and Gershwin
8. ___ and tired
9. Pharaoh's tomb
10. Garden soil
11. Motorcar
12. Difficult journey
15. Texas fare
21. Empty truck
25. Winglike parts
26. Snow shower
28. Arranging
29. Wails
30. Brilliance
31. Stage whispers
32. Knotlike
33. Coast
34. Diary
36. Lingerie item
38. Dejected
41. "And Then There Were ___"
44. Fanatics
48. Certain mushroom
50. "Sesame ___"
53. Egg cell
54. Tarzan's transport?
55. Black cuckoos
57. Branding ___
58. Sulk
60. Ice-cream thickener
61. Skin opening
62. Medieval slave
65. Baltic or Adriatic
66. Use poor judgment

PUZZLE 374 — Try-Angles

Fit the eight answers into the diagram, six answers across and one answer down each side from the top of the triangle to each outside corner. The clues are given in no particular order.

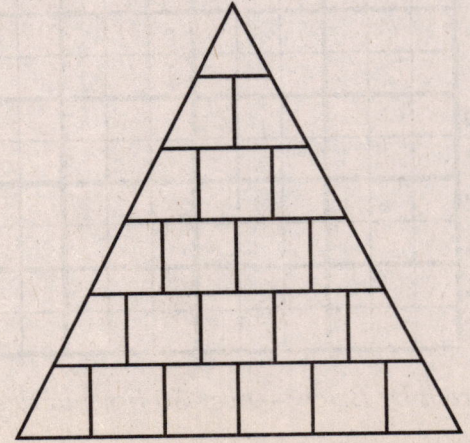

Prize

Cure

Coax

Film rating

Beret's kin

Bequest

Ceremony

That is: abbr.

PUZZLE 375

ACROSS
1. Container
5. Electrical measures
10. Circle sections
14. Major work
15. Domed home
16. Noose
17. Flees
18. Attracted
19. Molten rock
20. Limb
21. Appear
22. Sign
23. Hi-fi
25. Valuable
29. Uncooked
30. Auricle
31. Periodical, for short
34. Hauling
37. Dolt
39. Big wading bird
40. Lubricate again
42. Item
43. Funnyman
45. Herons
47. Spy
48. Leaders
49. Commercials
50. Tint again
52. Cafe
55. Flat-topped formation
58. Withdraw gradually
60. Stick
61. Painful
62. Wonderful
64. Shrill
65. Scat!
66. Seabiscuit, e.g.
67. Stake
68. Suburb
69. Affirmatives
70. Bambi, e.g.

DOWN
1. Soft drinks
2. Isolated
3. Gershwin tune
4. Curvy turn
5. Recorded movie
6. Meany
7. Andean animal
8. Drag
9. Junior
10. Parcel out
11. Wander
12. Small bay
13. Extent
21. Stitched
24. Lift up
26. Highway vehicle
27. Costly fur
28. Sooner than, to a bard
31. Vegetable soup
32. Touched ground
33. Retrieves
34. Twitches
35. Reed instrument
36. Pulverize
37. Electron-deficient particle
38. "Eating her ___ and whey..."
41. Elementary
44. "___ Hard"
46. Increase
50. Silklike fabric
51. Decorative jugs
52. Hay portions
53. 1 or 66
54. Weirder
55. Sail holder
56. Resonate
57. Movie
59. Choice word
62. Timid
63. Sadness
64. Chap

Crisscross

PUZZLE 376

Beside each diagram are six groups of scrambled letters. Rearrange each group of letters to form a word, and then fit the words into the diagram to read across and down in crossword fashion.

1.

IDTYNA
XEEICT
OPYADR
ERPRPO
DAORNI
EERCUD

2.

ETRAIT
OESNGP
NIOOTP
NCSAET
DNAREG
NCHESO

PUZZLE 377

DOUBLE TROUBLE

Not really double trouble, but double fun! Solve this puzzle as you would a regular crossword, except place one, two, or three letters in each box. The number of letters in each answer is shown in parentheses after its clue.

ACROSS
1. Reveal (6)
4. Fluent (4)
6. Minute part (6)
9. Wrist wear (8)
10. Sandwich mart (4)
11. Man's title (6)
12. Discard (4)
13. Forbid (3)
15. Motif (5)
17. Red gem (4)
18. Supposed (8)
20. Straight (6)
22. Germfree (7)
24. Sequestered (8)
26. Arrival (6)
27. Sparkled (5)
28. Flimsy (7)
31. Influence (8)
33. Jeopardy (6)
34. Dinosaur bone, e.g. (6)
35. Shrill (8)
38. Raise crops (4)
39. Show boredom (4)
41. Vivacity (5)
42. Dillydally (3)
44. Monarch (5)
46. Data (4)
48. Weld with plastic (8)
50. Discontinue (5)
51. Meaning (4)
52. Vacancy (7)

DOWN
1. Surpass (6)
2. Fishing rod (4)
3. Reversal (7)
4. Coast (5)
5. Cheerful (6)
6. Heavy hauler (4)
7. Build (9)
8. Kentucky ____ (5)
9. Cheeky (5)
14. Goose egg (4)
16. Intercede (7)
18. Persistent (10)
19. Crooked (9)
21. Superfluous (9)
22. Lieu (5)
23. Split apart (4)
25. Mexican "Rah!" (3)
27. Droop (3)
29. Melody (4)
30. Beneath (5)
32. In truth (6)
34. Recipe (7)
36. Ocean feeder (5)
37. Evolve (7)
38. Charade (5)
40. Doorway shelter (6)
42. Inner coating (6)
43. Colorful quartz (5)
45. Irish Gaelic (4)
47. Palm off (5)
49. Hymn finale (4)

PUZZLE 378

Changaword

Can you change the top word into the bottom word in each column in the number of steps indicated in parentheses? Change only one letter at a time and do not change the order of the letters. Proper names, slang, and obsolete words are not allowed.

1. BANK (4 steps)   2. HILL (5 steps)   3. PEAK (5 steps)   4. LAKE (6 steps)

DELL   MOOR   CAPE   REEF

PUZZLE 379
• THREE AMIGOS •

ACROSS
1. Somber
4. ___ machine
8. Circle overhead
12. Watch
13. Bills
14. With wings
15. Minister's subj.
16. Gaelic
17. Kind
18. Former Game Show Network program
21. DDE rival
22. Donahue of "Father Knows Best"
25. Islamic prince
28. ___ standstill
29. Gardner of film
30. Sirius B, to Sirius A
34. Flat hat
35. Pro's opposite
36. Phone starter
37. Unemotional
39. Nashville org.
41. Charles ___ of "Wings"
46. Leg bone
48. Debtor's notes
49. Plus
50. Beverly Archer role
51. Hosiery shade
52. Tiny meas.
53. Equal
54. Writer Zane ___
55. Pavement

DOWN
1. Medieval worker
2. Gloria Estefan song
3. Sandwich shop
4. Play episode
5. Fats
6. ___ buco
7. Also, in legalese
8. Vietnam city
9. Turn off, in a way
10. Fond du ___
11. Unrefined metal
19. Holliday's pal
20. Spanish dessert
23. Oblong
24. Infrequent
25. Portrays
26. Castle defense
27. Incapable of movement
28. French river
31. Nitric ___
32. Falling asleep
33. Buck
38. Type of eclipse
39. Vulgar
40. Amble
42. "On ___ Toes"
43. State, to Pierre
44. Capital of Italia
45. Tart
46. Little drink
47. Garden tool

PUZZLE 380
• FEATHERED PALS •

ACROSS
1. Relay portion
4. Tabby
7. Shadowbox
11. Egg cells
12. Sulawesi ox
14. Leaning-tower city
15. Goal
16. Garden items
18. Run away
20. Fly high
21. Hay quantity
24. Bedding
28. Warning sounds
30. Cry of discovery
31. Evergreen
32. "Star Trek" actor
35. Semi
36. Ampersand
37. ___ of history
39. Vacation spot
43. Nervous
44. "___ the Explorer"
46. Reed instrument
49. Do a nature-lover's hobby
54. Under the weather
55. ___ fixe
56. French dad
57. In medias ___
58. Fashion name
59. At present
60. Fawn's mom

DOWN
1. Bread unit
2. "Hear No ___"
3. Quail et al.
4. Taxi
5. "Wheel of Fortune" purchase
6. Craggy hills
7. Bowling score
8. Hole
9. Bat wood
10. ___ Dashan (Ethiopian peak)
13. Fusses
17. ___, humbug!
19. Musical sense
22. Allow
23. Hartmann of TV
25. Winner of the worm
26. The thing here
27. Slump
28. Trig ratio
29. Reggae's kin
31. Remote
33. Wind dir.
34. Not Dem. or Rep.
38. In the past
40. More unusual
41. Move a boat
42. Capture
45. Sun god
47. Butter substitute
48. Threat word
49. Offer
50. Dictator Amin
51. Olds auto
52. ___-hook
53. Chop down

PUZZLE 381

Diagramless crosswords are solved by using the clues and their numbers to fill in the answer words and the arrangement of black squares. Insert the number of each clue with the first letter of its answer, across and down. Fill in a black square at the end of each answer. Every black square must have a corresponding black square on the opposite side of the diagram to form a diagonally symmetrical pattern. Puzzles 381 and 382 have been started for you.

ACROSS
1. Curtain
6. Narrative stories
11. Gossip bit
12. Pertaining to ships
13. Went upward
14. Total points
15. Staffs
16. Guts
17. Math subject
20. So far
21. Above, poetically
22. Male turkey
25. Accommodated
30. Covers
32. Uncommon
33. Nitwit
34. Express grief
35. Sight or smell
36. Metal mold
37. Cornered
38. Tinters

DOWN
1. Theatrical production
2. Of the country
3. Amid
4. Sheriff's gang
5. Prior to, to a bard
6. Entangle
7. Tempo
8. Off-white
9. Sculpt
10. Frozen rain
18. Lifted
19. Civil War soldier
22. Coil
23. Command
24. Bangor's location
26. Satire's kin
27. Dial
28. Baseball bobble
29. Fender mishaps
31. Sit for a photo
34. Central

PUZZLE 382

ACROSS
1. Cried
5. Fitness farm
8. Sound
9. Hearty meat dish
10. Maple genus
11. Common duck
12. Fiercely
17. Cup handles
18. Bring home the bacon
19. In the back
20. Howl
22. Strong suit
23. Southern veggie
24. Frank's ex
27. Mother, to Gerard
29. Unclosed, poetically
30. Tame
34. Spanish surrealist
35. Skunk feature
36. Humdinger
37. Used to be
38. Pump purchase
39. Desert covering

DOWN
1. "____ My Line?"
2. Every person
3. Not guilty, e.g.
4. Aquatic flier
5. Author Gertrude ____
6. Toll
7. Puncturing tool
9. Sun, e.g.
12. Herbal drink
13. Clumsy fellow
14. Bit
15. River-mouth deposit
16. Back of the neck
20. Oxen's harnesses
21. Be wrong
22. Links cry
24. Skillful
25. Flying formation
26. Total
27. Burrowing rodents
28. Islamic chieftain
29. Rowed
30. Comic Carvey
31. Pulls
32. Belief
33. Maize
34. Pooch

PUZZLE 383

ACROSS
1. Kolkata dress
5. Top cards
9. Draft animals
10. Electrical unit
11. Municipal map
12. ___ monster
13. Greek vowels
15. Solid
17. Throbbing pain
19. Flag feature
21. Helpful hints
23. RBI, e.g.
25. Sports competition
27. ___ de Janeiro, Brazil
28. They wait for no man
32. Vigoda of "Fish"
33. Athletic squad
34. Grime
36. Heavy shoe
38. Look for
40. Baseball's Slaughter
42. Sketched
44. Harness part
46. Coral structure
48. Ali ___
50. Lollapalooza
51. English prep school
52. Decorate again
53. Apartment fee

DOWN
1. Soak in gravy
2. Wheel shaft
3. Lasso
4. Unblemished
5. Arith. mean
6. Hair style
7. Designer Perry ___
8. Commences
14. Sparkled
16. Wedded state
18. Kind of rapier
20. Sudden attack
22. Baltic, e.g.
24. Lower digit
26. Explosive initials
28. Young boy
29. Wading bird
30. Last mo.
31. Tall story
35. Great fright
37. Peanut
39. New Hampshire city
41. Glide over ice
43. Unwelcome plant
45. Black, in verse
47. To's partner
49. Picnic nuisance

Starting box on page 562

Loose Tile

PUZZLE 384

The tray on the right seemed the ideal place to store the set of loose dominoes. Unfortunately, when the tray was full, one domino was left over. Determine the arrangement of the dominoes in the tray and which is the Loose Tile.

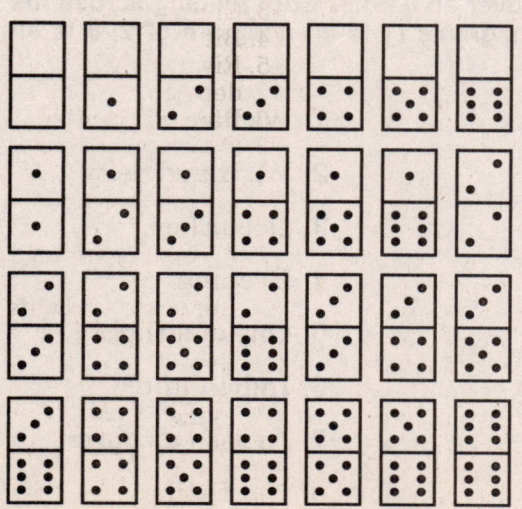

PUZZLE 385

ACROSS
1. Spat
4. Dad
5. Green ___ Packers
8. Pelts
9. Cartoon chipmunk
10. Tokyo's nation
11. Jet jockey
12. More certain
13. Coerce
14. Removable covers
15. African river
16. Highest card
17. Load heavily
18. Restaurant list
20. Works the land
21. Tug
25. Makes a touchdown
27. Sweet or chick
28. Misjudged
29. Say the rosary
30. Beg
31. Coastline
32. Overgrown
33. Graceful water birds
34. Acapulco coin
35. Holey cheese
36. "___ Miniver"
37. Plate of glass
38. Sailor's affirmative

DOWN
1. Tracking device
2. Ready for business
3. "How the West ___ Won"
4. Plumbing conduits
5. Mezzanine
6. Soothing succulent
7. Thus far
8. Solidify
9. Mournful tune
10. Breakfast drink
11. Small lakes
12. Close loudly
13. Shapes
15. Restored to health
17. Exposed
19. Without worth
20. Quick raid
22. Cooks' smocks
23. Approaches
24. Comedian Danny ___
26. Belief
29. Part of a process
30. Coworker
31. Hogs
32. Typing-speed abbr.
33. Rock to and fro
35. Recreation spot

Starting box on page 562

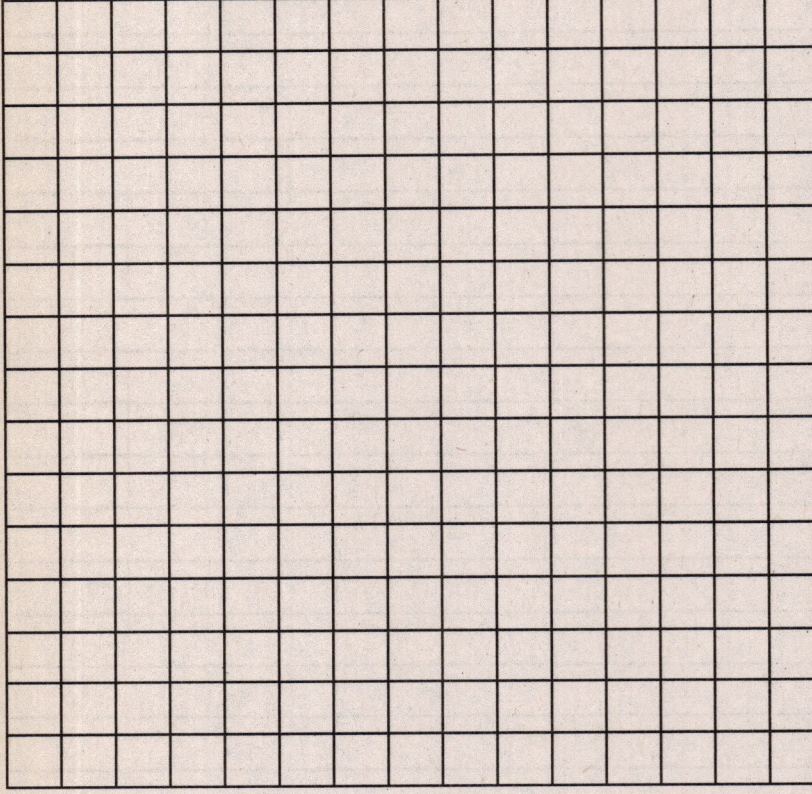

PUZZLE 386

Fan Words

Place the 5-letter answers to the clues into the fan to discover an 8-letter word reading across the outlined area. As an added help, pairs of answers are anagrams (1 is an anagram of 2, 3 is an anagram of 4, etc.).

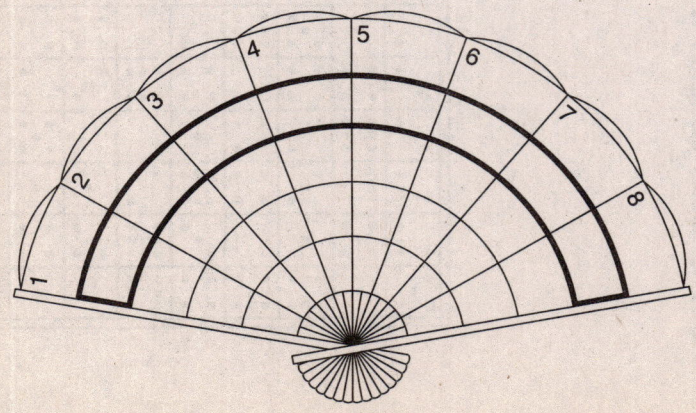

1. Wander off
2. Woodland deity
3. Doohickey
4. Evening
5. One of a flight
6. Indian lute
7. Artist's medium
8. Not fitting

PUZZLE 387

ACROSS
1. Fundamental
6. Present!
10. Dim
14. Coliseum
15. "___ the Roof"
16. Heed
17. Drudgery
18. Bauble
19. Reign
20. Heir
21. Be like Mike
23. Soak
25. Beam
26. Help
29. Jinx
30. Doctrine
35. Prone
38. Sense organ
39. Magnify
42. By way of
43. Reverence
44. Watchful
46. Purchase
48. Golf gadget
49. Light tap
50. Cargo weight
53. Blanket or underwear
57. Playful bite
59. Jacket
60. Verbal
62. Utter
64. Combat group
65. Parent
66. Hilo howdy
67. Depend
68. Seize
69. Belief

DOWN
1. Captures
2. Pointer
3. French river
4. Lodge
5. Scoundrel
6. Center
7. Rapier
8. Rove
9. Last
10. Raid
11. Border on
12. Strike out
13. Spud bud
22. Careless
24. Sunbathe
27. Polar sight
28. Clamor
29. Towel word
30. Soup veggie
31. Uncooked
32. Intense fury
33. Stratagem
34. Research room
35. Actress Gardner
36. Brooch
37. Do knot work
40. Obtain
41. "Look ___ ye leap"
45. Ex-soldier
46. Block
47. Ultimate
49. Insignificant
51. Edible bulb
52. Nook
53. Pitch
54. Salute
55. Operatic melody
56. Escapade
58. ___ moss
59. Nasty pooch
61. Gypsy Rose ___
62. Cauldron
63. Spanish hurrah

Starting box on page 562

Quotefinds — PUZZLE 388

In each diagram, start at the circled letter and draw one continuous path moving from letter to adjacent letter, horizontally, vertically, and diagonally, to discover a quotation. Each letter will be used once. The path does not cross itself.

1.

N	S	G	N	I
O	A	I	G	O
T	H	N	(S)	D
E	I	H	Y	A
R	E	T	I	N
N	O	S	I	G

2.

L	E	R	E	E
A	B	P	A	E
R	A	E	R	T
N	E	(S)	B	N
C	L	I	E	U
E	I	S	T	H

335

PUZZLE 389

ACROSS
1. Fido's foot
4. Fir's fluid
7. Sudden fear
9. TV spy drama
11. Sedan style
13. Beau or Jeff
15. Gallery contents
16. Thick piece
18. Slightly wet
19. Snaky swimmer
20. Croon
22. Ex's income
24. Refined woman
25. Views
27. Small boy
28. Diamond stats
29. Stoolie
30. Bush row
32. Deed
33. Cpl. Walter O'Reilly
35. Foe
37. Monotonous state
38. Boxer's option
39. Move stealthily
41. Planet
43. Born as
44. Wooden teal, e.g.
46. Goof
48. Tie together
49. Auto
50. Hilarious situation
52. Wooden strip
53. Family member
57. Part of PRND12
59. Farm animal
60. Bank transaction
61. Storage structure
63. Forest female
64. Awe-inspiring
66. "Extra! Extra!" crier
68. Like 2, 3, 5, etc.
69. Morpheus's domain
70. Gorilla, e.g.
71. Blue

DOWN
1. Associate
2. &
3. Mental acuity
4. Underskirt
5. Assistance
6. Elaborate spectacle
7. Seine straddler
8. Soda choice
9. Military forces
10. Tubers, bulbs, etc.
11. Owns
12. Chum
13. Prohibit
14. Crafty
17. Crab's large claw
18. Evade
21. Equipment
23. Humor magazine
24. Comedy legend
26. Had the lead
28. Aimless wanderer
30. Despised
31. Take pleasure in
34. Rightful
36. Auricle
39. Penny
40. Nut type
41. Lyricist's concern
42. Plumber's concern
43. North American river
45. Is able to
47. Rail foundation
48. Dirigible
51. "F ___"
52. Fancy resort
53. Departed
54. Tattered piece
55. Kegler's target
56. Pub options
58. West or Largo
60. C source
62. Strigiform birds
65. 90210, e.g.
67. Body of water

Starting box on page 562

PUZZLE 390 — Double Up

Each puzzle consists of four 5-letter words that use ten different letters exactly twice apiece. Thus, since there are already two P's in the first puzzle, you cannot use another P. There is only one N in that puzzle; think of a word using the second N.

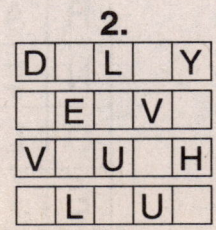

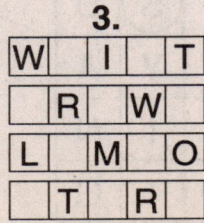

4.
S	E	F
	L	I
N		E
	O	N

PUZZLE 391

ACROSS
1. Dupes
6. "___ to Orpheus"
8. Deadlock
10. Eastern monk
14. Marshlike
15. Colorado Indians
16. Muslim official
17. Heidi's peaks
18. Split
19. Assembled
20. "___ Miserables"
21. Pungent gas
24. Eve's grandson
26. Hold up
28. Burden
30. Wicker baskets
31. Business promotion
34. Verifications
35. Call out
37. Certain Mediterranean lands
38. Consider
40. Nonbeliever
43. Ms. West
44. Barcelona bull
45. Show surprise
49. Take it easy
50. Consistent
51. Canadian prov.
52. Extraction sites
53. Exercise surfaces
54. Sailors' boxes
56. Makes from scratch
57. Fragrant compound

DOWN
1. Warty creatures
2. Merely
3. Individual
4. Arboreal primate
5. Assert
6. Greg, Peter, and Bobby, to Carol
7. British submachine gun
8. Moon pref.
9. Pieces of property
10. Warped wheels?
11. "___ Called Horse"
12. Skirt length
13. Locality
14. Breathing sound
22. Asian peninsula
23. Spread misinformation
25. Ate
26. Conscript
27. Shocking sorts
29. Minister to
30. Twig
32. Heating substance
33. Details
36. Contracts
37. Pride members
39. New York team
40. Kind of veto
41. Variable star
42. Pother
46. Baldwin or Guinness
47. Eyeball
48. Walks the floor
49. Platform
52. Distribute
55. Derby

Starting box on page 562

Mind Tickler

PUZZLE 392

A hundred coins (pennies, nickels, dimes, and quarters) add up to $2. If there are just as many nickels as dimes, exactly how many are there of each type of coin?

337

PUZZLE 393

ACROSS

1. Plumbing concern
5. Mushrooms
6. Went by cab
10. Public disgrace
12. "The ___ Ant Show"
13. Forceps
14. Take place
19. Rice dish
21. Perimeter
22. Mindless repetition
23. Picturesque
25. Earn a "C"
26. Many
27. Lucid
28. Charts
29. Beach hue
30. Russian emperor
34. Greek letter
35. Hide
36. Jacket parts
38. Strong chemical base
43. Retract
44. Contribution
45. Lace hole
47. Address
48. Elephant group
51. "We ___ Family"
53. Former mates
54. Unclose, to a poet
55. Long-legged wader
56. Chasm
58. Pot for paella
59. Narrow board
63. Beyond
66. Abound
67. Chianti, to Luigi
68. Fishing net
69. Did arithmetic
71. Tough fabric
72. ___ gin fizz
73. Maui instrument
75. Chopped
76. Teenagers' adjectives
77. Curly greens

DOWN

1. Sudden thrusts
2. Halts
3. Turkish title
4. Metric measure
5. Pointed teeth
6. Yaks
7. Of the ear
8. Distributes
9. Flow out
10. Degree
11. Musical conclusion
15. Muscle spasms
16. Some sodas
17. Perfect place
18. Soaks to soften
20. Decisive
24. Lincoln coin
30. Gave a hint to
31. Goofy
32. Cathedral section
33. Authentic
35. Cores
37. Caustic liquid
39. Sass
40. Leg hinge
41. Zenith
42. Clare Boothe ___
46. Postponed
47. Bun seed
48. Spanish hour
49. Heroic poems
50. Revitalize
52. Irritated
55. Little bit
57. Cotton cloth
59. Lithe
60. Ropes
61. Indigo
62. Large book
64. Shade of white
65. Spotted
70. Basketball shot
71. Double
74. New Zealand parrot

Starting box on page 562

DIAGRAMLESS DEVOTEES! *Delve into a special collection with loads of challenging puzzles in every volume of Selected Diagramless. To order, see page 159.*

PUZZLE 394

• FROM THE TOOLBOX •

ACROSS
1. Scope
6. Burst
9. Wiggling bait
13. Adjudged
15. Wildebeest
16. Muslim holy man
17. Fastener shooter
21. Portray
22. Russo of films
23. Car
24. Greek vowels
27. Moose's cousin
28. Small drinks
32. Makes a doily
34. Vocalist Sumac
35. Bar rocks
36. "Republic" author
38. Woosnam of the links
40. "___-Tiki"
41. However
42. Hexagonal tightener
46. Bit of wisdom
48. Certain ape
49. Cut of pork
51. Kindergarten class
52. Affirmative
53. Astern
54. Bind
55. Initial wager
57. Unit of corn
58. Average grade
59. Bikini part
62. Burn slightly
63. Showed the way
64. Grand ___ Opry
65. Chemistry suffix
68. Unlatch, in verse
69. Florida county
71. Sporting venue
73. Tropical tree
75. Phillips-head ___
81. The blue above
82. Bat wood
83. Spasm
84. Animated
85. Increases
86. American Olympics chant
87. Bit of matter
90. Retain
91. Every
92. Escapes
94. Mideast nation
96. Jazzy Fitzgerald
97. Diameter measure
99. Fancy wood cutter
105. Arabian gulf
106. Historic span
107. Message holder, possibly
108. Mood
109. Angry color
110. Fiddled

DOWN
1. Promos
2. Encountered
3. Arthur of "The Golden Girls"
4. Little devil
5. ___ Aviv
6. Nicklaus's gp.
7. A single time
8. Glazer's need
9. Electrician's snipper
10. Brunch choice
11. Military status
12. Mrs., in Rouen
14. Narc's org.
18. Kind of feeling
19. Stage-star Hagen
20. Paying heed
25. Quantity
26. What the stoolie did
28. Pedicure place
29. "___ Be Yours"
30. Buddy
31. ___ Anne de Beaupre
33. Pouchlike structure
35. European peninsula
37. Lennon's love
39. Penguins' assn.
43. Crooked, as a smile
44. "Norma ___"
45. Short dashes
47. Fence door
50. Western
55. Had a yearning
56. Teacher's union
59. It goes across the grain
60. Gets out of debt
61. Summer coolers
62. Ball-peen alternative
64. Black Sea city
65. Indignation
66. Dawn drops
67. Conclusion
70. Ballpark fig.
71. Circle or Ocean
72. Altar constellation
74. Carry
76. OSS successor
77. Type
78. Contest
79. Night before a holiday
80. Agt.
81. Morose
88. Spanish gold
89. Chart
91. Ray of "Inside Out"
93. Regal address
95. Bird's bill
96. Devour
98. Boy
100. Nary
101. Ronny & the Daytonas hit
102. Filthy home
103. Tavern quaff
104. Join in matrimony

Starting box on page 562

PUZZLE 395

ACROSS
1. Includes
5. Emcee
9. Metal fastener
14. Weary
15. Whale
16. Boorish one
17. Gusted
18. Light beige
19. Lying facedown
20. Faithful's age
21. Deck opening
23. Dress finely
24. Vessel
26. Perches
31. Sentence ender
33. Poser
34. Rainbow
35. Energy unit
36. Steel mill residue
37. Make right
40. Layer
41. Safecracker's soup
42. British noble
43. Ump's kin
44. Child
45. Ointment
47. Precede
50. Lackluster
51. Adverse fate
52. Exist
54. Bracelet item
56. Run away quickly
57. Arrive at
61. Reclines
63. Chantilly, e.g.
64. Assent
65. Chap
66. Wheel holder
67. Ladies
68. Bohemian
69. Hair colorist

DOWN
1. Monastery head
2. Small amount
3. Remove earth from
4. Attach a button
5. Tilling tool
6. Corsage bloom
7. Skinny one
8. Tight
9. Lab device
10. Caboose, e.g.
11. It comes after pi
12. Vast time
13. Sadness
22. Cliff projection
24. Finch, e.g.
25. Dutton TV series
27. At the location
28. Sailor
29. Skier's lift
30. Lily variety
32. Haphazard
33. Distorted
35. Sprite
37. Cinders of comics
38. Muffled cry
39. Ocean eagle
40. Coop
41. "Cheers" role
43. Opulent
44. As well
46. Moss's kin
47. Agitate
48. Milky Way, e.g.
49. Prophet
51. Not as wet
53. Muslim ruler
55. Seaweed, e.g.
57. Damp and cold
58. Id's cousin
59. Branch
60. 2.0 GPA
62. Messy abode
63. Junior

PUZZLE 396

ACROSS
1. Gush out
5. Children's game
8. Pony food
12. Federal ___
13. Arias
15. Fables
16. Formerly
17. Scout group
18. Doodle
19. Green soup
20. Humorous
22. Connecting link
23. Added wing
24. Metal deposits
25. Short trip
27. Poplar tree
29. Ballet move
30. All of two
32. Sticky stuff
34. Burn with liquid
38. Smells
40. Chalk up
41. Outdoor-meal site
42. French tam
43. Gun in neutral
44. Check
45. Marries
47. Express feeling
50. Dealer
53. Over
54. Snatch
57. Rink judge
58. Type of camera
60. "___ There Was You"
61. Something wicked
63. Sink
64. Loiter
65. Emanation
66. Grain towers
67. Some deer
68. Intense
69. Rating for Bo
70. Conjunctions

DOWN
1. Range
2. Instrument board
3. Mall conveyance
4. Like Willie
5. Oppressors
6. Healing plants
7. Virtuous
8. Secondhand
9. Heart line
10. Bride's following
11. Stitched
13. Inventory
14. Sales talk
20. Peace officer
21. Crunchy
26. Select new actors
28. Keen
29. Safety
30. TV's Barker
31. Lyric verse
33. Fear
35. Care
36. Stretch the truth
37. DeLuise of "Fatso"
39. Racehorse
46. Drabs' mate
48. Resources
49. Nocturnal hooter
50. Stomp
51. Variety show
52. Flaming
53. Corridor
55. Assisted
56. Grace word
59. Walking rhythm
62. Wind around
64. Lingerie item

PUZZLE 397

ACROSS
1. Embrace
6. Society newcomer
9. At once, on "ER"
13. Proportions
15. Hatchet
16. Foot part
17. Heaven
18. TV's McClanahan
19. Trig term
20. Guys
21. Internet surfer
23. Hook's companion
24. Scope
27. Baseball's Ruth
30. Wharf's kin
31. Salt additive
35. Of yore
38. Satire
41. Canine
42. Game cube
43. Influence
44. Cabin material
45. Precambrian, e.g.
46. Apportion
47. Onions' kin
49. African trip
51. Poker holding
53. Strike callers
55. Forget
59. Wild guess
62. Preposition
64. Grief
65. Health food
66. Banqueted
67. Senility
70. Petri-dish gel
71. Helium, e.g.
72. Brought to mind
73. Narrative
74. Picasso work
75. Ripeners

DOWN
1. Cookie-jar scrap
2. Future time
3. Do penance
4. Drink a little
5. South Seas staple
6. Be bold
7. Rural town
8. Bonnet dweller
9. Talked back
10. Cut shorter
11. Skin problem
12. You, once
14. Fry quickly
22. High-pitched
25. Impersonate
26. Clangor
28. "___ We Got Fun"
29. Young fellow
32. Laid-off
33. Secluded corner
34. Hen grenades?
35. Shelley offerings
36. Former Italian coin
37. Unheeding
39. Pooh's pal
40. Product
43. Buckle
46. Branch
47. "Mr. Peepers" aunt
48. Previous to, once
50. Reddish brown
52. Positive pole
54. Indian lute
56. Not sleeping
57. Actor Moore
58. Lacks
59. Collar insert
60. Galba's garment
61. Off yonder
63. Tree house
66. Eastern ruler
68. Caesar's meal?
69. Garb

PUZZLE 398

ACROSS

1. Parking timer
6. Feel bad
10. Wooden strip
14. Dynamic
15. Family
16. Engage
17. Ice pellets
18. Aerie
19. Bacon's mate
20. Fixed leftovers
23. Simple cabin
24. Vogue
26. Sends on a new course
28. Breeze
29. Eye cover
31. Sign gas
32. Hog's food
34. Game official
36. Withered
39. Flies alone
41. City transport
43. Wander away
45. Sailboat
47. Josh
49. Bygone days
50. Animal's nail
52. Bird cry
54. Dawn droplets
55. Auto repairman
59. Bent
61. Hatchet
62. Study
64. Go by horse
66. Jump
67. African mammal
71. Concrete piece
72. If not
73. Flawless
74. Seasoning
75. Color changer
76. Thick

DOWN

1. More, to Juan
2. Pipe shape
3. Connection
4. All possible
5. Say again
6. Teenager's woe
7. Erase
8. Quicken
9. Enrolled
10. That woman
11. Not heavy
12. Dispute
13. Experiments
21. Inheritor
22. Portals
24. Farm towers
25. Gnome
27. Oneness
28. Donkey
30. Society gal
33. Dog
35. Stole makings
37. Wear away
38. Provoked
40. ___ system
42. Attack!
44. Evergreen
46. Like some walls
48. Male pig
51. Prudently
53. Showy flower
55. Wetland
56. Outcast
57. Moth repellent
58. End
60. Scold
63. Impersonator
65. Flow back
68. Cage
69. Dads
70. Bravo!

PUZZLE 399

ACROSS
1. Dated ditty
6. Wound covering
10. Probes
14. Gaucho's rope
15. Legends
16. Narrow road
17. Wrong
18. Painful cry
19. Sunday response
20. Role for Ms. West
21. Cry in distress
23. Came to terms
25. Peeper woe
27. Get hitched
28. Energy
29. Sell
31. Pressure
35. Back streets
38. Direct
39. ___ Ane Langdon
40. Type of net
41. Chart
42. Punches
44. Printing liquid
45. Family vehicle
46. Absorb
47. More harsh
50. Spring peeper
51. Sweltering
52. Beverage for two
53. Slangy assent
57. Way of walking
60. Crude homes
62. In history
63. Bewail
64. Surprise attack
66. Lively
68. Upon
69. Skin breakout
70. Output
71. Turns to the right
72. Necessity
73. Binge

DOWN
1. Some exams
2. Speed ___
3. Morning paper
4. Part of TGIF
5. "___ Money"
6. Became tedious
7. Was able to
8. Circle section
9. Acted
10. Worries
11. Identical
12. Leg hinge
13. Remit
22. Holds title to
24. ___ rummy
26. Tied, as a race
30. Hurricane center
31. Incline
32. Land amid water
33. On the ___
34. Cozy spot
35. Sale term
36. Fasting period
37. Care for
38. Embargo
41. Spoil
42. Med subject
43. An omelet, e.g.
45. Experienced one
46. Mild oath
48. Horned animals
49. Head signal
50. Quarreled
52. Biblical pronoun
54. Nosher
55. Nimble
56. Large crowd
57. Fog and smoke
58. Sound pitch
59. Grade
61. Speaks
65. Whiz
67. Little drink

PUZZLE 400

ACROSS
1. Pout
5. Corrodes
9. Tastes
13. Matching
14. Vital fluid
16. Snag
17. Heredity factor
18. Knife part
19. Capri, e.g.
20. Off-center
22. Roy's wife
24. Mete out
25. Sound boosters
28. Arctic cover
30. Roofing goo
33. Mommy deer
34. Phooey!
35. Musical comedy
38. Carpet
39. Carve
40. Uneasy
42. Border
46. Abed
48. Lofty
50. Glass sheet
52. Light knock
53. Small dog
54. Paddled
56. Skirt type
57. Choose
58. Judge's wear
60. Fetter
65. Chap
67. Apple juice
70. Estate unit
71. Quick farewells
72. Rascal
73. Movie
74. Boat movers
75. Santa's ride
76. Biddies

DOWN
1. Heroic tale
2. Ho's instruments
3. Bond
4. Leg hinge
5. Decrease
6. Fully
7. Frogs' kin
8. Birch beer, e.g.
9. Glide over snow
10. Grasshopper, e.g.
11. Lively dances
12. Expensive
15. Sub shop
21. Slosh through water
23. Old lace hue
26. Modern inn
27. Mr. Rose
29. Keen
30. ___ the line
31. Likely
32. Type of room
36. Horned mammal, for short
37. Warhol's forte
38. Shine again
41. Tiny particle
43. Immerse
44. Large antelope
45. Chicken-to-be
47. Glance slyly
49. Grand
50. Tropical fruit
51. Buck's horn
54. Jazz group
55. Wharf
56. Award pin
59. Storage boxes
61. Jumble
62. Dull pain
63. Wrought ___
64. Brokaw's forte
66. Snaky letter
68. Eden dweller
69. Actor Skelton

PUZZLE 401

CODEWORD

Codeword is a special crossword puzzle in which conventional clues are omitted. Instead, answer words in the diagram are represented by numbers. Each number represents a different letter of the alphabet, and all of the letters of the alphabet are used. When you are sure of a letter, put it in the code key chart and cross it off in the Alphabet Box below the grid. A group of letters has been inserted to start you off.

1	2	3	4	5	6 A	7 M	8	9	10	11	12	13
14	15 P	16	17	18	19	20	21	22	23	24	25	26

Alphabet Box

A B C D E F G H I J K L M N O P Q R S T U V W X Y Z

PUZZLE 402

ACROSS
1. Bursts
5. Promise
9. Solid
14. "Aida" solo
15. Posterior
16. Wash away
17. Froster
18. Dole (out)
19. Head bone
20. Root vegetable
22. Mist
24. Golf stand
25. Curly's pal
27. Boat bottom
29. Balloon basket
32. Pond-scum ingredient
34. Judgment
37. Devoured
38. Wait on
40. Narrow board
42. Glimmer
44. Pitcher handle
45. Mimicry
46. Per
47. Exhausted
49. Genesis ship
50. Fair booth
53. Mythology
54. Seedy bread
55. Tress stuff
57. Talk over
58. Tree juice
61. Garbed
63. Claimed, as land
68. Nerve
70. It's tubular
72. Bright green
73. Distribute
74. Hot place
75. Horner's fruit
76. Nuzzled
77. Resounded
78. Not bad

DOWN
1. Couple
2. Humpback's kin
3. "The ___ Piper"
4. Delhi dress
5. Garment opening
6. Low neckline
7. Promise
8. ___ havoc
9. Plant again
10. Exasperate
11. Toe woe
12. At leisure
13. Remove from print
21. Destroy
23. Last letter
26. Heron
28. Speech defect
29. Paris eatery
30. Map book
31. Give answer
33. Be of profit
35. Cloudless
36. Dawdle
39. Inaccuracy
41. Small child
43. Persian king
45. Expert
48. Expunging
51. Needed
52. "___ Abner"
56. Shaving tool
58. Make a web
59. Part of a.k.a.
60. Cat
62. Opera star
64. Swiss peaks
65. Metric measure
66. Australian birds
67. Audition tape
69. Inkling
71. Five and five

PUZZLE 403

ACROSS
1. Haddock
6. Crest
10. Select
13. Stadium sound
15. Walk
16. Lock need
17. Loony
18. Formerly
19. Emulate Ice Cube
20. Hammerhead's end
21. Chair's support
23. Film again
25. Festivity
27. Slangy negative
28. Specialists
30. Watch
32. In case
35. Ocean
36. Country outing
39. Vigor
41. Decorative piece
42. Effigy
43. Begin, in poetry
44. Excavation
45. Collided
47. Above, to a bard
48. Observer
50. Yank's foe
51. Stare
53. The Bible, e.g.
55. Humpback's kin
57. Sign
60. Paid athlete
61. Rough file
65. Excessively
66. Toy with a tail
68. Hate
70. Selfish trip
71. Incessantly
72. Gulf's kin
73. Crazy
74. Ding
75. Transfer a daisy

DOWN
1. Freighter
2. Geometric shape
3. Got up
4. Fruit or color
5. Nick on "Cheers"
6. Excited
7. Fled
8. Very tiny
9. Belfry
10. Southern veggie
11. Pikes ___
12. Class
14. Squeal
22. Certain target
24. Football gadget
26. Burnt wood
27. Border on
28. Lofty abode
29. Slyly spiteful
31. Annul
33. Reel
34. Sioux dwelling
35. Drain
37. Gaseous mixture
38. Bad mark
40. Miles ___ hour
45. Bent
46. Grumpy's pal
49. Kind of tide
52. Service station
54. Popeye's love
56. Roster
57. Flower stalk
58. Exercise
59. Atmosphere
60. Brash
62. Overhead
63. Send away
64. Confined
67. Hamilton bill
69. Boat rower

PUZZLE 404

ACROSS

1. Cheerful
5. Lingerie item
8. Rates
13. Taboo
14. Row
15. Trial
16. Play parts
17. "We ___ Family"
18. Golf helper
19. Robber
21. Toward sunrise
23. "___ Got to Be Me"
24. "___ House"
26. British drink
28. Energy
29. Marbles
33. Raise
35. Govern
36. Saudi somebody
38. Jobs
42. Railroad rail
44. Fierce anger
45. Available
46. Raw-fish dish
47. Cat's comment
49. Allot
50. Faint
52. Accumulated
54. Wind around
57. "___ a Living"
58. Cut
59. Have bills
60. Detest
62. Assemble
67. Hors d'oeuvre
70. Shopworn
72. Fragrance
73. More giving
74. Once named
75. Clay square
76. Direct
77. Craving
78. Linger

DOWN

1. Biting bug
2. Scot's lake
3. Opposer
4. Reality portion?
5. Jungle snake
6. Fewer
7. Space
8. Notable time
9. Tack on
10. Immerse again
11. Unworldly
12. Snooze
15. Eight musicians
20. Rival
22. Hi-fi system
25. Function
27. Mobile prefix
29. Liberal ___
30. Pundit
31. Oy!
32. Mechanics, shortly
33. Warning wail
34. Bamboo eater
37. Champagne cocktail
39. Cease to go
40. Curly greens
41. Raced
43. Fuzzy fruit
48. "___ Done It?"
51. Alternate
53. Fleecy mama
54. Secures
55. Remain
56. Pasta option
58. Ruckus
61. Singer Bennett
63. Spoils
64. Polish copy
65. Soft drink
66. Deuce beater
68. Fruity quaff
69. Part of mph
71. Burrow

349

PUZZLE 405

ACROSS
1. Alter slacks
6. Newborn
10. Elsie's mom
13. "The ___ Cometh"
15. Burn remedy
16. Expert person
17. Pure
18. Spiffy
19. Split ___ soup
20. Sizzling
21. Library user
23. Long paddle
24. Foot woes
25. Astute
27. Stoneworker
30. Packed down
33. Atop
34. Confused
38. Nourished
39. Cozy room
40. Forest female
41. Guitar's kin
42. College group
45. Did in
46. Mesh
47. Dorm residents
48. Pollute
51. Metropolitan
53. Sprint
54. Pack animals
56. Extremely
59. "___ to Joy"
60. Actor O'Neal
61. It may be silver
63. Back talk
64. Killer whale
65. Tooth covering
66. Piece of land
67. Passing grades
68. Very stout

DOWN
1. Loaded
2. Repeat
3. Miami team
4. Some dashes
5. Married woman
6. Cutting tool
7. Toward shelter
8. Hog
9. However
10. Roaster
11. Watery expanse
12. Tired
14. Poetic contraction
22. Radio adjunct
24. Pro's opponent
25. Hand over
26. Cool drink
27. Blunder
28. Mimicker
29. Fizz water
31. Kind of exam
32. Scheme
34. "Titanic" foe
35. Law
36. Made do
37. Dawn droplets
39. Fender damage
43. Twice five
44. Exotic pets
45. Close relative
47. Gambling hall
48. Gnome
49. Sound
50. Incompetent
52. Bundle hay
54. Ancient harp
55. Doily material
56. Clock, as a race
57. Small numbers
58. Look amorously
60. Reel's mate
62. Catch

PUZZLE 406

ACROSS

1. '70s hairdo
5. Animal foot
8. List of thespians
12. Long lunch?
13. More authentic
15. Mannered
16. Jug
17. Swarm
18. Emit fumes
19. Frost
21. Clio nominees
22. Domesticated
23. Ski race
26. Agile
28. Asian weights
29. Captured
32. Misprints
34. Bugbear
35. Negative
37. Turkish rulers
38. Bread surface
40. Window part
41. Permit
42. Pub potable
43. Tribal medium
45. Esteem
47. Alpine ridge
48. Powerful person
50. Ornamental band
51. Soft drink
54. Every one
55. Average mark
56. Cultivating tool
57. Tutor
59. River sediment
63. Military employee
64. Invest
65. "Aida" solo
66. Crucifix
67. Ball holder
68. Require

DOWN

1. That lady
2. Chop roughly
3. Live
4. Apes
5. Debate side
6. Of hearing
7. June mergers
8. Monopoly
9. Square measure
10. Check
11. Little kid
13. Those people
14. Begins again
20. Price to pay
23. Be a thief
24. ___-than-life
25. Ventilate
27. Hurry
30. Tooth coating
31. Bestow
33. Make sour
34. "___ Town"
36. Principle
39. Fragrant
40. Pasta cheese
42. Kid's cry
44. Bunny's kin
46. Chewed on
49. Grass unit
50. Feel sore
51. Ship's pole
52. Meat stew
53. Dummy
58. Reminder
60. Annoy
61. Mislead
62. Small amount

PUZZLE 407

FLOWER POWER

Instructions for solving Flower Power puzzles are given on page 94.

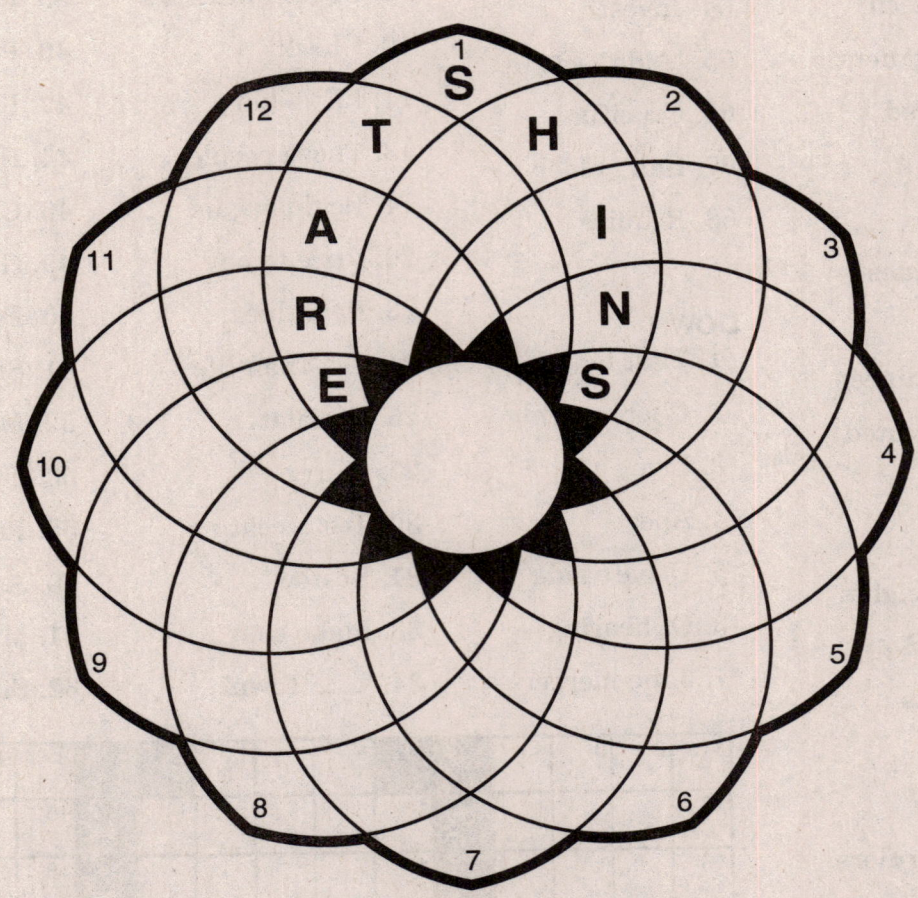

CLOCKWISE

1. Leg parts
2. Brisk
3. Hold responsible
4. Thrown
5. Fiend
6. Pulse
7. Holler
8. March proudly
9. Point total
10. Special utensil
11. Paddle
12. Smell

COUNTERCLOCKWISE

1. Fixed look
2. Armor opening
3. Verge
4. Walk stealthily
5. Goblet
6. Pound
7. Gleamed
8. Shoulder gesture
9. Bar seat
10. Scour
11. Gush forth
12. Baseball, e.g.

PUZZLE 408

ACROSS
1. Tons
6. Olympians
10. TV spots
13. Turn
14. Band
15. Pod content
16. Nail board
17. Shaving tool
18. Deer's kin
19. Campus digs
20. Skin
21. Ghostly
23. Happy face
25. Male
26. Astern
29. Everything
30. Rolled tightly
33. White, to Sajak
35. Old pronoun
36. Eye test
38. Topsoil
39. Life story
40. Dull finish
41. Opening
42. Amusing
43. Bleak
44. Expands
46. Office copy
47. Not subtract
48. Beam
49. ___ boom
51. Restless
54. Whip
55. Chops
59. Neither
60. Covered with vines
62. Confused fight
63. Brewed drink
64. Dressed to the ___
65. Plus factor
66. Stately tree
67. Nerd
68. Paces

DOWN
1. Went fast
2. Prom vehicle
3. Always
4. Fish bait
5. Pig's pad
6. A- or C+
7. Trickle
8. Twosome
9. Ranch
10. Rich Little, e.g.
11. Ham seller
12. Welfare
14. Barbecue
20. Sword handle
22. Make beloved
24. Crush
25. Merry month
26. High cards
27. Young horses
28. Hurl
30. Owl's query?
31. Bonus
32. Passe
34. Sea mammals
35. Shallow pan
37. Fix
39. Motor coach
40. Long skirt
42. Soar
43. Slam
45. Placing
46. Edible things
49. Glossy
50. Footlocker
51. Chip in
52. Mr. Coward
53. Trolley
54. Good
56. In a different way
57. Cry
58. Readies the table
61. Strive
62. Barker and Bell

353

PUZZLE 409

ACROSS
1. Rascal
6. Lively party
10. Haywire
14. Educator
15. Gifted
16. Approach
17. Wash away
18. Aspen lift
19. "___ Man"
20. 1,000,000, for short
21. Plot
23. In the know about
24. Singular
26. Bro, to sis
28. Not stereo
29. Flow-control device
33. Flirt
36. Stomach muscles
38. Word with store
39. Woodcutter's tool
40. Steeped drink
42. Pen's contents
43. Legislative body
46. Election winners
47. Fruit coolers
48. Slip away from
49. Bawdy
51. Museum handout
53. Buffed
57. Trucker's rig
60. Bright bird
62. Sense of hearing
63. Couple
64. Glimpse
65. Hunter's shelter
67. Capri or Royale
68. Set the tempo
69. Ranch guests
70. At no time, in verse
71. Imitator
72. Celebs

DOWN
1. Pipe parts
2. Trinket
3. Ring-shaped reef
4. In fashion
5. Voila!
6. Breakfast attire
7. Certain convent
8. Powerful dunk
9. "___ to Romance"
10. Circus gymnast
11. Whine
12. Disregard
13. Bingo's kin
22. Hors d'oeuvre
25. Small demon
27. "___ Got a Secret"
30. Deposited
31. Creeper
32. BPOE members
33. Florist's container
34. Skating feat
35. List of options
37. Go down the slope
38. Vend again
41. Witness
44. Fan
45. British ritual
47. Shoppers' readings
50. Handles
52. Momma's partner
53. Pie serving
54. "___ Gabler"
55. Zealous
56. Clothe
57. Twirl
58. Leisure
59. Miss by a ___
61. Gather
66. Away

354

PUZZLE 410

ACROSS
1. Swelter
6. Corn units
10. Tit for ___
13. Harmony
15. Hint
16. Hatchet
17. Artist's place
18. Loan
19. Animation unit
20. Cat or dog
21. Tableland
23. Island chain
25. Walk
27. Geisha's garb
30. Firedog
33. Show anger
37. Arrange troops
40. Confident
42. Frost
43. Print measures
45. ___ lizzie
46. Wisecrack
47. Varnish
49. Opportune
51. Israeli dance
52. Large knife
55. Black magic
57. Cruise et al.
61. Award
64. Alpha follower
67. Hawaiian offering
68. Develop
69. Callas, e.g.
72. Pictures in pictures
74. Tennis stroke
75. Hateful
76. Gazes
77. Snakelike curve
78. Clean
79. Rome's nation

DOWN
1. Scrapes
2. Four pairs
3. Intense
4. Grass
5. In good shape
6. Filled pastry
7. Andy Capp's drink
8. Hurry
9. Car
10. Mexican treat
11. Skating jump
12. Relate
14. Jane or John
22. Tackle moguls
24. Soybean curd
26. Companion
28. Zoo ditch
29. In a place
31. Director Coward
32. Electric generator
34. Twist one's arm
35. Breakfast, e.g.
36. Irritable
37. Platter
38. Mimic
39. Colleague
41. Fit of anger
44. Great number
48. Volcano's flow
50. Convened
53. Shade of blue
54. Tilling tool
56. Past
58. Verdi work
59. Highway inn
60. Ms. Spacek
61. Buck, e.g.
62. Self-images
63. Society newcomers
65. Song syllables
66. Not pro
70. "___ Always Loved You"
71. By way of
73. Posed for

PUZZLE 411

ACROSS
1. Without, in France
5. ___ tree (eucalyptus)
8. Hooters
12. Reprimand
17. ___ vera
18. Gay Nineties, e.g.
19. Trickle
20. Indian tea
21. Sidewalk surface
23. One, in Berlin
24. Showed again
25. Booby traps
26. Unwavering
28. "A Bug's Life" extra
29. Knights' transports
33. Sign up
35. Maximum limit
38. Panoramas
40. Stylist's task
44. Pueblo material
47. South American Indian
48. '60s do
50. Soccer feat
51. Ejection
53. Dress for a rani
55. Dead heat
56. Post-pasta drink
58. Chaplin role
60. Robust
61. Previous to, in verse
62. Inexperienced
64. Go ___ (explode)
66. Hair holder
69. Divvy up
71. Yearly register
76. Manipulate
77. Bigfoot's cousin
78. Violent windstorm
79. Mideast ruler, once
81. Conducted
82. Small: pref.
85. "___ Butterfly"
86. Very sweet
88. Hazard
89. Rock group's aid
90. Agency
93. Scope
97. Ruth's club
100. No kidding?
102. Wedding throw
106. Man with morals
108. "Clue" weapon
109. In flight
111. Fishing net
112. Like a dime
113. Hamilton, to Burr
114. On the ___ (quarreling)
115. "Stormy Weather" singer
116. Derbies
117. Certain pharaoh, for short
118. Bother

DOWN
1. Exhausts
2. King of comedy
3. Variable star
4. Forecasters
5. Barnyard fowl
6. Vessel
7. Scatter rug
8. Lyric poems
9. Jots down
10. Flax cloth
11. Javelin
12. In a nimble way
13. Piano key
14. Gumbo pod
15. Bank deal
16. Impression
22. Assembled
27. Extinct bird
30. Lesser of two ___
31. Clamor
32. Minute part: abbr.
34. Relay section
35. Custody
36. Dog-day drinks
37. Pageantry
39. Goof off
41. Tiny particle
42. ___ down (make final)
43. Delight
45. Operated a drill
46. For keeps
48. Former French coin
49. Hoop border
52. Adrift
54. "Just the Way You ___"
57. Eyed
59. ___ Alto, California
60. Redhead's rinse
63. Decompose
65. Curl job, for short
66. Kiss

356

PUZZLE 411

67. Like an unswept hearth
68. Get closer
70. Alkaline compound
72. Lopsided
73. Baby's father
74. Cartwright son
75. Caper
80. Wheel center
81. Ancient instrument
83. Fierce anger
84. Veto
87. Royal color
88. Sermonizer's stand
91. Big blue marble?
92. Hello or farewell
94. Florida bird
95. Catch a thief
96. Company
97. Bubble ___
98. Of flying: pref.
99. Emperor of old
101. Hankers
103. Correct
104. Tolkien creatures
105. Kick back
107. To each his ___
109. Sternward
110. Debtor's note: abbr.

357

PUZZLE 412

ACROSS
1. In addition
5. Yule drink
8. New York canal
12. Hardly early
13. Make watertight
15. Spoils
16. He tops the cake
17. Cook's smock
18. Pen fillers
19. Tire input
20. Female sheep
21. Swine
23. ___ thief
25. Boring tool
26. Clouds' region
29. Skirt panel
30. Friend
32. Broadside
34. Lounged
36. Reason for sneezin'
37. Tarts
40. With speed
42. Poetic works
43. Part of speech
45. Shrimp
47. Water birds
48. Porky's digs
49. Cut text
52. It has a drum
53. Etna residue
55. Bad BMW
57. Depressed
58. Halfway
60. For
61. Aquatic plant
64. Seedless orange
66. Sail pole
67. Foreteller
68. Take the wrong way?
69. Lily plant
70. Position
71. Chick's ma
72. Elapse

DOWN
1. False name
2. Corset fastener
3. Hi-fi system
4. Done, to Donne
5. Neck part
6. "___ Day Will Come"
7. Worldwide
8. Arab bigwig
9. Scurried
10. Bother
11. Snaky shape
13. Crow's call
14. Recognize
20. Stretched
22. Choir voice
24. Wakes up
26. Vended
27. Prayer supporter
28. Desires
30. School rally
31. Adjust
33. Fair-haired
35. Chemist's lair
36. Podded veggie
37. Errand boy
38. Inventor's start
39. Constantly
41. Wail
44. Authentic
46. Fuse
48. Blade case
50. Horned antelope
51. Trunks
54. Tans
56. Heeds
57. Stark
58. Nasty
59. Home sick
61. Beast of burden
62. Hilo wreath
63. Fetch
65. 22nd letter
66. Tourist's aid

PUZZLE 413

ACROSS
1. Monopolizes
5. Athenian vowels
9. Greek letters
12. Freshly
13. Secret bride
15. Footed vase
16. Highway hauler
17. Draw
18. Maui handout
19. Indy 500, e.g.
21. Office worker
23. Swipe
25. Thingamajig
27. Part of APB
28. Nostalgic
30. "Desire" trees
33. Girl
34. Dog-___
35. "___ of a Salesman"
37. Barely makes
39. Toga's kin
41. Dreadful
42. Naps
44. Kayak's cousin
46. ___ Quixote
47. Put on cargo
48. Plant disease
49. Printing measures
50. Break down
52. Tine
54. Magic word
57. Lip stick?
58. Loose
59. Word connector
62. Rubbernecker
66. Turkish bigwig
67. Effortlessly
68. Provide
69. ___-o'-shanter
70. Slate of names
71. Dill, formerly

DOWN
1. Holds
2. Small number
3. Masterpiece
4. Move in circles
5. Ms. Sommer
6. Sock tip
7. Fitting
8. Denominations
9. Hungarian dog
10. Infuriates
11. Bad mood
13. Confiscate
14. Made a verse
20. Realtor's unit
22. Steered a raft
23. Snow units
24. Most sick
25. Bomb
26. Antiseptic
27. Ripening agent
29. Cease-fires
31. Young miss
32. Powerful
36. Chickens
38. Curbs
40. Business
43. Enwrap
45. Aristocrat
51. Majestic
53. "The ___ Man"
54. City map
55. Indian melody
56. Large test
57. Cummerbund
60. Fraternity letter
61. That fellow's
63. Yang's mate
64. Garden dweller
65. Soak flax

PUZZLE 414

ACROSS
1. Teen woe
5. Type type
9. Batman's partner
14. Midday
15. False god
16. Aphorism
17. Miscalculates
18. Chance game
19. Food lists
20. Sopping
21. Fields
23. Tit for ___
24. Scraping tool
26. Love seat
27. Followers
28. Mocks
30. Andean climber
32. Grimm heavies
33. Mailed
36. Time period
37. Suffer
39. Check
42. Less pretty
43. Feel anxious
45. Minor role
47. Attentive
48. Light source
49. Ramble
53. Gun, as a motor
54. Cleopatra biter
55. Pharaoh's tomb
57. Subside
60. Not those
62. Like crazy
63. Algonquian
64. Toast word
65. Minstrel's strings
66. Patron
67. Sugary
68. Look
69. Dexterous

DOWN
1. Once more
2. Apple part
3. "___ Exposure"
4. Certain dashes
5. Highway
6. Thoughts
7. Apartment
8. Distant
9. Batters
10. Hymn of praise
11. Miniature chicken
12. Lizard
13. Bird beds
21. Note
22. Dance
25. Miner's yield
27. Trend
28. Boxer Frazier
29. Self-respect
31. Away from the wind
33. Maui meal
34. Attuned
35. Gawain's title
38. Praise
39. Cross over
40. Noah's boat
41. So long!
42. Ballpark judge
44. Part of IOU
45. Curved nut
46. Electrical unit
48. Strips of wood
50. Verbal exams
51. Merit
52. Gush
55. Nudnik
56. Element
58. Sirloin, e.g.
59. Ernie's chum
61. "___ No Evil"
63. Cow chow

PUZZLE 415

ACROSS
1. Greedy
5. Float
9. Narrow opening
13. Climbing plant
14. World carrier
16. Place for a gutter
17. Alan or Robert
18. Envelope sticker
19. Pulpit word
20. Snow coasters
22. Underling
24. Government levy
25. Punt
27. Pointed end
28. Moose's relative
29. Old soldier
33. Nutritious legume
37. Strike
38. Aphids
39. Indian, for one
40. Word before bag
41. Diamond or ruby
42. Music and dance, e.g.
43. Pat
44. Sent
45. Cleaning utensil
47. Movie, for short
48. Electric ___
49. Steal a look
50. Hoover, e.g.
53. Protected
57. Pigs
59. Possess
60. Of the nose
62. Performs in a play
63. Tavern tipples
64. Caption
65. Victory symbols
66. Towel marking
67. Missing
68. Duane or Nelson

DOWN
1. Stop, at sea
2. Spanish house
3. List in a book
4. Kaput
5. Lived
6. Assault
7. Container
8. Scottish caps
9. Safety straps
10. Tibetan monk
11. Kitchen appliance
12. Camper's cover
15. Small piano
21. Knitter's buy
23. Make a lap
26. Got the bug
29. By route of
30. Civil disturbance
31. Adolescent woe
32. Lack
33. Burden
34. Unbleached color
35. Butterfly catchers
36. Bland
37. Wise to the jive
40. Get brown
41. Punches
43. Capability
44. Bakery purchase
46. Canary, e.g.
47. Powers a bike
49. Pasta topping
50. Cubed
51. Added to the pot
52. Disorderly
53. Iranian ruler, once
54. Healthy
55. Always
56. Fence
58. Seashore sight
61. Type of serve

PUZZLE 416

ACROSS
1. ___ milk
5. Strong breezes
10. Nitrogen, e.g.
13. Mite
14. Neck scarves
16. Be indisposed
17. Exultation
18. Goober
19. Chaotic place
20. Rough
22. Marsh bird
23. Hardwood
24. Open container
26. Plot outline
28. Beg
32. Sly one
33. Casino game
34. Available
37. Engrave
41. ___ the knot
42. Jung topic
43. Deplore
44. Yukon vehicle
46. Knot
48. Affront
49. Question
51. Least
53. School recess
58. Trouser part
59. Tarry
60. On a ship's left side
62. Plumed bird
66. Screw up
67. Type of cord
69. "___ and Let Die"
70. Birthday concern
71. Of this matter
72. Dueler's tool
73. Ms. Wallace
74. Cut again
75. Scout groups

DOWN
1. Show relief
2. Soda-flavoring nut
3. Road for Cato
4. Liberace, to some
5. Crack
6. Manipulates
7. Looks over
8. Gin partner
9. Stun
10. Onlooker
11. Garlic mayonnaise
12. TV-replay method
15. Pool worker
21. Color
25. Pub
27. Woodcutting tool
28. Amphibians
29. Fastener
30. Dogwood or pine
31. Adolescent
35. Turkish general
36. College housing
38. Garnish
39. Caribbean country
40. Bounder
45. Hudson costar
46. Ship's captain
47. "Rugrats" tyke
48. Laughed lightly
50. Hiding place
52. Society page word
53. Beseech
54. Huge
55. Approve
56. Silk fabric
57. Sea eagles
61. Good-bye, in Soho
63. Mellow
64. Same amount
65. Casual shirts
68. Moo

PUZZLE 417

ACROSS
1. No ___, ands, or buts
4. Like Montel
8. Flower goddess
13. Set of two
14. Froster
15. More feeble
16. Poetic adverb
17. Deliver up
18. Sheathe
19. Plankton
21. Metal grate
23. Brooch
24. Patron
27. Columbus ship
28. Asian vehicle
31. Rim
33. Eon
34. 1,000,000
36. Addison output
40. Glum
43. Murphy's ___
45. Melody
46. Annoy a bunkmate
47. Green vegetable
49. Noise
50. Dancer's concern
53. Confronts
56. In order to avoid
59. Gave
61. Snake
62. Astonished
63. Borrow
67. Flashing light
69. Is unwell
72. Personal history
73. Flew high
74. Ballet exercise
75. Tall tree
76. Chose
77. Meted out
78. Okey-doke

DOWN
1. Concept
2. Give power to
3. Ditty
4. Arm muscle
5. Master
6. Headed
7. Coffee grounds
8. Guard
9. Varnish
10. Giraffe's kin
11. Amber, e.g.
12. Sports palace
15. Eerie
20. Beseech
22. Beluga dish
25. Electrical unit
26. Talon
27. Bird's home
28. Radiation units
29. Golf-bag item
30. Guitar adjunct
32. Goodness!
35. Lick
37. Lather
38. Mine passage
39. Deep longings
41. Hitherto
42. So far
44. Free slowly
48. Behave
51. Threw hen grenades
52. Not an amateur
54. Halted
55. Unpaired
56. Cowboy's rope
57. Legally bar
58. Jack ___ of rhyme
60. Yawning
62. Asleep
64. Pay heed to
65. Fabric nap
66. Cruise et al.
68. Mine find
70. Class
71. Fib

PUZZLE 418

ACROSS
1. Pipe part
5. Rosary piece
9. Clay brick
14. Roof feature
15. Force along
16. Woodcutter
17. Rotation center
18. Of course!
19. Radio part
20. Purple bloomer
22. Individual
24. Poker opener
26. Rabbit coop
29. Brazilian dance
32. Swindle
33. School dance
35. Ardently fond
36. Speedy car
39. Shad output
40. Regretful one
41. Court
42. Foretell
43. Traveler's stop
44. Wet completely
47. Warning
48. Parent
49. Bard's always
50. Single
52. Taco topping
54. Prom wheels
56. Cream-filled pastry
58. Rigid
63. Throw
66. Bad air
68. Breathing organ
69. Woody ___
70. Maine tree
71. Arrogant
72. ___ shooting
73. Eye woe
74. Wanes

DOWN
1. Emblem
2. City vehicle
3. Sinister
4. Flat hill
5. School vehicle
6. Burst
7. Be in accord
8. Buck
9. Surprise
10. Intimidate
11. "On My ___"
12. Social insect
13. Slip up
21. Hailed vehicle
23. Scram!
25. Slangy no
27. Metal finish
28. Like some sweatshirts
29. Finnish baths
30. Itinerary
31. Scar
32. Gator's kin
34. Hammer end
35. Network
37. Bill collector?
38. Cargo weight
42. Gift ribbon
44. Downfall
45. Earnest
46. Droning sound
51. Touch-me-___
53. Flood wall
54. Boundary
55. Satire
57. Poisonous serpents
59. Choice word
60. Anesthetized
61. Avoid
62. Souffle items
63. Holds
64. Lodge brother
65. Pub drink
67. Golly!

PUZZLE 419

ACROSS
1. Crop
5. In the know
8. Marble
13. Grad
14. Mine yield
15. Wall climber
16. Evil
18. More soaked
19. Brief brawl
20. Greek letter
22. Offs' counterparts
23. Nanny has three
24. Musical notes
27. Capri, e.g.
30. Projectile
31. Seismic wave
35. Unit of land
38. Antelope
40. Street urchin
41. Lunchtime
42. Slander
44. Moo juice
45. Heavy cord
47. Second of a series
48. Current
49. Forbidden by law
51. Epochal
53. Disburse
54. Moisture
55. Ostrich's kin
58. Thus
61. Citrus cooler
63. Portrayals
65. Type style
68. Sandbox pal
71. Comment
72. Electric atom
73. Roman road
74. Artist's garment
75. New England cape
76. Koppel et al.

DOWN
1. Not current
2. Weaver vehicle
3. Litter peewees
4. Radiate
5. Fiery
6. Animosity
7. Criminal
8. Expert
9. Heater
10. Choir member
11. Juvenile
12. Does wrong
15. From Geneva
17. Lounge
21. Positioned
25. Large boats
26. Tripped
28. Haul
29. Molar's coating
30. Hibernated
32. Betwixt
33. Balmy
34. Dark
35. Opposed to
36. Hooded garment
37. Muddy
39. Actress Ruby ___
43. Underdone
46. Id's companion
50. Alas!
52. Crooked
55. Gratify
56. Rationed
57. Customers
58. Knights
59. Short article
60. Like army garb, e.g.
62. Legendary story
64. Drop
66. Resin
67. Provoke
69. Card game
70. Also

PUZZLE 420

ACROSS
1. Birthday years
4. Hot tubs
8. Treaty
12. Those elected
13. Pillar
14. Healing plant
15. Facial hair
17. Vatican leader
18. Biblical boat
19. Straighten up
21. Lounge around
24. Black
26. Teach
28. Flavor
32. Yuletide drink
33. Publish
35. Shout of discovery
36. Wooded
38. Infuriates
40. Obligations
42. Identical
43. Ridicule
46. Third letter
48. Public melee
49. Recounted
54. Comedian Johnson
55. Tinter
56. "___ Got Sixpence"
57. Garden intruder
58. Hems a skirt
59. Cathedral seat

DOWN
1. Focus
2. Large antelope
3. Tee preceder
4. Ship's pole
5. Billiard goals
6. Fireplace dust
7. Office writer
8. Tropical fruit
9. Thanks ___!
10. Manage
11. High schooler
16. Powder mineral
20. Enroll
21. Church season
22. Fragrance
23. Winter Olympics event
25. Attack
27. Assisted
29. Epic tale
30. Those people
31. Relieve
34. Loosen by turning
37. Revised copy
39. Voyaging
41. Curves
43. Sketch
44. Shamrock land
45. Repetition
47. Misjudges
50. Popeye's yes
51. Bit of advice
52. Adam's mate
53. Dawn droplets

PUZZLE 421

ACROSS
1. Popular song
4. Extent
8. Musical symbol
12. Hubbub
13. Tempo
14. Jack rabbit
15. Diary
16. Concerning
17. Mimicked
18. Fire
20. Gambling numbers
22. "Desire Under the ___"
24. Accumulate
28. Locale
31. Italian wine town
33. Rush
34. Repeat showing
36. Prom date
38. Capp's Daisy ___
39. Snout
41. Deli loaves
42. Small silver fish
44. Threshold
46. Big cat
48. Not asleep
52. Killer whale
55. "The King and I" site
57. Marry
58. Rich soil
59. Pierced place
60. Finale
61. Author Ferber
62. Valuable lodes
63. Asian sauce source

DOWN
1. 50 percent
2. Folk hero
3. Roman garment
4. Sales talk
5. Shallow pot
6. ___-the-board
7. Necessity
8. Abyss
9. Pool circuit
10. Before, poetically
11. Gave lunch to
19. Oat ending
21. Podium
23. BLT dressing
25. Nautical hello
26. Royal address
27. Collections
28. Limbs
29. Paper amount
30. Dueling blade
32. Mounted on a peg
35. Against
37. Plane's personnel
40. Elder
43. Andes climber
45. Fun and ___
47. Norwegian port
49. Astounds
50. Lotto's relative
51. Whirlpool
52. Bullfight cheer
53. Closet bar
54. Pantry item
56. Mr. Vigoda

MOVIES & TELEVISION

PUZZLE 422

ACROSS
1. "____ and Loose"
5. A Smurf
9. "For Me and My ____"
12. Cow's comment
15. Actress Sheedy
16. Julia Child's prop
17. Intense fury
18. View starter
19. Admired actor
20. "Blood and ____"
21. TV's "____ World"
23. Actor Mitchum
25. Actor Beatty
27. Actress Balin
28. "Nine Hours to ____"
30. "A ____ in Harlem"
32. "High ____"
36. Objective
39. Actress Richardson
41. Actress Carol ____
42. "On Your ____"
44. "____, Voyager"
45. "Saturday Night ____"
48. Mouse's kin
49. Actress Tatum ____
51. Actor Davis
53. Actor's statement
55. Huey, to Donald Duck
57. Gary Cooper affirmative
59. Films
63. Actor Erickson
65. Break bread
67. Egyptian statesman
68. "____ the Dog"
71. Headliner
73. Actress Ullmann
75. Actress Gilbert
76. Tarzan's friends
78. Theaters
81. 007, e.g.
82. "One ____ Beyond"
83. Cartoon-dragon's friend
84. Actress Markey
86. Hooter
88. Actress Carol ____
90. Shortened, as a film
94. "The Story of Louis ____"
98. "____ at Sea"
100. "____ That Tune"
101. Tin Man's need
102. Actor Erwin
103. Actor Skinner
104. Part of "M*A*S*H"
105. Make a stab at
106. Babe
107. Actress Foch
108. Speaks

DOWN
1. Like Snow White
2. Actor Ray
3. Oscar Madison, e.g.
4. Mary ____ Moore
5. He always rings twice
6. "Evening Shade" role
7. Actor Sean ____
8. TV's Merry ____
9. Actress Scala
10. "L.A. Law" role
11. Actor Ames
12. "Speed" letters
13. Fay dirt
14. Byron's above
22. James Garner film
24. Akira Kurosawa film
26. Actress Arlene ____
29. Director Egoyan
31. Actor Max ____
33. Galley blade
34. Actress Munson
35. Accounting term
36. Bond's school
37. Naught
38. "____ Impact"
40. "Far and ____"
43. Comedian Mort ____
46. Enthusiasm
47. Shroyer's TV comedy
50. Actor Majors et al.
52. So-so grade
54. Gabor and Marie Saint
56. Funny one
58. "____ Rider"
60. Kaminska and Lupino
61. Lawman Wyatt ____
62. Command to Lassie
64. "____ the Nation"
66. "One Day at a ____"
68. Part of "TW3"
69. Bright
70. Command for Mr. Ed
72. Actress Hayworth
74. Ms. Redgrave
77. Speck
79. Rick or Willie
80. Comedian Caesar
83. Disney dog
85. Actress Merrill et al.
87. Actor Adam ____
89. French film comedian
91. King of "The Avengers"
92. Television award
93. "Love and War" actress et al.
94. Cook's item
95. Broadcast
96. Stallone, to friends
97. Furrow
99. Brooch

PUZZLE 423

ACROSS
1. Clog or pump
5. Raised platform
9. Choose
12. Genie's home
13. Made a cat's sound
15. Marked cube
16. Butter alternative
17. Gretzky's sport
18. Lodging place
19. Foul-weather gear
21. Abilities
23. Large lump
25. Aquarium attraction
26. Cotton fabric
28. Ornamental band
31. Grayish brown
32. Distrustful
34. Rowed
36. Touched ground
38. Indian term of respect
40. "The Seven ___ Itch"
41. Certain rays
43. Benefactor
45. Bawl
46. Calm
48. Callers
50. Settled up
51. Metal fastener
52. Chocolate dessert
55. "Rain Man" star
59. TV commercials
60. Musical interval
64. Gangster's girl
65. Tip of Italy
66. Approached
67. Athenian vowels
68. Make a boo-boo
69. Let it stand
70. "A ___ With Judy"

DOWN
1. Feed swill to
2. Saint's headwear
3. Forewarning
4. Geologic divisions
5. Batman and Robin, e.g.
6. Curved line
7. Exasperate
8. Sniffing bloodhound, e.g.
9. Lyrical
10. Cartoon-panther color
11. Decade numbers
13. Impostors
14. Powerhouse
20. Ship's bottom
22. Soothe
24. Massaged
25. Proverbs
26. Stubborn animals
27. Combine
29. Build
30. Drops of sadness
31. Dollop
33. 17th Greek letter
35. Not moist
37. Canvas covers
39. Rebounded
42. Add spice to
44. Type of admiral
47. Sibling's daughters
49. Foamed
52. Chess term
53. Stench
54. Purchaser
56. Pinch
57. Piece of wood
58. Differently
61. Do knot work
62. "Bells ___ Ringing"
63. Dobbin's doc

PUZZLE 424 — Rapid Reader

Twelve 5-letter words appear backward in these lines of letters. Can you find them all in four minutes or less? Underline each word as you find it, as we have done with the first word, ABIDE.

```
F L I T A E H W P A E D I B A M O O H S
A B O V E Y M I R G T R O K C A N S I G
N F O O L A W T A I D E M R E H C E R B
Y Z E C I L E R N E U Q W O R E Z I A M
E N T L U A V O W R E T U O T R E P I S
H T O N W A L R A N U N A G R O I R P O
```

DOUBLE TROUBLE

PUZZLE 425

Not really double trouble, but double fun! Solve this puzzle as you would a regular crossword, except place one, two, or three letters in each box. The number of letters in each answer is shown in parentheses after its clue.

ACROSS
1. Plait (5)
3. Seize (3)
5. Scamp (6)
8. Bargain (6)
9. Lurch (6)
11. Fall to pieces (7)
12. Boxers do it (4)
13. Be concerned (4)
14. Opportune (6)
16. Subject (5)
18. Go up (6)
19. Endure (4)
21. Quiet (7)
23. Blush (6)
24. Send payment (5)
26. Patio (7)
28. Roost (5)
29. Winding (7)
30. Future frog (7)
32. Butterfly trap (3)
33. Struggle (6)
35. Sheer (5)
37. Established (6)
38. Inaccurate (5)
39. Scratch (4)
41. Parody (5)
43. Swindle (5)
45. Like some submarines (6)
46. Authority (6)
47. Oracle (4)
48. Weight allowance (4)

DOWN
1. Boastful person (8)
2. Still (4)
3. Mother-of-pearl (5)
4. Uncovered (4)
5. With reckless haste (6)
6. Begone, cat! (4)
7. Kind of ego (5)
8. Door clasp (4)
10. Lure (6)
13. Sahara transport (5)
15. Repair (4)
17. Pause (8)
18. Determine (9)
19. Fire truck item (6)
20. Foul smell (6)
22. Go inside (5)
23. Full (7)
24. Pine product (5)
25. 17th-century dance (6)
27. Passed with a high grade (4)
31. Sheriff's gang (5)
33. Hot box (5)
34. Ponderosa, e.g. (5)
36. Paragon (7)
37. Benefit (6)
38. Move unsteadily (6)
40. Fashionable (4)
41. Rotated (4)
42. Pea envelope (3)
44. Soothe (4)
45. Perfume oil (5)

Letterdrop

PUZZLE 426

Discover the saying concealed in these lines. Drop one letter in each pair and decide where words begin and end.

WT HR EI CO NB AL EY MN DA NI QW HS OE WI AR NS

NP ET SE PV OD ZI OL TA BL EY AB ER FI NR EG LE

TI OH NU SI KZ YE DA WM JA OS UD CA LN TI AE RL

PUZZLE 427

BRICK BY BRICK

Rearrange this stack of bricks to form a crossword puzzle. The clues will help you fit the bricks into their correct places. Row 1 has been filled in for you. Use the bricks to fill in the remaining spaces.

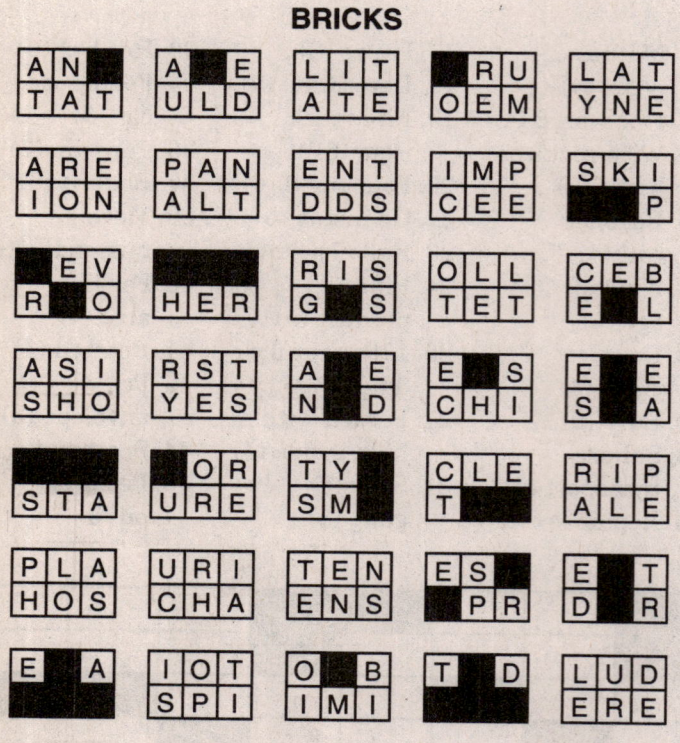

ACROSS

1. Stop
   Crazed
   Chapel nook
2. Japan's continent
   Evade
   Voyage
3. Took upon
   Chest noise
4. Decimal base
   Crude copper
   Outer ear
5. Guarantee
   Chew the fat
6. Ascend
   Pigpen
   Little rascal
7. Unaccompanied
   Division
   So-so grade
8. Glass pieces
   Aglow
   Occasion
9. Plane's ht.
   Babbler
   Gambling numbers
10. Slide downhill
    Monotonous routine
    Child's toy
11. Sonnet, e.g.
    Leash
12. Fake medication
    Prohibit
    "Chances ___"
13. Fire-truck item
    Restriction
14. Scintilla
    Tickle pink
    Formerly, formerly
15. Washer cycle
    Force units
    Favorable votes

DOWN

1. Quickness
   Mineral baths
   Frat letters
2. Pale
   Converse
   Circuit
3. Detroit team
   Appetizer courses
4. Sigma's follower
   Hankering
   Watery expanse
5. Petty of "Tank Girl"
   Buying frenzy
6. Set right
   Made a deep sound
7. Helm position
   Splendor
   Greasy
8. Prickly seedcase
   Popular song "The Invisible ___"
9. Inkling
   Located
   Nibble
10. Subtracts
    Gyrates
11. Reason's partner
    Actress Olin
12. Courtyards
    Electricity term
    Afternoon social
13. Rehearsed
    Shaggy
14. Threshold
    Fix
    Notched
15. Swordplay weapon
    Caresses
    Hires

PUZZLE 428

ACROSS
1. Battle of honor
5. Drummer Krupa
9. Grinding tooth
14. Gumbo essential
15. Immediately, of yore
16. Very stout
17. Brew, as coffee
19. Eats
20. Road bend
21. Medic
22. Whiskey blend
24. Do knot work
25. Remnants
27. "___ & Blood"
29. Copper coin
30. Sigma's follower
33. Country's Campbell
34. Throw off
36. Signs of drowsiness
38. Polynesian feast
39. ___ boom
41. Neural network
42. Force
44. Applied-science pro
45. Soldier's chow hall
46. Play the ponies
47. Heroic poetry
49. Piano-key wood
51. Relinquish
53. Accelerate in neutral
56. Personal quirk
57. Ed on "The Honeymooners"
58. Sols preceders
61. Legal excuse
63. Underling
66. Birchbark craft
67. ___ on (love excessively)
68. Meat stew
69. Door handles
70. Goggler
71. Earthen pot

DOWN
1. Dummy
2. Hawaiian instruments
3. Missteps
4. Varnish ingredient
5. Boots
6. Vote into law
7. Forget-me-___
8. Peppy
9. Humbleness
10. Kimono closer
11. Period before Easter
12. Voyaging
13. Musical symbol
18. Bards' verses
23. Money, in Osaka
25. Concert site
26. Coldness
27. Chute
28. Jumped
30. 'Twixt partner
31. Fidgety
32. Purposes
33. Fluent
35. President's procession
37. Tank feature
40. More jovial
43. Southpaws
48. Maui menu item
50. Cave dwellers
52. Garbage
53. Luggage holder
54. Verve
55. Chianti, to Luigi
58. Tumble
59. Indigo dye
60. Plato's porch
62. Mr. Hope
64. Nutritious bean
65. Also

Crossout Quote — PUZZLE 429

Cross out one letter in each box so that the remaining letters spell out a quotation reading across from left to right.

A/I	N/C	C/T	E/I	M/T	P/T	E/T		L/C	H/U	A/S	L/K
W/L	A/E	N/S	T/G	U/E	S/M			S/P	Y/O		T/C
R/H	A/U	T/N		Y/V	I/O	U/W		C/M	O/A		Y/C
	F/B	A/E	E/U	L/G		T/S	W/H	O/E		C/E	
X	A/H	L/L	I/E	L/T	A/R	E/A	N/D	T/E	I/O	R/N	T/Y
	O/I	S/F		V/J	A/I	C/M	I/P	T/O	A/R	R/L	Y/L

371

PUZZLE 430 — CODEWORD

Codeword is a special crossword puzzle in which conventional clues are omitted. Instead, answer words in the diagram are represented by numbers. Each number represents a different letter of the alphabet, and all of the letters of the alphabet are used. When you are sure of a letter, put it in the code key chart and cross it off in the alphabet box. A group of letters has been inserted to start you off.

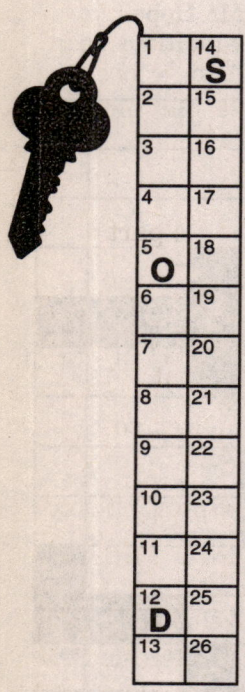

1	14 S
2	15
3	16
4	17
5 O	18
6	19
7	20
8	21
9	22
10	23
11	24
12 D	25
13	26

A	N
B	Ø
C	P
Ø	Q
E	R
F	Ø
G	T
H	U
I	V
J	W
K	X
L	Y
M	Z

LOVE CODEWORDS? *Enjoy hours of fun with our special collections of Selected Codewords! See page 159 for details.*

PUZZLE 431 — Piece by Piece

We have eliminated the spaces between the words in a message and divided all the letters into 3-letter pieces. Rearrange the pieces to reconstruct the message. The dashes indicate the number of letters in each word.

```
ARE  ETO  HEN  ISB  ITS  LAT
PAN  REW  SPA  THE  TOO  TRY
```

_ _ _ ' _ _ _ _ _ _ _ _ _ _ _ _ _ _ _ _ _ _ _

_ _ _ _ _ _ _ _ _ _ .

PUZZLE 432

ACROSS
1. "All That ___"
5. Well done!
10. Ms. Gardner
13. Section
14. Broadcasting
16. Dandy
17. Road Runner's remark
18. Furniture style
19. Drain opener
20. Manuscript mark
22. Authorize
23. Rower's blade
24. Newspaper features
27. Onager
28. Hero sandwich
30. Type of card
32. Furrow
35. Gourmet mushroom
36. Straightforward
37. Duel tool
38. Upset
39. Salamanders
43. Runt
45. Scorch
46. Feign
48. Gambling place
49. Former French coin
50. Go by plane
51. "___ Work"
52. Pitcher spout
53. Shade of color
56. Take a load off
58. Baseball arbiter
59. Captivate
61. Muslim leader
65. Ess follower
66. Plunging
67. Not stereo
68. Bungle things
69. ___ bear
70. Transmit

DOWN
1. Poke
2. Have being
3. Zorro's mark
4. Jolts suddenly
5. Most plain
6. Public disorders
7. Circle part
8. Cello's kin
9. Earlier
10. Buoyant
11. Journey
12. Monkey business?
15. Medieval
21. Follow
24. Zenith
25. Fall sharply
26. Baked
29. Some films
31. Intensify
32. ___ up (evaluated)
33. Sycamore, e.g.
34. Rosy
36. Sunup
38. Charge
40. Aluminum sheet
41. Sharp projection
42. Work hard
44. Engraved
45. Howls
46. Beginner's book
47. Coolio, e.g.
48. Ministry
49. Champagne glass
50. Fern leaf
54. Single part
55. Icicle locale
57. Clock
60. Central
62. Harriet, to Ricky
63. Tropical cuckoo
64. Clever remark

PUZZLE 433

ACROSS
1. Pond growth
5. Cartoon frame
8. Tent settlement
12. Gives off
17. Wasteland
18. Alfalfa
19. Bakery worker
20. Cowboy show
21. Buy
23. Moon's pull
24. Garnish
25. Swine's dwelling
26. United
27. Hard worker
29. Shade sources
30. Bear with
32. Motorless plane
34. Gush forth
37. Heroic
38. Quickest
42. Trying time
44. "___ Exposure"
48. Dent
49. Hawaiian necklace
50. Mouth edges
52. Before, to a poet
53. Glow with light
55. Unlock, in a sonnet
56. Astronomer's item
59. Press
60. Earth's center
61. Slippery critter
62. Cycle
65. Shark type
68. Free
71. Moth-eaten
74. Not fitting
76. Bad child
77. Capri or Skye
78. Kind of neckline
79. Congeal
80. Forefather, e.g.
84. Invisible
86. More sugary
88. Agts.
90. Very black
91. Most unusual
94. Magazine bigwig
96. Cut
99. Library stamps
101. Goof
102. Couple
105. Circle parts
107. Not stereo
108. Snatching
110. Spy
111. Formerly, formerly
112. Work onstage
113. Wickedness
114. Affirmatives
115. Cereal grains
116. Hive builder
117. Golden ___ Bridge

DOWN
1. Current measures
2. Oaf
3. Like a horror film
4. Curvature
5. Fancy light
6. Relax
7. Caustic stuff
8. Detroit, e.g.
9. Serving perfectly
10. Award pin
11. Basis
12. Historical epoch
13. "___ Romance"
14. Crowe, to some
15. Period of time
16. Inheritors
22. Deary
27. Art ___
28. Hound's trail
30. Sheep's ma
31. Wash lightly
33. Geologic ages
34. "Star Wars" pilot
35. Get ready
36. Adams or Falco
39. Asian official
40. Chirped
41. Playhouse locale
43. Choir voice
45. Voucher
46. Fish
47. In the know
51. Defendant's excuse
54. Cast
57. Cloth joints
58. Flows away
60. Dirty Harry, e.g.
63. Draw pictures for
64. Zealous
65. Russian jets

PUZZLE 433

66. Once again
67. Leafy veggie
69. Compete
70. Publicized
71. Yan's prop
72. Onion's cousin
73. Disclaim
75. Londoner's so long
81. Geek
82. Part of a tea set
83. Metallic rocks
85. Knight's designation
87. White weasel
89. Stab
92. Level of a building
93. Apprehensive
95. Eye
96. Waiter's need
97. Craze
98. Caesar's time
100. Spoils
102. Sills, e.g.
103. Military division
104. Look amorously
106. ___ in the bag!
108. Chat
109. Grovel

PUZZLE 434

ACROSS
1. ___ shot
5. Lament for Yorick
9. Sticky stuff
13. Geometric shape
14. Merit
16. Hairstyle
17. Small insects
18. Colorado ski spot
19. Regretful one
20. Encounter
22. Chilled dessert
24. Diamond girl
25. Golden ___
27. Tied
30. Advantageous
34. Hawaiian necklace
35. Thickness
37. Imitated
39. In addition
41. Fink
42. Bunch
43. VHS predecessor
44. Fruit drink
46. Born as
47. Mended socks
49. Created again
52. Enrages
54. Sound of a blow
55. Harness part
59. Likely
64. Loony tunes
65. Melodies
67. Chess piece
68. Public
69. Javelin
70. Plunge
71. Flower plots
72. Legal paper
73. Arctic transport

DOWN
1. Ripoff
2. By oneself
3. Poker-game starter
4. Mortar's mate
5. Helped
6. At the end
7. Greek vowel
8. "Curly ___"
9. Pundit
10. Major work
11. Keats wrote them
12. Read closely
15. Tangle
21. Triumph
23. Metallic rock
26. Rain-water channel
27. Caught congers
28. View
29. Ridicule
31. Marvy!
32. Turn on its head
33. Flood foiler
34. Testing area
36. Hippie home
38. Tint
40. Rower's paddle
44. Breakfast fare
45. Rested
48. Not a one
50. Noisy crowd
51. Medals
53. Book part
55. Soft lump
56. Lasso
57. Kind of tea
58. Knotts and Ameche
60. Competition
61. Cook in water
62. Passionate affection
63. Added to
66. Totally awesome!

PUZZLE 435

ACROSS
1. Disconcert
6. Weighty units
10. Tumult
14. Groovy
15. Be next to
16. Voiced
17. Barbecue site
18. Type of cotton
19. Neutral hue
20. Greek letter
22. Bikini top
24. Dearie
25. Mischievous being
28. Huey or Shelley
30. Baseball interval
32. Abundant
34. Library practice
36. Soon
37. Overlook
38. Snake
40. Dripped
41. Steal
45. Elaborate
47. Elvis, e.g.
48. Wood eater
50. Lodging places
52. Mounted gun
53. Small drink
55. Pub serving
56. Free (of)
57. Race (a motor)
59. Gaze at
60. Disembarked
62. "The ___ Piper"
64. Inferior
69. Taboo
70. Scoop
71. Develop
72. Consequently
73. Anglers' items
74. Adolescents

DOWN
1. Viper
2. Python's relative
3. Appear onstage
4. Enjoy a winter sport
5. To-do
6. Easy putt
7. Japanese belt
8. Insensible
9. Gazing intently
10. Adversary
11. Sea ___
12. Loose garment
13. Thrown
21. Portable trough
23. Peruvian peaks
25. Mosque official
26. Chatty bird
27. Formal dance
29. Crowed
31. Simpleton
33. Innate
35. Coastal bird
37. Campus gp.
39. Knight's protection
42. Intention
43. Sampling
44. Additional
46. Bowling club
48. Clothes maker
49. Wrapping up
50. Dried grass
51. Brunch dish
52. Wading bird
54. Remodelings
58. Ivy, e.g.
61. Overly
63. Immature newt
65. United
66. Advantage
67. Bask
68. Sure!

PUZZLE 436

ACROSS
1. Might
6. Belfry denizens
10. Shortcoming
14. Onto
15. Common metal
16. Portent
17. Pave again
18. Green fruit
19. Horseback game
20. Tag incorrectly
23. ___ room
24. Toy on a string
27. Hurting
28. Deluge refuge
29. Act like
30. Gun a motor
32. Not monthly
34. Elegant
36. Gained victory
38. Moistureless
39. Nonsupporters
41. Court
43. Aerie homes
47. "___ City"
49. Butt into
51. Royal title
52. Stable sounds
55. Douglas pine
57. Not many
58. Male or female
59. Carney et al.
61. Make orderly
63. Cool, formerly
64. Enraged
66. Suspicion
68. Locality
69. Feel
73. House wings
74. MTV watcher
75. Follow directly
76. Student's item
77. Drenches
78. Color changers

DOWN
1. Distant
2. Be beholden to
3. Squeal
4. Muscle ache
5. More creepy
6. Paper money
7. Opera melodies
8. Rowdy girl
9. Smirked
10. Cut
11. Without standards
12. Veggie stick
13. Rap
21. Cook slowly
22. Determine
24. Daddy
25. Fairy-tale word
26. Annoyance
31. Promise
33. Whiskeys
35. 45 player
37. Negative connector
40. Tales
42. Bumpkin
44. Comb through
45. Magnolia, e.g.
46. Stitched
48. Hazards
50. Maxi's cousin
52. Badger
53. Kicks out
54. Not mono
56. Let
58. Drew back
60. Brew tea
62. Torment
65. Mr. Christian Andersen
67. Consult
70. Function
71. Mutt
72. "___ So Shy"

PUZZLE 437

ACROSS
1. Penny
5. Spike of maize
8. Wingspread
12. Met piece
13. Pilot's realm
15. Choice word
16. Shopping plaza
17. Howdy!
18. Knight club
19. Ms. Meriwether
21. Checked the books
23. Lingers
26. Shaft
27. Print measures
28. Asta's foot
29. Tube
32. Agenda
34. Logger's tool
35. Thy, now
36. Ruckus
37. Skirt type
39. Steak choice
41. Drums
45. Iced brew
47. Yard event
49. Beer's kin
50. Draft
52. Unbarred, to a bard
53. Prosecute
54. Dunk
55. Chilly
58. Courted
60. Military vessel
62. Sports facility
63. Descended
64. Immature insect
67. Skillful
71. Settlement
72. Wilier
73. Eager desire
74. Chick's sound
75. Male or female
76. Souffle items

DOWN
1. Gear
2. Age of note
3. Not a one
4. Reckoning
5. Gain with effort
6. Suffer
7. Take a break
8. Big rig
9. Dishes
10. Climb
11. Lacks
13. "___-Devil"
14. Inner being
20. Detect
22. Hero store
23. Junk e-mail
24. Hired vehicle
25. Inspired
26. Spray can
30. A little bit
31. Tavern
33. Pen liquid
36. Take out
38. ___ a girl!
40. Doze off
42. Not west
43. Sticky stuff
44. Type of catalog
46. Engrave
48. Crosscurrent
50. Net tender
51. To swell, as music
54. Bog
56. Desqueaks
57. Milky gems
59. Stun
61. Footfall
62. Slender fish
65. Catcher's site?
66. Irritate
68. Entreat
69. Dillydally
70. Some railways, for short

PUZZLE 438

FLOWER POWER

Instructions for solving Flower Power are given on page 94.

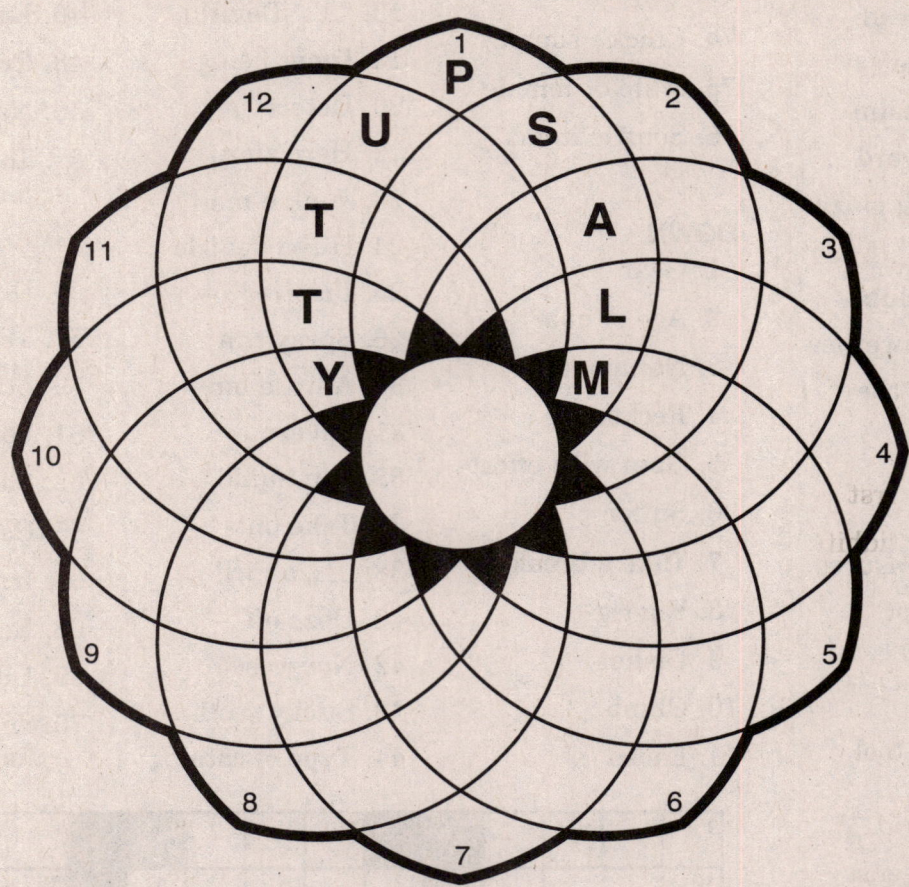

CLOCKWISE

1. Sunday song
2. Hint at
3. Separate
4. Lofty abode
5. Recites
6. Monet's need
7. Jiffy
8. Posh
9. Spoils
10. Pastry
11. Water lily
12. Hard to please

COUNTERCLOCKWISE

1. Glazing compound
2. Edition
3. Gather
4. Slather on
5. Empire
6. Juicy fruit
7. Characteristic
8. Prissy type
9. Joy
10. Feel
11. At liberty
12. Onward

FLOWER POWER FANS! *Fun is always in full bloom with every volume of Selected Flower Power. To order, see page 159.*

PUZZLE 439

ACROSS

1. Draperies
6. 100 percent
9. Make the grade
13. Alfresco meal
15. Four-in-hand
16. Female voice
17. Stampede
18. Of bad quality
20. Kicking stands
21. Bits of land
23. Mete out
24. Fix copy
25. Season's first
27. Feed-bag tidbit
30. Irritate
31. Men
32. Location
34. Taunt
36. Peppy
40. Shopping bag
41. Musical sense
42. Toward shelter
43. Circus animal
44. Mob
45. Laughing critter
46. Meat cut
48. Maui garland
50. Clio winners
51. Classify
54. Mets or Giants
55. Tennis-match call
56. Bear witness
58. Bridge term
62. Campers
64. Tempt
66. Anxious
67. Spoil
68. Closer
69. Magenta and cerise
70. Pig's pad
71. Craft

DOWN

1. Blemish
2. Zinfandel, e.g.
3. Farmland measure
4. African antelopes
5. Brother's sib
6. Leaning
7. Type of dance
8. Excluded
9. Bogey beater
10. Foreigner
11. Tend the fire
12. More painful
14. Scold
19. Notice
22. Sweet ___
24. Arden or Brenner
26. Student work
27. Decides
28. Hand-cream herb
29. Toodle-oo
31. Corsets
33. Violin's kin
35. Battle
37. Guilty, e.g.
38. Split
39. Affirmatives
44. Batters
45. That man
47. Verbal exam
49. Swallowed
51. Ritual platform
52. Wait on
53. Sedate
54. Grouchy
57. Step quickly
58. Play lead
59. Former Italian money
60. Excelled on
61. French mother
63. Egos' kin
65. Clear

PUZZLE 440

ACROSS
1. Skillful
6. Parlor piece
10. Finish off
13. Street shows
15. Stop
16. "___ Got Sixpence"
17. From that place
18. Spur
19. Garfield, e.g.
20. Abrade
22. Linger
23. Wise trio
26. Shortage
29. Leisurely
30. Rejoice
32. Gumbo
33. Kettle et al.
34. Discuss
35. Wharf rodent
37. Manhattan, for one
39. Tidal wave
41. Cravings
45. Pearly gem
46. Part of ENT
47. Green parrot
48. Roof goo
50. Insult
52. Not a child
54. Carry on
55. "Gandhi" garb
56. Chest noise
57. "___ Noon"
58. Wash
61. Off one's feed
62. Kind of bean
65. Female kin
69. Named formerly
70. Kitchen cooker
71. Release
72. Correlatives
73. Neck section
74. Less than four

DOWN
1. Paintings, e.g.
2. Morse-code word
3. Previous, in verse
4. Lead writer
5. Science pro
6. Hinge ailment
7. ___ Father
8. Pear-shaped fruit
9. Had a meal
10. Noisy insect
11. Profits
12. Picayune
14. Ocean
21. Small fleet
22. Windshield item
23. Pork, e.g.
24. Rotation center
25. Pundit
27. Standards
28. Baked buckwheat
31. Golf hazard
36. Accumulate
38. Old Italian bread?
40. Compass point
42. Ocean bird
43. Blab
44. Glut
48. Shadower
49. Intersections
51. Sophisticated
53. Wet completely
54. Horned mammal
59. Frat letter
60. Forage for game
62. Scion
63. Eggs
64. Slangy assent
66. Craggy peak
67. Deep anger
68. Increase

PUZZLE 441

ACROSS
1. Somersaults
6. Hunter and others
10. Bursts
14. Dashboard dial
15. Met melody
16. Graduate, briefly
17. Edit text
18. Cheeky
19. Former Italian money
20. Wood for ships
21. Mutton or veal
22. Make merry
23. Wintry
25. Begone!
27. Wriggler
28. Harshness
32. Amusing
34. "___ Girl Friday"
35. Seaman's shout
37. Weak
41. Premieres
43. Puppy's bite
45. Deport
46. Expire
48. Ale measure
50. ___ or never
51. Med subject
52. Some mints
54. Burro
57. Cheese
60. Mayberry woman
61. Threaten
63. Totals up
65. Not very busy
69. Sailing
70. Gerard's friend
71. Rock
72. Shack
73. Have a hunch
74. Birch tree
75. Popular songs
76. Authentic
77. Adult goslings

DOWN
1. Fuss
2. Like a bad excuse
3. Scheme
4. Little finger
5. Lay lawn
6. Adhesive
7. Territories
8. Beginning
9. Positioned
10. Lackluster
11. Green hue
12. Fruit pulp
13. Tiny
21. Invented story
22. Vegas wheel
24. Categorize
26. Not working
28. Split
29. Ready to eat
30. Operator
31. Hither's companion
33. Reject
36. Pup's cry
38. Certain skirt
39. Hog's food
40. Evergreens
42. Pen part
44. Photo
47. Tilling implement
49. Seizes
53. Snuggle
54. Embarrass
55. Fish meal
56. Freezing rain
58. Circus employee
59. Ta ta
62. Young fellows
64. Printer's term
66. Rich vein
67. Single bills
68. Lived
70. Fore-and-___
71. Wilt

PUZZLE 442

ACROSS
1. Price
5. Promise
10. Part of a pack
13. Battle song?
14. Curly, e.g.
15. Jewel
16. Cultivate
17. Mounted gun
18. Frozen cubes
19. Mahout's charge
21. Demon
23. Plus
24. Brandish
25. Yard tree
28. Try
30. Sign
31. Fido's rein
33. Red horse
35. Caesar's date
39. Narrative
40. Deck out
41. Near
42. Grand
43. "___ It Romantic?"
44. Church game
45. Tricked
47. Fodder storage
49. Needle feature
50. Crooked
53. Wheel tooth
54. Small chicken
56. Made like a teakettle
61. Posit ending
62. Territory
64. Sweep leaves
65. Door opener
66. Takes the fifth?
67. Kiln
68. Slow start
69. Logic
70. Family men

DOWN
1. Bistro
2. Uttered
3. Father
4. Pat down
5. Criteria
6. Refuses to
7. Eternity
8. Absorbed
9. Fame
10. Nimble
11. Pal of Beany
12. Change text
14. Meager
20. Brunch dish
22. Tiny two-piece
25. If not
26. Faith measure?
27. Wise trio
29. Windfalls
30. Tourist's stop
32. Scented bag
34. Jerusalem ___
36. Sup
37. Like an omelet
38. Wingtip, e.g.
40. Benefit
44. Marshes
46. Oscars, e.g.
48. Cuts of meat
50. Tolerate
51. Goalies' goals
52. Leg joints
55. Just
56. Achieves
57. Tramped
58. Rock on the roll?
59. Enlarged
60. Rumpus rooms
63. Martini base

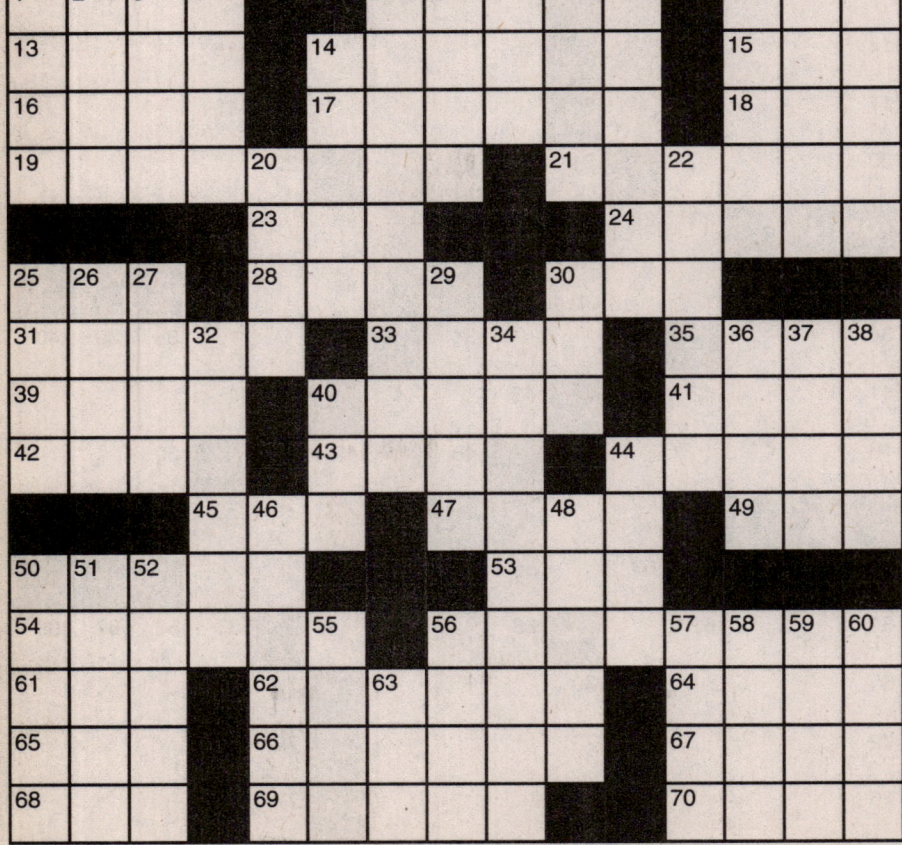

PUZZLE 443

ACROSS
1. Mineral springs
5. Needle's cousin
8. Already retired
12. Apiece
13. Overwhelm
15. Identical
16. Former Italian money
17. Stove
18. Infant's bed
19. Revive
21. Bed linens
23. List unit
25. Ink writer
26. Parodied
29. Forsake
33. Boneless cut
35. Spring flower
36. Menagerie
38. Outback birds
39. "M*A*S*H" clerk
41. Any moment
42. Dripping
43. Tall story
44. Smells
46. Lobby workers
48. Wallet bills
49. Not nope
50. Conceited
53. Gentlewoman
56. Perfume
61. Came down
62. National symbol
65. Challenger
66. Part to play
67. Cafe patron
68. Cake decorator
69. Verse contraction
70. Appropriate
71. Not as much

DOWN
1. ___-service
2. Couple
3. Farm measure
4. "___ Got a Way"
5. Level surface
6. Charged atom
7. Christmas drink
8. Rise
9. Nude
10. Radiate
11. Society entrants
13. Be distressed
14. Loses hope
20. Pelt
22. Egg producers
24. Young misses
26. Directed
27. Disney dog
28. Subways' kin
30. Lingerie buy
31. Atmosphere gas
32. Cozy corners
33. Not many
34. Crushed
37. Offs' opposites
40. Pub order
41. Moral wrong
43. Willow, e.g.
45. Clothes
47. Pearl bivalve
51. Riot
52. Consumer
53. Mend socks
54. Plant gel
55. 5,280 feet
57. Sermon topic
58. Friendly
59. OK grades
60. Goes astray
63. Help out
64. African antelope

PUZZLE 444

ACROSS
1. Coasted
5. Map volume
10. Powder
14. Child's steed
15. Relaxed
16. Matinee hero
17. Opponent
18. Dad
19. Say cheese
20. Sign gas
21. Uncertainties
23. Game caller
24. Clothes
28. Most hip
30. Mr. Hanks
33. Fertile soil
35. Bard's work
36. Unclose, in poems
37. In a foreign country
39. Peak
43. Mothers
45. Not offs
46. In trouble
47. Bungle
48. Theme song
50. Burro
51. Moray
53. Tiller
54. Golf peg
55. Frankfurters
59. Pig's dinner
61. Expert
62. Meshwork
63. Sharp
67. Doe's beau
69. Hooray!
73. Tempo
74. Pedro's dough
75. Rustic
76. Again
77. Let it stand
78. Change
79. Without

DOWN
1. Wingspread
2. Sole
3. Toward
4. Fading, as embers
5. French peak
6. Furthermore
7. Sever
8. Savory jelly
9. Shrimp, e.g.
10. Nib
11. Love a lot
12. Forfeits
13. Chin hollow
22. Turf unit
25. Sad word
26. Steal from
27. Nobleman
29. Table insert
30. Crypt
31. Pearly gem
32. Note
34. August, e.g.
38. Cigar remnants
40. Layer
41. Ponder
42. Besides
44. Astonished
46. Bullets, briefly
48. Math branch
49. Pipe shape
52. Geologic age
55. Fasteners
56. Group of eight
57. Taunt
58. Play a lute
60. From the Vatican
64. Staff
65. Sorbets
66. Dawn drops
68. Obtained
70. Common verb
71. Moving vehicle
72. Vintage

PUZZLE 445

ACROSS
1. Range
6. Mix
10. Mantle
14. Drying cloth
15. Area ___
16. Farm animals
17. Phony name
18. Reign
19. Tidings
20. Shipping weight
21. Asta's limb
23. Pledged to marry
26. Breaths
30. Food fish
31. Jam
34. Spigot
35. Repeating sound
37. Tough
38. Yes, cap'n
39. Talk to God
40. Delicate
41. Steep
42. Wagon track
43. Acts
44. Ox's harness
45. Decide
46. Voyage segments
47. Candle material
48. Fashion
50. Imitator
54. Search
58. Foamy drink
59. Small bug
62. Reside
63. Racing rowboat
65. Bothers
66. Bucks
67. Manet's stand
68. Adept
69. Jaunty
70. Songbirds

DOWN
1. Ohio or Iowa
2. Punctuation mark
3. Unpaid
4. Green veggie
5. Chicago trains
6. Fish
7. Trip
8. Immobile
9. Rod's partner
10. Cuban dance
11. Hatchet
12. Chapel seat
13. Type spaces
21. Supplied food
22. Like an omelet
24. Sore
25. Infant's sound
27. Bleak
28. Check endorser
29. Spit out
31. Gabs
32. Oahu garlands
33. Night animal
35. Blow up
36. Spiteful
37. Rocky cliff
39. Masters
40. Dues
41. Squat
43. Use a muscle
44. Babble
47. Grief
49. Slightest
50. Top
51. Bring about
52. Director Woody ___
53. Reveals
55. Make a splash
56. Boundary
57. Done
59. Rage
60. Invention
61. Sprite
63. Attach buttons
64. Auto

PUZZLE 446

ACROSS
1. Sen., e.g.
4. Tad
7. Barge
11. Uncover
15. Freudian word
16. Bristles
18. Father
19. Test
20. Rainbow shape
21. Baby hooter
22. Opponent
23. Agents, briefly
24. Ms. Helmsley
26. Heavens
27. Fall bloom
29. Blend
30. "Wyatt ___"
33. Sight
37. De-crease?
39. It bit Cleo
42. Average grade
43. Warden
44. Disintegrate
47. Trouser joint
48. Luau necklace
49. Called strikes?
50. Soared
53. Crooked
54. Sprites
56. Toon frame
58. Cocked
61. Bench
62. Remains
64. Rows
67. Did data entry
69. Label
70. Snarl
72. Swat
75. Concluded
77. Horned mammal
80. Connect
81. Join
84. Engaging
87. Sound system
88. Bass, e.g.
89. Ruby or Kiki
90. Applications
91. Wigwam's kin
92. Greek cheese
94. Donkey
95. Barbecue
98. Slangy turndown
101. Trapshooting
104. Not VHS
107. Advance
109. Distinctive time
111. Lobster eggs
112. Restraint
113. Glory
114. Exhausted
115. Motel
116. Plus
117. Ajar, in verse
118. Dehydrated
119. Sharp curve

DOWN
1. Toll
2. Shrek or Fiona
3. Train puller
4. Gab
5. Lubricants
6. Voyage
7. Fancy resort
8. Hors d'oeuvre
9. Decides
10. Linger
11. Juicy fruits
12. Tree feller
13. Tap
14. Double ens
16. Sham
17. Eye woe
25. Baseball team
28. Level
31. Perform
32. Rock ridge
34. Erupt
35. Binge
36. Military
37. Loiter
38. Spools
39. Mission
40. Food for dipping
41. Go before
43. New Zealand bird
45. Corroded
46. Cooling drinks
51. Chuckled
52. Nice summer
55. Snack
57. Illuminated
59. Trademarks
60. Seafarer
62. Race in neutral
63. Flit

PUZZLE 446

65. Spit
66. Babe, e.g.
68. Water sport
71. Limbs
72. Relish
73. Pot bet
74. Get ready
76. Aggravate
78. Great wrath
79. Once called
82. Pizza herb
83. Impolite look
85. Seine
86. Walrus tooth
88. Burning
93. Afresh
94. Pale
96. Data
97. Bound
99. Copied
100. Frost
102. Ages
103. Decades
104. Swimsuit top
105. Wriggler
106. Poetic contraction
108. Embarrassed
110. Weep

PUZZLE 447

ACROSS
1. Smack
5. Waves
9. Resort
12. Fables
13. Begin to bud
15. Large weight
16. Cooker
17. Movie house
18. Floor cover
19. Legume
20. Fragments
21. Undivided
23. Musical symbol
25. Contributor
26. Electing
30. Longed for
31. Tax inspection
32. Story starter
34. Promgoer
35. Provide with new guns
36. Epic tale
40. Choir member
41. Publicized
42. Fastener
46. Raced
48. Take it easy
49. Other than
50. Incidents
52. Italian peaks
54. Hit hard
57. Each
58. Ceremony
60. Well
61. Biblical zoo
62. Bureau
63. Rents
64. Sure!
65. Loathe
66. Applies

DOWN
1. Spill liquid
2. Made cloth
3. Part of a phone number
4. Finger count
5. Sputter
6. Footed vases
7. Lobster eggs
8. Seethe
9. Compete
10. Rained hard
11. Infuriate
13. Book type
14. Latin dance
20. Most favorable
22. Topple
24. Cut of meat
26. Felix, e.g.
27. Tint
28. Mr. Coward
29. Small flies
30. Skirt part
33. Field yield
35. Uncooked
36. Does wrong
37. Major roads
38. Exclamation
39. Do sums
41. Feels ill
42. Harsh
43. Salespeople
44. Managed
45. Surplus
47. Answer
48. Settle a debt
51. Moan
52. Uncle's wife
53. Shoestring
55. Poker opener
56. Army chow
59. Pekoe, e.g.
60. Winter woe

PUZZLE 448

ACROSS
1. Secure
5. Pigeon's home
9. Popular pops
14. Massive
15. Confines
16. Worship
17. Metals
18. Fastens
19. The press
20. Value
22. Available
24. Slender fish
25. Comrade
27. Cranny
29. Turf
32. Movie center
33. Lass
34. Dug
36. Fourposter
37. Yen
41. Oak offspring
42. Watch kids
43. Beam
44. Cradle rocker
45. Lou's pal
46. Calm down
47. Snub
49. Feel bad
50. Snaky sea food
51. Cracker type
54. Mire
55. And not
56. Wet sound
58. High-riser?
63. Helps a hood
65. Sore
67. Pilot or mobile start
68. Of sound
69. Stop!
70. Ship's gang
71. Cycle
72. Average
73. Turns left

DOWN
1. Display
2. Wallaroo
3. Ripener
4. In case
5. Jazz fan
6. Bird at bat
7. Minute
8. Bridge seat
9. Inhabi-tent?
10. Poem type
11. Resort
12. Opera solos
13. Scorches
21. Port
23. Waterless
26. Dominated
28. Scale
29. Junk e-mail
30. Pod member
31. Condemn
33. Acquire
35. Brazen
36. Offer
38. Ocean cycle
39. Holmes's tidbit
40. Cad
42. Tan
43. Sullen
45. Collide
46. Attack!
48. Pester
49. Novelist
51. Flying pests
52. Android
53. Bout site
54. Manly
57. Outside chair
59. Per
60. Nimbus
61. Irish ___
62. Pulls
64. Kiddie game
66. Sweet spud

PUZZLE 449

KID STUFF

ACROSS
1. Mop
5. Timetable abbr.
8. Health havens
12. Gooey stuff
16. Corporate symbol
17. ___ de Janeiro
18. Pawn
19. Speak wildly
20. Popular cookie
21. Probability
23. "The ___ Love"
24. Cake cooker
25. Evening entertainment
28. Academy ___
29. "Rhoda" mom
30. Flock mama
31. Big rig
33. Make merry
36. Tall tale
38. Matisse, e.g.
42. Woodsman's tool
43. Peculiar
45. Secures
47. Clinton's VP
48. Roast holder
50. Weekly wage
52. ___ and cons
53. Sincerity
55. Hurries
56. Belt locale
57. Monopoly props.
58. Entices
60. Miss Piggy's "me"
61. Extremely small
64. Pop quiz
65. Hand-thrown bomb
69. Jai ___
70. Elder escort
73. Insult
74. Meadow baby
75. Debtors' notes
76. Coin-toss option
78. Island garland
79. Shoelace holes
81. Grime
82. Outdated
84. Fencing foil
85. ___ Francisco
86. Rowboat item
87. Nina's sister ship
90. Parental pull-tabs
96. Winter fall
97. '70s hairstyle
99. Great ___ Lake
100. Recital piece
101. ___ time
102. Dealer's car
103. "The Raven" poet
104. "___ After"
105. Lower digits
106. Office table
107. Spring mo.
108. Rational

DOWN
1. Untidy person
2. Eroded
3. Mellowed
4. Baby shoe
5. Fragrance
6. Carousel, e.g.
7. Staffs
8. Coastline
9. ___ express
10. Winning serve
11. ___ lodge
12. Adolescent aches
13. Volcano output
14. Aloft
15. Await judgment
22. Audio system
26. Immobile
27. Hold title to
28. Pierre's pal
31. Tech. schematics
32. Relieve
33. Hotheaded
34. Annual show
35. Mineral deposit
36. Every twelve mos.
37. Feel poorly
39. Singer Amos
40. Love deity
41. Remainder
44. Corrodes
45. Rigid
46. Motels
49. Toddler term
51. Scribble
54. Theater abbr.
56. Sorrow
58. Sweetheart
59. Poisonous snakes
60. TV horse

PUZZLE 449

61. Fellow
62. "Now ___ me down ..."
63. Attended
64. The items there
65. Biting bug
66. "___ Fair"
67. Club payments
68. Canal of song
70. Mention
71. Horned animals, briefly
72. Above, in poems
77. Sail pole
80. Clean-air org.
81. The Beastmaster
83. Emerges
85. Scare
86. Marine mammal
87. Jr.'s exam
88. ___ thin air
89. No part
90. Munitions
91. California valley
92. Spatter
93. PBS science show
94. Small valley
95. Angered
97. Append
98. Service cost

393

PUZZLE 450

ACROSS
1. Quiz choice
6. Distant sun
10. Pile
14. Hilo hi
15. Remedy
16. Till, in verse
17. Coastal indents
18. Aid and ___
19. Poker choice
20. Football gadget
21. Decrease
23. Mouth wipers
25. Biscuit
27. Cause
28. Hornet
30. Time and again
32. "Dallas" name
36. Man or Wight
37. Hallow
39. Heavy twine
41. Peruse
42. Snaky swimmer
43. Muslim official
44. Sharpen
45. Noel
47. Dracula's wrap
48. Brief
50. Kind of trip
51. Again
52. Dry
54. Swiss sight
56. Leaked
60. Ox's kin
61. Lick up
64. Tease
65. Staffer
67. Old
69. Tankard fillers
70. Pork cut
71. Trace
72. Beef or lamb
73. Don't strike
74. Family auto

DOWN
1. Reality
2. Healing herb
3. Smooching spot
4. "___-Devil"
5. Art stand
6. Scratch covering
7. Bath place
8. Contest site
9. Recaptures
10. Perfume base
11. Opponent
12. Daze
13. Puts in grass
22. Lump
24. Flock's perch
26. Can gadget
27. Piloted
28. Dream
29. Wide scarf
31. Pet's peeve
33. Polar cover
34. Unclaimed area
35. Complain
38. Toil
40. Doodled
45. Breakfast foods
46. Mortgage
49. Plant juice
53. Dimwit
55. Desires
56. Liquid measure
57. Upset
58. Mental flash
59. Bother
60. Bloke
62. Pond growth
63. Hammer end
66. Spotted cube
68. Lace

PUZZLE 451

ACROSS
1. Make warm
5. Fitness club
8. Come again?
12. Data
13. Brag
15. Heavy cord
16. Fortune
17. Stand up
18. Minister's word
19. Drink cubes
20. Animal horn
21. Robin's roost
22. Belt
24. Air pollution
26. Rods
30. Church table
34. Iranian ruler, once
37. None
38. Constant
39. Government levy
40. Breeze
42. Ball peg
43. Warnings
46. Deep anger
47. Talk back
48. Western show
49. Graze
51. Only fair
53. Stern
57. Exchange
60. Filthy place
64. Have bills
65. Idol
66. Solitary
67. Among
68. Baking box
69. TV repeat
70. Warbled
71. The Grateful ___
72. Society miss
73. Leg joint

DOWN
1. Stereos
2. Pass laws
3. Following
4. Foot feature
5. Put in order
6. Water carrier
7. Rate
8. Argue
9. Baseball base
10. Tarzan's pals
11. Camper's abode
13. Embargo
14. Period
20. Fitting
23. Hearth residue
25. Kind of bran
27. Ifs, ___, or buts
28. Douglas pine
29. Style
31. Toodle-oo!
32. Summer quenchers
33. Certain breads
34. Sky twinkler
35. Angelic crown
36. Cut down
38. Simmer
41. To's associate
44. Answer
45. Additionally
47. Neptune's realm
49. Simmered
50. Bashful
52. Ship's pole
54. ___ numeral
55. Hogs
56. Shrub fence
57. Wearing boots
58. "___ Only Just Begun"
59. Region
61. Mr. Vidal
62. Rebuff
63. "___ Little Indians"
67. Beg

PUZZLE 452

ACROSS
1. Preserve
5. Dealer's car
9. Turn
13. Rotation center
14. Spring bird
15. Went by horse
16. Optical glass
17. Stroll
18. Always
19. Crafty
20. Hurry
21. Sirloin, e.g.
22. Dozing
24. Ding
26. Touch
28. Least powerful
33. 50 percent
36. Excavated
38. Glass panel
39. Unsociable
41. Hair tamer
43. Belief
44. Traveled
46. Periodical, shortly
48. Third letters
49. Populated
51. Stickum
53. Golf gadgets
55. Seed
59. Borders on
63. "___ Club"
65. Bagel topper
66. Manage
67. Liquefy
68. Animal skin
69. Press
70. Make right
71. Done
72. TV spots
73. Circus item
74. Fur

DOWN
1. Mexican sauce
2. Skating jumps
3. Plastic
4. Snaky letter
5. Capitol roof
6. Waned
7. Fungus mold
8. Single
9. Worry
10. Affection
11. Notion
12. Bonus
14. Chatted
20. View
21. Sedate
23. Try
25. Recent
27. Haul
29. Bumps
30. Border
31. A few
32. "___ the night..."
33. Bonnets
34. Healing plant
35. Oaf
37. Jewel
40. Soft fabrics
42. Loiter
45. Poor grade
47. Poured
50. Air out
52. Revenue
54. Warning sound
56. Vibrant
57. Pose
58. Put forth
59. Sour
60. Drill
61. Aware of
62. Perfect scores
64. Polite chap
67. ___ peeve
68. Jump

PUZZLE 453

ACROSS
1. Sharp blow
4. Desert spring
9. Sub shops
14. Be mistaken
15. Assemble
16. Live
17. Luau gift
18. Oarsman
19. Complete
20. Pie spuds
22. Skirt choice
23. Freshly
24. Intend
26. Lab tube
29. Drive away
31. Sparkling
35. Straighten
36. Previously
37. Support
39. Fellows
40. Guffaw
42. Busy insect
43. Dowel
44. Grain boxes
45. Strong rope
47. Balconies
50. Boric ___
51. Hound's prey
52. Coin a coin
54. Skillfully
57. Twirl
59. Large mop
63. Tragedy
65. Slants
67. Fury
68. Roof edges
69. Soap ___
70. Draw even
71. Stow away
72. Plant again
73. ___ Solo

DOWN
1. Bank (on)
2. Zone
3. Proper
4. Above, to a poet
5. Bakery feature
6. Needlework
7. Like some tea
8. Trying hard
9. Lawn moisture
10. Breathe outward
11. Big cat
12. Florida Key, e.g.
13. Mulligan ___
21. Haze
25. Long time
27. Craving
28. Took food
29. Icy forecast
30. Door hardware
32. Scoundrel
33. Synagogue figure
34. Road sign
35. Hi-fi item
38. Poor grade
40. Impostor
41. Forefather
44. Bikini piece
45. Food tin
46. Behaves
48. Verses
49. Beams
53. Preface
54. Picnic drinks
55. Terrible tyke
56. Hot stuff
58. Duct
60. Including
61. Formal solo
62. Has-___
64. Cinder
66. Noticed

PUZZLE 454

ACROSS
1. Pane stuff
6. Office sub
10. "___ So Shy"
13. Illuminate
14. Scuba ___
15. "On My ___"
16. Abrasive
17. Agreement
18. Luau necklace
19. Scents organ
20. Angular cut
21. Finest
22. Flirt with
24. Roman garb
26. Detective story
31. Unhook
35. ___-hop
36. Gin's partner
38. Midafternoon
39. Adds to
41. Rub clean
43. Soft drink
44. Aired again
46. "___, Dolly!"
48. Disfigure
49. Deletes
51. Normal quality
53. Large mop
55. A Stooge
56. Frolic
59. Barter
62. Flower jar
66. Propel a boat
67. Cello's kin
68. Coffee flavor
69. Poetic work
70. Signed
71. Additional
72. G-man
73. Affirmatives
74. Feats

DOWN
1. Secluded valley
2. Luxury auto
3. Grows up
4. Clever
5. Dirty place
6. Dye
7. Dispossess
8. System
9. Move with leverage
10. Doughnut feature
11. Flock mamas
12. Bad mood
14. Musical twosome
20. Forbidden items
21. Tub soakings
23. Ump's call
25. Fetch
26. At what place?
27. Backpacker
28. "Don Giovanni," e.g.
29. Part of a foot
30. Loses energy
32. Odor
33. Fragrant tree
34. Got word
37. Faction
40. Bold
42. Accuse
45. Recent
47. Yoko ___
50. Silky
52. Dedicate
54. Penniless
56. Univ. figure
57. Metal deposit
58. Inspired
60. Bitter brews
61. Papa
63. Throb
64. Tool hut
65. Sound organs
67. By way of
68. In fashion

PUZZLE 455

ACROSS

1. Scram!
5. Mangy mutt
8. Identical
12. Lira, now
13. Dummies
15. Fine
16. Help a criminal
17. Build
18. Attendant
19. Skirt type
20. Bask
21. Moneymaker
23. Read hastily
24. Dated
26. Antelope
28. Egg creations
33. Street name
36. Fielding muff
39. Departure
40. Thaw
42. Say further
43. Burning
44. Used up
45. Perfect
47. Get it?
48. Infinite
51. Carry
53. Swerved
56. Selects
60. Huey, to Donald
64. Single
65. Earth
66. Yard unit
67. Join
69. Locale
70. Smile
71. House units
72. Ocean oasis
73. Totals
74. Arid
75. Glimpse

DOWN

1. Clothing joints
2. Of volume
3. Stadium
4. Carrying
5. Reef stuff
6. Turn on its head
7. City athletic dept.
8. Float aloft
9. Alike
10. Assembled
11. Witness
13. Bypass
14. Type of heat
22. Consumed
25. Throng
27. Born
29. Hawaiian wreath
30. 24th letters
31. Car's "shoe"
32. Peeper woe
33. Brink
34. Mr. Spinks
35. Brains
37. Grow
38. Weird
41. Animation frame
43. Virus
46. Birches' kin
49. First female
50. One who stitches
52. Idle talk
54. Whirlybird blade
55. Foe
57. Dignity
58. Caption
59. Chic
60. Moans
61. Off-white
62. Proper
63. Coop birds
68. Show approval

PUZZLE 456

ACROSS
1. Fall fruit
6. Snakes
10. Skin woe
14. Kind of eel
15. Squadron
16. Clothed
17. Determine
18. Burger order
19. Dangle
20. Big rig
21. Posse
22. Certain street
24. Slick
26. Narrative
28. Outcome
31. Discuss again
35. Canine command
36. Tone
39. Of two parts
41. Upper crust
43. Card-game cry
44. Peevish
45. Secure
46. Sample anew
48. Female pronoun
49. Closing
52. Ascend
54. Sheep fat
56. Poor mark
57. Munchies
61. Copy
63. Medal color
67. Pillar
68. Backpack
70. Debate
71. Surrounded by
72. Level
73. Ms. Burke
74. Dole (out)
75. Split
76. Guide

DOWN
1. Bands' needs
2. Ponder
3. School formal
4. Posh
5. Gaze at
6. Sedan, e.g.
7. Snoots
8. Swine
9. Pawn
10. Hurt
11. Animal's nail
12. Granny
13. Fidgety
21. Invented story
23. Nope
25. Waste
27. Don't exist
28. Employs
29. Rice dish
30. Kind of book
32. Summer drink
33. Fish meal
34. Abhors
37. Consent
38. Dotted cube
40. Harp's kin
42. Decimal base
44. Class
47. Impolite
50. Invite
51. More luxurious
53. Rue
55. Confiscated
57. Junk e-mail
58. Alaskan city
59. Settled
60. Give up
62. Await judgment
64. Leer
65. Guitar's kin
66. Precious
69. "___ Gotta Be Me"
70. Promos

CODEWORD 2
PUZZLE 457

Codeword is a special crossword puzzle in which conventional clues are omitted. Instead, answer words in the diagram are represented by numbers. Each number represents a different letter of the alphabet, and all of the letters of the alphabet are used. When you are sure of a letter, put it in the code key chart and cross it off in the Alphabet Box below the grid. A group of letters has been inserted to start you off.

1	2	3	4	5	6	7	8	9	10	11	12 M	13
14	15 A	16	17	18	19	20 N	21	22	23	24	25	26

23	15	1	1	24		16	17	20	18		25	11	6	13
15	22	15	11	3		17	13	17	3		11	6	25	3
12	3	23	6	7	15	7	6	17	20		15	18	3	23
		19	6	18			23	11	15	12				
1	26	19	19		17	9	7	16	3	11		7	17	17
3	14	3			15	11	3		3	4	26	6	21
23	3	3	9		15	18	15		13	15	26	13	16	3
		7	15	11	15	20	7	26	16	15				
11	3	8	17	16	7		9	3	7		24	26	11	7
15	18	15	21	3		1	6	2			12	17	22
12	17	7		21	11	3	7	7	24		26	21	23	17
		22	10	6	12			15	16	16				
5	17	14	3		9	15	16	15	12 M	15 A	20 N	23	3	11
6	23	3	15		3	16	15	20		9	15	26	7	3
13	3	15	14		20	3	22	7		7	11	3	15	7

Alphabet Box

A̷ B C D E F G H I J K L M̷ N O P Q R S T U V W X Y Z

PUZZLE 458

ACROSS
1. Muslim leader
5. German physicist
8. Chronicle
12. Traveler's domicile
17. Carpentry joint
18. Stamping device
19. Granny
20. Previously, previously
21. Vain
23. Random try
24. Publicity ___
25. Kimono closer
26. Roadway hazards
28. Ginger cookies
30. Legal term
31. Paint finish
33. Switch settings
35. Of a historic age
36. Remark further
38. Roster
40. Former professors
45. More meager
49. Negate
51. Lollapalooza
52. Affected manners
53. Three x five
55. Clash
57. Unusual
59. Wrapped package
61. Stale
62. Bronzed skin
64. Angora fabric
66. Omelet ingredient
69. Brewing vessel
71. Teaser
75. Raised
77. Adage
79. Carbonated beverage
80. Legend
81. Fighting fish
82. Jet departure
84. Fireplace hook
87. Foyer
89. Wander
90. Seaweed extract
92. Kitty forfeit
93. Feudal peasants
97. Talk
100. Snoozed
102. Hindu prince
105. Cunning
106. End of a series
108. Crocus's kin
110. Italian bread
112. Fact
113. Main church part
114. Language suffix
115. Hit repeatedly
116. Dishonor
117. Chew
118. Caught ___-handed
119. Unoccupied

DOWN
1. Common phrase
2. Tree snake
3. Confess
4. Bovine bellow
5. Emotional poems
6. Sound of disapproval
7. Rock star?
8. Printer's measures
9. Squares of butter
10. Foolish
11. Minnelli film
12. Bothersome dispute
13. Many times, in verse
14. Guided trip
15. White-tailed flier
16. Reply to "Shall we?"
22. Exploits
27. Express derision
29. Shriver of tennis
32. Ankle bones
34. Exorbitant
37. Described
39. Nautical position
41. Rubbish
42. Division preposition
43. Snitch
44. Infuriated
45. Chump
46. As easy as ___
47. Circle section
48. Gaucho's lasso
50. Remove clothing
54. Thick shake
55. Comfy chair
56. Came down
58. Troubadour's strings
60. Graph
63. Compass point
65. Withdraw
66. Hitherto
67. Paraphernalia
68. Nuts
70. Sum
72. Kanga's baby
73. Pixie
74. "A Yank in the ___"
76. Lamb's dad
78. Bravery
81. Burning brightly
83. Baked buckwheat
85. "___ Bovary"
86. Braggart's problem
88. Moccasinlike footwear
91. Operated anew
94. Vied in a marathon
95. Ruffle
96. Frame of mind
97. Olympians
98. Indian maid
99. Phi ___ Kappa
101. Prima donna
103. Major-leaguer Canseco
104. Mastered
107. Bubble-blowing candy
109. Baste
111. Economist's abbr.

PUZZLE 459

ACROSS
1. Twitches
5. Remit
8. Gambles
12. Audition aim
13. Festive occasions
15. Type of sword
16. Molecule component
17. Kitchen emanation
18. Official decree
19. Illusionist
21. Loose overgarments
23. Prickly critter
25. Acid salt
28. Sopping
29. Rock's Steely ___
32. Cold and damp
33. Mexican moola
34. "___ on a Grecian Urn"
35. Ask for money
36. Canine coat
37. Sonata movement
39. "___ Got Sixpence"
40. Lean against
42. Sieve
43. ___ your request
44. Ruby or emerald
45. Finished
46. Made esteemed
48. Climax
51. "Concentration," e.g.
56. Rain heavily
57. Slice
59. Exploding star
60. Bruised
61. Work with dough
62. Humdinger
63. Formerly, formerly
64. Although
65. Meander

DOWN
1. Coal wagon
2. Minute amount
3. Drain obstruction
4. 18-wheeler
5. Easter march
6. "Take Me ___"
7. Certain tuberous root
8. Confuse
9. Grand-scale tale
10. Shipbuilder's lumber
11. Sinks below the horizon
13. Jollity
14. Cummerbunds
20. New Year's Eve bubbly
22. Auto procession
24. Large jug
25. ___ branch (peace token)
26. Subsequently
27. Ostrichlike animal
29. Person who receives gifts
30. Remarked further
31. Colorful sign gas
32. China flaw
33. Situate
36. Smoke
38. Surgery rms.
41. Adorn
42. Appeared
45. Neckwear
46. Plumed bird
47. Come to terms
48. Basilica section
49. Destitute
50. Belongs to us
52. Winter crystals
53. Fine-tune
54. Pizzeria appliance
55. Hospital division
58. "___ Wednesday"

Give and Take — PUZZLE 460

Change the 4-letter words on the left to the 5-letter words on the right by giving and taking letters. Add one letter to the word on the left to form a 5-letter word. Then subtract one letter from that word to form a new 4-letter word. Next add a letter to form a new 5-letter word; subtract a letter to form a new 4-letter word. Finally, add a letter to form the word given on the right. The order of the letters may be rearranged in forming new words.

Example: VEST, STOVE, TOES, THOSE, SHOT, SHORT

1. BRED _____ _____ _____ _____ REGAL
2. FAST _____ _____ _____ _____ TABLE
3. CHAR _____ _____ _____ _____ SMEAR
4. OVER _____ _____ _____ _____ ADDER
5. STEW _____ _____ _____ _____ SEPAL
6. SURE _____ _____ _____ _____ COURT

PUZZLE 461

ACROSS
1. Plant pest
6. Hindu ascetic
10. Bawdy
14. Circle portion
17. Audacious
18. Achieve
19. Petri-dish gel
20. Pine tree
21. Deride
22. Fox's dance?
23. Reproduction
24. Certain poem
25. Public vehicle
27. Coffee container
29. Put out
31. Timely
35. Nothing
38. "The Sun ____ Rises"
39. Linen fiber
40. Come ashore
42. Burdensome
44. Target
45. Anticipate
47. Soothed
51. Salespeople
53. Western lilies
54. Stops
56. Cassowary's kin
57. Marsh bird
59. Bounder
61. Facilitate
62. Three-bagger
65. Immediately
66. Notifies
68. Singer Stewart
69. Late
72. Help in wrongdoing
73. School wing
74. Pacific goose
75. Acts as usher
77. Choir section
81. Typed (in)
83. Receives
85. California fort
86. Save from danger
88. Look like
90. Poker variety
91. Train sound
94. Vouch
96. Sponsorships
98. Vended again
100. Healthy place
101. Freight measure
102. How ____ you?
103. Duane or Nelson
106. Gumbo must
109. Knot again
113. Craggy hill
114. Away from a storm
115. Harness
116. Water pitchers
117. Printer's concerns
118. Astute
119. Peek at
120. Force units

DOWN
1. Donkey
2. Baking vessel
3. Color shade
4. Vintage refrigerator
5. Waffle topping
6. So far
7. Long paddle
8. Hamburger meat
9. Beginning part
10. Natural resin
11. Conscious being
12. Elk
13. Prohibitionists
14. In trouble
15. Carnival features
16. Motto
26. Pliny's sun
28. Cashews, e.g.
30. Epic
31. From a distance
32. Ballet bend
33. Freeway entrance
34. Money vaults
36. Say hello
37. Laughing ____
41. Seasonal quaff
43. Snuggle
46. Embrace, as a cause
48. Brand
49. Discharge
50. Failures
52. Sample
53. Strainer
55. Brownish gray fabrics
58. Fair-haired
60. Type of lottery
62. Excursion
63. Actress's part
64. Leisurely
67. Athens vowel
70. Decree
71. Edit a film again
72. Lost
76. Gobbled
78. House sites
79. False's opposite
80. Chances
82. Thus
84. Average grades
87. Equestrian's need
89. Converged
90. Muscular
91. Jalopy
92. Great blue bird
93. Customers
95. Seed's kin
97. Pierced
99. Seep
104. Wallace of film
105. Itch
107. Split
108. A few
110. Bowling number
111. Bitter resentment
112. Racetrack curve

DOUBLE TROUBLE

PUZZLE 462

Not really double trouble, but double fun! Solve this puzzle as you would a regular crossword, except place one, two, or three letters in each box. The number of letters in each answer is shown in parentheses after its clue.

ACROSS

1. Conceited (4)
3. Quiet! (3)
5. Miner's stake (5)
7. Hostility (5)
10. Butterfly larva (11)
12. Small piece (7)
13. Remote (7)
14. Choir member (5)
15. Short ___ (quick work) (6)
17. Wedding member (5)
19. Twice five (3)
21. Colleagues (5)
23. Foolishness (8)
26. Unfortunate (10)
29. Trellis (7)
31. Block up (3)
32. Summer hue (3)
33. Antler covering (6)
36. Convert (6)
38. Nurture (7)
41. Purl, e.g. (6)
43. Ergo (9)
46. Engines (6)
48. Fireplace (6)
50. Apex (4)
51. Froth (5)
53. Big cheese (6)
55. Cross (9)
58. Repeat, lazily (7)
60. Fishing boot (5)
63. Surplus (5)
64. Submit (6)
66. French painter (5)
68. Formal name (5)
71. "The Jungle Book" bear (5)
73. Paper fastener (7)
75. Incisive (9)
77. Crave (5)
78. Poke fun at (5)
79. Tailor (5)
80. Zero (3)
3. Gambling decoy (5)
4. Severe (5)
5. Thunder noise (4)
6. Motivation (7)
7. Firewood support (7)
8. Exploit (4)
9. Speak wildly (4)
11. Omen (7)
12. Brandy glass (7)
16. Fully grown (4)
18. From this point on (10)
20. Capture (3)
22. Blind part (4)
24. Broadcast (4)
25. Cloth joint (4)
26. Door fastener (5)
27. Crueler (6)
28. Rank (5)
30. Fatigue (4)
34. Suit item (4)
35. Church donation (5)
37. Nothing but (4)
39. Doctrine (3)
40. Short-tempered (9)
42. Singe (4)
44. Concentrate (5)
45. Esteem (7)
47. Comic Bean (5)
49. Narrow (4)
51. Cowboy's prod (4)
52. Converge (4)
54. Hearty food (4)
56. Printed words (4)
57. Unstable (7)
59. Ring-tailed mammal (7)
61. Puff ___ (5)
62. Work measure (3)
65. Holdings (6)
67. Celestial (6)
69. Holier-___-thou (4)
70. Soup bean (6)
71. Large cove (3)
72. "Maude" producer (4)
74. Gladden (6)
76. Register (5)

DOWN

1. Move out of (6)
2. Student doctor (6)

LOOKING FOR DOUBLE TROUBLE? You've found it! Treat yourself to special collections of your favorite puzzles—over 50 in each! To order, see page 159.

405

PUZZLE 464
• RULE THE ROOST •

ACROSS
1. Silent type
5. Crows
9. Clip
13. Karate blow
17. Dalai ___
18. Disregard
19. Sherry or port
20. Verdi work
21. Greater than
22. Fable
23. Rembrandt, e.g.
25. Strict supervisor
28. Detroit eleven
29. Sinks down
30. Stock index, shortly
32. Mr. Carney
33. Olive center
36. Block up
39. Onion relative
41. British comic Hill
43. Obi, e.g.
44. Put into effect
46. Bulb planter
48. Pointed implements
49. Throw from a saddle
51. Required
53. Subdues
54. Pigeon coop
55. Purchase ___
57. Contest locale
59. Tiger's-___
60. Summit
61. Rugby play
63. Ex-Beatle Sutcliffe
66. European river
68. Photos
69. Sitting above
70. Capital of Jordan
72. Former's mate
75. Safe places
77. County festivities
78. A, B, and D, e.g.
80. Shirt size
81. Father's sister
82. Not tart
84. Russian parliament
86. Fast plane
87. Free (of)
88. Actress Claire
89. Dead or Red
91. Ms. Jaffe
93. Ridicule
95. Some secret agents
100. Commanding
104. Bridle strap
105. Sign of the future
106. Off-Broadway award
107. Ms. Lanchester
108. Otherwise
109. Skirt length
110. Inclination
111. Caraway or poppy
112. Zoomed
113. Sty fare

DOWN
1. Thicken
2. Volcanic flow
3. Iowa college site
4. Twain and Harmon
5. Advanced years
6. Accumulated
7. Wither
8. Spirited horse
9. Duet number
10. Rivulet
11. Sioux or Apache
12. Remembrance
13. Actress Peggy ___
14. Great success
15. Shelley poem
16. Golf goal
24. Fire or carpenter
26. Mediterranean landmass
27. Thief
31. Join by heat
33. Wage distributors
34. Cay
35. That's opposite
36. Tennis term
37. Pester
38. Plan skillfully
40. Types
42. Born
43. Mr. Laurel
45. Third letter
47. Sugar root
48. Originate
50. Shredded
52. Thrown missile
56. Folk dance
58. Hurry up
60. Deceives
61. Outbuilding
62. Removed the center of
64. Forceps
65. Agitated
67. Melissa Joan ___
68. Declares
69. Ms. Gardner
70. Distantly
71. Hawaiian landmass
73. ___ of Aquarius
74. Very, in Versailles
76. Ladd and Thicke
79. Guess
82. Sleep sounds
83. Equivocate
85. Whimpered
88. Cube or chest
90. After, to Jacques
92. Potent particles
93. Let it stand
94. Circuit breaker
96. Bark
97. Mr. Jannings
98. Western resort
99. Small piece
100. Unruly bunch
101. Vigoda of "Fish"
102. Wickedness
103. Lass's friend

407

PUZZLE 465 — DILEMMA

Except for 1 Across, there are two clues for each number and two identical sides in the diagram. Your Dilemma is to discover which answer goes on the right side and which answer goes on the left. Note: The heavy lines indicate the ends of words as black squares do in regular crosswords.

ACROSS

1. Baffling
9. Papal name / It climbs
10. Cellulose fabric / Bay window
11. Bill repository / Round projection
12. Sicily sight / Outdoor bed
13. Make a splash / Strokes
15. Him and her / Nudnik
16. Result / Sub finder
18. Poker decision / Negative link
20. Needle / Good hole card
22. Kin of a violin / Earth
24. Meager / Pacific
25. Frustrate / Anguish
26. Pads / Cools down
27. Ribald / Springiness
28. On edge / Sleep soundly?
31. Nuptial word / Be sociable
33. Water sport / Iterate
35. Moderate / Optimistic
37. Indeed / Have debts
38. Pluck / Of the moon
40. Extra / Stud fee?
42. Speaker's place / Durango dish
43. Windy mo. / Deuce
45. Resurgent / Me too!
47. Ames's locale / Curved molding
48. Close / Apportion
49. Dressed / Excite again

DOWN

1. Smack / Type
2. Island bird / Iniquity
3. Hosiery material / Diving birds
4. The sun / Ball
5. AAA handout / Dander
6. Nips / Marking post
7. Origin / Writer Deighton et al.
8. Happily / Crown
13. Let / Sacred songs
14. Draws (in) / Puppets
15. BMOC? / Pager noise
17. Vast amount / Brother's girl
19. Mediterranean fruits / Call forth
21. Take some courses? / Busy buzzer
23. Traipse / Reclined
27. Revolved / Refute
29. Introverted / Bullring shout
30. Part / Hue
32. Copied / Ugly thing
33. Charm / Lyrical
34. Fire / Night stalker
36. Garland / Spoke in public
39. Intense / Essential
41. Tough trip / Disseminates
44. Court / Allow to ripen
45. Agnus ___ / Heel
46. Traveler's stop / Kiwi's cousin

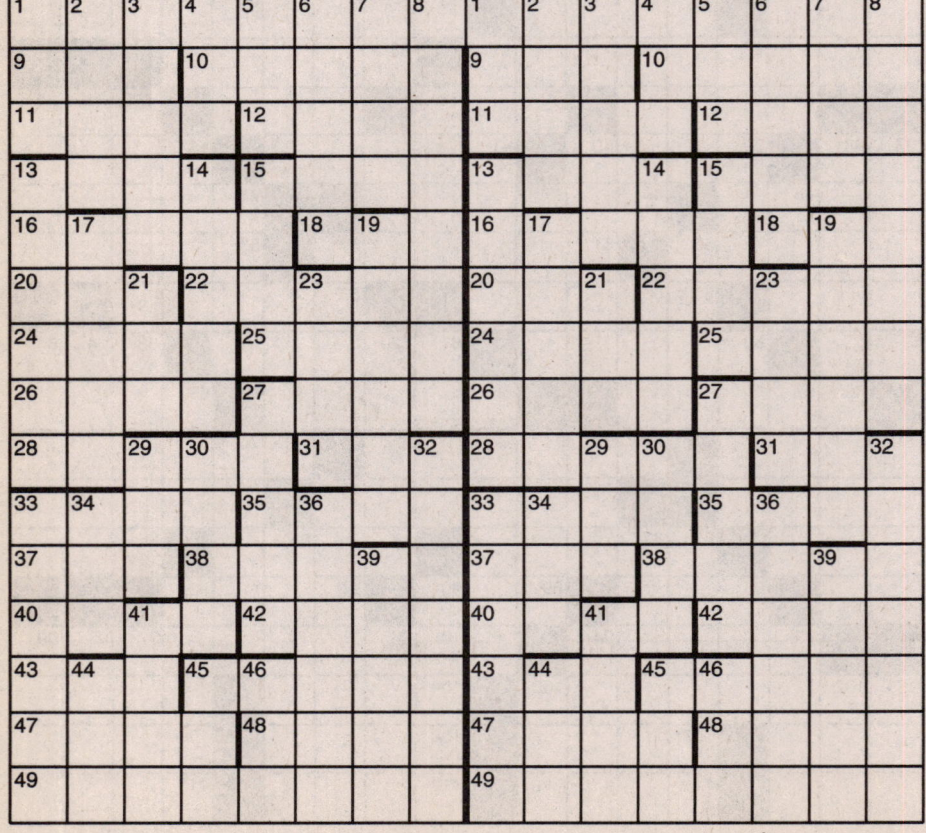

408

PUZZLE 466

• BODY LANGUAGE •

ACROSS
1. Protest event
6. Romanov title
10. Bumpkin
14. Cartoon Viking
19. Siouan language
20. Jazzy James
21. Knoll
22. Courtyards
23. Colorful
24. Mild reproofs
25. Salinger girl
26. Tolerate
27. Idyllic spot
28. Egg warmer
29. River horse
32. Play the wrong card
34. Council site
36. Water conduit
37. Like
39. ____ Antiqua
40. Subtle
41. Youth gp.
44. Certainty
48. Bullpen stats
50. Of 60-minute periods
52. Plenty, of yore
53. Trucker
55. Ocean fare
57. Moreno and Hayworth
59. True
60. Certain row house
62. Fur pieces
64. Nothing, to Juan
66. Rakes
67. Body of eau
68. Sabbatical
71. Au contraire!
72. Apply ointment to, formerly
74. Common couple
77. Blackthorn
78. Faucet trouble
80. Numb
84. Illinois city
87. Alcove
90. Play
91. Liqueur flavoring
92. First
95. Shipshape
96. Removed the center of
97. El ____
98. Unspecified place
100. Due's follower
101. Drat!
103. Minute
105. Singer Adams
106. Country home
108. Bamboo eater
110. Sex
114. Making lawful
118. Ship side
120. Broad
121. Gladden
122. Taken by mouth
123. Golden St. school
125. Boy of the street
126. Nautical direction
127. Diamond number
128. Is situated
129. Build
130. Convinces
131. Erstwhile Algerian governors
132. Basin
133. Staff pauses

DOWN
1. Transporter
2. Organic compound
3. Poe's bird
4. Insuperable barrier
5. Bamboozled
6. French pate
7. Risky feat
8. ABA member
9. Bacon serving
10. Inched
11. Speech problem
12. Fluid diffusion
13. Intensify
14. Dispatch
15. Perfume oil
16. Light weight
17. Japanese aborigine
18. X-ray dosages
28. Author Ben ____
30. Map within a map
31. Be obliged to
33. Reaction locale
35. Dealer in old cloth
38. Yesterday, in Nancy
40. Alda costar
41. Sweeper
42. Rhone feeder
43. Marsh tree
44. Sun. homilies
45. Module
46. Printing process, briefly
47. Highland negative
49. Returning, part of a payment
50. Hounded
51. O'er and o'er
54. Defames
55. Adult cygnet
56. Signed off
58. Becomes irate
61. Wood sorrel
63. Unguent
65. June bug
69. Emptiness
70. Sniggler's prey
73. Clay pottery
74. Ratify
75. Estate dwelling
76. Church topper
79. Polished
81. Be bold
82. Islamic leader
83. Handle
85. Compass dir.
86. Advance
88. Yoko ____
89. Glacial leftover
93. Dubuque native
94. Sill
97. Grassland
99. Golf's Michelle ____
101. MCII/II
102. Amaretto base
104. Swallow
106. Crucial
107. Objects
108. Stacks
109. Steve or Fred
111. Thin coins
112. Dictum
113. Gets a flat?
114. Meadows
115. Czech river
116. Scot
117. Wacky
119. Bridge hand
124. Labor inits.
125. Neighbor of Fr.

PUZZLE 467

• SPORT OR SPORTING? •

ACROSS
1. Shirt protectors
5. Heckler's cry
8. Bath bar
12. Region
13. Circle portion
14. Impulse
15. Safari member
18. Double curves
19. Distress letters
20. Respectful title
22. Cut, as prices
27. American Uncle
30. Female goat
32. Toward shelter
33. Followed convention
37. Kitchen extender
38. Half-dozen
39. Comedian Caesar
40. Eccentric
42. Aunt, in Madrid
44. Charged particle
47. Jumped
51. Wildlife refuges
56. Kiln
57. 151, to Brutus
58. Bit
59. Be pliant
60. Keyboard key
61. Water jug

DOWN
1. Baseball's Ruth
2. Spring flower
3. Implores
4. Wise people
5. Emeril's word
6. Mined metals
7. Siete y uno
8. Solar body
9. Food scrap
10. Generation
11. According to
16. Stage whisper
17. Prow letters
21. Wand
23. Fall behind
24. Woe is me!
25. Trucker's rig
26. Pay attention to
27. Hurried
28. Low female voice
29. Actor Dillon
31. Martians, e.g.: abbr.
34. Still
35. Sock
36. Banish
41. Puppy's bark
43. Nest on high
45. Killer whale
46. Actress Carter
48. Acknowledge
49. Singer Seeger
50. Romanov ruler
51. Sailor
52. "____ Maria"
53. Chess pieces
54. Intention
55. Roost

PUZZLE 468

• DON'T BREAK IT •

ACROSS
1. In favor of
4. Mr. Gingrich
8. Prohibit
11. French buddy
12. Opera tune
13. Hamlet, e.g.
14. Info-storage spot
16. Rural hotels
17. Verne character
18. Elicits
20. Sleeping
23. LTD's kin
24. Taxis
27. Center
29. Mimic
32. Actress Hagan
33. Leading
34. Cold and damp
35. Coop
36. Standard
37. Axlike tool
38. Scout Carson
40. Practice boxing
42. Adhesive
45. Stab of guilt
48. Feel sore
49. Section of Paris
53. School dance
54. Racetrack
55. Menlo Park inits.
56. Matched pair
57. Indiana steel town
58. Possess

DOWN
1. Passing fancy
2. Muscat's land
3. Sacrament
4. Influential person
5. Baseball stat
6. Triumph
7. Accept
8. Debit or credit voucher
9. Actress Archer
10. Famous loch
13. Singer DiMucci
15. Pearl divers
19. Strove
21. Alpine return
22. Achievers
24. Chalice
25. Consumed
26. Billiards feat
28. Inclined walk
30. La ____, Bolivia
31. Ram's mate
33. Naysayer
37. Fine steed
39. List component
41. With skill
42. Charts
43. Farm unit
44. Drain problem
46. Allied gp.
47. Chew
50. Ms. Longoria
51. Not nearby
52. Understanding

CODEWORD

PUZZLE 469

Instructions for solving Codeword puzzles are given on page 11.

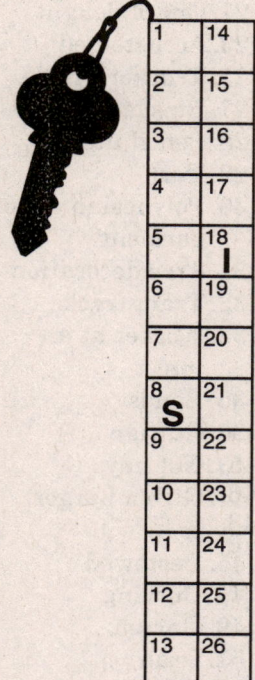

CODEWORD

PUZZLE 470

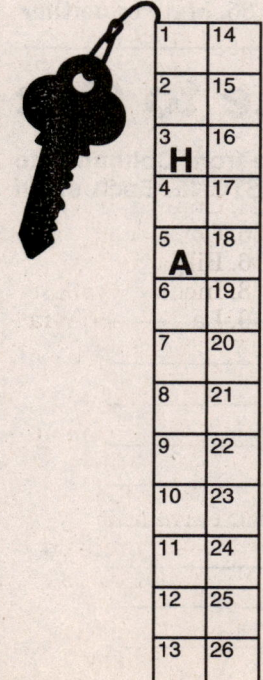

PUZZLE 471

ACROSS
1. Current measures
5. Egyptian snakes
9. Tendon
14. Encircle
15. Have feelings
16. Useful
17. Notion
18. Very eager
19. Yucca fiber
20. Foursome
22. Certain feathers
24. Doff
26. Gawker
30. Pressing need
34. Lined up
36. Twosome
37. Brewing need
38. Diminish
39. Ewer
40. Take a load off
41. Woeful
42. Curious
44. "The Most Happy ___"
46. Wagers
47. Leg's middle
48. In another place
50. Forest clearing
52. Sprinkle
53. Lyrical
56. Modernized
60. ___ macaroni
64. Affectionate
66. African goat
67. Made public
68. Berg
69. Zilch
70. Weeping
71. Lawn
72. Turns right

DOWN
1. Touched ground
2. Fashion
3. Bard
4. More meager
5. Private school
6. Wilt
7. Poke
8. Lily type
9. Prosecuting
10. "___ Magic"
11. Young bug
12. Building shape
13. Teensy
21. Cry of delight
23. Accustomed
25. Trucker's fuel
27. Bio class
28. Pencil utensil
29. Turn
30. Polynesian garment
31. Tree decoration
32. Train tracks
33. Worker at an inn
35. Bonds
36. Ruffian
43. Not nay
44. Give a burger to
45. Bestowed
46. Curving
49. Hasten
51. Drab
54. Doubtful
55. Kind of soda
57. Bassoon's kin
58. Hawaiian goose
59. Former spouses
60. ___ and run
61. False statement
62. Lingerie item
63. Byron's above
65. Mate of neither

PUZZLE 472 — Three to One

Starting with each word in Column A, add a word from Column B and then one from Column C to build ten longer words. For example, CORN plus ERST plus ONE is CORNERSTONE. Each small word will be used only once.

	A	B	C	
1.	WHEEL	MA	ADE	1. _____
2.	CAST	BAR	ABLE	2. _____
3.	PRO	SIT	HOLE	3. _____
4.	HIT	EON	TO	4. _____
5.	PIG	I	WAY	5. _____
6.	HE	A	ROW	6. _____
7.	DO	BIT	ON	7. _____
8.	HA	SUM	AT	8. _____
9.	SECT	HER	IN	9. _____
10.	AS	MEN	ANT	10. _____

PUZZLE 473

• GARDEN VARIETY •

ACROSS
1. Catch wind of
5. "No contest," e.g.
9. Diamond cut
13. Leave a mark
17. Loafing
18. Streamlet
19. Twist one's arm
20. Commandment pronoun
21. Anna's teaching post
22. Project
23. Teacup residue
24. "Seasons of Love" musical
25. Tall, thin guys
28. Lowers
30. Freight weight
31. Bona fide
33. Subpoena
34. Saratoga Springs, e.g.
37. Merit badge holder
40. Latin catchall
42. Cancel
45. Cauliflower ___
46. Door sign
48. Aphrodite's boy
50. "Yeah, right!"
51. Sermon topic
53. Potter pieces
55. "Days of Grace" author
57. Malleable metal
58. TV and radio
60. Some Angoras
62. West Texas city
64. Ocarinas
68. Buyer
71. Make Z's
72. Catches
76. Orchid wreath
77. False witness
80. Happening
82. D-Day beach
83. Thick hair
85. "The Odyssey," e.g.
87. Follow
89. Fast bird
90. Checks
92. Sonar signal
94. Word
95. Chanced upon
96. Rose Murphy's man
98. Mandlikova of tennis
100. In-between
102. Garb
105. Bronx cheers
111. NASCAR units
112. Part of LP
114. Lacerate
115. Crosscurrent
116. Rembrandt works
117. Dirk's kin
118. "Aurora" painter
119. John Lennon's son
120. Low card
121. Nurture
122. Mideast gp.
123. Equivalent

DOWN
1. Steam iron sound
2. Put in a good word?
3. Wing-shaped
4. Pay up
5. Like some pauses
6. Bough
7. Nobelist Wiesel
8. Bride's destination
9. Quiver
10. Browning's before
11. Elderly
12. Fix, as a hem
13. Melodies
14. Old jokes
15. First-rate
16. Tractor tracks
26. Snout
27. Once called
29. Suit top
32. Pasternak heroine
34. Appear to be
35. Make a road
36. Jejune
38. Outlaw's target
39. Laconian slave
41. ___ Altos
43. "Trinity" author
44. Singer Horne
47. Brings in
49. Vamoose!
52. Tilt
54. Jacob's pillow
56. Early garden
59. MP's concern
61. Potbelly, for one
63. Birthright seller
65. Buffalo's county
66. "___ We All"
67. Keyed up
68. Shady trees
69. Dinner entree, often
70. Hand grenade
73. Twosome
74. ___ duck
75. Closed
78. Tarzan's friend
79. Loaded
81. Curry ingredient
84. Diplomatic mission
86. Battle mount
88. Desert leader
91. Madam's mate
93. Stop ___ dime
97. Conger catcher
99. Jetson pet
101. Kind of code
102. More than enough
103. Two of a kind
104. Easy stride
106. Nest sound
107. Scourge
108. Hunch
109. Cracker topper
110. New Year's Eve word
113. PBS benefactor

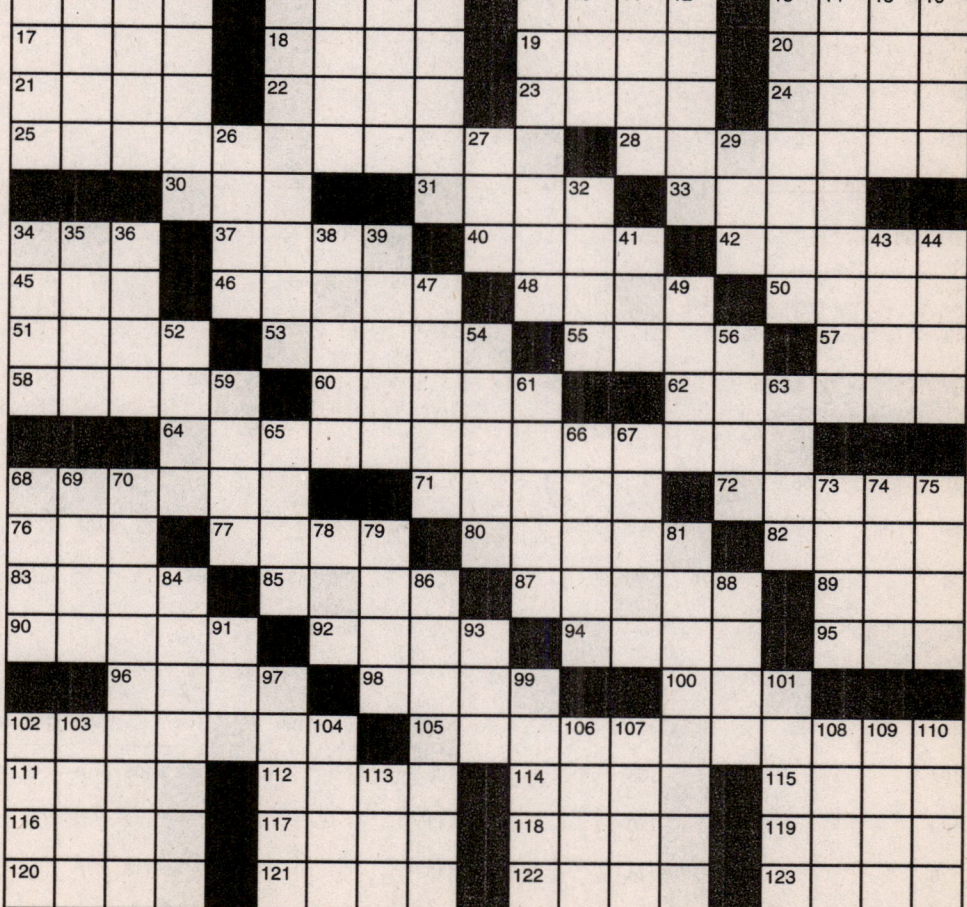

PUZZLE 474

• WHEN IN ROME... •

ACROSS
1. Not post
4. Straighten
9. Cheerleaders have it
12. Stationary
17. Opposite of terre
18. Grecian garment
19. Before now
20. Hero, to Leander
21. Psychic's gift
22. Ovid's gun?
24. Doddering
25. Garland's costar
27. Finback whale
28. Suit part
29. Walks the floor
30. Not in, in Glasgow
32. History muse
34. Secretary's sub
36. "___ Poetica"
37. Roman comic-book characters?
41. Rule
43. Educe
44. Ceremonial dinner
46. Cell terminals
49. Computer key
50. A tense
52. Hairpiece
54. Meir of Israel
55. Young newt
56. Proclaim
59. Mr. Simon
60. Indian title
63. Nero's last drink?
66. Beauty shop offering
67. Moonlight serenade?
69. Strikes hard
70. Entertainment-center item
71. Use
73. Broke bread
74. ___ noir
75. Ms. Massen
78. Old faithful, notably
80. Lauder of scents
83. Poet's foot
85. Quenches
87. Gable flick at the Colosseum?
89. Make a scene
91. Pound the keyboard
93. Tolkien tree creatures
94. Vote for
95. Barracks bigwig
97. Jai ___
99. Giant Giant
101. It marches on
104. Caveman's weapon
105. Pooh's home in Rome?
108. Cole or Turner
109. Rugged ridge
110. Biblical suffix
111. Membranes
112. Ancient Tokyo
113. Archaic
114. Bishop's domain
115. Ford failure
116. Study

DOWN
1. Shuck
2. Tabula ___
3. Pleasant-sounding
4. Off-road need
5. Pitcher Tiant
6. Arthropod
7. Anarchist
8. "Foucault's Pendulum" author
9. Party spread
10. Discharge
11. Baggage handler
12. Ready for takeoff?
13. Hebrides isle
14. Caesar's rendition of a Crests song?
15. Sniggler
16. Attire
23. Egg-shaped
26. Military initials
31. Clavell novel
33. Sculpture material, often
35. ___ culpa
37. Charge
38. Capp and Capone
39. Rods
40. Song units
42. Thug
45. Who's sorry now
47. Singer Brickell
48. Lot's wife, ultimately
51. Plant pore
53. Shady place
56. Bear witness
57. Female pronoun
58. Ploy
60. Carpet style
61. Roam
62. Certain iter?
64. Baptism, e.g.
65. Drab
68. Simpson sibling
72. Excelled in sports
74. Gave
75. Got
76. Soccer mom's trans.
77. "___ Lay Dying"
79. "Curious George" creator
81. Those people's
82. Bard's sunset
84. Proper
86. Parking spots
88. Bars legally
89. Hafez al ___ (Syrian leader)
90. Beloved director
92. Thrill
96. Airport exit
98. Head woe
100. Bear
102. Assembled
103. School for princes
106. Language suffix
107. Indian dish

PUZZLE 475

• WHOSE HUES? •

ACROSS
1. Sofa or bench
5. RBI, e.g.
9. Drug store abbr.
13. Way off
17. Close attention
18. Forest growth
19. Sprint
20. European capital
21. Craving
22. Shamrock land
23. Lab burner
24. TV horse
25. Marilyn Monroe, e.g.
29. Hesitation sounds
30. Writer Rand
31. Bullfight cheer
32. Glimpse
33. TV producer Griffin
35. Opposite of WSW
36. Slugger Slaughter
39. Pilot
42. Sunday lecture
46. Three voices
48. Gaelic
49. Commander's abbr.
52. Stowe's Legree
54. Spoiled child
56. Chimpanzee
57. King of Tyre
59. Cats have nine
61. Ranch
63. Creme de la creme
64. Vast plains
67. Picture puzzle
70. Humble
72. "Key ___"
73. Ripeners
74. Sta. listing
76. Stadium part
79. On the up and up
81. Bearded bloom
82. Study of topog.
84. Sign of crying
86. Regard highly
88. Good quality
90. Suggestive glance
92. "Cakes and ___"
93. Miscalculates
95. Atlas entry
97. "What Kind of Fool ___"
98. Tee preceder
101. Heidi's mountain
103. Beatles film
108. Principal role
110. Shakespearean monarch
111. Length x width
112. Genesis garden
113. Reject, as a bill
114. Bulk
115. Legal-exam letters
116. Rosary piece
117. Netman Arthur ___
118. Opening wager
119. Broadway auntie
120. Clumsy vessels

DOWN
1. Divers' gear
2. Too soon
3. Gaseous element
4. Young adult
5. Pittsburgh athletes
6. Clan
7. Dynamic beginning
8. Overruns
9. Gift
10. Biblical verb
11. Pimples
12. Empire
13. Limb
14. Kathleen Winsor work
15. Neighbor of Can.
16. 1981 Beatty movie
26. Finished
27. Honeycomb builder
28. Bandleader Brown
34. Hwy. choice
35. Inheritance
37. Globe
38. ___ Galahad
40. Sixth sense
41. Lady ruff
43. Wire measures
44. Exclude
45. Book of fiction
47. Klutz
49. Revolutionary Guevara
50. Need aspirin
51. Irresponsible plan
53. Himalayan nation
55. Scarlett's home
58. Encounter
60. Binge
62. System of government
65. Souffle items
66. "And ___ Goes"
68. New England college inits.
69. Draft org.
71. Pioneer Carson
74. Muslim title
75. Add.
77. Snakelike fish
78. "Norma ___"
80. Fellow player
83. Berlin's lang.
85. Deep regret
87. Director Kazan
89. Attempt
91. Untrained
94. Alabama city
96. Sacred song
97. From port to starboard
98. Down source
99. Prowl
100. Forwards
101. Thomas ___ Edison
102. Hollywood's Grant and Remick
104. Lacking fat
105. Endure
106. Major or Minor bear
107. Country's McEntire
109. Mommy deer

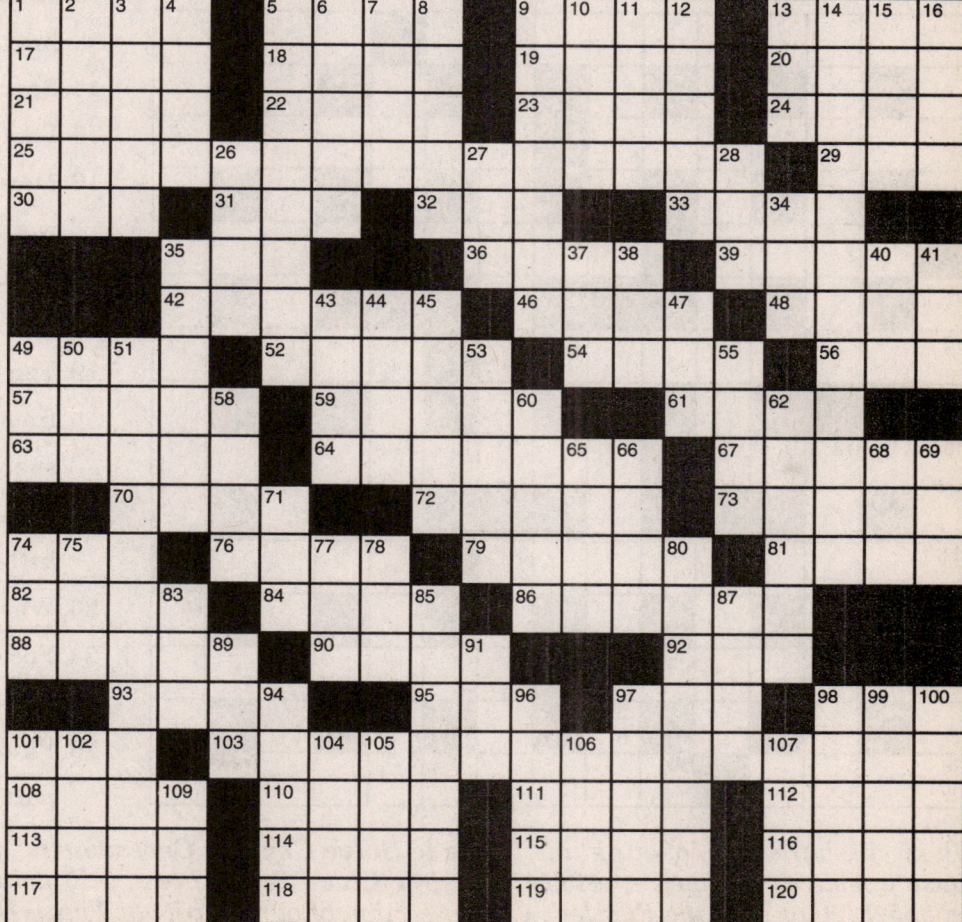

PUZZLE 476 — CRYPTIC CROSSWORD

British-style or Cryptic Crosswords are a great challenge for crossword fans. Each clue contains either a definition or direct reference to the answer as well as a play on words. The numbers in parentheses indicate the number of letters in the answer words.

ACROSS

1. Search for gold lines in organs (10)
6. Dish soaks when left (4)
10. Turner obtaining lower Italian fare (7)
11. U.S. ports redeveloped for some growth (7)
12. Eats noisily for so long (4)
13. Construction aids Sears, who's remodeled (9)
15. Speaker from Maine canyon put on edge (9)
17. "Rocky II" and "Country" (5)
18. Hard to fix name tag (5)
20. Exhausted even trade arrangement (9)
22. First person he spots grasping at dumbbells (9)
25. Denounce bar (4)
27. Sadly, roped to projectile in the water (7)
28. More cleverly devised raincoat (7)
29. Audibly regretted the misbehaving (4)
30. G-man Stein's difficult task (10)

DOWN

1. Pool recreation! (4)
2. One's tin glaze frames fitting inside (7)
3. Knotty rope urged to be assembled anew (9)
4. Like collecting mother's stock (5)
5. Train to stitch this spot, not this spot (9)
7. Made fast express change (7)
8. Tree saint planted amid Rod's bath accessories (10)
9. Jason's conveyance of limitless lingo (4)
14. Sanction a rum trip . . . I'm tipsy (10)
16. More than one switchboard worker works at Rocky Mountains (9)
17. Turn in adaptation (9)
19. The German telephoned from the east and snarled (7)
21. Cheat the French a little bit (7)
23. Whoops! (blushes) (4)
24. Fixed us his Japanese food (5)
26. Find fault with guitar part (4)

To receive a free copy of our guide, "**How to Solve Cryptic Crosswords**," send a self-addressed, business-sized, stamped envelope to Cryptic Clues, Penny Press, 6 Prowitt Street, Norwalk, CT 06855-1220 or visit the Puzzler's Corner section of our website at **PennyDellPuzzles.com**.

JUMBO PUZZLE BOOKS!

Order today and enjoy hours of puzzle fun with these 290-page volumes of top-quality Penny Press puzzles!

Family Favorites Variety Puzzles has all the variety puzzles you love including Cryptograms, Logic Problems, Syllacrostics, and much more. Hundreds of puzzles in each volume.

Family Favorites Crossword Puzzles delivers hundreds of top-quality Penny Press crosswords. Great enjoyment for the entire family!

To order, fill out the coupon below and mail it with your payment today, call TOLL-FREE 1-800-220-7443, or visit PennyDellPuzzles.com

---

PennyDellPuzzles™   Dept. PL • 6 Prowitt Street • Norwalk, CT 06855-1220

☑ **YES!** Please send me the _____ jumbo **Family Favorites** volumes I've circled below for just $4.95 plus $1.50 shipping & handling each. My payment of $_____ ($6.45 per volume, U.S. funds) is enclosed.

Name _____
(Please Print)

Address _____

City _____

State _____ ZIP _____

Variety Puzzles (VRFF):
Vol. 59   60   61   AUT17   SPR18

Crossword Puzzles (XWFF):
Vol. 60   61   62   AUT17   SPR18

Allow 4 to 6 weeks for delivery. **CT & NY residents:** Please add applicable sales tax to your total. **Outside USA:** Add an additional $5 shipping & handling and add applicable GST and PST (U.S. funds). Offer expires 8/31/19.

68-UXFJL4

PUZZLE 477

• DOUBLE FEATURES •

ACROSS
1. Musical windup
5. Hindu gentleman
10. Place for drawers
15. Food fish
18. Elliptical
19. Hippodrome
20. Last name in fashion
21. Tony's relative
23. With 25 Across, alien hunters being attacked?
25. See 23 Across
27. Good job!
28. Emotional piece
29. Purport
30. Sumerian deity
31. Prove human
33. Acquired kin
34. Attributes
35. A lot of spam
38. Premature
42. Draught
43. With 45 Across, Indian maid near a garden?
45. See 43 Across
51. "___ Do That"
52. Nut part
53. Hoarse
54. "Bali ___"
55. Cinema canine
56. Whit
57. Clarinetist Shaw
58. Loyalty
60. African lute
61. Raison ___
62. San ___, California
63. With 69 Across, Moroccan hotel?
69. See 63 Across
72. Poplar
73. "Teach Me Again" singer
75. 100 yrs.
76. Jeweler's item
77. Pursue
78. Like a lot
79. Zounds!
83. On-line giggle
84. Bay window
85. Malt drink
86. Contented sound
87. With 91 Across, rave?
91. See 87 Across
93. Secure
94. Huge
95. Hull abbr.
96. Sacristy
99. Spray
102. Met in session
104. Yale or Root
105. Serious
106. Slugger Ripken
109. Paroxysm
113. With 115 Across, obdurate Peace Corps workers?
115. See 113 Across
117. Med. course
118. Pee Wee, e.g.
119. Likeness
120. Form of address
121. Peer Gynt's mother
122. European viper
123. Put forward
124. Nice girl

DOWN
1. Toothed implement
2. Finished
3. Comic Carvey
4. Kicking
5. Anc. empire
6. Folk's Guthrie
7. Sweat unit
8. Without repetition
9. Furniture wood
10. Mean
11. Shrub for dye
12. Fund
13. Road's end
14. Gob
15. Neologism
16. Manuscript marks
17. 0 or 1
22. Congers
24. Bridge seat
26. Letter stroke
29. Former cable ch.
32. Many guests
33. Showy moths
34. Couple
35. Samoan port
36. Medicos
37. Buzz off!
39. Certain Iroquois
40. Unescorted
41. Cereal grass
42. Optic ailment
44. Literary olio
45. Singer Kitt
46. Houston player
47. Sales pitch
48. Delhi wear
49. Eroded
50. Japan, in Japan
53. Scottish explorer
58. Fed
59. Skate
60. Shawm, updated
61. Platforms
63. Arum lily
64. Remote
65. ___ Ste. Marie
66. Rock blaster
67. Indian statesman
68. French director
70. Most distant
71. Stages
74. Poulet seasoning
77. Neat
78. ___ ex machina
79. Emissions gp.
80. Intellectual guide
81. Abilities
82. Prohibitionists
85. Good, in Grenoble
88. Connoisseur
89. Summer show
90. Stable staple
91. Big bike
92. Whitney's partner
94. Halfway to
96. Ms. Wang
97. TV's Verdugo
98. "___ Marner"
99. Charger
100. Old hat
101. Stair feature
103. Subject
105. Snow slider
106. Lombardy city
107. Sad expression
108. Olympic event
110. Legitimate
111. Viva-voce
112. Salinger heroine
114. Refrain syllable
115. CEO, e.g.
116. Composer Rorem

PUZZLE 478

• TALK TO THE ANIMALS •

ACROSS
1. Glazier's product
5. Brown of renown
8. Durango digs
13. Actress Thompson
17. Busy as ___
18. Boat movers
19. Convert
20. Claw
21. How to lay an egg?
23. Serious
24. Bongo's kin
25. Always, in verse
26. Memo header
27. Kitty's character?
29. Salivated
31. Poet Hart ___
32. Meet defeat
33. Neither's correlative
34. Norman Vincent ___
35. Helm position
36. Presently
39. Picture puzzle
42. Easter flower
43. Thin coins
45. Persian sprite
46. Letters from Athens
47. Seville shout
48. Family man
49. Pseudonym
50. School gp.
51. Cote rooms?
55. "Taps" tooter
56. Least obvious
59. Shot container
60. Type of marten
61. Deteriorate
62. Infiltrator
63. Facets
64. Take long steps
66. Bakery enticement
67. Jib
70. Aesthetic judgment
71. Shows holding cattle calls?
73. "___ Send Me"
74. Cultural character
75. Outlaw
76. River of Spain
77. Allows
78. Author Uris
79. Nonplussed
81. Sr.'s exams
82. Diamond weight
83. Early dadaist
84. Leaf
85. James Joyce and his ilk
87. Even if, informally
88. Infield cover
89. Asserts
90. Board member
94. Serpentine dramatics?
98. Fiber source
99. Possesses
100. Neighborhoods
101. Hubris
102. Daffy ducks?
104. Vehicle with big tyres
105. Colorado's ___ Park
106. Workbook chapter
107. CSA's Robert ___
108. Till fillers
109. Takes wing
110. Giant Giant
111. Sean or William

DOWN
1. Walked up and down
2. More qualified
3. Biology beginning
4. Common Market letters
5. Landed Highlander
6. Celtic tongue
7. Compass dir.
8. Informal
9. Bedecked
10. British sword
11. Gorillas, e.g.
12. Sauntered leisurely
13. Rouen room
14. Asia's ___ Mountains
15. "___ Be Cruel"
16. Artist Warhol
18. Deed holder
20. Rib
22. Metric masses
27. Implore
28. Refusals
30. Burden
31. Paparazzi's target
34. Aviator
35. Hoard
36. Contrary filly?
37. Papal cape
38. Sager
39. D.C. figures
40. Caesar's cry
41. Place to get fleeced?
42. Unfettered
44. That is, in Latin
45. Assets
49. Remain
51. Hand over
52. Domed home
53. Chowder shellfish
54. Veranda
57. Poseidon's son
58. Mine veins
60. Cone producers
62. Subject
63. Recital pieces
64. Engraved pillar
65. Spud
66. Stun
67. Reliance
68. Whit
69. "___ for Life"
72. Vulgar
75. Scottish instrument
77. Vientiane's venue
79. Alda costar
80. Partition
81. Gentlemen
82. Slab
84. Dupe
86. Break
87. Pamphlet
88. Russian rulers
89. Singer Baker
90. Attribute
91. Rowboat pin
92. Devoured
93. Ruhr city
94. Overhead lighting?
95. It may be pumped
96. Bone-dry
97. Approximately
98. Baseball tap
102. Quid pro ___
103. Vigor

PUZZLE 479

WORDSWORTH

Fill in each row and column of the Wordsworth diagram with at least two words. The number of words in a row or column is indicated by the number of clues. Words are not separated by extra squares, so all the squares will be filled in when the diagram is completed.

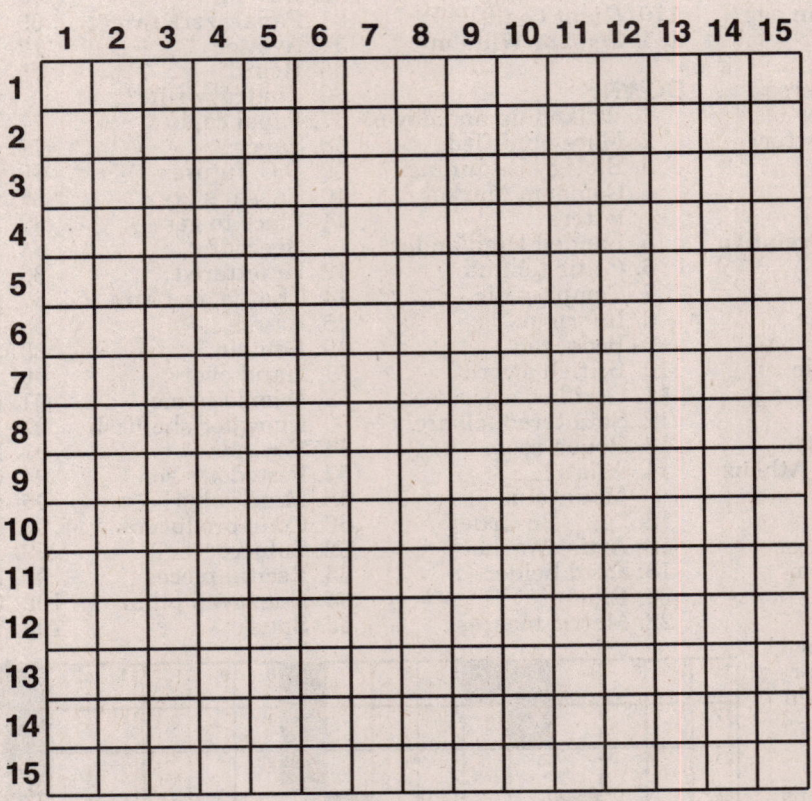

ACROSS

1. Crystal fixture • Live coal
2. Ancestry • Sufficient
3. Retinue • Rain drain
4. War god • Garden flower • Lorry wheel
5. Bike part • Fit • Maroon
6. Smell • Upper House • Hodgepodge
7. Ryan's daughter • Angle unit • Hires
8. Pee Wee ___ • Miscue • Actor Bridges
9. Nab • Jam fruit
10. Spanish deity • Legume • Novice • Hammer end
11. Butt • Auto • Maui goose • Fred's wife
12. ___ mode • Ruler • Dad • Chamber
13. Tiny • Sum • Wine region
14. Idiotic • Bruin great • Splendor
15. Male elks • Scarlett's place • Pooh's pal

DOWN

1. Antony's love • Plays
2. Impede • Trapeze artist
3. Remedy • Balkan nation
4. Inert gas • Tickles • Adhered
5. Smear • Gold cloth • Hot spot • Elevator man
6. Way out • Restraint
7. Alliance • Task • Hot spot
8. Othello's bane • Thankless one • Needy
9. Paradise • Poi source • Frank or Nancy
10. Sign up • Get ready
11. Liken • Jostle • Downwind
12. Mongrel • Ms. Esther ___ • Watery crime
13. Club • Elis' home • Mr. Hershiser • Norway city
14. Forever • San ___, Italy • Sea salt?
15. Altar screen • Nobel's invention

PUZZLE 480

• REDUNDANT TAUTOLOGIES •

ACROSS

1. Command by spell
8. Singaraja's site
12. With, in Arles
16. Rival
19. Excitement
20. Shortly
21. Jacob's son
22. Doctrine
23. Fresh start
25. Handel opus
27. Wrath
28. Awestruck
29. Combining form for "inner"
30. Map in a map
31. Asia's ___ Sea
34. Available
35. ___ Vista
37. French I verb
38. Uncovered
41. Hamlet
42. Scrape
44. Pacify
45. Taunting type
46. Nostalgia-inducing
48. Questioning sort
51. "___-Tiki"
53. Evenings in Paris
55. Sweetsop
58. Matisse, e.g.
59. Rotation center
61. Comic possum
62. ___ brulee
63. Fragrant compounds
65. Tiny terror
66. Sensational reading
67. Jail
69. Mild reproach
70. Skye cap?
72. Ripening
75. Day break?
76. Salt's assent
78. Ed or Julie
81. Swanky
82. Biographer Leon ___
84. Student's book
86. Canines, e.g.
87. Author Seton
88. Abram's wife
90. Mole
91. Influential folks
93. Pricked
95. Ohio Indians
97. Hiatus
102. "Diana" singer
103. Pro ___
104. Venerable person
106. Covenant
108. Reels
110. Martin or Kingsley
111. Captain's call
112. Bury
114. Soak, as hemp
115. Fateful date
116. Cobbler's tool
118. Maryland player
120. Unite
125. Sigma's follower
126. Tuftlike mass
127. On the calm side
128. Ruled
129. Shade provider
130. Phoenician port
131. Bits per second
132. Menu options

DOWN

1. Ax
2. Mined-over matter?
3. At once
4. Special celebration
5. Patron
6. Fashion
7. Samuel's mentor
8. Slammed
9. Negative particle
10. Extended
11. Gerund ender
12. Nearness
13. Bittern
14. Stowe character
15. Tubular pasta
16. Prime concern
17. Wicker willow
18. Play the ham
24. Scruff
26. Like a superstore
29. Triumphant cry
31. Arab garment
32. Knock on wood?
33. Dada pioneer
34. Dennis ___ of "Brewster's Millions"
35. Short cut?
36. Part of ETA
39. Egyptian president
40. Invite
41. Chopper
43. Political initials
45. Donate, of yore
47. Sheer fabric
49. Accumulated wisdom
50. Dance attire
52. Game for two
54. Sopping
55. Fleets
56. Furious fit
57. It'll never fly
60. Place for losers?
62. Films
64. Sprinkles
68. Have wings
71. Place
73. Woman governor of Connecticut
74. Article from Bonn
77. Sycophant's answer
79. Perplexed
80. Pottery fragments
83. Wash
85. Autocrat
89. Sign
92. Ring leader?
94. Argon or xenon
96. "___ Not Unusual"
98. Liturgical collection
99. "Somewhat" suffix
100. Nino's uncle
101. Tarzan portrayer
104. Augured
105. Cant
106. Please, to Helmut
107. Top center
109. Abbot's underling
110. Parting word
113. Great quantity
115. Beverly Archer role
116. Not fer
117. Took off
119. Employ busily
120. Poke
121. Barcelona bravo
122. Possess, to Burns
123. Somme time
124. Legal thing

PUZZLE 481

HERE'S TO HUE

ACROSS
1. Sicilian peak
5. Boat
9. Many
13. Scottish girl
17. Faulty
18. Robert or Alan
19. Turf
20. Killer whale
21. Roman road
22. Othello, e.g.
23. Like a cranberry
24. ___ Bator
25. Walker novel, with "The"
28. Ideas
30. Untamed
31. Hang ten
33. Once called
34. Guy's date
37. ___-control
39. Nerve
41. Book of maps
45. Nimble
47. Deer's kin
49. Ogle
51. William ___ of films
52. Glenn's group: abbr.
53. Fixed gaze
55. Past
56. Mr. Kazan
57. Blacktop alternative
59. Teases
61. Excellent
63. TV Tarzan
64. Tribal leader
66. Onassis, to pals
67. Cocker ___
71. Queue
72. Bank worker
76. Nobleman
77. Weep
79. Ms. Lauder
81. Verdi work
82. Tulsa native
83. Shredded
85. Generation
86. Get lost!
87. Baseball's Martinez
89. Sea weed
91. Make eyes at
93. Rock band's need
94. Batch of bills
96. Coral structure
98. ___ lamp
100. Lecturer
104. Nickname for the 1890s
109. Oaf
110. Cassette
112. Kernel
113. Defrost
114. Beast
115. Level
116. Eye woe
117. Seep
118. Dolt
119. Lease
120. French river
121. Some breads

DOWN
1. Heroic tale
2. Dorothy's dog
3. Mr. Coward
4. Dart
5. Try
6. Little nimbus
7. Scent
8. Twists
9. Of the side
10. Man ___ mouse
11. Sea bird
12. Crushed, in a way
13. Berle's "Batman" role
14. Singer Guthrie
15. Glance over
16. Without
26. Get up
27. Haul
29. Oolong, e.g.
32. ___ market
34. Mob
35. Culture medium
36. Ms. Kudrow
38. Oddball
40. Gams
42. Slow time
43. Diva's delight
44. Celebrity
46. Skin splash
48. Humpback's snack
50. Turn
53. Most cunning
54. Guitarist Van Halen
58. Mr. Wallach

PUZZLE 481

60. Feel
62. Before, once
65. Vintage-esque
67. Pig's dinner
68. Jab
69. Hot and dry
70. Watch
73. Former money, for Mario
74. Cheese
75. Incline
78. ___ Rabbit
80. Keen sight
84. Part of a whole
86. First name in golf
88. Common wood
90. Legume
92. Painter's step
95. Ward off
97. Particular
99. Role player
100. Untidy one
101. Walt Kelly creation
102. Italian money
103. Great review
105. Doggie docs
106. Marine greeting
107. Stupor
108. Farm females
111. Write

PUZZLE 482

ACROSS
1. Tiff
5. Brash
9. Coin openings
14. Guided trip
15. Opera highlight
16. Nun's garb
17. Palo ___
18. Diane or Cheryl
19. Bonus
20. Tiny shoes
22. Feel ill
23. "Roses ___ Red"
24. Swiss peak
27. Squid's camouflage
28. Scrooge
32. Longing
35. Future oaks
37. Poison
38. Class
39. Door complaint
41. Dad
45. Sing softly
47. Like some nuts
49. Soak
52. Hair tinters
53. Gear part
54. Cot, e.g.
55. Unhappy
57. Jet hotshot
58. Baked dessert
63. Dug
66. "Less ___ Zero"
68. Curved arch
69. Harness horse
70. Sobbed
71. Melody
72. Cleverly
73. Metallic deposits
74. Leak slowly

DOWN
1. Take a ___ at (try)
2. Explorer Marco ___
3. Sedan, e.g.
4. Jog
5. Lighter hued
6. Blotted out
7. Cast off
8. Smidgen
9. "___ Belongs to Me"
10. Lenient
11. Get
12. Exhausting
13. Flower stem
21. Draw a salary
24. On a boat
25. Connections
26. In favor of
28. Doily
29. Frozen
30. Food for dipping
31. Standing
33. Incident
34. Hint at
36. Make a goal
40. Highway
42. Had supper
43. ___ diem
44. Billboards
46. Chafe
48. Totals
49. ___ worker
50. Bureau
51. Flee
53. Pitches a tent
56. Em and Bee
59. Babes
60. Flu
61. Tennis's Lacoste
62. Low-pitched
64. Electric ___
65. Thirsty
66. 1 + 1
67. That girl

424

PUZZLE 483

ACROSS
1. Whisk
6. Come-___ (lures)
9. Gobs
13. Bakery units
15. Playmate
16. Glass sheet
17. Nab
18. Proof
20. Ink stick
21. Twister
23. Study
24. Make do
25. Gam
26. Baltic or Irish
28. Awry
30. Squash
34. Boring tools
35. Duel
36. Soup grain
38. Iffy
39. Spare
41. Noon, e.g.
42. Willow's kin
44. Cape ___
45. Deed
46. Look quickly
47. Embrace
48. Large vase
49. Snacked
52. Bluish green
54. More, Pedro
57. Involve
59. Army bed
62. Musical comedy
64. Anger
66. Trial
67. Coat sleeve
68. Draw idly
69. Gate
70. Sodium solution
71. Ayes

DOWN
1. Smack
2. Corroded
3. Gain
4. First mom
5. Green sauce
6. Bid first
7. Nautical
8. Skid
9. Mock
10. Terrain
11. Not twice
12. Young driver
14. Sojourn
19. Tenet
22. Mend again
24. Fortress
26. Plunge
27. Flee to wed
29. Bring
31. Cunning
32. Trickier
33. Macho term
34. Band aid
36. Vexed
37. So far
40. 1 or 66
43. With speed
50. Complete
51. Door
53. Tease
54. A la ___
55. Peak
56. Big rig
58. Attended
59. Rogues
60. Stare
61. Casual tops
63. Decompose
65. Shad delicacy

PUZZLE 484

ACROSS
1. Taunt
5. Fade away
8. Uniform hue
13. Curved support
14. Come what ___
15. Stringed instrument
16. Nobleman
17. Ogle
18. Assault
19. Make beloved
21. Tiny drink
23. Heaven
24. First man
26. "Cheers" regular
29. Word puzzle
31. Stair parts
34. Tuna tin
35. Take a gamble
37. Fixes text
39. Pretend
40. Confident
42. Neckline shape
43. Risk
45. Apartment
46. Sue ___ Langdon
47. 100 pennies
49. Seas
52. Kent's love
53. Back part
54. Peat source
57. Unusual
59. Cunning
63. Stuns
66. Reverent fear
68. Rational
69. Harsh
70. Pro
71. Break ___
72. Nasty smile
73. Pekoe, e.g.
74. Tidings

DOWN
1. Cassette
2. Small songbird
3. Glazed
4. Sewing cord
5. Green gems
6. Cooking leaf
7. Brief farewells
8. Tool set
9. Sizzling
10. Cry of lament
11. Punt
12. Very black
15. Mist
20. Say further
22. Situated within
25. Gauged
27. Coarse grass
28. Zany
29. Sped
30. Beginning part
32. Couch
33. British guns
34. Beret, e.g.
36. Gallop
38. View
40. "... and to ___ good night!"
41. And so on
44. Feeling rotten
48. Win by ___
50. Musical sense
51. Developed
54. Food fish
55. Warning sign
56. Donated
58. Foolish
60. Grotto
61. Was aware of
62. Desires
64. Final letter
65. Goof up
67. Sadness

PUZZLE 485

ACROSS
1. Impresses
5. Juan's dough
9. Camp beds
13. Hockey site
14. Alarm
15. Civil melee
16. Rafter's peril
17. Toast start
18. Water growth
19. Downed dinner
20. Fusses
21. Thesis
22. Crafty
24. Indian prince
26. Wreck-amended shop?
28. No longer is
29. A Tyler
32. Prig
35. Swerve, at sea
37. Readjust ivories
39. Vatican VIPs
41. Family
43. Potato pancake
44. Exhausted
46. Pen part
48. Unlockers
49. Bear burrow
50. Chewy buy
52. Enjoy
54. Legends
56. Connected
60. Of the sun
63. Resided
65. Rowboat need
66. Hateful
67. Unworldly
68. Nude
69. Skin woe
70. Reffed
71. Wrongs
72. Leave one laughing
73. Cause of hives
74. Inlets

DOWN
1. Zones
2. AAA or EEE
3. Finisher
4. Blue above
5. ___ Piper
6. Glitch
7. Teetertotter
8. Switch signs
9. Wreck
10. Lubricants
11. Roman wear
12. Stick with
14. Inferior
20. Pair
21. Studio stand
23. Waned
25. Crock
27. Chatty ox?
29. Old strings
30. Black
31. Pavlov pair
32. Tater
33. Face scenter
34. Outspoken
36. Gain
38. Seized
40. Glucose
42. None
45. Small dog
47. Charged
51. "___ Butterfly"
53. Young fox
54. Briny
55. Steal
57. Marsupial
58. Too soon
59. Clothing
60. Sutures
61. Ellipse
62. Pisa money, once
64. Dusks
67. Knob
68. Baby ware

427

PUZZLE 486

ACROSS
1. Basilica part
5. Formerly
9. Entranced
13. Small spots
14. Go secretly
15. Dressing gown
16. Pub drinks
17. In the know
18. Capacity
19. Skillet
20. Catch
21. Lemon drinks
22. Police officer
24. Whirlpool
27. Flower
29. Rainbow shape
32. Smell
35. Cafe list
36. Feather stole
37. Arouse
39. Rosy
40. Fasteners
42. Bungle
43. Copycat
45. Intertwine
46. Ocean
47. Chum
51. Locks' mates
52. Forsake
56. Lively party
59. Nay ending
61. Pasture mom
62. Killer whale
63. Should
64. Burro
65. Pikes ___
66. Releases
67. Mastered
68. Indian garb
69. Timespan
70. Acquires

DOWN
1. Adjust
2. ___ bear
3. Pool member
4. Snaky curve
5. Ahead
6. Close
7. Swayed
8. Mete out
9. Showing
10. Not bad
11. A woodwind
12. Rubies, e.g.
14. More rational
20. Hot spring
23. Grimm brute
25. Clamor
26. Paint
28. Abrasive
29. Skilled
30. Decays
31. Money
32. Is obligated
33. Confront
34. Gumbo must
38. Neck back
39. Encourage
41. Portent
44. Layer
48. Mischief
49. Aids a felon
50. Sticky stuff
51. Army fabric
53. Tennis score
54. Big-eyed baby
55. Lacks
56. Hits
57. Turf
58. Wound cover
60. Golden ___
63. Frequently, in verse
64. Periodical

FLOWER POWER

PUZZLE 487

Instructions for solving Flower Power puzzles are given on page 94.

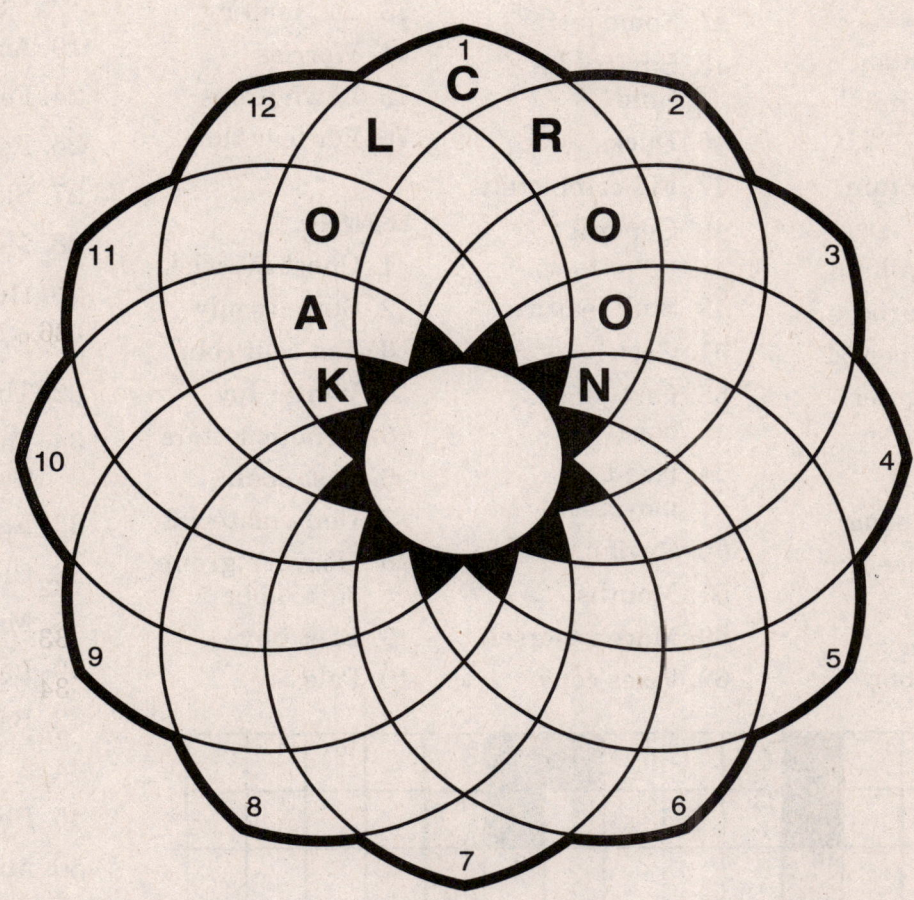

CLOCKWISE

1. Sing sentimentally
2. Skulk
3. Sink outlet
4. Feature
5. Impetuous
6. Hip bottle
7. Serenity
8. Hurrah
9. Metallic sound
10. Bundle of paper
11. Bend over
12. Sailboat type

COUNTERCLOCKWISE

1. Cape
2. Evidence of truth
3. Slouch
4. Girl Scout group
5. Muscle
6. Brittle
7. Simple
8. Creature
9. Stock-market dive
10. Loose
11. Remove whiskers
12. Court reporter

PUZZLE 488

CHAIRMAN OF THE BOARD

ACROSS
1. Cushions
5. Mr. Shannon
8. Road signal
13. Cruel
14. Ark's captain
16. Buffalo
17. Sinatra album
20. Greta Garbo, e.g.
21. Distinct period
22. Storm center
23. Promos
26. Sphere
28. Davis of song
31. Greek cheese
33. Station
37. West-coast school: abbr.
39. Leisure
41. Some jeans
43. Sinatra hit tune
46. Ducks
47. Fill completely
48. General Robert ___
49. Sink feature
51. Geek
53. Fast plane, once
54. Head movement
56. Caviar
57. Mouths
60. Mare's morsel
62. Fixes copy
67. Sinatra Grammy-winner
71. Skin woe
72. OK
73. ___ mater
74. Worries
75. Lawn drops
76. For fear that

DOWN
1. Chest muscles
2. State firmly
3. Ten-cent coin
4. Winter toy
5. Genetic letters
6. Vast span
7. Doily material
8. Hoover's group, once: abbr.
9. Beer buy
10. Pale
11. Italian city
12. Compass point: abbr.
15. Good guy
18. Unhearing
19. Actor Bond
24. Feat
25. Remains
27. Slacks support
28. Mongrel
29. Hurt
30. Erase
32. Thai, e.g.
34. Father, in Calais
35. Egg-shapes
36. Clocks
38. Ms. Nazimova
40. Lab compound
42. Barracuda
44. Z ___ zebra
45. Flying prefix
50. Midday
52. Judge
55. Papas
57. Leave out
58. Go on and on
59. Freshly
61. Dull sound
63. ___ citizenship
64. Wight or Capri
65. Conway et al.
66. Shoo!
67. Sounds of delight
68. Pack animal
69. Fury
70. Embroider

PUZZLE 489

STARTER COAT

ACROSS
1. Snaky letter
4. Kermit, e.g.
8. Hey, you!
12. Track circuits
14. Hearsay
16. Has unpaid bills
17. Pelvic bones
18. Overact
19. Jump
20. Oft-baked veggies
23. Islamic ruler
24. Fuss
25. Your, once
27. Towel word
28. Breezes
32. Scooter
34. Creep
36. Morays
37. Shuttle launch site
42. Baptism site
43. Take it easy
44. Some receptors
46. Charter
47. Truck's kin
50. Wrath
51. Hitting sound
54. Rear
56. Like the world of spies, e.g.
61. Chaotic condition
62. Worship
63. Finales
64. Arizona native
65. Oman's neighbor
66. Palm fruit
67. Singles
68. Stitches
69. ___ Angeles

DOWN
1. Actor Wood
2. Lunch meat
3. Seasons
4. Worry
5. Hind part
6. Melville story
7. Must, in slang
8. Horseback game
9. Climbing plant
10. Shore find
11. Kitchen measure: abbr.
13. Benefit
15. Understand words
21. Clear
22. Mr. Brokaw
26. Football measures: abbr.
29. Business word: abbr.
30. Bring up
31. Less wacky
33. Above, to bards
35. Curly veggie
37. Force
38. Gnu, e.g.
39. School group: abbr.
40. Singer Morrison
41. Additional
42. Spy organization: abbr.
45. Posh hotel
47. Motion
48. In the habit of
49. Poetic works
52. Sure!
53. Boggs et al.
55. Mature
57. Elevator name
58. Alaskan city
59. Sketched
60. Hideouts
61. Greek letter

PUZZLE 490

FIVE CARD DRAW

ACROSS

1. Oahu wreath
4. Snoozed
9. God
14. Mare's munchie
15. Pathway
16. Fury
17. Casserole veggie
19. Hawaiian geese
20. Waste cloth
21. Mother ___
23. Farm animal
25. Caller's kiosk
29. Prone
30. ___ du Diable
31. Kwon do start
32. Mr. Geller
33. Thieves
36. Right away: abbr.
37. Camera adjunct
41. Salamander
44. "1984" locale
48. Unlock, to bards
49. Helmut's exclamation
52. Guided
53. Pea's home
54. Daisy, e.g.
57. Foundation
58. Minnesota city
59. Handicraft
60. Italian city
62. Cash-stash site
67. Legally against
68. Famed cow
69. Mauna ___
70. Trite
71. Cherished ones
72. Hill insect

DOWN

1. Fireplace item
2. Jug handle
3. Utter again
4. Warbled
5. Women's ___
6. Compass point: abbr.
7. Texas town
8. Renter
9. German river
10. First month, to Juan
11. Lava rock, e.g.
12. Golf peg
13. Decade units: abbr.
18. Have a snack
22. Pekoe or oolong
23. Fuel
24. Choose
25. Not guilty, e.g.
26. Towel word
27. ___-la-la
28. Trendy
30. Unwell
34. Fore's mate
35. This lady
36. Arab cloak
38. Unit of hay
39. Patron
40. Business term: abbr.
41. Right away
42. Center start
43. Metalworkers
45. Kitchen tool
46. Cyclades island
47. Lime drink
49. Blazing
50. Actor Gulager
51. Nursery
55. Sand hills
56. Humpback, e.g.
57. Bikini top
59. Prayers
60. Drink slowly
61. TV chef Garten
63. Safety group: abbr.
64. White wine cocktail
65. Mr. Chaney
66. Make lace

432

PUZZLE 491

DRINKING SONGS

ACROSS
1. Form
5. Tracy's love
9. TV's Philbin
14. Winged
15. Hooked on
16. Have being
17. Hip bones
18. Elderly
19. Singer Simon
20. Buffett drinking tune
23. Skim
24. Suitable
25. Grudge
28. Actor Murphy
31. Cave flier
34. Modifies
36. Charged bit
37. Boo's cousin
38. Andrew Sisters drinking tune
41. Flees
42. Drumstick
43. Famous test pilot
44. Double curve
45. West Pointer
47. Ships' hands
48. Stately tree
49. Norse king
51. The Eagles drinking tune
58. California crater
59. Unseat
60. Stink
61. Formal songs
62. Devoted
63. Actor Penn
64. Extremely
65. Weakens
66. Swipe

DOWN
1. Injure
2. ___ podrida
3. Burrow
4. Strip vehicles
5. Jeweled crown
6. Motor
7. Editor's term
8. Baking ___
9. Cookbook entry
10. Glorify
11. Lass
12. Wight, e.g.
13. Dirty place
21. Sour
22. Futilely
25. Rich fur
26. Requests
27. Details
29. Sad song
30. John ___
31. Nonsense
32. Off-center
33. Russian rulers
35. Deli meat
37. Rime
39. Rosy
40. Pie nut
45. Awkward
46. 50/50 chance
48. Match
50. Minstrel's strings
51. Actress Reid
52. Ms. Bagnold
53. Loads
54. Atmosphere
55. Concept
56. Saturate
57. Sea eagle
58. TV's Dawber

PUZZLE 492

"B" PERSONALITIES

ACROSS

1. Breeze
5. OK marks
9. Dwindles
13. Hairless
17. Singer Tennille
18. Stag
19. Atmosphere
20. ___-friendly
21. Eternity
22. Skin woe
23. Tyrant
24. Those guys
25. Family outcast
28. Like bread, e.g.
30. Popular song
31. Ram baby
33. Once called
34. ___-relief
37. Office item
40. Courts
42. Knight's protection
46. Arm or leg
48. Scottish party
50. Pooch's name
51. Heroes
53. Easy as ___
54. Not me
56. Ford role, for short
57. Heathen
58. Elevate
61. Thinks
63. Feather wrap
65. Legumes
67. Droop
68. Uproar
71. "The Crucible" star
73. Rhythm
77. Mythology
78. Watch pocket
80. Western Indian
81. Fearless
82. Etch: abbr.
83. Wee ones
86. Arctic vehicle
87. Judges
89. Seethe
90. Sarge's pet
93. Printing measures
94. Grease
96. Ship part
98. Genetic letters
100. Ocean bird
102. Complainer
108. Fox's dance?
110. Promise
112. King Henry's number
113. Tot
114. Among
115. Ms. Sorvino
116. Press
117. Unlock
118. Lyrical poems
119. Charitable donations
120. Warbled
121. Modernize

DOWN

1. Brief attempt
2. Mr. Coward
3. Sulawesi ox
4. Nip
5. Pure
6. Every
7. White-tailed bird
8. Durable metal
9. Wolf down
10. Meddler
11. Dundee hillside
12. Wrap material
13. Klutz
14. Pale
15. ___ J. Cobb
16. Arid
26. Young goat
27. Ratchet device
29. Vast amount
32. Me, in Marseille
34. Radar image
35. Verdi work
36. Air problem
38. Wound reminder
39. Shish ___
41. Get lost!
43. Unearth
44. Gambling numbers
45. Mr. Rogers
47. Tattlers
49. More slippery
52. Snoot
55. Downs' mate
59. Speak
60. Invest
62. Metrical foot

PUZZLE 492

64. ___ Wiedersehen!
66. Spat
68. Sharpen
69. Entreat
70. Failure
72. Take a break
74. Story
75. Smooth
76. Beatty film
77. ___ Zeppelin
79. Reader
84. Fruit dessert
85. Commoner, to some
88. Man's title
91. Sampling
92. Munson of films
95. Pack animal
97. Strauss et al.
99. Keanu Reeves, e.g.
100. Dove's home
101. Mean
103. Former Italian money
104. Maned animal
105. Promote
106. Supplemented
107. Nevada city
108. Not quite three
109. Free (of)
111. Existed

435

PUZZLE 493

AUSTIN-TATIOUS

ACROSS
1. Outfit
5. Dunk starter
9. Repairs the lawn
13. Wise person
17. Hebrew month
18. Tickets
19. "Driving Miss Daisy" author
20. Crimp
21. Of flying: pref.
22. Astonished
23. Lend
24. For two musicians, to Mario
25. Annual arts fest
29. Clearance event
30. Hot spot
31. Mr. Kefauver
35. Seed holder
38. Evening in Venice
40. Writer Eugene ___
44. "Stargate" bad guys
45. Casual attire
47. It's at the foot of Lake Travis
50. Crucifix letters
51. Quantity: abbr.
52. Song syllables
53. Tropical tree
54. Tycoon
58. Golfer Hal ___
60. Maven
63. "360 Bridge"
67. Print measures
68. Surgeon's tool
70. Gives up
72. Loosen
73. That maiden
76. Actor Ziering
77. Military cap
81. Popular high spot
85. Medicine
87. Born
88. Clothing hole
89. Curly veggie
91. Witness
92. Serpent
94. Club
96. Animation units
98. Claim to fame
106. Stead
109. Milky gem
110. Tight
111. Hospital test
112. Blabbed
113. Frat garb
114. Church recess
115. Exhaust
116. Mr. Ellington
117. Being
118. Require
119. Jumps

DOWN
1. Steeped drinks
2. Bogus butter
3. Instructor
4. Some machines
5. Farm buildings
6. Dershowitz, e.g.
7. Eons
8. Windows predecessor
9. Muslim rulers
10. Oops' kin
11. Take a card
12. "Auld Lang ___"
13. German yachts
14. Assist
15. Antelope
16. Mete out
26. Biblical verb
27. Grimm word
28. Vend
32. As of now
33. Paolini novel
34. Carly and Paul
35. Greek letter
36. Have rights to
37. The, to Helmut
39. Jordan's capital
41. Salamander
42. Three, to Cato
43. Diminish
46. Objective
48. Court worker: abbr.
49. Spring for it: abbr.
51. Ms. Sothern
55. Copy
56. Makes do
57. Continental TV group: abbr.
59. Norse goddess
60. Female grad
61. Went by birchbark
62. Invested
64. Indigo plant
65. Blackboard writer

PUZZLE 493

66. Nebraska's neighbor: abbr.
69. Pro's mate
71. Shade of blue
74. Tiller
75. In the army: abbr.
78. Curve
79. Dessert item
80. Chill
82. Actress Hatcher
83. Galactic clouds
84. Airport postings: abbr.
85. Like some skirts
86. Give a hand to
90. Blame
93. Escape
95. A moon of Saturn
97. After fifth
99. Cast a ballot
100. Homeric work
101. Periodicals
102. Cod, e.g.
103. Small group
104. Seniors' group: abbr.
105. Caustic liquids
106. Restricted: abbr.
107. Letters for debtors
108. Forest animal

PUZZLE 494

IT'S NOT EASY BEING . . .

ACROSS
1. Mont Blanc, e.g.
4. Axe
8. Joyful
12. Anxiety
17. Briny expanse
18. Uncommon
19. Las Vegas rival
20. ___ Alegre, Brazil
21. Golfer's spots
24. Delicacy
25. Beatty film
26. Phantasmal
27. Night before
28. Provokes
31. Jittery
32. Flag
35. ___ d'oeuvre
36. Houston gp.
37. Weekly TV show
38. Take care of
40. Parrot
41. Weatherboard
42. Picks
44. Lab's lead
46. Damp
49. Franco ___
50. Shoe leather
51. Follow directly
52. Riot crowd
54. Largest island
58. "ER" group
59. Short simian
62. Dodge
63. Unbarred
66. Town official
67. Blow mark
68. Expands
71. Before a conflict
73. Healthy
75. Certain Buddhist
77. Derby holder
78. Gray of TV
79. Huron, e.g.
80. Yeast coffeecake
81. Cooped up
83. Like some submarines
85. Implore
86. Without restriction
87. Regal steed
88. Ostriches' kin
91. Southern staple
96. Road sign
97. Organic compound
98. Bright light
99. Bardot's water
100. Plus
101. Moistens
102. Colony dwellers
103. Caustic substance

DOWN
1. Type of snake
2. Romanian coin
3. Coach Riley
4. Hawker
5. Fieldworkers
6. Assns.
7. Dowel, e.g.
8. Sickly
9. Evil looks
10. "Tomorrow" musical
11. Portion
12. "___ Pupil"
13. Negative conjunction
14. Seuss's breakfast?
15. Barrel parts
16. Carrier
22. Bridge support
23. Della or Pee Wee
28. Exclamations
29. Votes against
30. Lambeau Field players
31. Faucets
32. Crib or cot
33. Wake up
34. Curtain cloth
36. Singer King Cole
37. Temptress
39. Above, in poems
41. Fountain order
43. Machine's tooth
45. Remove from text
47. Chewing stick
48. Word of assent
50. Aquatic mammal
52. Mother
53. Man-mouse link
55. Shine again

PUZZLE 494

56. Nonstop
57. June bug
60. Santa's Pole
61. Diving bird
64. Tiny vegetable
65. Hoop's site
68. Coasted
69. Author
70. Rice wine
72. Hit the jackpot
74. Sports ring
76. Slangy sleuth
77. Soothes
80. Hindu concept
81. Replica
82. Sanction
83. Specialized jargon
84. Mountain pools
86. Scored highly on
87. Mideast gulf
89. Beauty preceder
90. Complete group
92. Genetic transmitter
93. Slippery customer
94. Indeed
95. Bring legal action

PUZZLE 495

I "GOT" YOU, BABE

ACROSS
1. Spot
4. Fib
7. Permits
11. Like some houses
17. ___ Baba
18. Vast span
19. Solo for Callas
20. Lab organism
21. Hazard sign at the treasury?
24. Rue
25. Linden, e.g.
26. Annoys
27. Confuse
28. ___ bird
31. Majors et al.
33. Choose
36. Fencers' call
39. Sailor's OK
40. Tag-along's phrase
42. Dirty
43. Old-hat
46. Guard
47. Locales
48. Lozenges
49. Seats
50. Tennis great
51. Social class
52. Word game
53. Pro vote
54. Intercepted ciphers?
56. Folding bunk
59. No-goodnik
61. Cringe
62. Little bit
63. Letter carrier
65. Pearl hunter
66. Two-spot card
67. New York's ___ Island
68. Sovereign
69. Playground item
70. Navigational device
71. Forbid
72. Cleanser makers
73. Actor Danson
74. Ice-cream holder
75. Trademarks
77. Tired
80. Heidi Klum's mate
81. Every
85. Eave hanger
87. Ad for a Latin dance?
91. Recesses
92. Highest point
93. Elsie's call
94. Welcome item
95. Kelly, to Regis
96. Spheres
97. ___-de-France
98. Sooner, to Keats

DOWN
1. Batty
2. Winged
3. Liver product
4. Maui wreath
5. Charged atom
6. Motor
7. Tall and thin
8. Work units
9. Uncle, in Seville
10. Modeled
11. Trims
12. Coral structure
13. Thus
14. Neglected to attend the sit-in?
15. Mr. Vigoda
16. Wager
22. Fortune recipient
23. Fury
27. Hive dweller
29. Crude metals
30. Kooky
31. Glasgow girl
32. Ogle
34. Skin hole
35. Fiddles
36. School paper
37. Clamor
38. Batman's lunch buy?
40. Fixes
41. Inside: abbr.
43. Ski trail
44. Add to the pot
45. Crafter's tool
46. Passover meal
48. Morning Prayer
49. One who remains
51. Barbarian of films
52. Skiff mover
54. Video player

PUZZLE 495

55. Grotto
57. Writer Wilde
58. Muscles
60. Singer James
62. Type of diver
63. Furtive summons
64. Plains tribe
65. ___ buggy
66. Kaput
68. Managed
69. Inheritor
71. Lad
72. Deli meat
74. Peak
75. Glenn of talk et al.
76. Cheer
78. Sound return
79. Pub quaffs
80. Thrust
82. Wile E. Coyote's supplier
83. Burn
84. Loathe
85. Company's word: abbr.
86. VIP's job title: abbr.
87. U.S. Seal source: abbr.
88. Above, to bards
89. Army bigwig: abbr.
90. Garden tool

PUZZLE 496

BREAK A LEG!

ACROSS

1. Foot part
7. Amy Winehouse hit
12. Large home
18. Mosque roof
19. Florida city
20. Orchestra member
21. ___ dictum
22. Prankster's cup
24. Zero
25. Bayou bye
27. Carried
28. Room, to Pedro
30. Word form for egg
31. Sacred bull
33. Viewer's letters
36. Lots
38. Montgomery song, with "The"
42. Computer note
45. Meager
47. Ohio city
48. '70s British band
51. Head protectors
52. Bohemian
53. Makes cider
54. Loves to excess
55. God, to Cato
56. Nautical term
57. '60s protest
58. Mrs. Bundy
61. Gather
62. In a container
63. Actress Moore
64. Laments loudly
67. Virescent shade
69. Chopping down
70. Tank feature
71. Ancient region
72. Workplace no-no
74. Heat unit: abbr.
76. ___ de deux
77. Theories
78. Have the flu
79. Damsel
83. Port-au-Prince's site
86. People of Hokkaido, Japan
88. Old airline
89. Purchases that last
94. Praying insect
96. Writer Eugene ___
97. Of the snout
98. Slanders
99. Lords, e.g.
100. Cubic meter
101. Every 12 months

DOWN

1. Computer images
2. Red Sea region, once
3. Slosh
4. Tyke
5. Zeno's birthplace
6. Let off
7. Cowboy contest
8. Off-white
9. "Bali ___"
10. Mass apparel
11. Sinclair Lewis novel
12. Always
13. Warning
14. Painted metalware
15. ___ carte
16. Song syllables
17. Printing measures
23. Mislaid
26. Climbing plant
29. Friendship
31. Ladd et al.
32. Liquid measure
33. Exhaust
34. Londoner, e.g.
35. Woeful word
37. Each bit
39. Current following the wind
40. Ms. Burstyn
41. Workout sites
42. Zounds!
43. French mother
44. Against
45. "___ Marner"
46. Tranquil
49. Stoppage
50. Assume
51. Inn's cousin
54. Wholesaler: abbr.
56. Amid
57. Skater Yuka ___
58. Hammerhead's end

PUZZLE 496

59. China's ___ Shan mountain
60. Ms. Lollobrigida
61. Calais chum
62. Vegas freebies
63. Wry
64. Poker piece
65. Castor's mom
66. Pointed tools
67. Hat part
68. Jewelers' group: abbr.
70. Hands out
73. Location
74. Family
75. Graceless
78. Walkway
80. Rose-based perfume
81. Twist
82. Impudent
83. Frozen rain
84. Skilled
85. Troubles
86. Hebrew month
87. Identical
89. Singer Ho
90. One, to Miguel
91. Yank's foe
92. Stable bit
93. Sugar suffix
95. Teachers' group: abbr.

443

PUZZLE 497

COLLEGE MOVIES

ACROSS
1. Mama's mate
5. Slenderize
9. Kennedy's was 109
15. Movie whale
19. Auth.
20. Author Bombeck
21. Obligated
22. Anjou, e.g.
23. Pacific coll.
24. Ship's canvas
25. Sioux, e.g.
26. Toodle-oo!
27. Houseman college movie
30. Reno's st.
32. Chatroom giggle
33. Umberto ___
34. Eng. honor
35. Bee bite
37. Quick bite
40. Spanish aunt
42. Window ledges
44. Shirt arm
47. Belushi college movie
50. Gallery display
53. Russian leader
54. Tropical ant
55. Holy person
56. Provoke
57. Mexican farewell
58. Irate
60. Deli order
61. High point
63. Dilly
64. Rain cloak
66. Feudal serf
68. Future chicks
69. Latin being
70. Caine college movie
75. Butter squares
79. Rocker Brian ___
80. Canadian prov.
81. Bands
86. Santa's words
87. Waterways
89. Sis's sibling
92. ___ acid
93. Persian
95. Yacht wood
96. Empty
98. Saga
99. Rose essence
100. Botch
101. Broderick college movie
103. Survived
105. Hindu dresses
107. Vane dir.
108. Frequently, to Keats
109. Frenzied
111. Beer cask
112. UFO's crewmen
114. State
116. Actress Gabor
117. Roberts college movie
124. Big horn
126. Sum's part
128. Roman road
129. Rain in Spain?
130. Bond's alma mater
131. ___ network
132. Actor Singer
133. Glass and Moody
134. Nursery items
135. "Remington ___"
136. Insipid
137. Dish carrier

DOWN
1. Mope
2. Curve
3. Mound
4. Yawning
5. Plunders
6. Dies ___
7. Arabian ruler
8. Powder
9. Mutable
10. ___ Town
11. Invited
12. ___-Wan Kenobi
13. Ladd and Hale
14. Maxims
15. Pick
16. Kilmer college movie
17. Roman censor
18. Inland sea
28. Official records
29. Lift
31. Country home
36. Pine leaf
37. Civil rights gp.
38. Host's speech
39. Climber's spike
41. Moby Dick's foe
42. Solar-brewed drink
43. 1974 Nobel winner
45. String players
46. Follows
48. Not fem.
49. Lubricate
51. Hardship
52. Roman fountain
56. Used up
59. This lady
61. Indigo dyes
62. Gobbles up
65. Baltic Sea feeder
67. Barren
71. Wed
72. Screen
73. Anne's were green

PUZZLE 497

74. Government org.
75. Test tube
76. Heart artery
77. Martin/Lewis college movie
78. Musical piece
82. Author Philip ___
83. Texas mission
84. Rice dish
85. Smell
88. Jug handles
90. Ump's cousin
91. Rowing blades
94. Ms. Dunne
96. Dinnerware
97. Study
101. Roll
102. Backdrops
104. Sofas
106. Sans key
110. Academy student
113. Brainy
114. Printer's term
115. Sedan, e.g.
117. Pierre's mom
118. Branch
119. Romance lang.
120. Elisabeth Shue role
121. Mad doctor's helper
122. Moon goddess
123. Simple
125. Ques.'s reply
127. Payable now

PUZZLE 498

STATE CAPITALS, SORTA

ACROSS
1. Deli offerings
5. Bird's noise
10. Friendly Islands
15. Narrow valley
19. Fencing blade
20. Former French coin
21. The Hunter
22. Traveled
23. Iron Temple, in Vermont
25. Out near bog, in Louisiana
27. Captivate
28. Sudden flood
30. Western
31. Climbing vine
32. Mythical enchantress
33. Flair
35. Sofa
39. Simple
40. Listen to
41. Fast jet, once
44. Obvious
45. Ten room gym, in Alabama
47. Loafer, e.g.
48. Gambling town
49. Anguish
50. Writer Leon ___
51. Shade
52. Yoko ___
53. Halts a lease, in Florida
57. Apple, e.g.
58. European era
60. New York Bay island
61. Prop
62. Untruths
63. Fragrant shrub
64. Cloudburst
65. Injection sources
68. English poet
69. Agent
73. Trenches
74. Ringed flips, in Illinois
76. "___ There Was You"
77. Don Juan's mom
78. Wings
79. Castor's mother
80. Coal product
81. Remain
82. Scary tonic, in Nevada
86. Military coat
87. Egg source
88. Propelled
89. Blanches
90. Most peeved
91. Agenda
92. Cougars
93. "___ Pupil"
94. Proverb
97. Bargains
98. Breach of etiquette
103. Ever nip cod, in Rhode Island
106. Most arcane, in California
108. Reasonable
109. Primp
110. Les ___-Unis
111. Milan's lang.
112. Looker
113. Lifeless
114. ___ Jessica Parker
115. Master

DOWN
1. Dotted, in heraldry
2. Once's follower
3. Crooked
4. Actor Green
5. Stick
6. Not flat
7. Rotten
8. Before, in poems
9. Keep at it
10. Cigarette filling
11. Speechify
12. Nick at ___
13. Sticky stuff
14. Actress Blyth
15. Gripe
16. Boor
17. Brink
18. ___-do-well
24. Nosy type
26. Hearty laugh
29. Prude
32. Showy flower
33. Uncanny
34. Places
35. Atlantic fish
36. TV's Verdugo
37. Choir voice
38. Cosmic truth
39. Simmers
40. "___ Johnny!"
41. Yell
42. Of sound
43. Incisors
45. Guys
46. ___ to my ears
47. High-___
49. Book parts
53. Coin side
54. Alpine girl
55. Steve or Tim
56. Street talk
57. Sauteed
59. Clumsy
61. Lily type

PUZZLE 498

63. Entices
64. Thin
65. Mennonite group
66. ___ Carlo
67. Hymn of praise
68. Separate
69. Special menus
70. Do penance
71. Polynesian images
72. Pick
74. Incline
75. Soars
78. Perfect serves
80. Mongrel
83. Wealthy
84. Appoint
85. Groups
86. ___ pole
88. ___ Valley
90. Hanks movie
91. Suitor
92. Indiana cager
93. Chief artery
94. Church part
95. Medical photo
96. Actress Skye
97. Snick or ___
98. Wound memento
99. Put wood over
100. ___ thin air
101. Lead actor
102. Form
104. Resolution abbr.
105. Coastal eagle
107. ___ glance

PUZZLE 499

MUG SHOTS

ACROSS
1. Map book
6. Opposite of seld
9. Outfitted
14. Decorous
19. Window cover
20. Golf norm
21. Congregation
22. Diagram
23. Grimace
25. Confronted with
27. French island
28. Welt
29. Trivial
30. Gas pump number
31. Archer's aim
33. Aquatic flier
35. Slippery
37. Injure
38. Angler's tool
40. Speech imperfection
42. Tousle
44. Like lungs
47. Emit coherent light
49. Phony moniker
52. Powder ingredient
56. Moby's pursuer
57. Maintaining dignity
59. Dietary concern
60. Tedious
62. Pang
63. Isolated from others
64. Do a garden chore
65. Baseball deal
67. "___ Karenina"
68. Water down
69. Companies
71. Jumbo
73. Most faulty
74. Catches
76. Fruit peel
77. Strong string
79. Passing craze
82. Tex-Mex fare
83. Bundle
85. Debilitate
87. Becomes uniform
88. Happiness symbol
90. Elvis, e.g.
91. Ancient Persian
92. Tack
93. Wedding dessert
94. Sheds tears
95. Hollow
97. Rob Roy, e.g.
99. "Pygmalion" author
101. Lifetime
104. Lights
107. Entertain
109. Not purchased
113. Ball queens
115. Elevated
117. Red deer
119. Mama pig
120. From outward appearances
122. Mask
124. Pinch pennies
125. Time waster
126. Press covering
127. Splendid
128. Toots
129. Overgrown
130. Actress Arthur
131. Great!

DOWN
1. Fess up
2. Nonsense syllables
3. L.A. cager
4. Gibbon or gorilla
5. Ocean plants
6. Fiery stone
7. Element
8. Three, in Milan
9. Non-citizens
10. Deliver a diatribe
11. Kitchen gloves
12. ___ alcohol
13. Artificial color
14. Piles
15. Diplomat's skill
16. Nautical position
17. Ms. Massey
18. Yield respectfully
24. Lot
26. Central point
29. Minister
32. Diving bird
34. Additional
36. Vision
39. Woolly animals
41. Tarring
43. Snapshots
44. Wood slat
45. Akron's state
46. Brazen
48. Made a hole in one
50. Finch
51. Swenson of "Benson"
53. Reversal
54. Afforded
55. Algonquian
57. Molds
58. Scholarship winner
59. More just
61. Accent
66. Call forth
68. Gift receiver

PUZZLE 499

70. Did a laundry job
72. Feet joints
73. Reacts to pain
74. Stalk
75. Wheel hub
76. Male merinos
78. Frail
80. On the summit
81. Lairs
83. Biblical song
84. Mogul
86. Looks at
89. Suets
92. Indifferent
94. Meanders
96. Chooses by vote
98. Bright
100. Goth conquerors
101. Embarrass
102. Arrive at
103. Pixyish
105. Spanish museum
106. Famed opera soprano
108. Feudal lord
110. Orange choice
111. Provincial
112. Reside
114. Lean and ___
116. Litigates
118. Columnist Chase
121. Spirit
122. Tall tale
123. Infrequent

PUZZLE 500

"DEF" JAM

ACROSS

1. Prince of India
6. Evergreens
10. Ms. West
13. Valerie ___ of "Rhoda"
19. Author Zola
20. Pitching stats
21. "The Simpsons" clerk
22. Form a thought
23. Legal eagle for the people
26. Sent
27. Clerical robe
28. Santa's perch
29. Cupid's weapon
31. Gym teacher's deg.
32. Appear
34. Administrator
37. Greek Neptune
41. Swagger
43. "I cannot tell ___"
44. Water source
45. Painter Guido ___
46. Army privs.
48. Singer Bryant
51. Portentous
53. Soft shoe
56. "A Tale of Two Cities" villainess
60. Sugary suffix
61. Mr. Parseghian
62. Ret.
63. Mother ___
64. Dusky cuckoo
66. Veldt antelope
67. Fertile soil
69. Theater drops
71. Dynamic starter
74. Saunters
76. Terminal abbr.
78. Poet's dusk
79. Traces
81. Fit to ___
82. Recorded history
85. Pranks
87. Cheer
88. Muhammad ___
90. Tin Woodman's request
92. Tack
93. Big diamond?
94. Vaselike vessel
96. Military fortification
99. "___ Na Na"
100. Supporting musicians
102. Card's hero
103. RR locale
105. Keep it!
106. Babylonian storm god
108. Soggy
111. Wet snow
115. Recommendation
117. Fortified place
120. Confederate
121. To's opposite
122. Teams of oxen
124. Garble
126. ___ the mark
127. Make fair
130. The "HD" in "HD-TV"
134. Leave
135. Cool ___ cucumber
136. Motel room
137. Florida city
138. Deer horn
139. ID info
140. Be stuck (on)
141. Collect

DOWN

1. Go by again
2. Talisman
3. Horse that balks
4. Entirely
5. Offspring
6. Indiana Jones's hat
7. Irate
8. H.R.H.'s fliers
9. Vane dir.
10. Spanish mother
11. Copier
12. France's site
13. In style
14. Kind of brick
15. Breathe
16. Cracker topper
17. Summer abroad
18. Sunburned
24. Army bed
25. Dundee refusal
30. Tungsten
33. Coffee cup
35. Where Anna taught
36. Creed
38. Mine refuse
39. Heavy burden
40. Cairo's river
42. Opportune
44. Sealed, as a letter
47. Triangular Indian pastry
49. The ___ of March
50. Canonical hour
52. English drink
53. Molten rock
54. "Ripley's Believe It ___"
55. Vicious circle
57. Fourth letter
58. Old lace's pal
59. Foolish
65. Actress Martin
68. Having a stem
70. Unemotional types

PUZZLE 500

72. Attain
73. Actor Milo ___
75. Sniggler's prey
77. Alaska roadway, once
80. Small cays
83. 12:00 p.m.
84. Youth safety org.
86. TV's Rather
89. Theory
91. Craves
94. Cold War letters
95. Church ceremony
97. Eye drop
98. Coll. group
101. Everlasting
104. ___ carte
107. Maui greetings
109. Outcast
110. Courteous
112. Last syllable of a word
113. Sailboats
114. Laughing beasts
116. Path
117. Initiated
118. Fire remains
119. Sister
123. Smooch
125. Beatles' meter maid
127. Ms. Longoria
128. Martin ___ Buren
129. Apiece
131. Loser
132. Rocker Brian ___
133. Flat hat

PUZZLE 501

Diagramless crosswords are solved by using the clues and their numbers to fill in the answer words and the arrangement of black squares. Insert the number of each clue with the first letter of its answer, across and down. Fill in a black square at the end of each answer. Every black square must have a corresponding black square on the opposite side of the diagram to form a diagonally symmetrical pattern. Puzzles 501 and 502 have been started for you.

ACROSS
1. Fishhook part
5. Chow hall
9. Hero's award
10. Make up on the spot
12. Stopped sleeping
13. Gaucho's rope
14. Took a chance
15. Playful water creature
16. "Chances ___"
17. Shad eggs
18. Goods
24. Barnyard bird
25. Zilch
26. Raring to go
29. Tied
31. Adjusted musically
32. Active
33. Blot out
34. Dissuade
35. Amazed
36. Catches sight of

DOWN
1. Use caution
2. Worshiper
3. Garden implement
4. Seeped
5. Strand
6. Shortened, as a film
7. Thin board
8. Location
9. Lady's title
11. Soap cake
17. Hightailed it
19. Cracker topper
20. Rounded up
21. Provoke
22. Strainers
23. More mature
26. Somme summer
27. Atmosphere
28. Chew on, as a bone
29. Chaps
30. Out of the wind

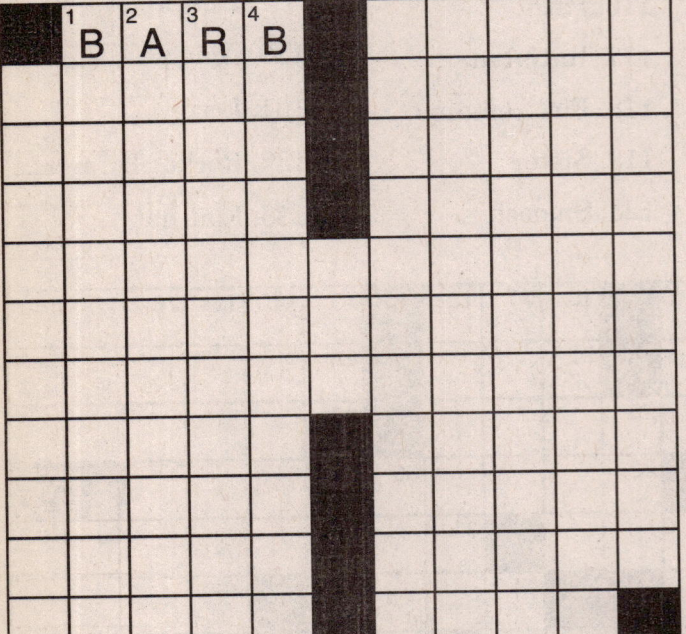

PUZZLE 502

ACROSS
1. Santa's staffer
4. Like Mother Hubbard
7. Aura
8. Hawaiian fare
9. Sneaky
10. Superman's chest letter
11. Ocean
12. Large bird
14. Feel
16. Cattle mark
18. Enfold
19. Byron's always
21. Former Milan money
23. Boat blade
24. Mature
25. Excess
26. Perfect place
28. Personal commitment
29. Actor Rob ___
30. Ravage
32. Clipped
34. Gentleman
35. Thanksgiving veggie
36. Tree fluid
38. Decimal base
39. ___ out (barely make)
40. Undivided
41. Repair with stitches
42. Spoil

DOWN
1. Relax
2. Purple bloomer
3. Cook in oil
4. Unfasten, in verse
5. Failure
6. Bleak
11. Hang gliders, e.g.
13. Unvarying
14. Cashless deal
15. Hoist
16. Steeps
17. Sketched
18. Deep suffering
20. Pride
22. Gulped down
27. Sounds
29. Temporary auto
31. Daddy duck
33. Laughing animal
37. Bench
38. Tabby's pop

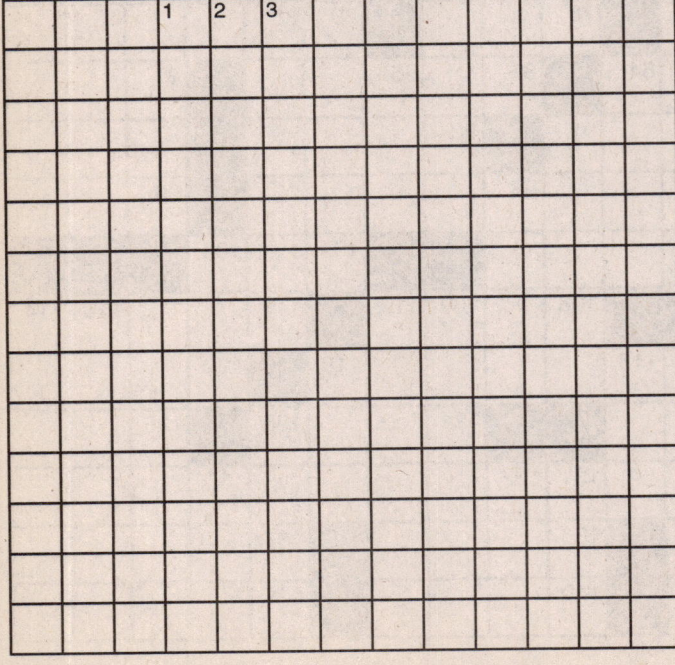

PUZZLE 503

ACROSS
1. Brooch
4. Walking aids
6. Little girls' hats
8. Preschooler
9. Freckle
10. Rarer than rare
11. Saute
12. Pepper type
13. Tint
14. Recuperate
15. Unflappable
17. Heavy metal
18. Difficult
19. Hair holder
20. Indefinite number
21. Seedcase
22. Loafer, e.g.
23. Purring pet
24. Popular song
25. Museum pieces
26. Sucker
27. Akin
30. Station
31. Embroider

DOWN
1. Prospect for gold
2. Roadside stop
3. "___ Things"
4. Foldup bed
5. Put away
6. Cereal dish
7. Filthy place
8. Lofty
10. Scan a book
12. Droplet
13. Coal bucket
14. Cackler
15. Made the scene
16. Pay dirt
17. Small boy
18. Owl's call
19. Soda containers
20. Liner
21. Peeled
22. Food fish
23. Bumper ___
26. Filming site
28. King Kong, e.g.
29. Haul

Starting box on page 562

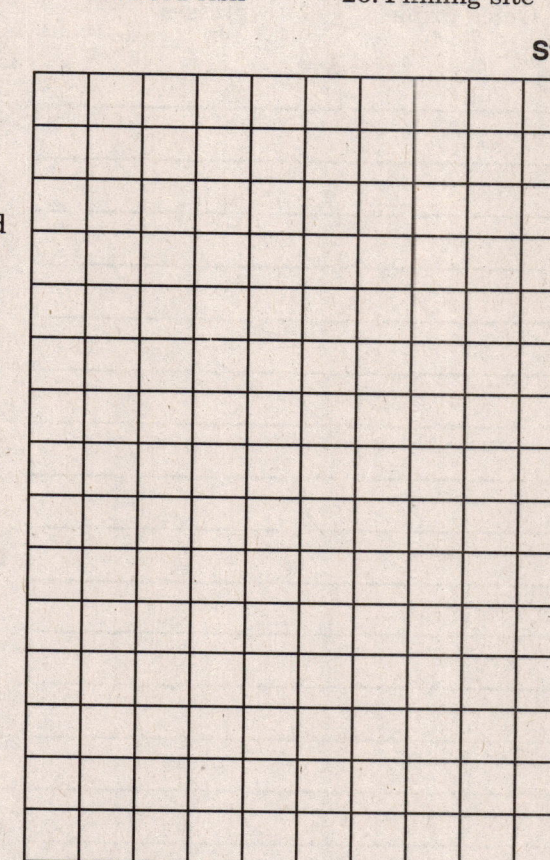

Nine of Diamonds

PUZZLE 504

Fill the small diamonds in the diagram with the 2-letter pieces in the box to form the answers to the clues. All answer words have eight letters and read clockwise around the corresponding number. Words overlap in the diagram so that a 2-letter piece may be used in more than one word.

AR	AS	BO	CA	CH	FI	HE	LE
LE	LL	MB	ND	OD	PA	RA	RD
RE	RE	SE	SE	SS	TE	TI	WO

1. Hearth fuel
2. Access code
3. Disconnect
4. Kit's companion
5. Unwearied
6. Scold
7. Register
8. Look like
9. Beach item

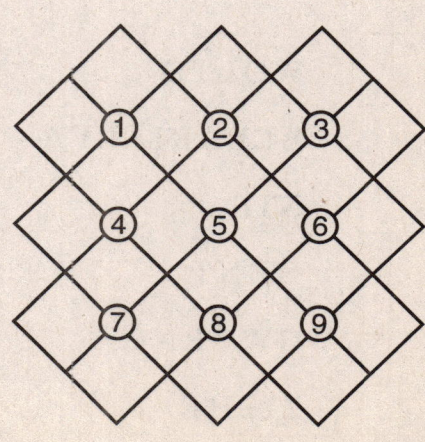

PUZZLE 505

ACROSS
1. Level
5. Corn core
8. Cotton bundle
9. Cry of despair
11. Exhale
12. Leases
14. Quick drink
15. Bambi's mom
16. Liability
19. Conform
21. Viewed
22. ___ Quixote
23. Type of glasses
26. ___ trip
27. Promissory note
30. Serious
34. Card game
35. Young chap
37. Veiled lady
39. Cleveland's state
41. Bit for Silver
42. Singer Morrison
44. Wide open
47. Shine's partner
48. Celebrity
49. Segment
50. Spud bud
51. Clutter

DOWN
1. Recedes
2. Genuine
3. Weds secretly
4. Recent
5. Auto
6. Fiesta shout
7. Kerchief
10. Halt!
13. Fixed
17. Movie swine
18. Thin branch
19. Hoopla
20. Snow White's pal
24. Enemy
25. Whopper
28. Norway's capital
29. Provo's locale
31. Disturb
32. Get ___ of
33. Compass pt.
36. Heavenly
37. Feather wrap
38. Tatters
40. Desert spring
43. Hair holders
45. Income
46. Poet's before
47. Island drink

Starting box on page 562

PUZZLE 506

Wacky Words

Rearrange each group of letters to form a word with one letter left over. When done correctly, these words form a wacky definition of the word formed by the leftover letters when read from top to bottom.

DEFINITION **WORD**

WOLTO

BLEARIALVA

NIE

HENT

GWORNC

ZISHE

PUZZLE 507

ACROSS
1. Mouth bone
4. Spanish gold
5. Quakes
9. Neptune's domain
10. Chip accompaniment
11. "____ sesame!"
12. Young male
13. Genesis name
14. Bronx attraction
16. Stamping tool
17. Persuade
18. Roll of cash
19. Parking field
20. Oliver's request
21. Total amount
22. Chunk of eternity
23. Cycle
25. Authorize
27. Anderson of "WKRP in Cincinnati"
28. Bitter anger
29. Hither and ____
30. Difficulty
33. Beluga delicacy
34. Sink in the middle

DOWN
1. Baseball's DiMaggio
2. Type of wrestling
3. Bin for logs
5. Abound
6. Conducted
7. ____ de Janeiro
8. Enemy agent
9. Baden-Baden, e.g.
11. "____ to Joy"
13. Military clerk
14. Zip along
15. Feed-bag tidbit
16. Shucks!
17. Piece of evidence
18. Court romantically
20. Space rocks
21. Descend Mt. Snow
23. Cannon sound
24. Lodging place
25. Rim
26. Botch things
27. Drain-cleaner chemical
31. Tropical snake
32. Voyage segment

Starting box on page 562

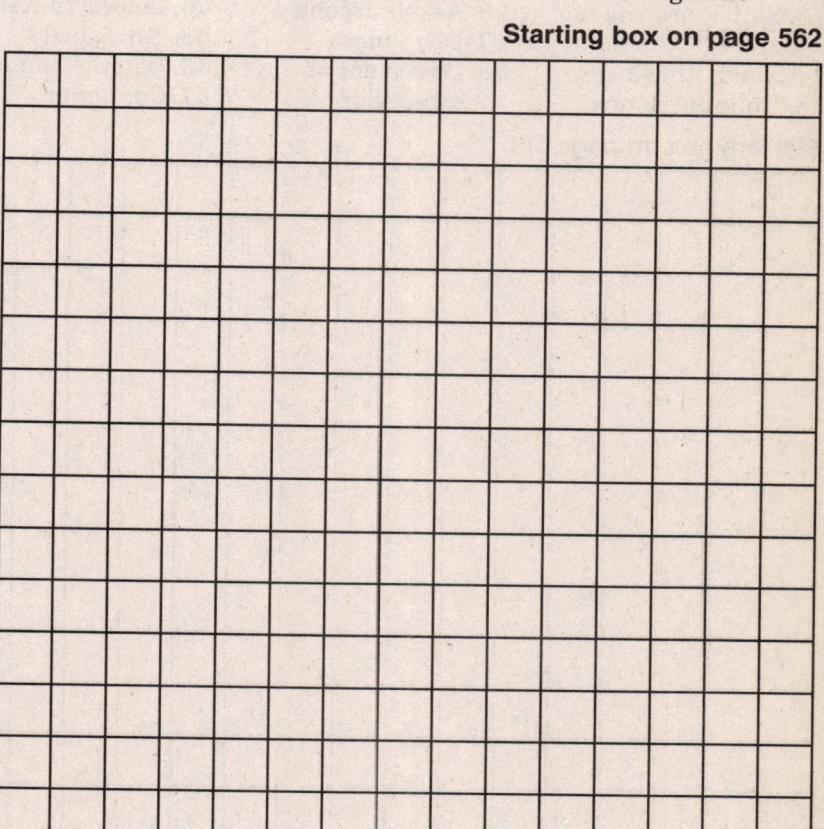

Foursomes

PUZZLE 508

In each puzzle the letters have different numerical values from 1 to 9. Four sums of combinations of four letters are indicated by the arrows. For example, in the first puzzle, 18 is the sum of the values of the letters L, A, I, and E. Find the values of the letters and place them on the correspondingly numbered blanks to spell a word or phrase. The center letter is entered to start you off.

1.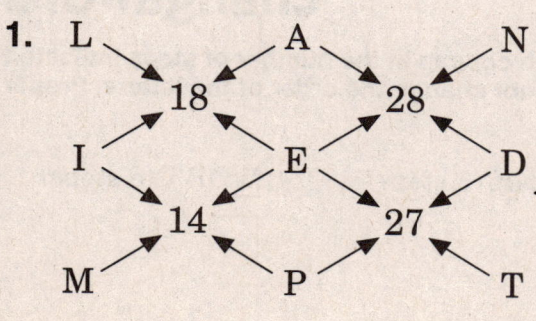

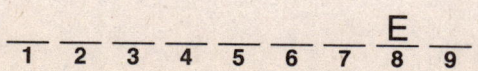

2.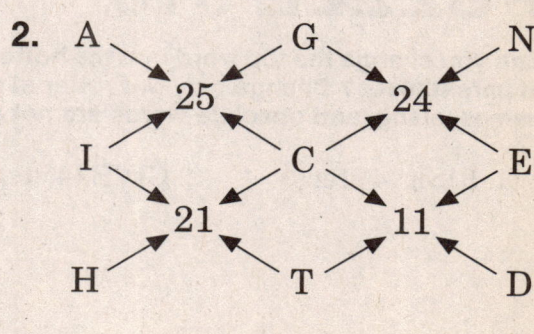

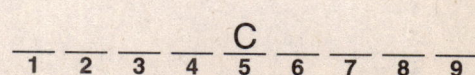

PUZZLE 509

ACROSS
1. Receive
4. Of fatty acid
6. Fourth notes
9. Benefactor
11. Dance
13. Skiff's propellers
14. XVII
17. Single thickness
18. Building annex
19. Retired for the night
21. Warm
22. Dough
24. Shorebird
25. Small cask
26. Asked urgently
27. Doe's mate
28. Document of ownership
29. He has it coming
30. Give up, as territory
31. ___ of passage
32. Cuckoo
33. Show relief
34. Cubed
37. Impress clearly
38. Ankle-length skirt
39. Boring
40. Before, to Keats
43. Tarnished
46. Botanic angle
47. Contempt
48. Extreme
50. Wilt
51. Swiss song
52. Hairstyling substance

DOWN
1. Magnificence
2. Poetic twilights
3. Scale notes
4. Certain gem
5. Bus. entities
6. Sharp tooth
7. Model Carol ___
8. Embezzle
9. Drench
10. Fuse again
11. Departed
12. Indian cow
15. Medicine bottle
16. Cravat
20. Gloom, in literature
21. Colored
23. Humpty Dumpty, e.g.
24. Great joy
26. Far East three-wheeler
27. Cain's brother
28. Strauss fabric
29. Towering
30. Lout
31. Wealthier
33. "___ Wars"
35. Former mates
36. Phonograph records
37. Zest
39. Ice mass
40. Be outstanding
41. Irani currency
42. Corner shape
44. Extinct bird
45. Dennis or Doris
46. Deputy
49. Lassie, e.g.

Starting box on page 562

PUZZLE 510 — Changaword

Can you change the top word into the bottom word in each column in the number of steps indicated in parentheses? Change only one letter at a time and do not change the order of the letters. Proper names, slang, and obsolete words are not allowed.

1. RISE (4 steps)
2. GIVE (4 steps)
3. SINK (6 steps)
4. WORK (6 steps)

FALL   TAKE   SWIM   PLAY

PUZZLE 511

ACROSS
1. Large parrot
4. Statesman Kissinger
6. Leader of the flock
9. Wile E. et al.
11. Trim of nonlean parts
13. Turn over ___ leaf
14. Descended from forebears
17. Bunk or cot
18. Depose
19. Pitfall
21. Difficult voyage
22. Sleep disorder
24. Bound firmly
25. Styling aid
26. Deviate suddenly
27. Sidewalk border
28. Sly glance
29. Speaker's platform
30. "___ Yesterday"
31. Heavy twine
32. "Pumping Iron" concerns
33. Dolt
34. Horse sound
37. Fabric joint
38. Flounder's cousin
39. Passing fashions
40. Hip-hop music
43. Least broad
46. Chalet feature
47. Portals
48. Tastier
50. Gesture agreement
51. Verbs' colleagues
52. Mule's father

8. A Von Trapp daughter
9. Pickup section
10. Noisy sleeper
11. Piece of office furniture
12. Diamond protector
15. Prompted
16. Listless
20. Equals
21. Cake layer
23. Mass robe

24. High schooler
26. Rendition
27. Tarot, e.g.
28. Ear projections
29. Adverse fate
30. Prohibit
31. Refined
33. Capitulate
35. Delighted
36. Long-legged wader

37. Carpentry tools
39. Mustang maker
40. "The ___ of Ranchipur"
41. Latin farewells
42. By means of
44. Pooh's pal
45. Wine cask
46. Big birds
49. Bird no more

DOWN
1. Entered data
2. Plenty, once
3. Gallery exhibit
4. Put an edge on
5. Word of assent
6. Sit a spell
7. Rearward, on a boat

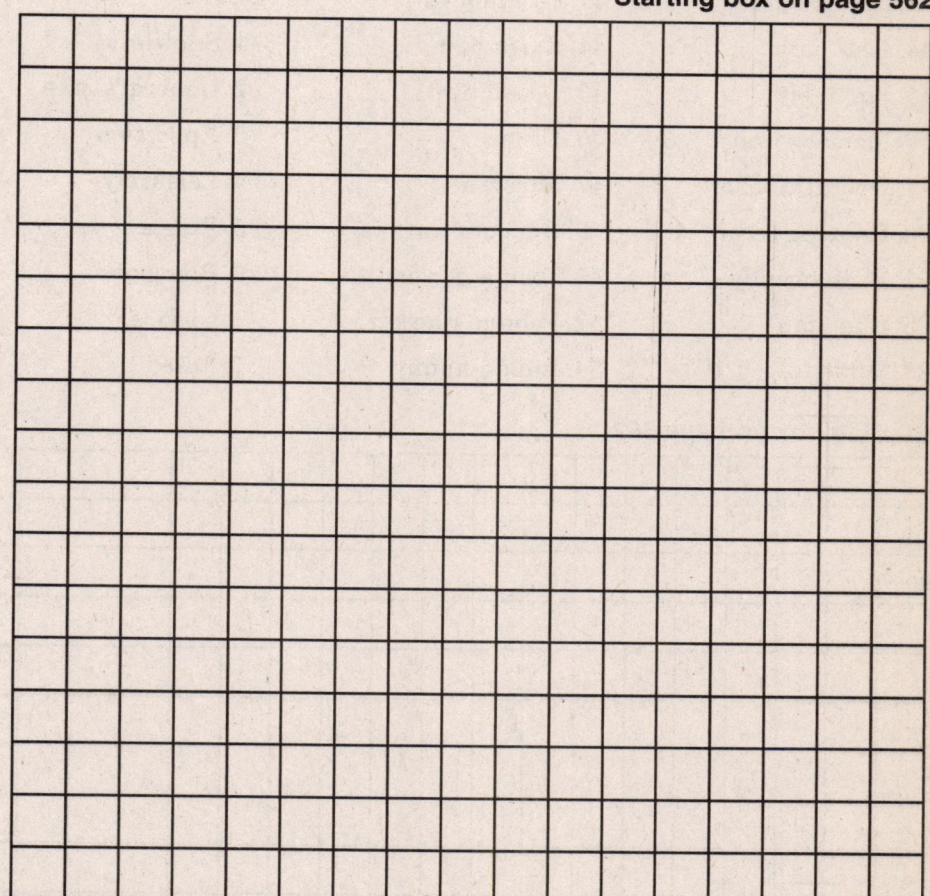

Starting box on page 562

Substitutions

PUZZLE 512

In these addition problems, letters are substituted for numbers. When the letters are placed in order from 0 to 9, they will spell a 10-letter word. The same code is used in all three problems.

```
   C O L D         A C T O R         P U L L
 + C O L A       + I D O L         + L O A D
 ─────────       ─────────         ─────────
   1 1 6 6 6     6 9 8 7 2         5 9 9 3
```

10-LETTER WORD: _ _ _ _ _ _ _ _ _ _
                0 1 2 3 4 5 6 7 8 9

PUZZLE 513

ACROSS

1. Dry watercourse
5. Fine dirt
9. Hurried
10. Hindu guitar
11. ___ wave
12. Aboveboard
14. Leaf part
15. Small bit
16. Memory unit
17. Operatic voice
20. Printing term
21. Walk heavily
25. Elmo fan
28. Verve
30. Corporate symbol
31. Dubuque native
33. Maxim
37. Time gone by
38. Deliverance
40. Stocking line
42. Techniques
44. Extra pay
45. Ocean bird
46. Drone
47. Moisten
48. Bigfoot's kin
49. Took a powder
52. Pointed marker
54. Indian nanny
58. Black cuckoos
60. Centers
61. Titles
65. Ills
66. Health worker
67. Insignificant
68. Reflex site
69. Peerless person

DOWN

1. Snowiest
2. General's man
3. Apportion
4. Leisurely
5. Finger
6. Being of service
7. Posed
8. Cut shorter
10. Alluring
11. Foreign farewells
12. Chemist's room
13. Throng
18. At sixes and ___
19. Auricular
21. Fabric layer
22. Impend
23. Folklore fiend
24. Biblical verb
25. Warty critter
26. Wise birds
27. Hebrew letter
29. Disorderly
31. Compound similar to another
32. Arrest
33. Forest sight
34. Total defeat
35. Lap pup, for short
36. Tense
39. Haul
41. ___ tai
43. Hawaiian dance
50. More brittle
51. Salad servers
53. Best
54. Blazing
55. Bullwinkle, e.g.
56. Teen woe
57. Part of HRH
59. Plunged
61. Showroom example
62. Level
63. Beget
64. Large cask

Starting box on page 562

PUZZLE 514

• STATES IN BLOOM •

ACROSS
1. Passing fancy
4. Units of work
8. Cry of discovery
9. Gather in
10. Rocky ledge
11. Halloween wear
14. Ready, ___, fire!
15. Graf's rival
18. Notre ___
20. Trail behind
22. Personal servant
24. Okra dish
27. Vermont's blossom
30. Astronaut Shepard
33. Gershwin brother
34. 43,560 square feet
35. Codlike food fish
36. "___ Man"
37. Make lace
38. Hot temper
39. Sees socially
41. Snakelike swimmer
42. Greek letters
43. Solidifies
44. No longer is
47. Run in neutral
51. Shortly
53. Kirk's crewmate
54. Indian gowns
55. Not well
58. Alaska's blossom
62. Absolutely!
63. Smallest amount
65. Nothing but
66. Went by jet
68. Boundary
69. Name
70. Hill's opposite
72. Clerical vestment
75. Gallivant
78. Friend, in Barcelona
80. Author Tolstoy
81. Shed tears
84. Reed instrument
86. Promise
87. Med. course
88. Night bird
89. ___ ho!
90. Nevada's blossom
92. "Bad Boys" costar
94. Indian, e.g.
97. Tree's anchor
98. ___ monster
100. Lift
102. CIA predecessor
103. Tropical storm
106. Differently
108. Without
109. Chew
110. Double curve
111. Tango numero

DOWN
1. Stiff
2. Gotcha!
3. Hounds
4. Unevenly worn
5. Legal matter
6. Hood's gun
7. Tater
10. Mythical enchantress
11. Cartoon frame
12. Louisiana's blossom
13. Cassowary's kin
14. Location
16. Occurrences
17. Shirt size
19. Give off
21. Nebraska's blossom
23. Road covering
25. Swimsuit part
26. Cereal grain
27. Umbrella weather
28. Eggshell
29. Lab container
31. Confederate general
32. Jungle animal
40. Moved in water
43. Infant's sound
45. Pub drink
46. Kansas's blossom
48. Withered
49. Pinocchio's misdeed
50. Curvy letter
52. Not seld
53. Sow's place
54. Fr. holy woman
55. Parisian island
56. Conducted
57. Dillydally
59. Type of antelope
60. Exile site
61. Mexican "Rah!"
64. Utah's blossom
67. Cashews' cousins
70. Armless sofas
71. Excited
73. Thompson et al.
74. Two together
76. Arab cloak
77. Wear
79. Kenyan tribesman
81. Fa follower
82. Have debts
83. Online journal
85. Tokyo, formerly
87. Came up
91. Promotes
93. Young bug
95. Picked
96. A long time
99. Lhasa ___
101. Prepared a golf ball
104. Old witch
105. Dollar bill
107. Thai language

Starting box on page 562

PUZZLE 515

ACROSS
1. Pronoun
4. Equal to the task
8. Short rests
12. Actor Knight
13. Linen source
14. Roll topping
15. Work measure
16. Musical sound
17. Travel endorsement
18. Sonnet
20. Yarn weaver
22. Compose
24. Aid
27. Boss, at times
32. Prevent
33. Foremost
34. Biological model
36. Goober
37. Take off
39. Helmet, e.g.
43. Irish river
47. TV's McBeal
48. Badger
50. Be sick
51. Frenzy
52. Soft light
53. Electees
54. Wood knot
55. Medieval serf
56. Bruce or Spike

DOWN
1. Phase
2. Idol
3. On the cutting ___
4. Rear, to Popeye
5. Fair-haired woman
6. Veranda
7. Strains
8. PBS science show
9. Came down
10. Mexican moola
11. Glide aloft
19. Tiny
21. Harvester
23. Aromatic spice
24. Shred
25. First lady?
26. Congress mem.
28. Short-billed flier
29. Cousins, e.g.
30. Australian bird
31. Steep
35. Appear
36. Release
38. Scoops
39. Listen
40. Panache
41. Pond organism
42. One who colors
44. Chair ___
45. Baseball count
46. At another place
49. Meadow muncher

PUZZLE 516

ACROSS
1. Leg
4. Unattached
8. Exam format
12. Be in hock
13. Trouser size
14. Chianti, to Luigi
15. Wager
16. "Christine" subject
17. Newts
18. Chemical compound
20. Loosen
21. Nuclear bit
23. European peak
25. Greek sandwich
26. Newspaper page
27. Social insect
30. Properly
32. Rally
34. Mythical bird
35. Like suntan lotion
37. On the pinnacle
38. Tennis point
39. Casino game
40. Stir again
44. Library stamp
47. Singles
48. Bugbear
49. Sleet, e.g.
52. Arena shape
53. Film segment
54. Birth-name word
55. Unit of force
56. Of a time
57. Set

DOWN
1. Clump
2. Fearful respect
3. Very rapid
4. Soho apartment
5. Scoundrel
6. Catch
7. Self-respect
8. Microwave, e.g.
9. Chasm
10. Oppositionist
11. Mislay
19. Urban woe
20. Hairstyle
21. Culture medium
22. Beginner
24. Tariff
26. Auricular
27. Changing
28. Sign gas
29. Misspelling
31. Deception
33. Body of water
36. Accounting book
40. Crucifix
41. Jealousy
42. Ornery
43. Wight, e.g.
45. Precinct
46. Reveal
48. Mined metal
50. Letter after bee
51. Electric fish

PUZZLE 517

• HOME FURNISHINGS •

ACROSS
1. Raced
4. Parisian season
7. End of the yr.
10. Activist Parks
11. Sermon subject
12. Trails
14. Inveterate channel-surfer
18. Tacit
20. Bodybuilder's pride
21. At any time, in verse
22. Regretting
24. ___ de la Cite
25. Layer
27. Most boorish
30. Pranks
32. Energy unit
35. Pound and Frost
36. Seer's letters
37. Ally of expediency
41. Annoyance
44. Nautical agreement
45. Jungle king
46. College cheer
47. Leasing
49. Operative
50. ABA member
51. ___-Magnon
53. Blot gently
55. In an abrupt manner
59. Under the weather
60. Polite address
61. Cote call
62. Humble
64. Fine carbon pigment
66. Palindromic sib
68. Attribute
71. ___ Paulo
72. Fracas
74. Desists
76. Cabbage salad
80. Drs. group
81. Exemplary
83. Engine additive
86. Psyche part
87. Probable
89. Rat
93. Plains dwelling
94. Drop the ball
95. Done
96. Blue
97. Society entrant
98. Singer Shannon

DOWN
1. Fabulous bird
2. Tennis great
3. Neck's back
4. Superlative suffix
5. Acapulco aunt
6. Main course
7. Hang freely
8. UFO crew
9. Board bigwig
10. Trick
12. Wordplay
13. Fine cloth
14. Popular pet
15. Kimono sash
16. Hockey legend
17. Force out
19. ___ Moines
23. "___ My Party"
26. Zebra
28. At the top of
29. ___ Jones Average
31. Egyptian cobra
33. Kindled again
34. Twinkle
37. Prohibit
38. Needle aperture
39. Cozy room
40. Daily record
42. Exhaust
43. Quaker pronoun
48. Poker-betting rule
51. Applauds
52. Latin dance
53. Obscure
54. Pub potion
55. Dull thud
56. Uncertain abbr.
57. Fond du ___
58. Jabber
60. Partner
63. Baby fox
64. Guitarist Paul
65. ___ Alamos
67. Dirty
68. Top card
69. Adriatic and Caribbean
70. Seasoned
72. Gal of song
73. Give off
75. Scale tone
77. Lascivious look
78. Before now
79. Triumphed
82. Fabric color
84. Walkman alternative
85. Reside
88. Ecology gp.
90. Wash. neighbor
91. Sphere
92. Hair application

461

PUZZLE 518

ACROSS
1. Type of duck or excuse
5. Quick attacks
10. Sculpture and dance
14. Angel's image
15. Boredom
16. Tree's anchor
17. Structural
19. Assess
20. Bind again
21. Infirm
22. Harbinger
23. Stuffs
26. Filthy place
28. Neural network
31. Snatched
33. Eternities
36. A Khan
37. Discord
39. Consume
41. ___ Lanka
42. Comprehend
43. Silent
44. It comes after pi
45. Cribbage piece
46. ___ of honor
48. Vitality
49. Anecdote
51. Emulate Estefan
52. Confederate soldiers
53. Carpenter's tool
55. Alto or soprano
57. Grassy expanse
60. Orangutan, e.g.
62. Running tracks
66. Felt obligated
67. Orderly
70. Prune
71. Sandwich requirement
72. Capri cabbage, once
73. Black-___ Susan
74. Rushlike plant
75. Whirlpool

DOWN
1. False witness
2. Complexion bane
3. Zoo ditch
4. Lure
5. Radiation unit
6. Tropical cuckoo
7. Front tooth
8. Twofold
9. Window ledges
10. Dry creek bed
11. Ramble
12. Shopping bag
13. Anna who played Nana
18. Above, poetically
24. Cruising
25. Choral compositions
27. Swarm
28. Grate
29. Heron variety
30. Subarctic forest
32. Honshu robe
34. Daring
35. Hindu title
38. Mushrooms
40. Male turkeys
42. Merganser's kin
47. Fastened like Rosie?
50. Came ashore
52. Insult
54. Flock babies
56. Adult scrod
57. Canter
58. On vacation
59. Existed
61. Pierre's papa
63. Digestive juice
64. Bacon residue
65. Kill with laughter
68. Crone
69. Pindar offering

PUZZLE 519   Squares

Each of the Squares contains an 8-letter word. It can be found by starting at one of the letters and reading either clockwise or counterclockwise. In the example the word STANDARD is found by starting at the letter S and reading counterclockwise.

Example:
```
D R A
S   D
T A N
```

1.
```
U O M
T   L
H F U
```

2.
```
E B A
I   C
W Z K
```

3.
```
S C R
Y   U
N I T
```

4.
```
H N I
C   D
A R A
```

5.
```
Y E N
T   T
A E R
```

6.
```
R U T
E   C
J U N
```

7.
```
E H E
M   V
E N T
```

8.
```
I L L
T   A
O L F
```

9.
```
N I L
M   O
A N D
```

PUZZLE 520

ACROSS
1. Exposed
6. Love seat
10. Sail pole
14. Familiarize
15. Knitter's thread
16. Trombone's kin
17. Map collection
18. Greek covered walk
19. Imitator
20. Envision
21. Narrow trail
23. Revolve
25. Wise guys?
26. Rubbish
27. Radioactive element
30. Constituting a reason
33. Marine hitchhiker
34. ___ Kippur
35. Name
37. Makes beer
38. Summer mo.
39. Point total
41. Deli sandwich
42. Piercing implement
43. Anchored
44. Lifelong citizen
47. Without direction
48. Australian marsupial, for short
49. Heron variety
50. Sesame paste
53. Track competition
54. Exasperate
57. District
58. Art ___
60. Put forth
62. Male monarch
63. Daring Knievel
64. Like decaying bread
65. Threat's final word
66. Accomplishment
67. Sporting blades

DOWN
1. Partiality
2. Chip in chips
3. Reign
4. Memorable period
5. Loses hope
6. Set of methods
7. Solemn promises
8. To's counterpart
9. Came, to acme
10. Kickoffs
11. Metamorphic stage
12. Assist in crime
13. Slightly cooked
22. Mexican water
24. "___ Send Me"
25. Winter forecast
27. City sections, shortly
28. TV repeat
29. Microscopic organism
30. Gear part
31. Cherish
32. Fishing decoys
34. Actor Brynner
36. Snoozing sites
38. Amazement
39. At a future date
40. Young horse
42. Shunned
43. Muck's partner
45. Determining medical priority
46. Electron-deficient particle
47. Ancient
49. Game-show host
50. Grab
51. Nutmeg coat
52. Roosters' mates
54. Wight, e.g.
55. Impolite
56. Lock openers
59. December 31, e.g.
61. Soak up

Bits and Pieces

PUZZLE 521

Can you identify these U.S. cities with two-word names from the Bits and Pieces shown in the boxes? The first words are always on the top and the second words on the bottom.

1. R G I / E A C
2. O R T / O R T
3. T O N / O U G
4. H I T / I N S
5. I T T / O C K
6. A N T / A R B
7. O L O / R I N
8. E D A / A P I

PUZZLE 522

ACROSS
1. Emanate
5. 2,000 pounds
8. Noble horse
12. Goose egg
13. "The ___ Express"
15. Smallville girl
16. Astringent substance
17. Certain protozoan
18. Against
19. Sport fish
21. Fireplace shelf
23. Sooner than, to a bard
24. Diamondback
28. Aphid devourer
29. Doctrine
32. Barren streambed
35. Checkup
36. Song from yesteryear
38. Gymnast
40. Doctor's customer
42. Absurd
43. Cato's road
45. Fabricate
46. Chair support
47. Amulet
50. Oak's apex
51. Islamic commander
54. Message recipient
58. Slanted font
60. Hand-cream ingredient
61. Rock bottom
65. "Paradise ___"
66. Slice off
67. Quickly
68. ___ wrestling
69. Click
70. Hurricane center
71. Bloodhound's trail

DOWN
1. Growing out
2. Wisdom tooth
3. Familiarize
4. Weather meas.
5. Male turkey
6. Bullfight shout
7. Arrest
8. Astronaut Shepard
9. ___ and rave
10. Gambling stake
11. Suspect's release money
13. Cure-all
14. Japanese noodles
20. Mouths, to Caesar
22. Slang
25. Woven material
26. Former airline
27. Most wilted
28. Bert Lahr role
29. Creative spark
30. Kitchen basin
31. Dispense
32. Moan
33. Skin condition
34. Pull behind
37. Describe
39. Midler of "The Rose"
41. Wardrobe
44. ___ the knot
48. Coliseum
49. Prone
51. Vocally
52. Gadget
53. Stage performer
54. Weakens
55. Lively spirit
56. Author Ephron
57. ___-dish pie
59. Furthermore
62. Orangutan, e.g.
63. "Queen for a ___"
64. Cover with frosting

PUZZLE 523 — Complete-A-Word

Fill in the dashes with the 4-letter answers to the clues to complete 7-letter words.

1. Dime, e.g.   __ __ M B __ __ E
2. Comrade   F __ __ __ A C __
3. Buffet   __ I N __ R __ __
4. Milky jewel   T __ __ S __ I __
5. Leash   __ __ L __ A __ T

6. Twine   P __ __ S __ __ R
7. Loud noise   __ E __ __ B A __
8. Loyal   S __ __ __ D __ L
9. Pursue   __ __ __ C T __ __ E
10. Fluctuate   __ __ __ S I T __

464

BRICK BY BRICK

PUZZLE 524

Rearrange this stack of bricks to form a crossword puzzle. The clues will help you fit the bricks into their correct places. Row 1 has been filled in for you. Use the bricks to fill in the remaining spaces.

ACROSS

1. Strike
   Female voice
   Egyptian snakes
2. Kauai porch
   Lout
   Marsh rail
3. Verbally
   Cartoon bear
   Make socks
4. Perfect scores
   Hart
   Summer quencher
5. King toppers
   Sharp ridges
6. Vote
   Warship fleets
7. Ankara official
   Roping
8. Beat
   Play part
   Violin's big brother
9. Advance stealthily
   Feel awful
10. Slugger's goal
    Pummeled
11. Gere's "American ___"
    Vacant
12. Misspeak
    Frenzy
    Hair goops
13. Lyric poems
    Math course
    Courtyard
14. Intense
    Tra-___
    Tree nut
15. Crosscurrent
    Fervor
    Chatty starlings

DOWN

1. Crib part
   Sosa's stick
   Hollow rock
2. Fella
   Develop
   Tracked sparrows, e.g.
3. Erelong
   Flee the law
   Gave consent
4. Responsible
   Acapulco money
   Eavesdrop
5. Little goat
   Sanders, e.g.
6. Zeta follower
   Chuckle
7. Chasm
   Delhi wrap
   Kazakh sea
8. Raid
   Broad tie
   Desert monster
9. Nero's garb
   Roster
   Started
10. Paper folding
    Apr. guru
11. Cattle farmer
    TV's Dawber
12. Interrogate
    Frontier
    Bequest
13. Brahms piece
    Not long.
    Bond's school
14. Lion groups
    Untruth
    Former Milan money
15. Gluts
    Ancient
    Mama's boys

BRICKS

| P E L | O R A | D E E | L L O | O R N |
| A R E | N I T | E D D | A I L | N A S |

| P   L | C E | A L A | I T | ■ A R |
| Y   E | C H | L A N | B | S S O |

| E R R | T E M | L O T | L A N | R   S |
| O D E | | L A | A L O | I   K |

| B A L | B O O | G | A C | S E H |
| A G A | Y O G | A R E | M Y | O L O |

| G | B A | S | T E N | E L S |
| P A | G I G | A C E | | T I O |

| M A D | A G E | A S | T E D | A D E |
| I N G | R I G | | | T E S |

| P O | R | A C T | A I | S T A |
| E N C | S T | R O A | U D | S |

DIAGRAM

	1	2	3	4	5	6	7	8	9	10	11	12	13	14	15
1	S	M	A	C	K	■	A	L	T	O	■	A	S	P	S
2															
3															
4															
5															
6															
7															
8															
9															
10															
11															
12															
13															
14															
15															

PUZZLE 525

ACROSS
1. Allege
6. Poor me!
10. Groovy!
13. Garden bloom
15. Let use
16. Adverse
17. Changes
18. Entrance
19. Mislead
20. Tiers
21. Hose, maybe
23. Barely earn
24. Printer's term
25. Approached
27. Aged
30. Bard's before
31. Door feature
32. Woods
34. ___ urchin
35. Movie whale
39. Oddity
40. Salary
41. Perfect
42. Stitches
43. Levy
44. Gladden
45. Inner selves
47. Annoy
48. Follower of cee
49. Seller
52. Singles
53. Grounded bird
54. Utters
56. Bolt
60. Squealer
61. Tent spikes
62. Acting company
64. Scrap
65. Border
66. Won a race
67. Foxy
68. Defeat
69. Grins

DOWN
1. Bygone ruler
2. Exec's wheels
3. Over
4. Hotels
5. Central
6. Pond plants
7. Drip
8. Feeler
9. Hi-fi
10. Secretary, e.g.
11. Identical
12. Extort
14. Affirm
22. Toledo cheer
24. Work surface
26. Home
27. Ons' counterparts
28. Folk tales
29. Depicted
31. Critical
33. Soothed
34. Jazz horn
36. Learned
37. Satchel
38. Tar's term
40. ___ de deux
41. Kinds
43. Undermine
44. Voila!
46. Scripture
47. Squid's fluid
49. Action words
50. Web note
51. Crazy
52. Desert springs
55. Omelet needs
56. Love excessively
57. Air
58. Canned meat
59. Biddies
63. Buff

466

PUZZLE 526

ACROSS
1. Crooner Crosby
5. Combat
8. Smack
12. Bouquet
13. Phony
15. Work
16. Pond plant
17. Blood passage
18. Motored
19. Answer
21. Joined
23. Hole
24. Composition
26. Varnish
30. Chex, e.g.
33. Calm
34. Legends
36. Dismiss
38. Wane
39. Brief life story
40. Female deer
41. Laced
43. ___ buddies
45. Model
46. Quake
48. Worker
50. Mushrooms, e.g.
52. Oxygen, e.g.
53. Appoint
56. Golfer's hazard
61. Halt!
62. Develop
64. Deep mud
65. Advance
66. Jeer
67. Pretends
68. Kind
69. Learn
70. Roost

DOWN
1. Wild hog
2. Still
3. Yule drinks
4. Wrestle
5. Romances
6. Concur
7. Groove
8. Wandered
9. Weave
10. Assistant
11. Begged
13. Small chicken
14. Back talks
20. Petroleum
22. Auricle
25. Teach
26. Let it stand!
27. Custom
28. Fire remnant
29. RoboCop, e.g.
31. Enthusiasm
32. Unfettered
35. Song syllables
37. Classmate
42. Rebellious
43. Easter hat
44. Fridge adornment
45. Letter carrier
47. Coffee cup
49. Faulty
51. Publish
53. Hole punches
54. Scat!
55. Fly
57. Em or Bee
58. Kind of pudding
59. Skills
60. Annoyance
63. Harass

PUZZLE 527

ACROSS

1. Plentiful
6. Carpentry tool
9. Cinema drink
13. Lasso
15. Produce fiction
16. Adored one
17. Cave
18. Bizarre
19. Like a cucumber
20. Deadly serpent
21. Quip
23. Military
24. Marble slice
26. Molt
29. Baby's father
31. Soak
35. Cherished
36. Ms. Hayworth
37. Contained
39. Force out
40. Part of MPH
41. Mediocre
42. Prospector's quest
43. Available
45. Lark
46. Fare dodger
49. Gentle
50. Travel stops
51. Combat group
53. Leno's prominence
56. Impersonate
57. Check
60. Chance
61. Clump
63. Perfect
66. Lotion lily
67. Leather punch
68. Eliminate
69. Fairy's rod
70. Handle
71. Ancient harps

DOWN

1. Pond plant
2. Spoils
3. Stage item
4. Illuminated
5. Gobble up
6. Walk heavily
7. Help out
8. Say "I do"
9. Buzzing insect
10. Air freshener target
11. Appear
12. Supporter
14. Roman cloak
22. Stomach muscles
24. Dot
25. Flee
26. Commotion
27. Cabin
28. Distinct time
29. Gushes
30. Plus
32. Sports facility
33. Rose spike
34. Soothed
35. Hiss!
38. Mommy deer
40. Fixed benches
41. Turning skewer
43. ___ up (confess)
44. Goat god
45. Alpine slider
47. Made like Babe
48. Slangy yes
52. Techie
53. Lobster appendage
54. Type of hoop
55. Church image
56. Competently
57. Cake layer
58. Poker move
59. Wax workers?
61. Cavity
62. It gives a hoot
64. Slippery fellow
65. Soar

ACROSS
1. Neckwear
6. Poetic contraction
10. Ensemble singer
14. Beach
15. File
16. Masterstroke
17. Obstruct
18. Anxious
20. Frenzied
22. Frozen water
23. Mothers
24. Feel
26. Acerbic
27. Forbids
28. Shag, e.g.
30. Substantial
34. Stubborn animal
35. Ogle
37. Make ready
39. Closed
41. Strange
42. Plow
43. Aesopian racer
44. Harmony
45. Winter ailment
46. Leavening
48. Blue above us
50. Porters
51. Sulk
53. Had
55. Fourth notes
58. Rural hotel
59. Department
60. Cravings
63. False
67. Lunch, e.g.
68. Beget
69. Chilling
70. Sins
71. Leader
72. Refine metal

DOWN
1. Hearth dust
2. That lady
3. Food fish
4. Wurlitzers, e.g.
5. Abounds
6. Excursion
7. Polish
8. Savory jelly
9. Sample
10. Routine
11. Rich earth
12. Bluefin ___
13. Selects
19. Relinquish
21. Opposite of neath
24. Strut
25. Guarantee
26. Abutting
27. Party
29. Hideous
31. Befitting
32. Knickknack
33. Cheered
36. Finch's portrayer
38. +
40. Afternoon drink
41. Amaze
47. Skewer
49. Distant
50. Rand novella
52. Loosen
54. Rubs
55. Reputation
56. Copier
57. Mast
59. Consumed
61. Chicago transports
62. Distinctive time
64. Crude mineral
65. None
66. To date

PUZZLE 528

PUZZLE 529

ACROSS
1. Backhand
5. Distant
8. Overacting actors
12. Kind
13. Like a mosaic
15. Gobs
16. Patron
17. Nimble
18. Bustle
19. Sealing ring
21. Rummy game
22. Border
23. Indemnifies
25. Torch
26. Tack on
29. Heir
30. Disclaim
32. ___ capita
33. Squealed
35. Assemble
39. Overjoy
41. "___ Send Me"
43. Fatigued
44. Harshness
45. Missteps
47. Soak up
48. Pesky bug
51. Beak
52. Flock member
53. Bounce back
56. Disaster
58. Spotted cube
59. Smidgen
60. Dash
65. Clutch
67. Eat away
69. Icicle spot
70. Hosiery hue
71. Less cooked
72. Malt drinks
73. Fathers
74. Mend
75. Variety

DOWN
1. Cozy
2. Ms. Kudrow
3. Pros
4. Bonus
5. ___ Newton
6. Adjust
7. Depended on
8. Cap
9. Maui greeting
10. Computer adjunct
11. Trample
13. Skin art
14. Compact
20. Asian
24. Lone
25. Old instrument
26. Impersonator
27. Hero store
28. Tow
31. Paper deliverer
34. Mommy deer
36. Luxury
37. Boast
38. Breed
40. Food order
42. Footed vases
46. Wealthier
49. Later
50. Crowns
53. Trimmed
54. Around
55. Understood
57. Cherish
61. Black-eyed ___
62. Ring of light
63. Always
64. Aerie, e.g.
66. "Speed" setting
68. Condensation

ACROSS

1. Greek treat
5. Pierce player
9. Stuffs
14. Cut of pork
15. Name word
16. Metal fastener
17. Bested
19. Corpulent
20. Sermonize
21. Observed
23. Texan Houston
24. Dark loaves
26. Topics for Freud
28. Zealous
31. Indicator
34. Sound booster
37. Scam
38. Stack
39. Circuit
41. Shanties
43. Lieu
44. Raced
45. Beige shade
46. Jaunty
47. Support
48. Deary
49. Confused
51. Cheek
52. Child
54. Gossip
56. Large antelope
59. Prepare to drag
61. Gloomy
65. Oblivion
67. Pleasant
70. Detach
71. Spoiled
72. Lamb's fabric
73. Peevish
74. Scads
75. Mends

DOWN

1. Sentimentality
2. "___ Cheatin' Heart"
3. Observance
4. Ahead
5. Song
6. Fortune
7. Payable
8. Common conjunctions
9. Mob
10. Josh
11. Blvds.
12. Butte's kin
13. Originate
18. Wintry
22. Telecasted
25. Seven-piece
27. Sodium chloride
28. Hurt
29. Affirm
30. Beginning part
32. Layers
33. Joyful
35. Bucks
36. Holes
40. Nails
42. Submerged
43. Shovel
50. Targeters
51. Sippers
53. Literary device
55. Shad ___
56. Excess
57. IX
58. Home bodies?
60. Gigantic
62. Reed instrument
63. Sluggish
64. Slippery ones
66. Nipped
68. Gunk
69. Dash

PUZZLE 530

471

PUZZLE 531

ACROSS
1. Joined
6. Random attempt
10. Bad actor
13. Missing links
15. Israeli dance
16. Kind of trip
17. Game tile
18. Deteriorates
19. Cleanse (of)
20. Fit of anger
21. See you!
23. Shoplifted
25. Smote
26. Corn piece
27. City railroads
30. Use an axe
31. Bread for filling
32. Mountain lion
34. Deary
35. Ruler mark
39. Seraglio
40. Picked up
41. Film's Doolittle
42. Bird of ill ___
43. Place
44. Scamp
45. Mend
47. Rowboat paddle
48. Sooner, to a bard
49. Rationally
52. Look-alike
53. Sea jewel
54. Males
55. Flourish
59. Coat sleeve
60. A woodwind
63. Appear
65. Fizzle out
66. Spat
67. Library stamps
68. Bard's always
69. Cuddly
70. Helium and neon

DOWN
1. Trends
2. Aware of
3. Large truck
4. Discharge
5. Cub Scout group
6. Nag
7. Also
8. Sculpture, e.g.
9. Hunting hound
10. Graceful wader
11. Nimble
12. Paragon
14. Grander
22. Evergreen shrub
24. Paths
25. Trickery
26. Cousins, e.g.
27. Canyon sound
28. Fertile soil
29. By all means!
31. Poker kitty
33. Sex
34. Peppery
36. Friendly
37. Russian ruler
38. Hearty
40. Smoking ___
41. Garner
43. Jimmy
44. Brought up
46. Divides
47. Have debts
49. Black card
50. Lofty abode
51. Title giver
52. Burglary
55. Kind of ray
56. Minerals
57. Grimm baddie
58. Private dining room?
61. Med subject
62. Not on
64. Periodical, briefly

DOUBLE CROSSER

PUZZLE 532

When you fill in the correct missing letters in the crossword diagram, those letters, transferred to the correspondingly numbered dashes below the diagram, will reveal a quotation. Make sure no word is repeated in the diagram. Proper names, abbreviations, contractions, and foreign words are not allowed. There are different possibilities to fill the diagram, but only one way will give you the correct quotation.

43	A	B	I	20	■	H	A	S	P	■	C	32	O	P
A	R	E	N	A	■	A	N	31	I	■	L	O	L	L
24	O	35	E	R	■	L	O	A	M	■	33	D	45	Y
E	M	I	R	■	P	O	6	T	I	F	F	■	■	■
M	A	13	T	R	A	■	■	5	E	L	■	28	D	O
■	■	■	■	1	D	O	34	■	N	U	4	G	E	10
C	8	U	M	B	■	14	E	A	18	■	L	I	29	T
L	U	T	25	■	21	E	L	L	30	■	7	L	S	E
O	M	11	T	■	U	N	I	T	■	38	N	36	E	R
19	O	L	E	M	2	■	C	O	27	T	■	■	■	■
E	R	41	■	16	C	37	■	■	O	Y	S	39	E	R
■	■	■	3	T	40	I	C	44	L	■	H	U	L	9
L	A	42	T	■	I	D	12	L	■	L	E	M	U	R
22	P	I	C	■	17	A	M	E	■	E	15	I	D	E
I	23	C	H	■	G	L	E	26	■	A	L	D	46	R

_ _ _   _ _ _ _ _ _ _ _ _ _
1 2 3   4 5 6 7 8 9 10 11 12 13

_ _ _ _ _ _   _ _ _   _ _ _ _ _ ;
14 15 16 17 18 19   20 21 22   23 24 25 26 27

_ _ _ _ _ _ _   _ _ _ _   _ _ _
28 29 30 31 32 33 34   35 36 37 38   39 40 41

_ _ _ _ _ .
42 43 44 45 46

PUZZLE 533

ACROSS
1. Dancing spot
6. Shut out
11. Flee
13. "Shoo!"
14. Thrilled
15. Aerie dweller
16. Encountered
17. Kinder
19. Cote female
20. Cultural
22. Bullfighter
26. Red dye
30. Skating jump
31. Slender stick
33. Alliance acronym
34. Chirps
36. Some journalists
38. Conflict
40. Append
43. Sprinted
44. Gorilla or gibbon
47. Departs
49. Idolized
51. Numb, as a foot
52. Paired
53. Trapshooting
54. Aridly

DOWN
1. Judge
2. Capri, e.g.
3. Ella's style
4. Mouser
5. Unwrapped
6. Sweetie
7. Breakfast favorite
8. Tree trunk
9. From the top
10. Network, as of nerves
12. Film cutter
13. Existed
18. Habitual
21. Deceives
22. Navigator's aid
23. Chopping tool
24. Informal shirt
25. European range
27. "Casablanca" character
28. Adherent's ending
29. Negative prefix
32. Vanquish
35. Boulevard
37. United
39. Grating sound
40. Word of regret
41. Student's need
42. Secluded valley
44. Military force
45. Citrus coating
46. Crosscurrent
48. Victory sign
50. Dinghy paddle

PUZZLE 534

ACROSS
1. Bullets, briefly
5. Pens' contents
9. Salon product
12. Sweetheart
13. Grandma
14. "We ___ Family"
15. Send forth
16. Roofed
18. Small blob
20. Afternoon event
21. Met songs
23. Angler's hook
27. Ship employee
30. Egypt's capital
31. Be in arrears
32. Weepy
34. Lousy grade
35. Nautical seepage
37. Trouser features
39. Optic problem
40. Fur scarf
41. Enjoy lunch
43. Churn
47. Flat broke
51. Give thanks
52. Single
53. Lower hinge
54. Place for a gutter
55. "Adios!"
56. Big name
57. Deli loaves

DOWN
1. Beneath the covers
2. Reminder note
3. Daily delivery
4. Fugitive
5. Motivate
6. Slangy turndown
7. Makes with yarn
8. Clear-thinking
9. Guy's date
10. Before, in verse
11. Directed
17. Overly enthusiastic
19. Speak formally
22. Conform
24. Attendant
25. Brood
26. Opponents
27. Blubbers
28. Dimwit
29. Slippery
30. Bike
33. Morning crower
36. Eccentric person
38. Caretaker
40. Feat
42. Torah cabinets
44. Serving platter
45. Possess
46. Storm centers
47. Type of haircut
48. Indefinite amount
49. Born
50. Soup ingredient

474

DOUBLE TROUBLE
PUZZLE 535

Not really double trouble, but double fun! Solve this puzzle as you would a regular crossword, except place one, two, or three letters in each box. The number of letters in each answer is shown in parentheses after its clue.

ACROSS
1. Links cry (4)
3. Provide funds for (5)
5. Get ___ of (3)
7. Fraud (4)
9. Frost (3)
10. Gull-like bird (4)
11. Good fortune (11)
13. Heavenly gift (8)
15. Flag site (4)
17. Trickle (4)
18. Hearten (9)
21. Ready to pick (4)
23. Spoken with ease (6)
24. Air duct (4)
25. Song part (5)
27. With it (3)
28. Thespian (5)
30. Page (4)
32. Land map (4)
33. Great open area (7)
35. Yearn (4)
37. Automatic response (6)
39. Pub feature (3)
40. Guidance (10)
42. Sequence (5)
44. Not that (4)
45. Spread throughout (7)
48. Newcomer to society (9)
51. Ill-humor (3)
53. Dryer fuzz (4)
54. Shelf's kin (5)
55. Wheat ___ (4)
56. Waistcoat (4)
57. Make airtight (4)

DOWN
1. Slight flaw (6)
2. Trial break (6)
3. Go in (5)
4. Heavy rain (8)
5. Stair part (5)
6. Thick (5)
7. Ocean vessel (4)
8. Friendship (5)
12. Withhold (7)
14. Unworldly girl (7)
16. Depart (5)
19. Get in touch with (7)
20. Mild (6)
22. Puzzle (7)
23. Impudent (8)
26. Chair, e.g. (4)
27. Curse (3)
29. Seer (6)
31. Anew (6)
34. Harbor (7)
36. Moor (5)
38. TV's dolphin show (7)
41. Mocking (8)
43. Disturb (7)
46. Suitcase (6)
47. Of teeth (6)
48. Remove from print (4)
49. Move a bit (5)
50. Time period (4)
52. Remainder (4)

Slide-O-Gram
PUZZLE 536

Place the seven words into the diagram, one word for each row, so that one of the columns reading down will spell out a 7-letter word that is related to the others. Each given letter is part of one word.

- Bolero
- Cloak
- Dashiki
- Dungarees
- Leggings
- Tunic
- Wrap

PUZZLE 537

ACROSS
1. Match
5. Sailor's mop
9. Of sound
14. Skin condition
15. Soft drink
16. Dote on
17. Zebras
18. Short leaps
19. Thanks, Pierre!
20. Thespian group
22. Multitude
24. Mother
26. Silly birds
30. Audio system
32. Most inactive
34. Skate runner
35. Name word
38. Destiny
39. Cookie grain
40. Classifications
43. Like a wet hen
44. Conscious of
46. Sandwich shop
47. Assists a crook
49. Put away
51. Catlike
53. Crack
54. Harplike instruments
55. Trim
57. On the wrong path
61. Quaking tree
65. Selves
67. Regatta
68. Stock portion
69. Record
70. Gumbo ingredient
71. Chopped
72. Snow glider
73. Predictor

DOWN
1. Section
2. Scorer on a serve
3. Facts, briefly
4. Started again
5. Plan
6. Romance
7. Greek vowel
8. Diamond corner
9. Packed down
10. Horatian work
11. Neither
12. Circle segment
13. Hawaiian gift
21. Peeling device
23. Growing older
25. Card game
27. Gnome
28. Mariners
29. Property
30. Slopes
31. Drum signal
33. Knight and Kennedy
34. Catcalls
36. Olive product
37. Join
41. Contributed
42. Low-price events
45. Night stalker
48. Cafes
50. Made level
52. Eliminated completely
54. Allowed
56. Attains
58. Gather leaves
59. Property measure
60. Decade unit
61. Fire remnant
62. "___ Stoops to Conquer"
63. Handle clumsily
64. Previously
66. Unlock, in poems

PUZZLE 538 — Pulling Strings

Place the answers to the clues into the squares. Squares that are connected with lines contain the same letter. Don't get tangled!

1. City of Light
2. Magnum opus
3. Quote
4. Wallop
5. Kudos

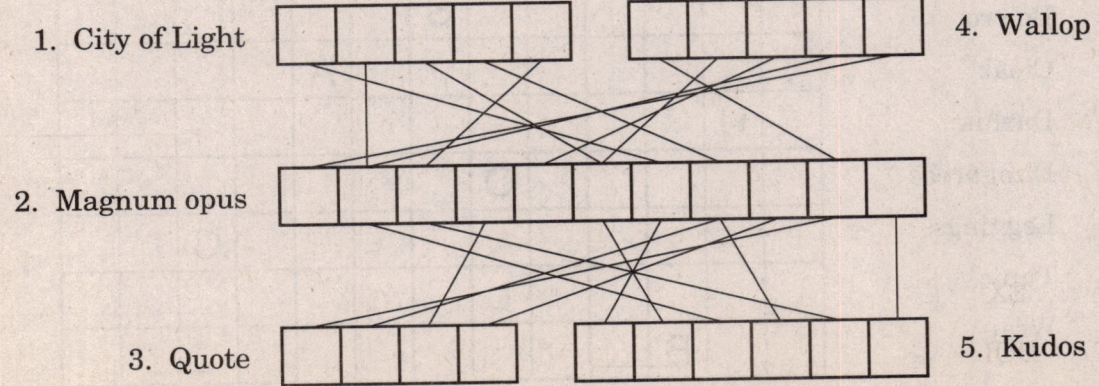

PUZZLE 539

ACROSS
1. Mimic
5. Level and smooth
9. Baseball hat
12. Arrived
13. Napped leathers
15. Lode's load
16. "Iliad," e.g.
17. Eager
18. Aglow
19. Make content
21. Ramblers
23. Tiny vegetable
24. Cactus's defense
26. Overlay
29. Armory
32. Self-conceit
33. Extremely small
35. Candy ingredient
37. Goof up
38. Hubbub
39. Ham on ___
40. Brief brawl
43. Disputes
46. Moray or electric
47. Become denser
49. Diner
51. Borrow, for a fee
52. In the past
53. Come into view
56. Deletion
60. Menswear item
61. "___ Son"
64. Mast
65. Unclose, in verse
66. Packed away
67. Ages
68. Corral
69. Observer
70. Irritated state

DOWN
1. Champs
2. Father
3. Discharge
4. Chef's formula
5. Wrath
6. Supervised
7. Lemon thirst-quencher
8. Agassi's forte
9. Soft drink
10. Very dry
11. Caresses
13. African trip
14. Pebbles
20. Look
22. Food list
24. Canned fish
25. Evidence of truth
26. Victory symbols
27. Wading bird
28. Compass direction
30. Be of the same opinion
31. Coat of paint
34. Actress Phoebe ___
36. Put trust in
41. Floor square
42. Pacific and Indian
44. Was scared of
45. Long narrative
48. Martial art
50. Flings
53. On the crest
54. Conduit
55. Hammer end
56. Constantly
57. Informed about
58. Rajah's mate
59. Formerly, formerly
62. Plaything
63. Great rage

Guess Who — PUZZLE 540

Change one letter in each word to form the name of a famous person.

Example: CLERK TABLE (**Answer:** Clark Gable)

1. BARK TRAIN _____
2. FELINE LION _____
3. LEAN MARGIN _____
4. ROVER EXERT _____
5. BIDDY DOLLY _____
6. ANTE VICE _____
7. TORT SWELLING _____
8. BORIC DECKER _____
9. BOX SAGER _____
10. MAP ZEST _____

PUZZLE 541

CAMOUFLAGE

The answers to the clues can be found in the diagram, but they have been camouflaged. Their letters are in correct order, but sometimes are separated by extra letters that have been inserted throughout the diagram. You must black out all the extra letters. Each of the remaining letters will be used in a word reading across and a word reading down. Solve ACROSS and DOWN together to determine the correct letters where there is a choice. The number of answer words in a row or column is indicated by the number of clues.

	1	2	3	4	5	6	7	8	9	10	11	12	13	14	15
1	H	U	A	N	N	D	G	L	E	S	C	R	A	W	P
2	O	P	P	O	U	A	S	E	M	H	V	U	I	L	A
3	B	A	P	Z	R	O	L	N	M	M	O	I	S	M	T
4	G	R	E	I	X	M	A	H	C	E	P	G	I	B	E
5	W	X	A	S	O	M	T	S	E	L	I	N	L	E	N
6	A	R	R	R	T	E	S	T	A	G	E	G	N	D	T
7	T	Y	E	V	A	R	K	N	E	V	H	U	I	C	T
8	S	U	L	E	N	U	T	H	H	E	R	R	L	O	R
9	H	A	M	I	R	D	T	O	M	D	P	E	N	S	E
10	D	G	E	M	E	K	A	N	O	R	P	L	E	A	A
11	A	T	H	U	T	E	M	P	T	O	M	O	I	R	L
12	S	L	E	A	I	P	C	L	I	F	A	B	R	S	T
13	B	A	G	G	K	A	I	H	N	O	R	I	Y	E	L
14	Y	S	U	E	E	J	N	U	G	R	S	K	E	L	M
15	B	O	L	M	E	W	A	S	K	P	E	T	T	T	Y

ACROSS

1. Manage • Fragment
2. Defy • ___-Hoop
3. Smock • Damp
4. Frown • Filled pastry
5. Squander • Bedclothes
6. Catch • Conclude
7. Hanker • Oust
8. Detective • Goof
9. Coiffure • Thick
10. Bearing • Supplication
11. Try • Grease
12. Bound • Fibbers
13. Once more • Window type
14. Beheld • Employ
15. Tooted • Solicit • Trivial

DOWN

1. Balderdash • Blot
2. Dodge (a punch) • World carrier
3. Garb • Lamprey
4. Din • Picture
5. Hard to find • Crossed letter
6. Arched ceiling • Impolite • Mutt's mitt
7. Made a lap • Staying power
8. Extended credit • Perplex
9. Host • Spicy • Squid squirt
10. Postpone • Sag
11. Office machine • Analyze
12. Spoil • Ignited anew
13. Silly • Ill-humor
14. Headed • Pamper
15. ___ leather • No kidding?

CODEWORD   PUZZLE 542

Instructions for solving Codeword puzzles are given on page 11.

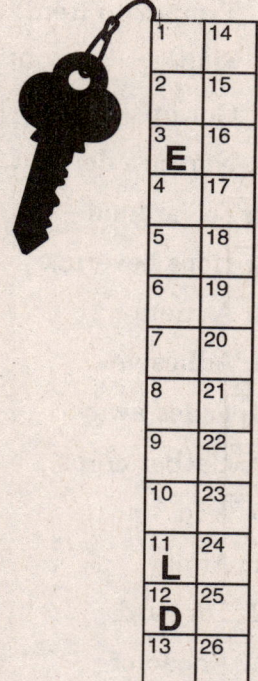

CODEWORD   PUZZLE 543

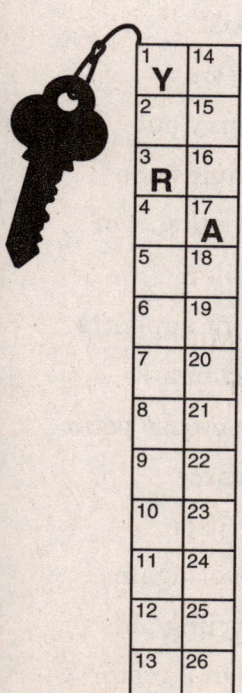

479

PUZZLE 544

ACROSS
1. Lieu
6. Make a web
10. Coarse file
14. Desert plants
15. Coloring
16. ___ code
17. Throbs
18. Ladder part
19. Cut, as a lawn
20. In addition
21. Fish lure
23. Slipped
25. High peak
26. Swine
27. Historic time
28. White fur
32. Wise one
33. Vandyke, e.g.
34. Made less tense
35. Mas' mates
38. River edge
39. Moisten
40. Building curve
41. Snoop
42. Evil spell
43. Likely
44. Comrade
45. Considered
46. Snake
49. Soar
50. Evergreen
51. Poured
53. Coral structure
54. Old witch
57. Story
58. Voiced
60. ___ layer
62. Nights before
63. Nil
64. Renegade
65. Intermission
66. Equal
67. Cats' cries

DOWN
1. Scram!
2. Mexican fare
3. Yodeling sound
4. Had a bagel
5. Separate
6. Remove
7. Sulk
8. Motel
9. Trousseau item
10. Slope
11. Got up
12. Norton's domain
13. Zoo animal
22. Hops beverage
24. Ancient
26. Adhesive
28. Fades away
29. Gather crops
30. A lot
31. Annoy
32. Forward
34. Ahead of schedule
35. Seniors' dance
36. Pimples
37. Molt
39. Level
40. Exist
42. Bistro
43. Carry out
45. Game cube
46. In pursuit of
47. Toiler
48. Tent supports
50. Criminal
52. Compass point
53. Scarce
54. Drifter
55. Over again
56. Styling aids
59. Gun a motor
61. Last letter

PUZZLE 545

ACROSS
1. Bankrolls
5. Housetop
9. Flatboats
13. Gate
14. Momma's man
15. Canned fish
16. Climb
17. Assessor
18. Abound
19. Eluded
21. Ring official
23. Stag's mate
24. Cobbling tools
25. Speaking
28. Consumer
31. What's the name?
32. Domain
35. Gear
37. Bungle
38. Squirm
40. Mimic
41. Except
42. Evade
43. Observe
44. Fundamental
46. Filter
50. Turf
52. Corn unit
53. Tool
56. Math branch
60. Scan
61. ___ de Leon
63. Third letters
64. Presented
65. Thick digit
66. Aquarium
67. Barely managed
68. Sensible
69. Lather

DOWN
1. No longer are
2. Pivot point
3. Plate
4. Unwavering
5. Street
6. Elect
7. Vocal drama
8. Cheerio!
9. Certify
10. Regretter
11. Leg joint
12. Ditto
14. Spruce up
20. Maui dish
22. Fire
25. Piece of greenery
26. Blood line
27. Mesh
29. Clear
30. Mellow
31. Part of WWW
33. Future chicken
34. Epochs
36. Wow!
38. Hums
39. Vouchers
45. Polished
47. Star
48. Tatter
49. Builds
51. Oahu greeting
53. Coax
54. Tropical wood
55. Overhang
56. Peak
57. Suitor
58. Split
59. Inquires
62. Sister

PUZZLE 546

ACROSS
1. Young cow
5. Among
9. Gathered
12. Belmont circuit
13. Neatens
15. Hew
16. PBS show
17. Sickest
18. Can metal
19. Exchange
20. Bar order
21. Harvest
23. Jolt
25. Spaded
28. Soap ingredients
29. Fleets
33. Hoodlum
35. Dog
36. Adversary
38. Mr. Hanks
41. Produce
42. Ref's count
43. Big
45. Study
46. Graded
48. Fragrances
49. Allot
50. Lawmaking bodies
52. Flat bread
55. Misjudge
57. Viper
58. Candid
60. Dinghy paddle
62. Crypt
66. Sever
67. Suppose
70. Saudi somebody
71. "Bells ___ Ringing"
72. Sired
73. Service
74. Bread grain
75. Songbird
76. Lamb dish

DOWN
1. Cheats
2. State
3. Kilauea's flow
4. Pancake
5. Determination
6. Loafed
7. Hitch
8. Stags
9. Pal at sea
10. Outcast
11. Leans
13. Royal headgear
14. Pig's pen
22. Kind
24. Cling
26. Inverts
27. Bazooka, e.g.
29. Mimicked
30. Ramble
31. Lunar body
32. Irish ___
34. Hosiery
37. Formerly called
38. Easy gait
39. Meany
40. Muddle
44. Connectors
47. Supped
49. Blemish
51. Having handles
52. ___ bear
53. Creamy white
54. Plains abode
56. Wake up
59. Roof goo
61. Prayer finale
63. Leave out
64. Bit
65. Steep
68. Cut
69. Elton's title

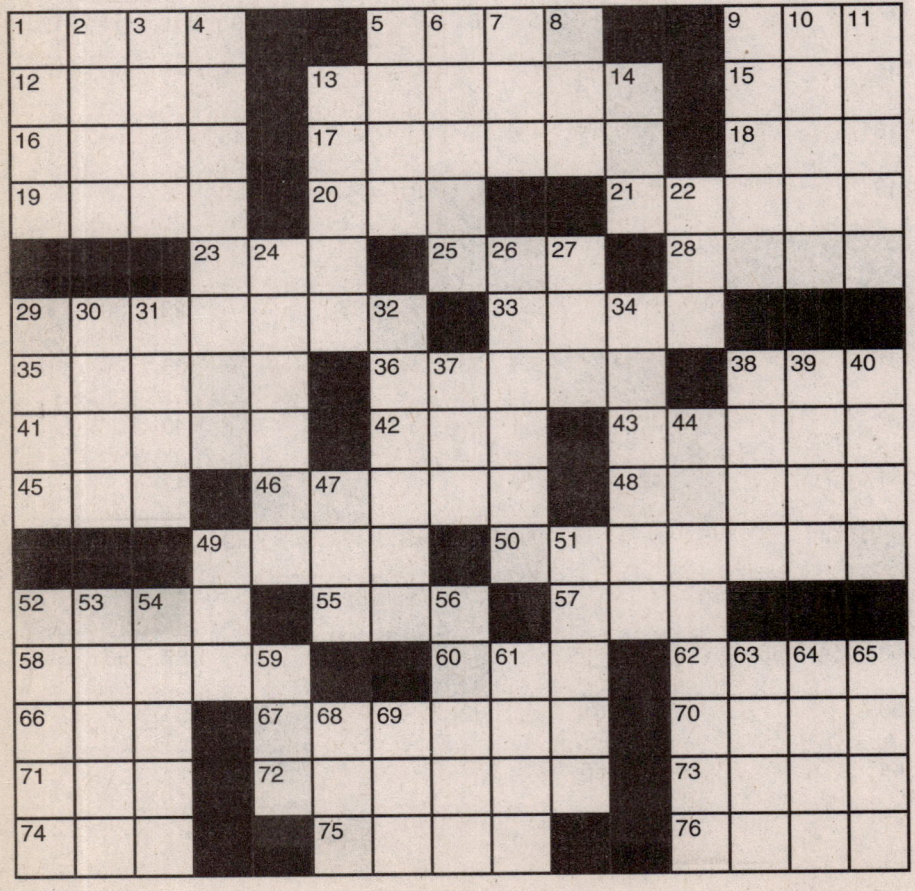

PUZZLE 547

ACROSS
1. Epic tales
6. Partly closed
10. Cheers, e.g.
13. Praise
14. Skinned
16. Fruit cooler
17. Mix of several metals
18. Doubly
19. Inkling
20. Engage gears
21. Mission
22. Aged
23. Fall bloom
28. Sharp
30. Restful resort
33. Irresponsible
35. Stir-fry vessel
36. Stopped lying?
37. Mauna Loa flow
41. Adjust
43. Bo's number
44. Nut
45. Cafe choices
46. Emcee's speech
48. Baby bug
49. Response
52. Type spaces
53. Ridiculous
56. Nightly need
58. Tennis-match call
59. Huge time span
61. Wrongs
65. Swimsuit section
66. Collision
69. Pry into
70. Keats's vessel
71. Indian shelter
72. Redhead's rinse
73. Frantic
74. Consider
75. Garden tool

DOWN
1. Baseball feature
2. Spindle
3. Guys' mates
4. Maui welcome
5. Pen
6. Suitable
7. Boxer's target
8. Operatic solo
9. Chef's secret
10. Breakfast strip
11. Mature
12. Like a marsh
15. Audition tapes
24. Look through
25. Frigate hand
26. Sensual
27. Begrudges
29. Wight or Royale
30. Took a dip
31. Fishing stick
32. Similar
34. Nutritious legume
38. Zits
39. Self-centered
40. Hill builders
42. Pundit
44. Corn bread
47. Costly appetizer
50. Build
51. Loved greatly
53. Photo book
54. Yogi ___
55. Put up with
57. Yearned
60. Neck back
62. Extended
63. Isolated
64. Mast support
67. Have in view
68. Skirt bottom
69. Not he

PUZZLE 548

FULL CIRCLE

To complete this circular puzzle fill in the answers to the AROUND clues in a clockwise direction. For the RADIAL clues move from the outside to the inside.

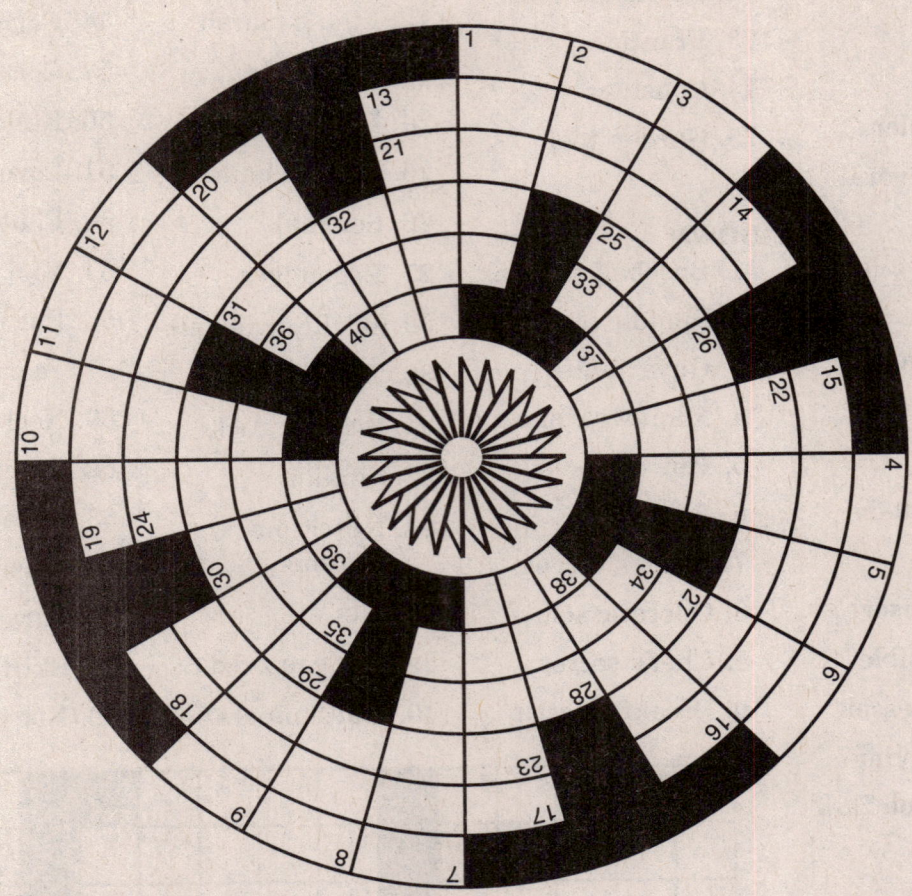

AROUND (Clockwise)
1. Marry
4. Legendary bird
7. Unhappy
10. Perform
13. Rebound
15. Train tracks
17. Land units
19. Sailboat
21. Desert plant
22. Brilliant success
23. Special favor
24. Coral island
25. Run to marry
27. Macaroni
29. Lariat
31. Interruption
33. Waste pipe
34. Hot vapor
35. Lock of hair
36. Express contempt
37. Lamprey, e.g.
38. Hearing organ
39. Pig's home
40. Finale

RADIAL (Out to in)
1. Bet
2. Time period
3. Pigeons' kin
4. Fast car
5. Lubricant
6. Applauds
7. Leave quickly
8. Exist
9. Handed out
10. Choir voices
11. Bird call
12. Bridge fees
13. Put in a box
14. Confused struggle
15. Repulse
16. Utah, e.g.
17. Perfume essence
18. Celestial bodies
19. Impudent
20. Aircraft
26. Be in debt
28. Ocean
30. Matched group
32. Writing tool

PUZZLE 549

ACROSS
1. Splash
6. Admiration
9. Waste metal
14. African animal
15. Careless
16. Wash away
17. Attentive
18. Semicircle
19. More sensible
20. Mimicking bird
21. Thing of value
23. Sample
24. Bath site
26. Catholic leader
28. Kid's game
31. Pull
33. Watered
36. "___ Town"
37. Newsy bit
39. Playground finds
41. Knot
43. Kindergartner
45. American bird
46. Reach
48. Power unit
50. Christmas ___
51. Grasped
53. Butter unit
54. Rumpus room
55. Adjacent
56. Chapel seat
58. Related
61. Put on hold
64. Cowboy's gear
68. Tusk material
70. Court
71. More mature
72. Birchbark vessel
73. Sprite
74. Aquatic animal
75. Dozed
76. Go bad
77. Work stations

DOWN
1. Farce
2. Tiger ___
3. Unfenced
4. Jack of rhyme
5. Burning
6. Woe!
7. Battles
8. Excluding
9. Make a quilt
10. Standards
11. Red bloom
12. Grape drinks
13. Brash
21. Border on
22. Foot appendages
25. Employ
27. Art board
28. Nero's garment
29. Fathers' sisters
30. Prepare cheese
32. Capture
34. Sidled
35. Probe deeply
38. Crop
40. Glimpsed
42. Downpour unit
44. Dance noisily
47. Tidy
49. Record
52. Dresser part
57. Pen
58. Nervous twitches
59. Arena shape
60. Solitary
62. ___ tie
63. Attic
65. Chooses
66. Glance
67. Goes astray
69. Although
71. Reel's mate

PUZZLE 550

ACROSS
1. Like Rubik's puzzle
6. Normal
9. Speech defects
14. Met event
15. Shelley work
16. Foot joint
17. Flame
18. Freddy's street
19. Check word
20. Some
21. Terraces
24. ___ tide
25. Yank's foe
26. Fault
28. Roofer
31. Pigment
32. Resort
35. Dunce
36. Margarine container
38. Belted
40. Excuse
42. Electric fish
44. Lasso part
45. Older
47. Silence
49. Ump's calls
50. Dangerous curve
51. McCourt book
53. Cave
55. Spokes
57. Wintry
58. Ranch unit
61. Tranquilize
63. Monkey
66. Fumble
68. Convene
69. Fables
71. Studio stand
72. Likewise
73. Available
74. Scent
75. Audio component
76. Touchy

DOWN
1. Pop
2. Aware of
3. Bunch
4. Animosity
5. Rug
6. Versifier
7. Go off-script
8. Shape again
9. Circuit
10. Trivial
11. ___ terrier
12. Guilty, e.g.
13. Drip
22. Prime a crime
23. Utters
25. Temple figure
27. Stingy
28. Shoe bottoms
29. Meat cuts
30. Bardot's street
32. Yell
33. Italian sauce
34. Thirst quenchers
35. Foundation
37. Panhandle
39. Ashy
41. Mite
43. Loiter
46. Disencumbers
48. Spunk
52. Nap
54. Spotted cat
55. Fend off
56. Common phrase
58. Lifetimes
59. Jam
60. Mrs. Kennedy
62. Straddling
63. Humanities
64. Soil additive
65. View
67. Gym wing
70. Buck

PUZZLE 551

ACROSS
1. Mock
6. Lament for Yorick
10. Jokes
14. Composition
15. Cessation
16. Recruit
17. Baked fruit
18. Edible shell
19. Emend text
20. "Me, ___ & Irene"
22. Ballpoint
23. Agents, for short
24. Common tree
26. Collar locale
28. Place for a pug?
31. Honor
33. Pocket fuzz
36. Ajar, to Keats
37. Hawaiian strings
38. Burger topping
40. Checkers side
41. Harvest
44. Woolly mama
45. Speech style
47. Bat wood
48. So-so grade
49. Type of gin
50. Prowl
52. Misjudge
53. Grade
55. Racket
56. ___ carotene
59. Done, to Donne
61. Like corduroy
66. Mowed area
67. Try
69. Coast
70. Misfortune
71. Light beige
72. Evade
73. Disclaim
74. Fillies and does
75. Blazer fabric

DOWN
1. Celtics, e.g.
2. Glimpse
3. Vipers
4. Auction
5. Shoelace hole
6. Painter's work
7. Bound
8. Climb
9. Large pebble
10. Pickle type
11. Attendant
12. Seize firmly
13. Movie locales
21. Tart start
25. Shark
27. Cluster
28. Feudal bigwig
29. Impersonators
30. Bike part
32. Car style
34. Brother's girl
35. Dominate
39. At no time, to a bard
41. Petition
42. Manipulated
43. Rocker, e.g.
46. Feminine
50. Doodle
51. Armor wearer
54. Popular blooms
56. Seeped
57. Chalet hanger
58. Duplicate
60. Unusual
62. Tooted
63. Linger
64. Brink
65. Action
68. Double-decker

PUZZLE 552

FLOWER POWER

Instructions for solving Flower Power are given on page 94.

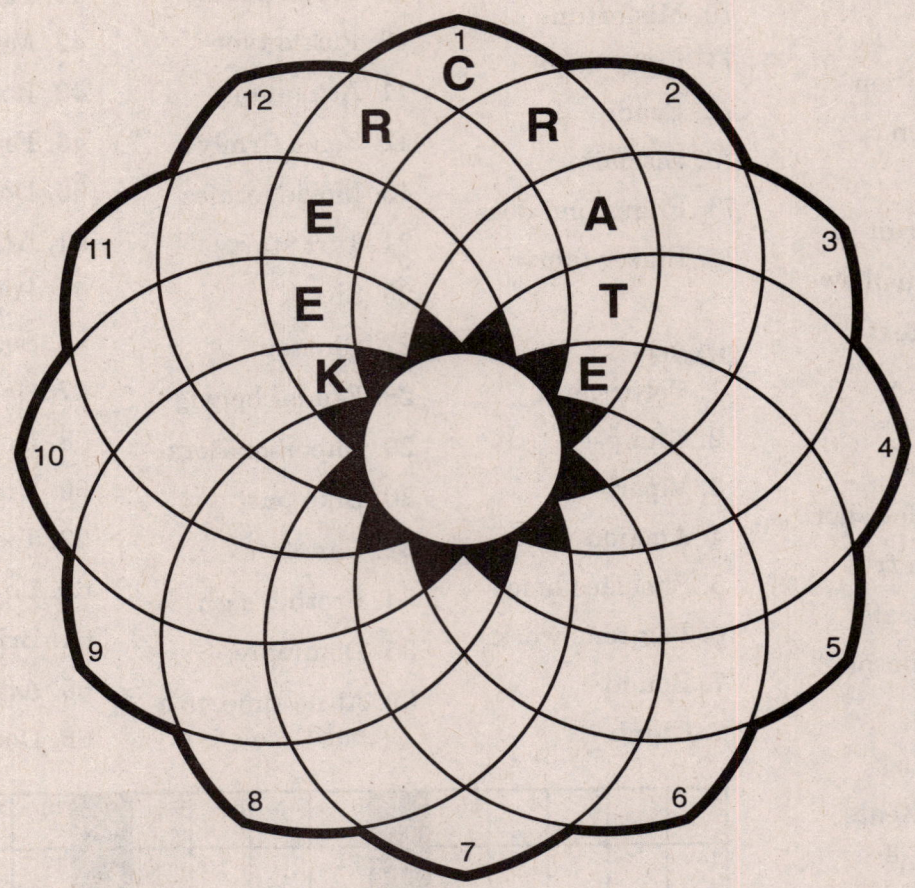

CLOCKWISE

1. Carton
2. Signal light
3. Atlanta player
4. Twist
5. Layered rock
6. Jostle
7. Hackneyed
8. Infuriate
9. Eskimo canoe
10. Diner customer
11. Kilt feature
12. Come about

COUNTERCLOCKWISE

1. Small stream
2. Monk
3. Explosive charge
4. Grind harshly
5. Catch
6. Remove whiskers
7. Stock unit
8. Coral ring
9. Jack
10. Majestic bird
11. Check endorser
12. Temple table

PUZZLE 553

ACROSS
1. Refuse
5. Glass sheet
9. Licks
14. Atmosphere
15. Declare
16. Sound
17. Await action
18. Hand over
19. Gamma follower
20. Question
22. Turf unit
24. Babble
25. Storm
29. Shade tree
31. Offspring
32. Psych 101 terms
33. Clarinets, e.g.
36. Cuddle
37. Jumped
39. Dozes
41. Bikini, e.g.
43. Excessively
44. Donkey
45. Savior
46. Rush
48. Chunk of eternity
49. Drooping
52. Buck
53. Carpet
54. Bauxite, e.g.
55. Spookiest
57. Jolly
60. Print measures
62. A few
63. Delight
65. Fascinated
68. Chills
72. Designated
73. Bare
74. Mr. Coward
75. Thesis
76. Tints
77. Like a slasher film

DOWN
1. Dupe
2. Signal
3. Large vase
4. Polite address
5. Parcel
6. Rd.
7. Doze
8. She-sheep
9. Duck's walk
10. Shade
11. Leisurely
12. Hummus holder
13. Detergent
21. Hex
23. Above, in verse
25. Ways to go
26. Sweater material
27. Nannies, e.g.
28. Embrace, as a cause
30. Remote button
31. Erstwhile king
34. Riskers
35. Shoot forth
38. Rich cake
40. Ballad
42. Trademark
44. Start
47. Carports' kin
50. Miserly
51. Itch
56. Watching
57. Unit of heredity
58. Woeful cry
59. Thanksgiving dish
61. Grit
64. Darjeeling, e.g.
66. Man
67. Certain poem
69. Dove's call
70. Always, in poetry
71. Cunning

PUZZLE 554

ACROSS
1. Nanny has three
4. Slide
8. Overflowing
13. By means of
14. Private
16. Horned mammal, shortly
17. Coop output
18. Long gun
19. Reef stuff
20. Thick rug
22. Peke pest
23. Before, to a bard
24. On the Baltic
26. Swiftly
30. Excuse
33. Team animal
35. Stick (out)
36. Female pupil
38. Most agreeable
42. Eternity
44. Clay brick
46. Sound
47. Negligent
49. Surly
51. Behold
52. Sculptor's tool
54. Makes tea
56. Least powerful
59. Grease
61. Vintage
62. Indication
64. Forehead
68. Crest
71. Observe
73. Pride
74. Strong metal
75. Beam
76. Large boat
77. Conditions
78. Once more
79. Odd couple?

DOWN
1. Arden et al.
2. Near
3. Narrative
4. ___ Lancelot
5. Blade
6. Incited
7. Strike out
8. Trajectory
9. Reporter's query
10. Televised
11. Dog's warning
12. Full of gaps
15. Raises
21. Yak
25. Ital. island
27. Having pimples
28. Luau treat
29. Craving
30. Cracked
31. Olympics sled
32. Columnist's entry
34. Dote on
37. Haven
39. Relaxation
40. Whole bunch
41. Cotton shirts
43. Fed up
45. News flash
48. This woman
50. Wane
53. Has room for
55. CSA soldier
56. Poorest
57. Choice
58. Snake
60. Pa's brother
63. Nursery cry
65. Study
66. Beast
67. Aroused
69. Diamond, e.g.
70. City trains
72. Use an axe

PUZZLE 555

ACROSS
1. Pares
6. Gigantic
11. Dally
14. Proportion
15. Limber
16. Dumbfound
17. Correct
18. Carrier
19. Edit.
20. Matriarch
21. Started
22. Dim
23. Earl Grey, e.g.
25. Voyaging
27. Drawing pencil
31. Hockey spots
35. Extremely
36. Cut
37. Secluded
38. Wheel center
39. Ballgame units
42. Stake
43. Metropolitan
45. Kolkata dress
46. Refrain syllables
47. Elegance
48. Placed trust
50. Operator
52. Mellow
53. "Mary Poppins" song word
56. Call on
59. Thicken
63. Barnyard female
64. Untangle
65. Shade of purple
66. Tick off
67. Flawless
68. Enrage
69. Shy
70. Nicks
71. Harsh

DOWN
1. Study hard
2. Monk
3. Component
4. Papier-mache figure
5. Lay lawn
6. Past due
7. Amazed
8. Custom
9. Valleys
10. Poetic contraction
11. Molten flow
12. Stunned
13. "Chicago" actor
21. Part of BLT
22. Flunk
24. Weasels
26. Expunging
27. Woo
28. Pastime
29. Possess
30. Licorice-tasting seed
32. Dignified
33. Massage
34. Gels
35. Therefore
40. Quick rest
41. Extraordinary
44. Graduate, briefly
48. Compelled
49. Pour
51. Sidestep
53. Trendy
54. Idol
55. Very black
57. Chair
58. Evils
60. Sled
61. Finished
62. Coastal bird
64. Unburden
65. Bell and Kettle

PUZZLE 556

HURRY UP!

ACROSS
1. Large bell
5. Army vehicle
9. Actor Stoltz
13. Capture
17. At a distance
18. Capri, e.g.
19. TV comic Jay ___
20. Circle dance
21. Abiding
23. Short-change
25. Bean curd
26. Drudge
28. Trunks
29. Without risk
32. Cut with an ax
33. Just
34. Swap
35. Crafted
36. Ripped
37. Booster
40. Classifieds
41. Type of jazz
43. Comic Mort ___
45. Actor's place
47. Round of duties
49. Shades
51. Baby's father
53. Aha!
54. Threw away
56. Food
58. Seasoned
60. Jaeger
61. Glides high
62. Bad mood
63. Broken-bone support
65. Shake off
66. Adult male fox
69. Hold on property
70. Halt
72. Platform
74. Merriment
75. The end
77. Ms. Parks
79. Chinese idol
81. Barbie's man
82. Draw on
83. Bound
85. Not this
87. Cooks
89. Remain
90. Wild pig
91. Path
92. Fisherman
95. Objectives
96. Leg part
97. Like some garments
99. Fixed position
104. Kitty's cry
105. Outfit
106. Booth
107. Sound return
108. Tall trees
109. Animation
110. Witnessed
111. Profound

DOWN
1. Fuel
2. Many times
3. Scottish negative
4. Prepared some cheese
5. Hurry
6. Famed fabulist
7. Raised trains
8. Stroked
9. Like a sprite
10. True
11. Those elected
12. Kind of pin
13. Coastline
14. Entre ___
15. Cartoonist Peter ___
16. Heaters
22. Hands out
24. Toe woes
27. Is in the red
29. Begin
30. Zeal
31. Snoozing
32. Loathe
33. Shape
35. Actress Adams
36. Defrosts
37. Slick one
38. Writer James ___
39. Must-have
42. Swindles
44. Worshipped
46. Fixing a shower wall
48. Probing
50. Ice-cream amounts
52. Rate

PUZZLE 556

55. Attila, e.g.
57. ___-been
59. Some
61. Sailboat
63. Opening
64. Type of cotton
66. Civil disorder
67. Coral structures
68. Firm
71. Cafeteria item
73. Not fully shut
76. Change
78. Bit of matter
80. Yell at
84. Outpouring of news
86. Trouble
88. Showed impatience
89. Delays
90. Please, to Wilhelm
91. Fixed a chair
92. Peak
93. Mr. Coward
94. Seize
95. Seeming to show
96. Coop
98. Ms. DiFranco
100. Fiddle
101. Maven
102. This lady
103. Summit

PUZZLE 557

• JEEPERS PEEPERS •

ACROSS
1. ___ Na Na
4. Vatican figure
8. Clarinet's kin
12. ___ Aviv
13. Sickens
14. Kissers
15. "You ___ My Love"
16. Calf's cry
17. Salamanders
18. Protective spectacles
20. Pigeon's call
21. Ordinary
23. Law officer
26. London district
29. African desert
31. Odors
34. Beams
35. Tranquil
36. Yo, buddy!
37. Dearie
38. Tempest in a ___
42. Train systems: abbr.
44. Single eyeglass
48. Opera highlight
50. Skirt style
51. Lenient
52. Cavort
53. "___ Around"
54. Mexican cheer
55. Jumble
56. Defeat
57. Tic-___-toe

DOWN
1. For men only
2. Sub sandwich
3. Shake ___!
4. Mr. Picasso
5. Tanker
6. Tissue: suff.
7. Guess: abbr.
8. Bogus butter
9. Dual-purpose lenses
10. Choose
11. 19th letter
19. Troll
20. Mollusk
22. Mule's kin
24. Metallic rocks
25. Gone by
26. Soft belt
27. Sandwich cookie
28. Tortoise-shell frames
30. African animal, shortly
32. Tiny insects
33. Watch
39. Juanita's friend
40. Traffic barriers
41. Divisions
43. Yaks
45. Lump
46. Tra follower
47. CEO
48. Sleeve
49. Lobster eggs
50. Wire measure

PUZZLE 558

• LENGTHY •

ACROSS
1. Decimal point
4. Venomous snake
7. Chicago summer hrs.
10. Trailing vine
11. Ski lift
12. Carnival
13. Cavity
14. Billion ender
15. Go upward
16. Faraway phone service
19. Sugar suffix
20. Debt note
21. Light-hued
24. TV notices
25. Every bit
28. World War II film
32. Took a seat
33. Large tub
34. Famed diamond
35. Tiny island
36. Teacher's org.
38. Mathematical process
44. Burn soother
45. Louts
46. Delivery truck
48. Santa's ride
49. Sleep time, to some
50. Ecology gp.
51. Holds
52. Like a fox
53. Fish snare

DOWN
1. Delve
2. Almost round
3. Spelling error
4. Tolerate
5. Rani's gown
6. Be chairperson
7. Genesis name
8. Part of D.J.
9. Sycamore
11. Labels
12. Berlin lady
17. Holiday tune
18. Throw
21. Gem wts.
22. Triumphant cry
23. Authorize
24. Rep.
25. Fuss
26. Lick up
27. Soap ingredient
29. Roman poet
30. Countries
31. Asian language
35. Ripened
36. Neat!
37. Latin being
38. Tie firmly
39. Earthen pot
40. Negative replies
41. Colorado resort
42. Food cooker
43. Neck part
47. Singer King Cole

494

STOPLINES

PUZZLE 559

A heavy black line, instead of the usual black square, is used to indicate the end of a word. When you have completed the puzzle, there will be a letter in every square.

ACROSS

1. Disney creation
16. Mull island neighbor
17. Hero's home
18. Justice Fortus
19. Kirghiz range
20. Transistors
21. Medieval workers
22. Set of three
23. Type of strap
24. Corroded
25. Young stallion
27. Clamp
28. Bellow
31. Black tea
33. Sprinkled
35. See eye to eye
37. Actor Washington
39. Po River feeder
41. Tutti-____
44. Proton's place
45. Jetson lad
46. One-sidedness
49. Ecclesiastical rule
52. Ms. Anderson
53. Teeter
54. Writer Seton
55. Strip
57. Must
58. Autumn apple
60. Jazzman Count ____
61. Afterward
63. Speechify
65. Public melee
67. Magazine bigwigs: abbr.
68. Exigency
70. Certain Nigerians
72. Passion
73. Soothsayer
75. Wells's aristocrats
76. Ms. Landers
77. Norwegian city
78. Headliner
79. Symbols

DOWN

1. Flattop
2. Ark captain
3. Kolkata's country
4. Leading
5. Hoopla
6. Examined
7. S. Grant's opponent
8. Breach
9. Camp boat
10. Adam's offspring
11. Legal matter
12. Make a doily
13. Oily liquid
14. Scull adjuncts
15. Fifteen-minutes-of-fame people
24. Do a takeoff
26. Author Gay ____
27. Small container
29. Fairy-tale baddie
30. Emeritus: abbr.
32. 1977 Best Actress
33. Brother of Romulus
34. Tokyo, once
36. Like some eggs
38. Colonial organisms
40. Clothe
42. Kindhearted
43. Arm of the sea
47. Clean-cut
48. Surfeit
50. Babylonian sky god
51. Kiln
56. Phantoms
57. "____ a Rebel"
59. Busybody
60. Maidservant, in Paris
62. Prefix for 100
64. Skillful
66. Hunter and Ziering
67. Orient
68. Judah ha-____ (Mishnah compiler)
69. Verve
71. Gentleman's address
72. More, in the Highlands
74. Go bad

PUZZLE 560

• MIDDLEMAN •

ACROSS
1. Force back
6. Begin
11. Ruth's club
14. Silly
15. Avid
16. Gold, in Madrid
17. British suitcase
19. Stereo component
20. Shade provider
21. Hornet's bite
22. Colorado Indians
23. Denounce angrily
26. Speaker's platform
28. Rigged, as voting districts
34. Swindle
36. Coliseum
37. Literary olio
38. Surgical beam
41. Type of rummy
42. Forty-____
45. Veto
48. Theater technicians
51. Mr. Sandler
52. Foot part
55. Even-steven
58. V-shaped bulwark
61. Classic car
62. NY clock zone
63. African mountain
66. Keanu, in "The Matrix"
67. Cordial flavoring
68. African republic
69. Twice five
70. Certain hardwoods
71. Feeds the pot

DOWN
1. Less green
2. "____ Gay"
3. Veal or eggplant
4. Tolkien creature
5. NASA's moon-lander
6. Transmitted
7. French film comedian
8. Schedule
9. He was the 40th
10. Play about Capote
11. Watercraft
12. Nice weapon
13. A-one
18. Stellar
22. Consumer
24. Dykstra of baseball
25. Country in S.A.
27. Ore.'s neighbor
29. Singer Sumac
30. Atomic particle
31. He's enrolled
32. Writer Bagnold
33. Native of Copenhagen
34. Without
35. Purl's partner
39. Ms. Peron
40. Saskatchewan's capital
43. Mild oath
44. Blushing color
46. Stimpy's pal
47. B&O et al.
49. Leatherneck
50. Fielding heroine
53. Scary
54. Spars' sources
55. Tepee
56. Words of comprehension
57. Harrow's rival
59. Manhole cover, e.g.
60. City in Iowa
63. "Krazy ____"
64. Hoopster's gp.
65. Romance-author Holling

PUZZLE 561

Word Ways

Hidden in each diagram are five 5-letter words beginning with the same letter. Draw a continuous line through the letters as you spell each word by moving in any direction from letter to adjoining letter without crossing your line. Each puzzle has a different starting letter.

1.

A	L	E	A	N
P	P	I	C	G
A	S	P	R	E
T	G	E	A	R
N	E	A	S	O

2.

H	C	L	B	W
N	B	W	O	N
E	E	L	O	B
B	N	B	R	A
O	G	I	E	Z

3.

A	P	A	R	C
H	M	W	O	A
L	C	L	L	C
O	O	C	E	O
C	R	A	N	C

DOUBLE TROUBLE

PUZZLE 562

Not really double trouble, but double fun! Solve this puzzle as you would a regular crossword, except place one, two, or three letters in each box. The number of letters in each answer is shown in parentheses after its clue.

ACROSS
1. Oarsman (5)
4. Trouble greatly (8)
7. Circle dance (4)
9. Tedious (6)
10. Tartan (5)
12. Teased (6)
13. Amuse (6)
14. Wizardry (5)
15. Slant (5)
17. Fate (7)
19. Touching (7)
20. Puccini work (5)
21. Not yours (4)
22. Dud (5)
25. Circuit (4)
27. Edgewise (7)
30. Notre ___ (4)
31. Affleck et al. (4)
33. Mo. neighbor (4)
34. "Bells ___ Ringing" (3)
36. Verified age (6)
38. Fused metal (7)
40. Take offense (6)
41. Beginning (5)
42. "Inferno" author (5)
44. High note (3)
45. Substitute (9)
47. Ascended (4)
48. Chances (4)
49. Clutter (4)
50. June or July (5)

DOWN
1. Mechanical (7)
2. Rumpled (8)
3. Joule's kin (3)
4. Exhibition (7)
5. Disastrous (6)
6. Drama segment (4)
7. Awful (8)
8. Under cover? (4)
11. Rats! (4)
14. Geologic deposit (7)
16. Mild (6)
18. Halt, legally (5)
19. Leather maker (6)
21. Bearing (4)
23. Trendy (3)
24. Reputation (4)
25. Fling (3)
26. Candid (4)
28. Guard (6)
29. Texas shrine (5)
32. Petrify (5)
35. Stagger (4)
37. ___ floss (6)
38. Accent (6)
39. "Cheers" star (9)
40. Plants again (7)
41. Native (6)
43. Fangs (5)
44. Adult scrod (3)
46. Word (4)
47. PC acronym (3)

Mini-Crosswords

PUZZLE 563

Fill in each of the diagrams with eight different 4-letter words to construct your own crossword puzzles. Only common English words are allowed. You may repeat letters as often as you wish.

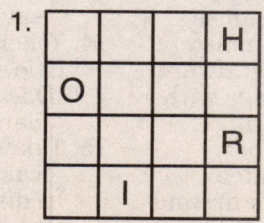
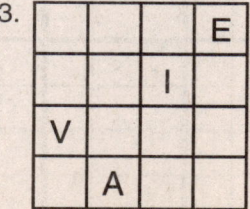

497

PUZZLE 564

BRICK BY BRICK

Rearrange this stack of bricks to form a crossword puzzle. The clues will help you fit the bricks into their correct places. Row 1 has been filled in for you. Use the bricks to fill in the remaining spaces.

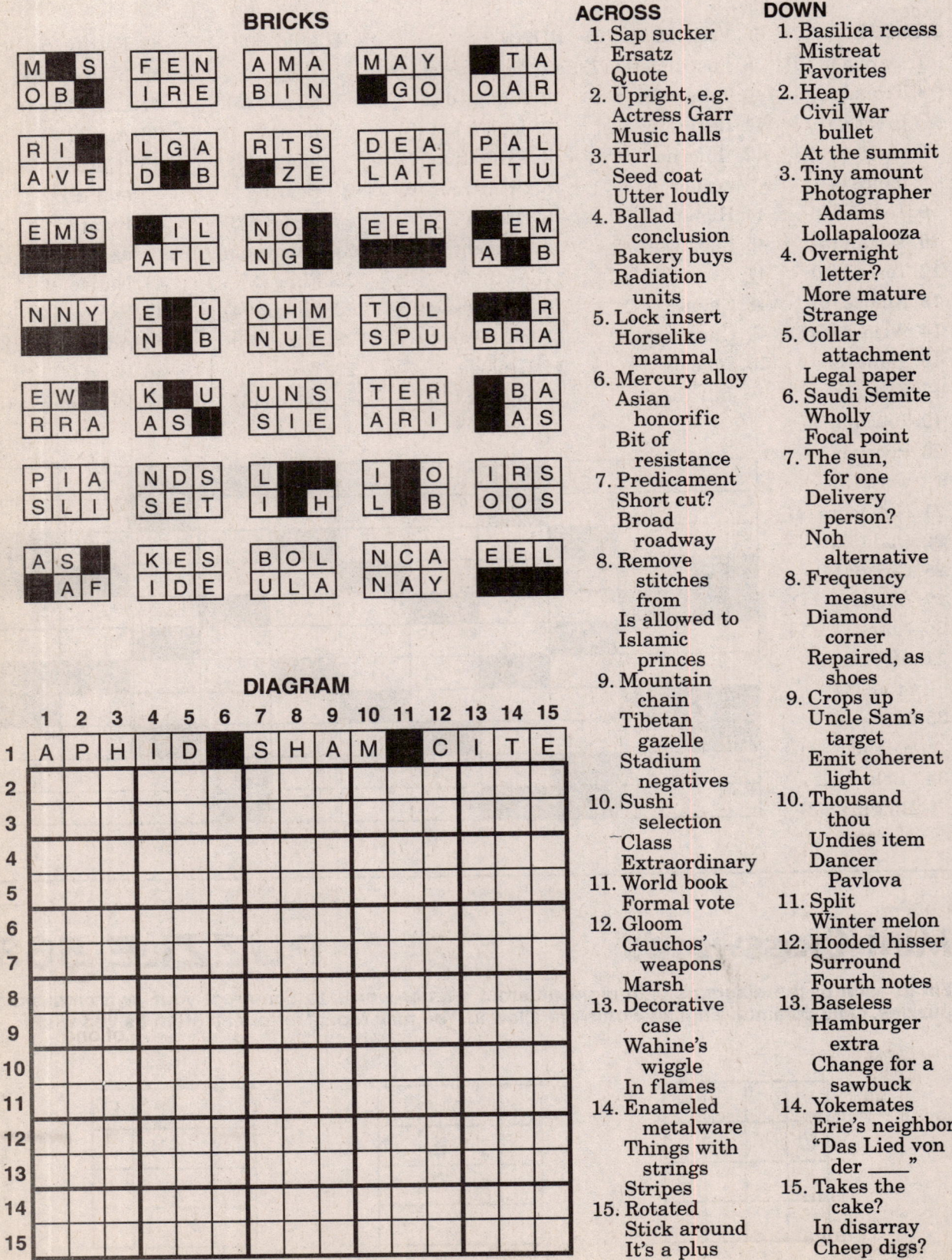

ACROSS
1. Sap sucker
   Ersatz
   Quote
2. Upright, e.g.
   Actress Garr
   Music halls
3. Hurl
   Seed coat
   Utter loudly
4. Ballad conclusion
   Bakery buys
   Radiation units
5. Lock insert
   Horselike mammal
6. Mercury alloy
   Asian honorific
   Bit of resistance
7. Predicament
   Short cut?
   Broad roadway
8. Remove stitches from
   Is allowed to
   Islamic princes
9. Mountain chain
   Tibetan gazelle
   Stadium negatives
10. Sushi selection
    Class
    Extraordinary
11. World book
    Formal vote
12. Gloom
    Gauchos' weapons
    Marsh
13. Decorative case
    Wahine's wiggle
    In flames
14. Enameled metalware
    Things with strings
    Stripes
15. Rotated
    Stick around
    It's a plus

DOWN
1. Basilica recess
   Mistreat
   Favorites
2. Heap
   Civil War bullet
   At the summit
3. Tiny amount
   Photographer Adams
   Lollapalooza
4. Overnight letter?
   More mature
   Strange
5. Collar attachment
   Legal paper
6. Saudi Semite
   Wholly
   Focal point
7. The sun, for one
   Delivery person?
   Noh alternative
8. Frequency measure
   Diamond corner
   Repaired, as shoes
9. Crops up
   Uncle Sam's target
   Emit coherent light
10. Thousand thou
    Undies item
    Dancer Pavlova
11. Split
    Winter melon
12. Hooded hisser
    Surround
    Fourth notes
13. Baseless
    Hamburger extra
    Change for a sawbuck
14. Yokemates
    Erie's neighbor
    "Das Lied von der ___"
15. Takes the cake?
    In disarray
    Cheep digs?

PUZZLE 565

ACROSS
1. Likewise
5. Field of study
9. GI's bullets
13. Cheerio
14. Ivan and Nicholas, e.g.
15. Don, as clothes
16. Excursion
17. Split ___
18. Pacquin of "The Piano"
19. "___ Got Sixpence"
20. Adventurous
21. Watery cereal
22. Measure of heat
24. Midas's metal
26. Tubular pasta
28. "___ Framed Roger Rabbit"
31. Cook slowly
34. Help a crook
35. Bunny motion
36. Litters' littlest
37. Stomach muscles
38. Pollute
40. Intoxicating drink
41. Onion, e.g.
43. Grabs
44. Lawn moisture
45. Affectionately linked
47. Travel stops
48. Incredible
52. Pottery fragment
55. Feathered friend
56. Judge's concern
57. Volcanic flow
58. Fur scarf
60. Religious service
61. Perched
62. Administered ointment
63. Kaput
64. Foreshadow
65. Tolerate
66. Flower plots

DOWN
1. Storage spot
2. Immature insect
3. Pittsburgh product
4. Acorn tree
5. Blooming bush
6. Sudden attack
7. Goof
8. Horse's relative
9. Academy ___ (actor's prize)
10. List of restaurant dishes
11. Lion's pride
12. Taken by mouth
14. Preference
20. Trumpet-and-trombone group
21. Sparkled
23. Eliminate
24. Heaps
25. Song from "A Chorus Line"
27. Synagogue official
28. Smart kid
29. Sharpen
30. Decides
31. Pitt of "Troy"
32. Govern
33. Afresh
37. Freewill offering
39. Purposes
42. Vaselike vessel
43. Became enraged
46. Carpenter, at times
47. Furious
49. Green shade
50. Defeated at chess
51. Decorative jugs
52. Cement chunk
53. Crown of light
54. Eager
55. Gaucho's lasso
58. Shed tears noisily
59. Bond
60. Burglarize

ABC's

PUZZLE 566

Use all 26 letters of the alphabet to complete the ten words. Each letter is to be used only once, and only one letter is used per dash.

A B C D E F G H I J K L M N O P Q R S T U V W X Y Z

1. S ___ U D ___ E
2. ___ O ___ I ___ C
3. A ___ ___ U I ___
4. ___ A B R ___ C
5. T ___ ___ L ___ E
6. ___ A S ___ E T
7. C A ___ D ___ R
8. ___ C O ___ C ___
9. L U ___ ___ R
10. ___ A ___ O ___ Y

499

PUZZLE 567

CODEWORD

Instructions for solving Codeword puzzles are given on page 11.

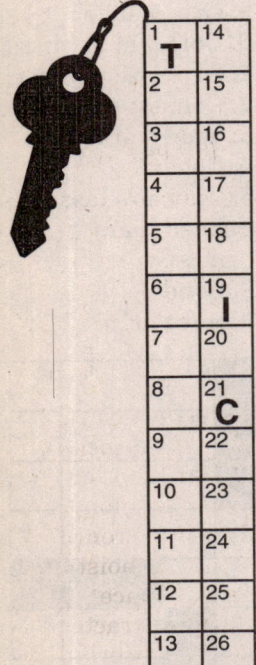

PUZZLE 568

CODEWORD

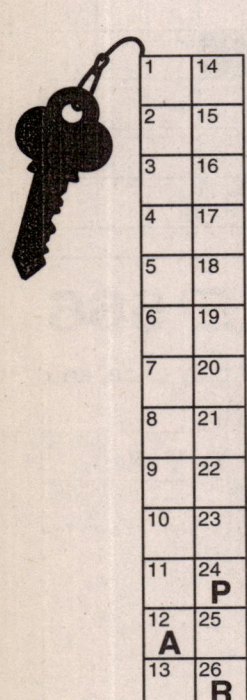

PUZZLE 569

• DAFFY DEFINITIONS •

ACROSS
1. Clerical vestment
4. Spider's snare
7. Possess
10. Baseball's Williams
13. Caribbean, e.g.
14. Epoch
15. Court amorously
16. Parisian pal
17. Coop dweller
18. Hall of frame?
23. Sister
24. Expensive
27. Eggs, to Ovid
28. Mork's planet
30. Cleopatra's undoing
31. Sorority members
33. Allow
34. Marsh bird
36. Clod
37. Varnish ingredient
39. Small hill
42. Crooner Vallee
43. Snoop
44. Pipe joint
45. Fencing sword
46. "___ a Wonderful Life"
47. Lawyer's charge
49. Under the weather
52. Down in the dumps
53. Mend, as socks
54. Chime
56. Western state
57. Green mineral
58. Director Preminger
59. Sandwich cookie
60. ___-relief
63. Personal pronoun
64. Traveler's stop
65. Garden tool
68. Canyon sound
70. Maple fluid
73. Mama's boy
75. Fine fabric
76. Bright lights
78. Freudian topic
79. Popular pet
80. Radio's Fibber ___
81. Former communications co.
82. "Silas Marner" author
84. ___ and aah
85. Decade
86. Publicize
87. Formal dress
88. Muscle spasm
90. Broken alarm clock?
96. Iron source
99. ___ de Cologne
100. Be in debt
101. One ___ time
102. "___ Gang"
103. Picnic pest
104. Unused
105. Tennis's Shriver
106. Named at birth

DOWN
1. Cigar residue
2. Golfer Trevino
3. Musicians' accessories?
4. Have on
5. Drop the ball
6. Cave denizen
7. Nocturnal predator
8. Misery
9. Neither's partner
10. Aquarium covers?
11. Ostrich's kin
12. Ruckus
19. Wacky
20. St. crosser
21. Soup scoop
22. Egg element
25. Catch sight of
26. Gorilla, e.g.
29. Actress Russo
31. Detroit product
32. "My Gal ___"
34. ___ Lanka
35. Threaded fastener
36. Roofless abode?
38. Barber shop?
40. Actress Thompson
41. Directed
47. Nickname for Arbuckle
48. Poetry Muse
50. Gain knowledge
51. Burdened
53. Couple
55. Lion's sign
60. Stiller of films
61. Perfect serve
62. GI's hairdo?
65. Midday on Mt. Everest?
66. Barcelona bravo
67. ___ out (barely make)
69. In the past
71. Ripen
72. Arctic
73. Contempt
74. Stable bit
75. Flat-bottomed boat
77. Beach material
80. Cattle call
83. "Richard ___"
87. Metric measure
88. Afternoon social
89. Writer Fleming
91. Extremely long time
92. Great reverence
93. Morning moisture
94. Empty space
95. Greek character
97. Regret bitterly
98. Before, to Shelley

PUZZLE 570

ACROSS
1. Broadway smashes
5. Pale
9. Fades away
13. Opera solo
14. More slippery
16. Bed part
17. Dog's relative
18. Gravy scoop
19. Epic
20. Lower joint
21. Relates
23. Ring official
24. Remains
27. Pronoun
29. Garden weeder
32. Totter
34. Saucer's partner
35. Mischievous child
36. Having handles
38. Losing strength
42. Charge for use
43. Crack
45. Mechanic's concern
46. Incompetent
48. Fiend
49. Unclose, in verse
50. Tease
52. Advanced
53. Fresh
54. Shoo!
57. Twiggy abode
59. Bunyan's chopper
60. Increases
63. Picnic crashers
67. Prohibits
69. Sedate
71. Questionable
72. Hosiery shade
73. Domingo, e.g.
74. Outskirts
75. Emanate
76. Oodles
77. Gather

DOWN
1. Peddle
2. Do a laundry chore
3. Piece of linoleum
4. "60 Minutes" man
5. Be sick
6. Strewed
7. Skin
8. Yowl
9. Snaky shape
10. Bellow
11. Roll with a hole
12. Personnel
15. Souvenir
22. Apprentices
25. Putting up
26. Burn to a crisp
28. Eavesdrop
29. Music system
30. Forewarning
31. Duel tool
33. Flat
37. Magnitude
39. Church picture
40. Scruff
41. Developed
44. Road marker
47. Golf teacher
51. Animal
54. Infants
55. Precise
56. Style
58. Lion handler
61. Thing
62. Granny
64. Lymph ___
65. Dress for Cato
66. Walk
68. Add
70. Parched

PUZZLE 571

Circle Sums

Each circle, lettered A through I, has its own number value from 1 to 9. No two circles have the same value. The numbers shown in the diagram are the sums of the circles that overlap at those points. For example, 15 is the sum of circles A and C. Can you find the value of each circle?

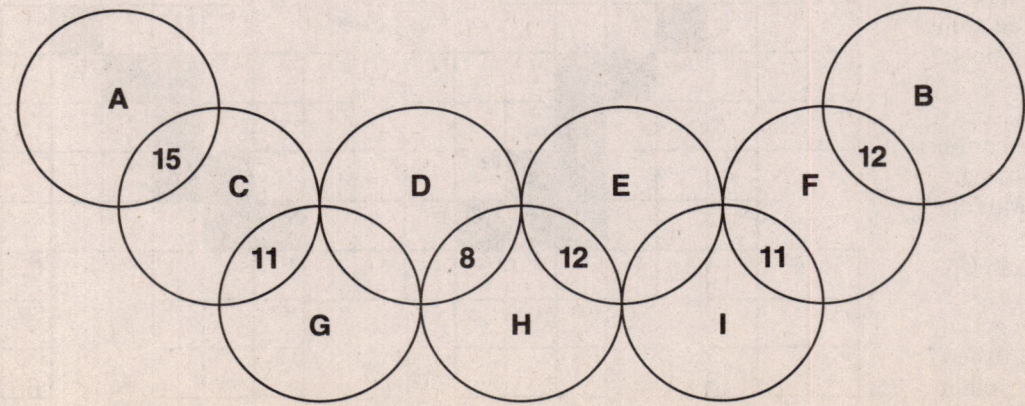

PUZZLE 572

ACROSS
1. Happy or Grumpy
6. Treaty
10. Annoy
14. Scarcer
15. German currency
16. Netman Nastase
17. Consolidate
18. Shock
19. Carnivore's diet
20. Ground grain
21. Condemn
22. Great artery
23. Big head
25. One in charge
27. City transport
31. Army color
34. Sheets, e.g.
35. Weeder
37. Craft
39. Torah closets
40. Bucks
41. Attracted
42. Hair tamer
43. Looks over
44. Soft, musically
45. Thick
48. Stray
50. Smidgen
52. Coop product
53. Adrenal, e.g.
56. Became shabby
59. Fictional fiend
63. Adult nits
64. Do roadwork
65. Pungent bulb
66. Forget
67. Uttered
68. Spoke wildly
69. Physique
70. Lazily
71. Make holy
22. Bonfire residue
24. Bar staple
26. Gumbo must
27. Fatigued
28. Bracelet locale
29. Seaman's shout
30. Hissed
32. Gold measure
33. Actress Dunne
34. Dawdle
36. Additional
38. Deuce
40. Encounter
41. Slanting
44. Ham on the hoof
46. Ripe old age
47. Grassy layer
49. Sign of triumph
51. Grant
53. Rounded lump
54. Exec's car
55. Sour substance
57. Arena shape
58. Depend
60. Contribute
61. Red deer
62. Last bits
64. Hawaiian fare
65. Ball

DOWN
1. Oil barrel
2. Dwindle
3. Diva's delivery
4. Muscle responses
5. Cook in fat
6. Pedro's dough
7. Driver's need
8. Food fragment
9. Brick poundage
10. Brunch cocktail
11. "The Sopranos" actor
12. Decree
13. Greek cheese
21. Sawbones

Progressions

PUZZLE 573

Can you follow the mathematical progression to find the fifth number in each series?

A.	47	39	33	29	____	19	13	9	7
B.	18	36	28	56	____	96	88	176	168
C.	25	28	34	43	____	58	64	73	85
D.	76	85	82	79	____	97	94	91	100
E.	83	77	70	62	____	43	32	20	7
F.	31	27	108	104	____	412	1648	1644	6576

PUZZLE 574 — CRYPTIC CROSSWORD

British-style or Cryptic Crosswords are a great challenge for crossword fans. Each clue contains either a definition or direct reference to the answer as well as a play on words. The numbers in parentheses indicate the number of letters in the answer word or words.

ACROSS

1. Cracked beer mugs in sink (8)
5. Surrounded by 500 in a fog (6)
9. Pair of clowns said, "Crowded" (9)
11. Woman's name I speak painfully in return (5)
12. Some linen Tom Brokaw put in a vault (6)
13. On parade, first of merrymakers making a bow (8)
15. Bullfighters moved to Madras (8)
16. Hide winter sports gear on the first of November (4)
19. Rabbit fur in the ear (4)
20. Using words extremely, describing comedian Lucille (8)
23. Idealistic Inca plot goes awry (8)
24. Clay I'd reshaped bitterly (6)
27. Exercising thinking, after the first (5)
28. Warrior ape's sound (9)
29. Maneuver okayed and knocked out (6)
30. Accursed, disorganized prompts for TV actors (3,5)

DOWN

1. Outspoken hitter in ball game (6)
2. Worst part of burnt nuts (5)
3. Guess I'm included in Eastern part of America (8)
4. Vice President Pierce (4)
6. Have a bite outside of one German town (6)
7. Gizmo that's impressive owned by the author of "Deliverance" (9)
8. First of turkeys flying is feeling some pain (8)
10. After Diana, a clan making an angry speech (8)
14. Sticking with advertisement on male jewelry (8)
15. Human quality of Tim Taylor changed (9)
17. Small squirrel's piece around 1 P.M. (8)
18. Choose most of rice with juice? (8)
21. Do some gardening with a GI hero (6)
22. Bly was breaking rules (6)
25. Front of lip caught in door causes grief (5)
26. Lover's tie mentioned aloud (4)

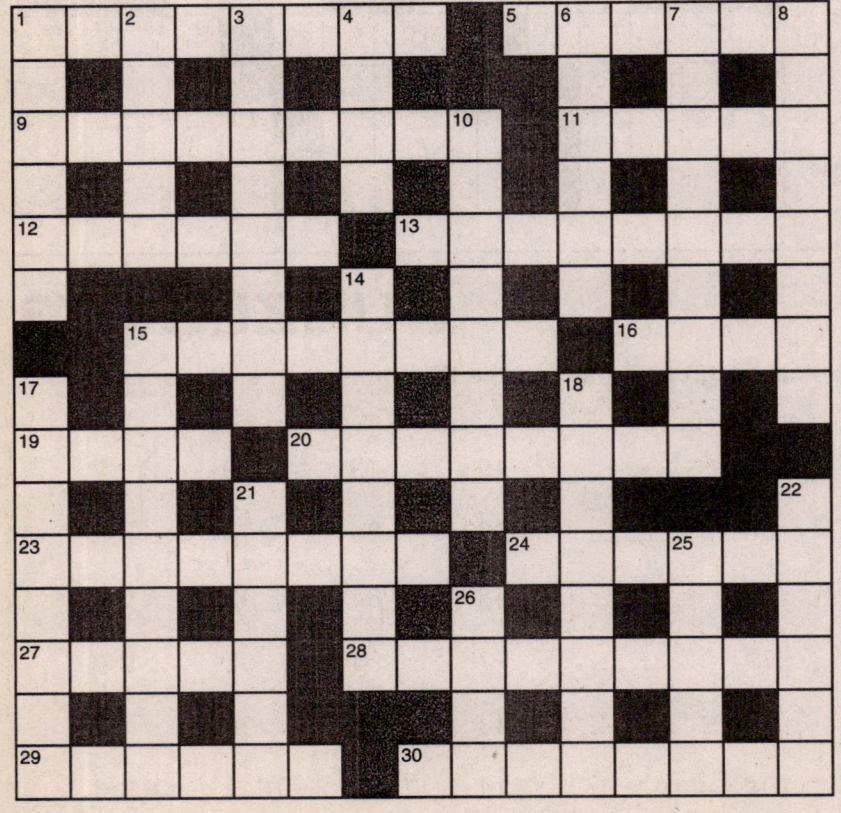

504

PUZZLE 575
• PET SOUNDS •

ACROSS
1. Furry foot
4. Bodybuilder's pride
7. Moselle feeder
11. Screen
12. Semicircle
13. Seating choice
14. Opposed
15. Dumb cluck?
17. Breadwinner
19. Togs
20. One way to stand
21. Hankered
23. Piglet's pal
25. High-pitched song?
27. Dead heat
29. Pant
32. Kept cold
34. Messy fellow
37. Choral voice
38. Breaks
40. Overwhelm
41. Bungled
42. Cuckoo
43. Feel (for)
44. Encountered
46. Up on the map
48. Graybacks
51. Kind of value
54. ____ roll (winning)
57. Half a folio
59. Larks
61. Barn dance?
64. Mademoiselle's mom
65. Parts to play
66. Noun suffix
67. Ohio lake
68. Barely made
69. Clear
70. Pumpernickel grain

DOWN
1. Certain code
2. Texas player
3. Horseplay?
4. Checkup sound
5. Ship's jail
6. Remnant
7. Formal address
8. Stat
9. Inter ____
10. Hire
11. Daisy or Fannie
13. Church official
15. Recognition
16. Specialist
18. Psyche part
22. A model may have it on
24. Basket case?
26. Yellow color
28. Ms. Fitzgerald
29. Chew the fat
30. Every bit
31. Restrain
33. Furnishings
35. Crew blade
36. Later!
39. Most tender
45. Relates
47. Baking meas.
49. Good grade
50. Glossy fabric
52. Suspicious
53. Spooky
54. Grimm heavy
55. Breakfast niche
56. Efficient
58. On the house
60. Envision
62. Rose plot
63. Morsel

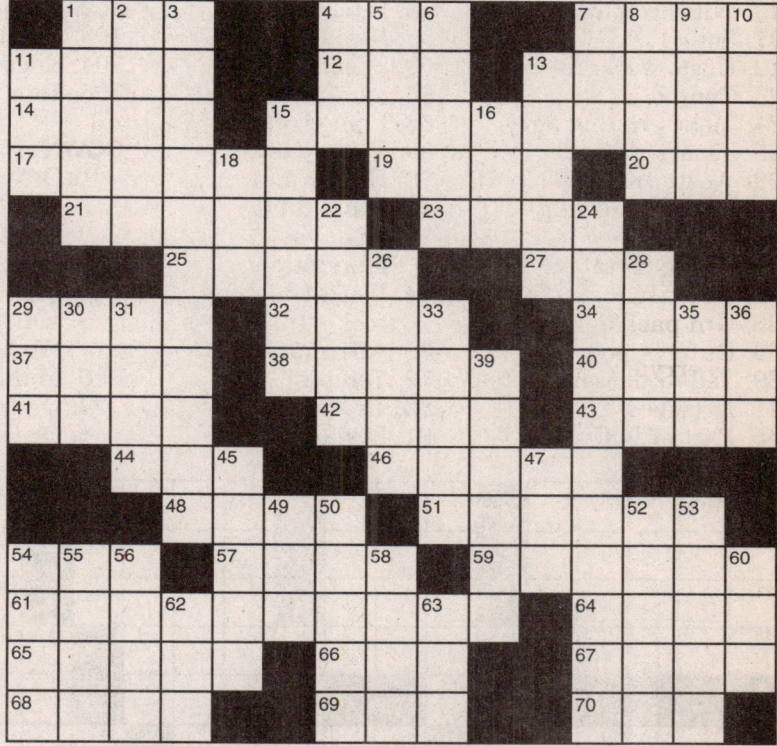

Place Your Number
PUZZLE 576

The large square below is divided into four smaller squares—A, B, C, and D—and each smaller square is divided into four sections—North, East, South, and West. Use the clues to number the sections. Each section will contain a different number from 1 through 16.

1. Within each square, the North number plus the South number equals 9.
2. All North numbers are odd.
3. The total of all West numbers is 53.
4. The total of all numbers in square C is greater than the total of all numbers in square B.
5. All numbers in square D are evenly divisible by D-North.
6. C-South is twice B-North and half A-South, which is the square root of B-West.
7. C-North is half A-East, which is less than C-West.

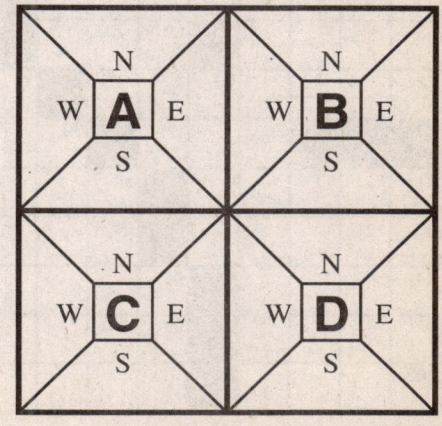

PUZZLE 577

• JUST THE TICKET •

ACROSS
1. Much, in music
6. Ripen
9. ____ up (admit)
13. NCOs
17. Basket material
18. Black gold
19. Compete
20. Witty remark
21. Sour
22. Hosp. workers
23. Coup d'____
24. Meat grading agcy.
25. Vacation time
28. Western film
29. Baltic or Bering
30. Close
31. Waste metal
32. Request
36. Group of eight
38. Duffer's peg
39. Yellow dessert
41. Deceived
45. Part of ICU
46. Spike ____
47. Asphalt
48. German article
49. Asian holiday
50. Kind of bouquet
53. Appealing sight
55. Ghostly hello
56. Scent
58. Internet co.
59. Resident
63. Spoof
65. ____-relief
68. Bone-dry
69. Victory letter
70. Hither and ____
71. Quite a bit
72. Highway foundation
74. Wood-finishing tool
78. Affirmative
79. Tempest
80. Or's mate
81. Dishonor
84. Small buffalo
85. "Diamonds ____ Forever"
86. Eagle's claw
87. Traffic offense
94. Tel ____
95. Rampage
96. A Gershwin
97. Kayak's cousin
98. Jacob's son
99. Seep
100. Melody
101. Swashbuckler Flynn
102. Leg joint
103. Belgian river
104. Encountered
105. Tour of duty

DOWN
1. Defensive ditch
2. ____-Umbrian languages
3. In ____ of
4. Dist.
5. "Oh, Pretty Woman" singer
6. Main artery
7. Dry spirits
8. Other than
9. Sudden overflow
10. Go to a restaurant
11. Paltry
12. Movie backdrop
13. Nutritional staple
14. Zest
15. Neap and ebb
16. Practices boxing
26. Antitoxins
27. Italian wine region
28. Performance halls
32. Touch against
33. Of sound mind
34. Weave yarn
35. Chew the ____
36. Run machinery
37. Cloudless
38. Needle's partner
40. ____-mo
41. Speak
42. Opposite of max.
43. Conclusion
44. Susan ____ of "L.A. Law"
47. Coffeehouse's kin
50. Vain man
51. Bread quantities
52. Cut off
54. Teasingly shy
55. Motion picture subgenre
57. Urban leader
59. Rower's propeller
60. ____-Magnon
61. Intelligence org.
62. Beatty or Sparks
64. Que. neighbor
65. Drab
66. Top-drawer
67. Young suffix
71. Laptop key
73. Existed
74. More portly
75. Jordan, in Biblical times
76. Wife of Zeus
77. Punctures
79. Nap
81. Stem
82. Place of safety
83. Animated
84. See ya, to Juan
85. Not together
88. Neeson of "The Haunting"
89. Pennsylvania city
90. Go-____
91. Cross initials
92. Midday
93. Moola
95. Rogers or Acuff

PUZZLE 578

• LAW AND ORDER •

ACROSS
1. Conduit
5. Mars, in Athens
9. Health havens
13. Bus rider Parks
17. Opera solo
18. French bridge
19. Apiece
20. Within
21. Law enforcer
23. Terrible
24. Hawk
25. The outdoors
26. Guide
28. Writing liquid
29. Newt
30. Draft
31. Electrified particle
33. Gush
36. Salty drop
37. Result
40. Eternity
41. Storage place
42. Mine tunnel
44. Pool circuit
46. Curtain holder
47. Germ
48. Chick and snow
49. Swiss river
50. Law enforcer
52. Fierce look
53. Spiritual
54. Standard
55. Overjoy
56. Astern
57. Assail
60. Unruly children
61. Law enforcer
65. First garden
66. Assistant
67. Romp
68. Eggs
69. Hazy
70. Consent
72. Balloon input
73. Outfit
74. Gauzy paper
76. Battery fluid
78. An Astaire
80. Flight
81. Graceful bird
82. Tavern drink
83. Before now
85. Sprinkle
88. Favor
91. Affirm
92. Harness part
93. Law enforcer
96. Feast
97. French waterway
98. Adam's grandson
99. Friendly
100. Polish border river
101. Give off
102. Bardot's head
103. Doodled

DOWN
1. Boot liner
2. Steam appliance
3. ____ colada
4. Parade or bonnet
5. Separated
6. Garment
7. Photography abbr.
8. Midler movie
9. Family car
10. Remitted
11. Land tract
12. Law enforcer
13. Steep valley
14. Augury
15. Basin
16. Calculate
22. Clump of hair
27. Corn portion
30. Hang fire
32. Frequently, to Keats
33. Spanish painter
34. Needy
35. Release
36. Layer
37. Let up
38. Social group
39. Weight allowance
41. Foamy drink
42. Stools
43. Tortoise's rival
45. For every
47. Squabble
48. China item
49. Con
51. Shop sign
52. Forest clearing
53. Doubtful
55. Spooky lake?
56. Remotely
57. Crib or cot
58. Red-pencil
59. "____-Tough"
60. Unclad
61. Rancid
62. Apple's middle
63. Sinister
64. Current fad
67. Discomfort
70. Sly ____ fox
71. Law enforcer
75. Not as fast
76. Dazzle
77. Floor covering
78. A Baldwin brother
79. Protect
81. Sugary
82. Get up
83. Ardent
84. Left
86. Injure
87. Prefix for all
88. Story line
89. Eastern ruler
90. Indy event
91. Fuss
94. Individual
95. Hot off the press

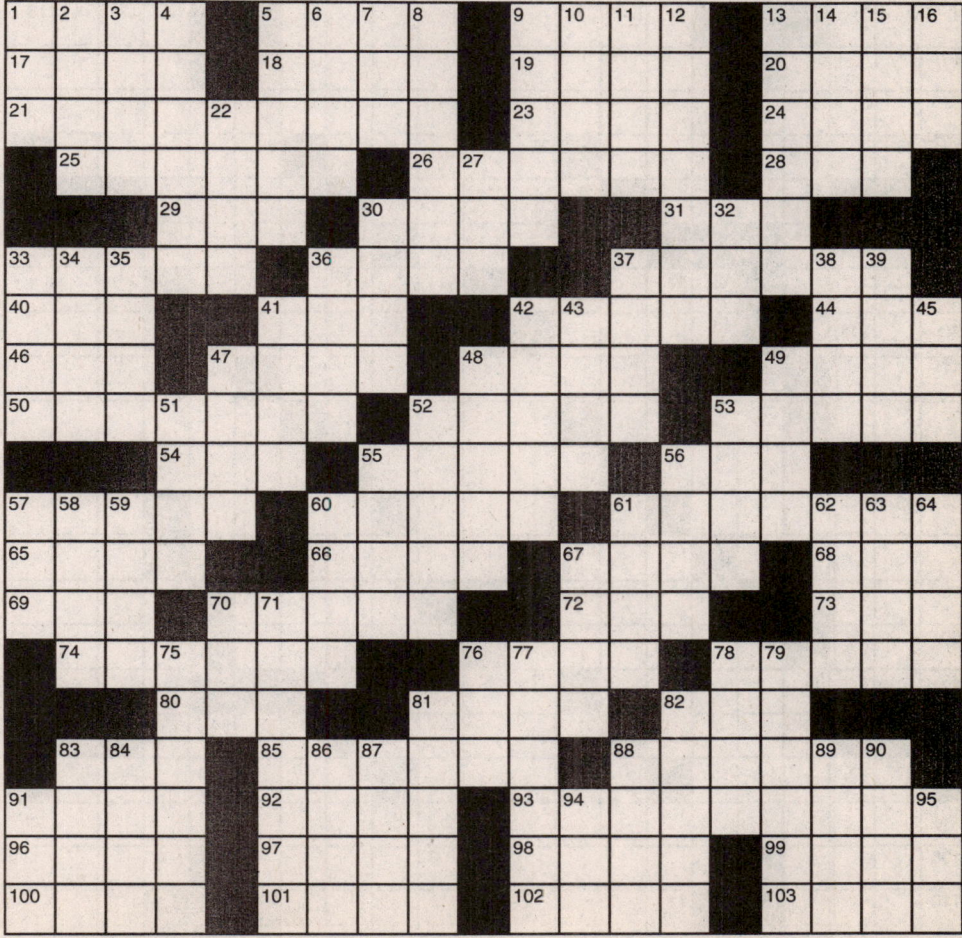

PUZZLE 579

• IN THE LOUPE •

ACROSS
1. Make a scene?
4. Bothers
8. Sewer lines?
12. Mama's boy?
16. Usher
18. Inconsequential thing
19. Iguana's kin
21. Farm team?
22. Bloodstone
24. Silicate mineral
26. Part
27. Cover words
29. Invoices
30. "Show Boat" composer
31. Senator Kefauver
32. Too
33. Marine mammal
36. Knock down
37. Velvety fabric
41. Mound
42. Edgar ___ Poe
44. Intrigue
46. ___ Lingus
47. Curing chemical
48. Pork piece
49. Narrow inlets
50. Boom, e.g.
51. Country's Ritter
52. Colorful gem
56. Idaho city
57. Big time
58. Islands in the stream
59. Nip and tuck
60. Composed
61. Frasier's brother
63. Decrees
64. Fish on the move
65. Police IDs
67. Fragrant resin
68. Aim
69. TV interruptions
72. Curly coifs
73. Large sapphire
75. Nada
76. Bete ___
77. What a koala isn't
78. Heels
79. Sushi favorite
80. Semi colon?
81. Mountain ridges
83. Hunt for water
84. Brilliance
85. Breastbones
87. Hammer ends
89. Venture
90. Elevator name
91. Mass measures
92. Rich earth
95. Some tangelos
97. "The Wreck of the Mary ___"
98. Strip
101. Translucent quartz
103. Faux jewel
106. Heraldic border
107. Ranch stray
108. Column style
109. North Carolina campus
110. Pair
111. Small dam
112. Mall habitue
113. Self starter?

DOWN
1. Wood for bats
2. Fair grades
3. Whopper
4. Airfield area
5. Decrease?
6. Splash lightly
7. Western topper
8. Derby producers
9. Organic compounds
10. Grimace
11. Type of camera, shortly
12. Hoi ___
13. Leaf angle
14. Writes
15. Hydrocarbon ending
17. Giggle provoker
18. Arouse
20. Tokens
23. Native suffix
25. Oise feeder
28. Japanese statesman
31. Rare antelope
32. Leading
33. Outpouring
34. Swiss peak
35. Variety of chrysoberyl
36. Trout lures
37. Crepe de ___
38. Deep-blue stone
39. Car contract
40. Goofed
42. Confederates
43. Bumpkins
45. Grouchy
50. Dirty
52. Makes hay while the sun shines?
53. More aloof
54. Memorable mission
55. Recurring theme
56. When repeated, Yale's fight song
60. Laud
62. Mr. Sikorsky
63. Roadside warning
64. Singer Rundgren et al.
65. Concert lineup
66. In progress
67. States, in French
68. Eats (at)
70. Merrill and Meyer
71. Paddle
73. Looks to be
74. Sacred images
77. Slightly injured
79. White ant
81. Ludicrous
82. Misting device
83. Misconduct mark
86. Tumbled
88. Pinna
91. Bottled spirits?
92. Russian revolutionary
93. Crude letters?
94. ___ gratia artis
95. "Driving Miss Daisy" author
96. Festive
97. Venetian official
98. Sup
99. Backyard burrower
100. Adam's grandson
101. Angler's catch
102. ___ Jones Average
104. Weeder
105. USNA grad

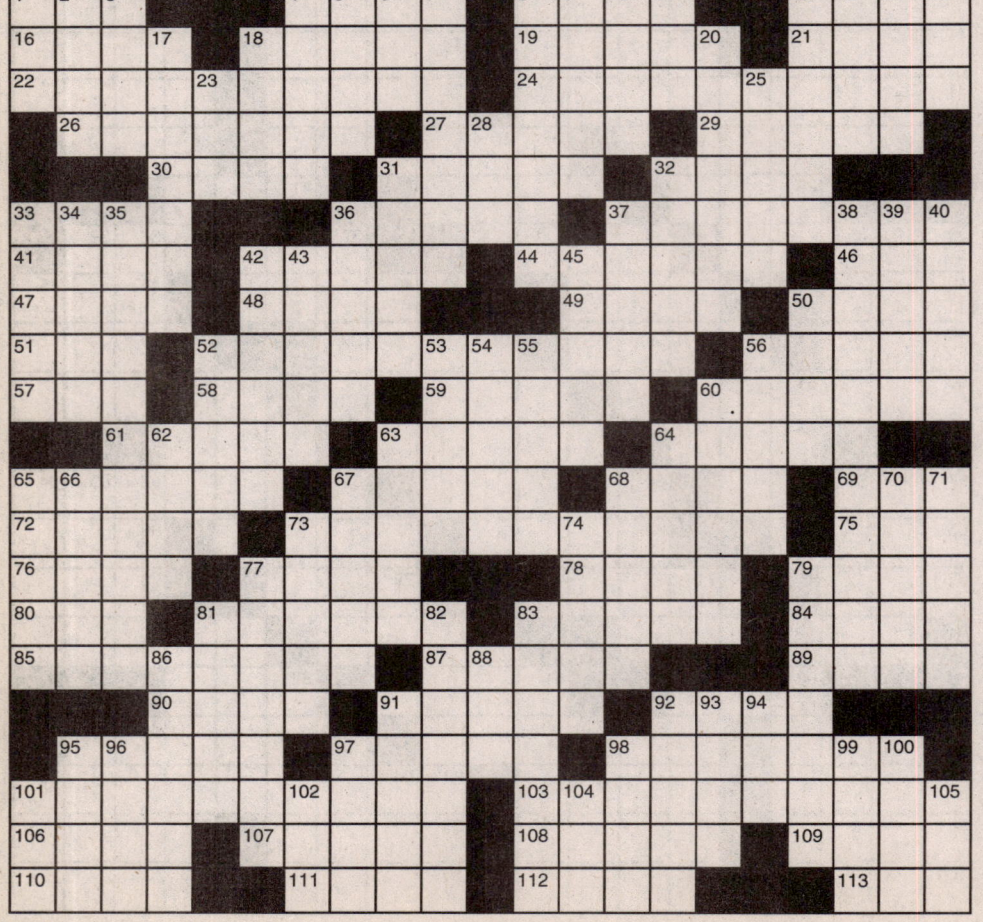

PUZZLE 580

• OF THE FEMININE PERSUASION •

ACROSS
1. Anxious
6. Beef or pork
10. Silly people
15. Influence
19. ___ costs
20. Curvature
21. Elude
22. Parable
23. Small sponge cake
25. Robin Hood's love
27. Extended family
28. "The Matrix" hero
29. Vices
31. Mouthfuls
32. Head flankers
34. Walking rhythm
35. Acquiesce
38. Scuffle
41. Calendar entries
42. Interstate
46. Licorice root
47. Seethe
48. Mule's kin
49. Poem of praise
50. ___-been
51. Stinging matriarchs
55. Zoo celebrity
57. Decide on
58. Tugs
59. Skin irritation
60. Requisition
61. Marseilles season
62. Needs aspirin
63. Thin and weak
64. Smirks
65. Shabby
67. Hazy
68. Sweet stuff
69. Assignments
71. Fruit pastries
72. Brisk wind
73. Woven network
76. Spotted horse
77. Margarine
78. Toronto ___ Leafs
79. Coronado's gold
80. TV host Funt
81. 1965 Presley film
83. Chinese leader
84. Turkey's Mount ___
85. Pod dweller
87. Comply with
88. Explosion
90. "Extra!" shouter
93. Lacoste and Descartes
95. Hags
96. Forest fillers
98. Pitcher Hershiser
99. Norway's patron saint
100. Mr. Agnew
103. Chum
105. Caesar's breakfast?
106. Accordingly
110. Hairline point
113. "The Alchemist" character
116. On the summit
117. Because
118. Eternally
119. Eaglet's lair
120. Chums
121. Knight's charger
122. Journeyed
123. Quarterback Favre

DOWN
1. Soft mineral
2. List ender
3. Nogales nothing
4. Cunning
5. Santa's aide
6. Lions' ruffs
7. Therefore
8. High card
9. Endanger
10. Relinquishes
11. Track shape
12. Dagwood's dog
13. Uncanny
14. Ministry sch.
15. Take long steps
16. Pause
17. Wings
18. Appetites
24. Regarding
26. Efficient
30. Contend
33. Pub beverage
34. Sports events
36. Uncertainties
37. Hesitation sounds
38. Sierra Nevada resort
39. Unfit
40. Brother's wife
41. Sword fights
43. Lynda Carter role
44. Venomous viper
45. "Through the ___"
47. Entirely
48. Pallid
51. Resigns
52. Avon River port
53. Directions
54. Detect
55. Silk fabric
56. Length x width
58. George C. Scott flick
63. Electrician, sometimes
64. Tarnish
66. Poker offering
67. Bamako's country
68. Succulent
69. Iberia
70. Diacritical mark
71. Roman wear
72. Yawns
74. Delete
75. "Puss in ___"
78. Silents' Normand
82. Melon variety
85. "The Raven" author
86. Hurricane center
88. Lingerie item
89. Haughtier
91. Barbers' sharpeners
92. Facial ridge
93. Swindled
94. Coastal predator
95. Applaud
97. Public spectacle
99. Blatant
100. Substitute
101. Pocket bread
102. False god
104. Dash or derby
105. Harbinger
107. Hound's quarry
108. Squadron
109. Don't strike!
111. Draft inits.
112. Deep hole
114. St. crosser
115. Experiment site

PUZZLE 581

AT 6'S AND 7'S

Clues to all the 6- and 7-letter entries in this crossword are listed first, and they are in scrambled order. Use the numbered clues as solving hints to help you determine where each one belongs in the diagram.

6-LETTER ENTRIES
Shudder
Insult
Hold back
Invent
Makes law
Filled pastry
Diminish
Groups of trees
Freight
Baltimore ___
Come forth
Beginnings
Lingo
Poisonous atmosphere
Misprints
Wall opening
Detailed account
Pub brews

7-LETTER ENTRIES
Isaac's wife
Food
Perfectly
Some explosives
More foamy
Wardrobe
Neglects
Extreme
Results
False names
Sillier
"Mommie ___"
Cover partly
Guiding lights

ACROSS
1. Yank
5. Auction word
15. Rectify
17. Stage of life
19. Compensate
20. Colonial insect
24. Propels
26. Eatery
27. Folktale monster
28. Eagle's nest
30. I-topper
31. Angler's scoop
37. Apron wearers
38. Coffee holders
40. Have a mortgage
44. Jazz style
45. French cheese
46. Keyboard
47. Handled
49. Listened
50. Masterwork
51. Italian volcano
54. Vroom
55. Lad's girl
56. Sharply bitter
61. Night person
64. Charged particle
65. Melodic sound
66. Pavarotti piece
67. Sow's opposite
69. On the briny
74. Bat wood
76. Electronic device
78. Oolong, e.g.
79. Sorrow
81. Hook shape
82. Darns

DOWN
4. Rascal
5. Sheep bleat
8. Staffs
9. Arden or Brenner
12. Musical symbol
13. Display box
14. Befitting
16. Go auburn
23. More secure
30. Fender flaw
32. Dayton's state
34. Reef material
35. Spin
36. Rundown
37. Swindles
41. To the left, nautically
42. More mature
43. Violet shade
44. Health resort
45. Rosary piece
49. Descendant
51. Profit
53. Boring tool
66. Spanish good-bye
67. Regulation
68. Blue-pencil
69. Martial ___
71. Supplement
72. Maple dripping
73. Swan song
75. Owns

PUZZLE 582

• THEME MUSIC •

ACROSS
1. Last word
5. Tote
9. Donaldson and Waterston
13. Sound boosters
17. Impale
18. Downwind
19. Door to ore
20. Corrida beast
21. Gymnast Korbut
22. Ivy, e.g.
23. Ike's ex
24. Sinful
25. "Designing Women" theme song
29. Rocks, in a bar
30. Song syllables
31. Broadcast
32. Developed
34. Lab container
38. Ovum
39. "___ 17"
41. "Catch-22" star
42. Honest one
43. Attic, maybe
46. Crew
47. Tease
48. Got word
49. Ms. Peeples
50. Voiced
52. Assess
53. Row
55. Lodestone
58. Twilled cloth
59. Go by
60. Unsociable
61. Capture
62. NASCAR driver
63. "Barney Miller" actor
64. Counterfeit
65. Hopper
66. Biblical pronoun
70. Line of bushes
73. Pouch
74. English guy
75. Westerns
76. Lad
77. Embroidery yarn
78. Tree extract
80. Pistol
81. Have being
82. Throw
83. "The Mary Tyler Moore Show" theme song
91. "East of Eden" actor
93. Actress Kedrova
94. Palindromic hour
95. Scram!
96. Optic problem
97. King of comedy
98. Sector
99. Breathing organ
100. Bridge hand
101. Charter
102. Mirrors
103. Surprised cries

DOWN
1. Eagerly expectant
2. Tunneler
3. Therefore
4. Get closer
5. Roe
6. Assumed name
7. Nevada town
8. Pre-adult
9. Lecher
10. "Experience is ___ lamp . . ."
11. Tiny
12. Norm
13. Lunched
14. "The Jeffersons" theme song
15. Cost
16. Fixed a shoe
26. Valley
27. Russian interceptor
28. Cowgirl Evans
33. Combat
34. Club
35. Browning's before
36. Police-blotter trio
37. Geisha's outfit
38. Decline
39. Phase
40. Sped
42. Hurt
43. Grasslike plant
44. Certain paints
45. Man
47. Fink
48. Run
51. Ump's kin
52. Denims
53. Cunning
54. Range animals
55. Pulverize
56. Sunburn application
57. "The Dukes of Hazzard" theme song
58. Winter weather events
59. Eternity
61. Famous restaurateur
62. Trivial amount
64. Bicuspid
65. Howl
67. Word of inquiry
68. Just manage
69. Wriggly swimmer
71. Butane, e.g.
72. Catchall abbr.
73. Windfall
74. ___ Rabbit
76. School vehicle
77. Derricks
78. Unconcerned
79. Heart conduit
80. Goliath, e.g.
81. Isolated
84. Contemptible
85. Brilliance
86. Circle
87. Cold capital
88. Slangy denial
89. "___, Nanette"
90. Collies, e.g.
92. Trawl

PUZZLE 583

• **REMEMBERING RUBY KEELER** •

ACROSS
1. Ship's jail
5. Research room
8. Kasbah dweller
12. Stiffly neat
16. Actress Turner
17. Aria, e.g.
18. Smoothing tool
19. "___ and the Swan"
20. Unique being
21. The Kingston ___
22. Singer Domino
23. Partially open
24. Odd
26. That woman
28. French river
30. Jolson/Keeler musical
34. Smear
37. Lock ___ (clash)
38. Devonshire city
40. Exclamation
41. Cornhusker St.
43. Eskimo settlement
45. Remove from print
46. "___ She Sweet"
48. Narrow cut
50. ___-thee-well
53. Tint
54. Decorator's decision
55. Dodge
58. Line of foamy water
60. Baxter/Keeler musical
66. Witnesses
67. Entire
68. New Mexican resort
70. Pausing sounds
73. On a voyage
75. German river
77. Sicilian peak
78. Bee ___ ('70s group)
80. Thick slice
83. Hebrew zither
85. Greek letter
86. Amiable
89. Intense dislike
91. Looking glass
93. Cagney/Keeler musical
96. Garden blooms
97. Sixth sense, briefly
98. Trap
102. Slide
104. Change direction suddenly
106. Newsman Sevareid
108. "Good Earth" heroine
109. Seeger or Best
110. Mr. Stanley Gardner
111. French philosopher Descartes
112. "The ___ in the Willows"
113. 365-day unit
114. Famous loch
115. Distress letters
116. Brooklyn cagers

DOWN
1. Lump
2. Hindu princess
3. Don Juan's mother
4. Sale site
5. Actress Sophia ___
6. Ms. MacGraw
7. Sobber's sound
8. Insult
9. Inlet
10. Preacher's platform
11. Next to
12. Devised
13. Rebuffed
14. Ms. Lupino
15. Impair
17. "The Empire ___ Back"
25. Horse color
27. Rochester's love
29. Jazz inst.
31. Flourish
32. American fliers: abbr.
33. Slithery
34. Fly high
35. Burglar
36. Composer's output
39. Arikara Indian
42. Consecrates
44. Bothers
47. Crags
49. Discretion
51. Fixed routine
52. Misjudge
56. Scooby ___
57. Being, in Barcelona
59. Holiday
61. Afternoon social
62. Sure thing!
63. Navigator Vasco ___
64. Cafe patron
65. Jay Silverheels role
69. German river
70. Ovum
71. Atoll
72. Madrid miss
74. Sleep like ___
76. Love affair
79. Crouching one
81. Sticks
82. Tiny amounts
84. Frees (of)
87. Captains' subordinates: abbr.
88. Football team's count
90. Shoe parts
92. Fame
94. French river
95. Control straps
99. "I cannot tell ___"
100. Talk wildly
101. Terminates
102. 007, e.g.
103. Actress Remick
105. Overhead trains
107. ___ Speedwagon

PUZZLE 584

• WEDDING PARTY •

ACROSS
1. Buddies
5. Flat hill
9. Egyptian canal
13. Transfer, as property
17. Captain's direction
18. And others
19. Nick and Nora's pooch
20. Dueling blade
21. Hearty laugh
22. Ladder step
23. Road's shoulder
24. Floppy ___
25. Jeanne Moreau movie
29. Anti's answer
30. Wager
31. Corn piece
32. Piano part
35. Apple middle
37. Relating to nitrogen
38. Retirement agcy.
41. Evelyn Waugh novel
46. Identical
47. Concealed
48. ___ pro nobis
49. Card game
50. Tic-tac-___
51. "The Time Machine" beings
53. Ladderlike in arrangement
55. Monstrous sequel, with "The"
61. Bedding
62. Gaelic
63. Hamelin pest
64. Florida Key, e.g.
65. Oklahoma Indian
66. Craggy peak
67. Circular course
71. Grimm tale
77. Pimple, slangily
78. Mr. Onassis, to friends
79. ___ majeste
80. Christens
81. Pay or view starter
82. Baby bloom
83. Little bit
84. Cary Grant comedy
92. Difficult
93. Elcar of "MacGyver"
94. Popular cookie
95. CSI portrayer George ___
97. Good golly!
98. Yalies
99. ___ even keel
100. Lives a cat has
101. Resembling twine
102. Cartoon chipmunk
103. Capitol roof
104. Romanov ruler

DOWN
1. Average
2. Tons
3. Ms. Remini
4. Lover's ballad
5. Jolly
6. Needle case
7. Beach soil
8. Branch of math
9. Belgian footwear
10. Patron
11. To be, to Fifi
12. African river
13. Moth repellent
14. Saga
15. Office item
16. Mouse-sighter's cry
26. Hay bundle
27. Garden invader
28. Asian country
32. Educat. network
33. Memorable period
34. Murky
35. Tribal leader
36. Ref. work
37. Haddad of Hollywood
38. Tasteless
39. Caravansary
40. Bedeck
42. Drives away
43. Arledge of television
44. Mr. Estrada
45. ___ first you don't succeed . . .
50. Twice five
51. Blooper
52. "Viva ___ Vegas"
53. Capture
54. Chi. clock zone
55. Overwhelming attack
56. Hindu sage
57. Narrow channel
58. Forest creature
59. Festival
60. Wear down
65. Kimono closer
66. Poetic contraction
67. Inclined surface
68. ___ Kippur
69. Caviar
70. Some dashes
72. Boat movers
73. Coated with crumbs
74. Melancholy
75. Sequoia
76. Snarl
81. Rice field
82. Apathetic
83. Steak choice
84. "Othello" villain
85. Shawl
86. Powers of "Hazel"
87. Indigo dye
88. Tuscan waterway
89. 500 sheets
90. Podium
91. Author Ferber
92. "___ Alibi"
96. Bk. in installments

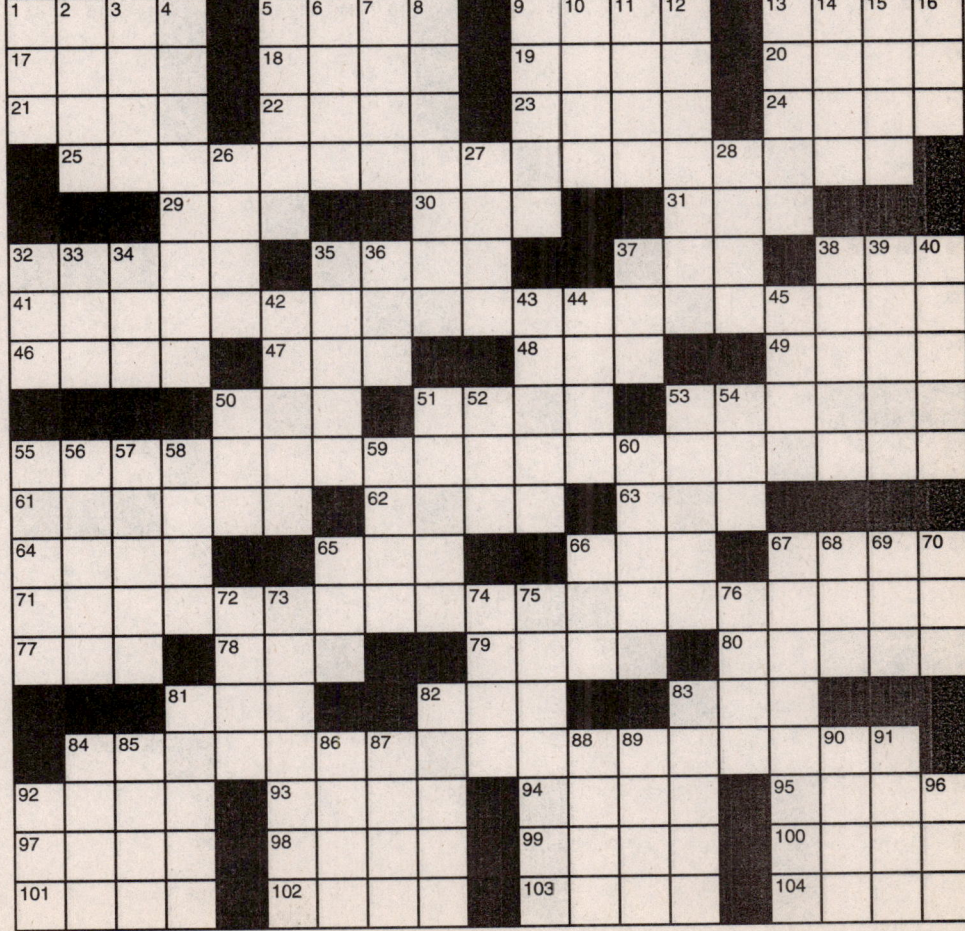

PUZZLE 585

• LIFT A FINGER •

ACROSS
1. Arithmetic
5. Hoaxes
10. Skier's tow
14. Golfer Ernie ___
17. 43,560 square feet
18. Diamond's weight
19. Bumpkin
20. Cherry center
21. Hitchhike
23. Greek war god
24. Egg cells
25. Skipper's OK
26. Sicilian city
27. Instigator
30. Fence door
31. Softball's Jennie ___
32. Representative
33. Hardy
36. "La ___ Vita"
37. Stout
38. Pronounce again
39. Present!
40. Melodious
44. The ___ of March
45. Social grace
46. Haul
48. Tender
49. Liberace's instrument
51. Billiards game
52. Struck
53. Mineral spring
56. Bourgeoisie
59. Part of rpm
60. Dutch flower
62. Achievement
63. Rosters
65. Persia, now
66. Wrath
67. Forfeit
68. Ship's wheel
72. Tranquil
74. Walking stick
75. Bank-check word
76. "The River Wild" prop
77. Low-heeled shoes
79. Mortar
80. Reeves of "Speed"
83. Hotel offering
84. Not aweather
85. Stationer's stock
87. At any moment
88. Rowdy crowd
91. Buck
92. Serve wine
93. Confirm a promise
96. Dine at night
97. Female voice
98. Jane Eyre's pupil
99. Cinema terrier
100. Young fox
101. Fret
102. Thrilled
103. Impudence

DOWN
1. Spy ___ Hari
2. Hurting
3. Factual
4. Sewn edge
5. Meager
6. Chili con ___
7. Elaborate solo
8. Loco
9. Aseptic
10. Daze
11. Scottish town
12. Biblical brother
13. Replaces a cap
14. Pindaric stanza
15. Energize
16. Commence
22. Small and round
28. Business abbr.
29. Kind of discrimination
30. Clutch
31. Army post
33. ___ Lanka
34. Journalist Koppel
35. Avail
36. Cryptologist
37. Summer mo.
39. Few
40. Illness
41. Chicken cage
42. Johnson of "Laugh-In"
43. Smirk
45. Mai ___ cocktail
46. Physician, briefly
47. Deodorant types
50. Scamp
51. Family animal
52. Atl. crosser
53. Arouse
54. Absolute
55. Hamlet's lament
57. Reclined
58. Opposite of NNW
61. Chant
64. Dishonor
66. Pelt
67. Behind schedule
69. View
70. Writer Deighton
71. Encountered
73. Blunder
74. Knot variety
75. Hammer ends
77. Shallow groove
78. Can cover
79. Sated
80. Sales booth
81. Boredom
82. Masterful
83. Fry quickly
84. Leg joint
86. Foal
87. Freshly
88. Tableland
89. Feed-bag morsels
90. Halters
94. Altar vow
95. "How the West ___ Won"

PUZZLE 586

• PAIRS •

ACROSS

1. Big cheese
5. Yukon transport
9. Stupor
13. Mr. Jannings
17. Fix film
18. Type size
19. Ms. Moran
20. Land unit
21. Roman fiddler
22. "East of Eden" actor
23. Camper cover
24. City haze
25. Tolstoy opus
28. Pantry items
29. Forte
32. Feminine principle
33. Totter
35. Before today
36. Spigots
39. Sicilian peak
42. Senator Specter
45. Hoover Dam st.
46. Methuselah's father
48. Anxious
50. GI's address
51. Recognized
53. Direct
55. Furry foot
56. Actress Markey
57. Gape
59. Slow mover
61. Substitute
63. Lon ___ (Cambodian leader)
64. Ford lemon
66. Velvet finish
67. Story hour
71. Seamstress
73. Pianist Watts
76. Coleridge work
77. Honshu wear
79. Mississippi or Ohio
81. Dumbfounded
82. Coach Parseghian
83. Lyrics
85. Locations
87. Curler's surface
88. Brusque
90. Stable fare
92. Miami's Junior ___
93. Booster
94. Ms. Moreno
96. Chimpanzee, e.g.
98. Gets some shuteye
100. Kingsley or Martin
102. John Garfield boxing flick
107. Medieval defense
108. Capacity
109. Thug
110. Mosaic piece
114. Border
115. "___ Christie"
116. Otherwise
117. Hot spot
118. Clairvoyant
119. "Buddenbrooks" writer
120. Tragic king
121. Must have

DOWN

1. Golfer Hogan
2. Verse form
3. Lady's man
4. Harriet Beecher ___
5. Lacedaemon natives
6. Turkish coin
7. Univ. course
8. Peachy
9. Political thaw
10. Geometric calculation
11. Galvanizing metal
12. Register
13. Parade occasion
14. Rock Hudson series
15. Fe, to a chemist
16. Staying power
26. Money to play with
27. Humble ___
29. Army vehicles
30. Realtor
31. Frank Sinatra song
34. Maize unit
37. Plant holders
38. Landscape
40. Pile
41. Petri-dish gel
43. Spectacular
44. Protuberance
47. Coin-toss choice
49. Mama sheep
52. Composed
54. Stage platform
56. Ms. Verdugo
58. Yale alum
60. Clark's partner
62. Tiny veggie
65. Weekend wear
67. Little monster
68. Beckett's homeland
69. Cattle call
70. Mediterranean feeder
72. Network of nerves
74. Summarize
75. Anthony and Barbara
78. Journalist Tarbell
80. "60 Minutes" name, once
83. Drenched
84. Apple variety
86. Takei role
89. Zsa Zsa, to Eva
91. Luxury hotel
95. James ___ Garfield
97. "Mary Tyler Moore" actress
99. First name in rock
100. Iowa town
101. Style
103. Charlie's wife
104. Bennett of "The Big Idea"
105. Distribute
106. Home-run champ
111. "___ Got to Be Me"
112. Grant's foe
113. Wrap up

PUZZLE 1

```
I D S   A I D E   D A L E   R A I N
N E W   B R A S   O P A L   O T T O
F E A T H E R S   T E D D Y B E A R
O P T I O N   A B N E R   E E E
      D R E   Y O U R S   R A S P S
L A C E S     P T S         O W E
O O H                     S W A N
U N I           R A D I O
D E N S E       E D E N S
    C P L       A I R
A C H E S       D E P O T
S H I N E           U M A
H I L T             F I B
E E L   F I G     R A F T S
    F A R E D   S L O O P   B E T
      E L O   C O U P E   A D O R E D
B E D P I L L O W   C A S H M E R E
O R A L   L I R E   O H I O   V I P
B A B Y   S E N D   S A L T   S E T
```

PUZZLE 2

```
H E M   R U D E   P R O D
I V E   A T O M   L A N E
S I N   H E L P   A N T E
S L U G   N E T   S T O P
    A S S   Y A M
D E S P A I R   W A S T E
E L K   L L A M A   P A Y
B L I S S   G A R B A G E
    O A T   S E E
F L E A   R E C   D A L E
L O C K   E X A M   W O N
A C H E   S I R E   A D D
P O O R   S T A T   Y E S
```

PUZZLE 3

```
W E B S   C L A P   A R M
E M I T   L A M A   B O O
T U B E   A X I S   L O T
    E L M   T E E T H
A M B L E   S H O E
V I E   I N T E R L U D E
I C E   O E R     N O D
D A R T B O A R D   D O G
    H A N D   I V O R Y
R I V E T   F E E
A D E   O G R E   N A M E
C E E   N E A R   O X E N
E A R   S E W N   M E N D
```

PUZZLE 4

```
F A D E   A B L E   H A N G S
L O W S   R A I L   U B O A T
O R E S   I C E D   M E R R Y
A T E   C A T   E D I T
T A B O O   E R R E D   G E E
    F L A R E   S O L E M N
    S A F A R I S   C R A N E D
C U R E   C A I N E   T I N S
A G E N D A   D O N A T E D
S A N D E D   U N T I E
    E R A   D E L E S   D R O O L
    M U S E   E R E   C R Y
M A G I C   V I N E   F E A R
A P A R T   E L S E   R A T E
Y E S E S   E K E D   O N E S
```

PUZZLE 5

Breton, Danish, French, Gaelic, German, Hebrew, Korean, Nepali, Pashto, Slovak.

PUZZLE 6

```
C A R P   P R O P   S P Y
A G E R   B L A R E D   W O E
M A D E   A E R A T E   A L L
P R O F   S T E T   L I B E L
    A N K H   O V E N
R A B B I   O G R E   F A S
H U E   G Y R O   G H O S T S
O D D   H E A R S A Y   K O I
S I E S T A   G O N E   E R R
O W E   R E E F   N U D E S
    L Y N X   T E A L
I S T L E   O V E R   T R A P
S P A   T O T I N G   R A L E
L U G   I B I S E S   A F A R
E N S   I C E D     S T E P
```

PUZZLE 7

1. Crayon, Pencil; 2. Button, Zipper; 3. Orchid, Zinnia; 4. Ginger, Nutmeg; 5. Mussel, Oyster.

PUZZLE 8

```
T O W E R   C H A R   S M O G
I M A G E   H A L E   T A K E
P I V O T   A R E A   E A R L
S T Y   A M I D   L L A M A S
    L I A R     L A M
W R I N G   G Y M   A R M
B E A N   I F F Y   A L G A E
L A C E   E R R     I R K S
O V E N S   R O O K   C E E S
W E D   T E N   I C I E R
    V I M   T W I T
A D V E R B   C H I C   W A R
L E A N   O D O R   A L I K E
A L S O   S O L O   D O R I S
S E E M   S C A B   A G E N T
```

PUZZLE 9
ARTIFACT

PUZZLE 10

```
G A R B   C R A M   A L B
A R E A   H E R E   L I E
B E V Y   I S M S   T E E
    O N C E   A B O U T
I S S U E   A P S E
T A P   N U L L   T O A D
E V I L E R   U S A B L E
M E N U   G I S T   I O N
    A G E D   U P S E T
F L O U R   E O N S
R U B   E D A M   A W A Y
A N I   T A T E   L O D E
Y E T   A M E N   M E O W
```

PUZZLE 11

```
A D E   S O F A   Y A W P
F U N   A P O D   E R A L
T O D D L E R S   T I L E
    W A N E   O I L E D
F E T E D   G A G
A C H E   D O V E   D N A
C H U B B Y   E E R I E R
T O G   R E A R   H A L T
    A R C   F I L L Y
L A V I N   C H I N
A C E D   P R I S O N E R
T R I O   A U N T   O W E
S E L L   N E T S   G E T
```

PUZZLE 12

```
C H E F   S O P   P R A M
A U T O   S Q U A T   S E G O
B E A U   P U N C H   A T O P
    R E L I C   I L L
D A B   N E N E   R E M I S S
E G O   J E T   A T E   N E E
B A B O O N   P R Y   S E T A
    S H Y   A O K   V E X
F I L M   P S I   B I C A R B
E V E   I R K   M A D   C U E
Z Y D E C O   F I R E   T E E
    G E L   A R R O W
J B A R   I N U R E   I F F Y
A O N E   X E N O N   F A R E
W A T T   W A R   E N O W
```

1-S, 2-G, 3-W, 4-L, 5-A, 6-X, 7-D, 8-E, 9-H, 10-T, 11-O, 12-B, 13-N, 14-F, 15-U, 16-M, 17-Z, 18-P, 19-R, 20-Q, 21-C, 22-K, 23-J, 24-Y, 25-I, 26-V.

PUZZLE 13

1. Indira Gandhi, 2. Alfred Nobel, 3. Mary Shelley, 4. Isaac Newton, 5. Miles Davis, 6. Phyllis Diller, 7. Martin Luther, 8. Leontyne Price, 9. Eugene Ionesco, 10. Mary Cassatt.

PUZZLE 14

```
I R E   C A R Y   R A T E
T A D   A L O E   E M I T
S H I R L E Y T E M P L E
    S E A L   I D O
    P E G S   A V I S
F A N   D O N A M E C H E
E G A D   B I N   D E A R
Z A S U P I T T S   D Y E
    S A F E   S E A T
    F E E   L I S T
R O B E R T M I T C H U M
O D E R   N A V E   A B E
D E N S   A P E D   D A N
```

PUZZLE 27
LUAU GRAB PAPAL / AKIN AURA ICILY / SEMI GEMS STEER / TBAR HOT DEE / ENDER ION / GEE ADS ILLEST / RIP SALAD SOLID / EGOS MIXES NAME / THROB NEAPS TIN / STRONG LAY ENS / EVE NUDGE / CAB ITS ARCS / OCEAN TAPE HIFI / INANE OWED EVEN / FEUDS WEDS RYES

PUZZLE 28
SPAS ISLE GATOR / WARP TWIN AWARE / ALTO SALT LENDS / PESO BARB GEE / NIB CEE SORE / RID GIG EASY / ARE NOEL MANTRA / CONDO LET ICIER / ENSURE GALL CAM / MEEK GOO SLY / HASP LIP WRY / ELK SNIT OPAL / ROARS DEAR DOLE / ONTAP ECRU ELSE / NEEDY REST LOOK

PUZZLE 29
WRATH MART BASS / AUDIO APER ABUT / KNEEL GAVE THEE / ESS DAIRIES ODE / REF TETHERED / NATURAL WORN / ACES RUB PUDDLE / BRATS GEM BORIS / SELLER GAB WARP / EWER RACEWAY / DEADENER BAD / REB RETAPES LID / ARIA WAVE TWICE / MIDI EKES LEMON / SEER DENT EBONY

PUZZLE 30
SHY LOOP STATE / TAI LURE DIALED / ALP ARTS EXTEND / BOSOM ONE STY / WARP AMEN / GUN OATH LUMP / FIT OPE AFLOAT / LATH MAMBO LULU / UNEASY PAR SET / TRUE JOLT TED / LAMA MAYO / POL UMP INPUT / EXOTIC ELSE ERR / RECOOK REEL AGE / KNOWN TIED KEY

PUZZLE 31
SPORT MASH ASPS / CAMEO ALTO WHET / ALERT SPAR LAKE / MENU IRE WOE / NAB GROVELED / DIM ROBE RES / ROE MOON STEEP / ETA ROUND BAR / WATTS IRIS BRA / OAR NAPE SLY / STAMPEDE SEW / LAD SHE OMIT / IRON ALSO GRADE / TORE STOW ASTER / STEW HAWN STEAM

PUZZLE 32
SCRAM AMEN CLAY / IRATE WALE HOSE / GENES OGLE ANEW / HAD ASK AREAS / STOP PERFORMS / EMOTE ALUM ONE / LAW VETO MOM / ALIEN DIE RUERS / SIN TRIO HES / PET REEL ADEPT / ERUPTION DIRT / STRUM ADD SUE / PING OWER OFTEN / ARAB WORE ROOST / RELY LORD MELTS

PUZZLE 33
ELM ICED ACED / BOA SNAKES DODO / BUM INDENT ALIT / STATE SIR PATE / ASP MIST / SMARTEST DISCS / HER ATLASES LEG / ODE AMP OER / PIN ZIPPERS SKI / CABIN SWEETEST / UGLY FRO / ROBS EAT VOICE / ABUT TREBLE DOG / FELL SNARED LOG / TYKE SLAT ELS

PUZZLE 34
RAG / IR / SOPPOSE / EEUL / SERMONTEASE / EVPETS / TRACELLARGESTEP / ESSESSEA / APERSONCENTERRY / EEIAUN / MELONERINKS / SVII / EVERSET / RE / TOW

PUZZLE 35
AREA COD GAVE / SYNC ADO AGAR / PEST BONELESS / SCARES SET / WEB ONSETS / IGUANA SILTED / FORDS MARRY / ESPIES DAMAGE / TRIVET MOD / ILL VEILED / COALESCE IOTA / EGGY TAT APOD / ROSE ARE LEND

PUZZLE 36
ALBS EAR LEIS / COOP DNA ACME / HOLY SKI CLAW / EKE MEANS AGE / DERAIL BELIED / DOUR HONORS / GATEWAY / SAUCER TACH / WHIRLS VOLLEY / ARM ETHER ACE / SOIL ION ASKS / TUNA FRO ISLE / EDGY YAM RYES

PUZZLE 37
WI SP CLAM OR PARA SOL / S ONG V ILL A FEST IVE / DOM E ST IC TE THE R SE NT / ALL LE GE ME MEN TO / PA TRO L STU B T UR MOI L / STO W RE LA TE ST UCK / R EL EA SE DE LL TE EN Y / CH AS TE ER RA ND / LA ST H AM PER V ER TI CAL / P IN AF ORE S POK EN T END / SE T TER ON ER OUS HE AR

PUZZLE 38
1. Window, 2. Letter, 3. Power.

PUZZLE 39
BEND DUCAT ACID / AVER INANE MACE / BICYCLISTS UPON / ELK HATE TALENT / RATE FAKE / CANINE LATITUDE / ADEPT BACON PAL / RAVE SABER PEND / AGE RESET DUNCE / TERMINAL BORDER / IDOL BANE / ANGLER GONE RIM / LEAD ILLITERATE / PALE TEASE ACES / SPAR ADDER GEMS

PUZZLE 40
1. Hailing cabs, 2. Cashew, 3. Teapot, 4. Marble cake, 5. Square meal.

PUZZLE 41

PUZZLE 46

PUZZLE 50

PUZZLE 42
1. Mozzarella, 2. Camembert, 3. Monterey Jack, 4. Limburger, 5. Parmesan, 6. Gruyere.

PUZZLE 47

1-D, 2-K, 3-G, 4-S, 5-O, 6-R, 7-X, 8-V, 9-P, 10-M, 11-H, 12-W, 13-C, 14-F, 15-Q, 16-J, 17-Y, 18-E, 19-B, 20-Z, 21-T, 22-A, 23-U, 24-L, 25-N, 26-I.

PUZZLE 51

PUZZLE 43

PUZZLE 48
A: 1. Crush, 2. Sable, 3. Laces, 4. Eking, 5. Nacre, 6. Reach, 7. Cease, 8. Speck.
B: 1. Rush, 2. Able, 3. Aces, 4. King, 5. Acre, 6. Each, 7. Ease, 8. Peck.

PUZZLE 52

PUZZLE 44

PUZZLE 49

PUZZLE 53

PUZZLE 45
Bag, Ban, Bat, Bib, Big, Bin, Bog, Bow, Boy.

PUZZLE 73
Escarole, Eggplant, Artichoke, Endive, Asparagus, Cucumber, Squash.
6TH COLUMN DOWN: Spinach

PUZZLE 76
1-F, 2-T, 3-W, 4-C, 5-N, 6-H, 7-L, 8-E, 9-R, 10-P, 11-Q, 12-V, 13-O, 14-Y, 15-D, 16-U, 17-Z, 18-J, 19-K, 20-A, 21-I, 22-X, 23-S, 24-M, 25-B, 26-G.

PUZZLE 77
Lightweight boxer

PUZZLE 80
1. Nail, 2. Well, 3. Bottle, 4. Pitch, 5. Base.
BONUS: Sugar (cane, maple, loaf, coat, plum)

PUZZLE 81

PUZZLE 85

PUZZLE 89

PUZZLE 82
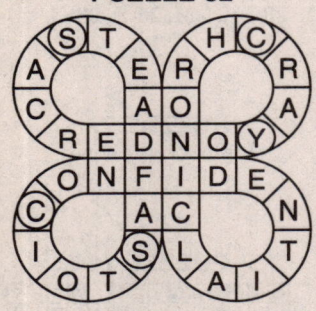

PUZZLE 86

PUZZLE 90
1. De/f/end/er, A/ma/t/eur, Et/h/n/ic, Fa/lte/re/d.
BONUS: De/ma/n/d
2. Cr/abg/ra/ss, Aut/oc/rat/ic, Ex/pl/odi/ng, Ad/mir/ab/le.
BONUS: Cr/oc/odi/le.

PUZZLE 87

PUZZLE 91

PUZZLE 83

PUZZLE 84
1. Notch, Guile, Clout, Hinge.
2. Decal, Adore, Mulch, Humor.
3. Robin, Inept, Pleat, Labor.
4. Grant, Oldie, Lingo, Tread.

PUZZLE 88

PUZZLE 92

PUZZLE 93

PUZZLE 97

PUZZLE 101

PUZZLE 94

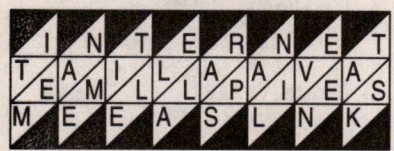

PUZZLE 98
SWIMMINGLY

PUZZLE 102

PUZZLE 99

PUZZLE 95

PUZZLE 103

PUZZLE 100

PUZZLE 104

PUZZLE 96
DIMINUTIVE

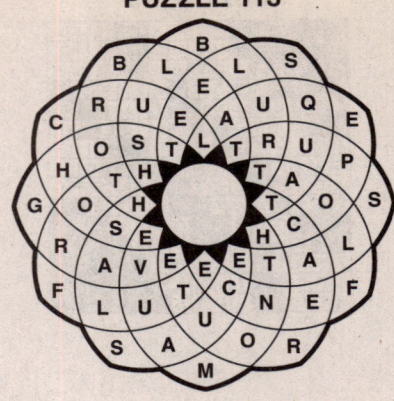
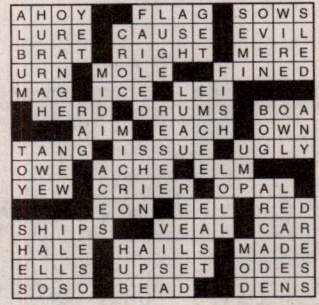

PUZZLE 117

DOCS POSH STAR ACME
AVOW RATE PITA LOON
MEMO ORAL ACED SUES
ENFOLD LEN IRON
OPED BOX LUAU SKI
EER DELE PEOPLE EEL
AUTO DISCOLOR DILLS
CREEP TEA SMOG COLA
HORRID TRY SORCERY
CEL DEB TAR
ASHAMED TAM DOMAIN
FREE OGRE RID CONDO
REARM MAGNETIC WELT
ANT ORANGE TEAM CEE
TAB LANK ESS TOAD
EWER ADE EMBOSS
OGLE IONS WHIR ATOP
WETS TREK EAVE TEAR
LEST YEWS DYER ESPY

PUZZLE 118

AMID TOP ERROL
MADE APE STOOGE
MALL SEW PEDDLE
OMELET FUR EER
TEN URNS
BIG CLEAN ALOT
OVERHEAD PLURAL
MINE STAIR MAKO
BERETS PROMPTER
DELE STENO ERE
SARI SOB
OFT RIB USEFUL
PARROT OWN WARE
AROUSE DOC EDGE
LEDGE DOE REEK

PUZZLE 119

SLEW ASPS APES
TAME SWEEP REEK
AGED SOWER ONLY
FOR MER POEM
FOG USED LATCH
NEWT REAL ROE
HES OAT DADA
SAFE PHOTO EYED
WREN RIP MUM
AIR TYPE ROOK
MANIA DRAG FED
SNOB AWE FRY
OVAL LARVA PINE
DELE DRYER ICER
EXES BEND GELS

PUZZLE 120

NECKS ALP CAVED
AGAIN BIO EXILE
GODDESSES LEASE
NAP DEAL LED
STAKE SON
HASP WARPS OPT
ALE ROLE ROAM
IOTA TOGAS MEMO
ROSS OMEN TEA
NEE RARER GIST
AIM ERECT
HAD VEND LEI
ALIBI EASYASPIE
MOVIE EMU CHURN
STAND REB TANKS

PUZZLE 121

SHES AWES SCAPE
PANT FIST CARLA
ALTO ALSO ANTES
STIRFRY PAR SAT
CEL ICE
EWE INS ALERTS
RIM PILAF EATS
APE BASIL PEP
SEND SHRUB EER
STENCH EGO SPY
BYE OFT
ADS LEG LIBERTY
HIPPO ACID LIRA
ONION ROLL LEEK
YETIS BYTE ASKS

PUZZLE 122

STASH CADS PAT
HAPPEN OMIT UKE
ENTIRE NINE MIX
ROAD SERVANT
PEA TRUSTEE
REAL HAT TONGUE
ERR WIDE URNS
BING DELES EATS
USER IRIS TIE
THROBS ZIP BEES
AUSTERE ODD
SPONSOR ECRU
HUB SLAP KINDLE
IRE EVIL SOCIAL
PRY DENY TEEMS

PUZZLE 123

TOTES HEMS FALL
AWARE ALOE OKAY
REBEL ISLE RISE
ERRED DENTS
TRACE STEM
FIESTAS HEAVY
EACH REPLY NAIL
ERA WEE CEE
TALC ENTER HALT
SLOBS REMINDS
MOST NESTS
CRUMB ELITE
HOSE SPIN KOALA
OPEN TEEN ENDED
PEST YENS REEDS

PUZZLE 124

ANTS MAMA STAB
REAP SOLOS PONE
IDLY HULLS LATE
ASK PAS DIVIDER
TOILED GIN
BRUNETTE NATURE
LURED RATE SNOW
ILK BARED IVE
NEED APER SAVER
DRYING SMOLDERS
PIP TIDIER
TRELLIS NOD SPA
YOYO POLAR GIRL
POEM EDITS ATOP
OKRA SALE GYMS

PUZZLE 125

ARIA SAC SLAT
GENT TIGER EASE
ABUT OXIDE ITEM
PARADE TEA NEAP
ERE ANTA LYE
PLAYTIME ORT
STOA ICON LAGER
TANGELO DEPLETE
OILER OMIT LEEK
PLY SANITARY
FED SEGO EFT
THOU OFF EDIBLE
RIOT BRIAR DOOR
ORZO EERIE ONUS
TEEN EEL LYRE

PUZZLE 126

SETS ROAR UMP
TRAP ELSE TAR
ARTY PITS ORE
ROT SLOE PRY
TROUPE RATIOS
SONATA THAW
PRELATE
PIES SPIRAL
BARGED PREPAY
EGO RILE ICE
TON WADI LEIS
ADE EPEE ACNE
SAD BEAD BEGS

PUZZLE 127

RASP BOP DOCS
ARIL AGE ERAL
TREY YEA WIRE
EEN FOES ERE
LANDAU OCELOT
RAIN SUREST
STOPPER
CICADA CINE
ALMOND CHEERS
GAB BORE GOT
ARIA ALE FADE
REBS LED ITEM
STEP LOO BEDS

PUZZLE 128

CAVE SALE ELLE
OLIVE ELUDE TOAST
MOTEL DAVIDCARUSO
ONA EDEN TIA RAW
ELINOR NOEL AYN
VAN NOR LAB
PETE GUNS ROSE
AMOS ALTE FLOWERS
PIT AMES FRAN RIO
ALADDIN GRIM EVEN
ELIA SLED NESS
EMP QUE MII
SOS ALUM SANDER
UNA MIA AIDA LAS
DENNISFRANZ NADIA
SITAR TERSE EWING
LANE STAR ENSE

PUZZLE 129
(crossword solution grid)

PUZZLE 134
(crossword solution grid)

PUZZLE 139
(crossword solution grid)

PUZZLE 130
1. Aromatic, 2. Comedian, 3. Daughter, 4. Delicate, 5. Bandanna, 6. Inactive.

PUZZLE 135
1. Cold gold, 2. Phony crony, 3. Cross boss, 4. Stuck truck, 5. French bench.

PUZZLE 140
(crossword solution grid)

PUZZLE 131
(crossword solution grid)

PUZZLE 136
(crossword solution grid)

1-N, 2-J, 3-P, 4-G, 5-X, 6-C, 7-O, 8-Q, 9-D, 10-W, 11-V, 12-U, 13-T, 14-Y, 15-L, 16-Z, 17-R, 18-S, 19-M, 20-I, 21-K, 22-B, 23-H, 24-F, 25-E, 26-A.

PUZZLE 141
(crossword solution grid)

PUZZLE 132
1. This world is but a canvas to our imaginations. (Henry David Thoreau)
2. Friends are the family we choose for ourselves.

PUZZLE 137
1. Funnel, Tunnel; 2. Debate, Debase; 3. Warren, Warden; 4. Strode, Stroke; 5. Squeak, Squeal; 6. Pocket, Socket; 7. Stable, Staple; 8. Valley, Volley.

PUZZLE 133
(crossword solution grid)

PUZZLE 138
(crossword solution grid)

PUZZLE 142
(crossword solution grid)

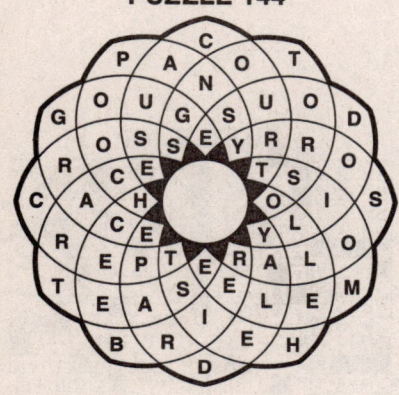

PUZZLE 163

1-L, 2-Q, 3-T, 4-G, 5-S, 6-Y, 7-K, 8-I, 9-B, 10-H, 11-A, 12-O, 13-P, 14-F, 15-N, 16-J, 17-M, 18-W, 19-U, 20-X, 21-Z, 22-C, 23-V, 24-E, 25-R, 26-D.

PUZZLE 166

1. EVERGREEN: Hemlock, Spruce, Redwood, Cypress.
2. FINANCE: Dividend, Balance, Capital, Interest.

PUZZLE 167

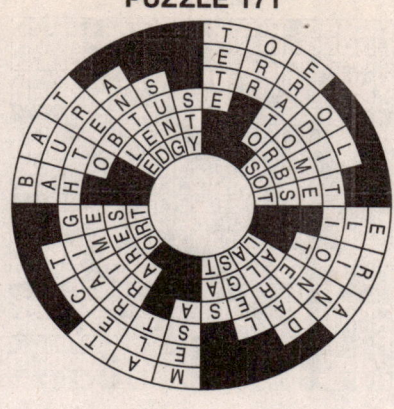

PUZZLE 168

PUZZLE 169

PUZZLE 170

PUZZLE 171

PUZZLE 172

PUZZLE 173

PUZZLE 174

PUZZLE 175

1-M, 2-L, 3-T, 4-E, 5-N, 6-C, 7-W, 8-I, 9-A, 10-D, 11-X, 12-S, 13-R, 14-P, 15-B, 16-Z, 17-G, 18-H, 19-O, 20-F, 21-K, 22-Y, 23-J, 24-V, 25-Q, 26-U.

PUZZLE 176

1-Z, 2-R, 3-W, 4-M, 5-H, 6-B, 7-Q, 8-Y, 9-L, 10-N, 11-D, 12-F, 13-J, 14-A, 15-P, 16-S, 17-V, 18-E, 19-G, 20-X, 21-I, 22-K, 23-U, 24-C, 25-T, 26-O.

PUZZLE 177

PUZZLE 178

1. Shuttle, 2. Sparkle, 3. Strange, 4. Shingle, 5. Subside, 6. Suppose, 7. Sublime, 8. Sizable, 9. Spindle, 10. Stature.

10-LETTER WORD: Transplant

PUZZLE 179

RASP SHAD SHOP SALE
OVER CORE TOUR AMOK
MERE ROTE ANTE FIRE
PRECOOK PARE TRADED
AND WENT BEAR
PRISE JEST PREVIEWS
LECT CURT SHANE VIP
ODE BORE FLAGS BELA
DESTROY BLISS BERET
RAP GRACE DOE
SPLIT FRAME VANTAGE
TEAM PEACE WORE LOW
EAT ARTIE BITE PINE
PRECLEAN CODE ORDER
AAHS RAGE ARE
AHORSE TETE PREPAID
WILT AVON YEAR ALTA
EDGE TARE ERGO CLEF
DEAR STOW DREW KYAT

PUZZLE 183

SATIN SPAR SLOPE SPAN
ELIDE WEVE TIMER ELSE
CLASSMATES AMALGAMATE
TAR TONE PARENT LINED
SHARED SLICED MITERS
IDES ARID CHOKE
CHIC CASED MOUSE FAD
LONE VOTE CARET MILE
OAT BOWL SPANKS CARVE
PRIMAL ASTERN BURSAR
MELT STINTED ABIT
SLATES ACCEDE SEAMED
LATER BARKER AMID AVA
AVER MUSTS ENOS STAR
BED MARKS BRASS TENT
FERNS MAAS SOME
BUSILY SETTER MOTELS
ANKLE SONNET EMIT VIP
STALEMATED LEGITIMATE
KITE OUTRE EGAN LADEN
SEER PLODS SOLE EXERT

PUZZLE 187

BRAD ATOM KALE FIRE
EAVE IRAE AGER IDOL
AKIN RITE RAIN SLOE
KEVINCOSTNER SCHEME
MER SEE TAN
BAG LASS OMAR RECAP
ERROLFLYNN MINOTAUR
LAID TYRE ANAT IRE
ALTOS IASI STE NAY
RICHARDGREENE
CAT DOE SILO ERROR
USA ELAN OCOA NOSE
PALISADE JOHNCLEESE
SPENT SEGO ASHE SAD
VET ANT INA
ESCAPE BRIANBEDFORD
TOOL RYAN KIEV OREO
AUDI SALE ELLE RATS
SLED EMIT NETS ELSE

PUZZLE 180

OLEO ASTA STAB HELP
PULP CHOP TARA EVEL
ESSE ROMP ORAN LIVE
CHARLIEBROWN AMELIA
AID ODE ANON
PASTE ALVA STARWARS
ARNE TREE GTO THREE
DNA CULT AROMA EINE
SOPRANO SCAR SWEDEN
URN BETTE LIL
GAMBLE ALOE LESSONS
OBEY LASER PEEP VAT
ERATO LIS HEAP MESA
SATURATE NOAH DONAT
ENNA NOR OAR
CLOSET JOHNNYBGOODE
HOLD LAIT EASE CRAW
ARIA ELLE TRES CARE
DENY RATS SERE OLES

PUZZLE 184

CABS AGLET MAST GLAD
IDEA NOONE ABLE PRONE
DOGDAYAFTERNOON LARGE
ERE LOTTO OGRE CANNED
RETAINS MOOT CANTER
CEE QUID STAVES
RAVEN CURD AMES SAG
USER MOANS CAPER ZOLA
THEBLACKSTALLION EDAM
SER ALOE GEER BRASS
GILA PROMS MIRO
UNSER SOAR SALA SMU
NEER CATONAHOTTINROOF
IONE EVERT ORATE ARNO
TNT OMEN PARE BITTS
AVERSE PELT GAS
REGENT FRED RENEWAL
COVERT AFAR SPENT AME
AMEND CROCODILEDUNDEE
LENTO SERE ALIVE BEND
MOTS TATS STEER ARTS

PUZZLE 188

IMP WAS SHOWS
VEE LOFTS PEKOE
OLD ANTIC AWARE
REACT FAST YEN
YELLED FLOUR
EXAM POLECAT
LAMA BAR TAMALE
ACING TOT SAGAS
INTERN TOP REST
RETREAT WEAK
SEMIS TRENDS
PIC NEAT IDIOT
ERASE ROOFS EWE
LITER APPLE CEE
ESSAY STY ELL

PUZZLE 181

SLOB GASH CHAP SMOG
LIME RHEE REDO PORE
ARAB EARL URAL LUNA
MAROONBELLS MARINER
PGA OATS RENT
OAR ADAS PELE OTHER
SPA MALTA DIVA SOLE
LOCO LANG MALL OLE
OPERA AGILE SANDAL
CLINGMANSDOME
PLEATS ASTIR EASEL
OIL OLEO SETI TACO
ONCE EATS RAVEL SRO
REALM RIOT REVE HUM
PEON SLAB EAP
GLIMMER DIAMONDHEAD
RATE GOBI TOTO OGLE
IRAN EPEE ETTU NAME
PANT VEER SOOT EDAM

PUZZLE 185

BARB SCAT CHASM
ASEA KALE AORTA
CHAR ISLE PREEN
HERB ION TRAPS
EBONY GOO
ESCUDO NARRATE
AROUND LIP WAS
OGLES OIL SCALP
NOV OWE VERILY
ETERNAL SANITY
AUK MINTS
ADMIT HEM PURE
DEISM EDIT IRON
OLDIE MALE EGAD
SLING PLEA REDS

PUZZLE 189

BETS GASH MUST
AKIN ANGLE ISLE
DECO BARES DEED
RIOTED AIRED
UPEND EGOS SKY
PRO NEW EASE
AGOG SIR FEVER
RECAP NAB TENOR
SHRUG YOU SAGE
BLAB ANT CUD
ASH SLAB TASTE
STALE BIKINI
COVE EBBED EDGE
OVEN ALLEY VANS
TENS TEEN EMUS

PUZZLE 186

SLAM PAST MASC CLARET
HOMO ARTA ALAR ALLUDE
ALBS PERU LALO RABBIS
GILLIANANDERSON MEETS
STEEL TITO MANOWAR
ADMIT TENS SERE TUBA
ARI DORA DIAPERED
SLEDDING RIDE AVAILED
HORA ACRES INC ERN
AVIV LION CEDAR ISSUE
LECID TOMCRUISE STATS
TRADE EVERY VIVA ERIK
LAP ESE SENOR IOLE
ANGELIC HERA OLEANDER
FRITTERS DOLT TNT
CANT TOAD OARS ALBUS
ELAPSES MEAL AUNTS
ADORE SHELSILVERSTEIN
NORMAN IMAM LADE TALE
ENCASE METE INGA ESTA
WEANED IDEE STEP DESK

PUZZLE 182

ACTUALLY JARRED
N R C O S E
DOUGHNUTS TRACT
R M I T U R C E
EXPELS PREACHES
W L T F Y A T
OVERHEAD OBOE
M P S R C P L D
APED REHEARSE
R N O A S I G
INHABITS INSTAL
N O J E O T O A
ELUDE NEXTOFKIN
R S C E U E C
SHEATH INSTANCE

PUZZLE 190

CALL PER SAGA
AWAY COMIC AXED
RARE HIPPO LINE
ARK ANT ROASTS
TEST STY RAM
WHEY MARINAS
ABROAD PAL ILL
LEAST POP IGLOO
TAN NET STREET
OUTGREW SOSO
RAP GEM GARY
AWEIGH LAB LEI
CHAP ELITE SIRE
HOSE WADER OVAL
EATS WED BEND

PUZZLE 191

RADAR HERB CLAW
EXUDE APER HALE
BEBOP MINI EMIT
ROD CON EATS
GEESE WEPT
WON ELFIN EAST
OFT TAR SHARD
OER CABARET FOE
DRAMA TEX AWE
SPAR GENES RED
IDLE REOIL
OVAL IRA TAP
FILM ABLY RECAP
FLOE RITE ERODE
SEEN SLOT DATER

PUZZLE 195

ACMES ADIT ROSA
LOOSE RUNE EPIC
GLASSSNAKE DART
ATTESTED DASHES
ESS IRS MORE
HOUSEOFCARDS
FLAUNT ALF IOU
LILTS OTT ROPED
EMS SHE COWERS
WOODENINDIAN
OLIO ODD HBO
LAPTOP EYESTALK
EXIT PAPERTIGER
ALEE EVEN ELENA
NERD DEES RENDS

PUZZLE 199

RAJAH OBEYED ADAGES
ELENA REMORA BEWARE
BIRTHDAYSUIT EMERGE
BISON REEF ODD
EDO EGIS OWN ESS
LEAST EDEN LEO ONLY
MYSTIC ENTRY OMEGAS
ALOHASHIRT ERNST
ABLY MALE BERRA OHO
IRA WEB ION MEL
RAW ARILS PALL CEDE
MINOR TEATROLLEY
ALBUMS FLOOR STATUS
SLOT ART ROTC ENURE
SEW STY FARO NIX
LAW ETCH EASED
SAILOR HOUSEOFCARDS
IGNORE UNREAL AVAIL
REGENT SEDATE TESTY

PUZZLE 192

AMID TRAM LOST
LICE GAILY IDEA
OXEN URBAN NEAR
HEM UMP SANE
ARABS ENTER
SNEEZE RAW RAY
GREATEST IRE
YENS BROTH DONS
EVE PREMIERE
TEA LAD ENABLE
INTRO STERN
IDOL PEP ARE
LOAN GALAS SPAR
AWLS LIONS PEND
GLEE EDGE ADDS

PUZZLE 196

ASS SUE SOY REP
LIT ENS THERETO
EGOTRIP RATECAP
CHARITYRARITY
ONE EYE CRI
ANY ADS MELON
SPA PALP HERALD
TERRIBLEPARABLE
EXCESS NOTE LOX
LEIGH SCI HEN
ESS ALI SKI
SANDALSCANDAL
CHINOOK CORDAGE
AUSTERE ANA TEN
TEM LED BET ADD

PUZZLE 200

WREN OHOS REST SHAR
HALO BALL EVER WIRE
IMAM EDEA META OLLA
ZANANDJAYNA SCALLOP
DII SAND ELL
OST NEAL IDES TEASE
PHILANDLIL ATTENDED
TELE TMAN NEER ARE
SALAD MARA NAE RAN
FREDANDGEORGE
SON ECO EARN ONION
URI ACNE EELS INRE
EASEMENT BERTANDNAN
SLIME ANOA ODIE SSE
ERR ALBS GEE
SPARSER DATAANDLORE
LEDA FARE ELSA IDOL
OPEL EROS REIN SOCK
TEND RENT NEAT ERAS

PUZZLE 193

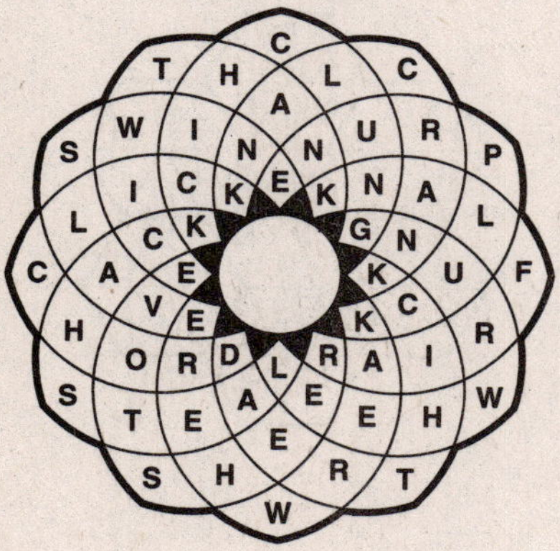

PUZZLE 197

SKA MAC NOT SPA
PAD ELL ABE KOP
EPA TOE DECRYPT
APPLEPOLISHER
RATIO ERE LOG
TRENT BICEP
CAFE BOOTLICKER
OTR TON HOG ESE
BROWNNOSER STEP
BISON POESY
ATM SEE ANGLO
BACKSCRATCHER
HEINOUS USE OVA
OAT OLA HIE SET
DUE SLY RAN TEE

PUZZLE 201

PIE EKE TORAH STOP
URN DIN HUMANE CHAR
PADDINGTONBEAR AERO
OUT WEAR DOLMEN
LARGESSE ERA ELUDE
ITS DOCENT OBERON
DEER RADIO SSA PST
HARRYPOTTER ETRE
STORE LIEN IDEAS
RAH ELITE ORTON RDS
OPERA MILS POSSE
NOSE MARYPOPPINS
RID AGA UNION SHED
MALTED NOOSES ERE
AMPLE SEW NESTEGGS
PESETA UGLI OLE
ODOR SHERLOCKHOLMES
RENT PULSES AIL OWE
TASS STATE YES NEE

PUZZLE 194

BAJA JADES AJAR
ALUM AMUSE SALA
NEMO COSTA IMAM
JUBILANT SEDANS
OTO ARGOS LEI
TVA FUJI CAP
ADJOIN FRA RANI
FRIENDS ENTENTE
RATS ACT IRISES
OTT TSAR TIN
ERA BORON JET
STREWS JEREMIAH
TUBE AMATI ONTO
ONUS MANIA AGES
WAGE EDSEL TONE

PUZZLE 198

CHIT GANG OMEN ASPS
AIDE ALOE TOGA RHEE
PROPELLER HEAD ROLE
EELER LAKE DERIVED
ENDS HELM RAVE
CLOSEOUT ALEC MELBA
HOT TREE OLIO SHOW
ERIC SERVE TSAR ARE
RECAP REDO CHEATED
PUSHINGAROUND
ENDORSE TETE TIRED
DOR ETNA DELES TALI
ERIN SCUP RIPE BAN
NAVEL ENOS COERCING
ETAT TAPE SPAR
PARTYER CALM TIARA
ORAL NOAH FORCEPLAY
LINE SOLE IRAE ESME
EATS EKES NENE SOPS

PUZZLE 202

JAVA ACE MAYA ASHE
ATONE RANSOMED PEAL
ROCKYMTNATIONALPARK
MELEES MARY OASIS
ERA MOTE VAIL
BEETS HERE SAWN PUB
REVS TESS SALES INA
ARE HORA SARIS SKIS
SORTIE BOLAS POETS
GARDENOFTHEGODS
SPRIT LOOTS ELAPSE
PEEL PETTY SHAY EON
ERE CAVES HEAR DART
DUN OVER MEAT PEKES
GMEN BOAT ELS
AGREE SENT ELAINE
MOUNTOFTHEHOLYCROSS
ERLE RELATERS EERIE
SEES ODOR NEE EAST

PUZZLE 203

PUZZLE 207

PUZZLE 212
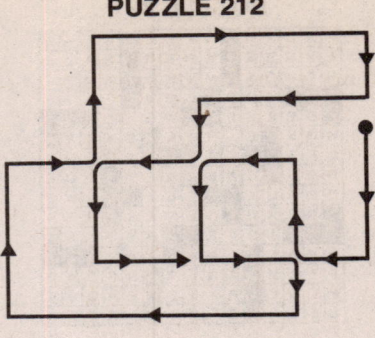

PUZZLE 204

PUZZLE 208

PUZZLE 213

PUZZLE 205

PUZZLE 209

PUZZLE 214
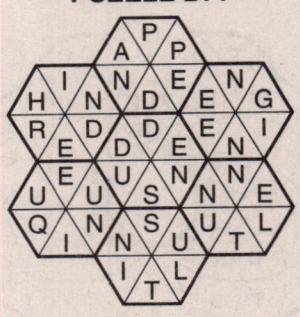

PUZZLE 210
1. Least, 2. Clear, 3. Fuel, 4. Travel, 5. Mediate.

PUZZLE 206

PUZZLE 211

PUZZLE 215

PUZZLE 216

Archers: One girl.
Bensons: One boy, one girl.
Campbells: One boy, two girls.

PUZZLE 217

PUZZLE 218

ADIJKX, BELUWZ, CHMNPY, FGOQRS.

PUZZLE 225

1. Whirlybird, 2. Fragrance, 3. Toadstool, 4. Inventive, 5. Sauerkraut, 6. Lovelorn, 7. Sandbank, 8. Bourbon, 9. Palatial, 10. Pompous.

PUZZLE 227

1. Elvis Presley, 2. Percy Faith, 3. Gene Chandler, 4. Chuck Berry, 5. Bobby Goldsboro, 6. Marvin Gaye, 7. Freddy Cannon, 8. Ray Charles.

533

PUZZLE 229
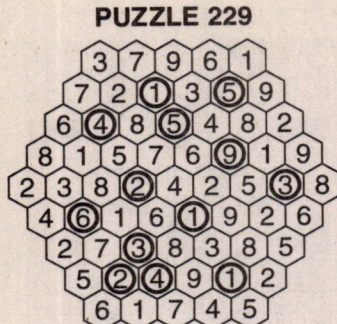

PUZZLE 233

PUZZLE 237

PUZZLE 230
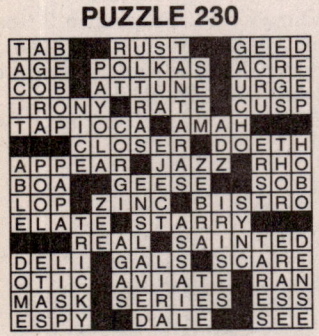

PUZZLE 234
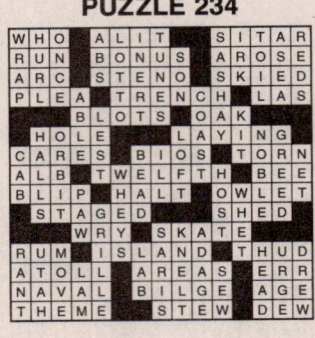

PUZZLE 238

PUZZLE 231
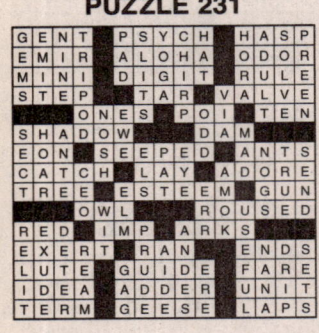

PUZZLE 235

PUZZLE 239

PUZZLE 232

PUZZLE 236
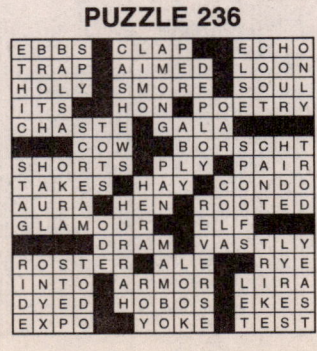

PUZZLE 240

PUZZLE 241

```
ACT   TWAS  ABED
DUO   REST  BOLA
SENSIBLY   EAST
   POSE   TREE
AMMO       ERAS
GEER   UPON  ERS
EMOTES  STRAIT
ROW   EELY  ORCA
   UNDO   ASHY
GOWN       NEWS
AVOW   REMITTED
FAKE   ALIT   AYE
FLED   MYTH   PEN
```

PUZZLE 242

```
STEM   ASPS   AFT
HAVE   SNAP   PEA
OXEN  SINISTER
PINUP   VENT
       ATE   AMEN
SHE   GULP   NOPE
COBWEB   OODLES
ABBE   ATOM   LET
ROSE   ALE
       DELL   NUTTY
LADYLIKE   SIRE
AIR   KEEL   EDIT
PLY   SURF   SEMI
```

PUZZLE 243

```
SE RE NE   RAN CH ER      RE AR
NA M ED       S EA R ING   GUL CH
TE EM   INT AC T      RA DI ATE
   BER S ER K      CA TE R
      EA VE   STA VE      TY CO ON
MA IN      NE GO TI AT OR   RE LY
RES TO RE      LI ON   DI NE
      BE NE ATH   TE NA B LE
COL L AR   PO ET RY      AC TU AL   LOY
DA LE   BY STAN D ER         ME RE LY
TA CT      LE ER ED
```

PUZZLE 244
TH/E LE/TTE/R T

PUZZLE 245

```
CROP   PRAM   ACMES
ROTA   RAGA   MOOSE
OUTSPOKEN   PLANE
ATE   OBESE   USER
KERNEL   DORM
   AMEBA   DANDLE
STOP   MOTHER   EAR
OAKEN   ARE   EDEMA
BUR   ADRIFT   OPAL
STARVE   ATOLL
       EYED   NOTATE
ELLE   RELIC   BIG
KOALA   IMAGINING
ENDED   PITH   EDGE
DEEDS   STET   WEED
```

PUZZLE 246
GOPHER

PUZZLE 247

```
GOAL   SOLO   LEAPS
ABLE   ARID   ANVIL
LOGO   TALE   STOLE
SEATBELT     OWED
     ARE   SERUM
SOPRANO   AIRBUS
APED   BATON   NAT
ITS   OMELETS   BBB
LIT   GAYER   GILA
   COLLIE   SPEEDER
     LENDS   INN
TATA     CASSETTE
AROMA   SENT   RAIL
BEGAN   INTO   AXES
SASSY   REEL   LIRE
```

PUZZLE 248
Two may talk together under the same roof for many years, yet never meet, and two others at first speech are old friends.

PUZZLE 249

```
COMEDIANEGATE
OVERACTANAGER
LEROYETIGRESS
ONEDDYELLAPSE
NEVERENEIGHTS
EGADELTASEERA
LOGIAMISHEMOM
STORMOVEUGENE
PICTURENLARGE
RAHOSEDRAWALK
ATOMSAGOPALEE
NENEAREBENDAS
GAGILLSEXTANT
```

PUZZLE 250

```
REC   PIQUE   KEG
E Z A   U L   H A
JEANS   AWKWARD
E R H V     K G
CLIMATE   OXIDE
T N   R A   T
   KAYAK   AFFIX
  S   D O   N B
HERTZ   BRUSQUE
A E   J   B U L
DRIZZLE   ORIEL
O G   O C A   R O
WIN   OCTET   YAW
```

1-W, 2-X, 3-D, 4-B, 5-M, 6-A, 7-P, 8-K, 9-V, 10-T, 11-I, 12-R, 13-H, 14-C, 15-Q, 16-U, 17-F, 18-J, 19-G, 20-L, 21-Z, 22-Y, 23-N, 24-E, 25-S, 26-O.

PUZZLE 251

```
ASCOT   SET   FOB
R A   H I   O A   E
RELIEVE   FLUFF
O Y   T V   U N   O
WAXPAPER   FANG
  D   R U   E   Y
ZITI   OHM   RILL
  E I M   X B A   O
QUIP   YEARLING
L   N M   N A   N E
IMPLY   JAVELIN
C U   T O   E E   I
KIT   HAY   LETHE
```

1-V, 2-H, 3-M, 4-E, 5-T, 6-Q, 7-A, 8-J, 9-D, 10-G, 11-Y, 12-S, 13-R, 14-U, 15-F, 16-N, 17-P, 18-C, 19-K, 20-O, 21-I, 22-B, 23-Z, 24-W, 25-X, 26-L.

PUZZLE 252

```
LOPER   PEAR   SNAP
AWAKE   ARIA   PAPA
SLYER   REDPLANET
       ASK   ERASE
MANNA     ERAS
POLE   WANDERERS
LOUT   BEGAN   AWL
ARM   DERAILS   SEA
YEN   ROUTE   SCAT
   DAVENPORT   OATH
     EAST   IMPLY
ASTER     LEI
STORYLINE   ADAPT
PONE   IRON   MEDIA
SPED   DART   INDEX
```

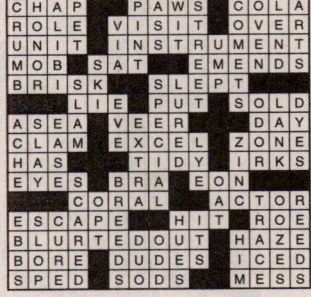
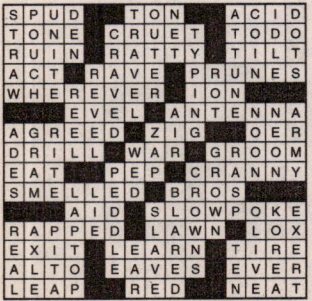
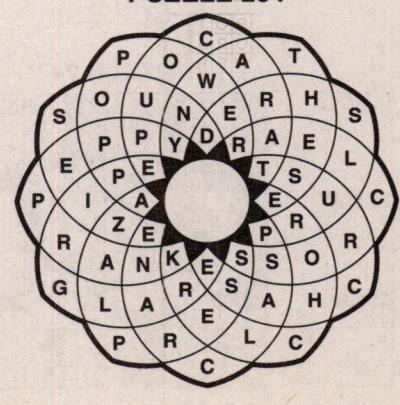

PUZZLE 275
1. Water fountain, 2. Crew neck, 3. Stadium blanket.

PUZZLE 277
BARBARA STANWYCK

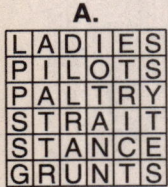
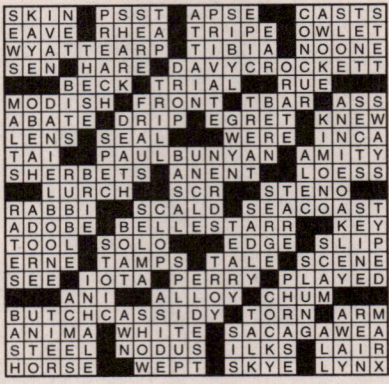
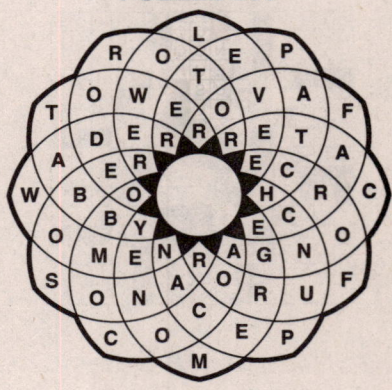
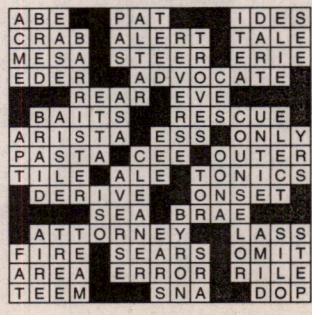

PUZZLE 291
FABRICS: Tweed, Taffeta, Khaki, Challis, Organdy.
FEATHERED FRIENDS: Mockingbird, Kookaburra, Kiwi, Albatross, Booby.
WORLD CITIES: Madrid, Alexandria, Hanoi, Paris, Calgary.
CLOTHING: Leotard, Parka, Bikini, Dress, Jersey.
MOUNTAINS: Mount Hood, Mount Shasta, Mount Fuji, Mount Olympus, Mount McKinley.

PUZZLE 299
1. Creak, Croak, Crook, Brook, Broom, Bloom.
2. Merry, Marry, Parry, Party, Pasty, Pasta.
3. Thane, Thank, Shank, Shack, Shuck, Stuck.
4. Along, Alone, Clone, Crone, Crane, Craze.

PUZZLE 301
National-Guard, On-Off, Number-One, Easy-Difficult, Water-Nymph, Solar-Eclipse, Inscribe-Write, Seven-Seas.
SAYING: No news is good news.

PUZZLE 303
Cookie, Menace, Missed, Rabbit, Swanky, Wither.

PUZZLE 305

G	E	L	■	C	A	R	B	■	C	U	T	E
A	P	E	■	A	X	E	L	■	A	K	I	N
P	I	E	■	R	E	P	O	■	M	E	N	D
S	C	R	A	P	■	O	■	A	C	H	E	■
■	■	■	D	E	L	I	■	O	O	M	P	H
S	A	R	I	■	E	R	O	S	■	Y	E	A
P	L	A	T	E	S	■	K	E	E	N	E	R
A	I	R	■	S	T	A	R	■	Y	A	R	D
S	T	E	E	P	■	G	A	P	E	■	■	■
■	T	Y	P	E	■	O	D	D	L	Y	■	■
B	A	T	H	■	O	N	E	R	■	R	O	O
A	L	O	E	■	E	D	G	E	■	A	S	K
D	E	E	R	■	T	A	G	S	■	T	E	E

PUZZLE 306

F	L	U	■	F	R	O	■	F	O	E	■	S	I	B
A	I	M	■	J	A	R	■	I	R	K	■	H	O	E
T	A	B	■	O	W	N	■	G	E	E	■	A	D	S
E	R	R	O	R	■	A	S	H	■	D	A	V	I	T
■	■	E	N	D	■	M	E	T	■	T	E	N	S	■
S	A	L	E	S	M	E	N	■	E	R	O	D	E	■
O	W	L	S	■	I	N	S	■	M	O	M	■	■	■
P	E	A	■	E	X	T	I	N	C	T	■	G	A	L
■	■	■	R	Y	E	■	T	O	E	■	T	A	X	I
■	S	P	E	E	D	■	I	T	E	M	I	Z	E	D
S	O	L	E	■	E	V	E	■	I	M	P	■	■	■
Q	U	A	K	E	■	W	E	B	■	L	E	A	P	T
U	R	N	■	A	T	E	■	O	L	D	■	C	R	Y
A	C	E	■	S	I	R	■	O	I	L	■	H	O	P
B	E	T	■	Y	E	S	■	K	E	Y	■	O	W	E

1-B, 2-O, 3-P, 4-M, 5-J, 6-N, 7-S, 8-U, 9-Y, 10-Z, 11-H, 12-I, 13-T, 14-E, 15-L, 16-V, 17-X, 18-F, 19-R, 20-W, 21-A, 22-C, 23-Q, 24-G, 25-K, 26-D.

PUZZLE 307

Area, Card, Care, Char, Cite, Czar, Dare, Dark, Daze, Dodo, Down, Drag, Drew, Each, Earl, Ewer, Gala, Gaze, Glad, Hard, Hare, Hark, Haze, Lard, Lark, Laze, Mica, Mien, Mite, Near, Nerd, Newt, Odor, Okra, Oral, Rare, Raze, Read, Real, Rear, Rent, Teal, Tear, Tent, Tier, Wear, Went, Were, Word, Wore, Work, Wren, Zeal, Zero.

PUZZLE 308

A	D	O	■	S	A	R	I	■	C	O	L	D
M	E	X	■	M	I	E	N	■	A	L	A	N
A	L	E	■	I	D	E	S	■	M	E	S	A
S	I	N	G	L	E	F	I	L	E	■	■	■
■	■	■	R	E	D	■	D	O	O	D	L	E
A	B	B	A	■	■	M	E	G	■	O	E	R
D	O	U	B	L	E	C	R	O	S	S	E	R
I	R	S	■	E	L	I	■	■	L	E	S	S
T	A	S	S	E	L	■	■	P	H	I	■	■
■	■	■	T	R	I	P	L	E	P	L	A	Y
S	A	G	O	■	P	I	E	R	■	A	G	O
I	D	O	L	■	S	C	A	D	■	M	U	G
P	A	T	E	■	E	A	T	S	■	P	E	A

PUZZLE 309

P	A	T	S	■	S	P	E	T	■	H	O	Y
A	S	E	A	■	A	L	T	O	■	E	D	E
S	C	A	M	■	F	O	R	W	A	R	D	S
T	U	M	B	L	E	W	E	E	D	■	■	■
A	S	S	A	I	■	■	■	R	A	B	A	T
■	■	■	M	I	N	I	■	■	G	A	G	A
S	L	I	D	E	F	A	S	T	E	N	E	R
S	A	L	E	■	■	S	E	M	I	■	■	■
S	C	A	P	A	■	■	■	N	O	I	S	E
■	■	■	T	R	I	P	H	A	M	M	E	R
R	U	S	H	M	O	R	E	■	B	A	R	O
A	P	E	■	O	T	I	C	■	E	G	O	S
P	S	T	■	R	A	N	K	■	R	O	W	E

PUZZLE 310

S	T	A	K	E	■	M	E	S	S	■	O	P	T	S
C	A	N	O	E	■	A	C	N	E	■	A	R	I	A
A	T	T	A	R	■	S	L	U	R	■	F	I	L	L
M	A	I	L	■	A	B	U	T	■	V	E	T	■	■
■	■	■	A	S	C	O	T	■	M	A	L	A	D	Y
A	M	P	■	A	R	K	■	■	■	C	A	T	■	■
R	O	O	S	T	E	R	S	■	F	O	R	E	S	T
E	R	I	C	■	■	P	A	P	E	R	■	■	V	E	T	O
S	E	N	A	T	E	■	Y	E	A	S	A	Y	E	R
■	■	S	L	Y	■	■	■	L	I	P	■	E	W	E
S	T	E	P	P	E	■	B	Y	L	A	W	■	■	■
A	R	T	■	O	G	R	E	■	■	A	R	M	S	■
M	I	T	E	■	G	A	I	N	■	A	X	I	A	L
B	A	I	L	■	E	R	G	O	■	G	E	N	R	E
A	D	A	M	■	D	E	E	D	■	A	D	D	E	D

PUZZLE 311

O	L	D	■	B	R	I	M	■	R	E	F	S
F	U	R	■	L	A	V	A	■	O	M	I	T
F	L	U	■	O	N	Y	X	■	D	U	T	Y
S	U	M	A	C	■	■	■	I	C	E	■	■
■	■	■	S	K	I	■	L	O	V	E	R	■
S	T	O	P	■	T	O	T	O	■	E	V	E
C	O	B	■	S	C	R	A	P	■	A	I	L
A	G	E	■	P	H	E	W	■	A	L	L	Y
B	A	Y	O	U	■	■	■	S	I	X	■	■
■	■	A	R	T	■	N	E	W	S	Y	■	■
O	D	O	R	■	E	V	E	N	■	A	C	E
F	I	N	E	■	M	I	R	E	■	V	A	N
T	E	E	D	■	P	E	E	R	■	E	N	S

PUZZLE 312

A	N	E	W	■	S	N	A	P	■	A	P	T
L	I	M	O	■	O	U	C	H	■	G	O	O
P	L	U	M	■	U	N	T	O	■	E	G	G
■	■	■	A	W	L	■	T	O	D	O	S	■
C	H	I	N	A	■	W	O	K	■	■	■	■
L	O	T	■	S	A	V	E	■	A	L	S	O
A	P	E	R	■	D	I	P	■	Y	A	W	N
D	E	M	O	■	D	A	T	A	■	V	I	E
■	■	■	B	U	S	■	S	L	A	M	S	■
C	R	E	E	P	■	S	K	Y	■	■	■	■
O	E	R	■	P	A	P	A	■	I	D	E	A
P	A	R	■	E	W	E	S	■	N	E	O	N
E	L	S	■	R	E	P	S	■	G	E	N	T

PUZZLE 313

G	R	I	T	■	S	W	A	B	■	O	A	T
O	U	C	H	■	L	I	R	A	■	D	I	E
O	B	E	Y	■	I	N	K	Y	■	O	D	E
■	■	■	M	U	T	E	■	O	A	R	E	D
S	H	Y	E	R	■	■	C	U	D	■	■	■
H	U	E	■	N	O	V	A	■	S	A	G	A
I	L	L	■	■	N	I	L	■	■	R	A	M
P	A	P	A	■	L	E	F	T	■	I	M	P
■	■	■	S	T	Y	■	■	O	K	A	Y	S
I	T	C	H	Y	■	■	S	E	M	I	■	■
D	O	E	■	P	I	T	A	■	N	O	E	L
L	Y	E	■	O	V	E	R	■	G	I	V	E
E	S	S	■	S	E	W	N	■	S	L	E	D

PUZZLE 314

R	A	W	■	V	E	S	T	■	D	R	A	M
A	C	E	■	A	R	E	A	■	O	I	L	Y
S	H	E	■	D	A	W	N	■	S	L	I	T
P	E	K	O	E	■	■	■	T	E	E	T	H
■	■	■	P	R	A	Y	E	R	■	■	■	■
M	A	S	T	■	C	O	M	E	■	O	W	N
A	L	P	■	S	T	U	C	K	■	W	O	O
P	L	Y	■	L	O	N	E	■	S	E	E	D
■	■	■	■	U	R	G	E	N	T	■	■	■
W	R	I	N	G	■	■	■	E	Y	E	R	S
H	O	S	E	■	S	L	A	W	■	D	I	M
I	D	L	E	■	P	A	W	S	■	G	N	U
P	E	E	R	■	A	B	L	Y	■	E	G	G

PUZZLE 315

O	A	F	■	F	E	E	T	■	M	O	P	E
F	R	O	■	R	A	G	E	■	A	G	E	D
F	E	W	■	I	R	O	N	■	D	R	A	G
S	A	L	S	A	■	■	■	G	E	E	S	E
■	■	■	C	R	A	B	B	Y	■	■	■	■
I	D	E	A	■	C	L	A	M	■	C	A	R
V	E	R	B	■	T	A	B	■	M	O	R	E
E	W	E	■	O	O	Z	E	■	A	B	E	D
■	■	■	■	D	R	E	S	S	Y	■	■	■
S	L	A	V	E	■	■	■	M	O	W	E	R
W	I	N	E	■	V	E	T	O	■	A	C	E
A	R	T	S	■	A	M	O	K	■	S	H	E
M	E	E	T	■	T	U	N	E	■	P	O	D

PUZZLE 316

R	A	F	T	■	W	H	I	P	■	R	A	N
A	L	O	E	■	I	O	T	A	■	A	G	O
G	E	R	M	■	S	A	S	S	■	I	O	N
■	■	■	P	I	E	R	■	T	A	N	G	O
S	P	O	O	N	■	■	■	S	C	A	M	■
E	O	N	■	F	L	E	A	■	M	A	U	L
C	U	C	K	O	O	■	B	L	O	U	S	E
T	R	E	E	■	S	O	S	O	■	T	E	A
■	N	E	E	R	■	■	■	A	C	O	R	N
M	O	T	O	R	■	D	A	D	A	■	■	■
A	G	E	■	R	E	E	L	■	P	A	P	A
I	R	E	■	O	R	A	L	■	E	D	E	N
L	E	D	■	R	E	L	Y	■	S	E	A	T

PUZZLE 317

A	S	S	■	A	S	P	S	■	C	H	O	W
W	H	O	■	P	O	L	O	■	H	U	L	A
L	O	W	■	O	D	O	R	■	O	B	E	Y
S	O	N	A	R	■	W	E	A	R	■	■	■
■	■	■	I	T	S	■	■	L	E	E	C	H
A	M	E	N	■	W	I	S	P	■	A	R	E
R	I	O	T	■	A	M	P	■	D	R	A	W
I	N	N	■	T	Y	P	O	■	E	L	M	S
D	I	S	C	O	■	■	T	I	E	■	■	■
■	■	■	E	M	I	T	■	S	P	I	N	E
B	E	L	L	■	O	R	A	L	■	D	E	B
O	V	A	L	■	T	O	N	E	■	L	O	B
D	E	M	O	■	A	D	D	S	■	E	N	S

540

Believe only half of what you see and nothing that you hear.

PUZZLE 330
PUZZLE 331
PUZZLE 332
1. Don't burn your bridges.
2. Great minds think alike.
3. Rats desert a sinking ship.
4. Honesty is the best policy.

PUZZLE 333
PUZZLE 334
1. Teheran (Iran), Nail, Llama, Amherst, Target.
2. Damascus (Syria), Safe, Elephant, Tufts, Shuttlecock.
3. Seoul (South Korea), Locker, Rhinoceros, Smith, Helmet.
4. Beijing (China), Grill, Leopard, Drew, Whistle.
5. Bangkok (Thailand), Key, Yak, Kent State, Earplug.

PUZZLE 335

PUZZLE 336
1. Yale, 2. Brown, 3. Colby, 4. Smith, 5. Bates, 6. Babson, 7. Brandeis, 8. Amherst, 9. Williams, 10. Simmons.

PUZZLE 337
PUZZLE 338

PUZZLE 339
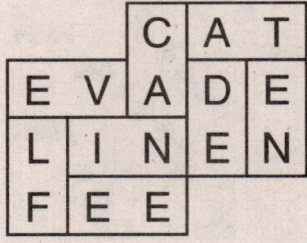

PUZZLE 340
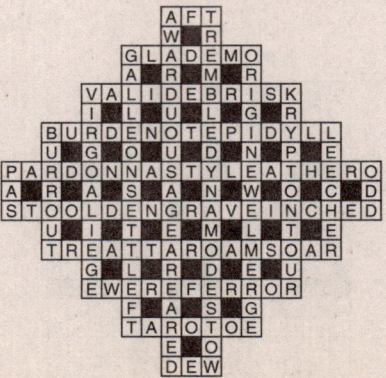

PUZZLE 341

1-P, 2-Q, 3-R, 4-H, 5-B, 6-Z, 7-D, 8-Y, 9-O, 10-K, 11-C, 12-T, 13-J, 14-E, 15-M, 16-F, 17-V, 18-G, 19-W, 20-L, 21-X, 22-N, 23-I, 24-U, 25-A, 26-S.

PUZZLE 342
1. Deduce, 2. Dieter, 3. Salmon, 4. Carpet, 5. Salute, 6. Beacon.
6-LETTER WORD: Dimple

PUZZLE 343
PUZZLE 344
PUZZLE 345

543

Puzzle Answers

PUZZLE 367
1. Gaelic, 2. Whiskey, 3. Shamrock, 4. Colleen, 5. Stout, 6. Banshee.
BONUS: Brogue

PUZZLE 370
1-M, 2-J, 3-Q, 4-N, 5-B, 6-P, 7-E, 8-X, 9-F, 10-Y, 11-C, 12-S, 13-A, 14-R, 15-Z, 16-D, 17-L, 18-I, 19-V, 20-K, 21-W, 22-O, 23-U, 24-G, 25-H, 26-T.

PUZZLE 371
The first American president to attend a major league baseball game
BENJAMIN HARRISON

PUZZLE 372

PUZZLE 377

PUZZLE 382

PUZZLE 378

1. Bank, Balk, Ball, Bell, Dell.
2. Hill, Mill, Mild, Mold, Mood, Moor.
3. Peak, Perk, Park, Pare, Care, Cape.
4. Lake, Lane, Land, Lend, Rend, Reed, Reef.

PUZZLE 373

PUZZLE 383

PUZZLE 379

PUZZLE 374

```
       R
   I   E
   T A M
   U R G E
 A W A R D
L E G A C Y
```

PUZZLE 384

The 3-5 is the Loose Tile.

PUZZLE 385

PUZZLE 380

PUZZLE 375

PUZZLE 386

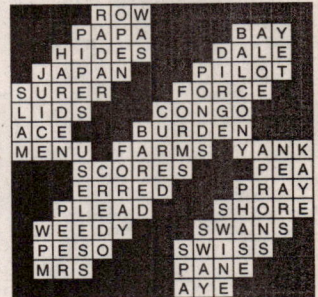

1. Stray, 2. Satyr, 3. Thing, 4. Night,
5. Stair, 6. Sitar, 7. Paint, 8. Inapt.
8-LETTER WORD: Tahitian

PUZZLE 381

PUZZLE 376

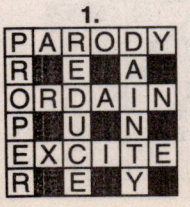

PUZZLE 387
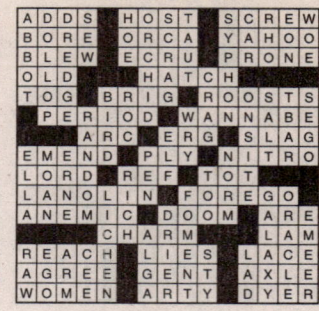

PUZZLE 391

PUZZLE 395

PUZZLE 388
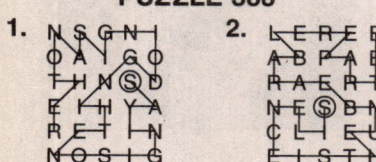

1. Saying is one thing, doing is another.
2. Silence is the unbearable repartee.

PUZZLE 392
Ninety pennies, four nickels, four dimes, and two quarters.

PUZZLE 396

PUZZLE 393

PUZZLE 389

PUZZLE 397

PUZZLE 394

PUZZLE 398

PUZZLE 390
1. Prong, Upset, Genus, Aorta.
2. Delay, Heavy, Vouch, Cloud.
3. Waist, Brawl, Limbo, Storm.
4. Shelf, Fluid, Noise, Hound.

546

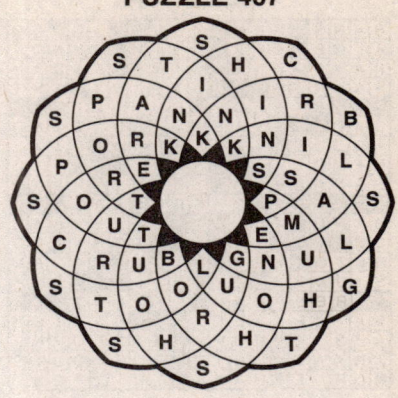

PUZZLE 411

```
S A N S   G U M   O W L S   S C O L D
A L O E   E R A   D R I P   P E K O E
P A V E M E N T   E I N E   R E R A N
S N A R E S   S T E A D Y   A N T
      S T E E D S   E N R O L L
C A P   V I E W S   D Y E I N G
A D O B E   I N C A   F R O   G O A L
R E M O V A L   S A R I   T I E
E S P R E S S O   T R A M P   H A L E
      E R E   G R E E N   A P E
B A N D   A L L O T   C A L E N D A R
U S E   Y E T I   T O R N A D O
S H A H   L E D   M I N I   M A D A M
S Y R U P Y   P E R I L   A M P
      B U R E A U   E X T E N T
B A T   R E A L L Y   G A R T E R
A E S O P   R O P E   A I R B O R N E
T R A W L   T H I N   F O E   O U T S
H O R N E   H A T S   T U T   P E S T
```

PUZZLE 412

```
A L S O   N O G   E R I E
L A T E   C A U L K   M A R S
I C E R   A P R O N   I N K S
A I R   E W E   B O A R
S N E A K   A W L   S K Y
  G O R E   P A L   T B O N E
    I D L E D   P O L L E N
P I E S   A P A C E   O D E S
A D V E R B   P R A W N
G E E S E   S T Y   E D I T
E A R   A S H   L E M O N
    B L U E   M I D   P R O
A L G A   N A V E L   M A S T
S E E R   S T E A L   A L O E
S I T E   H E N   P A S S
```

PUZZLE 413

```
H O G S   E T A S   P I S
A N E W   E L O P E R   U R N
S E M I   S K E T C H   L E I
  R A C E   T Y P I S T
F I L C H   G I S M O
A L L   R E T R O   E L M S
G A L   E A R E D   D E A T H
E K E S   T U N I C   D I R E
R E S T S   C A N O E   D O N
S T O W   E D E M A   E N S
  P A R S E   P R O N G
P R E S T O   B A L M
L A X   H Y P H E N   E Y E R
A G A   E A S I L Y   G I V E
T A M   L I S T   A N E T
```

PUZZLE 414

```
A C N E   P I C A   R O B I N
N O O N   I D O L   A D A G E
E R R S   K E N O   M E N U S
W E T   M E A D O W S   T A T
    H O E   S O F A   F A N S
J E E R S   K E N O   L L A M A
O G R E S   P O S T E D
E O N   A G O N I Z E   T A B
    U G L I E R   W O R R Y
    C A M E O   A W A K E
L A M P   R O V E   R E V
A S P   P Y R A M I D   E B B
T H E S E   A L O T   C R E E
H E R E S   L U T E   U S E R
S W E E T   S E E M   D E F T
```

PUZZLE 415

```
A V I D   W A F T   S L O T
V I N E   A T L A S   E A V E
A L D A   S T A M P   A M E N
S L E D S   A S S I S T A N T
T A X   K I C K   N I B
    E L K   V E T E R A N
L E N T I L   H I T   L I C E
O C E A N   T E A   S T O N E
A R T S   T A P   P O S T E D
D U S T P A N   P I C
    E E L   P E E K   D A M
S H E L T E R E D   S W I N E
H A V E   N A S A L   A C T S
A L E S   T I T L E   V E E S
H E R S   L O S T   E D D Y
```

PUZZLE 416

```
S K I M   G U S T S   G A S
I O T A   A S C O T S   A I L
G L E E   P E A N U T   Z O O
H A R S H   S N I P E   E L M
    T U B   S C E N A R I O
E N T R E A T   F O X
F A R O   R E A D Y   E T C H
T I E   E G O   R U E
S L E D   S N A R L   G I B E
    A S K   M I N I M A L
P L A Y T I M E   L E G
L A G   A P O R T   E G R E T
E R R   S P I N A L   L I V E
A G E   H E R E T O   E P E E
D E E   R E S A W   D E N S
```

PUZZLE 417

```
I F S   B A L D   F L O R A
D U O   I C E R   W E A K E R
E E N   C E D E   E N C A S E
A L G A E   G R I D   P I N
    S P O N S O R   N I N A
R I C K S H A   E D G E
E R A   M I L   E S S A Y
M O P E Y   L A W   E T U D E
S N O R E   P E A   D I N
    S T E P   A C C O S T S
L E S T   G R A N T E D
A S P   A G O G   A D O P T
S T R O B E   A I L S   B I O
S O A R E D   P L I E   E L M
O P T E D   E K E D   Y E S
```

PUZZLE 418

```
S T E M   B E A D   A D O B E
E A V E   U R G E   S A W E R
A X I S   S U R E   T U N E R
L I L A C   P E R S O N
    A N T E   H U T C H
S A M B A   C O N   H O P
G A G A   H O T R O D   R O E
R U E R   W O O   B O D E
I N N   D R E N C H   O M E N
D A D   E E R   U N W E D
S A L S A   L I M O
    E C L A I R   T E N S E
H E A V E   S M O G   L U N G
A L L E N   P I N E   S M U G
S K E E T   S T Y E   E B B S
```

PUZZLE 419

```
P A R E   H I P   A G A T E
A L U M   O R E   S C A L E R
S I N I S T E R   W E T T E R
S E T T O   P S I   O N S
E N S   F A S   I S L E
    D A R T   T S U N A M I
A C R E   K U D U   G A M I N
N O O N   S M E A R   M I L K
T W I N E   B E T A   E D D Y
I L L E G A L   E R A L
    D O L E   D E W   E M U
S I C   A D E   R O L E S
I T A L I C   P L A Y M A T E
R E M A R K   I O N   I T E R
S M O C K   C O D   T E D S
```

PUZZLE 420

```
A G E   S P A S   P A C T
I N S   P O S T   A L O E
M U S T A C H E   P O P E
    A R K   N E A T E N
L O L L   E B O N Y
E D U C A T E   T A S T E
N O G   I S S U E   A H A
T R E E D   E N R A G E S
    D E B T S   S A M E
D E R I D E   C E E
R I O T   N A R R A T E D
A R T E   D Y E R   I V E
W E E D   S E W S   P E W
```

PUZZLE 421

```
H I T   S P A N   C L E F
A D O   P A C E   H A R E
L O G   I N R E   A P E D
F L A M E   O D D S
    E L M S   A M A S S
A R E A   A S T I   H I E
R E P L A Y   E S C O R T
M A E   N O S E   R Y E S
S M E L T   E D G E
    L I O N   A W A K E
O R C A   S I A M   W E D
L O A M   L O B E   E N D
E D N A   O R E S   S O Y
```

PUZZLE 422

```
F A S T   P A P A   G A L   M O O
A L L Y   O V E N   I R E   P R E
I D O L   S A N D   A N O T H E R
R O B E R T   N E D   I N A
    R A M A   R A G E   N O O N
E N D   N A T A S H A   K A N E
T O E S   N O W   L I V E   R A T
O N E A L   M A C   L I N E
N E P H E W   Y E P   M O V I E S
    L E I F   E A T   S A D A T
W A G   S T A R   L I V   S A R A
A P E S   C I N E M A S   S P Y
S T E P   P E T E   E N I D
    O W L   A L T   E D I T E D
P A S T E U R   S A P S   N A M E
O I L   S T U   O T I S   A R M Y
T R Y   T O T   N I N A   S A Y S
```

PUZZLE 423

PUZZLE 428

PUZZLE 432

PUZZLE 424
Abide, Wheat, Snack, Grimy, Media, Aloof, Maize, Relic, Outer, Vault, Prior, Organ.

PUZZLE 429
Accept (the) challenges, so that you may feel the exhilaration of victory. (General George S. Patton)

PUZZLE 433

PUZZLE 425

PUZZLE 426
The only man who wasn't spoilt by being lionized was Daniel.

PUZZLE 430

1-C, 2-V, 3-Z, 4-E, 5-O, 6-U, 7-L, 8-B, 9-J, 10-R, 11-G, 12-D, 13-F, 14-S, 15-H, 16-Y, 17-N, 18-T, 19-K, 20-X, 21-P, 22-Q, 23-A, 24-W, 25-M, 26-I.

PUZZLE 434

PUZZLE 427

PUZZLE 431
It's too late to spare when the pantry is bare.

PUZZLE 435

PUZZLE 436

F	O	R	C	E		B	A	T	S		L	A	C	K
A	W	A	R	E		I	R	O	N		O	M	E	N
R	E	T	A	R		L	I	M	E		P	O	L	O
			M	I	S	L	A	B	E	L		R	E	C
P	U	P	P	E	T		S	O	R	E		A	R	K
A	P	E		R	E	V		Y	E	A	R	L	Y	
P	O	S	H		W	O	N		D	R	Y			
A	N	T	I	S		W	O	O		N	E	S	T	S
			F	A	T		R	A	M		S	I	R	E
	N	E	I	G	H	S		F	I	R		F	E	W
S	E	X		A	R	T	S		N	E	A	T	E	N
H	E	P		S	E	E	T	H	I	N	G			
I	D	E	A		A	R	E	A		T	O	U	C	H
E	L	L	S		T	E	E	N		E	N	S	U	E
D	E	S	K		S	O	P	S		D	Y	E	R	S

PUZZLE 440

A	D	E	P	T			S	O	F	A		C	A	P
R	A	R	E	E	S		Q	U	I	T		I	V	E
T	H	E	N	C	E		U	R	G	E		C	A	T
			C	H	A	F	E				W	A	I	T
M	A	G	I			L	A	C	K		I	D	L	Y
E	X	U	L	T		O	K	R	A		P	A	S	
A	I	R		R	A	T		I	S	L	E			
T	S	U	N	A	M	I		T	H	I	R	S	T	S
			O	P	A	L		E	A	R		K	E	A
	T	A	R		S	L	U	R		A	D	U	L	T
R	A	N	T		S	A	R	I			R	A	L	E
H	I	G	H				B	A	T	H	E			
I	L	L		S	O	Y	A		A	U	N	T	I	E
N	E	E		O	V	E	N		U	N	C	O	R	K
O	R	S		N	A	P	E			T	H	R	E	E

PUZZLE 444

S	L	I	D		A	T	L	A	S		T	A	L	C
P	O	N	Y		L	O	O	S	E		I	D	O	L
A	N	T	I		P	O	P	P	A		P	O	S	E
N	E	O	N					I	F	S		R	E	F
			G	A	R	B		C	O	O	L	E	S	T
T	O	M		L	O	A	M		O	D	E			
O	P	E		A	B	R	O	A	D		A	C	M	E
M	A	M	A	S		O	N	S		A	F	O	U	L
B	L	O	W		A	N	T	H	E	M		A	S	S
			E	E	L		H	E	L	M		T	E	E
H	O	T	D	O	G	S		S	L	O	P			
A	C	E		N	E	T					A	C	I	D
S	T	A	G		B	R	A	V	O		P	A	C	E
P	E	S	O		R	U	R	A	L		A	N	E	W
S	T	E	T		A	M	E	N	D		L	E	S	S

PUZZLE 437

C	E	N	T			E	A	R			S	P	A	N
A	R	I	A		S	K	I	E	S		E	L	S	E
M	A	L	L		H	E	L	L	O		M	A	C	E
			L	E	E			A	U	D	I	T	E	D
S	T	A	Y	S			A	X	L	E		E	N	S
P	A	W		P	I	P	E			L	I	S	T	
A	X	E		Y	O	U	R		D	I	N			
M	I	D	I		T	B	O	N	E		K	E	G	S
			T	E	A		S	A	L	E		A	L	E
	G	U	S	T			O	P	E	D		S	U	E
S	O	P		C	O	O	L			D	A	T	E	D
W	A	R	S	H	I	P			G	Y	M			
A	L	I	T		L	A	R	V	A		A	B	L	E
M	I	S	E		S	L	Y	E	R		Z	E	A	L
P	E	E	P			S	E	X			E	G	G	S

PUZZLE 441

F	L	I	P	S		T	A	B	S		P	O	P	S
R	A	D	I	O		A	R	I	A		A	L	U	M
E	M	E	N	D		P	E	R	T		L	I	R	A
T	E	A	K		M	E	A	T		R	E	V	E	L
			I	C	Y		S	H	O	O		E	E	L
C	R	U	E	L	T	Y			F	U	N			
H	I	S		A	H	O	Y		F	L	I	M	S	Y
O	P	E	N	S		N	I	P		E	X	I	L	E
P	E	R	I	S	H		P	I	N	T		N	O	W
			B	I	O			C	A	T	N	I	P	S
A	S	S		F	E	T	A		B	E	E			
B	U	L	L	Y		A	D	D	S		S	L	O	W
A	S	E	A		A	M	I	E		S	T	O	N	E
S	H	E	D		F	E	E	L		A	L	D	E	R
H	I	T	S		T	R	U	E		G	E	E	S	E

PUZZLE 445

S	C	O	P	E		S	T	I	R		C	A	P	E
T	O	W	E	L		C	O	D	E		O	X	E	N
A	L	I	A	S		R	U	L	E		N	E	W	S
T	O	N			F	O	R	E	L	E	G			
E	N	G	A	G	E	D				G	A	S	P	S
			C	O	D		C	L	O	G		T	A	P
	E	C	H	O		C	H	E	W	Y		A	Y	E
P	R	A	Y		F	R	A	I	L		B	R	E	W
R	U	T		F	E	A	T	S		Y	O	K	E	
O	P	T		L	E	G	S		W	A	X			
S	T	Y	L	E				C	O	P	Y	C	A	T
			E	X	P	L	O	R	E			A	L	E
F	L	E	A		L	I	V	E		S	C	U	L	L
A	I	L	S		O	N	E	S		E	A	S	E	L
D	E	F	T		P	E	R	T		W	R	E	N	S

PUZZLE 438

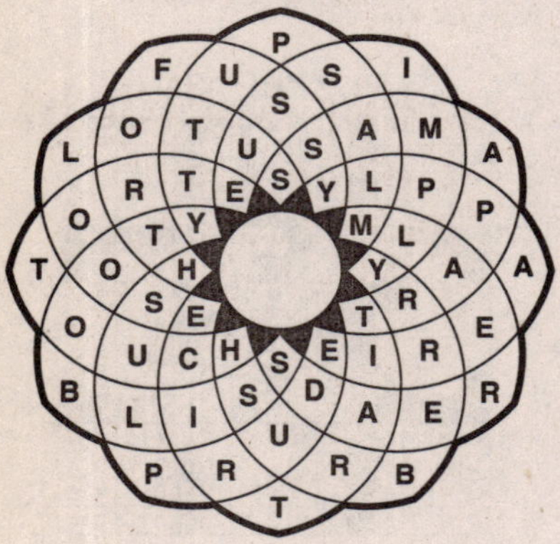

PUZZLE 442

C	O	S	T			S	W	E	A	R		A	C	E
A	R	I	A		S	T	O	O	G	E		G	E	M
F	A	R	M		C	A	N	N	O	N		I	C	E
E	L	E	P	H	A	N	T		G	O	B	L	I	N
				A	N	D				W	I	E	L	D
E	L	M		S	T	A	B		I	N	K			
L	E	A	S	H		R	O	A	N		I	D	E	S
S	A	G	A		A	D	O	R	N		N	I	G	H
E	P	I	C		I	S	N	T		B	I	N	G	O
			H	A	D		S	I	L	O		E	Y	E
A	S	K	E	W				C	O	G				
B	A	N	T	A	M		W	H	I	S	T	L	E	D
I	V	E		R	E	G	I	O	N		R	A	K	E
D	E	E		D	R	I	N	K	S		O	V	E	N
E	S	S		S	E	N	S	E			D	A	D	S

PUZZLE 446

P	O	L			J	O	T			S	C	O	W		B	A	R	E
E	G	O		H	A	I	R	S		P	A	P	A		E	X	A	M
A	R	C		O	W	L	E	T		A	N	T	I		R	E	P	S
L	E	O	N	A		S	K	Y			A	S	T	E	R			
		M	I	X				E	A	R	P			V	I	S	T	A
I	R	O	N		A	S	P		C	E	E		K	E	E	P	E	R
D	E	T	E	R	I	O	R	A	T	E			I	N	S	E	A	M
L	E	I		U	M	P	E	D		F	L	E	W			W	R	Y
E	L	V	E	S			C	E	L		A	T	I	L	T			
	S	E	A	T		R	E	S	I	D	U	E		O	A	R	S	
			T	Y	P	E	D		T	A	G			G	R	O	W	L
Z	A	P			O	V	E	R		R	H	I	N	O		T	I	E
E	N	R	O	L	L			I	N	T	E	R	E	S	T	I	N	G
S	T	E	R	E	O		A	L	E		D	E	E		U	S	E	S
T	E	P	E	E			F	E	T	A				A	S	S		
			G	R	I	L	L			N	A	H		S	K	E	E	T
B	E	T	A		N	E	A	R		E	P	O	C	H		R	O	E
R	E	I	N		F	A	M	E		W	E	A	R	Y		I	N	N
A	L	S	O		O	P	E	D			D	R	Y			E	S	S

PUZZLE 439

S	W	A	G	S			A	L	L		P	A	S	S
P	I	C	N	I	C		T	I	E		A	L	T	O
O	N	R	U	S	H		I	N	F	E	R	I	O	R
T	E	E	S		I	S	L	E	T	S		E	K	E
				E	D	I	T		O	P	E	N	E	R
O	A	T		V	E	X		G	U	Y	S			
P	L	A	C	E		T	W	I	T		S	P	R	Y
T	O	T	E			E	A	R			A	L	E	E
S	E	A	L		H	E	R	D		H	Y	E	N	A
			L	O	I	N		L	E	I		A	D	S
A	S	S	O	R	T		T	E	A	M				
L	E	T		A	T	T	E	S	T		S	L	A	M
T	R	A	I	L	E	R	S		E	N	T	I	C	E
A	V	I	D		R	O	T		N	E	A	R	E	R
R	E	D	S		S	T	Y			T	R	A	D	E

PUZZLE 443

S	P	A	S			P	I	N			A	B	E	D
E	A	C	H		F	L	O	O	D		S	A	M	E
L	I	R	E		R	A	N	G	E		C	R	I	B
F	R	E	S	H	E	N			S	H	E	E	T	S
				I	T	E	M		P	E	N			
	A	P	E	D			A	B	A	N	D	O	N	
F	I	L	L	E	T		I	R	I	S		Z	O	O
E	M	U	S		R	A	D	A	R		S	O	O	N
W	E	T		T	A	L	E		S	T	I	N	K	S
	D	O	O	R	M	E	N			O	N	E	S	
			Y	E	P		S	M	U	G				
D	A	M	S	E	L			E	S	S	E	N	C	E
A	L	I	T		E	A	G	L	E		V	I	E	R
R	O	L	E		D	I	N	E	R		I	C	E	R
N	E	E	R			D	U	E			L	E	S	S

PUZZLE 447

S	W	A	T			S	U	R	F			S	P	A
L	O	R	E		S	P	R	O	U	T		T	O	N
O	V	E	N		C	I	N	E	M	A		R	U	G
P	E	A		B	I	T	S		E	N	T	I	R	E
		C	L	E	F					G	I	V	E	R
C	H	O	O	S	I	N	G		H	O	P	E	D	
A	U	D	I	T		O	N	C	E					
T	E	E	N		R	E	A	R	M		S	A	G	A
					A	L	T	O		A	I	R	E	D
	S	C	R	E	W		S	P	R	I	N	T	E	D
R	E	L	A	X					E	L	S	E		
E	V	E	N	T	S		A	L	P	S		R	A	M
P	E	R		R	I	T	U	A	L		F	I	N	E
A	R	K		A	G	E	N	C	Y		L	E	T	S
Y	E	S			H	A	T	E			U	S	E	S

JUMBO PUZZLE BOOKS!

Order today and enjoy hours of puzzle fun with these 290-page volumes of top-quality Penny Press puzzles!

Family Favorites Word Seek Puzzles brings you hundreds of your favorite Penny Press word seek puzzles. Enjoy hours of relaxation with Missing Vowels, Wizard Words, and more!

Family Favorites Spotlight Word Seek Puzzles delivers hundreds of word seek puzzles highlighting movies and television shows.

To order, fill out the coupon below and mail it with your payment today, call TOLL-FREE 1-800-220-7443, or visit PennyDellPuzzles.com

---

PennyDellPuzzles™ Dept. PL • 6 Prowitt Street • Norwalk, CT 06855-1220

☑ **YES!** Please send me the _____ jumbo **Family Favorites** volumes I've circled below for just $4.95 plus $1.50 shipping & handling each. My payment of $_____ ($6.45 per volume, U.S. funds) is enclosed.

Word Seek Puzzles (WSFF):
Vol. 59 60 61 62 AUT17 SPR18

Spotlight Word Seek Puzzles (SWFF):
Vol. MAY16 MAY17 NOV17 MAY18 NOV18

Name _____
(Please Print)

Address _____

City _____

State _____ ZIP _____

Allow 4 to 6 weeks for delivery. **CT & NY residents:** Please add applicable sales tax to your total. **Outside USA:** Add an additional $5 shipping and handling and add applicable GST and PST (U.S. funds). Offer expires 12/31/19.

88-UGFWLL

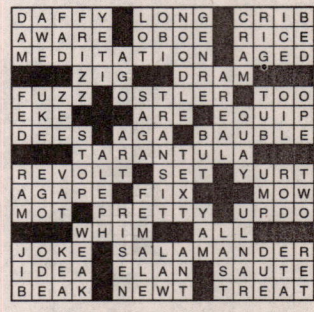

PUZZLE 460

1. Bred, Beard, Dare, Grade, Gear, Regal.
2. Fast, Feast, Seat, Stale, Late, Table.
3. Char, March, Cram, Cream, Mare, Smear.
4. Over, Drove, Rode, Adore, Dear, Adder.
5. Stew, Waste, Sate, Paste, Apse, Sepal.
6. Sure, Curse, Cure, Truce, Curt, Court.

PUZZLE 469

1-U, 2-L, 3-J, 4-Z, 5-K, 6-E, 7-D, 8-S, 9-O, 10-T, 11-N, 12-V, 13-H, 14-P, 15-Q, 16-W, 17-B, 18-I, 19-X, 20-A, 21-G, 22-R, 23-Y, 24-M, 25-F, 26-C.

PUZZLE 470

1-O, 2-J, 3-H, 4-E, 5-A, 6-V, 7-Y, 8-U, 9-X, 10-I, 11-B, 12-P, 13-L, 14-Z, 15-C, 16-K, 17-R, 18-W, 19-T, 20-D, 21-Q, 22-M, 23-F, 24-S, 25-N, 26-G.

PUZZLE 472

1. Wheelbarrow, 2. Castaway, 3. Promenade, 4. Hitherto, 5. Pigeonhole, 6. Hesitant, 7. Domain, 8. Habitat, 9. Section, 10. Assumable.

PUZZLE 496

PUZZLE 497

PUZZLE 498

PUZZLE 499

PUZZLE 500

PUZZLE 501

PUZZLE 502

PUZZLE 503

PUZZLE 504

1. Firewood, 2. Password, 3. Separate, 4. Caboodle, 5. Tireless, 6. Chastise, 7. Calendar, 8. Resemble, 9. Seashell.

PUZZLE 505

PUZZLE 506
WRENCH: tool available in the wrong size.

PUZZLE 507
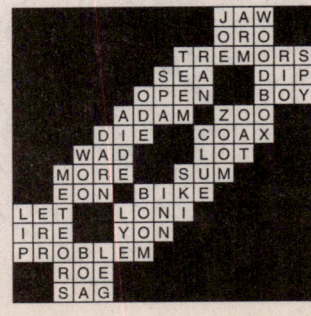

PUZZLE 508
1. Implanted, 2. Detaching.

PUZZLE 512
DUPLICATOR

PUZZLE 509

PUZZLE 513

PUZZLE 516

PUZZLE 510
1. Rise, Rile, File, Fill, Fall.
2. Give, Gave, Cave, Cake, Take.
3. Sink, Sank, Sand, Said, Slid, Slim, Swim.
4. Work, Pork, Perk, Peak, Peat, Plat, Play.

PUZZLE 514

PUZZLE 517

PUZZLE 518

PUZZLE 511

PUZZLE 515

PUZZLE 519
1. Mouthful, 2. Zwieback, 3. Scrutiny, 4. Arachnid, 5. Entreaty, 6. Juncture, 7. Vehement, 8. Flotilla, 9. Mandolin.

PUZZLE 520

PUZZLE 521
1. Virginia Beach, 2. Fort Worth, 3. Baton Rouge, 4. White Plains, 5. Little Rock, 6. Santa Barbara, 7. Colorado Springs, 8. Cedar Rapids.

PUZZLE 522

PUZZLE 523
1. Coin/Combine, 2. Ally/Fallacy, 3. Meal/Mineral, 4. Opal/Topsail, 5. Rein/Reliant, 6. Rope/Prosper, 7. Bang/Beanbag, 8. True/Strudel, 9. Tail/Tactile, 10. Vary/Varsity.

PUZZLE 524

PUZZLE 525

PUZZLE 526

PUZZLE 527

PUZZLE 528

PUZZLE 529

PUZZLE 530

PUZZLE 531

PUZZLE 532

One generation plants the trees; another gets the shade.

PUZZLE 561

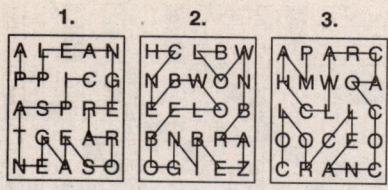

1. Apple, Anger, Arose, Agent, Aspic.
2. Blown, Braze, Bingo, Below, Bench.
3. Color, Clean, Cocoa, Crawl, Champ.

PUZZLE 567

1-T, 2-U, 3-F, 4-Y, 5-V, 6-K, 7-R, 8-M, 9-E, 10-G, 11-Z, 12-H, 13-N, 14-W, 15-P, 16-A, 17-J, 18-S, 19-I, 20-B, 21-C, 22-X, 23-L, 24-Q, 25-O, 26-D.

PUZZLE 568

1-H, 2-X, 3-L, 4-U, 5-D, 6-N, 7-T, 8-W, 9-Q, 10-F, 11-E, 12-A, 13-Y, 14-V, 15-K, 16-C, 17-M, 18-B, 19-J, 20-I, 21-Z, 22-O, 23-G, 24-P, 25-S, 26-R.

PUZZLE 571

A=6, B=4, C=9, D=1, E=5, F=8, G=2, H=7, I=3.

PUZZLE 573

A. 27 (-8 -6 -4 -2 -8 -6 -4 -2)
B. 48 (x2 -8 x2 -8 x2 -8 x2 -8)
C. 55 (+3 +6 +9 +12 +3 +6 +9 +12)
D. 88 (+9 -3 -3 +9 +9 -3 -3 +9)
E. 53 (-6 -7 -8 -9 -10 -11 -12 -13)
F. 416 (-4 x4 -4 x4 -4 x4 -4 x4)

PUZZLE 566

1. Smudge, 2. Zodiac, 3. Acquit, 4. Fabric, 5. Twelve, 6. Basket, 7. Candor, 8. Scorch, 9. Luxury, 10. Jalopy.

PUZZLE 576

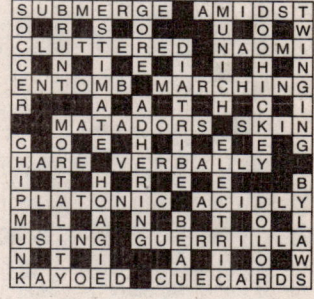

DIAGRAMLESS STARTING BOXES

Puzzle 89 starts in box 7
Puzzle 91 starts in box 1
Puzzle 93 starts in box 7
Puzzle 95 starts in box 8
Puzzle 97 starts in box 10
Puzzle 99 starts in box 13
Puzzle 100 starts in box 4
Puzzle 209 starts in box 10
Puzzle 211 starts in box 8
Puzzle 213 starts in box 7
Puzzle 215 starts in box 2
Puzzle 217 starts in box 14
Puzzle 219 starts in box 6
Puzzle 220 starts in box 14
Puzzle 383 starts in box 1
Puzzle 385 starts in box 5
Puzzle 387 starts in box 1
Puzzle 389 starts in box 3
Puzzle 391 starts in box 5
Puzzle 393 starts in box 5
Puzzle 394 starts in box 1
Puzzle 503 starts in box 11
Puzzle 505 starts in box 1
Puzzle 507 starts in box 11
Puzzle 509 starts in box 3
Puzzle 511 starts in box 3
Puzzle 513 starts in box 13
Puzzle 514 starts in box 7

PUZZLE 538
1. Paris, 2. Masterpiece, 3. Cite, 4. Cream, 5. Praise.

PUZZLE 540
1. Mark Twain, 2. Celine Dion, 3. Dean Martin, 4. Roger Ebert, 5. Buddy Holly, 6. Anne Rice, 7. Tori Spelling, 8. Boris Becker, 9. Bob Seger, 10. Mae West.

PUZZLE 536
Dashiki, Wrap, Dungarees, Cloak, Tunic, Leggings, Bolero.
7TH COLUMN DOWN: Sweater

PUZZLE 543
1-Y, 2-C, 3-R, 4-H, 5-J, 6-U, 7-M, 8-T, 9-W, 10-E, 11-Q, 12-P, 13-D, 14-I, 15-L, 16-X, 17-A, 18-V, 19-F, 20-Z, 21-K, 22-G, 23-S, 24-B, 25-O, 26-N.

PUZZLE 542
1-R, 2-Z, 3-E, 4-F, 5-X, 6-S, 7-C, 8-W, 9-K, 10-Y, 11-L, 12-D, 13-P, 14-A, 15-T, 16-J, 17-B, 18-U, 19-Q, 20-H, 21-V, 22-O, 23-I, 24-M, 25-N, 26-G.

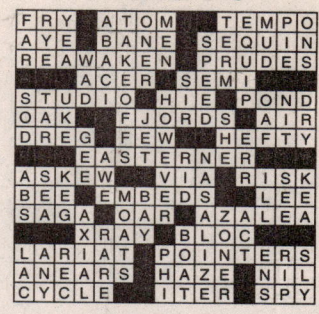

559

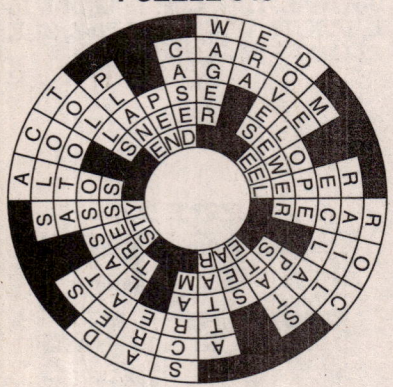
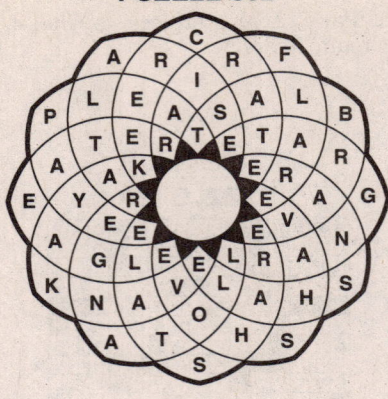